Christmas 1989

To Alasdair.

                                    ...ting'

David Prince

THE NEW WILDFOWLER

THE NEW WILDFOWLER

THIRD EDITION

Edited by Eric Begbie

ASSISTANT EDITORS
John Harradine, Tony Laws, Peter Mayhew

Foreword by H.R.H. The Duke of Edinburgh

Introduction by The Viscount of Arbuthnott

Preface by Sir Peter Scott

Illustrations by John Paley

Published under the auspices of the
British Association for Shooting and Conservation

STANLEY PAUL
London Sydney Auckland Johannesburg

Stanley Paul and Co. Ltd

An imprint of Century Hutchinson Ltd

Brookmount House, 62–65 Chandos Place
Covent Garden, London WC2N 4NW

Century Hutchinson Australia (Pty) Ltd
88–91 Albion Street, Surry Hills, NSW 2010

Century Hutchinson New Zealand Limited
191 Archers Road, PO Box 40-086, Glenfield, Auckland 10

Century Hutchinson South Africa (Pty) Ltd
PO Box 337, Bergvlei 2012, South Africa

First published (as *The New Wildfowler*) by Herbert Jenkins Ltd in 1961
Reprinted in 1963

Revised edition (*The New Wildfowler in the 1970s*) published by
Barrie & Jenkins in 1970
Reprinted in 1979

Revised edition (*The New Wildfowler, Third edition*) published in 1989

Copyright © The British Association for Shooting and Conservation,
1970, 1989

All rights reserved

Set in 'Monophoto' Photina by Vision Typesetting, Manchester
Printed and bound in Great Britain by Butler & Tanner Ltd, Frome, Somerset

British Cataloguing in Publication Data
The New Wildfowler.—3rd ed.
1. Great Britain. Wildfowling
I. Begbie, Eric   II. The new wildfowler
in the 1970's
799.2′44′0941

ISBN 0 09 172642 5

ACKNOWLEDGEMENTS

The B.A.S.C. gratefully acknowledges the valuable
assistance of the following:

Tom Brown, David Gray, Graham Howe, Alan Jarrett,
Peter Keyser, Julian Novorol, Jill Nicholls,
Paul Oakley, John Paley, Trefor Phillips,
Margaret Rowson, Paul Walkden

CONTENTS

BUCKINGHAM PALACE

The first version of The New Wildfowler appeared in 1961, followed by an up-dated edition in 1970. That yet another edition is to be published in 1989, suggests that there is a continuing and very welcome interest in sensible and responsible wildfowling.

Wildfowling, like stock-farming, takes advantage of the surplus production of animal species, but in the case of wildfowling, the species are wild and they form part of an integrated natural system. If this system is to continue to function efficiently, and if wildfowl are to continue to breed a surplus, it is absolutely essential to protect their nesting habitats and migratory routes and to ensure that no more than the surplus production is taken by wildfowlers. This is the essence of conservation.

This book is intended for wildfowlers, but I hope it will also be read by many others interested in the conservation of nature.

1989

LIST OF CONTRIBUTORS
(in alphabetical order)

John Anderton OBE, VRD – Hon. Secretary of WAGBI from 1957–1964 and Director of WAGBI/B.A.S.C. from 1964–1988. Member of the Nature Conservancy's Wildfowl Conservation Committee from 1957–1973 and the Department of the Environment's Wild Birds Advisory Committee from 1961–1981.

The Viscount of Arbuthnott CBE, DSC, MA, JP – President of the B.A.S.C.; Deputy Chairman of the Nature Conservancy Council and Chairman of its Advisory Committee for Scotland from 1980–1985.

Robert Baker – Professional wildfowl keeper at the Pensthorpe Wildfowl Trust in Norfolk. Secretary of the Wells and District Wildfowlers' Club.

Bernard W. Barker – Founder member and first Hon. Secretary of the Eden Wildfowlers' Association. Life member of the B.A.S.C.

Bill Beckett – Northern Ireland Editor of Ireland's *Shooting News* and country sports correspondent for Northern Ireland's independent local radio station. The B.A.S.C.'s Hon. Regional Public Relations Officer for Northern Ireland.

Eric Begbie – Former Chairman and Secretary of the Eden Wildfowlers' Association. Served on the B.A.S.C.'s Wildfowling Liaison Committee. Author of several books on wildfowling and a regular contributor to the shooting press.

The late William Brotherston – WAGBI's Hon. Legal Adviser from 1966–1979.

Arthur Cadman OBE – Author of several books on sporting shooting. Has served several terms on the B.A.S.C.'s Council. He was a member of the Department of the Environment's Wild Birds Advisory Committee (Scotland) from 1969–1981.

Turlough J. Coffey – Hon. Secretary and Treasurer of the Wexford Regional Game Council, Ireland.

James Douglas – Professional gundog trainer and author of several books on sporting shooting.

Veronica Downing – As the wife of a keen wildfowler, an accomplished wildfowl cook.

Nick Frearson – Member of B.A.S.C.'s Council from 1983–1988 with special responsibilities for punt-gunning.

David Garrard – Regular contributor of cartridge loading articles to the shooting press. Committee member of the Wells and District Wildfowlers' Club.

Rick Goater – Reserve Ranger/Naturalist for the Scottish Wildlife Trust's Montrose Basin Local Nature Reserve. Previously, Refuge Manager at the Wildfowl Trust's Slimbridge reserve.

David Guild – The B.A.S.C.'s Scottish Legal Adviser.

Dr John Harradine – Head of Research at the B.A.S.C., member of the Wildfowl Trust's Scientific Advisory Committee and Co-ordinator of the International Waterfowl and Wetlands Research Bureau's Wing Study Group.

Dr David Hill – Senior Ecologist at the Royal Society for the Protection of Birds. Previously studied duck and gamebird population dynamics at the Game Conservancy.

The late Henry James – a past member of WAGBI's Management Committee and also Chairman of Frodsham and District Wildfowlers' Club.

Alan Jarrett – Member of the B.A.S.C.'s Wildfowling Liaison Committee and Chairman of the Kent Wildfowling and Conservation Association. Author of wildfowling books and regular contributor to the shooting press.

Dr Peter Knights – Former Hon. Secretary of the Pembrokeshire Wildfowlers' Association; currently Deputy Regional Officer for North-East England with the Nature Conservancy Council.

Tony Laws – Director Conservation and Research at the B.A.S.C. Served on the Nature Conservancy Council's Specialist Waterfowl Group from 1982–1984. Serves on numerous wildfowl reserve management and advisory committees.

Andrew Macfarlane – An accomplished taxidermist and member of the B.A.S.C.'s Conservation and Research Committee. Chairman of the Upper Forth Wildfowlers' Association.

Dr Peter Mayhew – Head of Conservation at the B.A.S.C. and Secretary of the B.A.S.C.'s Wildfowling Liaison Committee. Previously carried out research on wigeon at the Wildfowl Trust's Caerlaverock reserve.

Desmond Mills – Qualified gunmaker, having served with both James Purdey and E. J. Churchill. Regularly writes on sporting guns in the shooting press.

Dr Myrfyn Owen – Assistant Director (Head of Research) with the Wildfowl Trust and a member of the B.A.S.C.'s Conservation and Research Committee. Author of several books about wildfowl.

Richard Porter – Head of Species Protection at the Royal Society for the Protection of Birds.

John Richards – a former Sales Director on the Board of Holland and Holland Limited and Vice-Chairman of the Gun Trade Association. Formerly Director Development with the B.A.S.C.

David Salmon – Research Officer with the Wildfowl Trust. Organiser of the National Wildfowl Counts.

The late Noel M. Sedgwick – Co-editor of, and contributor to, the first two editions of *The New Wildfowler*. A former WAGBI Vice-President and editor of *Shooting Times*.

Professor Norman Seymour – Professor of Biology at St Francis Xavier University, Nova Scotia. A wildfowl researcher for over 15 years and keen wildfowler on both sides of the Atlantic.

Dr Colin B. Shedden – Head of National and International Affairs with the B.A.S.C.; Secretary of the UK Federation of The Hunting Associations of the EEC (FACE).

John Swift – Director of the B.A.S.C., member of the Nature Conservancy Council's Advisory Committee on Birds and Vice-Chairman of the UK Federation of FACE.

Dr Gareth Thomas – Head of Reserves Ecology at the Royal Society for the Protection of Birds.

Peter Turner – The B.A.S.C.'s Hon. Legal Adviser from 1964–1979 and Vice-Chairman from 1979–1983. Trustee of both the B.A.S.C.'s Wildlife Habitat Trust Fund and the Youth and Education Countryside Trust.

Peter Whitaker –Life member of the B.A.S.C.; co-editor of, and contributor to, the first two editions of *The New Wildfowler*. A regular contributor to the shooting press.

INTRODUCTION
THE VISCOUNT OF ARBUTHNOTT

My earliest wildfowling memories around Montrose Basin are still evoked, albeit vicariously, by the sight or sound of the geese lifting off the mud as I wait at the station on a winter morning for the first train south. The clamour of the grey geese as they rise contrasts with the sharper and deeper quack of mallard or the occasional whistle of wigeon. Ten minutes or so later, on a still morning, one hears the first thump of a magnum fired by an expectant gunner in the hinterland on Garvock, Dun, Usan or Kinnaird wherever geese are known to be feeding.

Recently I have been thinking of the changes that have occurred for wildfowlers over the fifty years I have known the Basin and, particularly during the last sixteen years, since the second edition of *The New Wildfowler* was compiled. My predecessor as President of the Wildfowlers' Association of Great Britain and Ireland (WAGBI), the late Lord Mansfield, wrote in his introduction of the essential need for co-operation between wildfowlers and naturalists. He was absolutely right and how much more difficult it has become to forge that harmonious collaboration!

Since that time WAGBI has become the British Association for Shooting and Conservation, emphasising a wider than wildfowl shooting interest and the significance placed on conservation practices by all who shoot and are members of the Association. Nevertheless the grass roots of the membership remain firmly established below the sea wall or around the inland marshes.

The wildfowler of today might well look askance at these changes. They include not only the WAGBI name change, but, as at Montrose Basin, the advent of the permit with bye-law control of shooting areas and sanctuaries on many a foreshore previously open to all sportsmen. I was closely involved in the pioneering plans for such an area at Caerlaverock on the Solway and have seen many others develop since. How much better a regulated shooting opportunity for the increasing numbers of sportsmen with more time and greater mobility than no chance to shoot at all.

The 'cowboys' condemned by Lord Mansfield still occasionally bring shooting into disrepute and wildfowlers still have to put up with them and the additional restrictions imposed by hard weather bans, Site of Special Scientific Interest conditions and the multifarious competition for wetlands from agricultural and industrial development and the acquisitive voluntary conservation organisations.

Now farming may have to take a lower profile and the reclamation of tidal areas for any other purpose may become less attractive even for nuclear power stations, but the steady erosion of wildfowling grounds seems to go on.

Our need to manage our wildlife resources in collaboration with those of mainland Europe was always apparent to the discerning few, but the UK accession to the European Economic Community in 1973 brought many more of those issues into focus. European Community law and practices have been seen to become a reality with every prospect of their influencing our own shoot management. Derogation from EEC regulations was and is always possible for the UK Government and it is incumbent on all of us to see that the best UK practice is not submerged simply for the sake of uniformity with other European conventions. Wildfowlers need allies in Government, and indeed amongst the conservation bodies, to ensure that the age-old skill and sporting practices of wildfowling are not gradually eliminated.

Thirty years ago the Nature Conservancy and everyone else with a dedication to waterfowl and wetlands used to meet for 'tea parties' at 19 Belgrave Square in London, during which much that had seemed suspicious or threatening dissolved in the course of successive discussions on topics of mutual interest. Then later, even within WAGBI/B.A.S.C. itself, wildfowlers began to feel a lack of sympathy and support from those from whom they most expected it. In recent years therefore the annual Wildfowling Conference organised by the B.A.S.C. has again appropriately focused on the need for consultation and a better appreciation by us all of the threat that hangs over shooting. It is one thing to try to regulate geese or duck populations by restricting the amount of shooting they sustain and quite another to secure their breeding, roosting and feeding areas in perpetuity. The former control is a blunt weapon that does little good and the latter is frankly much more difficult to achieve but eventually so much more rewarding. It needs continuous patience and co-operation with all those interested in wildfowl to achieve success. Wildfowlers should always subscribe to the safeguarding of habitat allied with a responsible shooting regime within it.

We also want to concentrate on the issues where we can find common ground and dismiss those that only lead to fruitless confrontation. Our closer links with Europe and indeed the world conservation movement have made it more than ever apparent that the British Isles lie on the western-most migratory route for a host of bird species. Many of these are quarry species which winter with us but breed elsewhere. As we depend on sub-Saharan Africa for so many of our songbirds so we rely on the rest of north and western Europe, Greenland and Iceland, for virtually all our migratory wildfowl. A mutual responsibility for the welfare of all these species must be a first duty. Wildfowlers have seen how the greater popularity of their own sport has brought its constraints, but they have also been the first to recognise the advantage of sensible control of wildfowl stocks by better protection of their chosen habitat. In return wildfowlers would wish to be recognised as a race of people who can bring to every debate about their future exploitation a wide experience and deep appreciation of the inland and coastal waters they enjoy.

I hope those talents will be engaged as a further means of safeguarding the wild and sporting countryside we all feel is part of our fragile heritage and that this book will awaken a larger public to an appreciation of the sport of wildfowling.

PREFACE

SIR PETER SCOTT

The rapid growth of the human population, the progressive drainage of marshland, the spread of industry, and the means and leisure for people to travel widely; all these are factors bearing heavily on the interests of wildfowl, not only in Britain but throughout the European flyway and indeed many other parts of the world. In the face of such pressures, the continued existence of adequate wildfowl stocks can no longer be taken for granted. If we want to have them in the future, now is the time for all those who are interested to band together and ensure that it shall be so. In such a campaign the wildfowler has strong allies among the birdwatchers, the photographers, the painters, and even the less specialised nature lovers, all of whom would like to see more rather than less birds. Surprisingly, despite all the threats they face and the disappearance of so much of their habitat, the stocks of wildfowl in this country have increased over the last two decades. This may be largely due to a changing attitude towards conservation principles.

The basic problem, from which all others stem, is not so much a shortage of ducks as the growing scarcity of habitat. In the old days, if a place was too much disturbed the birds were able to move elsewhere for a while. Now there are fewer places for them to move to and much greater care must be taken of those that remain. At the same time there is already not enough room for everyone to go wildfowling just whenever and wherever they please.

As a start, therefore, let us continue to make sure that everyone who wants to shoot wildfowl really has the interests of the sport at heart. Already most genuine wildfowlers have realized that the privilege of shooting on the foreshore is too precious a right to squander on hooligans who cannot be bothered to learn the manners and customs of their sport. People who do not know what they are shooting at (and there are still some unfortunately), nor what is the effective range of their weapons, should not be allowed to endanger this ancient heritage (or, for that matter, their neighbours at flight time). With this book there is no longer any excuse for ignorance; the standards have been set and wildfowling must (and with the aid of B.A.S.C. I believe quite easily can) keep its house in order.

Secondly, let us look after every available acre of wetland habitat. If we can increase the capacity of our countryside to accommodate breeding duck in summer, and migratory duck in winter, it will at least help to compensate for the places irrevocably lost to development. The key to the problem lies, of course, in food supplies. Provided that these are adequate, even quite small roosts, so long as they are free from disturbance, will suffice for many thousands of birds. Research into the biology of wildfowl is thus of paramount importance as a prelude to habitat improvement.

The problem now is to integrate wildfowling, birdwatching and other leisure pursuits in our major wetlands. This means co-operation between those on all sides to devise sufficient well-managed refuge areas so that the birds can coexist with the other activities and whatever short-term disturbance they may cause. We must encourage the trend towards habitat restoration and less intensive use of agricultural land.

In the meantime, however, there is still the urgent need to stop, wherever possible, the present wastage of prime habitat. In a hundred years much more than half the country's marshes and wildfowl habitat have gone; yet even now there can be few places in Britain where one has to travel more than a dozen miles to find a duck, or more than fifty miles to see a wild goose, and this is surely as it should be. It would be small comfort to a Londoner to be told that the only remaining geese were in Scotland, or to an Aberdonian that he must go to Cheshire to see a pintail. Our task must, therefore, be to maintain our stocks of wildfowl not only in their present strength, but in their present distribution. One way of achieving this, and I am sure the best, is to have a network of refuges at key-points throughout the country. The strongholds can then carry the nucleus of the local population, and the other resorts would carry the overflow. Any such plan must, of course, be based on a detailed knowledge of conditions in every part of the country, and to this end in the early 60s the Wildfowl Trust undertook a full survey of wildfowl and wildfowl habitat in Great Britain (*Wildfowl in Great Britain*, 1963). The help and advice of the B.A.S.C. was sought and freely given at every stage. This survey was updated with the publication of the second edition of *Wildfowl in Great Britain* in 1986.

With this strategy to work on, all those with an interest in wildfowl are able to come together to plan constructively for the future. Let us be clear about it, the main object of these refuges is to increase the stocks. As a natural resource wildfowl can be regarded as a legitimate crop, and wildfowling is, of course, the traditional way of harvesting it. We must only be sure that the harvest is there to gather, and that it is not harvested too heavily.

Since the publication of the last edition of this book the number of duck breeding in the lowlands has increased considerably, on the new habitats provided by reservoirs and gravel pits. Feral geese have also expanded – there are now estimated to be 40,000 Canadas and 12,000 feral greylag in Britain and Ireland.

The first publication of this extremely comprehensive and authoritative book in 1961 marked the beginning of a new era of mutual confidence and respect between WAGBI as it then was and the Wildfowl Trust. The chapters that follow show how close the link now is, and how dependent we are, one upon the other. So long as these bonds of common interest remain, the future of wildfowl and wildfowling is, I believe, assured; and with the same excitement of anticipation on a wild morning long hence our grandchildren will be able to see the skeins of wild geese coming in from the shore.

EDITOR'S NOTE
ERIC BEGBIE

Of all country sports, wildfowling is the pursuit which most relies upon the ability of the hunter to come to terms with his quarry in truly wild conditions. The marshes, saltings and mudflats below the sea wall constitute one of the last areas of true wilderness to be found in the British Isles and it is to those remote places that the true fowler repairs when wild duck and geese are in season.

The wildfowler does not measure success by the size of his bag nor does he gauge his enjoyment according to the social intercourse which occurs over lunch or between drives. His pursuit is that of the lone gunner. With a faithful retriever as his sole companion, he relishes the peace and solitude of the coastal marshes. It is a world which he shares with the wildfowl and a world which he must learn to respect. The storm winds of winter are part of his sport, and the wilder the weather, the more likely he is to finish the flight with a bird to take home for his dinner.

Perhaps it is because the wildfowler experiences such a deep and profound communion with nature, because he must fully understand the habits and habitat of his quarry, that he has led the entire shooting community towards a meaningful partnership with conservation interests. The first edition of *The New Wildfowler* in 1961 was a milestone along the road to developing this partnership. By the time that *The New Wildfowler in the 1970s* was published nine years later, the link between sporting shooting and practical conservation was well and truly forged.

That *The New Wildfowler* played such a vital role in that process is a lasting tribute to the editors of those two editions. Sadly Jeffery Harrison and Noel M. (Tim) Sedgwick are no longer with us, but they are fondly remembered by everyone who has regarded *The New Wildfowler* as the 'fowler's bible' during the past quarter of a century. It is fitting that Jeffery Harrison has joined the 'famous wild-fowlers of the past' in Chapter 34 and that Noel Sedgwick's contribution on inland marsh shooting has been retained in this edition. The third member of the original editorial trio, Peter Whitaker, has revised his chapter about clothing and equipment and, thus, retains his link with *The New Wildfowler*.

Much has changed in the nineteen years since the second edition was published. Wildfowling as a sport has become even more popular and, due largely to the influence of clubs and associations, better regulated. Major legislative change, in the form of the *Wildlife and Countryside Act 1981*, has reduced the number of species which legitimately may be shot by the fowler and, to a minor extent, has restricted the types of weapon which may be employed. Perhaps most significantly of all, the Wildfowlers' Association of Great Britain and Ireland – founded in 1908 by Stanley Duncan and known to generations of fowlers as WAGBI – has undergone a change of name and become the British Association for Shooting and Conservation (B.A.S.C.).

The growth in size and influence of the Association is reflected in the format of this book. Unlike previous editions, many of the new chapters have been written by members of B.A.S.C.'s large and expert staff. These chapters are complemented by contributions from colleagues employed by the Wildfowl Trust and the Royal Society for the Protection of Birds. There has remained, of course, a very real place for the contributions of practising wildfowlers and it is appropriate to record the willingness and enthusiasm with which so many sportsmen and naturalists responded to the invitation to prepare material for this book.

The enlarged format has also provided an ideal medium for the superb artwork of John Paley. His illustrations have done much to enhance this volume and as his colour paintings show, he is an experienced wildfowler as well as an accomplished artist. Another accomplished wildfowling painter, Julian Novorol, kindly consented to the use of 'Pinkfeet over the sands' and 'Mallard flighting in' for the jacket illustrations.

In thanking all those who have helped to produce this third edition of *The New Wildfowler* we must make special mention of John Anderton, who retired as Director of the British Association for Shooting and Conservation in 1988. His dedication to the cause of WAGBI/B.A.S.C. is unparalleled and his contribution to the well-being of shooting sports in general and wildfowling in particular will continue to reap dividends for many decades to come.

That wildfowlers continue to lead the movement to protect and maintain the essential balance between country sports and wildlife conservation has been demonstrated by their support for the inauguration of B.A.S.C.'s Wildlife Habitat Trust Fund. This concept germinated in the mind of David Gray, an enthusiastic practical wildfowler, was nurtured by B.A.S.C.'s Wildfowling Liaison Committee and was publicly endorsed by a B.A.S.C. wildfowling conference. It is with great pleasure that I can record that all those concerned with the production of this book – editor, contributors, photographers and artists – have given their services without fee in order that royalties from the publication and sale of *The New Wildfowler* may be paid to the Wildlife Habitat Trust Fund.

1

THE BRITISH ASSOCIATION FOR SHOOTING AND CONSERVATION

JOHN ANDERTON

The Wildfowlers' Association of Great Britain and Ireland, known as WAGBI, was founded by Stanley Duncan of Hull. He was an engineer. He was also a highly experienced wildfowler and naturalist and well known and regarded for his knowledge of wildfowling and related matters. His object in forming the Association was threefold. He sought to help the professional wildfowlers, then eking out a meagre living on our coasts; he was becoming alarmed at the increasing drainage and subsequent development of much excellent wildfowl habitat and he realised that as time went by it would be necessary to defend the sport of wildfowling against factors that were moving contrary to its interests, namely the growing enthusiasm of extremists bent on total protection of wild birds.

Today there are no longer any professional fowlers other than for a few guides. But there is a new breed of protectionist and, thus, the threats to wildfowling grow stronger – much more so than was the case in 1908 when , having canvassed and obtained the support of far-seeing and experienced sportsmen, our founder called an inaugural meeting in his wildfowling hut, which, until destroyed by floods, stood at Patrington Haven, not many miles from Hull. Rules were adopted, Stanley Duncan became the Association's first Honorary Secretary which office he held for forty unbroken years. The famous wildfowler and sporting author Sir Ralph Payne-Gallwey, Bt. was elected President.

WAGBI, with the support of a small committee, built up a system whereby there would be, in every wildfowling district, officials capable of giving advice and able to represent and support wildfowling and associated interests whenever they became threatened or were likely to be so.

Largely as a result of Stanley Duncan's tremendous enthusiasm, dedication and the high regard in which he was held by the sporting public through his writings, drawings, sporting achievements and knowledge, WAGBI became recognised within wildfowling circles and accepted as the authoritative and representative voice of all such interests in this country.

The war of 1914–18 meant that the Association and its activities had to be placed, virtually, in cold storage. Its activities immediately after that war were on a modest scale, Stanley Duncan confining his activities to enrolling as members such persons as were interested, and dispensing advice whenever it was sought.

Between the wars, as he had foreseen, the sport was subjected to increasing pressure from organisations who wished to suppress or curtail the shooting of wildfowl, and in the years immediately prior to the outbreak of the Second World War the Association gave ground to pressure from the protectionists. This resulted in legislation being passed that curtailed the season at both ends.

In those years, immediately prior to 1939, when the control of wildfowling lay substantially in the hands of county councils, there was a growing body of opinion in the country that laws relating to the sport should be put on a national basis and that decisions as to which species of birds could or could not be shot, and when, should be made at that level.

The Second World War had an immediate effect on the amount of support wildfowlers could give to the defence of their sport, as most young and active men interested in wildfowling were serving their country in the armed services. With the cessation of hostilities, however, wildfowlers returning from war service soon realised that in their absence the protectionists, invariably part of an older generation, had not been idle and the initiative had passed to their 'side'. If wildfowling was to enjoy any future then WAGBI must be prepared to fight – in particular for the rights of its members.

The first WAGBI meeting place – Stanley Duncan's Black Hut at Patrington

In 1947 the call went out urging such members of WAGBI as had survived the war to attend a meeting at Hull, at which plans to revitalise the Association and prepare for the coming struggle were laid. After a further meeting held the following year in Manchester, Stanley Duncan, now visibly ageing, resigned the office of Secretary and went into retirement, taking with him the sincere gratitude and deep respect of all wildfowlers. At this meeting new rules were adopted, a new committee appointed and the foundation of the modern WAGBI laid.

THE THREAT TO WILDFOWLING

The long expected attack on wildfowling came in 1953, when legislation which the Association regarded as both unfair, unnecessary and very restrictive, was introduced in Parliament.

Although a strictly voluntary organisation, with no paid staff, a small group of public-spirited men gave considerably of their time, energy and private funds, determined that the interests of wildfowlers be given a fair hearing and their beliefs recognised and upheld. Many meetings were convened and thousands of letters written, whilst there was considerable lobbying of Members of both Houses for, in the opinion of those serving the WAGBI cause, there had been very considerable misrepresentation of the true facts.

'In the events that followed' – as the lawyers say – the ultimate outcome was the *Protection of Birds Act 1954*. The Act was something far removed from the original Bill and WAGBI accepted it as, on the whole, fair and reasonable. Even so there remained certain clauses that did not and still do not appeal to all wildfowlers, although prior to the *Wildlife and Countryside Act 1981*, such views were confined to a very small minority.

Having participated in the protracted and sometimes heated deliberations culminating with the 1954 Act, WAGBI, 35 years ago, did everything possible to ensure that sportsmen respected and, as appropriate, enforced the provisions of the Act. This policy has also been followed with the *Wildlife and Countryside Act 1981*.

While acknowledging the tremendous contributions made by that handful of dedicated Association officials, it was equally important that full credit be given to the Editor and staff of the *Shooting Times*. It would be wrong to assume that the *Shooting Times* came to our aid only at that time, for this excellent weekly magazine has, in fact, acted for an unbroken period of close on eighty years as the Association's official organ, and more recently its official weekly magazine. It has disseminated sound advice week by week and has never shrunk from the truth, particularly in its down-to-earth editorials and correspondence columns. The space it at one time devoted entirely to WAGBI was more than a mere noticeboard. WAGBI had at all times been granted great strength and support by its Editor-in-Chief 'Tim' Sedgwick and Editor, Philip Brown. We hope that the bond of friendship, trust and confidence which existed then between our two organisations will again prosper and continue far into the future, so providing a lasting marriage of ideas and beliefs.

The effect of the publicity and behaviour that preceded the 1954 Act was so profound that throughout the country there developed a determination that never again should genuine sportsmen find themselves in similar circumstances. All over the country those who valued their sporting heritage and its future began to seek membership, and many of them, with WAGBI's help and advice, set about forming local clubs and associations, thus bringing together many who, individually, could do little to safeguard that future, but collectively could and would – if it became necessary. This did not mean, however, that wildfowlers would cease to follow their sport singly or with a companion or two as they did in Stanley Duncan's day.

WILDFOWL CONSERVATION

In 1949 the Nature Conservancy, incorporated by Royal Charter and responsible to the Committee of the Privy Council for Nature Conservation, came into being. Subsequently it became an integral part of the Natural Environment Research Council, since which time it has become the Nature Conservancy Council. Its functions, of relevance to wildfowlers, were to provide advice on the conservation, control or protection of natural fauna and to establish, maintain and manage nature reserves in Great Britain, many of which embraced shooting zones jointly created and managed with WAGBI.

When the Conservancy was first formed it was felt that the cause of wildfowling had been ignored whilst the naturalists were well represented and, therefore, decisions would be made and discussions would be held without reference to our opinions. Ultimately a meeting was arranged between the two bodies at which there was much plain speaking, which in turn led to the establishment of an informal wildfowl discussion group (known as 'tea parties') under the Conservancy's auspices and at which all shades of opinion were represented. It is to the great and lasting credit of the then Director-General (E. Max Nicholson, CB, CVO, now a B.A.S.C. Vice-President) that he saw the real need for such a meeting.

This group, founded at a time when wildfowlers were full of bitterness and suspicion at what they considered to be the 'scheming and unfair propaganda' that had taken place behind the scenes prior to the 1954 Act, became the recognised and fully established Wildfowl Conservation Committee in 1960.

It constituted a formal gathering of many interested bodies with a genuine interest in the future well-being of wildfowl and their habitat, whilst providing its members with regular opportunities for discussing a wide range of concerns. From a beginning fraught with suspicion and mistrust grew, among many things, complete accord and confidence, with the chair alternating between the Wildfowl Trust and WAGBI. The Committee and WAGBI fully appreciated that 'our' wildfowl are shared with other European countries. They are common to all and, unlike we foolish humans, do not recognise political or national barriers. Hence the development of national nature reserves and wildfowl refuges that are a part of a broad European pattern.

THE GROWTH OF WAGBI/B.A.S.C.

In 1950 WAGBI had five affiliated organisations, namely Southport & District Wildfowlers' Association (1887), Morecambe Bay Wildfowlers' Association (1929), Blakeney and District Wildfowlers'

Association (1927), Frodsham and District Wild-fowlers' Club (1938) and the Tay Valley Wildfowlers' Association (1949). Subsequently it has grown into a huge organisation comprising some 100,000 members, over 1000 affiliated clubs and registered shooting syndicates and a staff of no fewer than fifty-eight dedicated and hard-working enthusiasts, its first paid employee having been appointed as recently as 1961.

In 1981 WAGBI changed its name to the British Association for Shooting and Conservation (B.A.S.C.). This change was agreed at the Annual General Meeting of that year in recognition of the fact that shooting sports required a single representative body and that WAGBI was the most suitably placed organisation to take on that role.

The formation of local affiliated organisations, now covering all forms of sporting shooting and not merely wildfowling, with the support and backing of their parent body, B.A.S.C., has provided much-needed common meeting grounds. The clubs share the responsibility for education of the newcomer, operating the B.A.S.C.-recommended practical conservation schemes that embrace the improvement of habitat and the purchase or lease and subsequent management of land and sporting rights over fresh and salt water marshes, foreshore, agricultural land, forest and merse, together with wildfowl restocking programmes. Local associations also arrange social occasions, including film shows, illustrated talks and lectures, clay-bird shooting and organised pest control shoots, which are of benefit to the farming community.

Joint Councils co-ordinate and represent the interests of clubs within laid-down areas, encourage sporting competitions, maintain a watch on developments which are or might not be in their best interests and generally relieve national headquarters of certain responsibilities better dealt with on a regional basis by members with local knowledge. However, support, help and guidance is provided by full-time Regional Officers centred on the North, East and South East, South West, with Wales and West Midlands, not forgetting, of course, Scotland (which country has had its own B.A.S.C. office for the past twelve years) and Northern Ireland.

National Headquarters, responsible to Council, which is elected by the Association's members, is very much a full-time and professionally administered operation. Under the Director, it comprises five divisions covering Administration and Finance, Regional Development, Conservation and Research, Firearms and External Services (which includes Education and Training, and Public Relations), and Scotland. In addition, specific departments have responsibility for international affairs, membership and computer services, and sales. The voluntary and honorary aspect happily remains well to the fore, consisting of specialist advisers covering the law, conservation, public relations, publications, education, etc. All elected members of Council serve in an honorary capacity.

Some noteworthy achievements have been the authority granted to the Association by the Crown Estate whereby a member, whilst carrying a gun over land in their ownership and not already subject to a lease of shooting rights, cannot be proceeded against for the criminal offence of armed trespass under the provisions of the *Firearms Act 1968*. Wherever possible the B.A.S.C. has, for obvious reasons, encouraged local associations to purchase or lease shooting rights, appoint wardens, and accept responsibility for the shooting conduct and conditions in those areas. Recognition by the Sports Council came in 1968 with subsequent financial grant aid.

The Association is represented on, or works most closely with, many committees and organisations, including British Field Sports Society, British Shooting Sports Council, Central Council of Physical Recreation, Clay Pigeon Shooting Association, County Conservation Trusts, Crown Estate, Duchy of Cornwall, Duchy of Lancaster, Game Conservancy, Gun Trade Association Ltd., International Council for Bird Preservation, International Waterfowl and Wetlands Research Bureau, National Trust, Nature Conservancy Council, Royal Society for the Protection of Birds, Water Recreation Sub-Committee of the Regional Sports Councils, Wildfowl Trust, national, regional and local nature reserve committees, and FACE (UK) (Fédération des Associations de Chasseurs de la CEE), for which we provide the secretariat, Council for Country Sports and the Standing Conference on Countryside Sports. The last three 'umbrella' organisations the Association helped to found.

It might be wondered why the Association is working in the European field. As already intimated wildfowl are migratory in the main and therefore are common to and shared by many countries. This calls for joint responsibility. It is at EEC level that decisions in future will be made with regard to possible (blanket) laws concerning lengths of season, methods of taking fowl and game and, in fact, virtually every aspect of the sport, including firearms and gun legislation. Obviously British sporting interests must be cared for and the B.A.S.C. is the one organisation equipped to do so. It is worthy of mention that in the European mind the triumvirate comprising the Nature Conservancy, Wildfowl Trust and WAGBI in the 1960s/70s was regarded as being a blueprint that was ten years ahead of the remainder of Europe. It has helped us ever since.

There have been other changes. In 1975 the Gamekeepers' Association of the United Kingdom (founded in 1900) became a part of the Association, and, as previously mentioned, in 1981 WAGBI became the 'British Association for Shooting and Conservation'. This led many 'purist' wildfowlers to believe that wildfowl, wildfowl habitat and wildfowlers had been 'relegated to the third division'. This feeling was understandable but wholly incorrect. It is an undeniable fact that those three named have, since 1981, enjoyed a far superior service and interest than ever before. Indeed, they have their own Wildfowling Liaison Committee made up of fowlers drawn from all points of the compass, enjoy their own Wildfowling Conference plus an increased full-time staff who are efficiently and wholeheartedly working for and representing their best interests at all levels, whether it be in Brussels, Westminster or at local authority level. Thus such doubts and fears that there may have been should no longer be acceptable.

The foregoing is only a very brief account of, first, the Wildfowlers' Association of Great Britain and Ireland, latterly, the British Association for Shooting and Conservation, which really deserves a volume – or three! But it will point to 80 years of service, firstly to the fine sport of wildfowling and, in more recent years, all disciplines of sporting shooting, including deer stalking – in addition to wildfowling and fowler who, let it never be forgotten, were the *cause célèbre* of WAGBI!

The Association's current work, responsibilities and aspirations are complex, broad-based and becoming more so as the world shrinks, the

Marford Mill – B.A.S.C. headquarters

countryside changes and the people demand greater access to it. Agriculture and forestry policies are undergoing change previously believed unthinkable. In addition, we are a part of Europe – with all that that means and portends.

Nevertheless, this brief survey adds up to an essential background to a book which ably represents what has been and is being achieved, and covers virtually every aspect of what is undoubtedly an ancient and honourable sport that the B.A.S.C., as was the case with WAGBI, is determined to maintain for future generations as well as its current devotees. Whilst the Association works tirelessly in the best interests of all forms of sporting shooting there can be no doubt that wildfowl are the quarry species by far the most in need of care and long-term thought and planning since, being migratory in the main, they are subject not only to the risks of weather, in all its forms (not least on the northern breeding grounds), but 'progress' which embraces drainage, development, disturbance, certain herbicides and insecticides and pollution. In addition to countering the 'protect everything' brigade much time and effort is devoted to public relations, not least in a bid to disseminate the truth and try to have the general public understand that their magnificent and varied countryside is as it is thanks to generations of landowners, farmers, foresters and field sport devotees and those among them who shoot, in particular.

Although the past has led to a better understanding of present needs for wildfowl and wildfowling, the future is overshadowed by the unfortunate and growing trend towards mass thinking based on the media's attitude towards urban rather than rural understanding. The countryman, or the town-dweller who has a real appreciation of country life, is therefore in a minority and at a disadvantage in the face of emotionalism easily inspired by press, radio and television. Whilst it is from the former that the B.A.S.C. has gained its strength, a growing number of thinking naturalists have realised that only through practical conservation allied to reasonable harvesting of the surplus can the future of wildfowl and wildfowling be assured.

There are those who might at one time have been against the wildfowler, through ignorance or lack of understanding, but are today supporting the B.A.S.C. in increasing numbers as the constructive policies it has inaugurated – and which are outlined in this book – bear fruit. This, surely, is the right attitude not only for today but for the future if we, as a nation, are to preserve our wildlife in an ever-decreasing countryside that more and more is being spoiled by man in his demand for 'progress'.

2
THE NATURAL HISTORY OF WILDFOWL

MYRFYN OWEN

Much of this book describes specific aspects of wildfowl, mainly in Britain and mainly as they affect the numbers and distribution of the birds. This chapter serves as a general introduction to the group and covers aspects of their general biology and lifestyle that may not be applied specifically to the interests of the wildfowler, but nevertheless determine how the birds survive and move in their environment and how changes might affect them. The term 'wildfowl', in the most common usage in Britain, is applied to birds of the family *Anatidae*, namely ducks, geese and swans: 'waterfowl' is the equivalent term in North America. Waterfowl are defined by the International Waterfowl and Wetlands Research Bureau, as birds 'ecologically dependent on water' and includes grebes, divers, cranes, herons, etc., as well as wildfowl. In this account I use the term in the narrow sense; this includes most of the quarry species of interest to wildfowlers.

Wildfowl are generally large birds which associate with water to some extent throughout their life cycle. They have long necks and rather short legs, which gives them a distinctive appearance in flight. They are relatively heavy for the area of their wings, i.e. they have a high wing loading, which means that they must fly fast, with a continuous flapping flight. Although its speed has not been measured accurately, its wing loading suggests that the eider duck is the fastest bird in level flight.

The wildfowl body is covered with a layer of down beneath the outer layers of waterproof feathers. This is plucked by the female during incubation to cover and insulate the eggs. Wildfowl nest on the ground or in tree holes and lay white or pale green, pale blue or brownish eggs. The newly-hatched young are covered with down and are able to fend for themselves from the first day or two. Whilst the adults might stir up submerged invertebrates and uproot underwater plants for their chicks they do not feed their young directly.

A characteristic which they share with a number of other waterbirds is the simultaneous moulting of the flight feathers. They become flightless for 3–6 weeks during the summer months just after breeding when the young are relatively independent. There are a very few exceptions, all in the southern hemisphere.

SWANS AND GEESE

Swans and geese are very closely related and are put, with the exclusively tropical whistling duck, into the subfamily *Anserinae*. The swans are large herbivores, the only vertebrates to rear their young entirely on vegetable protein. They are characteristically monogamous, the sexes are similar in plumage and both help to care for the young. Families migrate together and in many species young associate with their parents until the next breeding season approaches. They are long-lived and generally do not breed until they are at least two and, in some cases, four or five years old.

All but the South American coscoroba swan belong to the genus *Cygnus*. The mute swan is only partly migratory and the cob is one of the world's largest flying birds. Otherwise, all the northern hemisphere species are migratory. The two migratory species encountered in Europe, the whooper and Bewick's swans, are very similar. All are white with black bills with a variable amount of yellow on them, and all have bugling or trumpeting calls. They are less dependent on water than the other swans; the Bewick's especially is well able to gather its food from land.

All true geese occur in the northern hemisphere; they are split into the grey geese in the genus *Anser* and black geese, *Branta*. The grey geese have white (snow geese), brownish or grey plumage with pink, yellow or orange legs and pink or orange on at least part of the bill. Black geese have grey or brown bodies and all-black bills and legs. They include the most southerly of all geese – and the rarest of the species – the Hawaiian goose or nene. All geese walk well on land and feed largely while standing. Their voices are a variety of honks, barks and high-pitched cackles.

The black geese include the largest of the group – the large races of Canada geese, which can weigh up to 8 kg, and the smallest – the brent and red-breasted goose, which at just over a kilogram are about the size of a mallard. Most are migratory and many breed in the high arctic and travel thousands of kilometres to their temperate wintering grounds.

DUCK SPECIES

The ducks, subfamily Anatinae, are much more variable than geese and swans and are separated into seven tribes. Wildfowl are descended from land birds, so the more adaptations they display for an aquatic existence the more advanced they are considered evolutionarily. There are a few long-legged, land-based duck, but most have short legs and are rather ungainly on land, walking with a distinct 'waddle'. In most duck the sexes are dissimilar, the males being brightly coloured. Courtship rituals involve elaborate displays and pair bonds generally last only for a few months prior to and during the breeding season. Duck generally have two body moults including one after breeding is over, when the males change into their cryptic 'eclipse' plumage, and resemble the drab females. Most species have a brightly coloured speculum, an iridescent area on the secondary feathers of the wing that is conspicuous in flight. A characteristic of all duck is that they have an enlarged chamber or 'bulla' on the side of the windpipe of the males.

The most similar ducks to the geese and swans, and hence the most primitive, are the shelduck (the *Tadornini*) which include the sheldgeese of the tropics and the southern hemisphere. They have long-lasting pair bonds, both sexes care for the young and in all but two species the male and female resemble each other in plumage. They have long legs and walk well; the sheldgeese have evolved to a similar land-based existence, as have

the true geese. The young of the shelduck are characteristically patterned, brightly blotched or striped in black or dark brown and white. The steamer ducks (the *Tachyeres*) are restricted to the southern hemisphere and are put in a tribe of their own.

The perching ducks (the *Cairinini*) are a diverse group of surface-feeding ducks, some resembling geese and others true duck. There are no native European perching ducks but the mandarin duck now has a sizeable feral population in southern England. They are mostly forest birds, readily perching in trees and nesting usually in holes or on platforms well above ground. They include probably the rarest of wildfowl species – the white-winged wood duck of the Far Eastern rain forests.

By far the largest tribe, and the most familiar, is the *Anatini* – the dabbling ducks. The 'puddle ducks' of North America, they are ubiquitous wherever there is shallow freshwater. They feed by picking, grazing or filtering particles of food from the shallows with their broad bills, most well developed in the shoveler. The sexes are usually very dissimilar in plumage and the males engage in elaborate courtship – a common sight in winter. The females of all species are similar to each other – rather dull, brown birds, well camouflaged when incubating. Dabbling ducks are a vocal group – the decrescendo quacking of a female mallard is one of the most familiar sounds of the marsh. Other species have a variety of quacks, chirps and croaks.

The remaining ducks are specialised divers, the least advanced of which is the *Aythyini* – the pochards. They are rounded duck with broad bills and are largely found on freshwater. They inhabit rather shallow waters and include the redheaded pochards, the tufted duck and the estuarine scaups. Their soft parts are generally black or blue. Pochards are not very vocal; females have low grunts and burps, while males whistle or hiss softly, mainly during display.

The sea ducks and sawbills are put together in the *Mergini*. They are specialist divers, and their legs are set well back, which makes them most ungainly on land. All are carnivorous, feeding on molluscs, crustaceans and fish. The tribe is very diverse, including the widespread eiders, scoters, goldeneyes and the fish-eating sawbills.

The most advanced of wildfowl are the stifftails (the *Oxyurini*), which have an almost completely water-borne existence. Their legs are so well back

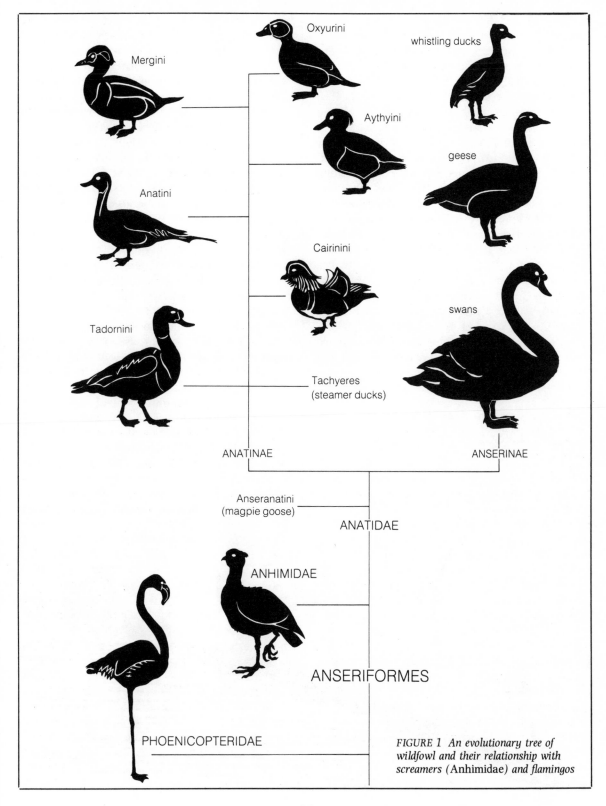

FIGURE 1 *An evolutionary tree of wildfowl and their relationship with screamers (Anhimidae) and flamingos*

on the body that they can hardly walk on land and their stiff tail feathers help in steering underwater. The only European representative is the rare whiteheaded duck, but the introduced North American ruddy duck is now a familiar sight on many enclosed freshwaters of England and Wales.

The group, then, have adapted to use all the watery habitats from the shallowest marshland and even dry land to the open sea. Water, though usually safe from most predators, is often cold, salty and rough; the birds have developed a range of adaptations to cope with these disadvantages.

Wildfowl are among the most well insulated of birds. Their outer feather layer is waterproof – the dense feather filaments, kept well organised and supple by preening, do not allow water to pass between them. Underneath is the down, which provides another dense layer – the insulation qualities of eiderdown are well known, and this has not yet been matched by any man-made substitute. A layer of thick subcutaneous fat, especially below the waterline, is an added barrier against the cold. Feathers cover most of the body, but the legs, in contact with the cold water, are poorly supplied with blood vessels so that the

FIGURE 2 A diagrammatic representation of the feeding niches of freshwater wildfowl. The diving pochard reaches seeds and vegetation up to 5 metres, whilst the mute swan, by upending, can reach nearly 1.5 metres. The pintail has a longer neck than the mallard and teal so they are separated though they have similar diets. The wigeon is a herbivore and grazes around the water margin

minimum of heat is lost. The feet are tucked into the flank feathers while resting; in swimming birds one foot may be tucked in while the other paddles to keep the bird facing the wind.

Wildfowl adopt a variety of feeding methods. Swans generally feed while floating on water by submerging the head and neck and upending. This way they can graze underwater vegetation over a metre down, or pull up aquatic plants to be consumed at leisure on the surface. Geese are all grazers at some part of the year, but at others various specialisations help them to coexist in the same geographical area. Some species – the snow geese of North America and the greylag of Europe – are rooters, having thick, tough bills with a vice-like grip which can uproot the most firmly established rhizomes and tear into fleshy plant storage roots. The long-necked species reach seeds from trees or tall grasses, whilst the short-billed grazers can peck at up to 200 pecks per minute and feed on the finest and shortest of swards.

In water many species of dabbling ducks live together on flooded marshland, but the differences in the length of their necks and their feeding methods reduce competition between them when food is scarce. The diminutive teal forages in the shallowest of water, usually feeding by submerging its head and bill at the water margin. The long-necked pintail can reach deeper foods than the mallard, which is highly adaptable, turning to any source of nutriment in adversity.

The diving ducks are similarly separated by differences in their diving abilities and as a result

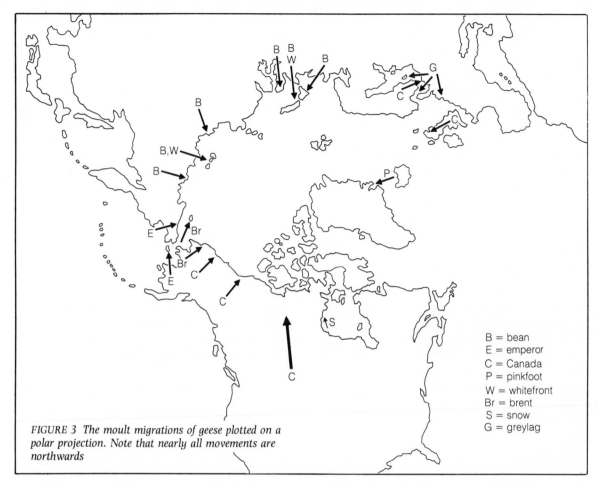

FIGURE 3 *The moult migrations of geese plotted on a polar projection. Note that nearly all movements are northwards*

B = bean
E = emperor
C = Canada
P = pinkfoot
W = whitefront
Br = brent
S = snow
G = greylag

MIGRATION

Shallow water, even if saline, often freezes and wildfowl have developed movement and migration patterns which enable them to use habitats which are only temporarily available. Many species make very long migrations during their annual cycles. The most well known are those that take swans, geese and duck from breeding grounds in the high arctic to wintering places in the temperate zone.

The long migrations of geese and swans are closely related to their herbivorous habit. In comparison with animal food, plants are low in protein and have also developed strategies of combating

some are able to cope better than others with saltwater. The pochards are generally duck of shallow, freshwater, whilst the maritime long-tailed duck, the best diver of all, can reach depths of 20 metres or more.

predation by animals. Chief among these is the reinforcing of their cell walls with fibre. Fibre is not only itself difficult to digest but it inhibits the digestion of other elements of the diet. Herbivores must therefore graze vegetation which is at an early stage of growth, when it has least fibre. In spring grass is at its most nutritious, and, as the quality of the herbage declines, the birds move northwards, or in some cases upwards in altitude, to capitalise on a later spring there. Geese and swans have staging grounds between wintering and breeding areas where they can refuel and they time their movements to coincide with the start of growth there. In the arctic breeding grounds the flush of new growth is at its most concentrated, having a sufficiently high protein content to enable the young to grow adequately on vegetation alone.

Many of the migrations of geese and swans cover vast distances, some brent geese and Bewick's swans travel more than 5000 km. Those that nest in the high arctic are vulnerable to the severity of the northern weather; in some years they fail to rear any young at all.

Though their requirements are different, duck also make spectacular journeys in the course of the season. To rear their young successfully they need a plentiful supply of insect food and these are available in the wetter parts of the arctic – the blackflies and midges that are so troublesome to the northern traveller. On some lakes, as in Myvatn in Iceland, hundreds of pairs of many species gather in the summer to breed. On arrival the females dabble or dive in the shallow water, feeding on the larvae and pupae of the insects, and when the young hatch they paddle swiftly along the water surface catching the emerging flies. Some of the pochard and wigeon wintering in Britain travel over 5000 km to breed in central Siberia, but by far the most spectacular of duck journeys is the trans-Saharan movement of garganey from their wintering grounds in West Africa to their breeding lakes in Europe and Asia.

These long journeys consume large quantities of energy, which the birds carry with them in the form of fat reserves. Flying is a costly activity, taking about twelve times the amount of energy that the bird uses at rest. For geese and swans, not only must fat be laid down for migration, but also there must be sufficient reserves left to lay and incubate the eggs. When the birds arrive there is very little food, and sometimes none, in the still frozen tundra. They have to nest early so that the hatching of the young coincides as closely as possible with the concentrated growth of the arctic plants.

These migrations are predictable and take place in response to seasonal events. Sometimes, especially in winter, conditions can change quickly and birds may be forced to move. In severe winters there may be movements both to and from Britain. Geese and many dabbling duck cross the North Sea to winter on our east coast estuaries when it freezes in Denmark and the Low Countries. If conditions are severe here, the birds continue westwards and also move south into France and Spain. Different species show different degrees of vulnerability. In general the smaller a species the more it suffers from the cold, so that the teal has to move quickly whilst the larger mallard can wait for a few days for the weather to improve. Feeding habitats are also important: the greylag digs through the snow for

roots, whilst the pinkfoot, which is largely a grazer, is forced to move in prolonged cold spells. In general, because of the large amounts of energy involved, a bird only moves as far as is necessary to find a suitable climate and feeding conditions.

Wildfowl are vulnerable during the flightless period, which lasts from three weeks in the smallest duck to six in the swans. Some make special journeys known as moult migrations. The most spectacular involving a British species is the mass movement of shelducks from all over north-west Europe to the massive mudflats of the Heligoland Bight in the German Wadden Sea, but the males of most ducks migrate to moult once the females are on the nest. Their main requirement is an area safe from predators with a good food supply rich in the amino-acids necessary for feather growth.

Some geese also undertake a moult migration, and this is almost invariably northwards. Canada geese, imported into Britain centuries ago, have re-established the habit and birds from the Midlands of England move to the Beauly Firth in north-east Scotland specifically to moult. Their northwards movement is probably related to food as well as safety since their plant diet is not rich in the amino-acids they need (they can capitalise on yet another spring by moving north).

One of the most obvious features of wildfowl during the non-breeding season is their gregariousness. In some situations they are forced together because the food supply is concentrated, but even when this is not the case they still gather in flocks. In goose flocks it has been shown that birds flying overhead pick up clues about feeding conditions from the behaviour of other birds on the

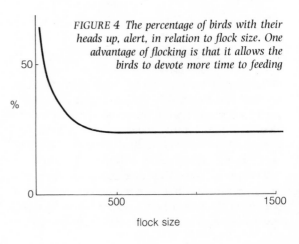

FIGURE 4 *The percentage of birds with their heads up, alert, in relation to flock size. One advantage of flocking is that it allows the birds to devote more time to feeding*

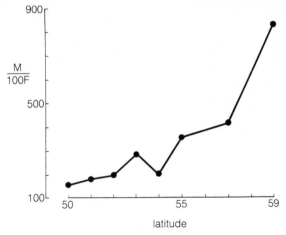

FIGURE 5 *The sex ratio, expressed as males per 100 females of pochard wintering in Britain, in relation to the latitude of the wintering site*

ground. The fact that they are there at all during the day is an indication that there is food, and the more of the group actively feeding the more likely are the flying birds to join them. The more birds are in a group the less time each individual has to spend in the guarding role, so each bird benefits by increasing the time it has for feeding.

Once in a flock, the individuals compete for the best feeding positions, and the largest and the strongest obtain the best foods. In overwintering duck, this leads to an imbalance in the sex ratio of some species. The pochard is the most extreme British example: in most flocks drakes outnumber the ducks by three to one. The farther north the wintering area, the higher the proportion of males. This is because the closer the birds are to the breeding area (usually the farther north and east) the greater the advantage when it comes to moving back there. The competition is greatest in the north and the larger males displace females which have to winter farther south. Males outnumber females in most duck populations and this may be because this displacement leads to some mortality at some season. Females are also, of course, more vulnerable during the nesting period.

In goose and swan flocks things are slightly more complicated in that birds are not always acting only as individuals but also as part of a pair or a family. The larger the group the more powerful it is as a unit, so a pair can displace a single individual and a family a pair. The most dominant of all are the largest families – a pair with five or six young. Geese and swans pair for life and

we have found with barnacle geese that a bird which stays with the same mate is several times as likely to breed successfully in the following year than one which changes its mate through death or separation. This explains why divorce is such a rare event among geese and swans. Just as significantly, the later in the year a separation occurs the less is the chance of breeding. Birds which are not paired in the crucial period when reserves are being laid down for migration and breeding have little or no chance of success. This is one reason why spring shooting can be so damaging to the breeding success of wildfowl.

Goslings inside a family group are fatter than orphaned ones, so presumably they survive better in adverse conditions. Their parents invest time and effort in their care, mainly by taking on the whole of the vigilance burden and allowing the young to feed continuously. The parents do not suffer unduly since being in a larger family unit allows them access to the best feeding because they can displace all smaller groups. It is advantageous, therefore, for all its members to remain in a family during the winter. Conflict occurs in spring, when the parents are preparing for the next breeding effort and they force their young away. In swans and some geese the bonds are, however, so strong that the family reunites again for the following migration and winter season.

During the breeding season the gregariousness disappears to a large extent. Although the patchy food supply or the shortage of good nesting areas may force birds to nest densely, most are territorial, especially when it comes to defending a food supply. Geese protect an area around the nest, and in duck species, drakes may maintain an exclusion zone around their mates to prevent them being disturbed or harassed by other drakes.

If we are to conserve wildfowl, or exploit them without causing damage to their populations, we must understand what makes them what they are and know what their requirements are at all stages of their life cycle. We must give them full protection when they are most vulnerable, such as during prolonged severe weather, and ensure that there is little disturbance to their feeding areas in the build-up to the coming breeding season. Crucially, we must co-operate internationally to make sure that wetlands are available wherever they are needed on the breeding and wintering grounds and along the migration routes between them.

3

MIGRATION OF BRITISH DUCK AND GEESE

COLIN B. SHEDDEN

One may think that an update of Hugh Boyd's chapter in *The New Wildfowler in the 1970s* would be unnecessary, or merely a question of cosmetics, since migration is a fairly stable phenomenon. Fortunately, Boyd himself stated that 'the distribution of birds is a dynamic process so that our knowledge is continuously changing and will probably always be obsolescent'. Consequently, after nineteen years there is a great deal to add to the framework of wildfowl migration he ably laid.

Additionally, he alluded to the developing concept of flight corridors, or flyways, evolving in North America at that time. By transferring this thinking to Europe I hope that a considerable advancement of the state of the science can be achieved, that 'insular impressions' can be put 'in a continental context'. Ideally, therefore, I would hope to allow the modern fowler to put the local arrivals and departures of his migratory quarry in an international context, so that he not only understands but appreciates the complexity and marvel of this topic.

Traditonally, migrations of our ducks and geese have been studied through the collection and analysis of ringing recoveries. Birds ringed as young or adults on their breeding grounds in the spring and summer, or on staging grounds in the autumn, carry their rings to Britain and, if shot or found dead and the ring reported, a general picture of that species' migration can be elucidated. This can be further refined by using both wildfowl counts to pinpoint the areas used as wintering grounds and wing studies, which give a good indication of not only sex ratio but age composition of the migrants as well. Long-established wing studies, particularly in Britain (by the B.A.S.C.) have revealed interesting features about wigeon, for instance, that might otherwise have remained unknown. The current expansion of these studies through the International Waterfowl and Wetlands Research Burerau (IWRB) Wing Research Group is bound, through the initiation of collections in other countries, to reveal more detail on the migration patterns of duck in particular. This contribution to the study of migration by European hunters is greatly appreciated by scientists and those attempting to manage these populations.

On top of this, we now have detailed ornithological studies which generally look at part of a population, or race, of a wildfowl species and attempt to individually colour-ring as many birds as possible. In this way family groups can be studied on their wintering grounds and can also be followed to their breeding grounds and identified there. They can also be located on staging grounds and, therefore, the complete migratory route can be revealed, again with important implications for management. This is especially relevant for some goose populations which are seemingly dependent upon only a few staging or wintering sites.

There are, therefore, a number of ways by which the migratory patterns of our ducks and geese can be revealed, though the base of this is surely ringing studies. It must be remembered that these rely on the amount of effort at the ringing site. A widely scattered and effectively unmarked breeding population of duck in the remote areas of north-east Europe may well be wintering in Britain, but without ringing recoveries we know little of their origins or movements. Therefore, on all figures in this chapter the breeding ranges of these birds are marked to indicate the possible area from which birds could be attracted to Britain as a wintering site. Additionally, wintering ranges are shown, though I suggest looking at the British Trust for Ornithology *Atlas of Wintering Birds in Britain and Ireland* for a more detailed picture of our wintering wildfowl's distribution.

GEESE

British geese can effectively be subdivided into the grey geese, the most important quarry species, and the black geese, which are now, with the exception of the introduced Canada goose, fully protected, though some can be controlled to protect crops.

PINKFOOTED GOOSE *(Anser brachyrhynchus)*

This goose is represented by two discrete breeding populations, one in central Iceland and on the west coast of Greenland and the other on Spitsbergen, north of Norway (Figure 6). Ringing studies have shown that the two populations effectively winter in separate areas; those from Greenland and Iceland in Scotland and England, with only a few in Ireland, and those from Spitsbergen on continental Europe, especially Denmark, West Germany, the Netherlands, Belgium and occasionally northern France. A few individuals of this Spitsbergen population may reach eastern England during periods of severe weather. The Greenland birds leave during early September, join the Icelandic population and normally reach Britain in the first half of October. Departure is usually in April, extending into May.

With this species, it is clear that the British population is almost entirely made up of Icelandic/Greenland birds, which remain broadly faithful to their traditional wintering haunts. Changes do take place, however, in response to food availability and disturbance. In recent years the numbers have increased, with some 170,000 counted in the UK in November 1987. As Britain's most abundant wintering goose, it is not surprising that this is also the most frequently shot goose, the harvest perhaps being about 10% of the population.

The Spitsbergen population is not as large, comprising about 25,000 wintering individuals with a harvest of about 1000 taking place in Denmark.

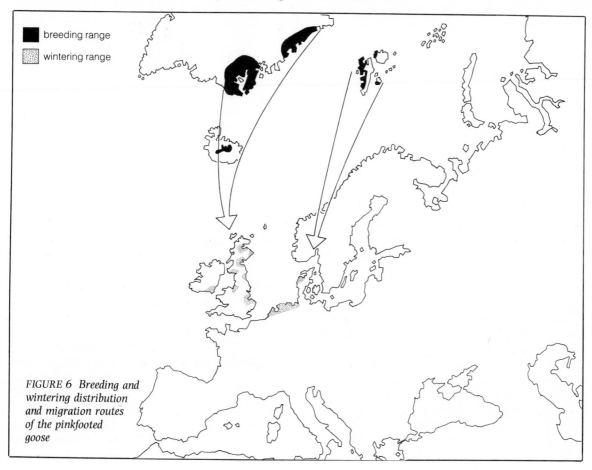

FIGURE 6 *Breeding and wintering distribution and migration routes of the pinkfooted goose*

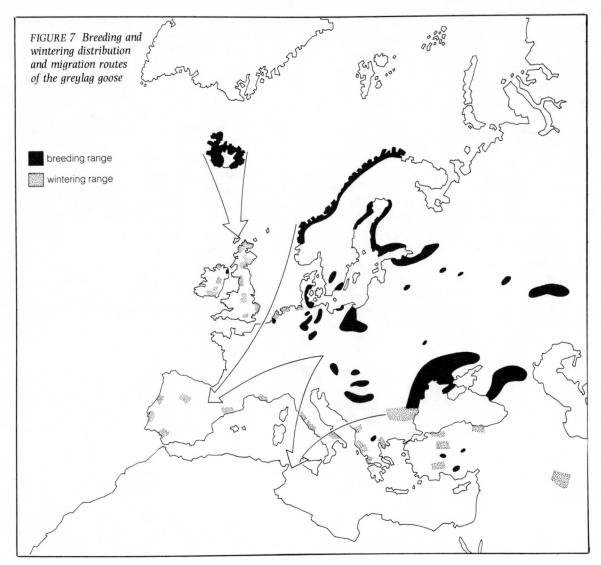

FIGURE 7 Breeding and wintering distribution and migration routes of the greylag goose

breeding range

wintering range

GREYLAG GOOSE (Anser anser)

The greylag is our largest goose, with the exception of the introduced Canada goose, and also our second most abundant wintering species. Like the pinkfoot, Britain's wintering greylag come predominantly from breeding grounds to the north-west rather than from the continental population. The Icelandic population, numbering about 18,000–19,000 pairs, moves to Scotland and northern England in October and November to traditional haunts, where they may mix with home-bred birds (Figure 7). The total wintering population in Britain was some 130,000 in 1987/88, with as many as 30,000 in southern Ireland as well. Greylag tend to leave Britain in March and

April, slightly before the departure of pinkfeet. It is estimated that again about 10 % of these geese are shot annually. However, like the pinkfoot, this population is increasing, thought to be due mainly to reduced shooting mortality and perhaps helped by the greater availability of food in the form of winter cereals.

The continental population is patchily distributed over much of northern and eastern Europe, seemingly breeding on remnants of suitable habitat. A wintering population of approximately 45,000 birds is found extending from the Netherlands to France, Spain and Portugal. Only a few of these continental birds have been known to cross the North Sea and winter in Britain.

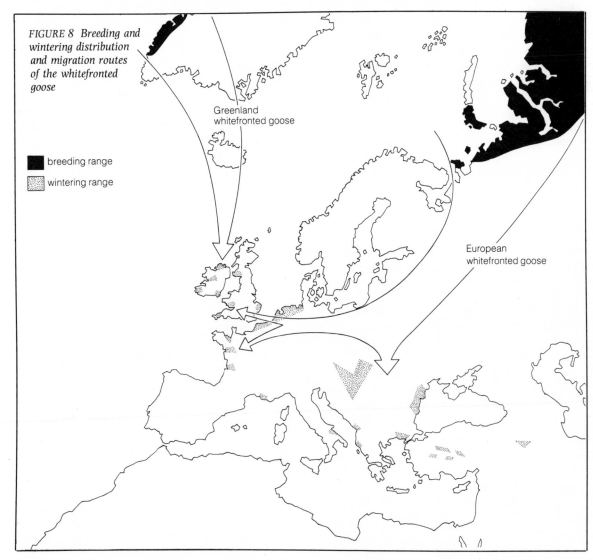

FIGURE 8 Breeding and wintering distribution and migration routes of the whitefronted goose

Greenland whitefronted goose

European whitefronted goose

■ breeding range

░ wintering range

WHITEFRONTED GOOSE (Anser albifrons)

Once again we have here a goose whose population is divided into sub-groups with distinct wintering grounds. The continental population (the European whitefronted goose) breeds entirely in Russia, in the north of that country west of the River Khatanga (Figure 8). In addition, there is a smaller breeding population in south-west Greenland (the Greenland whitefronted goose) which winters in Ireland and western Scotland, with declining numbers in Wales (21,000 birds in total). This smaller population is fully protected in Scotland and Ireland, though a short experimental season was opened in Wexford, Ireland, in the 1985 season. The continental population, number-ing perhaps 150,000 breeding adults, winters in north-west Europe, particularly in the Netherlands, with a small number in England and Wales (5800). These are a quarry species for English and Welsh fowlers who harvest a few hundred per year. The total north-west European wintering population is at least 200,000.

These birds arrive in southern Britain from early October onwards, with return passage starting in March. The Greenland population arrives at the same time, after resting in Iceland. As with all goose species, the wintering numbers depend on the success of the preceding breeding season, and the severity of the winter dictates their movements, either to or indeed from Britain.

The Greenland population is showing little change in numbers, though there may be an underlying decline, whereas the continental population is apparently showing an increase in numbers. How much this is due to a shifting population, favouring the Dutch wintering grounds to those areas traditionally used in Greece, Yugoslavia and Rumania, rather than a genuine population increase, is not yet clear. However, unlike the other grey geese, the Greenland population is protected while the continental population does winter in small numbers in the UK and is a quarry species.

BARNACLE GOOSE *(Branta leucopsis)*

Although not a quarry species since full, year-round, protection was afforded in 1954, this species is still of great interest to fowlers due to its prominent place in the history of the sport. Three distinct breeding populations exist, two of which rely on northern Britain and Ireland for their wintering grounds. The eastern Greenland popu-lation, which in winter numbers 24,000, spends these months entirely in the west of Scotland and Ireland, after stopping off in Iceland at the end of September/early October (Figure 9). Their arrival in Scotland usually occurs in late October. The traditional haunts of the Hebrides are the main sites used, especially the islands of Islay and Colonsay. The more northerly Spitsbergen population winters entirely on the Solway Firth, concentrated around the Caerlaverock National Nature Reserve. Over 5000 individuals have been counted on this one estuary. They arrive in Scotland earlier than the Greenland population, usually late September/early October. Their departure is usually in the second half of April.

The Russian population which breeds on Novaya Zemlya and Vaygach Island, winters primarily in the Netherlands, though severe weather can and does drive them south, although not to Britain. This sub-population can number as many as 45,000 individuals.

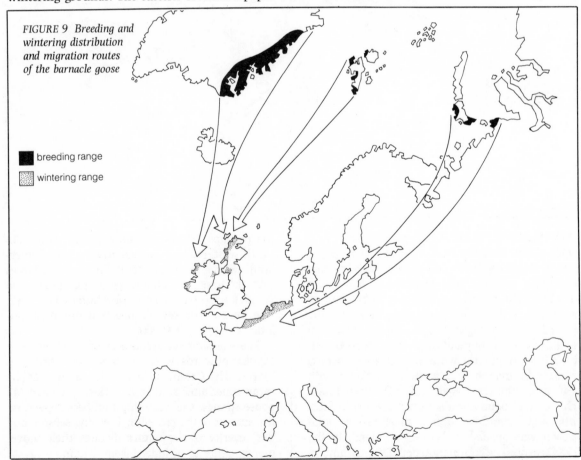

FIGURE 9 *Breeding and wintering distribution and migration routes of the barnacle goose*

■ breeding range

▨ wintering range

BRENT GOOSE (*Branta bernicla*)

Again, this goose is not a quarry species in the UK, though moves are afoot to have its former quarry status reinstated. This is the result of a substantial increase in one of its races, the darkbellied brent (*Branta bernicla bernicla*), from a population low of 16,500 in 1955 to around 180,000 in the 1980s.

The darkbellied race breeds in the high north tundra of western Siberia and winters around the North Sea, with about half of the population in south-east England and the rest in the Netherlands and west France (Figure 10). They arrive in Denmark in October and then move on to their wintering grounds. Their return begins from England in March, gathering on islands off the German/Dutch/Danish coast until the main departures in mid-May.

The other population, the lightbellied brent (*Branta bernicla hrota*), breeds in north Greenland and arctic Canada and winters in Ireland (currecently some 19,000), particularly on Strangford Lough (about 15,000). The importance of Canadian birds to this migration has only just been realised, it generally being assumed that all North American birds wintered on that continent. Additionally, another lightbellied population – on Spitsbergen and Franz Joseph Land – moves to Denmark in September/October and thence to Lindisfarne on the Northumberland coast. Extreme weather in Denmark pushes the majority of this population, which recently numbered 3400 birds, to Lindisfarne which, in recent years, has regularly been used by up to 3000 birds.

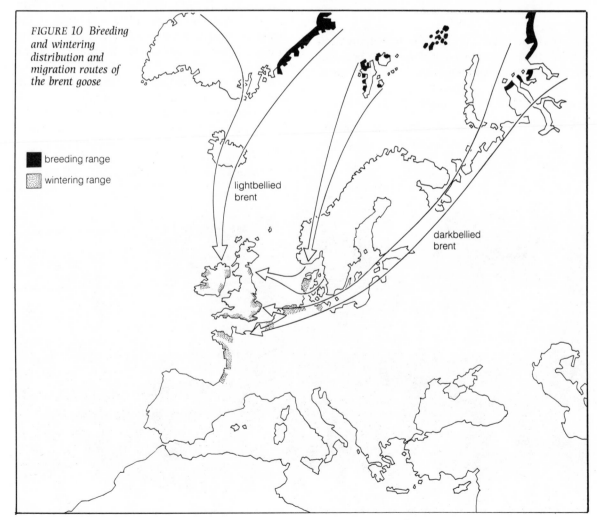

FIGURE 10 Breeding and wintering distribution and migration routes of the brent goose

breeding range
wintering range

lightbellied brent

darkbellied brent

CANADA GOOSE *(Branta canadensis)*

Although this bird is regarded as migratory in North America and vagrants may even turn up in Ireland and the west of Scotland, the introduced British population is largely sedentary, though groups do show northward moult migrations. This is especially the case for Yorkshire non-breeders which have regularly moved to the Beauly Firth since 1950 in April/May, returning in August/September. The British population is expanding rapidly and has exceeded 40,000 birds, particularly in the southern half of the country.

On the Continent, Swedish breeding birds migrate to Germany and the Netherlands in November, returning in March. Other small populations exist in Norway and Finland, with smaller numbers in France and the Netherlands.

DUCK

Whereas the geese that migrate to Britain each winter have reasonably well-defined breeding areas, the same cannot be said for the duck. Iceland, Greenland, Scandinavia, eastern Europe and the high Russian tundra all hold widely scattered breeding populations which are assumed to migrate to Britain. Ringing studies give an indication of the range of these breeding populations and the known areas from whence the British duck have come, but there are still many unknowns when it comes to breeding ranges, the sizes of these populations and their actual migratory routes.

WIGEON *(Anas penelope)*

Although perhaps 400 pairs of wigeon breed in northern Britain, perhaps some 400,000 individuals of this species over-winter on our major estuaries and inland marshes. Their breeding distribution is extensive, ranging from Iceland, through Britain, to Norway, Sweden and Finland, and then eastwards over much of northern Russia (Figure 11). The total winter population of over one million birds ranges widely over much of the North Sea and Atlantic coastline, as well as having concentrations around the Mediterranean and the Black Sea.

Most of the Icelandic population is known to winter in Britain and Ireland, though a few move as far as the Low Countries, France and Spain. The bulk of our birds come, however, from Scandinavia

Wigeon flushed from a saltmarsh gutter (Julian Novorol)

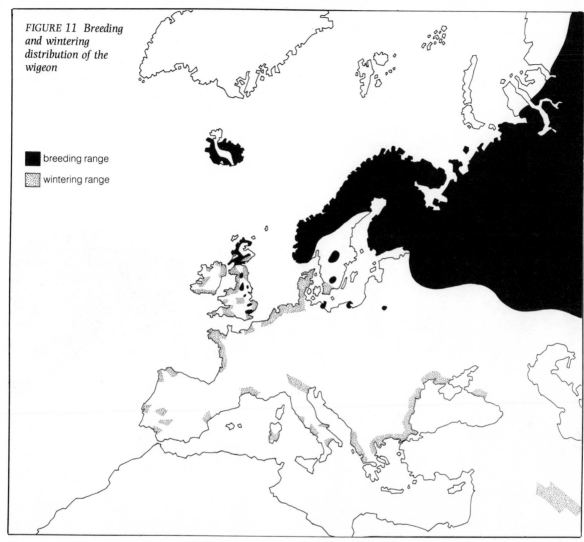

FIGURE 11 Breeding and wintering distribution of the wigeon

■ breeding range
▧ wintering range

and Russia, as far east as the Yenisay Basin, and those breeding farther to the east in central Siberia winter around the Black Sea and the Mediterranean. Males generally leave their breeding grounds first, joining non-breeders in moulting localities and eventually reaching wintering grounds in October/November. Females then catch up with them, but overfly to winter farther south in Europe, probably as a result of competition between the sexes. This behaviour was first revealed by the B.A.S.C. wing studies and has been confirmed since by ringing recoveries. The peak British count is usually in January, this being due to our mid-winter influx of continental-wintering birds, pushed across the North Sea by the colder continental climate. Departure for

breeding grounds typically takes place in mid-March to early April, though in mild winters this can take place earlier.

The importance of this species to the coastal fowler needs no emphasis, since at least 70,000 are shot annually. Its status is relatively unchanged in western Europe, though this in itself may be of some concern since most other dabbling ducks have been increasing over the past fifteen years. Local shifts in population, particularly in relation to sanctuary areas, affect their regional abundance. The shooting of wigeon, more than any other duck species, is very closely related to their migratory pattern, and more particularly to their movement in response to severe weather in north continental Europe.

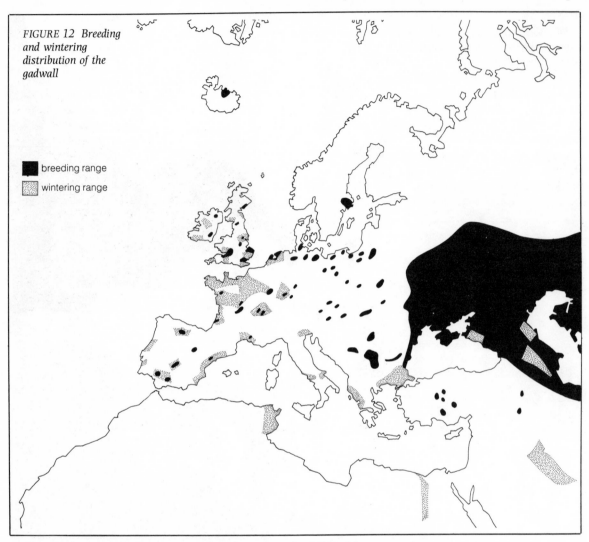

FIGURE 12 Breeding and wintering distribution of the gadwall

breeding range
wintering range

GADWALL (Anas strepera)

This duck is infrequently encountered by wildfowlers in Britain, since it is estimated that fewer than 3000 winter here. Most of the birds that come here to join our native stock (500 pairs) do so from the Netherlands and central Europe, with a small number from Iceland (Figure 12). The breeding range of this species is patchily distributed over central Europe, though is more continuous in southern Russia. The bulk of these Russian birds winter in the Black Sea/Mediterranean area where it is estimated that there are 50,000 individuals, compared to only 10,000 in north-west Europe. Gadwall are, however, one of the world's most numerous wildfowl species with vast numbers in North America and Asia.

TEAL (Anas crecca)

The teal breeds in Britain, perhaps around 3000 pairs doing so each year, but wildfowlers rely greatly on migratory birds from the rest of Europe.

Its breeding range is extensive, covering most of northern Europe and Iceland (Figure 13). These birds extend from Iceland and Britain, through north-western Europe, all of Scandinavia and most of Russia. Breeding numbers are hard to ascertain, due to its dispersed distribution and generally inconspicuous behaviour, but there are thought to be at least one million breeding birds in Europe.

Ringing has revealed a number of overlapping flyways. Icelandic birds winter almost exclusively in Britain and Ireland, and those from northern Russia, the Baltic and Scandinavia winter around the North Sea (chiefly in Britain and the Netherlands), whilst others from west central Russia and west Siberia also migrate south-west but through central Europe to Spain, France and Italy. Those birds breeding in central Russia and the Ukraine have a flyway running through the Black Sea to Greece and western Turkey, and those from central and southern USSR to Iraq and Iran. During migration males tend to arrive before females, generally in October/November for most of Europe. The bulk of the return migration occurs in March and April. Consequently, and in summary, our teal come from Iceland, Scandinavia, the Baltic states

and north-west Russia, northern Poland and northern Germany.

Numbers and distribution of this duck can be markedly affected by severe winter weather, as with the case in 1978/79 when the numbers wintering in Spain increased dramatically. It was thought that these birds came from north-west Europe. Closer to home, the severity of continental weather dictates to a great extent the numbers of birds in Britain. In mild winters as many as 50 % of the north-west European population will remain on the Continent, north of Belgium, with just 40 % in Britain and Ireland. In severe weather only 13 %

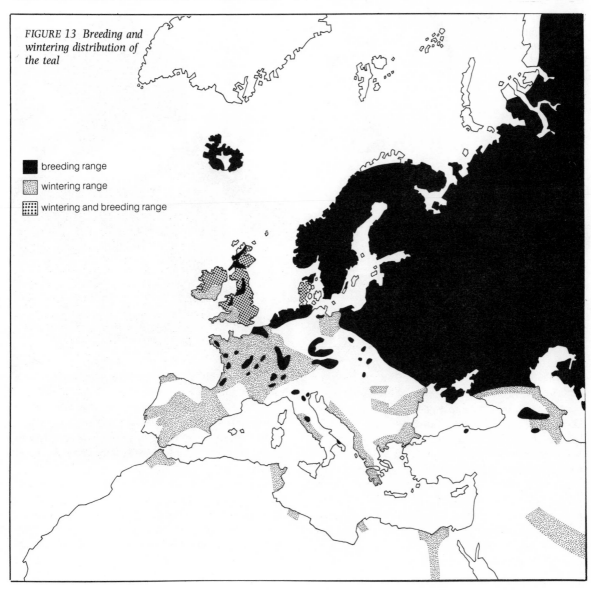

FIGURE 13 Breeding and wintering distribution of the teal

breeding range
wintering range
wintering and breeding range

may be left on the Continent, more than 50% in Britain and Ireland, while the rest move to French and Spanish coastal areas.

Although our smallest duck, the teal is clearly very mobile and its normal migration can be greatly affected by climate. A good series of mild winters clearly helped this species, whose population in north-west Europe has increased by 178% between 1967 and 1983. This is remarkable, considering the threat that much of its favoured habitat is faced with, and shows a little of the species' adaptability.

MALLARD (*Anas platyrhynchos*)

As our commonest breeding duck, wintering duck and wildfowl quarry species, the mallard surely deserves particular attention. We can estimate (for the UK) 200,000 breeding birds, at least 500,000 counted wintering birds (in mid-winter) and perhaps 700,000 birds shot each year. These figures clearly display a discrepancy between the numbers wintering and the numbers actually shot, but when one takes into consideration turnover of migratory and migrating birds through the season, the fact that many are shot early in the

FIGURE 14 Breeding and wintering distribution of the mallard

■ breeding range

▨ wintering range

▦ wintering and breeding range

season, as well as the large numbers of hand-reared mallard released into the wild for sporting purposes (estimates here range between 300,000 and 500,000 per annum), our understanding of the situation is clarified. At the European level the mallard is the most abundant wildfowl species. Its wintering range overlaps its breeding range, with many breeding birds, especially those of south-west Europe, being largely resident (Figure 14). Birds from Scandinavia, the Baltic countries and north-west USSR winter in Denmark, south and west France and Britain. The Icelandic birds again follow the normal path and winter in Britain and Ireland. Central European birds tend to move to the Mediterranean and the Adriatic, while some go as far as North Africa. The mallard's tolerance to inclement conditions is such that the birds do not peak on their wintering grounds till November/December, and they depart as early as February.

Extensive ringing of this species has shown that the mallard, within Europe, uses numerous flyways from breeding to wintering areas, but that the overlap between breeding and wintering populations, as well as overlap of wintering ranges, makes clear definition of these flyways difficult. Birds wintering in Britain may therefore be birds that breed, or were bred, in either Britain itself, Iceland, north-west Russia, Scandinavia, or the Baltic regions, including north Poland and north Germany. Those birds breeding farther to the east tend to winter around the Black Sea, Adriatic coast, Mediterranean and even North Africa, including Egypt, and those that breed even farther east, well into Russia, are known to winter around the Caspian Sea and into Iran, Iraq and the Persian Gulf. Of all of these eastern and southern countries, Rumania is thought to hold 21% of the wintering population, with 8% in Bulgaria, 3% in Greece, 6% in Turkey, 17% in Hungary and 5% in southern France.

Therefore, mallard migration shows a broad front moving from northern/central Europe to wintering grounds as far apart as Britain and Denmark to Iraq and Egypt. The concept of flight corridors could therefore be superimposed upon this migration, dividing it into three ranges covering the western European flyway, the central European flyway and the eastern European flyway. However, there will always be overlap between adjoining flyways and distinct geograph-

ical boundaries could never be drawn. It was estimated in 1982 that three million mallard existed in the north-west European component of this population with a further two million in the more eastern component. The western population is known to be increasing, while at present the southern European/eastern population is stable. But the enormous numbers of hand-reared birds released makes the mallard a very difficult species to describe in these terms with any certainty.

PINTAIL (Anas acuta)

Unlike the duck species already discussed, the pintail's winter distribution within Britain is patchy, concentrating around our major estuaries. Our breeding numbers are low and consequently all sport is provided by migratory individuals.

Once again, Icelandic birds migrate to Britain and Ireland, though some of these birds move farther on to the Continent (Figure 15). However, the bulk of the birds wintering in Britain originate in Sweden, Finland and northern Russia, as far east as north-west Siberia and as far south as the Baltic states. The bulk of these birds, as many as 50,000, winter predominantly in the UK and the Netherlands, but some move farther south to France, Spain, Portugal, Italy and even north-west Africa. The bulk of the breeding population in eastern and central USSR winters around the eastern Mediterranean, Black and Caspian Seas, Africa and as far as the Indian sub-continent. Greece and Turkey are notable for their large wintering populations. Additionally, a small number of Canadian ringed birds have been recovered in Britain, indicating perhaps that a larger number of birds regularly undertake this long migration, than has been thought.

The timing of migration is from mid-August to early September from both breeding grounds and moulting areas, with a peak from mid-September to November. Wing collections have shown that males arrive before the females. Like most duck species, further movements can be dictated by periods of severe weather. Departure from the UK wintering grounds takes place towards the end of February or March.

Although this is not a numerically important species from the fowler's point of view, comprising under 2% of their total duck bag, it is locally an important quarry species. The north-west European population does fluctuate in numbers,

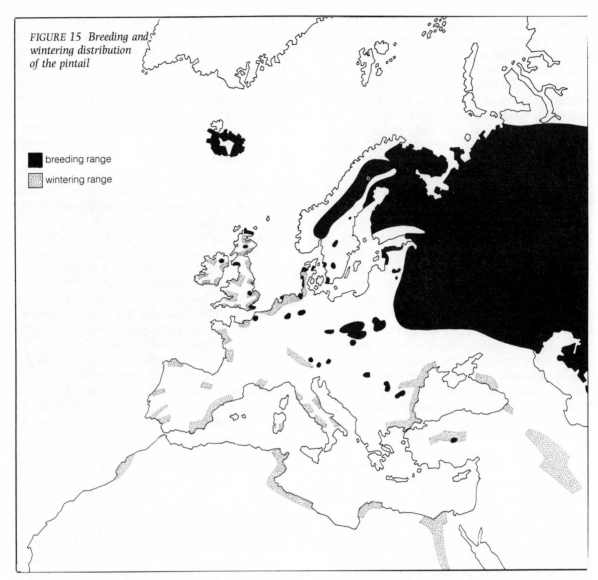

FIGURE 15 Breeding and wintering distribution of the pintail

■ breeding range

▨ wintering range

related to the severity of the winter to a great extent, but it is reassuring that there have been recent increases in the numbers. However, the southern European population, though much larger than the north-west European one, has shown a decline in recent years.

SHOVELER (Anas clypeata)

Although a more common breeding bird in Britain than the pintail, it is less common in winter. Two hundred and fifty pairs breed in Britain and yet our wintering birds only number 6700. It is thought that the small Icelandic population of between 30–60 pairs winters in Britain or Ireland, but at the same time our breeding population moves to southern France and Spain, northern and central Italy and even as far as Africa (Figure 16). After our birds have left (by the end of October) the main arrivals of birds from Scandinavia and west USSR begins. These birds winter in the Netherlands, Britain and Ireland, extending down to France and the north of Spain. Therefore, the pattern of migration of shoveler to Britain closely follows the pattern we have already seen for most of our other ducks.

The bulk of Europe's breeding population from much of central and southern USSR winter around

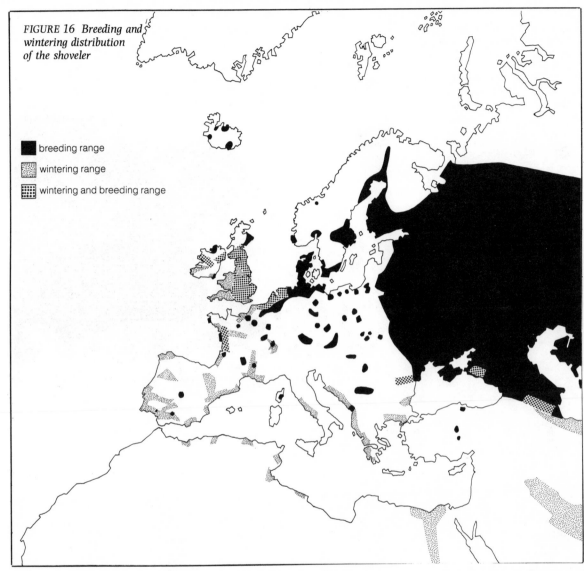

FIGURE 16 *Breeding and wintering distribution of the shoveler*

breeding range

wintering range

wintering and breeding range

the Caspian, Black and Azor Seas, and in the Mediterranean countries of Turkey, Greece and Italy. There is, however, overlap between the two flyways when birds from each intermingle in North Africa and, to a lesser extent, in the Mediterranean.

The early migration of this species (chiefly through Europe in September/October) reflects a degree of reduced tolerance to severe weather compared to other species of duck, and its preference for more southerly wintering grounds is greater than among other species. Overall, the species is doing well in Europe, showing one of the largest increases of all European waterfowl. This is reflected in the increasing mid-winter population in Britain as well.

POCHARD *(Aythya ferina)*

Although diving duck differ greatly in their behaviour from dabbling duck, once again their migration reflects much of what we have seen already. Since only 400 pairs of pochard breed in Britain our wintering population of around 45,000 birds (16% of the north-west European population) is migratory, coming chiefly from southern Scandinavia including Denmark, north Germany, Poland, the Baltic states and western Russia (Figure 17). This breeding population also winters

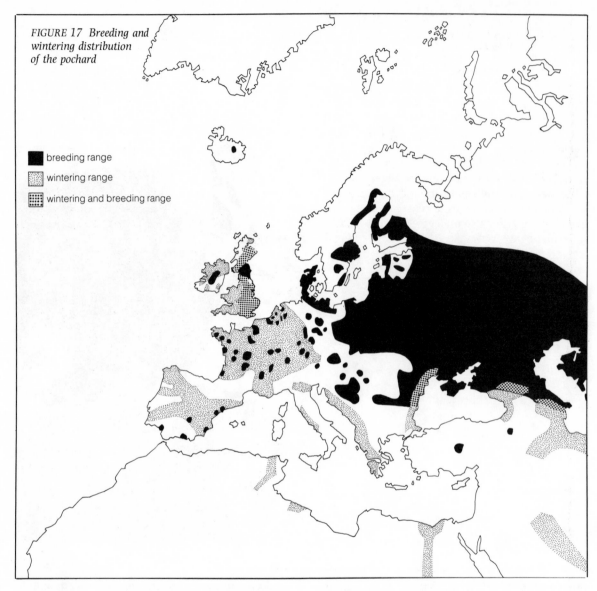

FIGURE 17 Breeding and wintering distribution of the pochard

breeding range
wintering range
wintering and breeding range

in other parts of western Europe, central Europe, Spain and Portugal. The extent of the movements of our own breeding birds is uncertain, but some are known to migrate south at least to France. The bulk of the continental breeding population (found in central USSR) winters in Tunisia, Greece, Turkey and around the Black Sea.

Once more the males tend to migrate about two weeks before the females. Migration is usually in October/November in western Europe, a little earlier in central and eastern Europe. The males and the females are often geographically separated

by their migratory behaviour, in that the males tend to become established at the first suitable waters they reach, the later-arriving females moving farther to find suitable habitat. The return to the breeding grounds takes place in March/early April.

Overall, this species has declined slightly in Europe in recent years despite an overall increase in suitable wintering habitat, i.e. reservoirs and gravel pits. Severe winters obviously take their toll, but factors affecting the breeding grounds may also be responsible.

TUFTED DUCK *(Aythya fuligula)*

As our commonest breeding diving duck, and the diving duck most commonly encountered by the fowler in Britain, the tufted duck is undoubtedly popular, both from a sporting and general interest point of view. With 5000 breeding pairs in Britain, a population which is increasing, we once again rely greatly on migratory birds for most of our wildfowling.

The large Icelandic population (the tufted duck is probably the most abundant freshwater duck in Iceland) mainly moves to Ireland in the winter, though some do come as far east as Britain. The British population also undergoes some migratory movement, with the Scottish birds moving to Ireland, while the majority of English birds remain sedentary. Again the bulk of the north-west European population from Scandinavia, the Baltic region, Poland and Germany migrate south-west to the Netherlands, Britain and Ireland (Figure 18).

Movement as far south as Spain and Portugal is not uncommon, especially during severe winters. Those breeding in central and south USSR and west Siberia use the Mediterranean and Black Sea areas as wintering grounds, especially around Greece and Turkey. Both sexes start arriving in winter quarters in early October, although in Britain the peak numbers may not be reached until January/February, as they may be pushed out of wintering grounds on the Continent by cold weather. Between late February and mid April the return migration is undertaken, the males preceding the females. Unlike pochard, the tufted duck has taken full advantage of new habitats in Europe and, in conjunction with the spread of the zebra mussel (an important food source), this duck has shown a dramatic increase in numbers in countries such as Switzerland. Overall in Europe the numbers are stable.

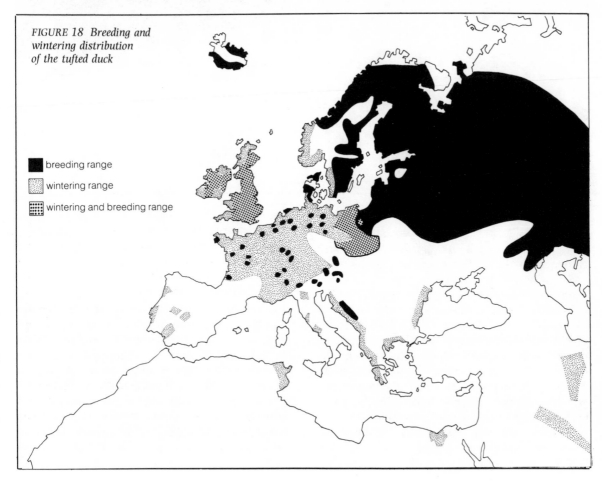

FIGURE 18 *Breeding and wintering distribution of the tufted duck*

■ breeding range

▨ wintering range

▦ wintering and breeding range

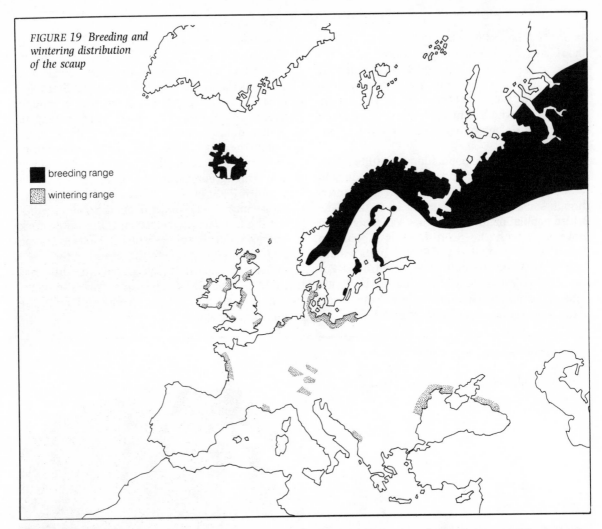

FIGURE 19 Breeding and wintering distribution of the scaup

breeding range

wintering range

SCAUP (Aythya marila)

Although no longer a quarry species in Britain, this duck is still shot in Northern Ireland and consequently deserves inclusion in this chapter.

Scaup are very much a species of northern climes, as seen from its breeding range covering only Iceland and northern and Baltic coasts of Norway, Sweden, Finland and USSR (Figure 19). The Icelandic population moves to Britain, Ireland and the Netherlands, as well as a few to Denmark, France and Germany. Some Scandinavian birds may stay on nearby coasts over the winter months, but most of these northerly breeding birds winter in the west Baltic and in cold winters move to the Netherlands, the east coast of Britain and France. Others move overland to winter in the east of the Mediterranean around Yugoslavia and west

Turkey with many birds from west Siberia in the Black Sea area. Birds do not arrive on British coasts until late October, returning to their breeding grounds in mid-March.

GOLDENEYE (Bucephala clangula)

The goldeneye is another diving duck of northern climes, both in breeding and wintering range. Absent in Iceland, it does breed in small numbers in Scotland (15 pairs), but the bulk of Europe's breeding population is found on forest lakes in Norway, Sweden, Finland and USSR (Figure 20). The western component of this population winters around the Baltic (in mild winters), Denmark, the Netherlands, Britain and Ireland, with small numbers extending through Belgium to southern France. Central Russian birds winter in south

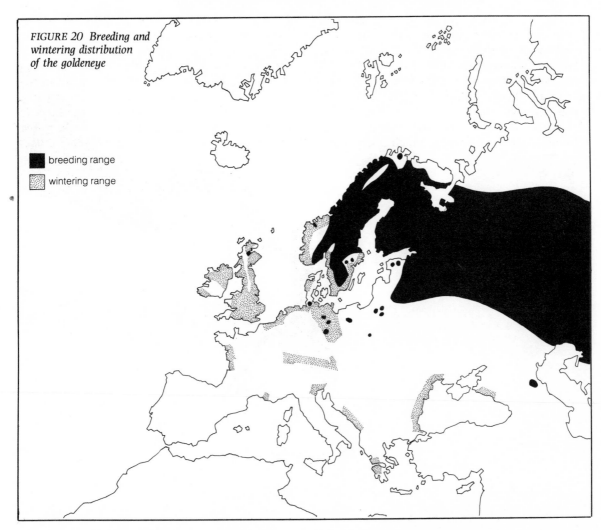

FIGURE 20 *Breeding and wintering distribution of the goldeneye*

■ breeding range
▓ wintering range

Russia around the Black Sea and in Greece, Turkey and around the Caspian Sea.

Autumn migration begins in late August, though in North Sea areas the peak is not reached until November. Interestingly, adult males move the least distance and the juveniles move the greatest distance. Most wintering areas are abandoned by the end of March. Goldeneye numbers in Europe have been stable over the past couple of decades, but there is now concern that breeding populations in Scandinavia may be affected by the acidification of their lakeland habitat.

DISCUSSION

This brief summary of the migration of our quarry species does, I hope, put the important role that Britain plays as a passage and wintering area for waterfowl into context. Furthermore, I hope that it gives the wildfowler a deeper understanding of the migratory behaviour of his quarry, not only to increase his knowledge when out on the foreshore or marsh, but also to increase his understanding of these birds when he is involved in conservation planning and management, as most modern wildfowlers are.

This explanation of the concept of flyways hopefully will make him or her more readily aware of the possible origins of birds either in the field or in the bag. A summary of this concept could be constructed to separate the flyways into those from (a) Greenland/Iceland to Ireland and Britain and thence on to western and southern continental Europe; (b) Scandinavia, north Russia and Siberia, down through the Baltic and north-west Europe to Britain; (c) western Russia and the Baltic states through north-west Europe to Britain and Ireland; (d) western Russia and Baltic states through north-west and central Europe to the western Mediterranean and North Africa; (e) central and south Russia through the Black Sea to the eastern Mediterranean, Red Sea and North Africa. Although there is, of course, much interchange between these flyways, they are distinct enough to serve some useful purposes. The main purpose in this chapter is to illustrate the importance of Icelandic, Scandinavian, Baltic and north and west Russian birds to the fowler in Britain and to ensure that the necessary management of these populations at the international level continues to benefit not only these birds but all that enjoy their arrival on our shores each autumn and winter.

4

POPULATION DYNAMICS OF WILDFOWL

DAVID HILL

What do the words 'population dynamics' mean? 'Population' is the collective noun defining the number of inhabitants of a given area. 'Dynamics' implies movement either in the total size of the population or of certain classes of inhabitants or of any other quantitative aspect of the population.

Populations change in size from year to year as a result of recruitment, i.e. the production of young, and mortality, i.e. losses due to death. An imbalance between them will result in increase or decrease. Other factors also apply. Immigrants may arrive to add to winter populations and some of these may try subsequently to breed. Others emigrate and may not return. Such 'dispersal' has an important role to play in determining numbers in a breeding population – which is usually the starting point for population dynamics studies.

Additionally, the larger species of wildfowl such as swans and geese exhibit delayed maturity. They do not breed while nesting sites are filled by established breeders. They have to wait for a site to fall vacant. Removal of established breeders allows less experienced birds to take up a place in the breeding sector of the population. The workings of these factors and their interrelations constitute the 'dynamics' of populations.

An understanding of the population dynamics of quarry species is fundamental to determining the effects of shooting on populations. If, as some believe, shooting losses simply add to natural mortality and are not compensated by a decline in natural mortality (that is compensatory survival), a cessation of shooting would lead to an increase in survival and an increase in the breeding population. If, however, compensation occurs, the breeding population is unaffected. Breeding numbers will be set by other factors. The factors which thus 'regulate' populations are those which ecologists describe as 'density dependent'. They cause recruitment or mortality to change at a rate which is disproportionate to any change in population numbers. Thus, if the population doubles in size mortality triples, thus preventing increase. If the population falls to half, recruitment per breeding female goes up, thus preventing decline. Compensatory survival relies on such density-dependent factors.

This chapter aims to outline the general population dynamics of wildfowl. While this draws mainly on studies of mallard, the implications for harvesting wildfowl populations in general are also discussed.

Table 1: Estimates of winter and breeding populations of wildfowl in Britain and Ireland (Sources: Lack 1986, Sharrock 1976)

Species	Winter	Breeding
Mute swan	20,000	5000–6000[5]
Bewick's swan	16,000–16,500[4]	0
Whooper swan	5000–6000[1]	0
Bean goose	200–300	0
Pinkfooted goose	101,000	0
Whitefronted goose (Greenland)	16,000–17,000	0
Whitefronted goose (European)	6000[2]	0
Greylag goose	100,000	700–800
Canada goose	30,000–35,000[4]	10,500[1,4]
Barnacle goose	33,000[4]	0
Brent goose (lightbellied)	610	0
Brent goose (darkbellied)	92,600[4]	0
Shelduck	65,000–73,000[4]	20,000[5]
Wigeon	300,000–350,000	600–1000
Gadwall	4000[2,4]	500
Garganey	0	100–200
Teal	130,000–250,000[4]	7000–12,000
Mallard	600,000[1,3]	140,000–300,000
Pintail	32,000[1]	100
Shoveler	17,000[4]	2000
Pochard	80,000	400–800
Tufted duck	60,000–80,000[4]	12,000–14,000[4]
Scaup	5000–10,000[6]	10
Eider	72,000	30,000–50,000
Longtailed duck	20,000	0
Common scoter	25,000–30,000	300–400
Velvet scoter	2500–5000	0
Goldeneye	10,000–15,000[4]	10
Smew	100[6]	0
Redbreasted merganser	11,000[4]	4000–6000
Goosander	5000[4]	2000–4000
Ruddy duck	1380[4]	350[1]

1 – Definitive underestimate
2 – Marked between-year variations
3 – Influenced by the release of hand-reared birds
4 – Increasing dramatically
5 – Excludes non-breeders
6 – Decreasing

POPULATION SIZE

Britain and Ireland are host to some thirty-two regularly occurring species of wildfowl during the winter months, twenty of which have resident breeding populations (Table 1). Numbers of all species are boosted in winter by immigrants from Scandinavia, Iceland, Greenland, USSR and other parts of the Continent. Many individuals of our resident breeding species leave in winter, particularly during hard weather, to visit parts of southern Europe and North Africa, where conditions are less harsh.

The wintering populations of some species are relatively 'closed', that is to say that very few foreign birds join breeding birds on their winter quarters in Britain and Ireland. An obvious example of this is the Canada goose, in which the winter population is composed of surviving breeding birds, surviving non-breeding individuals, and the year's production of young. At the other extreme our rarer British breeding species of wildfowl may be joined by a large influx of migrants during the winter. An example is the wigeon, in which a 600–1000 breeding population is joined by a large influx of individuals migrating from their northern breeding grounds stretching from Iceland to the Russian Urals, making a total winter maximum population of perhaps 400,000 birds.

According to the Wildfowl Trust's National Wildfowl Counts most species have shown some increases in Britain and Ireland during the past two decades. Little, however, is known of whether this is a true increase or the result of other factors such as habitat losses elsewhere in their range. Mallard and tufted duck have readily exploited the recent expansion of water bodies such as gravel pits and reservoirs. Increases have occurred not only in winter but also in breeding populations, as shown by the National Wildfowl Counts for March and the farmland Common Bird Census conducted by the British Trust for Ornithology.

The importance of long-term counting and survey programmes will be stressed later, when we consider the dynamics of harvesting and the identification of trends in population numbers.

ANNUAL SURVIVAL AND BREEDING PERFORMANCE

The evolution of species has resulted in an infinite variety of 'strategies' for survival and success, not least in wildfowl. In general the life history strategies of wildfowl species range, for example, from those with large body weight (high annual survival, small clutch size and delayed maturity) to small body weight (low annual survival, large clutch size and breeding maturity reached at one year of age). Some data for regular breeding species in Britain and Ireland are given in Table 2. For example, eiders, weighing an average of 2250 g (males) and 2000 g (females) have an annual survival of 80%, lay an average of 4.6 eggs with 75% of nests hatching successfully and do not

Table 2: Survival rates, weight and various breeding statistics for 19 species of wildfowl (after Cramp & Simmons, 1977)

Species	Annual survival rate (%)	Weight (g) ♂	♀	Mean clutch size	Nest success (%)	Hatched young reaching fledging (%)	Delayed maturity
Mute swan	72	11,000	9000	5.5	58	50	✓
Canada goose	78	4800	4400	5.9	55	65	✓
Greylag goose	72–76	3500	3100	5.9	nd*	69	✓
Eider	80	2250	2000	4.6	75	25	✓
Goosander	60	1600	1400	9.4	72	68	✓
Redbreasted merganser	nd*	1200	950	9.2	77	20	✓
Shelduck	80	1300	1150	9.0	76	24	✓
Common scoter	76	1100	1050	7.0	82	nd*	✓
Mallard	52	1100	980	9.6	68	55	—
Goldeneye	63	1050	730	9.3	51	51	✓
Scaup	48	1000	1100	9.7	68	nd*	—
Pochard	55	900	800	9.0	56	62	—
Pintail	52	850	750	8.3	76	56	—
Tufted duck	54	800	700	10.5	57	30	—
Gadwall	nd*	800	650	10.0	60	60	—
Wigeon	47	750	550	9.0	55	34	—
Shoveler	56	650	550	9.2	54	24	—
Garganey	nd*	400	350	9.0	nd*	nd*	—
Teal	47	350	300	10.0	nd*	45	—

*no data

reach breeding maturity until three years of age (sometimes two years in females). They have life history strategies more akin to seabirds than to duck. By contrast teal which weigh 350 g (males) and 300 g (females) have an annual survival rate of 47 %, lay an average of ten eggs, and breed at one year of age.

These differences in breeding performance and life history strategy are compounded by other factors. In some years eider ducklings, for example, may suffer heavy mortality during their first two or so weeks as a result of food shortage. Female eider may not even breed when the likelihood of success is small and the cost of failure could affect the following year's production (Coulson, 1984). Differences may exist between individuals of the same species in different habitats and parts of the breeding range. For example, mallard breeding on flooded gravel quarries, which are generally poor in food for young ducklings, exhibit lower productivity than those breeding on insect-rich chalk streams in southern England (Hill, Wright and Street, 1987).

Breeding performance is, of course, affected by a large number of factors, such as nest success, duckling survival and predation. In order to look at these factors in operation we shall examine a species in more detail.

One of the most widely studied wildfowl species is the mallard. It has a distribution covering the middle latitudes of the western Palearctic from arctic tundra to the sub-tropical zone, and its commonness, together with its popularity with sportsmen, has made it one of the best known of all wildfowl.

In Britain the mallard breeds on lakes, rivers and farmland. From a survey of shooting activities conducted by the British Association of Shooting and Conservation, it was estimated that mallard constitute 60 % of the 875,000 ducks shot annually in Britain during the winter months, the majority being shot inland (Harradine, 1983). Approximately one-third of these are thought to be wild birds, the rest having been reared and released.

In order to quantify both the mortality which causes the main fluctuations in numbers, and the survival which is most able to compensate for additional losses, data were analysed for the numbers and productivity of mallard breeding on the Sevenoaks Wildfowl Reserve, covering the 15-year period 1962–76 inclusive (see Hill, 1984).

The annual counts conducted by Jeffery Harrison consisted of (1) the number of breeding pairs; (2) the number of broods hatching; (3) the number of fledged young produced from those broods and (4) records of carrion crows and foxes killed on the reserve.

There were three main stages at which mortality was known to occur: predation of the clutch, mortality of ducklings and overwinter loss of adults. For convenience of analysis overwinter loss was considered to include all unknown natural mortality. In order to find out which of these factors were density dependent mortalities can be expressed as 'k' values (obtained by mathematical calculation outside the scope of this chapter, but which, in effect, define the proportion of a population surviving a mortality-causing factor). The calculation of 'k' values is a fundamental first step in any population dynamics study.

Immigration to the Sevenoaks Reserve of more northerly breeding birds from northern Britain, Scandinavia, Iceland and parts of Siberia occurs from October onwards. These birds spend the winter months in southern England along with resident birds which only exhibit short-range movement in severe weather (Boyd and Ogilvie, 1961). Northward emigration is usually completed by early March, although this can be delayed in cold weather.

Tuite (1981) showed that in most years mallard numbers in September were not influenced by immigration. He further showed that the percentage of sites on which mallard were present was very similar in March to that in April through to July. Harrison counted paired mallard on the Sevenoaks reserve in late March to mid-April. The estimates of overwinter loss are therefore considered reliable because migrants were excluded. With the kind permission of the Wildfowl Trust, I have analysed, and shall present, overwinter loss values for 35 other lakes on which counts under the National Wildfowl Count Scheme were conducted (Atkinson-Willes, 1958, Atkinson-Willes and Frith, 1964). I chose sites on the basis of at least seven years' continual data during the period 1960–80.

Figure 21 shows that the number of breeding pairs of mallard increased at Sevenoaks after the majority of gravel extraction ceased. This growth is characteristic of populations following colonisation of habitat, where available habitat had

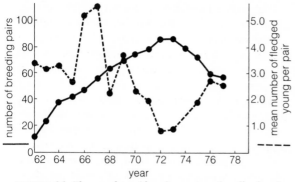

FIGURE 21 *The number of breeding pairs of mallard and the mean number of young produced per pair at Sevenoaks during 1962–77*

previously been fully occupied. At Sevenoaks the breeding mallard population peaked in 1972 and 1973, thereafter it declined to about 50 pairs. The number of young fledged per pair declined over the period, indicating that losses of young (or the production of fewer young) were related to breeding density (Figure 21). In order to investigate this, annual individual mortalities and total mortality (sums of the different mortalities for each year) are

FIGURE 22 *Key factor analysis of the Sevenoaks mallard population*

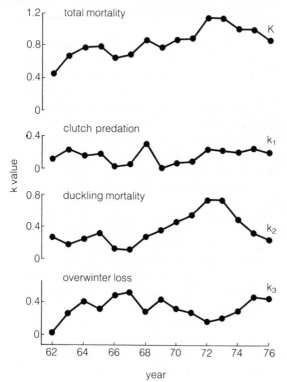

presented in Figure 22. Total mortality (K) was highest in 1972 and 1973, due mainly to high duckling mortality (k_2).

Clutch predation (k_1) was weakly correlated with total mortality, while duckling mortality was the key factor, explaining 58 % of the change in total mortality. Between years overwinter loss (k_3) was not correlated to total mortality but was negatively correlated with duckling mortality, i.e. when overwinter losses were greater duckling mortality was smaller (and vice-versa).

It was mentioned earlier that mortality factors which operate density dependence, i.e. when their extent varies disproportionately to population size, are very important to the dynamics of populations. This is because if density is reduced there is a disproportionate reduction in mortality. Of the three mortalities identified for Sevenoaks mallard, clutch predation and overwinter loss were density dependent (Figure 23). Duckling mortality was not related to the number of broods. During the years 1966, 1967, 1969, 1970 and 1971, clutch predation was particularly low, with values ranging from 0 % to 18 %. Significantly ($P < 0.02$) more carrion crows were killed during this time (mean $\pm$ s.e. = 59.8 $\pm$ 4.7) than before or after this period (31.8 $\pm$ 8.0). The number of foxes killed each year at Sevenoaks during the period 1960–76 remained relatively constant (mean = 23.9 $\pm$ 3.1). Consequently the control of clutch predators, particularly crows, can have an important effect on productivity.

The main 'regulatory' factor at Sevenoaks was found to be overwinter loss. By this we mean that when breeding populations are at the 'carrying capacity' of the habitat, and if preceding autumn populations are high, perhaps most commonly as a result of high duckling survival that summer, a greater proportion of birds will die or disperse than if the September population had been low as a result of low duckling survival. Carrying capacity is the term given to the number of birds the habitat can support based on the resources available. Only density-dependent factors can regulate populations. Density-independent factors such as weather will not regulate numbers over a long period of time. They cause a certain proportional mortality unrelated to the density of individuals upon which the mortality acts. The finding that overwinter loss holds the main power to regulate the mallard population has very important impli-

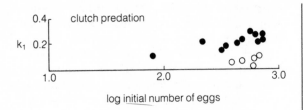

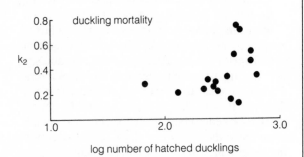

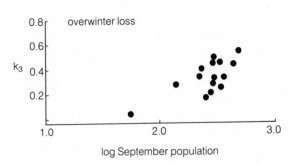

O = years 1966, 1967, 1969, 1970 and 1971 when predators were controlled more heavily

FIGURE 23 *Testing clutch predation, duckling mortality and overwinter loss for density dependence*

cations for harvesting dynamics, and for the debate about whether shooting and natural mortalities are additive or compensatory. We shall return to this shortly.

It is not surprising that variations in duckling mortality cause variation in autumn numbers. Mallard ducklings, particularly during their first 12 days, are susceptible to cold weather in spring (Koskimies & Lahti, 1964). The abundance of their food, adult chironomids emerging from the water (Chura, 1961, Bengston, 1975, Street, 1977), is determined by temperature, wind speed and rainfall (Titmus, 1979). The number of young in any

autumn therefore depends on spring weather conditions (and this number is then 'regulated' by overwinter losses).

One very significant point when considering the dynamics of the Sevenoaks mallard population is that the number of breeding pairs did not fluctuate in relation to duckling mortality between years. This was because overwinter loss, the main regulatory factor, was able to buffer between-year fluctuations in the production of young, which therefore prevented large-scale variations in the number of breeding pairs. Podoler & Rogers (1975) have shown that when a key factor is followed by a density-dependent form of mortality, the two are usually inversely related in this way.

FURTHER EVIDENCE OF DENSITY DEPENDENCE IN POPULATIONS

A detailed study of 35 'wildfowl count sites' in which overwinter loss was calculated in the same way as described above, showed that mallard populations were largely regulated by density-dependent overwinter loss factors, whereas those of tufted duck, for example, were not (Hill, 1982, 1984). This is supported by the fact that breeding and wintering mallard populations appear to have reached an equilibrium point, showing no further increases, suggesting that breeding habitat is limiting numbers. An unpublished report by the Game Conservancy showed, from ringing returns since the 1950s to the present time, no significant trend in survival rate. This supports the argument that density-dependent overwinter loss is regulating the mallard population at a national level. Tufted duck on the other hand are still increasing in numbers, largely because of their exploitation of gravel pits, which readily become colonised with their major food items, the molluscs *Potamorpyrgus jenkinsi* and *Dreissena polymorpha*.

The detection of other density-dependent factors in wildfowl populations has received less attention. Several studies have shown that shelduck productivity (number of fledged young) decreases with an increase in breeding density, and that proportionally fewer young fledge from birds nesting in 'colonies' than from those on more dispersed breeding areas. This is due to lower duckling survival at high density as a result of interference between breeding pairs and an increase in the levels of intraspecific clutch parasitism between individual nesting birds (Pienkowski & Evans, 1982).

Other work on shelduck has suggested that populations are regulated by competition for feeding space in late winter flocks, through the formation of a dominance hierarchy and the exclusion of subordinate birds. However, Evans and Pienkowski (1982), could find no evidence of density-dependent dispersal and suggested that passage of birds through the area gave rise to the results of the previous study.

Dispersal of individuals results from two kinds of movement: that from the place of birth to somewhere else in the breeding range, which is called natal dispersal, and that between successive breeding attempts, which is called breeding dispersal. In most bird species these kinds of dispersal are female biased: that is females move further than males. In wildfowl such dispersal is male biased. Lessels (1985), for example, showed male-biased dispersal in Canada geese. Dow & Fredga (1983) showed that female goldeneye which failed to breed successfully were less likely to return to the same nestbox than were females that had previously been successful. Furthermore, moving away from the vicinity of a nestbox in which the female had previously been unsuccessful was advantageous because boxes in which clutches were destroyed by predators in one year were more likely to be preyed upon the following year.

Dispersal is therefore an important additional component of the dynamics of wildfowl populations, and it has implications for harvesting.

HARVESTING POPULATIONS AND THE ROLE OF COMPENSATORY SURVIVAL

Density-dependent overwinter loss in mallard populations has fundamental implications for consideration of the effects of shooting on populations. The complicated manipulation of hunting regulations in the United States depended on the theory that wildfowl numbers were regulated on the breeding grounds. In mallard two regulating factors could be: (i) the abundance and distribution of feeding areas for laying females being actively defended by males or, less likely, (ii) the abundance and distribution of nest-site vegetation. Pospahala et al. (1974) suggest that breeding mallards space themselves in relation to available habitat. When a limit has been reached, the ducks without es-

tablished territories enter less favourable habitats (Bellrose et al., 1961, Crissey, 1969, Dzubin, 1969). The removal of an individual in any way, including being shot, will therefore release breeding sites which can potentially be exploited by other individuals which might otherwise have left the area or died from other causes.

This gave rise to a management approach involving the precise manipulation of hunting regulations (hunting methods, season dates, bag limits and season lengths) based on the assumption that this has a direct effect on the size of the harvest, and in turn that variations in the harvest will ultimately affect the size of the subsequent breeding population. In other words that natural winter and hunting mortality are additive Geis et al. (1969). Rogers (1979), Martin & Carney (1977) and Nichols et al. (1984) have provided much evidence to show, however, that natural mortality can compensate, to a threshold level, for increases in hunting mortality. Anderson & Burnham (1976)

FIGURE 24 *Annual survival rate as a function of hunting mortality rate under the compensatory mortality hypothesis (from Nichols* et al., *1984). Up to a threshold point (C), an increase in hunting mortality rate (K) creates no change in total annual survival (S). Beyond C an increase in hunting mortality cannot be compensated for by an increase in non-hunting mortality. Consequently total annual survival begins to decline as hunting mortality rate is increased*

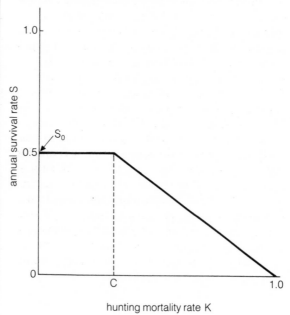

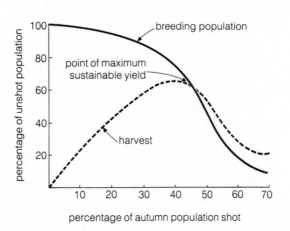

FIGURE 25 The number of mallard harvested and the size of the breeding population from a computer simulation model incorporating density dependent overwinter loss, with an increase in the shooting mortality rate

suggested that annual manipulation of harvest rates which lie below some threshold level would have no effect on population size. The compensatory survival hypothesis is shown in Figure 24.

When compensation for shooting takes place in this manner, an increase in the hunting rate (or mortality due to shooting) leads simply to an increase in the number of mallard harvested. This is presented in terms of predictions from a population model (Figure 25). At the point at which non-hunting mortality can no longer compensate for the high mortality due to shooting, the breeding population and the harvest decline to zero. The shooting mortality rate at which the yield is maximised is the point of 'maximum sustainable yield'. For the Sevenoaks population a computer simulation model showed that the maximum sustainable yield would be achieved by shooting between 35–40% of the autumn population. Under variable breeding conditions harvests should always err on the conservative side. Consequently an 'optimum sustainable yield' could be achieved by shooting about 30% of the autumn population.

POPULATION DYNAMICS AND MANAGEMENT

There are no other good data from which to calculate sustainable harvests for other species. Even for mallard it is important to know the size of winter populations in order to describe harvesting regimes or produce guidelines. The difficulty of counting makes this an enormous task, although for those species, particularly the geese, which have a more local distribution at their wintering grounds, the problem ought to be less extensive. For example, counts of young and adult European whitefronted geese on their wintering grounds have suggested that breeding success is dependent on the winter population size (Owen et al., 1986). Restrictions on hunting, resulting in a decrease in winter and spring mortality, appear to have contributed substantially to an increase in numbers which, in some countries, may have been exaggerated by an increase in the availability of cereal food supplies. Breeding populations, however, appear not to have increased in the same way, and individuals within the population respond by not breeding until later in life. However, knowledge of the population dynamics of many wildfowl species, their key factors and how density dependence operates are still largely unknown and yet are crucial to future conservation and management.

There is one important consideration. It is impossible to 'stockpile' a species which is regulated by density-dependent losses caused by a limiting resource. An increase in numbers can only be achieved by providing more of that resource through, for example, habitat management which creates more breeding sites. In order to know which factor to improve we must know what is causing density-dependent losses. For most wildfowl this is unknown. In Britain at least, many species are increasing. Much of this increase may be due to the creation of disturbance-free reserves (Owen, Atkinson-Willes & Salmon, 1986), although the creation of reserves often only results in a redistribution of birds and an appearance of increase rather than a true growth of populations. In tufted duck, breeding and wintering habitat have increased through the exploitation of flooded gravel quarries and the corresponding spread of favoured foods. Some of the increase might be due to changes on their breeding grounds far away from Britain. Only by rigorous routine monitoring, supported by long-term studies at breeding sites, will we gain the knowledge necessary to (a) detect long-term trends and (b) improve management programmes.

REFERENCES

Anderson, D.R., & Burnham, K.P., 1976. *Population ecology of the mallard: VI.* 'The effect of exploitation on survival'. US Fish and Wildfowl Service Research Publication *128*.

Atkinson-Willes, G.L., 1958. 'National Wildfowl Counts' in *Wildfowl Trust Annual Report 10*, 21–3.

Atkinson-Willes, G.L., & Frith, J.C., 1964. 'Trends in the population of British wintering ducks 1961–64' in *Wildfowl Trust Annual Report 16*, 21–9.

Bellrose, F.C., Scott, T.G., Hawkins, A.S., & Low, J.S., 1961. 'Sex ratios in North American ducks', *Illinois Nat. Hist. Surv. Bull. 21*, 391–471.

Bengtson, S.A., 1975. 'Food of ducklings of surface feeding ducks at Lake Myvatn, Iceland', *Ornis Fenn. 52*, 1–4.

Boyd, H., & Ogilvie, M., 1961. 'The distribution of mallard ringed in southern England' in *Wildfowl Trust Annual Report 13*, 125–36.

Chura, N.J., 1961. 'Food availability and preferences of juvenile mallards' in *Trans. 26th N. Am. Wildl. Conf. 2*, 121–34.

Coulson, J.C., 1984. 'The population dynamics of the Eider duck, *Somateria mollissima*, and evidence of extensive non-breeding by adult ducks', *Ibis, 126*, 525–43.

Cramp, S. & Simmons, K.E.L., 1977. *The Birds of the Western Palearctic, Vol. I* OUP, London.

Crissey, W.F., 1969. 'Prairie potholes from a continental viewpoint', in *Saskatoon Wetlands Seminar*, 161–71. Can. Wildl. Serv. Rep. 6.

Dow, H., & Fredga, S., 1983. 'Breeding and natal dispersal of the goldeneye, *Bucephala clangula*', *J. Anim. Ecol. 52*, 681–96.

Dzubin, A., 1969. 'Assessing breeding populations of ducks by ground counts' in *Saskatoon Wetlands Seminar*, 178–230. Can. Wildl. Serv. Rep. 6.

Evans, P.R., & Pienkowski, M.W., 1982. 'Behaviour of shelducks, *Tadorna tadorna*, in a winter flock: does regulation occur?', *J. Anim. Ecol. 51*, 241–62.

Geis, A.D., Martinson, R.K., & Anderson, D.R., 1969. 'Establishing hunting regulations and allowable harvests of mallards in the United States', *J. Wildl. Manage., 33*, 848–59.

Harradine, J., 1983. 'Sporting shooting in the United Kingdom – some facts and figures', Proceedings of 2nd Meeting Int. Union Game Biol. Working Group on Game Statistics, Doorwerth, Netherlands, 6–7 October 1982, Ed. by Frans Leeuwenberg and Ian Hepburn.

Harrison, J., 1974. *The Sevenoaks Gravel Pit Reserve.* A conservation publication of WAGBI in co-operation with Redland Ltd and the Harrison Zoological Museum Trust, Marford Mill, Rossett, Clwyd.

Hill, D.A., 1982. *The comparative population ecology of mallard and tufted duck.* Unpubl. DPhil thesis, University of Oxford.

Hill, D.A., 1984. 'Population regulation in the mallard', *J. Anim. Ecol., 53*, 191–202.

Hill, D.A., Wright, R., & Street, M., 1987. 'Survival of mallard ducklings and competition with fish for invertebrates on a flooded gravel quarry in England', *Ibis, 129*, 159–67.

Koskimies, J., & Lahti, L., 1964. 'Cold hardiness of the newly hatched young in relation to ecology and distribution in ten species of European ducks', *The Auk, 81*, 281–307.

Lack, P., 1986. *The Atlas of Wintering Birds in Britain and Ireland.* Pub., T. and A.D. Poyser, Town Head House, Calton, Staffordshire.

Lessels, C., 1985. 'Natal and breeding dispersal of Canada geese, *Branta canadensis*', *Ibis, 127*, 31–41.

Martin, E.M., & Carney, J.M., 1977. *Population ecology of the mallard: IV.* 'A review of duck hunting regulations, activity and success, with special reference to the mallard'. U.S. Fish and Wildlife Service Research Publication *130*.

Nichols, J.D., Conroy, M.J., Anderson, D.R., & Burnham, K.P., 1984. 'Compensatory mortality in waterfowl populations: a review of evidence and implications for research and management', *Trans. N. Amer. Wildl. Nat. Res. Conf., 49*, 535–54.

Owen, M., Atkinson-Willes, G.L., & Salmon, D., 1986. *Wildfowl in Great Britain.* Pub. Cambridge University Press.

Pienkowski, M.W., & Evans, P.R., 1982. 'Clutch parasitism and nesting interference between shelducks at Aberlady Bay', *Wildfowl, 33*, 159–63.

Podoler, H., & Rogers, D., 1975. 'A new method for the identification of key factors from life table data', *J. Anim. Ecol., 44*, 85–114.

Pospahala, R.S., Anderson, D.R., & Henny, C.J., 1974. *Population ecology of the mallard: II. Breeding habitat conditions, size of breeding population and production indices*, Res. Publ. 115 of U.S. Bureau of Sports Fisheries and Wildlife.

Rogers, J.P., Nichols, J.D., Martin, F.W., Kimball, C.F., & Pospahala, R.S., 1979. 'Can ducks be managed by regulation?', *4th N. Am. Wildl. for Nat. Resources Conf.*, 114–26.

Sharrock, J.T.R., 1976. *The Atlas of Breeding Birds in Britain and Ireland*. Pub. British Trust for Ornithology, Beech Grove, Tring, Hertfordshire.

Street, M., 1977. 'The food of mallard ducklings in a wet gravel quarry and its relation to duckling survival', *Wildfowl, 28*, 113–25.

Titmus, G., 1979. *The ecology of Chironomidae*. Unpubl. PhD thesis, University of Keele.

Tuite, C., 1981. *The impact of water-based recreation on the waterfowl of enclosed inland waters in Britain. A report to the Sports Council and the Nature Conservancy Council*. Publ. by the Wildfowl Trust, Nature Conservancy Council and Sports Council.

5

WILDFOWL IDENTIFICATION IN WILDFOWLING CONDITIONS

BERNARD W. BARKER

The art of wildfowl recognition in the field does not come easy to either fowler or birdwatcher. Simply reading a few thousand words in a book or looking at coloured illustrations, however true to life, will not replace the need for positive effort. The object of this chapter is to point the direction of this effort and offer as much advice as space allows. There are no secret formulae, which is a good thing. There are, however, short cuts to success and fairly clear directions which will, in the long run, save time. Anyone ignoring these could spend a lifetime in the proximity of wildfowl and yet end up with very little knowledge to show for it. On the other hand, a person willing to study can be reasonably proficient in a remarkably short time.

The coloured photographs in the many bird books available are intended to assist positive identification of species. Of course, in field conditions, it is often difficult to detect these clear shapes and sparkling colours, and – in the wildfowler's case – it is almost impossible at flight times. It is one thing to observe the static duck or identify it from the static picture; quite another to determine the identity of something whistling by at dusk against, perhaps, a dark background. For this we need to look for clues (subconsciously), assemble evidence and come to conclusions. Unless we do, we have not identified the bird and, for the wildfowler, the quarry species is not proven no matter the circumstantial evidence.

Unfortunately, some people try to identify birds in field conditions when they could not do so with certainty even if they were actually holding the bird in the hand. So I do stress the first rule of identification: get to *know* the bird. This means learning to identify it with certainty, given most of the evidence such as shape, size and colours. If this cannot be done, then there is no point in making it harder by standing in a cold and muddy estuary in the middle of a winter blizzard, waiting for the lights to go out. For the fowler in particular, the aim should be to identify all the quarry species, and any others likely to cause the slightest confusion. Better still is the genuine fowler, who makes time to continue the study throughout the years of his sport.

Obviously, good binoculars are a must, but why leave the book at home? In reasonable conditions, like September on the foreshore, a polythene bag will keep a book clean and, if there is a chance to study it, the time will be well spent. Indeed, a trip without the gun will ensure maximum concentration and you are not restricted to seasons. This is an area where a local expert can be a most useful companion. Responding to your enthusiasm, he will be only too happy to help you avoid many mistakes and indicate details not at first obvious. To sit still on a foreshore and have a dozen shelduck ducklings running over your feet is one of life's treasures and part of the magic for fowler or birdwatcher prepared to make an effort. A comfortable summer activity one might say, but rewards come from any season of the year.

POSITIVE IDENTIFICATION

I live on a farm which is overflown by geese, attracts duck and nesting waders and collects varying numbers of assorted gulls, herons, corvids and the like. I also have my own wildfowl collection with many free-flying duck and geese. This is probably the ideal way to learn to identify birds in all their plumages and become thoroughly familiar with most of the flight and voice mannerisms. Not everyone can be so situated, but there are many wildfowl collections and most are worth a visit. Those in zoos are good for close-ups but usually have a broader world coverage. It should, though, be natural for any fowler or birdwatcher to be enthusiastic about the incredible spectrum of fowl and waders from all regions. Most birds in zoo collections will be pinioned to stop them flying away, the only fliers being uninvited mallard. A private collector will probably have more free winged birds and native species and any reasonable request to view is unlikely to be refused. Most serious collectors have observed something unusual and have been involved in interesting confidences with their charges. By such close proximity, it is possible to understand much of the vocal side, and attitudes which have been observed in the wild at a distance become identifiable practices when close to.

An extremely good place to observe all manner of fowl can be the local park water. Some parks will be home to a mere token force of rapidly hybridising and inbred mallard and domestic duck. But others attract such numbers and variety of fowl as to have regional or national importance, a fact not perhaps appreciated by some local authorities. The most important aspect of a good park water is that most of the birds can be seen at close quarters and yet are free flying; in all probability they are simply wild birds attracted to the habitat or just to a free feed of bread. This is of extreme importance to the novice spotter, especially when an odd-looking duck comes in to land after three or four fast circuits and presents easy and certain identification. Do not be embarrassed to sit with a well-illustrated bird book and binoculars. Indeed, why not take a camera and start a collection of slides and prints. But – beware the trap of the flying shot. It is merely a point frozen in time and is not at all reliable. Such pictures are misleading unless they are reasonably close and clear.

The last positive means of identification is the carcass. Here we have two extremes: the mounted specimen or the simple study skin. I would strongly advise all but the experienced to be cautious of the bird department of a museum. The best collections of mounted birds are likely to be with good professional taxidermists or discerning collectors and will be housed to avoid natural light and damaging organisms. By their very purpose, museums must present good displays to the public and thus are frequently forced to put some of the collection at risk. The worst will be sun-bleached, moth-eaten, mislabelled and all mounted to look either like penguins, or – if penguins – mounted to look like bean bags! Many will clearly not abide by the rules dictated by the centre of gravity. So,

although I am sure there are some splendid examples in museums, I cannot stress enough the risk of seeking knowledge in this way. It is not only easy to stuff a bird the wrong shape; it can also be made the wrong size by a wide margin. Neither is it unknown for legs and beaks to be painted the wrong colours and the glass eyes can be entirely wrong.

Museums might, however, have a thoroughly first-class collection of 'study skins' not on display but available for inspection. Most serious students will use such study skins, which are simply the whole fully plumaged skin with only a light packing inside to give slight reinforcement. A clear label should give all necessary details of the bird, including plumage identity, such as male, female, eclipse, hybrid, plus date and collection area. There are no eyes and the bare parts are unpainted. Such collections are kept in large drawers which are moth-proofed and exclude light. Some wildfowling clubs build their own collection of quarry species, which is extremely easy to do without spoiling the meat. If such skins are to be used for group study, such as a club night, I strongly suggest that they be enclosed in clear polythene bags for safety.

Wildfowlers should study their quarry once retrieved, or even ask to examine the bag of another fowler. Handle the carcass, see how the wings and legs fold; compare ratios of head, neck, wings and body. Even take the weight and certainly ensure you are able to identify both species and sex.

FIELD IDENTIFICATION

Having outlined how to brush up the positive and easy side of identification, we now come to the obscure and difficult 'in-field' observation.

Take an experienced pigeon shooter who sits for hours behind a spread of decoys. He is just lighting his pipe or pouring a warmer from a flask when he spots some specks in the distance. He finishes lighting his pipe or continues pouring, having dismissed the specks as crows. Now if those specks had been frozen in a photograph it is doubtful if he could have told the difference between pigeon, crow or approaching aircraft. They were after all specks with no obvious shape and were all black.

FIGURE 26 (opposite) *Flight patterns of wildfowl*

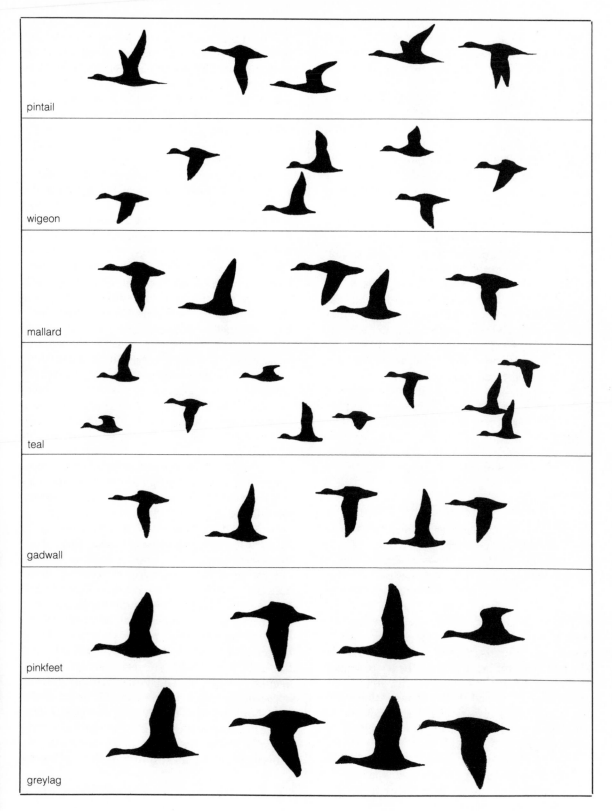

pintail

wigeon

mallard

teal

gadwall

pinkfeet

greylag

In my own efforts at identification of flying fowl from photographs, I noted that those I could identify were no clearer or more obvious than the others. Even where I knew that two pictures showed the same bird, one I could say looked like the species, the other looked like nothing more than a flying sock! I came to the conclusion that since my identification rested on clues, the freezing of the motion had killed a significant number of these. I could identify some of the 'frozen frames' because I could judge the shape against the true species, and I could recognise the other few characteristics which the sparse detail allowed. But movement, form and colour were all restricted to the one chosen point in time.

In the case of the pigeon shooter, I conclude that many hours, days and, perhaps, years had trained the man's brain to deduce from experience the identity of the birds, simply because he had seen the same thing many times before and, when they got close enough, he could give positive identification. He detected clues at a distance sufficient to distinguish between pigeon and crow; in this case I think it would have been speed and manner of flight rather than any particular wing flap which was the giveaway. This way of evaluating clues is available to us all, but it is easier to assimilate if we prepare the ground by knowing *what* we have when we detect the clues. Let us now examine the areas from where these clues might come.

FLIGHT CHARACTERISTICS

There are as many flight variations for birds as there are differences in shape and size. This, of course, is due to the process of evolution, which served to fit the bird into a particular niche or way of life. Hence, a bird which does not need to fly will, in the course of time, lose the power to do so. Evolution has also given us the long-distance fliers such as terns and swifts with their long, narrow wings and very light bodies. Conversely, the average farmyard hen will be too heavy to sustain flight and it uses its flying ability mainly for roosting. There are all shades between these, and any good illustrated book will clearly indicate the differences in wing shapes and the ratios between wing and body.

The science of aerodynamics started with observations of bird flight and the same basic principles apply to each. With aircraft, we refer to 'lift', weight, wing chord, aspect ratios, dihedral and so on. With birds, it is enough for us to know that these principles exist and influence the flight characteristics. For example, the short, wide rounded wings of a pheasant linked with a high body weight, put it firmly in the home-loving camp, where rapid acceleration and relatively short bursts of power to escape from predators are all it demands of its wings. Most of us will develop this theme somewhat with observations of the birds we see most and come to our own conclusions. But we should consider too, how basic life styles can also influence the way birds fly.

If a bird needs a long neck and is as bulky as a swan, it will find it difficult to keep the body still when flapping its huge wings. Here, then, is one of our clues, for overall shape differences may influence body movement in flight. The result may be undulation of the neck, marked enough for the observer to notice from some distance. With many birds, the action of flapping the wings actually causes the whole body to rise and fall in a constant cycle; this and the degree of rise and fall are a clue. Another characteristic is the 'angle of attack' which the wings, but more often the whole body, make with the line of flight. Something else to look for is the way a bird takes off. Does it simply leap into the air or expend great energy on a long take-off run?

The last basic movement is the degree of flap, where the wings perform varying amounts of an arc when flapping in normal flight. In other words, not all species merely flap their wings up and down, nor do they flap at the same speed. Seen from the front, a mallard will raise its wings above the body about the same amount as it lowers them, but without their touching each other. A pigeon does the same, but the movement covers a longer arc and the wing tips frequently touch, especially in rapid changes of direction or accelerating. We all know the 'clap' of the pigeon's wings and this is the reason. Of the two, the mallard flap is faster and the body line steady. The pigeon has a slower average air speed, which means that the two approaching birds can be readily distinguished.

It should be noted at this point that I know of no published work concerning the relative wing arcs of birds; the exact degree of arcing and other movement is for some future student to determine

FIGURE 27 (opposite) *Flight silhouettes of shore birds*

– with plenty of time, expensive camera equipment and a research grant at his disposal.

Not all birds give equal amounts of up and down flap and our mental picture might offer examples such as partridge, grouse and waders as having a decided low arc, yet a photograph will clearly show all of these birds with a whole range of wing positions. The probable reason for this is that these particular birds do have a low arc for part of the flight when not actively flapping and frequently adopt the glide or semi-glide attitude. Paintings of packed grouse, in a low arc posture, are therefore technically correct, but since they depict a non-power wing position, only half the picture.

A last but important flight characteristic is the glide. First, not all birds glide and that in itself is a basic clue. Then, angle of wings to body and duration of glide can distinguish between, say, a curlew and a gull. The curlew can hold its wings very high in a glide, which is broken by flapping to regain lost height. The soaring gull has a negative or low arc and may regain height by little or no flapping. It is also possible for some birds to 'semi-glide' whilst still flapping their wings. In doing so, they are merely flying on 'reduced power' or like a propeller, 'windmilling' with little or no thrust. The average duck will do this when in cruising flight by reducing the amount of arc above the body. The basic flight clues are therefore:

(a) Variations from line of flight and undulation of neck
(b) Angle of attack of body and wings
(c) Speed of wing flap
(d) Forward speed of bird
(e) Degree of wing arc
(f) Manner of glide

FORMATIONS

There are a number of clues in birds' flying formations, as well as a number of pitfalls. The commonest mistake is thinking that a vee formation must be duck or geese. Seagulls are probably responsible for most vees seen because, for some species, it is a common flying practice. Groups of duck are more likely to be in bunches than vees and are prone to changing formation quickly. Curlew can fly in steady vees, bunches or broken groups. Geese certainly form up in vees but mostly so shallow as really to be lines.

The purpose of such formation is now clearly understood. It is now known that the 'turbulence' or 'slipstream' behind each bird provides 'lift' for those immediately following. One particular feature of the goose formation is the tenacious way each bird holds the line. The leaders often change in flight, the assumption being that the stronger adults are supporting the younger birds. This again is not proven, but the observation that changing leaders do not necessarily move to the end of the line, is certainly suggestive. On take-off and when gaining height quickly, there appears to be no need for formation and we usually see just a mass of birds lifting. Over an estuary, however, geese may not seek to gain height so fast and the formation we see is a long line of approaching birds lifting above the horizon. This is a positive clue because, unlike similar formations of gulls, geese will maintain these lines, whereas gulls often break and re-form, a frustrating but clear gull clue. Also, the goose line is usually much longer. Some goose species, such as barnacle and brent, rarely have an identifiable formation, being seen more often in bunches. A swan formation is not distinct, but the birds' manner of flight is a giveaway.

A common formation, particular to coastal habitats, is the dense mass. This is often a flock of waders, the smaller species like knot, appearing similar to fast-drifting clouds of smoke. These birds are best studied at rest, whilst the larger waders such as lapwing and oystercatcher give enough flight clues.

Duck formations are mostly tight, fast-flying groups of small numbers, the commonest probably in single figures with a maximum of thirty to forty individuals. A formation above this number will split into many small groups rather than, say, two large packs.

VOICE

Despite highly vocal bird gatherings, it is surprisingly difficult to spot an individual actually giving voice. Some species offer very clear voice clues and are generous in the frequency. Others may only call in particular situations or at specific times such as during the breeding season or when taking off in alarm. Most birds have a purpose for any noise they make. Records of wildfowl calls are not common, those available being usually on mixed bird discs from which selected species can be taped

Golden plover
Pluvialis apricaria

Lapwing
Vanellus vanellus

Golden plover
Pluvialis apricaria

Woodcock
Scolopax rusticola

Snipe
Gallinago gallinago

Jack snipe
Lymnocryptes minimus

JOHN PALEY

Inland waders: with dusk fast approaching, small flocks
of waders fly across an inland marsh

Mallard
Anas platyrhynchos

♀

♂

Pintail
Anas acu...

♂

♀

Wigeon
Anas penelope

♀

Garganey
Anas querquedula

♂

♂

♀

♀

Pochard
Aythya ferina

♀

♂

Tufted duck
Aythya fuligula

♀

♂

JOHN PALEY

Surface feeding and diving ducks: a misty morning on
an East Anglian river provides a fleeting glimpse of
wildfowl on the wing

Gadwall
Anas strepera

♂

♀

Teal
Anas crecca

♂

♀

Shoveler
Anas clypeata

♂

♀

Goldeneye
Bucephala clangula

♂

♀

Common scoter
Melanitta nigra

♂

♀

♂

♀

Velvet scoter
Melanitta fusca

Scaup
Aythya marila

♂

♀

Sea duck: a freshening wind as the tide turns, moves
these sea duck to more sheltered waters

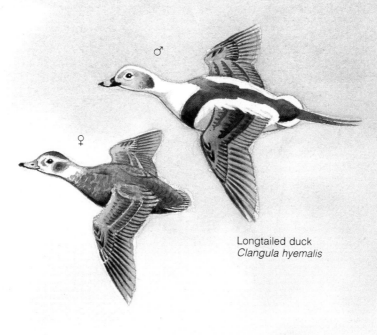

♂

♀

Longtailed duck
Clangula hyemalis

♂

♀

Common eider
Somateria mollissima

JOHN PALEY

Geese: highlighted by the first rays of the morning sun.
A mixed skein of geese drop in to join others already
feeding on the autumn stubble

Pinkfooted goose
Anser brachyrhynchus

Canada goose
Branta canadensis

Bean goose
Anser fabalis

Greylag goose
Anser anser

European whitefronted goose
Anser albifrons albifrons

JOHN PALEY

Shore waders: against the grey sky of a winter's day this small flock of waders in winter plumage await the turn of the tide

Curlew
Numenius arquata

Whimbrel
Numenius phaeopus

Oystercatcher
Haematopus ostralegus

Blacktailed godwit
Limosa limosa

Bartailed godwit
Limosa lapponica

Avocet
Recurvirostra avosetta

Grey plover
Pluvialis squatarola

Greenshank
Tringa nebularia

Dunlin
Calidris alpina

Knot
Calidris canutus

Sanderling
Calidris alba

Redshank
Tringa totanus

JOHN PALEY

for easier reference. A word of warning about decoy callers. They will range from excellent in good hands to diabolical with the buffoon. Simply blowing a call neither guarantees the correct species note, nor the right 'come hither' call for the quarry.

SIZE AND COLOUR

In my early days of watching fowl, I thoughtlessly dismissed the usefulness of relative size in trying to identify a bird in less than good field conditions. In particular, birds seen in the drab wintry dawns of an estuary could not be measured against anything for scale and so a high mallard could, in theory, be mistaken for a low teal. This I have found to be true, but only when conditions are so poor that my eyes are unable to give a good focus. The time of greatest confusion is the pre-dawn murk when I believe most of us will find distance difficult to judge; fog and mist also influence our judgement of range. Apart from these exceptions, I believe we can discern size fairly accurately and certainly within normal shooting ranges. Of course, good identification could be obtained through the use of other clues, both visual and aural, which would subconsciously help us to judge size, since we do not expect to see a greylag as small as a teal nor a giant redshank.

With colour, the same poor estuarine conditions turn all but the most sparkling white plumage into shades of grey. With good light it is certainly possible to detect colours, especially those of great contrast, but we really must take that as a bonus and not expect to see any colour detail with the flying bird. Even on the water, colour is elusive and it can be quite a surprise when, on a fine day, a bird shows most of the colours found in our bird book. Remember too, a bird flying overhead may show that part of its anatomy which has possibly the least colour and even then it may well be shaded. Things to note are the areas of dark and light, plus the points of demarcation between them. The so-called 'black geese' can be distinguished by the amounts of black in their plumage, which also distinguishes them from the grey geese. With duck, contrasts between head, neck and body shades help pick out drake mallard, pochard, goldeneye, tufted and scaup, the males being the easier. The problem ones are females, males in eclipse or stages between, and, of course, hybrids. There is also the possibility of a rare visitor. A king eider, for example, could turn up in a northern firth, swimming alongside the common variety.

BODY SHAPE AND STANCE

If we attempt to identify birds which are static and give no colour, voice or shade clues, we are forced to consider the shape and stance only. To gain practice in this skill, it is useful to re-examine the illustrated books and try to visualise all the birds as silhouettes. Better still, trace a selection, ink them black and label them. Certain features will soon become very obvious and can readily be related to the field. A crest, for example, may appear in silhouette to alter the shape of the head or neck and become the most significant diagnostic feature, yet appear secondary in full light. Also notice the apparent centre of gravity and how the legs are angled to the body. Coupled with length of leg, this feature assumes great importance with many birds. For example, the vertical legs of geese differ clearly from the angles of nearly all duck. I am sure that most of us have far better analytical brains than we are willing to admit and that given even tiny fragments of visual information, we are able to rationalise the facts so long as we know the bird in the hand. The beak is a case in point. Despite its usual smallness, it can frequently be seen at a good distance.

On water, shape is notoriously difficult to define not only because the background can be poor but the bird may move a lot as well. In this situation, notice how high the bird sits on the water, the obvious shape, the position of head and tail and, finally, its activity. A bird very low in the water with no tail showing and an obvious diving ability, could be a diving duck which has a short neck, a grebe with a short to medium neck, or a cormorant with a very long neck. The latter can become so saturated as to sink to the neck, making repeat dives easier and, thus, identification easy. A stout-necked diving bird might be one of the named divers – redthroated, blackthroated or great northern, in which case head carriage is a good clue, even at a considerable distance. A high floating bird with a prominent cocked tail and no obvious neck is most likely to be a seagull. The duck and geese range between these extremes. Some are easy to identify but in general the identification of wildfowl on water is more difficult than when they

FIGURE 28 Birds on water

mallard   herring gull   wader   razorbill

greylag   grebe   cormorant

eider   diver   goosander   dabbler

FIGURE 29 Birds on land

godwit   oystercatcher   curlew   lapwing

greylag   moorhen   heron   brent   woodcock

scoter   shelduck   teal   herring gull

guillemot   snipe   crow   tern   sandpiper

are in flight. The delightful auk family, commonly mixed with sea duck, are short-bodied with a very distinct body form in flight. Although we may only see a silhouette of the bird, even simple movements may give helpful clues. The act of diving is one, another is the way a bird walks. Have a good look at the way a crow or rook struts. They often turn up in wildfowl habitats, and can be distinguished easily.

Lastly, there is the 'illusion' of a shape which can be a most helpful clue. This comes about through an overpowering feature blinding us to the *true* shape. In this way, I for one see a fast-flying goldeneye as a distinct body blob led by a head blob but no neck or clearly defined wings. Such clues or 'keys' are in the eye of the beholder and I urge individuals to identify their own if they exist. Another example for me is the impression lapwing give of 'figure of eights' in their leisurely flight. An even sillier illusion is the group of 'swastikas' I see perched on distant sea rocks, which are cormorants hanging their wings out to dry. Never mind how absurd this sounds; even one's personal illusion is an aid to correct identification and should not be dismissed lightly.

Both duck and geese are tidy birds in flight, with their legs tucked tight into their bodies or even hidden altogether. Any bird, therefore, with legs hanging down or trailing clearly behind, must be something else such as heron, rail, coot, moorhen, crane, stork, bittern, corncrake or a wader. One last point on shape is the sleeping bird on land. It is a fact that birds that normally sleep standing on one leg can, and frequently do, sleep sitting down. Duck and geese are obvious ones, but watch for the long-legged bird which does this, because sitting down with their heads in and beaks under wing feathers can make dissimilar species look confusingly alike.

COLLATION OF CLUES

GEESE

Geese have a strong unlaboured flight and excellent aerobatic ability which differentiates them straightaway from swans, sawbills and divers. Their ability to 'whiffle' or drop out of formation is a well-known means of losing height very quickly and is just about unique. They are supposed to do this so as to allow them to approach their roost from a safe height, but my own geese appear to do it also from a sheer sense of fun. The neck to body ratio is short to medium, ranging from the brent to the Canada, which is about the longest and which enhances this impression by being smaller at the shoulder. In active flying, the wings have a definite crank and the general impression is of a backward sweep when viewed from the side. With sudden direction changes or when landing, the wings straighten, no doubt to maximise lift or braking effect. The heron at a distance can be similar only in colour, for it is slower, has a large wing area and obvious legs. The carriage of the heron's head is not reliable seen at a distance, being uniquely folded back rather than straight.

Geese are highly vocal and, with practice, it is possible not only to distinguish between species, but also to understand the meaning of some of the calling. It is common for some geese to make a lot of noise whilst feeding or at roost and then to alter the tempo shortly before take-off. The greylag is often said to call like a barnyard goose and both barnacle and Canada to imitate 'puppy dogs'. It all depends on how you interpret these other sounds, but at least listen to a true domestic goose first.

It is important to get practice with goose identification, but I think most will find it soon becomes very easy to differentiate geese from other birds, either by sight or sound. The hard part is to tell the species apart, especially when they can cheat by not calling at all. The grey geese are very similar, but look out for the pinkfoot, which is smaller in the head and neck than the greylag. When pinkfeet are standing in a field, the brown in the plumage, particularly in the head to chest area, is very noticeable. The whitefront displays dark chest bars and, in the Greenland race, the *whole* plumage is darker. I also think the body is longer in the latter, but that is purely my own opinion. Whitefronts are also known as 'laughing geese' in reference to the call, and, of course, the Americans call them 'specklebellies'. The barnacle might be thought to be most easily confused with the Canada, but this is not so. In silhouette, it could double for a pinkfoot and I have seen one or two mixed in with these grey geese in wild flocks. Bear in mind, too, that geese can vary in size *within* the species, a fact commonly known by wildfowl keepers. Beans are similar to pinkfeet but coarser and now quite rare in Britain. The brents are distinctive and highly localised and can be easily confused with duck in poor light. If the common geese are efficiently identified, rarities or vagrants will readily stand out.

DUCK

As with geese, it is worth making a list of all the native species and working at their positive identification. We can divide duck into two distinct groups, *surface feeders* and *divers*. Recognising this difference in the field naturally halves the identity problem.

(a) The surface feeders or dabblers

Duck such as pintail, wigeon and teal can dive, but do so only in play or to escape danger if unable to fly. They feed on land and in shallow water by upending. The mallard, the most famous of the 'dabblers', might be taken as a datum for the group. Deviations from this norm range from the grazing wigeon to the filter feeding of the shoveler. The latter is very distinctive on land or in flight because of its huge beak, but the pintail can be difficult. The long, thin neck distinguishes it from wigeon if seen clearly enough, and the pointed tail from mallard. Much practice is needed on what, to wildfowlers, is the most important quarry group. For voices, the mallard again is the best, with a nice range of quacks from the female. The cock wigeon is another distinctive caller with a lovely whistle, enabling us to identify the whole pack without another single clue. The shelduck can be a problem bird for, although it is boldly marked and is not a fast wing flapper, it can be confused in a stormy pre-dawn. Watch out for the nippy little teal which can so rapidly change direction. It can switch from level flight to the vertical without *seeming* to lose any speed. Teal will also move their heads a lot more in flight than others and this is a good clue if you can see it. Other species also swivel the head, but I have not seen any bend the neck as much as teal. In good light, the gadwall can be identified by the unique parts of the plumage such as black tail and white speculum. In poor light, the bird is lighter in the belly and has thinner, more pointed wings than the mallard, which it resembles the most.

(b) The divers

Diving duck actually do dive for food and can stay submerged for some time. Most divers appear to me like animated bullets in flight, yet I believe the surface duck have recorded the highest speeds, so this may be an illusion. Pochard, tufted and goldeneye can give problems and I suggest attention to the obvious areas of dark and light plumage as a first step. The eider is an easy one, with its head shape and body bulk quite clear. It is also much the easiest to spot around its coastal habitat because it spends a lot of time very close to the shore and, when flying, is generally slow and low to the water. Note also the angle of attack of the body in flight. The longtailed duck always appears to me as a cruciform shape, whilst scoters are kind enough to be so tame as to allow reasonable recognition of both sex and species. The head of the male common scoter is distinct with its bill knob, and the velvet is often helpful enough to display its white wing speculum. Scoters are infrequent fliers, being happy to live a lot of their lives drifting with the tides. Notice how divers sit in the water and the clear difference in stance on land when compared with surface feeders, which indicates their preference for floating rather than standing. The scaup is a tough one and some practice is needed, especially to distinguish it from the similarly plumaged tufted.

Under the general heading of divers, we must consider those great fishers, the sawbills. The main areas of confusion come with the redbreasted merganser and the larger goosander. Both can be confused with other duck, especially mallard. They are fast, direct fliers and even their formation is mallard-like. The pointed head and beak can be detected, however, and the large area of light-coloured underbody is another clue. I have even spotted the pink hue of the goosander but would not rely on this. On the water, their heads are usually held quite differently from other duck.

WADERS

This is where the binoculars come into their own and, because it is easy to confuse so many varieties, I would suggest using a process of elimination. First, make a list of the common waders from any good book and mark those you can identify for certain. The remainder must be worked on until the list is exhausted. In the first instance, lapwing, curlew, whimbrel and oystercatcher might go, followed perhaps by ringed plover, godwits and golden plover. Before we know it, half the list is gone and we are left with sandpipers, shanks and others where there are less obvious distinctions. Here we will find the greatest dependence on binoculars for finer detail and, despite distinct calls, this end of the wader group takes much practice.

Once competent with 'in hand' identification, it is then possible to relate what we know to those intimidating clouds of wader in the field. The way to go about this is to secrete oneself close to a good habitat like an estuary or saltmarsh in order to watch flying birds and formations land and take off. Choose fine weather and low tide because this is the time of greatest wader movement and there is no point starting this game in either poor light or uncomfortable conditions. 'In flight' identification of waders may not be as easy as for duck or geese, and there is greater emphasis on flock formation and voice than any other group. It is also worth noting that some wader flocks have an overall colour impression. A notebook in which the voice or individual call of each known species is written down phonetically can be a great help with voice identification. In other words, if the call of a redshank sounds to you like 'chiefy chiefy', then write that. I will give no more examples because my own are quite ridiculous!

OTHER SHORE BIRDS

Many other birds use the habitat of wildfowl, although only a few will confuse identification. The woodcock is one, sometimes using the estuary at dawn and dusk as well as inland flight ponds. Its carriage and flight pattern should clearly mark it for what it is, but note the beak held low and wing tips not so sharp, plus a wing flap different from most waders. Swans can and do turn up where a waiting wildfowler might be expecting geese and there should be no difficulty in spotting their slower, measured wing beats, if not the huge size, glowing white plumage and over-long neck. They can also make a noise and it is quite an experience meeting your first whooper swans with their enchanting call. Even the mute swan cannot get away without making a 'zip zip' noise, which comes from the wing feathers. Of the large birds which might be confused with geese, none are quite the same distinctive shape and many look more cross shaped in flight, i.e. the divers, gannet, shag and cormorant. Coot and moorhen are mostly on inland waters, being the perennial bane of fishermen. With its legs hanging down, the moorhen is a very poor flier, but the coot can get up quite a respectable speed, although it should always be obvious for what it is.

CONCLUSION

It is possible to meet with such surprises as domestic duck, albinos and hybrids, especially the mallard crosses. In darkness, a half white mallard is still a mallard. The fowler, in particular, should be aware of such likely meetings, and in coastal areas, be on guard for rare visitors or migrants in transit. Identification is not a one time thing but something to work at and build upon. Even old hands at the game can be surprised, as with the line of geese which become oystercatchers, or the bursting flock of dawn starlings that turn out to be teal! Granted, the percentage of error will diminish with experience, but there appears to me little chance in average field conditions of differentiating between some birds, for example, the teal tribe. In this country, the difference between the common teal and the rarer garganey males in full plumage is as obvious as that between red and white wine. See them flying on a murky coastal dawn, or compare females, and, like the midnight alcoholic, it's all much the same. If that seems an extreme example, there are grades between the obvious and the obscure, where each of us will find our own ability level. Suffice to say that for the fowler, the bird must always have the benefit of the doubt.

6

THE ECOLOGY OF ESTUARIES

PETER J. KNIGHTS

An understanding of the processes which mould estuaries and the reaction of birds to the various physical and biological features of intertidal land is acquired rather than consciously learnt by most wildfowlers – it comes as a natural consequence of pursuing quarry in conditions to which they are adapted and man is not. More so than for any other branch of sport shooting, it is an appreciation of ecological processes which contributes to success and moreover to the enjoyment of estuary wildfowling. At the same time, an understanding of ecological processes within estuaries provides an insight into why they are so important to wildfowl, what the requirements are for conserving their integrity and what opportunities exist to maintain and enhance their value to wildfowl through practical management.

This account presents a very generalised picture of the estuarine environment since space is simply not available to consider the full range of variation which this country is still fortunate enough to possess. It is intended to provide a framework of knowledge against which personal observation and experience can be set in context.

Estuaries in this country invariably represent drowned river valleys, inundated by a rise in sea level following the last glaciation around 3000 years ago. It is the ongoing process of siltation through the deposition of river-borne debris and marine material which gives rise to the present-day intertidal flats and saltmarshes. They are typically lacking in sharp relief, and the rigours imposed by the cycle of tidal flooding and exposure severely limit the range of animals and plants which are to be found. However, estuaries are one of the most productive ecosystems in the world in terms of the sheer abundance of life. The huge populations of wildfowl and waders which they support in winter are one proof of this.

The principal features of the environment which determine the physical form of intertidal land within an estuary are the degree of exposure to wave action, the strength of water currents, the nature of the sand or silt that is building up and the vertical extent of tidal influence. The shape and size of the estuary is decided by the way in which each of these factors operates. The distribution of animal and plant communities will additionally be influenced by less conspicuous features such as gradients in salinity – that is the saltiness of the water through the tidal cycle – and by the degree of aeration and waterlogging in the sediments – which affects the level of available oxygen.

Most estuaries contain areas of both sand and mud, with coarser, sandy material characterising areas around the mouth of the estuary subject to greatest wave action and tidal scour and with silt and fine organic matter being deposited in the central and upper reaches. The degree to which wave action and tidal scour penetrate an estuary will depend upon the width of the estuary mouth while the strength of tidal scour will be influenced by the shape, size and length of the estuary and the vertical extent of the tidal cover. Generally speaking, the estuaries of our northern and western coasts tend to have a preponderance of coarser sandy sediments whilst estuaries of the east and south coasts are dominated by muddy substrates.

Sand flats tend to be unstable with features such as channels and banks being short-lived and subject to swift changes, for example under storm conditions. Because of their instability, vegetation is absent or sparse, perhaps comprising occasional clumps of brown seaweed, such as the bladder wrack (*Fucus vesiculosus*) which find anchorage on exposed bedrock, boulders or the ubiquitous lumps of concrete.

Open sandflats characterise the seaward portions of estuaries (Nature Conservancy Council)

VEGETATION

In areas of silt deposition, stability is sufficient to permit colonisation of the surface by a variety of algae, including particularly species of the green algae *Enteromorpha*. An important early colonist of open mudflats in some estuaries is eel grass, principally *Zostera noltii*. Substrates with a high lime content are particularly favoured by *Zostera* and extensive areas are to be found, for example, at Lindisfarne, Chichester and Langstone habours, and on the estuaries of the Essex and north Norfolk coasts.

Less obvious to the human eye but of critical importance as a component of the estuarine food chain is the abundance of bacteria and microscopic algae as diatoms that occur within and on the surface of the open mudflats. It is these that give mudflats a green or olive hue at certain times of year, and their presence reflects the high levels of organic matter in the sediments. These microorganisms represent the initial decomposers of this material and have a position at the very beginning of the estuarine food chain.

The lowest unvegetated mudflats are poorly consolidated and have a gently undulating appearance. Creeks are generally wide with shallowly shelving banks and have a shifting pattern largely determined by wave action and water currents. These newly deposited muddy sediments, although very soft, are not necessarily deep, sometimes forming only a superficial layer on the basal sands. Where vegetation in the form of *Enteromorpha* and *Zostera* begins to appear, accretion accelerates, a process which the presence of vegetation itself promotes. Invariably this is a zone of deep glutinous mud. Here the creeks are deeper in cross section and more permanent and the pattern of creeks is not so much determined by the action of waves and current but by drainage from the upper marsh.

Apart from supporting food plants of grazing wildfowl in the form of algae and *Zostera* the open mudflats within an estuary are characterised by an abundance of invertebrate animals which are the principal food of many wading birds and certain wildfowl such as shelduck, pintail and to a lesser extent teal. It is for this reason that mudflats are the single most important component of the estuarine habitat for birds.

Another early plant colonist which, where *Zostera* occurs, will overlap with and succeed it at higher tidal levels, is marsh samphire or glasswort (*Salicornia* spp.). Whilst *Zostera* has a weak structure to its stems and leaves and simply lies limply across the mud surface when exposed, marsh samphire has an upright form and is regarded as the pioneer of saltmarsh development, occupying a level on the shore immediately below mean high water mark. Its characteristic fleshy, cylindrical stems and lack of leaves are adaptations for survival at the leading edge of the saltmarsh. In common with other opportunist plant species, it is an annual and produces large numbers of relatively big seeds which are an important food for wildfowl. Following swiftly in succession and often itself pioneering saltmarsh development where substrates are sandier, is common saltmarsh grass (*Puccinellia maritima*). The dense creeping stems of this grass further accelerate accretion and individual plants grow rapidly to form flat-topped hummocks which eventually coalesce to form ridges and ultimately an uneven lawn. Whereas many of the open depressions between hummocks infill with vegetation, especially on better drained substrates, some remain as water-filled pools long after the ebb tide has receded. These 'pans' have a tendency to persist and remain unvegetated, through subsequent succession of the saltmarsh.

This emerging saltmarsh dominated by *Puccinellia* and lying around mean high water mark is the zone of maximum accretion within the saltmarsh succession and rates of accretion may exceed 10 cm per year, although it is more usually under 1 cm per year. Creeks become deeper and their banks steeper, a feature accentuated by the fact that higher rates of silt deposition take place on the immediate edge of creeks so as to give them an embanked appearance. These raised drier banks are often made more conspicuous by being colonised by species from the upper marsh, such as sea-purslane (*Halimione portaculoides*). They also form a favourite access for wildfowlers. A typical associate of *Puccinellia* in this zone is annual sea-blite (*Suaeda maritima*). Like marsh samphire, this is an annual producing abundant seeds which are also an important food for wildfowl. A less welcome associate and competitor is the cord grass (*Spartina anglica*). Because of its impact on estuarine habitats *Spartina* is considered in more detail later.

Above mean high water mark a more varied plant community develops which, although subject to continued inundation on higher tides, is much more terrestrial in appearance. Particularly towards its landward edge there are found species of grass such as red fescue (*Festuca rubra*) and creeping bent (*Agrostis stolonifera*) which are commonplace in a variety of habitats not least suburban parks and gardens. However, species which are typically estuarine predominate in what may be regarded as the mature saltmarsh and these include sea-purslane, sea-lavender (*Limonium* spp.), thrift (*Armeria maritima*) and marsh arrow-grass (*Triglochin maritima*). Many of the plants here are perennials, but gaps in the sward are filled by annuals such as orache (*Atriplex* spp.) and annual sea-blite. At higher levels in the mature saltmarsh taller species such as sea rush (*Juncus maritimus*) and common reed (*Phragmites communis*) may appear.

Where stock grazing takes place the dominance by tall shrubby species gives way to a close-cropped turf in which *Puccinellia maritima* resumes prominence together with red fescue and in some situations creeping bent. This has particular benefits for grazing wildfowl in winter. Where stock grazing is too heavy, however, the general lack of cover greatly impairs the value for breeding waders.

The development of new saltmarsh (Nature Conservancy Council)

SALTMARSH DEVELOPMENT

There is a general levelling of the surface in the mature saltmarsh with creeks losing their former embanked appearance. Because of the height of the marsh and the consequential reduction in tidal flooding, accretion rates are lower and erosion rather than accretion comes to take precedence. This is apparent in the undercutting and slumping which takes place along the margins of creeks and particularly in the cutting back and multiple branching of creeks at higher levels in the mature marsh. This is referred to as creek head ramification and has the effect of dividing up the marsh into many discrete blocks of vegetation. At the same time this process leads to some surface channels being cut off and these remain as ribbon-like semi-permanent pools.

Although succession from saltmarsh to terrestrial habitats such as sand-dunes, freshwater marshes, fens and woodland is to be found on some estuaries, the uppermost point of the saltmarsh is often artificially determined by a sea bank. Irrespective of these differences, it is very often marked by a relatively bare strip of ground which is the strandline of spring tides. This quite distinct line, which may appear almost like a well-worn footpath around an estuary, is created when the estuary is full by water-borne debris crushing the vegetation which might otherwise become established.

The phases of saltmarsh development outlined above are expressed both as a zonation across the intertidal area and as a succession in time. Whereas succession may be a gradual affair estuaries are dynamic, youthful habitats and it is equally possible for the succession from highly mobile sand flats to mature saltmarsh to take place very rapidly. At the same time, however, an apparently stable saltmarsh can be eroded away just as swiftly as a result, for example, of a major shift in the course of the river channel.

Notwithstanding the inexorable process of siltation which is taking place in all estuaries, the greater part of the change observed at any one point in time represents the redistribution of material from place to place within the estuary. This is particularly the case where an estuary is unaffected by recent enclosure of the upper marsh or where there is no interference with the central river channel by draining or dredging. Both these activities tend to promote a more permanent stabilization of form within an estuary. Where the central river channel is not artificially constrained it changes course freely, swinging from one side of the estuary to the other in the manner of a dog wagging its tail. In doing so it will bring about erosion on one side and accretion on the other. Evidence of active erosion in this way is seen in the cliff-like edge to a saltmarsh and this may be associated with spectacular slumping of the former marsh surface. This is particularly so where movements in the earth's surface are causing the coastline to rise. Successive phases of erosion and accretion sometimes give a stepped appearance to a saltmarsh where erosion has only proceeded partway through a former marsh system and again where coastlines are rising mature saltmarshes may display marked terracing.

This perpetual cycle of rejuvenation is a fundamental characteristic of estuaries and one which maintains a balance in the distribution of open mudflats and vegetated saltmarsh. A consequence of this is that saltmarshes are predominantly recent in origin and many are less than 200 years old.

INVERTEBRATES

Estuaries support only a relatively small range of invertebrate animal species, but these may occur in extraordinary numbers and it is upon these that populations of waders and certain wildfowl prey. Most of the important invertebrate prey species for waterfowl belong to three main groups, the molluscs (e.g. gastropod snails and bivalve mussels), annelid worms (e.g. ragworm) and crustaceans (e.g. shrimps), and primarily occupy the muddy, sparsely vegetated substrates rather than either the coarser sands of the outer estuary or the consolidated soils of the mature saltmarsh.

A feature of almost all estuarine invertebrates is that they live largely or wholly beneath the surface of the flats, some in semi-permanent holes or tubes. This adaptation is one which permits avoidance of drying out and extremes of temperature when the flats are exposed by the tide and avoidance also of predation by birds. Estuarine invertebrates tend to feed most actively when the tide covers the flats. Some, such as the bivalve molluscs, stay permanently beneath the sand or mud surface drawing water from above and filtering out organic debris and plankton. Important representatives of this group in muddy sediments include peppery furrow shell (*Scrobicularia plana*), and the Baltic tellin (*Macoma balthica*) whilst the cockle (*Cerastoderma edule*) and thin tellin (*Tellina tenuis*) prefer more sandy areas close to the estuary mouth. The mussel (*Mytilus edulis*) also occurs where marine influence is strong, usually on rock outcrops or consolidated gravel banks, and differs from the aforementioned in living on the surface.

Although the bivalve molluscs of muddy sediments, particularly *Macoma*, feature in the diet of shelduck and pintail, from the point of view of wildfowl, mussels and thin tellins are of greater importance, the former for eider and the latter for common scoter.

The most important representative of the gastropod molluscs is the laver spire shell (*Hydrobia ulvae*). This small snail, some 2–4 mm in length, emerges from the near surface sediments as the tide floods and feeds either by grazing algae, which cover the mud surface, or by floating in the water, where it traps plankton and suspended organic matter in a mucilagenous secretion. *Hydrobia ulvae* is a principal food of shelducks and small waders such as dunlin and is favoured also by pintail and teal.

Amongst the annelid worms two species of very different life styles are of particular importance, the lugworm (*Arenicola marina*) and the ragworm (*Nereis diversicola*). These are major foods of larger waders such as curlew and godwit. The lugworm, best known for the distinctive casts it leaves on the surface, lives permanently beneath the surface and effectively eats its way through substrates rich in organic debris. In contrast the ragworm is an active scavenger and predator of smaller creatures both on and beneath the mud surface. Where they occur in high densities, smaller annelids may be significant prey, such as *Tubifex* and *Scoloplos armiger*. The most valuable crustaceans are the shore crab (*Carcinus maenas*), another active scavenger on the mud surface, and the small amphipod *Corophium volutator*. Crabs are recorded as a frequent food of goldeneye when feeding in estuaries.

Because these animals show their greatest activity when the tide covers the flats it is at this time that they are both more easily detected by predators and also more easily caught, since they are closer to or on the mud surface. This behaviour of the prey, which makes them more available to predators, is reflected in the distribution of wading birds and duck which tend to concentrate their own feeding activity at the tide's edge. As the time after exposure of the flats increases, the activity of the invertebrates diminishes and they move deeper into the substrate. Thus, only an hour or so after exposure, there may be few feeding birds at all on the upper parts of the mudflats, particularly if they are well drained.

Since invertebrate animals are 'cold blooded' their activity is reduced and may virtually cease at low temperatures, and creatures capable of doing so will burrow more deeply as the flats are exposed during cold weather. They will also respond in these ways more quickly the lower the air temperature is and the net result of this behaviour is to reduce their availability to waders and wildfowl. As a consequence of this, birds must feed for longer periods of time on each tide to satisfy their own increased daily food requirements under cold conditions, and it is this relationship which underlies the perceived need for restraint on the part of wildfowlers during prolonged severe weather.

Reference to the densities at which key invertebrate animals can occur illustrates the enormous food resource which our estuaries represent for overwintering waders and wildfowl. Amongst the molluscs the Baltic tellin may occur at densities in excess of 5000/m², whilst the laver spire shell frequently reaches between 20,000–30,000/m². The most abundant crustacean, *Corophium volutator*, may exceed 50,000/m². Of the larger annelid worms the lugworm populations may be in the order of 200–250/m², whilst ragworm can exceed 1000/m². The smaller representatives of the annelids such as *Tubifex costatus* has been recorded at densities of over 1 million per square metre where levels of organic pollution are high, and these situations can attract large numbers of wildfowl, including shelduck and pintail.

These densities do not of course apply to the same square metre of mudflat, for there is a zonation between low- and high-water levels and from the mouth to the upper reaches of an estuary. In addition, the distribution of invertebrates is exceedingly patchy. Important factors determining distribution are the nature of the substrate, the height of the shore, the amount of organic material in the sediment, gradients of salinity and aeration, and the degree of waterlogging. Within a single estuary it is usually the case that only a relatively small number of species will reach high densities and then principally in a handful of locations, and it is these same factors which determine the presence or absence and the differences in abundance which are found to exist between estuaries.

Because estuary birds tend to have particular food preferences and specialisations, some of which have been referred to, the zonation and patchiness of invertebrate distribution within an estuary has a marked influence on the feeding dispersion of waders and wildfowl and on their movements during the course of the tidal cycle. Thus, particular locations within an estuary will be noted for holding, say, shelduck, whilst in another location there will be large numbers of curlew. To a great extent, it is this same relationship which makes one estuary good for certain species of wader or wildfowl but poor for others.

On the flood tide, estuaries become valuable feeding grounds for fish, in particular for flatfish such as dabs, plaice and flounders. These too are dependent upon the exceptional abundance of invertebrate prey and are themselves a significant food resource for fish-eating birds such as goosander, merganser and cormorant.

SPARTINA

No description of estuarine ecology would be complete without reference to the impact of the

*The enclosure and reclamation of mudflats threatens
many estuaries* (Nature Conservancy Council)

cord grass, *Spartina anglica*. This is a hybrid species
which arose naturally between our native *Spartina
maritima* and a North American species, *S. alterni-
flora*. Hybrids are typically robust and vigorous in
their growth and *Spartina anglica* is no exception.
More unusually, however, it is fertile, indeed
highly so. The presence of this hybrid and of the
non-fertile cross, *S. townsendii*, was first recorded in
1870 in Southampton Water, from where it has
spread naturally and artificially by transplants to
estuaries all around our coast, being reported as far
north as the Outer Hebrides. Whereas *Spartina* can
invade parts of the mature saltmarsh it is principally a pioneer species, readily colonising open
mudflats and early stage saltmarsh below mean
high-water mark.

Once established from a seed or from a buried
stem fragment growth takes place by way of long
radiating underground rhizomes which sub-

sequently send up aerial shoots giving the typical
mass of upright stalks, invariably in a distinctive
circular hummock. These circular clones continue
to extend, sometimes by up to ten centimetres a
year, until they eventually coalesce to form a
continuous sward. This process has been aptly
described as 'meadowing'. It is the speed of this
process, the ability of the developing meadow to
trap silt and moreover the ability of this aggressive
plant to displace other valued vegetation (e.g.
Zostera, *Salicornia* and *Puccinellia*) and open mudflats which makes it so notorious.

Although *Spartina* may provide some shelter for
wildfowl it is often avoided by waders for roosting
and its seeds and vegetative parts are not a
significant food. Its presence in an estuary is
rightly regarded as undesirable and great efforts
have and continue to be made to prevent its
establishment and to control its spread in locations
where it already has a foothold. Undoubtedly
Spartina invasion poses a considerable threat in

estuaries where extensive, relatively level mudflats exist, such as on the Mersey and at Lindisfarne.

The picture, however, is not entirely one-sided, for as early as the 1920s, die-back in *Spartina* meadows was reported in estuaries where it first became established in the latter part of the last century. Now, widespread decline of *Spartina* has been recorded in many estuaries on the south and east coasts, with a consequential erosion of the raised marsh that it had created and a return to open mudflats at a lower level. This has been accompanied in some instances by a resurgence in populations of *Salicornia* and *Zostera*.

Wide-scale die-back has been attributed variously to excessive waterlogging, the development of anaerobic conditions and accumulation of litter. In fact, it is probable that several factors are involved. Certainly increased waterlogging and the associated creation of slurry-like surface muds is prevalent within *Spartina* swards and this in itself will lead to the development of anaerobic conditions. More local reduction in extent may come about as the result of wave action at the seaward edge of a *Spartina* sward and at its landward edge there is invasion and displacement by mixed marsh species such as sea purslane and saltmarsh grass. A further feature in areas of wide-scale die-back is a reported decrease in the vigour of individual plants. Since *Spartina anglica* is, as far as we can see, here to stay, this change in its character gives some hope for the future and perhaps in time it will be viewed as simply another component of the pioneer saltmarsh community.

In the preceding account of estuarine habitats, emphasis has been placed on the relationships which exist between the physical form of an estuary, the distribution and abundance of invertebrate animal and plant species and the feeding ecology of waders and wildfowl. A knowledge of these relationships can make a valuable contribution to the management of estuary land, for example, in the determination of sensible shooting and non-shooting zones, and the assessment of practical management opportunities.

Since the processes of erosion and sedimentation operate on an estuary-wide basis, it is in practice impossible to manage just part of it so as to perpetuate a given arrangement of mudflats and saltmarsh. Desirable though this might seem in the short term, perhaps where a valued saltmarsh is being eroded away, the continued cycle of natural change signifies the health of an estuary and should therefore be accepted. The quality and attractiveness of habitats for overwintering and breeding wildfowl and waders can, however, be maintained and enhanced by judicious on-the-ground management. This may include the local control of *Spartina* so as to prevent its invasion of particularly important sections of mudflat, but it is likely that practical effort will focus on the mature saltmarsh, where there may be scope to re-introduce stock grazing, manipulate grazing levels or introduce mowing so as to extend and improve the quality of the sward for grazing waterfowl.

All around the coast of Britain, enclosure and reclamation for agriculture and industry, together with developments such as road crossings, coast protection schemes, waste disposal and marinas, continue to bring about the attrition of estuarine habitats. It is an unfortunate fact that mudflats and saltmarshes have a low economic value in their semi-natural state and there seems to be no shortage of proposals to put them to more 'beneficial' uses. What is also important within an estuary is that development in these ways can radically affect the processes of erosion and accretion over large parts of an estuary and can bring about changes quite literally miles away. This underlines the principle that the management of one part of an estuary cannot be seen in isolation from the whole and that defence of an estuary's integrity is fundamental.

7

WILDFOWLING AND THE LAW IN ENGLAND AND WALES

PETER TURNER

(Revised November 1988)

Legal technicalities are probably anathema to most wildfowlers. It is, however, an inescapable fact that the privilege, or right, to enjoy the pursuit of fowl in the splendid wilderness of the marshes depends for its continuance upon the law. By the same token the law imposes duties upon those who enjoy its privileges. To neglect these duties is to run a grave risk of ultimately losing their concomitant rights. The prudent wildfowler will therefore carry out meticulously the duties which the law and traditions of his sport impose. At a lower level a more than passing interest in the law is required of the wildfowler who wishes to avoid trouble for himself or to protect his shooting rights. Certainly no official of the great preponderance of B.A.S.C. clubs which maintain a reserve can afford to be without a working knowledge of the law.

LICENCES AND CERTIFICATES

No wildfowler, or any other shooting man, may lawfully possess, purchase or acquire a shotgun without holding a shotgun certificate authorising him to possess shotguns under the provisions of the *Firearms Act 1968* and related legislation.

To obtain a shotgun certificate, application has to be made on a prescribed form (obtainable from police stations) to the chief officer of police for the area in which the applicant resides. The legislation requires the chief officer of police to be satisfied that the applicant is not prohibited by the Act from possessing a shotgun and can be permitted to possess a shotgun without danger to the public safety or to the peace before granting a certificate. For most practical purposes a prohibited person is one who has been imprisoned for three years or more, or who applies for a shotgun certificate within five years of being released from a term of imprisonment for three months or more but less than three years.

An applicant who is aggrieved by the decision of the chief officer of police has a right of appeal to quarter sessions. On the determination of an appeal the court may make such order as it thinks fit as to payment of the costs of the appeal. It cannot be said with certainty that a successful appellant would obtain an order for costs against the chief officer of police; but it is possible. A great deal would depend upon the circumstances of the appeal.

Once granted, a shotgun certificate continues in force for three years unless cancelled or revoked. No conditions other than such as may be prescribed by the Secretary of State may be imposed on the grant of a shotgun certificate. The only conditions prescribed (as at November 1988) are that the certificate holder must sign it in ink and report to the police the loss or theft of any shotgun in his possession.

There are exceptions which enable certain persons to use or have in their possession a shotgun without holding a certificate. Probably the two most important from the wildfowler's point of view are, first, that which enables a person to borrow a shotgun from the occupier of private premises and to use it on those premises in the occupier's presence and, secondly, that which enables a person who does not hold a shotgun certificate to use a shotgun at a time and place approved for shooting at artificial targets by the chief officer of police for the area in which that place is situated.

A police constable is entitled to demand the production of a shotgun certificate from any person whom he believes to be in possession of a shotgun. Failure to produce the certificate enables the constable to seize the gun and to require the person who has failed to produce the certificate to declare his name and address. It is prudent therefore to carry the certificate on all occasions when a gun is carried.

It is an offence to sell or transfer to any other person, other than a registered firearms dealer, any Section I firearm or a shotgun unless that other person produces a certificate authorising him to purchase or acquire it. It is, therefore, essential when selling a gun to examine the purchaser's shotgun or firearm certificate. Similarly when taking a gun for repair the firearm or shotgun certificate must be produced to the repairer.

Possession of a shotgun without holding a certificate is punishable on conviction with a maximum fine of £2000 and/or six months' imprisonment.

Since the use of rifled weapons for wildfowling is contrary to the spirit of the sport and is discouraged by the B.A.S.C., it is probably only necessary to say that a firearm certificate is necessary to possess any rimfire or centrefire rifled weapon or ammunition, certain air weapons and shotguns (see below). Similarly for most types of distress flare cartridges a certificate is required; even if they are fired from a shotgun.

The *Game Licences Act 1860* requires a person who shoots pheasants, partridges, grouse, blackgame, moorgame, hares, snipe, woodcock, rabbits or deer to hold a game licence. This licence is obtainable as of right at any main Post Office on payment of the duty, but it is only valid from the hour of issue. An annual licence costs £6 and runs from 1 August to 31 July following. A licence running from 1 August to 31 October costs £4. A licence from 1 November to 31 July costs the same. A licence for any continuous period of fourteen days costs £2.

Only the annual licence gives the holder the right to sell game, and then only to a licensed dealer. Nowadays game is defined in the *Game Act 1831* as pheasant, partridges, grouse, blackgame, moorgame and hares. No licence is needed to deal in certain wild duck, pigeon, snipe, woodcock or rabbits.

The law provides so many exceptions to the rule of having a game licence to shoot rabbits or deer that, in practice, the sportsman can almost always do without one. The *Game Licence Act 1860* itself provides that all those who kill rabbits or deer on any enclosed land whatever by permission or order of the tenant or owner need not hold a game licence. Similar provisions exempt a person lawfully exercising his rights under the *Ground Game Act 1880* and the *Hares Act 1848*.

The game licence of a person convicted of trespass in pursuit of game under Section 30 of the *Game Act 1831* is automatically invalidated. Pursuit of game without holding a game licence constitutes two offences. First under the *Game Act 1831* and secondly under the *Game Licences Act 1860*. Proceedings can be instituted under both Acts in respect of the same offence, but only the local authority can prosecute under the latter Acts, unless the appropriate procedure under Section 4 of the *Finance Act 1961* to enable the police to prosecute has been put into effect. Anyone can prosecute under the former Act. The penalties are cumulative and the maximum fine under the former is £5, under the latter £20. The offence under the *Game Act 1831* can only be committed in respect of game as therein defined.

An owner or occupier of land, or a police officer, or a person who himself holds a game licence can demand to see the licence of a person doing any act for which such a licence is necessary. Refusal to produce the licence and to give one's name and address on request constitutes another offence for which the maximum penalty is £20.

A gundog is a faithful companion. He should always be under close control. The chasing of stock could lead to claims for damages (John Paley)

DOGS

The dog owner should take out an insurance policy to indemnify him against loss or damage caused by the dog. Chasing of sheep and poultry by dogs can lead to substantial claims for damages. It is an offence under the *Wildlife and Countryside Act 1981* for a dog to be not on a lead or otherwise under close control in a field or enclosure in which there are sheep, with the exception of *inter alia* working gundogs.

MINORS

The *Firearms Act 1968* consolidated the law concerning possession and use of firearms by minors. Formerly the law on this topic was somewhat difficult to discover, being scattered amongst several different statutes.

The first point of importance is that it is an offence for a person under the age of seventeen to purchase or hire *any* firearm. Although this provision does not prevent the gift or loan of a firearm to such a person, a different section of the Act prohibits a gift or loan of any Section I firearm or ammunition therefore to persons under the age of fourteen. Section I applies to all firearms and ammunition, except a shotgun as defined, and air weapons not of a type declared by the Secretary of State to be specially dangerous, and normal ammunition for use in such weapons. A similar provision makes it an offence to part with the possession of such a firearm or ammunition to a person under fourteen years of age subject to limited exceptions of little importance to the wildfowler. Similar rules concerning the purchase and sale, hiring, and parting with possession apply to air weapons; but with fewer exceptions.

So far as shotguns are concerned it is an offence to make a gift of such a weapon or ammunition to a person under the age of fifteen. It should be noted that a loan is not prohibited and therefore a boy under the age of fifteen may be lent a shotgun and ammunition. If he has no shotgun certificate it can be used only in the circumstances mentioned earlier relating to exemptions from holding a shotgun certificate. If, however, a boy under fifteen years of age is the holder of a shotgun certificate he can be lent a shotgun and ammunition; subject to the proviso that it is an offence for a person under the age of fifteen to have an assembled shotgun

with him except whilst under the supervision of a person aged twenty-one or over, or while the gun is so covered with a securely fastened gun cover that it cannot be fired. Shotgun certificates have been granted to boys under fifteen as there is nothing in the Act to prohibit such a step. The Act does not therefore prevent a father from educating his son in the use of a shotgun from whatever age he considers appropriate; provided that it is done under the supervision upon which any wise parent would insist.

Air weapons are treated differently from shotguns and Section I firearms. The basic rule is that it is an offence for a person under the age of fourteen to have an air weapon or ammunition for an air weapon with him. There is an exception to this rule permitting a person under the age of fourteen to have an air weapon with him while he is under the supervision of a person aged twenty-one or over; even so, if the weapon is used to fire a missile beyond the premises on which it is being used an offence is committed both by the person who fires the missile and the person who is supervising the youngster concerned.

It is also an offence for a person under the age of seventeen to have an air weapon with him in a public place except an air-gun or an air-rifle so covered with a securely fastened gun cover that it cannot be fired. It should be noted that the exception does not extend to air-pistols.

GUNPOWDER AND CARTRIDGES

In order to purchase gunpowder for muzzle-loading weapons and loading black cartridges a permit, issued by a chief constable, is needed by virtue of *Statutory Instrument No. 1598 of 1953* made under the *Emergency Powers Laws (Misc. Provs.) Act 1953*. No permit is needed for percussion caps. Anyone holding a stock of shotgun cartridges for sale needs to have a permit for storage from his local council, but if the cartridges are for the holder's own use no permit is required.

FIREARMS (AMENDMENT) ACT 1988

This Act received Royal Assent on 15 November 1988 and introduces some important changes to the firearms legislation, not least as it affects shotguns. As at November 1988 the full details of how those changes will be administered and the timetable for their introduction has not been finalised, so in any case of doubt the B.A.S.C. or the police should be consulted.

However, the changes will include:

(a) A new definition of 'shotguns'.

(b) Increased police powers relating to the grant of a shotgun certificate including the applicant having to provide a 'good reason' to possess a shotgun ('good reasons' are listed in the Act), and the descriptions and serial numbers of shotguns to be listed on certificates, though there will be no limit on the number of guns which may be possessed.

(c) Applications for certificates will have to be accompanied by photographs.

(d) If a shotgun is lent to another for more than 72 hours, the transfer will have to be notified to the police.

(e) Semi-auto and pump action shotguns with a magazine capacity of more that 2 cartridges, will in future be classed as Section 1 firearms, and require a firearms certificate.

(f) A shotgun certificate will have to be produced to purchase cartridges.

It is likely that there will be a statutory requirement to notify change of address and to provide security for shotguns when not in use.

FORESHORE SHOOTING

The myth, at one time widely believed, that any member of the public has a right to shoot on the seaward side of sea walls has been finally exploded by the case of *Beckett v. Lyons (1967) 1 AER 833.* That there is no public right to shoot on the foreshore there is no doubt. Nor is there any doubt that such a right cannot be acquired by custom or usage by the general public. The only public rights over the foreshore are for purposes ancillary to navigation or fishing. As a consequence anybody on the foreshore is a trespasser unless he has permission from its owner or is exercising his right of navigation or fishing. The true significance of the principles so clearly enunciated in *Beckett v. Lyons* can only be appreciated when viewed against the background of the trespass provisions of the *Firearms Act 1968*. This act makes it an offence for a person who has a firearm with him to enter or be on any land as a trespasser and without reasonable excuse (the proof whereof lies on him).

For the purpose of this section 'land' includes land covered with water. Thus, not only does the wildfowler trespassing on the foreshore render himself liable to a civil action for trespass, but he also renders himself liable to prosecution under the Act.

B.A.S.C., on behalf of its members, has negotiated a form of authority entitling its members to be on foreshore in the ownership of the Crown. Members of B.A.S.C. having shotguns with them on foreshore so owned do so with the consent of the owners and, therefore, commit no offence under the section. The authority does not extend to foreshore owned by any other person or body or which has been let to any other person or body by the Crown Estate without reserving the sporting rights. In all other cases permission must be obtained in some form or another if the risk of prosecution or proceedings for armed trespass are to be avoided. In this connection it should be noted that there are substantial stretches of coastline where the Crown, which in the absence of evidence to the contrary, is presumed to be the owner, has either granted the foreshore absolutely, or a lease of it, to a subject.

This authority does not convey shooting rights to B.A.S.C. members but is a privilege enabling traditional wildfowling to continue within the law on uncontrolled Crown foreshore. It is not adequate to make a wildfowler on the foreshore into an 'authorised person' for the purposes of the *Wildlife and Countryside Act 1981*. He can only shoot the duck, geese and waders listed in Part I of Schedule 2. He must not shoot birds in Part II of Schedule 2; such birds include pigeons and crows.

Whilst considering the question of armed trespass in relation to the foreshore it is important that it should be properly defined. The standard definition is that the foreshore is that part of the sea shore which is more often than not covered by the flux and reflux of the four ordinary tides occurring midway between springs and neaps. For most practical purposes this can be construed, so far as the landward limit of the foreshore is concerned, as the medium line of ordinary tides midway between springs and neaps.

This definition excludes most green marshes, saltings, or merses (call them what you will) which lie on the seaward side of the sea wall in many places. Hence the wildfowler must not shoot there unless he has permission.

Access to the foreshore can only be lawfully had over public rights of way. There is not necessarily a public right of way along a sea wall. Even if there is a right of way along a sea wall or elsewhere such a right is exactly what it says and no more. Thus, although it may be lawful to carry an unloaded gun along a public right of way, the minute a person fires a gun whilst exercising this right of passage he becomes a trespasser as against the owner of the soil over which it passes.

Modern Ordnance Survey maps indicate public rights of way, where space is available, as shown on the Definitive Maps of such rights which local councils are now obliged to maintain. In the absence of any indication on the Ordnance map inquiry should be made of the local council in whose area any alleged public right of way is thought to exist.

TRESPASS – OTHER THAN
ON THE FORESHORE

Anyone who enters on another person's land without permission or lawful authority is a trespasser and renders himself liable to a civil action

Below high water mark. Wildfowlers must know the definition of foreshore (Pamela Harrison)

for damages, or for an injunction to restrain a further trespass, or (if he has a gun with him) to the criminal proceedings, discussed in the section on foreshore shooting, under the *Firearms Act 1968*. In addition anybody who can be proved to have been trespassing in the daytime in pursuit of game, woodcock, rabbits or snipe can be prosecuted under Section 30 of the *Game Act 1831*.

Although no reasonable neighbour would stop a person from retrieving a dead bird which had fallen over the boundary he has a perfect right to do so and it is just as much trespass to enter on somebody else's land for this purpose as any other. The only proper thing to do is to be courteous and seek permission. Should this not be possible because the landowner concerned is not available, or for some other good reason, it is prudent to leave one's gun on one's own land. Failure to do so increases the risk of prosecution under the *Game Act* and makes it virtually certain under the *Firearms Act 1968*.

The *Game Laws (Amendment) Act 1960* has substantially increased the powers of the courts and police in relation to trespassing and poaching offences. For example, upon conviction for trespass in pursuit of game in the daytime a court can order the offender to pay a fine of up to £20 and confiscate his gun. The police are empowered to

enter land without invitation if they have reasonable grounds to believe that a person on that land is committing an offence under Sections 1 or 9 of the *Night Poaching Act 1828*, or Sections 30 or 33 of the *Game Act 1831*. Such a person may be arrested and searched. Any game or gun found in the course of the search may be seized.

The *Poaching Prevention Act 1862* as amended by the 1960 Act enables a police constable who has good cause to suspect a person of poaching game to stop and search him and any vehicle on any road or public place and seize any game, guns or ammunition which he finds. If the search discloses sufficient evidence the constable must bring the charge under the Act. Upon conviction the offender can be fined up to £50 and any game or guns found in the search may be confiscated. For the purpose of the 1862 Act game includes pheasants, partridge, grouse, blackgame, moorgame, their eggs, and hares, rabbits, woodcock and snipe.

The *Night Poaching Act 1828–44* make it an offence unlawfully to take or destroy any game or rabbits by night on any land, open or enclosed, or on any road or path or in any gate or entrance-way on a road or path, or unlawfully to enter by night on to any land with any gun, net, engine, or other instrument in order to take game. For the purpose of these Acts 'game' means the same as in the *Game Act 1831*. Only the owners or occupiers of land or their gamekeepers and the police have powers of arrest for the purposes of this Act.

HIGHWAYS

Although there is no express rule to prohibit shooting on the highway it is (apart from the question of safety) a hazardous thing to do.

First, Section 19 of the *Firearms Act 1968* makes it an offence for a person without lawful authority or reasonable excuse (the proof whereof lies on him) to have with him in a public place a loaded shotgun or loaded air weapon or any other firearm (whether loaded or not) together with ammunition suitable for use in that firearm. Whilst possession of a shotgun certificate may well amount to lawful authority, and the fact that one has the sporting rights on the land on one or both sides of the highway concerned may constitute a reasonable excuse, these defences are by no means certain. The prudent shooting man will therefore avoid having a loaded shotgun in a public place unless

he wishes to become the subject of a leading case. Until the courts have given a ruling the not uncommon practice of driving birds to guns standing on the highway is of doubtful legality.

Secondly the *Highways Act 1959* makes it an offence to discharge a gun without lawful authority or excuse within fifty feet of the centre of the highway which consists of or comprises a carriageway, and thereby to endanger, injure, or interrupt any person using the highway. To constitute the offence it is essential to show that someone using the highway was endangered, interrupted, or injured and unless this can be proved it is no offence under this Act to shoot birds from the highway. That this provision was not repealed by the *Firearms Act 1968*, may be a useful point to make in a case concerning that Act in the circumstances described in the preceding paragraph.

THE WILDLIFE AND COUNTRYSIDE ACT 1981

The days when all legislation designed to protect birds was strongly opposed by sportsmen have long since gone. The B.A.S.C. representing wildfowler-conservationists is proud to have made positive suggestions for improved conservation which are incorporated in the legislation.

The Act is basically simple in that it makes it an offence to kill, injure, or take any wild bird. An attempt to do these things is also an offence. Similar protection is given to nests and eggs.

Having created overall protection the Act then creates some exceptions to this general protection by listing many species of birds in Schedules to the Act and making special provisions with regard to those birds. Except for Sections 5 and 16 of the 1981 Act gamebirds are not given any protection beyond that given to them by the *Game Acts*.

Thus Schedule I lists birds which are rare, or which for some other reason need special protection. Birds listed in this Schedule are protected by a special penalty. This Schedule is itself divided into two parts. Part I contains a list of birds specially protected throughout the year. Those only so protected during the close season are listed in Part II of Schedule 1. Part I of Schedule 2 lists the wildfowler's legitimate quarry. The birds in this Schedule may be killed or taken outside the close season. Shooting of wildfowl on Christmas Day and Sundays in Scotland is prohibited. In England

and Wales it is illegal to shoot wildfowl on a Sunday in the following counties (or parts of counties in existence before the 1974 reorganisation): Anglesey, Brecknock, Caernarvon, Carmarthen, Cardigan, Cornwall, Denbigh, Devon, Doncaster, Glamorgan, Great Yarmouth County Borough, Isle of Ely, Leeds County Borough, Merioneth, Norfolk, Pembroke, Somerset, North and West Ridings of Yorkshire. Part II of Schedule 2 lists such agricultural pests as pigeons and such enemies of the game preserver as the carrion crow and these may be killed by authorised persons at any time, except in Scotland on Sundays and Christmas Day, and in England and Wales in counties where Sunday shooting of Schedule 2 birds is prohibited. Authorised persons are the owners or occupiers of the land on which the killing, etc. takes place; the person having the sporting rights over the land; a person having the permission of such persons to shoot over the land; and persons having the written permission of the Local Authority and certain statutory bodies. A trespasser 'only after a few pigeons' therefore commits an offence under the Act; as does a wildfowler shooting Schedule 2 Part II birds on the foreshore unless it is owned by or let to his club. Game birds are not included in these schedules. The open seasons created by the Act are indicated in the table on the next page.

If it can be shown to have been necessary to prevent *serious* damage to crops, vegetables, fruit, growing timber or any other form of property, or to fisheries, the killing of birds in the close season or of birds enjoying the general protection of the Act is lawful. This defence does not apply in the case of birds listed in Schedule I and the onus of proof is on the defendant. The Act, however, also provides for licensed shooting of birds causing damage to crops but it is advisable to seek such a licence from the appropriate authority before taking any action.

The Secretary of State can vary the open season, but only to make it shorter. In this connection it should be noted that the 1981 Act also enables him to sign an order preventing the shooting of the birds in Schedule 2 Part I during prolonged severe weather for periods of up to fourteen days. There are adequate safeguards in the procedure for the shooting man, but at the same time the fowl can be given protection speedily at a time when no responsible sportsman would wish to shoot them (see Chapter 28).

On the topic of wildfowl shooting between 1 and 20 February two important points must be mentioned. First, the area where this is permitted by no means coincides with the area previously defined as 'foreshore', which is much more restricted. It certainly includes saltings which are flooded by ordinary spring tides. Secondly, the extension does not apply to waders; only to ducks and geese.

A final point on the general working of the Act is that the Secretary of State can add birds to or remove them from the Schedules. He may also declare certain areas as sanctuaries. This power is in addition to that contained in any other statutes. Before he makes any of the orders which the Act empowers him to make the Secretary of State must consult an advisory committee, provide for the submission of objections and representations, and, if he thinks fit, hold a public inquiry.

The pattern of the Act is, therefore, of strict protection, whilst at the same time recognising the legitimate right of the sportsman to take the harvestable surplus; coupled with a degree of flexibility to enable natural fluctuations in the bird populations to be catered for.

Having assimilated the general nature of the Act the wildfowler should attempt to obtain a good working knowledge of the important detailed provisions which affect his sport.

Section 5 of the 1981 Act prohibits certain means of taking or killing any wild birds, including game birds. It is illegal to use or set in position any spring, trap, gin, snare, hook and line, any electrical device designed to frighten birds, any poisoned, poisonous or stupefying substance, a floating container holding explosives or use any gas, net, baited board, bird lime or similar substance. Live decoy birds may not be used if they are tethered, blind or maimed. Shotguns having an internal diameter at the muzzle of more than one and three-quarter inches may not be used to kill wild birds. Except in order to find a wounded bird the use of an artificial light for killing or taking birds is unlawful. Section 5 also makes it an offence to use any automatic or semi-automatic weapon with a magazine capable of holding more than two cartridges. A licence under Section 16, however, allows the unrestricted use of semi-automatic shotguns for the purpose of killing pest species, i.e. those listed in Part II of Schedule 2. The courts have yet to decide whether pump-action weapons are considered to be 'semi-automatic'.

Table 3: Open seasons for wildfowl and waders (all dates inclusive)

Species	Shooting	Sale (of dead birds)
Wild duck of the following species: mallard, teal, wigeon, pintail, tufted duck, pochard, goldeneye, gadwall	*Inland:* 1 Sept–31 Jan next *Below high water mark of ordinary spring tides:* 1 Sept–20 Feb next	1 Sept–28 Feb next the following species: mallard, teal, wigeon, pintail, tufted duck, pochard, shoveler
Wild geese of the following species: pinkfooted, greylag, whitefronted (England and Wales only), Canada	*Inland:* 1 Sept–31 Jan next *Below high water mark of ordinary spring tides:* 1 Sept–20 Feb next	Totally prohibited
Woodcock	*In England and Wales:* 1 Oct–31 Jan next *In Scotland:* 1 Sept–31 Jan next	1 Sept–28 Feb next
Common snipe	12 Aug–31 Jan next	1 Sept–28 Feb next
Golden plover	1 Sept–31 Jan next	1 Sept–28 Feb next
Coot and moorhen	1 Sept–31 Jan next	1 Sept–28 Feb next (coot only)

The use of a mechanically propelled vehicle or boat, or an aircraft in immediate pursuit of any wild bird for the purpose of driving, taking or killing it is prohibited.

The 1981 Act has extended the restrictions on the sale of dead wild birds. It is now an offence to sell not only the geese species listed in Part I of Schedule 2 but also gadwall and goldeneye. The other species may be sold from 1 September to 28 February. Of the species listed in Part II of Schedule 2 only woodpigeons and feral pigeons may be sold dead at all times.

Prior to the *Wildlife and Countryside Act 1981* it was permissible for the eggs of a wild duck, goose or swan to be taken from a nest in the wild for the purpose of causing them to be hatched. That provision was not included in the 1981 Act in order to reduce the risk of the eggs of rare species being taken by mistake. A general open licence under Section 16 of the 1981 Act issued by the Nature Conservancy Council now allows mallard eggs to be taken from the wild before 31 March in England and Wales (10 April in Scotland) so long as they are hatched and their progeny returned to the wild before 31 July. Eggs taken from the wild may not be sold.

Any ringing of mallard reared from eggs taken from the wild must be done under licence from the Nature Conservancy Council.

The police have substantial powers under the Act and a constable can stop and search any person found committing an offence and search any vehicle or boat which that person is using. He can also arrest the person if he fails to give his name and address to the constable's satisfaction. Wild birds, and any weapon or other article capable of taking a wild bird, may be seized. Upon conviction of an offender the court must confiscate any wild bird, egg, skin, or nest, and the offender may forfeit any weapon, decoy bird, or other article by means of which the offence was committed. This is in addition to any fine or imprisonment which the court may order. Except in cases to which the special penalty applies, the court can order a fine of up to £200 per bird. The special penalty is up to £1000 per bird or egg.

INSURANCE

Whilst no sum of money can provide adequate compensation for a life lost or a body maimed, every shooting man should insure against third-party liability.

CONCLUSION

This summary of the law is only sufficient to inform the wildfowler about the more common legal points which are likely to crop up in his shooting career. Those who wish to be better informed must study the statutes and cases for themselves. A recommended text covering all aspects of the law as it affects shooting and the countryside is *Fair Game* by Charlie Parkes and John Thornley published by Pelham Books in 1987. All should be scrupulous in their own observance of the law affecting the sport and vigilant to see that others do likewise. Failure in this respect can only damage the sport. The right to shoot is too precious to be lost as a result of the failure of a small number to honour their obligations.

8

WILDFOWLING AND THE LAW IN SCOTLAND

THE LATE WILLIAM BROTHERSTON
(REVISED BY DAVID GUILD)

Scots law differs in many respects from English law including to some extent those branches of the law which affect the activities of wildfowlers. It is the purpose of this chapter to outline the most important aspects of the law which are of interest to wildfowlers, and particular attention will be paid to those rules which differ from the English ones.

The first important question is: where can wildfowling be done? Most obviously, one can shoot wildfowl on one's own land, or on land over which one has permission to shoot. The problem in law arises in relation to other land. Then it is important to consider the law of trespass. Trespass consists in temporary intrusion on to land or other heritable property, such as a private loch, without the owner's permission or other legal justification. A public or private right of way would constitute such justification to get to an area of land where shooting was permitted.

Trespass is dealt with both by the civil and the criminal law, but the civil law ways of dealing with it are cumbersome. The owner of the land over which the trespass is being committed is entitled to order or conduct the trespasser off his land, but he is not entitled to use force to achieve this end, unless it is made necessary by the use of force on the part of the trespasser; and even then the landowner's force must be only as much as is reasonably necessary. The use of such preventive devices as man traps and spring guns is not permissible.

Unless actual damage is caused, the landowner cannot sue the trespasser for damages. He can, on the other hand, obtain from the courts an order of interdict, which prohibits the trespasser from trespassing again. The usefulness of interdict is, however, severely limited. It only prevents future trespass by the same trespasser. It will only be granted if repetition of the trespass is feared, and is in any event only granted in the discretion of the court.

More important, in practical terms, are the various statutory criminal offences relating to trespass. There are a number of old statutes dealing with trespass, and in particular trespass in pursuit of game. There is no general definition of game in Scots law, and it is necessary to look at the terms of particular statutes to determine their scope. For that reason, the only such statute which is of importance to wildfowlers is the *Game (Scotland) Act 1832* (otherwise known as the Day Trespass Act) which applies to trespass in search or pursuit of 'game or of woodcocks, snipes, wild duck or conies' (but not wild geese). Such a trespass during the hours of daylight (i.e. from the last hour before sunrise to the first hour after sunset) is an offence. If a bird is shot from one's own land, but neither killed nor mortally wounded, it is an offence under the Act to pursue it on to neighbouring land. Only if the bird is killed, or rendered moribund, may it be recovered without contravention of the Act. The offence under the Act may also be committed by sending one's dog on to land in pursuit of game, even when the dog's owner does not himself trespass. This Act is notable in respect of two procedural anomalies. Private prosecutions, not normally allowed in Scotland, are specifically provided for in the Act, and conviction may proceed on the evidence of a single witness. (The *Night Poaching Act 1828*, which deals with the period of the day not covered by the Act of 1832, defines 'game' in such a way as not to concern the wildfowler).

A more modern offence is that created by Section 20 of the *Firearms Act 1968*. Under that section it is an offence for any person, who has in his possession a firearm, to enter or be on any land as a trespasser and without reasonable excuse (which he must prove). It should be noted that this offence is committed whatever the purpose of the trespass may be. In terms of penalty, too, it is a much more serious offence.

There is one apparent exception to the law of trespass in Scotland which is of particular importance to wildfowlers. That exception relates to the foreshore. The basic rights in the foreshore, like other land, belong in feudal theory to the Crown. But the Crown's right in relation to the foreshore is different from that in respect of other land. Even where the foreshore is owned by private individuals there remains in the Crown certain rights which are held in trust for the public. The public is therefore entitled to resort to the foreshore for certain purposes, including recreation. In this connection, recreation may be regarded as including wildfowling. It is therefore generally legitimate in Scotland (so far as questions of trespass are concerned) to engage in wildfowling on the foreshore. The foreshore in Scots law means that area lying between the high- and the low-water marks of ordinary spring tides. (The definition of foreshore in England and Northern Ireland is slightly different.)

Some limits on the public right exist. It may be taken away by statute in particular cases. This applies to Nature Reserves and Country Parks, and bye-laws regulating the use of the foreshore may be made under the *Civic Government (Scotland) Act*

1982. The practical limitation to the public right is that it may be difficult to get to a stretch of foreshore over land without trespassing.

Open and close seasons and the methods of killing and taking wildfowl are governed by the same statute in Scotland as in England, *viz*: *Wildlife and Countryside Act 1981.* There are some variations of the rules as they apply to Scotland. By virtue of a special limitation of Section 2 of the Act, it is not permissible to shoot wildfowl (or various other birds) in Scotland on Sundays, even in the open season, or on Christmas Day. Whitefronted geese are protected in Scotland.

It is thought that the word 'game' in the *Game Licences Act 1860* does not include wildfowl, and accordingly such a licence is not required by a wildfowler. Firearms are dealt with by the *Firearms Act 1968* and the *Firearms (Amendment) Act 1988* which apply equally to Scotland and England. An appeal against a refusal to grant a shotgun or firearms certificate is dealt with by the Sheriff Court.

9
WILDFOWLING AND THE LAW IN NORTHERN IRELAND

BILL BECKETT

WILDFOWLING IN NORTHERN IRELAND

Like many of our counterparts in the rest of Britain, we wildfowlers in Northern Ireland would claim that wildfowling in the truest sense of the word means shooting in coastal waters where, for our part, the main quarry is wigeon, mallard, pintail and grey geese. I suppose that could be looked upon as a fairly contentious statement from whatever side of the Irish Sea it originates, and one which would be challenged by those members of the shooting fraternity who pursue wildfowl on inland waters. However, as one who regularly shoots duck on inland flight ponds and flood meadows, I would still argue that I wildfowl below the high-water mark and merely shoot duck inland!

Ireland, both North and South, was once a land rich with game and fowl, but today Ireland is facing problems in respect of pollution, drainage and general loss of habitat, just as any other region where agriculture and industry are forced to co-exist. The change of use of many of our once remote coastal areas, increased leisure activities and shooting pressure itself are cited as contributing to the decline of game in Ireland. The noticeable decrease in numbers of some feral and migratory wildfowl has even led to bans, voluntary and mandatory, on certain species, most notably whitefronted geese. But it is not all such a bleak picture; there are, of course, many areas, some quite sizeable too, where wildfowling and other shooting sports can be pursued in much the same fashion as they have for generations.

To understand wildfowling in Northern Ireland one must first know something about the topography of the areas in which most of the fowling is carried out and something of the habitat likely to be encountered. For a country as small as ours, we have a considerable length of coastline and quite a diverse one at that, if we consider the rough, rugged cliffs of north Antrim, the coves and headlands of the eastern counties and the long, sandy beaches and secluded inlets in the extreme south. Not all, admittedly, perfect wildfowling terrain, but within those areas there is potential for some of the finest wildfowling in these islands. Areas where the sport is actively pursued each winter by hundreds of Northern Irish wildfowlers, many of whom can trace their links with the sport through generations, to the days when grandfathers used punt guns, or hid in the channels or rocky promontories for the flights of geese coming to the grazing offered by rich pasture and cropped fields which led down to the water's edge. Many shooters acquire wildfowling skills, but the best of them are born into the sport!

Three areas in Northern Ireland stand out in particular when we talk about fowling, and the common denominator is they are all sea loughs, rich in feeding and with this history of wildfowling. The least known or maybe least recognised of these is Larne Lough, situated north of Belfast, perhaps better known for the town of Larne, which stands at the northern edge of the lough and one of the principal passenger and cargo ferry terminals in Ireland, looking, as it does, across the narrow North Channel towards Scotland, quite clearly visible some twenty miles away, even on the worst of days! Obviously some disturbance is caused in the north end of Larne Lough with the continual coming and going of shipping, and the huge power station on the peninsula opposite, which forms the eastern shore of the lough. Fine shooting still can be had, however, especially in the south and east of the lough, by those who are familiar with the region.

Local knowledge is, of course, the key to successful wildfowling anywhere along our shore line in

89

the UK and that premise would hold fast for the other two principal regions in Northern Ireland, Lough Foyle and Strangford Lough. Both are areas of outstanding natural beauty, but like so many such areas there is a more sinister side in terms of tide and wind; areas so picturesque yet so dangerous for the inexperienced or unwary.

The Foyle for most of its length forms a natural border between Northern Ireland and the Irish Republic in the form of the neighbouring county of Donegal. It is a huge inlet along Ulster's Atlantic coastline, rich in fowl and fowlers alike. As we go to press, B.A.S.C., local wildfowling clubs, R.S.P.B. and D.O.E. Northern Ireland, are negotiating a management scheme on Lough Foyle.

PERMITS

The third and, possibly, the most important wildfowling area in Northern Ireland has a shooting permit scheme in operation. The National Trust controls the shooting on Crown foreshore around Strangford Lough, as well as many of the islands which are dotted along the length of this long finger of sea which projects into the coastline of eastern County Down. The Strangford Lough Wildlife Scheme was created by covenant between B.A.S.C. and the National Trust. Strangford is one of the most striking features of that county with only the Mountains of Mourne, immortalised in song by one of her favourite sons, Percy French, outgunning it as the region's top tourist and recreation attraction. Having as it does over 150 miles of coastline, it is a most important wildfowling area, but like Lough Foyle, Strangford's beauty can be misleading, and its toll of unwary sportsmen lengthy. Barely one-third of a mile wide at its narrowest point, an estimated 350 million cubic litres of water pour through the 'narrows'

Shooting from a 'scance' on Strangford Lough (Bill Beckett)

during each tidal cycle. The tidal range is between three and four metres, and with the current running in excess of seven knots (approximately ten mph) it is thought to be one of the fastest currents in northern Europe. Add to all that some 115 islands, and in excess of 1000 tidal rocks, many of which are shootable, and one can imagine the potential for wildfowling on this long sea lough.

Wildfowling is, as we earlier agreed, about shooting the intertidal area around our coast, and that immediately throws up the problem of defining the limits of that area, as trespass and particularly armed trespass is a serious offence on both sides of the Irish Sea. It is not good enough to assume all foreshore below the level at which the foreshore grasses occur are below the mean high-water mark. Many of the grasses will quite happily exist below that mark and the shooter making that assumption in unfamiliar terrain could be laying trouble in store for himself. Rule of thumb, and it's a fairly accurate one too, is find where the living seaweed is attached to the stones of the foreshore, and that will certainly be below the mean high-water mark.

The National Trust permit scheme, which has been in operation on Strangford Lough, is now in its twenty-first year and has about 500 shooters participating. By far the overwhelming majority of these are members of the five B.A.S.C. affiliated clubs which, along with the National Trust, formed the Strangford Lough Wildlife Scheme in 1966. Today these clubs make up the Joint Council of Wildfowling Clubs for Strangford Lough. Private permit holders number about 50, although it is possible to obtain a visitor's permit, basically a one-day or weekend permit, by simply applying to the National Trust at their Northern Ireland Headquarters. The criteria for obtaining these is fairly informal requiring only a few days' prior notice. However, the officials at the National Trust will want to assure themselves the applicants are competent wildfowlers, are preferably in the company of other permit holders, and hold valid insurance, such as the type held by all B.A.S.C. members. Visitors from outside the province, but still residents of the UK, must apply for a permit to bring sporting weapons into Northern Ireland, and again this is quite a simple operation whereby application is made to the Royal Ulster Constabulary, Firearms Branch, Belfast. This permit is, of course, read in conjunction with the applicant's

shotgun certificate and is valid for the period specified, and covers all weapons as indicated.

THE LAW

It is not sufficient, though, to let a shooter, be he wildfowler, rough or game shooter, resident or visitor to Northern Ireland, pack his gun and dog in the car and simply go shooting. Obviously, we in Northern Ireland live in a completely different situation from our contemporaries on mainland Britain. Restrictions are placed upon shooters this side of the 'water' as to the number of guns which can be owned, methods of purchase and re-sale, storage, calibre and variety of weapons we can legally possess. Whilst we realise the need for such tight control of firearms we still feel aggrieved that the shooting community bears the brunt of these restrictive measure when here, as in Britain, statistics show a very low proportion of crimes are committed with sporting firearms. One of the big differences in Northern Ireland is that we do not have shotgun certificates; all weapons, sporting or otherwise, must appear on the full firearms certificate, and that includes air-guns. All variations to the certificate must be approved by the RUC in advance, with the make, number, calibre, model and from whom purchased verified by a registered firearms dealer.

The Firearms (Northen Ireland) Order 1981 and *1983*, and certain provisions in the *Firearms (Amendment) Act 1988*, set out the requirements for possessing firearms in this country. For example, it is an offence to acquire or sell firearms or ammunition without holding a current firearms certificate or to possess ammunition in greater quantities than that specified on the certificate. A constable can ask any person whom he believes to be in possession of firearms or ammunition to produce his certificate; failure possibly leading to the firearms and ammunition being seized, and the person prosecuted. The Order extends beyond the possession of sporting weapons to those who are entitled to use them and at what age. Under Part II of Article 26 it is generally an offence for any person under the age of eighteen to purchase acquire, or have in their possession a firearm or ammunition. It is not an offence for any person of sixteen years or over:

(a) to have with him a firearm or ammunition for sporting purposes, where he is in the company and under the supervision, of another person of eighteen years or over who holds a firearm certificate in respect of that firearm or ammunition; or

(b) to purchase, acquire or have in his possession, a shotgun or any other firearm of a calibre not exceeding .22 inches and ammunition there for the purpose of destroying or controlling animals and birds. . . .

  (i) on agricultural lands occupied by him, or,
  (ii) on agricultural lands on which he works and also resides.

Quite clearly anyone under the age of sixteen may not use a shotgun or, indeed, any other weapon in Northern Ireland under any circumstances. Even with these firearms restrictions, there are currently on issue an estimated 120,000 firearms certificates with approximately 50,000 for live quarry shooting.

There are, of course, many differences in the law between Scotland and Northern Ireland and the rest of Britain. Some laws can trace their roots through many centuries, and I suppose quite a number of them should be updated to take into account today's changing situation. Two of the most talked about variations, as far as we in Northern Ireland are concerned, are those relating to the ban on moonlight shooting, a fairly recent legislative change, and the absence of the extended season for foreshore fowling, those twenty days mainland shooters have in February. The moonlight shooting ban has curtailed wildfowling for a number of years, and few of today's generation of wildfowlers in Northern Ireland will have the experience unique to flighting fowl under the moon. That aspect of fowling is, I am afraid, destined to fade into the annals of wildfowling history in the Province, and the present unrest would appear to be the biggest contributing factor here. The law as it presently stands allows shooting from one hour before sunrise until one hour after sunset. As in Scotland wildfowling is also prohibited on Sundays in Northern Ireland.

The other complaint the Province's wildfowlers make, and have made to a succession of B.A.S.C. representatives and, indeed, their WAGBI forerunners. is the non-extension of the fowling season on the foreshore in Northern Ireland to include those days in February. Some have even suggested a change in the wildfowling season, whereby it would open a month later, 1 October, and continue until 20 February. It is not a suggestion without some foundation either. In Northern Ireland, we depend greatly upon the influx of migratory fowl which would make up a considerable proportion of the total number of birds shot. As a rule, this influx does not occur until the latter part of the present season and the birds remain here until well into March. Sound an argument as it may be, it really will take much lobbying to make such changes because, let's face it, when compared with the pressures shooting throughout the UK is facing, it is only a minor point within the broader perspective.

QUARRY SPECIES

The law regarding shooting in Northern Ireland is, as it is on the mainland, continually being assessed and new legislative measures being taken to provide guidelines for the benefit of quarry, habitat and shooter alike. Recently the *Wildlife (Northern Ireland) Order 1985* became law after a fairly lengthy passage through the various committee stages and the amendments agreed upon by Government and interested parties alike. Some might regard it as the definitive work, whilst others, myself included, would regard it as the basis for future legislation, which would be flexible enough to allow change when it became necessary. Whether or not this can be achieved remains to be seen, but all must surely agree it is a step in the right direction and has given wide-ranging powers to those enforcing it. Like all legal documents, it is worded in such a manner as to render it incomprehensible for the first-time reader, only with study do the salient points flow. Under the Order, all wild birds are afforded some level of protection. It can be further split into two sections or schedules. Schedule 1 lists those birds which are protected by special penalties; Schedule 2, those birds which may either be killed or taken outside the close season (under Part I) or by authorised persons at all times (under Part II). It may be noted that some quarry species occur in both schedules, being given special protection during the close season.

For illustration only those species which would be of some interest to those using the foreshore have been included in Schedule 1 below. Schedule 2 is given complete.

SCHEDULE 1

Birds which are protected at all times by special penalty

Dotterel	Greenshank
Dunlin	Heron
Garganey	Scoter, common
Godwit, blacktailed	Swan, Bewick's
Goosander	Swan, whooper
Grebe, blacknecked	Whimbrel

Birds which are protected by special penalty during the close season

Gadwall	Pochard
Goldeneye	Scaup
Pintail	Shoveler
Plover, golden	Wigeon

SCHEDULE 2

Part I *Birds which may be killed or taken outside the close season*

Curlew	Pintail
Duck, tufted	Plover, golden
Gadwall	Pochard
Goldeneye	Scaup
Goose, Canada	Shoveler
Goose, greylag	Teal
Goose, pinkfooted	Wigeon
Mallard	

Part II *Birds which may be killed or taken by authorised persons at all times*

Crow, hooded/carrion	Pigeon, feral
Gull, great blackbacked	Pigeon, wood
Gull, herring	Rook
Gull, lesser blackbacked	Sparrow, house
Jackdaw	Starling
Magpie	

In many respects the *Wildlife (Northern Ireland) Order 1985* is modelled on the mainland's *Wildlife and Countryside Act 1981*. Thus the Order goes on to detail restrictions on lifting eggs of wild birds and the licences which are available for this purpose, particularly first clutch mallard eggs, which is a common practice by wildfowlers. It lays out criteria for setting up refuges and penalties which can be imposed on persons killing, injuring or taking any wild bird within those designated areas. Restrictions on the methods of killing and taking wild birds are also similar including the prohibition of the use of automatic and semi-automatic shotguns which will hold more than two rounds in the magazine. The sale of all wildfowl is illegal in Northern Ireland except under licence.

So, all-in-all, a fairly comprehensive document, and one which should be in the possession of all shooters in Northern Ireland. There is no doubt it is quite difficult to understand exactly the meaning of some of the items contained within the Order, but the Department of Environment, Countryside and Wildlife Branch, have, within their ranks, some excellent people at the other end of the telephone who will and, indeed, very often have, cleared up misunderstandings, or misinterpretations in the Order. Copies of the Order are obtainable from HMSO, Belfast.

So there we have it; wildfowling in Northern Ireland. Not that different to that conducted on foreshore, saltmarsh, mudflat or island around any other part of the British coastline. Some of the terminology is certainly different, as is some of the quarry, but the characters involved in the sport are very much the same as they are anywhere else. It takes, I suppose, a certain temperament to become a wildfowler. We have in Northern Ireland those who dabble in the sport, who venture out on a few occasions every season, and think of themselves in the same light as others who guard jealously their haunts around the foreshore, who never give too much away about their forays in weather which would make most pull the bed-clothes over their heads again! But that's wildfowling and wildfowlers for you. Shooters yes, but surely something more!

10
INTERNATIONAL LEGISLATION

COLIN B. SHEDDEN

Any chapter entitled 'International Legislation' is bound to receive scant attention from readers, who will either expect a plethora of rather dry, complex detail or scant summary of the obvious. I hope to avoid both these categories and, by taking a middle path, illustrate how fowling in the 1980s is becoming increasingly influenced not only by our own national government but directly and indirectly by supranational government and a number of truly international conventions, to which the United Kingdom is a ratifying party.

Firstly, however, it should be pointed out that international legislation at present influences what quarry species we can shoot, how we can shoot them, when we can shoot them and even, to some extent, where we can shoot them. Consequently, even though many of these measures are enforced via national legislation, we should be aware that many of the recent changes to the relevant statutes have arisen through international initiatives.

The most glaring level of international intervention in the British way of life is, for most people, the European Economic Community (EEC) or the Common Market. As I hope to explain, this influence reaches as far as the wildfowler.

EEC

In March 1957 the Treaty of Rome was signed by six European countries, establishing the EEC, whose aim was to create a large area with a communal economic policy, allowing continuous expansion, increased stability and an accelerated rise in the standard of living. The accession of the UK, Ireland and Denmark followed in 1973, Greece in 1981 and Spain and Portugal in 1986, making the Community one of twelve member states.

We are all aware of the power and influence that the Community has over many aspects of our lives and this does not extend only to areas of trade, development, agriculture and internal security.

When the Treaty of Rome was being drafted in the 1950s environmental considerations were certainly not as prominent as they now are and, in fact, the Treaty does not contain any provisions for an environmental policy. However, Article 235 of the Treaty stipulates that, if Community action appeared necessary without the Treaty having provision or the powers of action requested, the Council of Ministers could make the appropriate arrangements. It is through this Article that a large number of environmental measures have been introduced, sometimes in conjunction with Article 100, which deals with the 'harmonisation of national measures'. These steps are now superseded by a new act, the Single European Act, which, in unifying the concept of a Common Market, gives the Community direct responsibility for environmental matters.

The chief EEC document that concerns us is, of course, the 1979 Directive on 'The Conservation of Wild Birds' (79/409/EEC). (A directive is binding on each country as far as the results to be achieved are concerned, but leaves open the method of attaining the defined objectives.) The Birds Directive effectively rules on the matter of bird protection, limits the number of species which can be shot or taken, as well as the means of taking them, restricts the trade in certain species and lays down certain general measures concerning the protection of habitats.

What did this mean for the fowler? Firstly, it meant that the UK government was obliged to amend its national legislation within two years of the Directive coming into force so that all of the Directive's provisions could be incorporated. The direct result of the 1979 EEC Directive on Wild Birds, in the UK, was the *Wildlife and Countryside Act 1981*. This Act took on board all the provisions of the Directive and also covered areas not mentioned by the Directive, such as wild plants and animals. The main provisions of the Directive reflected in the *Wildlife and Countryside Act* meant:

(1) The loss of certain quarry species to the British fowler such as curlew, whimbrel, bartailed godwit, grey plover, redshank, jack snipe, common scoter, velvet scoter, garganey, longtailed duck, scaup and the bean goose. In this case, although the Directive inspired the *Wildlife and Countryside Act*, the Directive still gives the UK the right to treat all of the above mentioned species as sporting quarry. However, the *Wildlife and Countryside Act* actually afforded all of these species complete protection. In fact, the only British quarry species afforded protection under the Birds Directive was the stock dove. This is now recognised as being an error and efforts to seek its reinstatement as a legitimate quarry species are being pursued by the Department of the Environment.

(2) The recognised need to establish Special Protection Areas (SPAs). Here, the Directive was far-sighted and recognised that habitats important for birds need as much protection as the birds themselves do. Consequently, all species listed in Annex 1 of the Directive (74 species in 1979, increased to 144 by an amendment in 1985) are those whose habitats are the object of special conservation measures. This annex includes such species as the barnacle goose, Greenland whitefronted goose and the golden plover. (It may seem strange that an Annex 1 species like the golden plover can still be

shot as legal quarry, but this just identifies the important point that Annex 1 deals with the protection of the habitat of these species and not the species themselves.) It still remains to be seen whether SPAs will actually affect the fowler any more or less than the present national system of Sites of Special Scientific Interest.

(3) Annex III (1) stipulates that, of the fowling quarry, only the mallard can be exploited commercially, i.e. sold in all member states, although Annex III (2) and III (3) does allow for permission to be granted to individual member states for the sale of other species. Britain is authorised, under these Annexes, to permit the sale of seven duck species as well as snipe, woodcock and golden plover.

(4) The methods and means of taking these wild birds are outlined in Annex IV of the Directive, which prohibits the use of mutilated birds as decoys, semi-automatic shotguns whose magazine contains more than two cartridges, and the use of boats 'driven at speed exceeding 5 kilometres per hour'. (However, the *Wildlife and Countryside Act* has gone further, prohibiting the use of any mechanically propelled boat in immediate pursuit of wildfowl.)

Thus, the Birds Directive has had a profound effect on all shooting, not only fowling, in the UK as well as throughout the EEC. Despite the length of

The Wash, numerically the most important area in Britain for wintering wildfowl, has been designated as a SPA and Ramsar site (Alan Jarrett)

time since its first appearance, this Directive still causes much debate and controversy. Many EEC member states, such as Italy, France, West Germany and Belgium, have been taken before the European Court of Justice for supposed failure to implement it. Italy and Belgium have been found guilty and consequently not all national legislations are regarded as being truly in line with the Directive. Much depends upon interpretation, though, particularly over Article 9, which allows for derogations (specified exceptions) to protect public health, safety, prevent serious damage to crops and fisheries and protect other fauna and flora. Licensed shooting of brent geese in southeast England, for instance, is one example of such a derogation, another being the shooting of crows, etc. As long as EEC countries interpret this Article in different ways, there will continue to be not only confusion, but also loopholes by which the European Commission and member states will criticise each other. Fortunately, there are no moves afoot to charge the UK government with failure to implement the general provision of the Directive, since the *Wildlife and Countryside Act* recognises all the points the Directive demands. However, conservation and preservation organisations have used the habitat protection provision of the Directive to put pressure on the UK government over the drainage of Duich Moss, a roosting site for Greenland whitefronted geese on the island of Islay.

COUNCIL OF EUROPE

The second political institution in Europe that must be recognised is the Council of Europe, which was founded in 1949 to achieve greater unity between the democratic European states. Its aims specifically include environmental matters and consequently, since 1962, it has worked to unify and harmonise the policies of its 21 member states, which include the UK. The direct result of this institution's involvement with environmental legislation has been the Berne Convention 'Concerning the Conservation of Wildlife and the Natural Habitat of Europe'. This came into force in June 1982 and has been ratified by both the UK and the EEC. The contracting parties undertake to take all measures necessary to protect the habitats of wild species of flora and fauna, paying particular attention to those areas which are of importance for migratory species. Appendix 2 of this convention

lists the birds and animals that are to be strictly protected (such as the barnacle goose and the shelduck) and effectively all others can be 'exploited', though deserving a certain level of protection such as close seasons and regulation on their sale, etc. Interestingly, the Berne Convention exempts species such as the crow, magpie and jay from any protection, recognising them as pest species even though the 1979 EEC Birds Directive does not. Additionally, Appendix 4 also lists prohibited means of taking birds, very much in accord with Annex IV of the Birds Directive.

The Council of Europe's 'Committee of Experts for Training and Education in the Environment' has, since 1983, been looking at the role of hunting examinations in its member states. This committee had recommended to the Committee of Ministers of the Council of Europe the adoption of a 'hunting examination' (mandatory shooting test) in all member states. However, the UK has always stood firm on this point and, influenced by the B.A.S.C. and its voluntary training programme 'The Proficiency Award Scheme', has no intention of implementing this Council of Europe recommendation in the UK.

Two other international conventions affect the fowler in the UK, or should I say affect fowlers' quarry and their favoured habitat – wetlands.

BONN CONVENTION

The 'Convention on the Conservation of Migratory Species of Wild Animals' was brought into force in November 1983, after being signed by 28 states in 1979. So far, only 15 states have ratified the Convention. Through two annexes, this Convention hopes to seek international agreements on the immediate protection of threatened migratory species (Annex 1) and conservation and management of species who have 'an unfavourable conservation status' (Annex 2). This latter annex includes all 'migratory species of ducks, geese and swans' and consequently this Convention could be one that could be of interest to the British fowler since all his quarry species are included. However, since it came into force in 1983 this Convention has effectively achieved very little, mainly due to its working basis being one of voluntary international co-operation, which often takes time. However, if the number of contracting parties increases then this Convention does have great potential and it should be borne in mind that a working group under this Convention has already been formed to look at the particular situation relating to migratory duck and geese in Europe. Thus our particular group of quarry species could be among the first to benefit from the Bonn Convention.

RAMSAR CONVENTION

The 'Convention on Wetlands of International Importance Especially as Waterfowl Habitat' was brought into force in 1975 and so far over 39 states have ratified it. Each contracting party must designate at least one wetland, selected in accordance with its international role from an ecological point of view (but above all its importance to waterfowl), to be included in a list of wetlands of international importance. Additionally, each contracting party must bear in mind its responsibilities on the international scale for the conservation, improvement and rational exploitation of migratory populations of waterfowl, as well as favouring the conservation of wetlands and wild birds by creating reserves in these wetlands.

Obviously, this Convention does affect the British fowler, since many sites of fowling importance are now British Ramsar sites. Of the thirteen sites in the UK, such as Lindisfarne, the north Norfolk coast, Ouse Washes and Loch Leven, many are well known to fowlers so, obviously, Ramsar designation does not automatically exclude sporting shooting as an acceptable activity.

The preamble to the Ramsar Convention states that one of its objectives is 'to stem the progressive encroachment on and loss of wetlands now and in the future'. To achieve this, the Convention seeks to promote the wise use of wetlands and their fauna and flora. These, surely, are among the aims and objectives of any thinking fowler. There are actually very few legal obligations with respect to sites placed on the Convention's 'list of Wetlands of International Importance'. These, roughly, are the promotion of the conservation of these wetlands and their waterfowl and the creation of reserves in these wetlands. Since more than 80% of the sites on this international list are already within nature reserves (in 1980) it is usually found that existing hunting legislation is not modified by a site becoming designated under the Ramsar Convention. In fact, far from restricting the activities of the fowler, the Ramsar Convention has played an important role a number of times in the UK in the protection of important wetlands against development, drainage and subsequent damage.

The arena of international legislation is further filled with a large number of conventions and organisations that have small impact on the sportsman in Britain. It is not necessary to go into these in detail since the three conventions and two governmental bodies mentioned above are those of direct relevance. It should be mentioned that both the EEC and the Council of Europe have been, or currently are, involved with proposed legislation affecting not the fowler's quarry, nor its environment, but affecting his weapons and to a lesser extent his ammunition. The Council of Europe, in 1986, pepared a draft convention designed to harmonise national legislations on firearms. This was never implemented, but recently, as part of the EEC's goal of 'completing the market', in other words making the Community one where customs and trade barriers would be redundant by 1992, a draft Directive on 'The Control of the Acquisition and Possession of Weapons' has been prepared. Designed to allow free movement of legally held weapons in the Community, but to prevent movement of illegal weapons, many of its ramifications could once again affect the British sportsman, including the fowler, through any resultant changes in national legislation.

We have, therefore, seen that the shooting man in Britain is not sheltered from international legislation and is directly affected by the national legislation it demands. This applies probably more so to fowlers than any other group of sportsmen since fowlers' quarry species are migratory and as such do not respect international borders, and thus demand some level of international management. We have seen how the EEC's Bird Directive influenced the *Wildlife and Countryside Act*, how the Council of Europe's Berne Convention strengthens many points contained in the Directive and how both the Bonn and Ramsar Conventions focus international attention on waterfowl and wetlands. With the growing awareness of environmental issues by the public and the Single European Act giving the EEC direct competence in environmental matters, it is surely inevitable that the destiny of fowling in Britain will be decided, to some degree, in the corridors of power in Brussels and Strasbourg or in the convention secretariats in Switzerland or Germany.

11
PROFILE OF A WILDFOWLING CLUB

ALAN JARRETT

As long ago as 1953 the Kent Wildfowlers Association (KWA) was founded in the front room of a modest house in Gillingham, barely more than a stone's throw from the Medway Estuary. At that early stage it was simply the gathering together, within a club framework, of like-minded men who shared a common interest. Those interests were succinctly summarised in the KWA Rules drawn up at the inaugural general meeting, held on 26 September 1953, and attended by around 30 members. Although some 35 years have elapsed since that evening, those interests and aims remain virtually unchanged to this day.

Rule 2 of the KWA Rules states:

The objects of the Association shall be:
(a) To protect the interests of wildfowlers.
(b) To maintain and uphold the best interests of sportsmanship in wildfowling.
(c) To maintain a proper conservation of all wildfowl.
(d) To provide facilities to encourage a better understanding of wildfowling as a sport.
(e) To provide social and other amenities for its members.

Really these objectives sum up why we have wildfowling clubs and what the aims of these clubs are today. As we shall see, the wildfowling club has frequently developed into a vast and complex organisation, so far removed from its 1950s base as to be virtually unrecognisable, yet the objectives still remain the same – the perpetuation of the sport and the quarry via landholding, conservation and education.

During those early years the KWA had the task of formulating a coherent policy, and moving forward toward what was hoped would be a bright future. A first subscription of 10s. 6d. per annum was paid into the Association's new bank account opened in November 1953, and the KWA was on the road and running. An early concentration of effort was to be centred on social aspects, conservation and political activities. An early and crucial fight to defeat proposals to ban Sunday shooting in the county was ultimately successful and, even though the KWA could in no way take full credit for such a victory, the united wildfowling front had a bearing on the eventual outcome and showed that here was a new voice which was determined to make itself heard.

CONSERVATION

A heavy conservation theme ran through the club's work right from those earliest days, with the formation of a Conservation Sub-Committee as early as 1954. This, together with liaison with the Wildfowl Trust, clearly demonstrates that even 35 years ago Kentish wildfowlers fully understood how vital the cause of conservation was to the future of their sport. It is a theme which has proved central to the administration of the club ever since.

Perhaps surprisingly, it was not considered an early priority to provide exclusive shooting rights for club members. In the present day and age such facilities are fundamental to what running a wildfowling club is all about. But in the 1950s social and conservation aspects received first attention, perhaps because there was less pressure being applied to the foreshore, with a virtual free-for-all, in wildfowling terms, being the norm. The real scramble for foreshore shooting rights was still a long way off.

Yet within 4 years, by 1957, the KWA had already provided the basic ingredients required for operating a complete club: 1955 – clay shoots established; 1956 – first club dinner, mallard and Canada geese released, whilst the first two reserves were acquired; 1956 – first exclusive shooting rights and newsletter launch.

Social aspects were strongly favoured and popular. As well as the annual dinner, there were monthly general meetings at which members could get together, come to know each other and exchange yarns. Wildfowlers have always been great story tellers, even if certain crucial details will be left to the listeners' imagination! Indeed any excuse for a gathering, whether it be meeting, clay shoot or impromptu assembly at the marsh head, serves as a means of strengthening the social bonds so essential if a young club is to grow and flourish. Such social gatherings were also a means of spreading the word that the KWA existed, and was open for membership, and during those early years many of the country's foremost wildfowlers entered the fold. Pre-1957 the KWA had comparatively little to offer its members in material terms, save for their affiliated membership of WAGBI, and there was little call for anything else. In the main, members sported over the foreshore of the Medway and Thames Estuaries and in the Swale Channel, and there was little pressure to disturb the status quo.

1957 was a good year. Membership was increasing steadily, a new reserve near Faversham was established and, most noteworthy of all, the club acquired its first exclusive shooting rights. Nor Marsh, a substantial island off the southern shore of the Medway near Gillingham, was leased from the Gillingham Borough Council – Nor Marsh is today an RSPB reserve.

Interestingly, even though many see the more restrictive wildfowling regimes of today as a thoroughly modern trend, the first club shooting over Nor was subjected to a self-imposed limit of three days' shooting per week. This restriction was designed to reduce any tendency towards overshooting and to provide a period for assessment. Subsequently the restriction was lifted, with the resultant increase in wildfowling opportunity having no detrimental effects on the quality of sport.

Thus from day one of leasing land the KWA was engaged in active and responsible management of the wildfowl resource. Such management continued during the close season, with raiding parties aimed at rat control in support of the many bird species attempting to breed on the island.

FACING A THREAT

In the late 1950s the KWA was left largely to its own devices to build the club virtually unfettered by outside interference. But in 1960 the interest of the local county naturalist trust in acquiring land was noted with some alarm, so that the officers of the club realised that unless some action was taken many prime wildfowling areas could be lost. As a result most of the area known as Stoke Saltings in the Medway Estuary was leased for one shilling an acre, and this area too remained under club control for a period of 21 years.

A limit on membership of 500 had been set, and throughout the 1960s the club grew in size. There was still plenty of 'free' shooting with the club's exclusive rights acting as a centrepiece of activity around which members could revolve. The next great watershed to affect wildfowlers nationwide was *The Firearms Act 1968*. This, almost at a stroke, with the advent of the new offence of armed trespass – with severe penalties available to deal with transgressors – brought an effective end to free-for-all wildfowling. Now landowners became more aware of the land under their control and were prepared to use the new law against hitherto rather blasé trespassers. Thus the pressure was really on for clubs to provide more exclusive shooting rights for members, many of whom were now being increasingly denied access to traditional wildfowling areas.

For the KWA with 500 full members the potential problem was considerable, and was only resolved by some diligent committee work, a great deal of hard labour and one or two lucky breaks. By the early 1970s the club had acquired additional areas on the southern shore of the River Thames, in the Medway Estuary and a vast area of foreshore in the Swale Channel. In the short term at least the shooting future of the club seemed assured. Still the old ways of paying a nominal membership fee continued, and only after much soul-searching were subscriptions increased in line with current needs accepted by the members. Indeed a series of 100 % increases soon took the subscription rate to £16.00 per annum. A firm commitment to adopt inflation-linked annual increases as the norm later in the decade allowed the club to record a reasonable surplus of income over expenditure.

In 1972 the KWA bought its very first piece of land – fifty-one acres of creek bed and surrounding marsh. The area was at Yantlet Creek and lay between the rivers Thames and Medway on the Hoo Peninsula. It was a valuable wildfowl roost and, as such, has remained an unshot reserve ever since. Later a further purchase of seventeen acres of adjoining salting was added and Local Nature Reserve status was attained.

Increasingly with the passing of time, and as the clamour for more recreation grew, the security of wildfowling tenure became a pressing problem for clubs throughout the land. Mostly clubs held their shooting rights on tenuous agreements, so that each summer club officers would be faced with the task of renegotiating shooting licences. The lucky ones managed to tie up land in various leasehold arrangements, although even these were apt to be of fairly short-term duration – in many instances representing little more than a stay of execution.

It was becoming ever more apparent that real security of tenure could only lie in freehold ownership. The KWA were to become one of the pioneers in the field, although the purchase of the 450 acre Bridgemarsh Island by the South Essex Wildfowlers' Club as long ago as 1963 was very much a torch to light the way for others to follow.

FINANCE

Of course the key to long-term wildfowling security was to lie in finance: only those clubs large enough, and forward-thinking enough, to formulate viable fiscal policies would be able to compete

in the land purchase field when the opportunity arose. In the early 1970s the KWA embarked on the road to providing secure shooting by setting aside £5000 per annum to be placed in a land purchase fund.

History now shows this to have been a crucial time for the KWA, for in the early part of this decade the club was to lay the foundations for what were to be spectacular land-buying feats that would shake the wildfowling world. Yet the intervening fifteen years were to prove a minefield for such an amateur organisation as a wildfowlers' association, totally dependent as it was on voluntary officers, with much money wasted and many blind alleys to be overcome.

Wildfowl over the north Kent marshes (Alan Jarrett)

The 1970s were infamous for the raging inflation which almost devastated the British economy. Paradoxically this aided the KWA's fund-raising schemes, for the inflation-linked subscription went up annually in leaps and bounds – something which did little to endear the system to those obliged to put their hands in their pockets! Aside from subscriptions most clubs generate a modest income from other sources: clay pigeon shooting, raffles, dog trials and sundry receipts. For the KWA the second largest income was from the monthly summer clay pigeon shoots and, of all income, this source was most likely to produce a much increased yield with some investment and hard work.

In 1978 the KWA purchased its Detling clay shooting ground, and once the dust had settled on various exchange deals with neighbouring landowners the club was left in possession of a valuable thirty-one-acre site. Much work and investment was to follow, indeed this still occurs to the present day, but the net result is that there now exists a club facility capable of providing an annual income which provides a valuable back-up to the revenue raised from subscriptions.

On the conservation front the club added another reserve area in 1974, this time the 1100-acre Cliffe Pools site, so that the KWA now controlled strategically placed reserves adjacent to the Thames and Medway, and as far east as Canterbury. In 1975 duck release reached a peak with over 2000 mallard put down on club reserves and adjacent sites; this feat was never again repeated, as a gradual shift in conservation priorities from duck-rearing and release to habitat protection and management was taken up by sportsmen.

The KWCA's clay shooting ground – an important source of income for land purchase and other projects (Alan Jarrett)

GREYLAG GEESE

However, 1975 saw the KWA join in a scheme already being run by WAGBI and local farmers to re-establish greylag geese as a breeding bird in Kent. This was done in two ways: a complete moratorium on the shooting of these birds on club land and a programme of releasing hand-reared birds – from Scottish eggs – onto selected sites. This work was to prove a complete success, so that eventually feral greylags reached sufficient numbers to allow a limited annual cull by club members. The KWA had contributed some 200 released birds to the re-establishment scheme, and this, together with what was to become a ten-year moratorium on shooting, was to prove of great importance to the scheme's ultimate success.

The KWA's objective of land purchase was not solely aimed at providing secure wildfowling, but to allow the club to embark upon an integrated land management programme for both shooting and conservation. The actual legalities of land-holding were anything but straightforward, for it was not permissible for such a loose-knit body as a wildfowlers' association to hold land, or to borrow

the sort of substantial sum which might be necessary to effect a sizeable purchase. There were alternatives, and the club had to decide upon the method most likely to suit its purposes. In the mid-1970s it was necessary for the KWA to thoroughly prepare itself for the future, in order that any future investments might proceed smoothly.

LIMITED COMPANY

Eventually the club took the option of forming its own company – to be called the KWA Ltd. This would have its own memorandum, articles, directors and council of management and would hold KWA ownerships, both leasehold and freehold, in trust for the members of the Association. On the face of it this seemed the ideal set-up, but would eventually prove to be a dead weight around the club's neck and the cause of much grief and argument.

The late 1970s and early 1980s saw a great wind of change beginning to sweep the wildfowling land, with others besides wildfowlers taking an increasing interest in our coastal wetlands. This, allied with the relentless advance of changing agricultural practices resulting in vast drainage programmes, really began to cause problems for wildfowlers who, by and large, were still relatively ill-prepared for a fight. The protectionist camp was able to carry a lot of political weight, and things became progressively more difficult for those seeking to carry out their sport in peaceful isolation. For the KWA, in possession of substantial parts of the highly prized ornithological paradise of the North Kent Marshes, the problems began to stack up. The Royal Society for the Protection of Birds, the Nature Conservancy Council and the Kent Trust for Nature Conservation all held land in the area. Around the turn of the decade their attentions meant more and more land being either lost to sport or the subject of increasing pressures.

CRISIS

Yet the KWA of the early 1980s had long shed its tiny skin of 1953 and had blossomed into a vast organisation with substantial land holdings, a large membership supplying a considerable annual sum and in excess of £50,000 in the bank. Yet this was to be no guarantee of continued shooting for, during 1982, the club lost the shoot-ing rights of Nor Marsh, most of Stoke Saltings and some fourteen miles of foreshore on the Thames. As a result many members drifted away and the club was in grave danger of heading into an unstoppable downward spiral.

The 1982 AGM, held in September, elected a new committee and officers. It was to be the committee's task to halt the slide and once again steer the club back to its rightful position of high standing in the national wildfowling community. The club's task in 1982 was one of halting a period of relative decline. Many of its prime functions were in limbo, with only the enlargement of the land purchase fund proceeding with anything like its former momentum. It was a time for the new committee to evaluate and determine the policy for the immediate future.

For wildfowlers on a national scale 1981–2 was a critical time anyway. With the *Wildlife and Countryside Act 1981* reaching the statute book the pressure was immediately applied, with many sporting aspects under siege. For the KWA this additional challenge could scarcely have come at a worse time, for it meant a re-evaluation of all shooting practices and, in many instances, a considerable alteration to normal modes of operation.

Fortunately the B.A.S.C. (formerly WAGBI) was on hand to advise and support. Much hard work now needed to be done in drawing up the necessary management plans which would serve to govern the club's shooting methods for the foreseeable future. I shall not dwell on this facet of club management, for it can be found thoroughly covered elsewhere in this volume. Suffice to say that such management planning is now fundamental to the running of the modern-day KWA.

In simple terms the KWA had to decide on a new direction and purpose which would see it move smoothly into the remainder of the decade; to decide on its conservation strategy, its land-buying priorities and such matters as membership recruitment and fund-raising. In many ways a new, stronger and more purposeful club was about to emerge from the near ruin of the old. In such times of desperate pressures from protectionists, what was needed was a clear sense of purpose and togetherness and to this end the KWA's general meeting of 13 April 1983 was a turning point for the club. At this meeting the following resolution was adopted:

WE RESOLVE THAT: We the members of the Kent Wildfowlers Association do and hereby reaffirm our commitment and dedication to the cause of conservation,

AND THAT: The Committee is hereby directed that this must be a very important principle in the formulation of the policy of the Association and the general conduct of its affairs.

AND THAT: This be publicly acknowledged by the change of name of the Association to the Kent Wildfowling and Conservation Association (KWCA) at the annual general meeting next.

This change of name was duly adopted at the 1983 AGM, and the committee now had a clear road along which it would travel. Of equal importance was the setting up of an alternative means by which the club could hold land and this was done through the legal framework of appointing trustees. Trustees were appointed in 1982 and the necessary rule was added to the club's constitution.

The KWA Ltd was still in existence and, because of tax implications, must remain so into the future. But with new directors and council of management and no effective trading anyway, the original intention of asset holding could be adhered to. Henceforth the new assets of the club could be handled through the trustees as directed by the committee who, after all, were responsible in the best democratic manner to the general membership for their activities.

So the KWCA engaged on a programme of shooting within the framework of management plans over land almost wholly contained within various Sites of Special Scientific Interest (SSSIs). The constraints of shooting over such land will also have been dealt with elsewhere, but under such circumstances the KWCA did well to retain sport in a form more or less of its own choosing.

It was felt worthwhile to virtually abandon duck release as a conservation means, *per se*. Instead it was a case of falling in line with a national trend of protection and enhancement of natural habitats, something which had been allowed for within the framework of the management plans anyway. A drive to make the general public aware of the indivisible link between wildfowling and conservation was a priority and the initial campaign of being present via displays at local shows was to lead to the launch of a joint KWCA/British Field Sports Society annual Detling Country Sports Fair. This was to become an invaluable part of the club's public relations campaign.

Land-buying plans remained and, even though the membership fell during the post-1982 period to below the 500 mark, there was still a considerable annual financial input. The Sports Fair and a revamped clay pigeon operation ensured that the funds kept rolling in, whilst a general settling-down period took place during 1983 and 1984.

Land acquisition is never an easy task, especially in the increasingly cut-throat world of wetland sites. More than once the KWCA was baulked in its attempts at purchase; sometimes by ill-fortune, whilst at other times by its own naïvety! A new impetus was required.

The loss of much valuable land in the Medway Estuary, notably at Stoke Saltings, had been a dagger-blow to the club for, despite other land-holdings, it had always considered the Medway as 'home'. Eventually, in 1985, after intense lobbying, Blue Circle Industries announced the sale, by tender, of 710 acres of prime wildfowling land. Here at last was the chance the club had been waiting for – with the consequences of failure dire for the future well-being of the KWCA. Quite simply, if the KWCA wished to retain a substantial presence within the Medway Estuary the tender bid had to succeed.

Competition came from purist conservation bodies, and as with all tender offers the actual money aspect was difficult to decide upon. The future use of the land was also to be taken into consideration by the vendors, and in this direction the KWCA's management planning was to stand it in good stead, for the club's future plans for this land had already been well documented as part of the above mentioned lobbying.

A bank balance of some £70,000 was a good start, but was still way short of the estimated value of the land. A further complication was the time-scale, with only one month available from tender acceptance to completion. It was to be a case of make the offer first, based on the £70,000, and worry about raising the extra cash later! Fortunately for the KWCA their tender offer was successful. Now came the task of raising the money and, as the offer had been one of £130,000, this was to be no small task, with £60,000 needed in four weeks!

Again fortune favoured the brave, for those years of fiscal wisdom were bound to impress the bank manager, whilst various money raising schemes eloquently presented ensured that the full amount became available on an overdraft facility within the specified time. Thus the land was bought and paid for; but the club was now broke and, notwithstanding a substantial annual surplus of over £10,000, unable to instigate the speedy erosion of the massive overdraft unaided.

LOANS

The B.A.S.C., despite its own financial constraints, weighed in with a substantial £5000 interest-free loan. Many KWCA members also rallied round in a spontaneous show of support – £20,000-worth of loans of varying size and duration, plus the many small donations which came in, showed the depth of feeling within the membership – although the overdraft, attracting interest at an almost crippling $15\frac{3}{4}\%$, was still positively huge. What was needed was a financial commitment from the whole membership, rather than piecemeal voluntary support.

The 1985 AGM in May found the club fighting for financial solvency, although with such valuable assets as the Detling clay pigeon ground there would never be any question of going to the wall. But the committee had further aspirations in the land-buying field, and did not wish to use all its options on this initial purchase. At the AGM the chairman apologised unreservedly to the members for abandoning democratic procedures in purchasing land without referring back. The reason had been sound, the purchase successfully completed and the club now had the sort of security of tenure which it had long worked for.

With virtually no dissent the meeting set about the task of financing the removal of the overdraft. It was the committee's wish to do this without an increase in the annual subscription, whilst being keen to remove any disparity with some members paying extra and others not. What was needed was some sort of levy, across the board, and if this could be applied to all 350 members the problem would disappear at a stroke.

Eventually the following resolution was overwhelmingly accepted: 'That £100 be paid as an interest-free loan, in instalments, to the KWCA. This loan to be repayable on leaving the Association, after 5 years' service has been completed.' This would be binding on all present and future members, and although more legalities had to be tidied up at the 1986 AGM the problem was solved. The KWCA had won through, thanks to the foresight and determination of the general membership.

Land purchase had been found to be fraught with problems, most of which were the direct result of inexperience. Such problems related mainly to correctly worded resolutions, finance and the provision of adequate securities. The KWCA learned many valuable lessons in the 1985–6 period, and because of this many other clubs should be able to avoid similar pitfalls.

Late 1985 saw a second purchase of 190 acres, also in the Medway Estuary, this time involving a sum of £35,000. Again the deal was arranged without recourse to a subscription increase, this time via a term-loan arrangement with the association's bankers. Even so, the members decided upon a £10 subscription increase for the next year at the 1986 AGM, in order to facilitate additional land purchase when the occasion arose. Other sources of income were also healthy, with money being the crucial key to the club's future well-being.

But any club is only as strong as its membership, and the KWCA's membership is healthy and flourishing. The club has much to offer as we approach another decade and, with membership vacancies, there is every opportunity for those who do not mind paying a modest sum for almost unlimited sport.

As we move forward to the 1990s only those clubs willing to adopt a more professional approach to their affairs seem likely to survive in the long term. Wildfowling is no longer sport on the cheap, run by a few enthusiastic, although often muddle-headed, elder statesmen. Our wetlands form a complex environment, while the maintenance of worthwhile sporting opportunity is no less complex. Much opportunity still exists nationwide for those wishing to enter the sport, despite charges that wildfowling clubs operate a 'closed shop'. Many clubs run a permit scheme for visiting wildfowlers, whilst many also have membership vacancies. Anyone interested in obtaining details of permit schemes or of how to join a club can do no better than contact the B.A.S.C.

12
SAFETY AND ETIQUETTE ON THE MARSHES

ARTHUR CADMAN

The great majority of townsfolk, who know very little of country life, are surprised to learn that country sport has a long history of first-class sporting behaviour and traditional etiquette. Thus, over the ages, our game laws came into being before those of any other country. Good sportsmanship is a British tradition and it behoves everyone who follows the great sport of wildfowling to uphold that tradition. (The word 'sport' originally referred to country field sports and not to games such as cricket and football!) It is essential to know and to uphold not only the letter of the law

When crossing an obstacle, the gun should be unloaded

but also the spirit thereof. The game laws, the close seasons and the *Wildlife and Countryside Act 1981* must be understood and observed. Club rules must be obeyed.

Next in importance is safety in gun handling. The beginner must be taught every aspect of safety by an experienced hand and one of the first lessons is to see a gun discharged at an object (an empty cartridge carton is suitable) placed on the ground, in a safe place, at about 10 ft distance. The disintegration of the carton and the hole in the soil resulting from the discharge illustrate what could happen to a friend's stomach through careless handling.

A gun should be treated as if loaded at all times and *never* be pointed at anyone. Of course there are very many occasions when the gun must *not* be loaded. It must become an automatic reaction to check that the gun is unloaded when entering a house, building, car or other vehicle or boat or even if being put down. Under some circumstances it may be permissible to use a gun from a boat, but extreme care is required.

When crossing an obstacle – fence, ditch, plank over ditch, creek – or very rough or difficult ground, the cartridges must be taken out. It is not enough merely to open the breech. It is not good enough to be safe. You must be seen to be safe and therefore the gun should be carried open at the breech when not in use. When handing a gun to another person the gun should be empty. Although it is permissible to hand a 'broken' gun over a fence, it is better to demonstrate that it is empty, close the breech and then hand the gun to the other person with the barrels pointing directly upwards.

A gun is an expensive weapon. It is easily damaged. A novice should regard the barrels as if made of glass. Quite a small tap will cause a dent. It follows that a gun should never be put down leaning against a fence or wall where a dog, or even stormy wind, can cause it to fall. Nor should it be put down on the roof of a car. If it does fall the barrels and stock are likely to be damaged.

Anyone who handles his gun carelessly or dangerously, whether he be prince or pauper, should be sent home by the senior member of the party. If he is an outsider he should be spoken to in no uncertain terms.

A gun should be kept unloaded until you are sure it is ready for a likely shot, i.e. either lined up for walking-up or in position in hide or butt. When shooting in the company of others it is essential to keep a straight line and *never* to swing through the line. The gun must be carried safely at all times and the two acceptable positions are either pointing at the ground or elevated at a safe upward angle. This applies particularly to carrying a gun on the shoulder, a perfectly acceptable practice provided that the barrels are not more or less level. The practice of carrying a gun cradled in the crook of the left arm is dangerous. Anyone to the left will find himself looking down the barrels.

Never fire at a bird or beast if the land beyond it is not seen to be safe. A bush or hedge may conceal man or animal. Make sure you know where every other person is placed in the shooting field and also where someone else may be hidden. Wildfowling often takes place in a poor light and it behoves every wildfowler to be extremely cautious. You may think that you are the only person on the shore – but that black lump may be another fowler lying under a camouflage sheet.

Everyone who shoots should look through his barrels frequently, especially before loading the

Mud is always a hazard – keep your barrels up (Ian McCall)

gun and after crossing obstacles. This is even more important for the wildfowler because it is so very easy to get mud into the muzzle. You do not have to dig the barrels into the mud, as a dollop of mud can be splashed into the end of the barrels. Snow is also a serious hazard. Always carry a pull-through and however many geese are pouring low over your head, do not attempt to fire until the last speck of mud or snow has been cleared. Better to return home with both hands intact and no geese.

That great wildfowler Bill Powell of the Solway, wrote: 'Wherever you are, or whatever you are doing, the observation of common conventional

Another method of crossing an obstacle. Care should be taken that the unloaded gun cannot fall

Check the barrels frequently for any obstruction

courtesies and consideration makes the marsh a more agreeable place . . . the code (of etiquette) is simple common sense, good manners and consideration for others.' I would add that etiquette costs you nothing (and, today, anything worthwhile that costs nothing is priceless!). Also of equal importance is consideration and respect for the quarry species. Geese are magnificent birds. The sight of one thousand geese whiffling down from one thousand feet up, all calling, far out on the shore, gives untold pleasure to many and one does not have to be a wildfowler to be thrilled by this incomparable spectacle of nature.

When visiting a new area, do not go blundering out onto the shore without first finding out if a local club has the shooting there. Even if it is all right to shoot there, the correct accesses must be found. After that the behaviour of the local wildfowl must be studied. It is an unfortunate fact that the lure of goose shooting, which to many is the cream of all shooting, sometimes brings out the worst in those whose only thought is to bag a goose. Some, who would never put a foot wrong when pheasant shooting, forget all the tenets of good behaviour. Greed and selfishness replace all other sentiments!

The geese settle on a private field, where they should be safe to feed in peace. All too often some visiting fowler will creep up a ditch, or hedge, without permission from the owner or sporting tenant, in the hope of getting a shot – sometimes they carry a rifle: often they will shoot at the geese on the ground! A few geese sometimes feed on the shoot which I share with others, where we give complete sanctuary to the feeding geese. When the geese 'are in' constant patrolling is necessary to keep poachers at bay. That is the extreme form of bad behaviour. Crossing private land, without permission, in order to reach the shore, is nearly as bad. If a gun is carried both these serious offences are punishable by law.

Always respect other people's interests, especially those asleep in nearby houses. Unnecessary noise is unacceptable. It is thoughtlessness which causes offence to other sportsmen, to farmers, to birdwatchers and to the general public. If a car is left across a gateway, preventing a farmer from using his field, then he will be very put out. If the gate is left open, so that his domestic stock escape, then that is very serious. Apart from the trouble of recovering the farm animals, they may cause serious damage to crops or serious accidents on a public road.

The fowler who arrives late for the morning flight should go home. Why should he risk spoiling the sport of others by moving about, when they are already well concealed? A very frequent mistake, which may be seen daily around the shores of Britain, is to march in full view (often talking to others in a loud voice!) along the top of the sea wall. Even experienced fowlers sometimes commit this offence. I am reminded of 'the invisible man', as we call him – one who strolled about in full view during the morning flight. 'They'll no see me!' was his excuse and he believed it too! It is also obvious that brightly coloured clothing should be avoided. If there is another fowler already concealed in your favourite place when you arrive, that is your bad luck. Find out if there are others with him, nearby, and set up well away from them (not less than one hundred yards) so as not to spoil their sport. Don't position yourself the other side of another fowler's decoys, in his line of fire or downwind of them to intercept the birds he is pulling in.

Do not let your dog roam all over the marsh. Few things are more infuriating than to fire a shot, successful or not, and to be joined almost at once by a wild labrador dashing here, there and everywhere, whilst you own dog is sitting obediently beside you. On the other hand, if another fowler without a dog is searching fruitlessly for a duck or goose which he has shot, an offer to help with your dog will be appreciated.

If, by chance, you pick a bird shot by another, do not stuff it in your bag and hope that he has not noticed. Take it to him and give it up with good grace. The remark. 'That was a nice shot of yours', fosters goodwill, even if it was not so! In the bad old days at Wells, it used to be said that you needed a

108

greyhound to reach your goose, a bulldog to hold on to it and an Alsatian to keep other eager gunners at bay until it was safely in your bag! To shoot a duck and have it claimed by someone else is most annoying. It happens sometimes that the other person genuinely thinks it is his. Then it is not worth an argument. The fact that it is picked and not left out on the marsh, wasted, is something.

The fowler who does not attempt to conceal himself may be a good conservationist, but he will spoil the sport of others. Also, if he is ill-concealed, he may only get very wide chances and be tempted to fire very long shots. Many goose shooters get carried away and fire at incredible ranges. That may not hurt the geese, but it causes frustration all round. If he fires hopeful, but long, shots the result may be wounded geese, which is abominable. Neither of these 'shooters' is a sportsman.

Large bags of duck or geese are not often possible on the shore. When the wonderful chance does happen, possibly only once or twice in a lifetime, then, maybe, it is permissible to take a fair toll. That must be left to the individual's conscience. The man who goes out every day of the week and shoots nothing may cause more disturbance and do more harm than the man who has one good flight! What is reprehensible is to shoot one or two geese and then throw them into a ditch because they may not be sold. That is a dreadful thing to do, but it does happen. If I caught anyone doing that, I would feel like throwing him and his gun into the ditch too.

Shooting duck inland may result in excessive bags. Much depends upon the size of the water, the frequency of shoots, the number of guns shooting and the presence or not of hand-reared duck. Normally the host or shoot leader will decide what may be shot. Goose shooting at morning flight over decoys on their feeding grounds is a very different event. Restraint is essential. Greylag and pinkfeet are very numerous and they may be doing some harm, but, even so, an excessive bag is not good sportsmanship. Either a bag limit per gun should be imposed or a time limit. I prefer a strict time limit with all shooting being stopped at, say, thirty minutes after sunrise.

If geese are shot on their roost, then the inevitable result will be to drive them away. It is my belief that geese should *never* be shot on their roost on the shore. To do so is selfish and greedy and spoils the whole area for all other fowlers. Inland it is not wise to shoot a roosting loch, even once in six weeks. It is far preferable to shoot them as they come off in the morning or to shoot them at evening flight a quarter of a mile away, choosing a windy evening. On many club areas there is a club rule that no digging in out on the sand or mud flats is allowed and that rule must be observed. But there are areas where there is no such rule for a part of the shore well away from the roost. It is far better to be well concealed, either dug in or in a suitable hide, than to stand up and act like an armed scarecrow, thus spoiling the sport for all others.

The use of a torch is something which needs discretion. Personally I never use one. It destroys night vision. However dark the night, it is a poor fowler who cannot reach the place of his choice without the use of a torch – and he should know where he intends to go before he leaves his bed. But it is very important that he should consult tide tables on every outing and he must know what effect the wind will have on the tide in his area. So know your marsh thoroughly and, even so, never take risks. It is wise to tell someone to what part of the shore you are going.

On the large saltmarshes of the east coast, and elsewhere, a compass is useful. Fog can be very dangerous and it is wise to stay near the sea wall under foggy conditions. Duck often do not flight during dense fog. Geese in fog put off flighting in the morning until late and then they tend to follow the shoreline. If you do get lost, or even misplaced, under foggy conditions, do not panic. Stop and think very carefully. You may be able to hear sheep or cattle or the sound of traffic from a known main road or a train. If you know that the tide is ebbing, move up the creeks or channels. If it is flowing, start for the sea wall in very good time. If you do get drowned you will cause a lot of trouble to a lot of people! You may even cause someone else to lose his life.

If you get badly stuck in mud (or quicksands, which should be known and avoided, because such places are not all that common), the only hope is to lie on your back with your arms outstretched and work your way out backwards, even abandoning thigh boots in the process. Panic will not help.

As already said, respect for the quarry species is a hallmark of good sportsmanship. To shoot a duck or a goose so that it will fall where it cannot be picked up is a stupid waste of life. Every fowler should have a dog, not only because the dog can gather fowl which might otherwise be lost but also because the pleasure of shooting is greatly enhanced by the companionship of a good dog.

Alas, birds are wounded, but there is no excuse for shooting at duck or geese out of fair killing range. It is often thought that the poor shot is responsible for many wounded birds, but usually he has a clean miss or an occasional unexpected good kill! It is the good shot on an off-day who is liable to place his shots too far back, especially on tall geese. The answer is to stop shooting, but it is a natural human fault for him to think that he can place his shot on target at the next chance. Whatever the reason for a wounded bird, every effort must be made to pick it up quickly and to despatch it efficiently.

Every fowler should carry field glasses. The extra pleasure that they provide is one good reason, but the need to watch a wounded bird also justifies the need to carry them. To enable efficient picking up, it is necessary to understand the behaviour of a wounded bird. If you hear the pellets strike, usually the sound is the result of pellets striking the outstretched primary feathers. But one or more pellets may have struck the body, so the bird should be watched as long as it is in sight. Sometimes a goose will parachute down and that indicates that it is stunned. In both cases the bird must be approached at once with the gun ready in case it takes off again.

If a bird falls with one wing flapping, that means that the other wing is broken at the shoulder. The bird will run, at once. A duck or goose which comes down slanting at a steep angle is usually wing-tipped. Unless it is also struck in the body, it will run. A wing-tipped duck or goose, if kept alive, will very soon become tame in captivity. A winged duck or goose, falling in dense cover, may creep into a tussock and stay still. If it does move, it should leave a good scent, but it is likely to go a long way if the dog does not get onto it at once. A winged goose can run as fast as a cock pheasant.

If either duck or geese fall near water, they will make for the water. If a duck does not see the shooter it may hide under the bank, but a goose is more likely to make for the centre of the area of water, especially if there is an island there. On the shore a winged goose is likely to make for the tideway, although sometimes they will walk about apparently without any sense of direction at first. That is where there is no cover – bare sand or a grass field. A duck that falls in water usually makes for the shore and hides in suitable cover.

When the wingbeats of a wounded goose or duck become shallow and the flight appears to be flat, then the bird will drop dead within a hundred yards or so. Duck or geese do not 'tower', as game birds do, and this flat flight may be the equivalent of a towering game bird, which is caused by internal haemorrhage, not by a pellet in the lungs, as is generally believed. Geese are such powerful birds that even if they appear to fall dead at the shot, it is better to let the dog pick them up quickly unless they can be clearly seen to be lying dead.

It should be an unwritten rule that a wounded goose or duck calls for a second shot to finish it off and, anyway, it should be watched until it is either down or out of sight in preference to shooting at another. Many people find it hard to despatch a wounded goose efficiently. The bird should be picked up with its head held between the first and second fingers of one hand. Immediately the body should be rotated fast. The neck will be dislocated at once and death follows instantly. A mallard may be despatched in the same way, but smaller duck can be killed by knocking the head hard against a stone or other hard object. A 'priest' is useful for this purpose.

One pleasure of every outing is the close examination of the bag afterwards. Young and old should be sorted out and noted. Unusual plumage should be noticed. Wildfowl should be hung by the neck – not by the feet. Respect for the quarry applies also after death. One wing from each bird provides valuable information for the B.A.S.C.'s shooting surveys.

One final point. It is the bounden duty of any sportsman who witnesses dangerous behaviour, abuse of the law or of club rules or selfish unsportsmanlike activity, to remonstrate with the offender. Wildfowlers are a grand race and wildfowling is a great sport and we who indulge in it gain much pleasure therefrom. There is no room at all for the small minority who cause unpleasantness to other wildfowlers and bring their sport into disrepute. There is enough ignorance and criticism of all country sports, and every wildfowler, by his example and by his tolerance of other folk's interests, should foster a better understanding of his sport.

13

BELOW THE SEA WALL – DUCK SHOOTING

ALAN JARRETT

If one learns anything at all from a lifetime in pursuit of wild duck it is that this sport can be an exceedingly complex affair! Indeed, duck shooting on the shore is as widespread and diverse a subject as one could hope to include in a single chapter. Just where does a fellow begin if he wishes to discuss shooting wild duck on the shore?

To define what we mean by 'shore' is the first obvious step. The legal definition of foreshore is given elsewhere in this book (pages 81 and 88), but by tradition the foreshore is defined as all that land on our coasts and estuaries which lies below the mean high-water mark (MHWM) and above the mean low-water mark. This is the intertidal zone, which encompasses mudflats, sandbanks and the lower areas of saltmarsh. It is that seemingly inhospitable area, inundated by every tide, beloved by a multitude of wild birds and by the hardy sportsmen who pursue this wild quarry.

Yet to many wildfowlers the shore will be regarded as all that land which lies on the seaward side of the sea wall. Truly, in many instances, the MHWM will often reach the foot of the sea wall itself. Equally, there will be many occasions when vast stretches of higher mature saltmarsh separate the sea wall from the intertidal zone, so these areas can scarcely be excluded from any discussion of the shore.

Even the sea wall itself will often occupy a substantial portion of the wildfowler's time, especially when the biggest tides make even the high saltmarsh untenable. Therefore to complete any meaningful analysis of the wildfowler's pursuit of duck on the shore it will be necessary to include all that land which lies below the sea wall and to include the sea wall itself.

Procreation aside, wild duck are basically simple creatures that want nothing more than to feed and roost in relative peace and quiet and to feel reasonably safe while so doing. Here lies the wildfowler's first task if he is to achieve success with any sort of consistency. He will need to ascertain where the birds are feeding, where they are roosting and, thereafter, work out a plan of campaign which will put him on terms with his potential quarry.

For the sake of simplicity it can be said that wild duck roost during the day on the sea or some other large expanse of water or exposed tidal flats, only moving off to feed as evening draws on. Having sated their appetite they will once again head for the security of the roost at dawn. Thus, dawn and dusk will be the times for the wildfowler to lie in ambush for his quarry. His knowledge of the area and the movements of the birds will determine the precise point of ambush and this in turn will be affected by various factors such as time of year, weather, moon and state of tide.

QUARRY SPECIES

The wildfowler's principal quarry on the shore will be dabbling duck – mallard, wigeon and teal in the main, but with locally common species such as pintail, shoveler and even gadwall to add variety to the bag. The diving ducks will feature irregularly, but can be excluded from pre-flight planning in the great majority of cases. All the dabbling duck may feed on the shore at some time or other and the wildfowler must be alert enough to take advantage of each change as it occurs.

The botanical/invertebrate make-up of the estuary is dealt with in Chapter 6, but briefly it can be said that the shore is divided roughly into zones which are basically dependent on the degree of tidal cover. Thus on the lower shore – the flats – such plants as *Zostera* may be found, with *Enteromorpha* and other algae being commonplace, and these will need to be most tolerant of such saline conditions.

As we move up the shore typical saltmarsh plant succession will be found: the *Salicornia* of the salting edges; the sea aster and *Spartina* zones of the middle salting; the shrubby sea purslane of the creek edges and finally to the *Puccinellia*/fescues and thrifts of the higher saltmarsh. A variety of invertebrates and molluscs will be present on the flats and among the lower saltmarshes and these, too, can provide food at various times.

Of course not every shore is made up in this manner, but the above will serve as an example of saltmarsh plant succession, most of which can produce potential food for duck. Once the wildfowler has acquainted himself with what his local shore has to offer the duck, then he will be far better equipped to put a bird or two in the bag.

Yet on a great majority of occasions the birds will be feeding inland beyond the sea wall and the wildfowler will have to adjust his strategy accordingly. Thus, if the birds are feeding on the shore itself, the fowler must move out from the sea wall to set his ambush in the feeding grounds. Alternatively, if they are flighting inland to feed, an ambush on their line of flight may be used, a strategy which can prove highly effective at times.

Such flightlines will often be well established and used regularly year in and year out. There are vital reasons for this, with the shortest route from roosting to feeding grounds being the most common. Yet flightlines can alter due to such factors as wind and tide and the wildfowler must remain flexible enough to note any such changes.

Unless 'green' birds are involved – either early-season or freshly arrived migrant birds – flightline shooting will be heavily dependent upon weather conditions. The birds are apt to fly high out of range, especially so in those areas where regular shooting takes place, but a good headwind can soon alter this and bring the birds within range of the hidden gunner.

Such flighting will often take place from an ambush point in the saltings, on sea walls or banks or among dunes – in short, anywhere that can be found to afford reasonable cover. It is probably fair to say that this is the least inspiring form of wildfowling, save in times of wild windy weather when the sport can be fast and furious.

The true essence of the sport lies out on the shore itself, 'flighting' birds as they come to the flats or salting to feed. Many species of duck may be encountered in this way. Wigeon, a grazing duck, will come to the flats to graze on *Zostera* and algae and to those areas of higher saltmarsh where the sward is short and sweet due to the grazing activities of cattle. Sometimes they will come in huge numbers, offering the wildfowler some quite superb sport.

The open flats offer little in the way of cover for the wildfowler and the wigeon are sharp-eyed and adept at evasive action. Tradition decrees that a tub or pit be used to shoot from, whilst a good 'flock' of decoys in any adjacent pool will be an invaluable aid. To this day the combination of gunning tub and decoys remains the only realistic way of putting together a decent bag. Where wigeon are feeding on the sward of the higher saltmarsh the problems encountered will often be less acute, with pools for decoying and creeks in which to hide being present in most places.

When birds are kept on the move by windy conditions, a few well placed decoys can pay dividends

Teal, mallard and pintail, together with wigeon, will come to the lower saltmarsh to feed on *Salicornia*, the dropped seed from such plants as sea aster and *Spartina* and the tiny snail *Hydrobia* which is a firm favourite in some parts. The wildfowler who is able to predict where the birds will come from to feed will often be rewarded with some incredibly exciting shooting at dusk and, on occasion, a decent bag.

CONCEALMENT

Actual cover in the saltmarsh is usually fairly good. Some wildfowlers use lightweight portable hides consisting of a few bamboo-type poles and a flimsy shroud of netting, but in many instances this will not be necessary. The tall saltmarsh plants, sea aster and *Spartina*, will provide good enough cover, especially in the half-light of the evening flight, whilst the many creeks and gutters which dissect most saltings will form a ready-made hide. When waiting for duck any hide, no matter how rudimentary, should allow the wildfowler to have his feet on a lower level than that enjoyed by his backside! Otherwise manoeuvrability will be severely impaired. Always, whether sitting or lying full length, face the estimated line of flight so that the gun can be moved smoothly to left or right – thus making the most of an inevitable restriction on movement.

DECOYS

The use of decoys requires brief elaboration at this point. Although the employment of artificial duck should not be considered essential in every situation, there will be many occasions when their use will swell the bag considerably. Most wildfowlers seem to favour using as big a 'flock' as they can, thereby multiplying the drawing power of their set-up. There will, however, be instances when a simple pair of decoys, astutely placed, will prove deadly. Here is another example of the wildfowler's need for adaptability.

The normal duck movements described above can alter significantly during times of rough, stormy weather. The open-water roosts are especially liable to disruption, with the birds seeking out more sheltered parts until the storm abates. Here local knowledge will play an important part in determining success or failure, for this can be another time of fine sport for the alert wildfowler.

Any calm water, whether this be a sheltered bay, estuary or creek, can attract massive numbers of birds. Under such circumstances a well-placed decoy pattern, and some straight shooting, will often pay dividends. This sort of abnormal movement will frequently occur during daylight hours, so the wildfowler must remain alert to just such a possibility.

Many estuaries possess a complex system of mud flats, creeks, and fragmented saltmarsh islands, and there are some particularly fine examples of this on the east coast in Kent and Essex. Here the full range of foods described earlier will be available, although in a less uniform manner due to the complex estuary system. There are bountiful food supplies for the ducks to scoop up and there is likely to be ample opportunity for sport.

This is where our duck shooting story is complicated still further, for duck will frequently move with the flooding or ebbing tide in order to take advantage of both food and shelter amongst the islands. Wildfowlers need to be specially adaptable to take advantage of this type of sport, with decoys and artificial hides as fundamental items of equipment.

The importance of a dog to the wildfowler is covered in Chapter 20, but it cannot be stressed often enough just how important a good retriever is in this sport. This is especially so when shooting birds under such tide-bound conditions as the estuary islands and saltmarshes which our coasts are likely to offer.

SAFETY

A good deal of our wildfowling will take place, of necessity, on exposed pieces of saltmarsh, which are frequently cut off by the advancing tide. Indeed, many of those salting islands will be tiny once isolated at high tide. It will at once be seen that wildfowling can be a potentially hazardous pastime and extreme care should be taken at all times.

Inevitably, local knowledge plays a big part in determining where and when it is safe to pursue the sport, for each piece of shore has its own idiosyncrasies. Access to and, critically, from the saltmarsh will be all-important and this must be clearly established before any attempt at shooting takes place.

Yet local knowledge is not the be-all and end-all of safe wildfowling, for, as long as the sportsman obeys certain well-established criteria, he should manage to avoid falling foul of the elements. Wildfowling can be an arduous sport and adequate equipment and survival aids are as important to the wildfowler as they are to the potholer or the mountaineer for, in many instances, our sport is every inch as great a test of resilience and endurance.

Three of the most fundamental requirements are a tide table for the chosen locality – this may be obtained from a harbour-master or newsagent – together with a reliable wristwatch and a compass. Obviously, there is a need to understand the intricacies of any tide table and to relate this to the area concerned. The watch is a necessity where there is a need to be back to the safety of the sea wall by a certain time and the compass for finding the correct direction especially in fog or heavy mist.

Many saltmarshes and saltmarsh islands will be separated from the sea wall by creeks or gutters. These will often seem innocuous enough at low water, when they will be devoid of water. However, it is a very different story when the tide is surging through and providing a formidable barrier to anyone seeking safe passage off the marsh. Such obstacles will mostly prove too deep to wade and too wide to leap once the tide is in full flood. To say that such a situation can be one of life or death is not overstating the case. Many a wildfowler has felt the cold stab of fear at finding his escape route blocked – and too many have paid the ultimate penalty for this act of misjudgement or bravado.

Of all the factors affecting both sportsman and quarry the tide is the most relentless. It will often prove an unwitting and valued ally in the pursuit of duck, for its movements are largely predictable and its effect upon the shore birds fairly uniform. Yet the tide can at once be a pitiless killer of those unwary enough to dismiss the potential danger for more than an instant.

Therefore, before venturing away from the sea wall onto any exposed section of shore it is necessary to establish: (a) time and height of high water; (b) which, if any, parts of the saltmarsh will remain above water on that height of tide and (c) how long after low water can be safely spent on the marsh before any gutters start to flood. Also leave word with someone in case your return should become overdue.

Many saltmarshes will be fairly safe on the neap (smallest) tides, whilst the springs (largest) will often flood everything below the sea wall. Any quotation of actual height is largely academic, as each area has its own tidal levels. For instance, the Medway Estuary in Kent, where I mostly shoot, will give neaps as low as 4.4 metres and these will flood only the flats, creeks and lower saltmarsh, whilst the largest springs of say 6.5 metres will flood everything save the very largest islands – and there are precious few of those! Neap tides do not retreat as far as the springs, nor flood as high, so that there is the minimum of fluctuation between high and low water. Springs are the other extreme, frequently exposing low-water banks seldom otherwise seen.

Tides will be influenced by three factors: moon, barometric pressure and wind. Spring tides occur on the new and full moons, with the largest tides being during the period of the full moon. Barometric pressure, if there is a marked variation between low and high pressures, can cause tides to vary considerably from the predicted height. Always bear in mind, however, that tide tables provide nothing more than a prediction – albeit mostly fairly reliable – and one would be unwise to gamble one's life by treating these predictions as sacrosanct. Yet such variation pales into insignificance beside the effect sometimes exerted by the wind.

WIND AND GALES

Certain winds will have differing effects, dependent upon the area concerned. For example, an onshore wind can both drive in the tide earlier, thereby flooding access points prematurely, and add extra height to the tide. One does not need to be clairvoyant to appreciate just what effect this can have. Similarly, strong offshore winds can hold back the tide and even depress the height. Of course, this type of wind is less likely to be the sort of potential killer that its onshore counterpart might be.

A classic example of raging north-westerly gales was the east coast floods of 1953. Here many sea defences were breached, thousands of acres inundated and many lives lost; there have been less spectacular examples since, but these serve to remind the wildfowler of the awesome power of wind and tide combined.

The duck-shooting wildfowler will find actual access to the shore constrained by factors other than the tide. A legal right to shoot and have access is an obvious and fundamental constraint, though not part of this writer's remit (but see Chapters 7–9). The actual state of shore is often the single biggest arbiter after the tide. In many areas the muds are composed of almost bottomless sediments over which access by foot is near impossible, similarly in other parts there might be isolated soft patches or even quicksands. Many creeks will be a morass of glutinous mud and the ability to move about effectively on the shore is seen to be just another facet of the wildfowler's skill.

The use of mud pattens is favoured in some parts, but in the main a stout wading pole, some astute 'reading' of the shore and a good pair of lungs are the main requirements. Much vegetated mud will be safe to walk on, but one must be careful to differentiate between vegetation and algae for much algae-festooned mud is soft and dangerous. A combination of sticky mud and incoming tide can be a potential killer and the speed of an incoming tide must never be under-estimated. Mud walking is a slow and tortuous process for the most part – with a mile or so on the shore apt to seem a very long way indeed.

BOATS

An assortment of small craft is often used by wildfowlers; less frequently to actually shoot from, but rather as a means of access to remote saltings and islands. Punt, canoe or dinghy are all used, whilst less commonly larger craft are employed by the more affluent. Mostly access by boat will be more of a luxury than a necessity, although there are those areas which are totally inaccessible by foot. A good example is Poole Harbour, in Dorset, where the northern-based wildfowlers are obliged to traverse the harbour by boat to reach their extensive southern wildfowling grounds.

Boating throws up its own significant problems, such as transportation, launching, propulsion and safety. It should also be noted that the use of a mechanically propelled boat in immediate pursuit of wildfowl is illegal. It is a subject which could occupy much space, but I will content myself with a few comments on elementary safety.

One sees many extremes in wildfowling craft. Some will be quite excellent whilst others are horrendously dangerous and totally unsuitable. When contemplating acquiring a boat for wildfowling one must make certain that the craft is at least seaworthy; basically this means being of sufficient length, beam, draft and buoyancy so that it will not be easily swamped or overturned.

A life-jacket would seem to be a commonsense requirement for anyone going afloat, but is sadly still neglected by too many. More than one wildfowler owes his life to an investment totalling no more than a few pounds. A compass, a necessity for any wildfowler, is a vital part of a boat-owner's

In some situations the shoulder gunner can make use of a punt (John Paley)

equipment, for it is remarkably easy to become disorientated in conditions of darkness and/or fog when afloat. Finally, it is well worth investing in some sort of distress flare against the day when an emergency might arise.

No matter how good the craft, it must be remembered that it will be no match for the sea in murderous temper. Any wind exceeding force four is likely to pose problems and when wind is running against tide even shallow onshore waters can become a maelstrom. Under such circumstances it is far better to stay afoot – even if this may mean foregoing some sporting opportunities.

It will be noted increasingly during my narrative that wildfowling is constantly influenced by, and at the mercy of, the elements. Few other sports are so intimately tied up with the natural forces of weather, tide and moon. Some of these factors must be considered in any discussion concerning the shooting of duck on the shore. The traditional concept of the wildfowler out in some raging gale, gamely doing battle with ghostly wind-blown packs of fowl, has much relevance. Indeed, as I mentioned earlier, under such circumstances as flightline shooting and decoying amongst sheltered estuary waters, wild weather can be a distinct advantage.

Yet anyone who thinks that it is only worth venturing out when the weather is rough could be making a big mistake. There will be many occasions when the sky is clear and starlit at evening

flight and a sharp frost plucks at the cheeks. This is often the time to get amongst the ducks feeding in the saltmarsh or on the open flats. Such exposed feeding sites might well prove inhospitable to duck during stormy weather, so that sport may actually be disrupted by the advent of 'ideal' wildfowling weather! Such perversities once again demonstrate the importance of understanding what goes on locally and serve to underline just how idiosyncratic the sport can be.

Long-term weather conditions play an all-important part in determining the wildfowler's degree of success. Generally speaking, nothing ruins sporting prospects on the shore quite like excessive autumn rains, which will in turn create generous inland floods and thereby abundant feeding sites. Thus the great majority of duck will be inland, forsaking the saltmarshes and frustrating wildfowlers near to distraction.

HARD WEATHER

Always awaited with great anticipation by wildfowlers, periods of frost and snow will be especially welcome at such times. Frosts need to be severe and prolonged if they are to effectively freeze the bulk of inland floods and drive the duck to the shore to feed. Snow can play its part in covering food and, once the fields are covered, the wigeon will be forced to the saltmarsh to feed. Of course, the shore too is liable to freezing and snow cover

but the twice-daily inundation by the tide may serve to make a certain amount of food available. At such times duck will take any available food, including that with less nutritional value than might be considered ideal.

Under such circumstances birds can lose some of their natural caution. This can be the time for the wildfowler to make a decent bag, although he will always conduct himself with due moderation and consideration for his quarry. If extreme conditions persist, however, no wildfowler worthy of the name will shoot large numbers of hard-pressed birds.

Once a thaw sets in the snow begins to vanish from the fields, the frozen floods begin to unlock and, once again, abundant food becoming available, duck will sometimes flight to and from the shore with gay abandon. He who finds himself in the right place at such a time can enjoy some of the best sport on offer. However, such sport is likely to be short-lived, perhaps only lasting for a single day before the thaw becomes more advanced and the duck once more settle into a more regular pattern.

MOONLIGHT FLIGHTING

Moonlight shooting is the *crème de la crème* of wildfowling, given suitable conditions. However, such conditions are not necessarily forthcoming and, in a poor season, it can be difficult to have any good moonlighting at all! Ideal conditions consist of a moon near the full, a sky filled with white fluffy clouds and a strong enough breeze to keep the clouds moving across the face of the moon. At such times it will be possible to see duck a long way off and, when the duck are on the move, this can be an incredibly exciting time.

No matter how bright the moon, the absence of cloud cover makes it near impossible to see the birds, with the constant whicker of wings in an inky void frustrating in the extreme. Admittedly, one might snatch the odd glimpse as duck dash across the moon itself, but this is scarcely a formula for success. The exception may occur where the moon is still low enough in the sky to create an aura from mud or water against which it will be possible to pick out low-flying birds, and this circumstance can give exciting, if fairly short-lived, sport. Where the cloud cover is too dense and dark,

so as to totally blot out the moon, the wildfowler will be well advised to stay at home and wait for another night.

Much the same rules apply for moonlight shooting as exist for the evening flight, with birds flighting either to their inland feeding grounds or to the saltmarsh. In mild, settled conditions the duck are often loath to move, being content to loaf out on the tideway half the night – a frustrating time for the wildfowler ensconced in the salting listening to merry whistling and quacking from the roosting hordes. However, if the tide is flooding during the evening, as the moon rises, there can develop a procession of birds moving before the tide. Where this occurs all the facets of duck movement outlined earlier come into play and this is likely to be a stimulating challenge for the sportsman.

The presence of a moon will often disrupt normal duck flighting patterns. For instance, when the moon is in the sky at dusk, the evening flight will often be a long-drawn-out affair with birds being able to flight at their leisure. This can keep the wildfowler on the alert for many hours into the night and will be an enthralling time. When the moon is on the wane – rising after dark – there may occur two distinct movements of birds: a traditional evening flight, with a separate flight developing once the moon has risen. The waning moon will eventually remain in the sky at dawn, and this is likely to encourage duck to flight to their roost before dawn. These conditions will invariably make the traditional morning flight a complete waste of time and many a disappointed wildfowler can bear testimony to this fact.

Most moonlight flighting will take place a few days either side of the full moon. Indeed some clubs prohibit any night shooting other than during something like seven nights around the full moon. The reasoning behind this is clear enough, particularly as the whole concept of night shooting is under the microscope. Because of this pressure, those responsible for administering the sport are most anxious to ensure that any night shooting which does take place is simply a retention of wildfowling tradition. The arrival of concentrated industrial sites close to many of our estuaries has created a now familiar red glow in the sky which, in some areas, is extensive, and most certainly ample to shoot duck by. It is this fairly modern phenomenon which wildfowlers must spurn if they are to ultimately retain credibility and fight off the challenges to their sport.

As I have attempted to convey to readers throughout these pages, wildfowling is a very special sport. The pursuit of wild duck on the shore is filled with variables and imponderables, and is a wonderfully stimulating challenge for those who choose to make this potentially hazardous environment their hunting place. It is totally dissimilar to any other sphere of shooting. Wildfowlers are a race apart – strange lonesome souls, who want for nothing more than to be down on the shore with dog and gun and perhaps a duck in the bag as reward for their often herculean efforts.

Wildfowlers hail from every walk of life, whether this be city financier or local countryman. They are united by a common bond or calling, a calling which for some strangely indefinable reason is in the blood. It is a calling which can seldom be resisted or discarded for very long, for the call of the shore is strong and the wild duck the very spirit of these lonely places.

14
BELOW THE SEA WALL – GOOSE SHOOTING

ERIC BEGBIE

Having risen from the comfort of his bed long before daybreak and travelled through deserted country roads to reach the estuary, a lone wildfowler experiences a primordial thrill when, with his ageing labrador close to heel, he crosses the sea wall and hears the murmuring of geese rise above the unremitting howl of a cruel December gale. Buffeted by the wind he picks a careful path through the dense, swaying fringe of faded reeds and then stops to listen before stepping out on to the rutted marsh grass. There is no mistaking the music of the greylag as they preen in preparation for morning flight.

With the first pale streaks of dawn already lightening the eastern sky the fowler must take great care to avoid alarming the birds on the roost. A deep gully provides the only chance of cover on an otherwise featureless shore so, oblivious to the liberal coating of mud which he picks up on his backside as he slides down into the gutter, the fowler takes advantage of the channel to make his way closer to the sound of the geese.

Stooping to walk along the deeper sections and crawling in six inches of water in other parts, the fowler progresses for almost a quarter of a mile before a branching in his creek provides a likely spot from which to survey the marsh. Cautiously peering over the gully he discovers that his calculations have been accurate and the flock of restless birds is grouped on the mud a few hundred yards in front of his position. To attempt to creep closer would be to risk disturbing the fowl, so he settles down against a slimy bank and awaits the flight.

The tide has just turned and its flow, far out on the mudflats, disturbs small trips of waders which rise and circle to find drier ground. The high-pitched piping of the dunlin and redshank grows in intensity as the incoming water covers more and more of the shore. That, coupled with the continuing talk of the greylag, is music to the fowler's ears.

As daylight strengthens an occasional soloist plays a brief passage in the symphony. The whistle of a wigeon, replete from a night grazing the succulent *Zostera*; the quack of a mallard duck as she leads her drake to their roost on the mudbanks after a feast on nearby barley stubbles. Then, in the climax of the first movement, the snare drum rattle from the wings of a thousand fieldfares sweeping low over the saltings.

Half-buried in the ooze of his deep gutter, the wildfowler ignores a trickle of icy brine which has found a way inside his left wader. He knows that the movement of the small thrush-like birds behind him frequently coincides with the flight of the first geese on their hazardous daily journey from the foreshore to feed on the waste potatoes in the fields above the sea wall.

Each chamber of his magnum is now loaded with an ounce and a half of No. 3 shot – he scorns the heavier American cartridges with their BB pellets – and he waits for the sounds which will announce that the greys are leaving their roost.

The rising crescendo from a large group in front of his position sets his pulse racing and he risks another quick glance over the edge of the channel to see them rise from the shore and pass inland a hundred yards to his right.

For almost thirty minutes parties of geese leave their roosting places and flight over the mud, but none comes closer than that first skein. Eventually, having checked that no greys remain on the tideline, he removes the cartridges from his gun, makes a rueful comment to his labrador and carefully picks his way back towards firmer ground and another day's toil.

It has been his fifth morning flight of the season and he still has to fire his first shot. When geese are the quarry, wildfowling can be like that. One does not speed a fortune on cartridges, but the satisfactions are probably greater than in any other

119

branch of shooting sport. Occasionally the fowler may even be rewarded with a plump greylag or pinkfoot.

THE QUARRY SPECIES

The principal quarry species from amongst the grey geese are the greylag and the pinkfooted goose. In England and Wales the European white-front may legitimately be shot, but in Scotland, which is visited by the Greenland race, white-fronted geese are protected. In addition to grey geese, the Canada goose may be shot throughout the British Isles.

GREYLAG GOOSE *(Anser anser)*

One of the larger grey geese, the greylag is the stock from which most of our farmyard geese are descended. Both sexes are brownish-grey with noticeably paler grey forewings and white barred tail coverts. The bill, which is particularly large and heavy, is orange while, in the western race, the legs range between pink and flesh colour.

A number of greylag geese nest in the Hebrides and many feral flocks are established in other parts of Britain. The major winter population, however, migrates to our shores from Iceland with over 100,000 birds making the annual journey over the North Atlantic to spend the colder months in east and central Scotland. Smaller numbers winter around the Solway and in north-west England.

PINKFOOTED GOOSE *(Anser brachyrhynchus)*

Somewhat daintier and smaller than the greylag, the pinkfooted goose is characterised by a chocolate-brown head and neck. The body is paler brown with bluish-grey tinges in the wing coverts and darker grey in the tail. The rump, in common with that of all grey geese, is white. The bill of the pinkfoot is smaller and neater than that of the greylag, being pink coloured with variable black markings at base and tip. The feet and legs are pink.

The western population of pinkfeet migrates each autumn to Britain from Iceland and eastern Greenland. Like the greylag, numbers wintering in Britain have steadily increased in recent years and currently (1988) stand at around 170,000. The winter population is more widely dispersed than that of the greylag goose and, although eastern

and central Scotland are again favoured, significant flocks are to be found in north-west England, the Solway and north-east Scotland.

A second population of pinkfooted geese breeds in the Spitsbergen area and winters in Denmark, the Netherlands and northern Germany. Occasionally birds from this population may turn up in south-east England.

WHITEFRONTED GOOSE *(Anser albifrons)*

There are two distinct races of whitefronted geese in Europe. A population of around 21,000 birds breeds in Greenland and winters on the Wexford Slobs in Ireland, on the Hebridean island of Islay

Pinkfooted geese flight inland to feed (Eric Begbie)

and throughout western Scotland. A much larger population of European whitefronts breeds in Siberia and migrates to Germany, the Netherlands, Belgium and France with around 4000 birds coming to southern England. The Wildfowl Trust refuge at Slimbridge is a major haunt of this species.

The Greenland whitefront is a dark goose, predominantly grey-brown with black transverse bars across the lower breast and belly. Adults have a distinctive white forehead. The bill and legs are orange. Birds of the European race tend to have an overall lighter plumage and a pinkish bill. They share the characteristic black barring and white forehead of the Greenland race.

CANADA GOOSE *(Branta canadensis)*

In North America there are over a dozen distinct races of Canada goose, but those which exist in Britain are probably descended from one or two of the larger races, possibly including the giant Canada *(Branta canadensis maxima)*. It is currently the only black goose on the British shooting list and the current population in this country is around 40,000, largely in southern England, the Midlands and Yorkshire.

The head and neck of the Canada goose are black with a white patch circling from cheek to chin. The back is brown and the belly greyish brown with variable transverse barring.

FLIGHTING PATTERNS

With the exception of flight pond shooting, most wildfowling is dependent upon calculating the flightlines of the duck or geese and lying in wait to ambush them as they fly past. Whereas a few notable fowlers of yesteryear adopted stalking tactics using horses or cattle as mobile blinds or, more commonly, taking advantage of the natural gutters and creeks to get within gunshot range of resting fowl, the shooting of sitting birds would today be considered unsporting. A large part of marshcraft, therefore, lies in developing the skill to predict where and when the quarry will fly within range of a waiting gun.

Although there are many exceptions to the general rule, it is normally accepted that duck roost on the marsh or on open water by day, flighting inland to feed at dusk, while geese reverse this procedure and roost by night, flying off the saltings at dawn to graze on agricultural land and pasture.

Conditions vary on different estuaries, but, by and large, grey geese favour roosts which allow them to spend the hours of darkness in relatively calm conditions and secure from predators or disturbance. Where there are sandbanks a few hundred yards offshore these will frequently be used and geese generally are not averse to spending part of the night on water in instances where the banks are covered at high tide. Similarly, in locations where the uncovered foreshore extends sufficiently far from the sea wall to offer reasonable safety, geese will often roost at the tide edge, taking to the water when the incoming flow pushes them too close to civilisation.

WEATHER AND TIDES

One of the perpetual problems facing the shore-based wildfowler is the height at which geese normally flight over the sea wall. There is, therefore, considerable benefit in becoming familiar with the conditions that are likely to bring them lower.

It is often claimed that wild, windy weather is most suitable for fowling. Not only does a good gale tend to make the geese fly at lesser altitudes, such weather also renders roosting on open water somewhat uncomfortable. By choosing a windy morning when the tide will be approaching full at around the time of dawn, the prudent fowler can draw additional advantage from the likelihood that the starting point for the flight will be closer to high-water mark than is normally the case.

The timing of morning flight is similarly subject to a fair degree of variation and the experienced wildfowler should be able to make an educated guess at both the time and duration under different conditions. On a calm, relatively cloud-free morning, geese may flight from their roosting areas at

when the fields are covered by deep snow. Conversely, during periods of the full moon geese, especially pinkfeet, may feed throughout the night and, as a result, be less pressed by hunger pangs in the morning. It is at the full moon that the flock movements are least predictable and the wise fowler will avoid such times when selecting dates for his annual goose shooting vacation.

One other important point in relation to the effects of wind and tides upon flighting patterns is that on calm nights, when the tide is well out just prior to dawn, geese tend to congregate in large roosting flocks on the water or open marsh. Under those conditions they will frequently flight in a single large skein of 200 or 300 birds and the fowler who lies underneath their path may be unlikely to

any time between one hour before sunrise and one hour after. Dirty weather will delay the lightening of the sky and may consequently postpone the movement of the birds. If, however, tide conditions are pressing, high winds may cause the geese to flight earlier to avoid sitting on choppy seas. All other factors being equal, geese which are resting on saltmarsh may flight earlier when being inched along by a flowing tide than they would during the ebb.

Hungry birds are liable to leave the roost earlier than normal and this factor may become important in times of food shortage such as can occur have a second chance that morning. On the other hand, when the elements are approaching storm level and the tide is well advanced at flight time, the geese are apt to be found in small scattered groups, each of which will flight separately over an extended period and may provide the waiting fowler with a succession of sporting opportunities for a shot.

EVENING FLIGHT

Just as geese leave the roost at dawn and provide the longshore gunner with the chance of a shot as they flight inland to feed, so do birds returning to the roost at dusk offer another opportunity for sport. It is, however, very unusual for geese to fly over the sea wall in the afternoon at a height which would give the sportsman much hope of a successful outing. Typically the birds will flight at a safe altitude until they are almost above their chosen roosting area and they will then tumble from the sky with that marvellous 'whiffling' action.

This presents a problem. If the only place where a successful shot may be taken is on, or very close to, the roost there is clearly a danger that the disturbance from shooting may unsettle the geese and cause them to forsake the area in search of more peaceful surroundings. Around the coast of Britain there are many marshes which were once favoured as goose roosts but which are now rarely used due to disturbance of this type.

On balance, it is probably wiser not to attempt to shoot geese at evening flight unless it is possible to do so from a position at least half a mile from the roosting area.

CAMOUFLAGE AND CONCEALMENT

Whether he seeks his sport at dawn or at dusk, the fowler who pursues geese on the shore must learn how to conceal himself so as to remain hidden from his quarry until they are within range of his armament. The wariness of geese is legendary and, especially in localities where the shooting pressure is heavy, they become astonishingly adept at spotting and avoiding a human ensconced on the marsh.

For this reason, some attention must be paid to the clothing which the fowler will wear for an expedition to the estuary. In addition to choosing garments which will blend into the background, it is vital to ensure that there are no bright metal buttons or buckles which might flash in the light of the rising or setting sun.

Many manufacturers now produce waxed cotton or synthetic fibre shooting coats in a camouflage pattern. Where possible this type of jacket should be worn as the standard olive green colour tends to be far too dark when worn in the faded straw-coloured surroundings of a midwinter marsh. A hat with a good broad peak is another essential.

On the shore, natural camouflage should be used as much as possible and, when flighting close to the sea wall, it is frequently a simple matter to throw together a hide from the flotsam and seaweed which normally litters the high-water mark. Artificial hides using army surplus netting or one of the tangleproof leafscreen products are useful in some situations, but, as with clothing, a green and brown camouflage net is worse than useless when erected amongst the pale vegetation of winter. A man-made hide, whether of a temporary or permanent nature, will be less obvious if it is constructed against some natural feature such as an eroded banking or a fallen tree.

Irrespective of the type of hide or the materials from which it is built, the cardinal rule is that it must not be silhouetted against the sky when viewed from the direction from which the fowl will approach. In suitable locations a permanent hide has the advantage that it can be left unused until the geese have become accustomed to it and, additionally, it can be made more comfortable than a temporary erection. Where circumstances do permit the construction of this type of hide, the fowler will find that timber pallets are exceptionally useful as they are not only conveniently sized but, being strong and hollow, they can be filled with soil and mud to weight them down and to provide a substrate for the growth of grasses and other plants in future years.

Unfortunately it is not always possible to have the luxury of a hide from which to shoot. Most of the time it will be necessary for the wildfowler to conceal himself as efficiently as possible by using such areas of shade, clumps of weed and natural gutters as he might find upon the shore. In this event it is vital to get as low as possible and it is worth bearing in mind that the human form is less obvious when crouched in front of a dark backdrop than when peering over the top of it.

Keeping as still as possible is also important. Whether sitting in a comfortable hide, painfully crouched in a damp creek or merely attempting to attain invisibility in a bed of seaweed on an otherwise featureless shore, the fowler should try to avoid moving once he is in position. The slight motion of a human head turning to survey an arc of 180° will be sufficient to flash a warning to any goose which may be approaching. Experienced marsh gunners have developed a method of scanning the horizon by eye movement alone.

GUNS AND CARTRIDGES

Chapter 17 gives some excellent advice about the care of wildfowling guns, but it is perhaps apposite to mention here the range of weapons which might be considered for use when geese are the quarry.

Because wild geese habitually seem to fly at a safe height, the wildfowler is often tempted to attempt to achieve the maximum possible range by choosing a large-bore shotgun and the heaviest cartridges his weapon will fire.

Any survey of the literature relating to the 'good old days', when geese and duck reputedly blackened the sky above every fen, marsh and estuary, will leave little doubt that the hard gnarled fowlers of yesteryear went in for big guns in a big way. The 8-bore was commonly regarded as the smallest gauge which could be legitimately described as a 'fowling piece' and 6-bores and 4-bores were not exactly rare. Even when the professional fowler was joined on the foreshore by a new breed of gentleman gunner, the obsession with heavy guns did not disappear.

Over a period of several decades, however, the popularisation of wildfowling as a sport and the simultaneous development of the 12-bore magnum shotgun led to a decline in the use of those large weapons. During the middle years of the 20th century the magnums held sway and the shot load which they could safely handle gradually increased.

In more recent times there has been a tendency for wildfowlers to view the choice of gun more objectively and many experienced sportsmen favour the use of an ordinary game gun for use below the sea wall. At the same time, there has

been something of a revival in the use of larger-calibre shotguns due to the importation of relatively inexpensive 10-bores, 8-bores and even a single-barrelled 4-bore. Add to that range the options of over-and-under, side-by-side, pump action and semi-automatic, together with an almost infinite variety of barrel length, chamber length, choke boring and other such details and it is clear that the wildfowler of today has a bewildering selection from which to choose.

Fowling is a sport in which there is plenty of room for individuality and the sportsman who wishes to use a large-bore, heavy gun should feel free to do so. Similarly, if one's confidence is boosted by having magnum capacity, then there is no reason why a shotgun of this type should not be employed.

To some extent the choice of shotgun will depend upon whether it is to be used solely for goose shooting or for a range of other quarry. In the latter case, there is likely to be merit in opting for a general-purpose 12-bore rather than a specialist goose gun.

Another consideration is the cost of ammunition. It is generally accepted that No. 3 shot is the best all-round choice for geese and this size is available in everything from a standard 12-bore game load, through a variety of magnum cartridges to shells for the larger-bore shotguns. It should be borne in mind, however, that magnum ammunition is disproportionately expensive and the price of commercially loaded 10-bore, 8-bore and 4-bore cartridges is prohibitive. The man or woman who plumps for a large calibre weapon should, therefore, be prepared either to pay heavily for cartridges or to settle for reloading their own empty cases.

ETHICS

Wildfowling in pursuit of geese is perhaps the ultimate shooting sport, but, unfortunately, 'goose fever' can occasionally bring out the worst in some so-called 'sportsmen'.

The most commonly committed offence is probably that of shooting at out-of-range birds. Geese are large and it is tempting to try a chance longshot at a skein which is 60, 70 or even 80 yards high. The danger of wounding geese at such ranges is considerable and, to avoid unnecessary suffering, it is incumbent upon the fowler to learn

It is incumbent upon the fowler to restrict his shooting to distances which are well within the capacity of his gun and cartridge combination

to assess range and then to restrict his shooting to distances which are well within the capacity of his gun and cartridge combination.

Linked to this problem is that of striving to achieve kills at long ranges by using large shot sizes. Some fowlers swear by BB shot and it is not unknown for AAA pellets to be employed. The indisputable fact is that the effective range of a 12-bore magnum load of BB shot is less than 45 yards as the pattern density required to ensure a clean kill fails before this distance is reached. To use BB at a greater range is to run the serious risk of wounding geese and the use of AAA or larger shot is sheer irresponsibility. For general purposes, No. 3, No. 4 or, in very heavy loads, No. 1 shot should be employed when geese are in prospect.

A third ethical consideration is that of excessive bags of geese. Although the populations of the quarry species are at a healthy level, much bad publicity comes from a few reports each year of wildfowlers killing large numbers of geese. Usually those incidents arise when gunners who do not appreciate the ethics of wildfowling set up decoys on the inland feeding grounds of the geese. There may be very occasional opportunities for the shore shooter to kill more geese than is considered decent and a wise rule would be to set oneself a personal bag limit of three geese per flight. It has to be said that, on public or Crown foreshores, this limit is rarely likely to be achieved.

The respect which true wildfowlers have in the eyes of non-shooting conservationists derives very largely from the code of conduct and self-restraint which characterises the sport. It is vitally important that newcomers to the pursuit wholeheartedly espouse those well-established ethics and do nothing to endanger the future of the art.

An estuary where the goose roost is protected by local nature reserve bye-laws (Eric Begbie)

15
PUNT-GUNNING
NICK FREARSON

When invited to contribute to *The New Wildfowler* I was confronted with the task of condensing into a single chapter all that should be written about punt-gunning, a sport that itself would easily fill a book. With such limitations on space and the need to both describe and explain the sport and in addition provide some guidance for the newcomer to this branch of wildfowling, literary considerations have been somewhat cast aside in an attempt to include all that is necessary.

INTRODUCTION

Historical research has shown that the development of punt-gunning into the sport that is known today probably took place in the first decade of the 19th century. Before this various methods of attaching guns to boats for the purpose of shooting wildfowl had been used for some time. It therefore appears that true punt-gunning has been practised for about one and three-quarter centuries with much of the equipment still being used remaining little changed in design. Although wildfowling has altered considerably over this period, punt-gunning is still an important and integral part of the sport.

Today's punt-gunners are drawn from a broad cross-section of society and are pursuing their activity on tidal waters for sport, the days of the professional wildfowler having long since passed. Those professional gunners, who operated on both inland and tidal waters, had very different objectives, the principal one being to harvest an important food source. Their practices must be considered in the context of the times in which they lived, times before the existence of a welfare state as we know it today.

That it has much interested some of the great naturalists and ornithologists of the past is quite understandable, the opportunities to study birds and their habits being almost unique. One only has to read the works of men such as Abel Chapman, J. G. Millais, Frank Southgate, E. T. Booth and other great wildfowl authorities to realise that punt-gunning has many more attractions to its devotees than just as a shooting sport. In fact, anyone wishing to take up punting purely for the shooting aspect will very soon find himself sadly disappointed.

Punt-gunning played a most important role in securing the modern wildfowling of today. The BASC (formerly WAGBI) was founded by punt-gunners, the legendary Stanley Duncan becoming the Association's first honorary secretary and Sir Ralph Payne-Gallwey (perhaps the most prolific author on the sport) becoming its first President. Analysis of those wildfowlers attending the famous inaugural meeting on 7 April 1907 at the Imperial

Hotel in Hull shows a high proportion of punt-gunners. If these men had not had the foresight to form such an Association, that was to develop over the years a national supporting structure of affiliated wildfowling clubs working together and in partnership for the same ends, one wonders how the sport might have suffered.

In 1967 came time of crisis, when WAGBI, under the leadership of its Director, John Anderton, and supported by punt-gunners of the time, fought a three-month battle and saved the sport from a political death: a clear demonstration that the Association would always support and fight for its members' rights and interests.

THE SPORT

Punt-gunning is a highly selective and tactical stalking sport involving the use of a combination of the weather, the tides, the light and wildfowl habits. It is a stalking sport that is carried out in full view of the quarry, unlike other stalking sports (for example, deer stalking) when normally cover or dead ground is used. The puntsman has to propel his craft lying in the prone position and exceptional skill, strength and physical fitness are required to manoeuvre along a tactical course, so achieving an imperceptible approach to the birds.

Success is achieved when an effective shot is fired after lesser opportunities have deliberately been allowed to pass, the puntsman sometimes making only one shot after a number of days' effort afloat. Such is his selectivity that on many occasions he will stalk birds that ultimately will not be shot at. This challenge without doubt renders the sport the most difficult means of bagging wildfowl, and for this reason alone has always in the past, does now and will in the future only interest and attract a very small number of wildfowlers.

The shore gunner has to locate a flightline, then endeavours to intercept the fowl and to bag a number of birds with a number of shots. The punt-gunner has to locate the fowl, then endeavours to stalk them and bag a number of birds with a single shot. Both aspects of wildfowling involve their own particular skills to bring success, measured in terms of number of birds bagged either by a series of shots fired by a shoulder gun or by a single shot from a punt-gun.

The punt-gunner has constraints imposed upon him that do not affect the shore shooter. The type of craft used places great restrictions on his sport, as the few inches of freeboard of a gunning-punt can render impossible many a trip in rough weather. In addition, the sport can only be pursued when the tides are at a certain height at a certain time. These restrictions mean that there are only two or three days during the fortnightly tide cycle when it is possible to punt in one particular estuary and these days, of course, can coincide with gales. A general strategy is to depart with an ebbing tide after dawn, returning with the flood before dusk, so enabling the punting and land-fall to take place during the hours of daylight.

Mallard, wigeon and teal are the principal quarry species of the puntsman, geese being very seldom shot as their daytime inland feeding habits render them most unlikely to be in the estuary when he is afloat. The puntsman's actions are always governed by modern sporting ethics and a desire to follow such a traditional pursuit in a thoroughly proper and responsible manner.

THE GUNNING-PUNT

Gunning-punts are either single or double-handed, the latter usually carrying a slightly larger gun as two people are aboard to carry out its propulsion and the firing of the gun. Sir Ralph Payne-Gallwey gave us some basic designs for gunning-punts and, a hundred years later, his ideas are still an excellent starting point for building a punt. Different versions of his plans are published in several of his works, the dimensions used in this chapter being taken from *Shooting Moor and Marsh*, a volume in the Badminton Library.

Without doubt, Sir Ralph Payne-Gallwey's designs have since been improved by a number of individual puntsmen, increasing both the invisibility and seaworthiness of the punts that they have built. Up to 6 inches flare on the sides will make a punt much drier in a sea and give her more lift from the waves. Four feet of beam, which might be considered as the minimum for a double punt, should be carried well forward if she is to float a heavy gun, so placing adequate buoyancy underneath its weight. Larch, yellow pine and marine plywood are all excellent timbers for the purpose, as are modern glues, epoxy resins and fixings.

In some areas, notably Norfolk and Essex, local traditional designs of punt have been in existence for a very long time, these craft often being

A single-handed punt for sculling and using a setting-pole, to take a gun of from 80 lb to 120 lb weight

Total length	18′ 0″
Length on floor	17′ 3″
Extreme width on floor	2′ 9″
Extreme width across decks	3′ 4″
Height of stem	0′ 5½″
Height of stern	0′ 8″
Length of fore-deck	7′ 3″
Length of after-deck	3′ 6″
Greatest width of cockpit	2′ 2″
Each side flared out at most	0′ 3½″
Width of side decks at half length of cockpit	0′ 6½″ each
Round of deck at gunbeam	0′ 3″
Coaming forward ($\frac{3}{8}$″ thick)	0′ 3″ high
Coaming aft	0′ 2½″ high
Spring on floor, fore and aft	0′ 2¼″
Round athwartships or kammel	0′ ¾″

Floor timbers, 14 in apart, and a pair of elm knees ($\frac{5}{8}$ in. to $\frac{3}{4}$ in. thick) to each alternate one. Floor timbers of elm, 1¼ in wide on surface by $\frac{3}{4}$ in. deep.
Three aft and five fore-deck rafters, $\frac{3}{4}$ in. on surface, by 1¼ in. deep.

Floor planks	$\frac{3}{4}$″ yellow pine
Sides	a full ½″ yellow pine
Decks	$\frac{3}{8}$″ yellow pine

For a gun not more than 100 lb this punt may be 2 ft 8 in across floor, and 3 ft 2 in over decks; all else the same as above.

Double-handed punt for paddling, sculling, or using a setting-pole, to take a gun of from 130 lb to 170 lb weight

Total length	22′ 5″
Length on floor	22′ 0″
Greatest width of floor	3′ 2″
Greatest width across deck	3′ 11″
Height of stem	0′ 5½″
Height of stern	0′ 8″
Length of fore-deck	8′ 3″
Length of after-deck	4′ 2″
Greatest width of cockpit	2′ 6″
Width of side decks at half length of cockpit	0′ 9″ each
Each side flared out at most	0′ 4½″
Round of deck at gunbeam	0′ 3¾″
Coaming forward (½″ thick)	0′ 4″ high
Coaming aft (½″ thick)	0′ 3″ high
Spring on floor, fore and aft	0′ 2½″
Kammel or round athwartships	0′ $\frac{7}{8}$″

Floor timbers 14 in. apart, and a pair of elm knees ($\frac{3}{4}$ in. to $\frac{7}{8}$ in. thick) to each alternate one. Elm floor timbers, 1$\frac{1}{8}$ in. on surface by 1 in. deep. Three aft and five fore deck rafters, 1 in. on surface by 1½ in. deep.

Floor planks	$\frac{3}{4}$″ yellow pine
Sides	$\frac{5}{8}$″ pine or elm
Decks	$\frac{7}{16}$″ fir

undecked, which I consider greatly reduces their seaworthiness. Apart from ease of construction and the resultant saving in cost, one can see little advantage in such a type.

Gunning-punts are painted a shade of pale grey similar to that of a kittiwake's back. Variations of this colour will produce greater invisibility depending on the structure of the estuary punted, as glistening wet mud or dry sand do give different light reflections along a tide edge. An off-white hat and clothing should be worn as, like the punt, its occupants are silhouetted against that area of sky that merges with the water.

STALKING, SETTING AND METHODS OF PROPULSION

Of the two great skills in the sport, one is the handling of the punt, the other being the firing of the gun (described later). One has to control and propel the punt with a minimum of noise and movement and with a maximum of speed, special attention being given to the head and to the arm that is driving the craft, seamanship also being involved. Movement, particularly of the head, is the largest single cause of the quarry spotting the approach and it is essential that one should lie down and start the stalk from a distance at which the birds are oblivious of one's actions – generally a greater distance than is appreciated.

Do not start your approach until you are fairly certain that you can float into range, as you are most unlikely to get more than one chance, although this may involve waiting for the flood tide. If your stalk fails on account of running aground or you decide that it is inappropriate to fire and the birds still remain settled, depart as carefully as you approached, so leaving them undisturbed. Should the stalk fail with the birds seeing you and lifting, remain motionless in the punt until they disappear, so causing them little alarm.

It takes several seasons to develop the skills of controlling the punt and to learn that tactical course that gives an imperceptible approach to your quarry. In simple terms, the punt is propelled along a heading just slightly off the birds, so concealing the movement of the arm until the moment when a direct course is taken, just as the required range is being reached. Up-wind stalks are generally more successful than down-wind ones.

There are three main methods of propulsion used when stalking. Sculling with a single oar through a rowlock on the stern can be used in deep water, but its disadvantages are the difficulty in concealing the moving hand and its lack of power in strong winds and tides. Again in deep water, side paddling is a means of manoeuvre when a small hand paddle is held in either hand, the strokes being made entirely under water by feathering of the blades. Such paddles are generally 2 ft 3 in. in total length, with a blade length of 1 ft 8 in. and width of $3\frac{3}{4}$ in., being weighted so they float vertically. Again the disadvantage of this method is lack of power combined with the fact that there is a moving arm to conceal on either side of the punt.

Setting-poles are the third and most powerful and controlled means of driving the punt, provided that the bottom can be reached by one of the varying sizes usually carried aboard. The setting arm operates through a hinged or removable section of cockpit coaming and poles of the following lengths are generally considered suitable: 2 ft 6 in., 4 ft, 4 ft 6 in., 6 ft, 6 ft 6 in., 7 ft, 8 ft. Such poles have two prongs and should be weighted so they sink to the bottom and then stand vertically, a four-pronged version being necessary for use on

FIGURE 30 1. *Hand paddle: 2ft 3in. in total length, blade length 1ft 8in. and width $3\frac{3}{4}$in. to be weighted so it floats vertically*

2. Setting-pole head: four pronged type for use on soft mud

3. Setting-pole: for use on hard or sandy bottoms. Flat section with tapered edges approx $2\frac{1}{2}$in. in width. Suitable overall lengths are 2ft 6in., 4ft, 4ft 6in., 6ft, 6ft 6in., 7ft, 8ft

Setting-poles should be weighted, so they sink to the bottom and then stand vertically

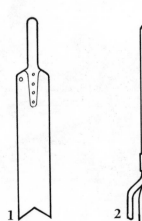
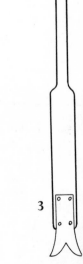

1   2   3

soft mud. A lead shoe reduces noise on a bottom of rock or gravel. These setting-poles should be of flat section with tapered edges, approximately $2\frac{1}{2}$ in. in width up to the handle, as apart from lateral thrusts steering the punt, the trailing of the pole between strokes acts as a rudder.

Rowing and sailing are the two means of covering large distances; 8 ft oars work well for a double punt and 7 ft ones for a single. A leg o' mutton sail is the least complicated rig, and with a little ingenuity, a spare oar can be used as a mast, so reducing the amount of equipment on board: a sail with a luff of 6 ft 6 in. and a foot of 6 ft drives a double punt satisfactorily.

Current legislation prohibits the use of a mechanically-propelled boat in the immediate pursuit of any wild bird for the purposes of driving, taking or killing it. There is certainly no place for an outboard engine in punt-gunning today and there has not been one by tradition either. The use of an engine, apart from bringing the sport into disrepute, directly conflicts with the ethics of modern puntsmen who wish to preserve a pure and traditional pursuit for the future.

THE PUNT GUN AND ITS FIRING

A punt-gun is simply a big-bore shotgun generally too large to be discharged from the shoulder and therefore fired from a punt. However, this is not always the case as 4-bore is normally considered to be the smallest size of punt-gun.

The other great skill is in firing the gun, which may be either breech- or muzzle-loading, both types performing equally as well if correctly loaded and primed. Some muzzle-loaders have had their ignition systems converted for the use of a black powder revolver blank, generally of .32 or .38 size, as commonly used in the making of a breech-loader's cartridge, a modification that has improved their reliability. Muzzle-loaders are usually slightly lighter in weight than their breech-loading counterparts, not having a breech plug and action. They are more complicated both to clean and load, but just as effective as the breech-loader that is more commonly in use today. Efficient cleaning is of great importance, hot or boiling water being a most satisfactory method of removing black powder fouling from the barrel.

Punt-guns are built using the same standard formula as for smaller shotguns, namely that a minimum of 6 lb of ordnance is required to deliver one ounce of shot. The following table quoted from *The Complete Wildfowler Ashore and Afloat* by Stanley Duncan and Guy Thorne provides a very useful guide to dimensions and loads, although variations of these standards undoubtedly work well. By law a punt-gun is limited to a maximum of $1\frac{3}{4}$ in. diameter internal bore measurement, with most punt-guns in use today being considerably smaller in size.

Punt-guns may look like large shotguns to those unaccustomed to seeing them. However, per head accounted for, their shot charge is probably no greater than the accumulated total of shot charge of a number of much smaller cartridges fired by a shoulder gun. In short, a large shotgun to shoot a number of birds with one shot, as opposed to a number of birds being shot by a series of shots from a smaller shotgun.

Size of bore	Weight	Length of barrel	Charge of shot	Charge of black powder
1 to 1¼ in.	50 to 75 lb	6 ft 8 in. to 7 ft 6 in.	8 to 12 oz	1½ to 2½ oz
1⅜ to 1½ in.	80 to 120 lb	7 ft 9 in. to 8 ft 0 in.	16 to 20 oz	3 to 3¾ oz
1⅝ to 1¾ in.	130 to 150 lb	8 ft 0 in. to 8 ft 6 in.	22 to 28 oz	4 to 4¾ oz

A fact often overlooked when considering large-bore guns is that the effectiveness of such guns decreases with size; the greater the load, the smaller the percentage of pellets reaching the target as a result of distortion and friction during passage through the barrel. Dr Charles J. Heath (a past president of WAGBI) addressed his thoughts to this matter amongst other problems and developed his famous chamberless design for wildfowling guns: the modern plastic cup wad used in standard cartridge manufacture assists with this same problem.

The screw-plug action is probably the most common and simplest type, having been made in several forms. One design uses a dovetailed head on the cartridge base that slides into a corresponding slot in the striker face, so enabling both action and cartridge to be screwed into the breech as one unit.

Punt-guns are loaded with coarse-grained black powder, oakum providing excellent wadding and BB as the best all-round shot, No. 1 being the smallest size recommended.

Two 16 oz breech-loading punt guns each with screw plug actions, the dovetail enabling the action and cartridge to be screwed into the breech as one unit. Both central and side lever cocking systems are employed on these guns. One, built by Messrs T. Bland and Sons (Gunmakers) Ltd, London, has provision for the breeching rope to be threaded through the stock itself, the other being fitted with trunnions on the barrel

There are basically two methods of absorbing the recoil of punt-guns, the boot-jack system having now more or less been consigned to history. The simplest arrangement is the use of a breeching rope passed through a hole in the stem of the punt, laid along her foredeck and attached to trunnions on either side of the gun's barrel and positioned approximately 10–12 in. behind its point of balance. Some guns have provision for the rope to be threaded through the stock itself. Nylon rope with that fibre's shock-absorbing properties serves the purpose well, as does hemp manilla.

Also used is Colonel Peter Hawker's recoil spring system, later adapted by Sir Ralph Payne-Gallwey. Here the barrel is mounted on a spring-loaded swivel stanchion which drops into a sliding block on the punt's floor, the block itself being attached to the punt's stem by a breeching rope led underneath the foredeck. This more complicated system has several advantages: the gun is automatically balanced when shipped on account of the fixed position of the stanchion. With the absence of trunnions sighting can be done along the side of the barrel rather than along the top of it, so lowering the gunner's head; and in the event of a capsize, the gun immediately falls off, so relieving the stricken punt of its weight. In this context every gun when aboard should have a buoy-line attached to it, the rope being of sufficient length and strength to raise it from the bed of the estuary. The only disadvantages lie in the maintenance of the springs and the breeching rope that is concealed under the decking and which requires regular inspection.

The elevation of the gun, which is mounted in a gun-crutch, is adjusted by use of a long-handled gun rest that slides along the slope of the foredeck, so raising or lowering the muzzle: the gun can either be fired with the barrel supported on the rest (best taken the instant the duck raise their heads) or, as in the case of a flying shot, with the barrel swinging above the rest and controlled by downward pressure on the stock. Another elevating

A single-handed gunning-punt equipped with breeching rope recoil system attached to trunnions on the gun's barrel

Right: *A double-handed gunning-punt with gun mounted on Col. Hawker's underdeck recoil spring breeching system. Note watertight inspection hatch in foredeck for access to breeching rope*

system involves the movement of the breech end by a threaded stanchion revolved by a rope and pulley block. In the single punt, there is little option to firing the gun on the rest and aiming it with the punt, one hand only being available for this task, the other being employed for setting.

Generally speaking, there is only a split second in which to pull the trigger lanyard, any delay often resulting in failure. It is in fact remarkably easy to miss with a punt-gun, as chronicled in many books on the sport, although perhaps hard to understand by those who have not tried their hand at it.

A punt-gun should never be discharged unless you are absolutely certain, right up to the very moment of firing, that it is correct so to do. Many factors can affect this decision – that you are certain no protected species are involved (easily determined by use of binoculars at the short range involved); that the quarry are placed in a way that will produce a clean shot; that you will be able to collect your bag and that it will not be swept away by wind or a fast tide; that your actions will not spoil the chances of any shoulder-gunners.

Every puntsman should set himself a personal standard of when it is worth firing a shot, realistically related to the size of his gun, and to both the potential and circumstances of the area where he is afloat. If ever in doubt, do not shoot, particularly if one is unable to see clearly.

Above all, you must be certain the range has been correctly judged, as this is the most important factor in ensuring a clean shot. This can be particularly difficult when lying so close to the water level, distances often appearing less than they really are. As in all wildfowling, the skill is to get well within range of the quarry and not in achieving a spectacular long shot. Sixty yards is an ideal range and shots at over seventy yards should not be taken. If BB shot is used and the pattern correctly placed on the quarry, it will be found that at sixty yards distance, the birds will mostly all be cleanly killed. It should not be forgotten that the effective range of a punt-gun does not vary substantially from that of other large-bore shoulder guns.

When considering the range, remember it is the distance to the furthermost duck at the back and not to those at the front that matters. Shots at birds floating on the water, particularly if rough, are rarely satisfactory, the most successful ones being made at lifting or flying birds. If fowl rise time after time and just out of range, do not pursue them, as the stalk is most unlikely to succeed and is only moving them unnecessarily. Birds floating and resting at high tide should be left.

AFTER THE SHOT

When a punt-gun is fired at the correct range, loaded with BB shot, and its pattern placed correctly by a true aim, birds are cleanly and instantly killed. It is possible, and by no means always the case, that one or more duck may have been struck by the charge, but are not dead, as can happen in all types of sporting shooting. Such birds are traditionally and, I feel, most unfortunately, known as 'cripples', referred to in similar cases as 'pricked', 'runner' or 'winged'.

If there is a winged bird it must immediately be gathered, before those that are dead. In this task,

the puntsman is very well placed as amongst exposed mudflats and in estuary channels there are few hiding places. He is afloat, able to cross channels and carries a standard 12-bore shoulder gun in his punt so enabling a bird to be shot, should this prove necessary. The experienced gunner prides himself on never knowingly losing a wounded bird and indeed this should be the case. Departing fowl should be closely watched as sometimes a bird which has been shot cleanly in the heart or lungs will collapse after a matter of several seconds, quite dead, and is easily collected. These have been described as 'droppers'.

SAFETY

The dangers in correctly practised punt-gunning are few, certainly no more than in many other sports, and such dangers that can arise generally result from ignorance, folly or poor seamanship. The loading, unloading and handling of a punt-gun requires great care, especially if carried out with cold hands or in adverse conditions, but is after all only a matter of common sense.

The weather and particularly wind speeds perhaps pose the puntsman with his greatest dilemma for it is often in bad weather and strong winds that the best chances are to be found. A punt with a combination of its low freeboard and considerable overall length cannot survive a big sea, although it is surprising just how much a well-designed hull can cope with when handled well.

If encountering bad weather, it is essential that water is baled or pumped out as fast as it is shipped and not allowed to accumulate. The gun is best brought inboard to trim the craft and stowed on the floor, so lowering the position of its weight. A tight and well-fitting cockpit cover should always be carried to keep out large waves, in which she cannot live, the only option then being to walk the punt along in shallow water to shelter. With a correctly made cover, she should not ship water and will float the gun and the gear whilst the seas break over her: it is essential that the cover has a skirt of approximately $2\frac{3}{4}$ inches lying on the decks in addition to its fall down the side of the coamings. If it is not so made, it will be found that waves rolling up the decks and slamming against the coamings tend to squirt water upwards between the coamings and the cover and thus, of course, inboard.

Remember that the predicted heights and times of tides, as published in tide tables, can be affected considerably by the weather and particularly by strong winds. This is of great importance in estuaries where the tide may flood as a bore. A compass, baler or pump, waterproof torch, distress flares, first-aid kit, spare oar and rowlock are all items that should be carried, as are a suitable anchor with adequate length of warp. Mud pattens may be needed for areas of quicksand and very soft mud, but such places are better left unvisited. A life-jacket of the modern slim type is comfortable to wear and helps to retain body warmth in cold weather. The correct and proper maintenance of a punt, punt-gun and all equipment is an essential to overall safety.

THE DISTURBANCE OF WILDFOWL

The word 'disturbance' is becoming more commonly used by those opposed to sporting shooting and particularly to wildfowling, its convenience being obvious: however, it has to be determined exactly what constitutes 'disturbance' and when that is decided, whether or not it significantly affects the birds.

The twice daily flooding tide, splashing and playing seals, birds of prey, mobbing greater black-backed gulls and other predators all move wildfowl, but is this 'disturbance'? I suppose it probably is as birds are 'disturbed', but then their lives are always on the move whether it be in their daily habits or greater factors such as migration.

Shipping, commercial fishing, aircraft, bait digging, shell-fish gathering, dredging, water sports of many types, gunnery ranges – the list is endless – can again move fowl, particularly when newly arrived. But is this really creating significant difficulties for the birds in achieving their essentials of feeding and resting? It is encouraging how some of our estuaries with their factories, oil refineries, power stations and other industrial developments hold substantial populations that appear to be living satisfactorily in such circumstances and how birds have shown their adaptability by changing habits, when necessary.

As mankind changes the environment, perhaps it should be considered satisfactory if wildfowl also change their habits in order to cope with the altered conditions. This they largely appear to be achieving and, speaking in general terms, the populations of quarry species have suffered no drastic declines.

But what of punt-gunning in this debate? In carrying out this stalking sport, the puntsman will try to create a very minimum of 'disturbance' to wildfowl and the surrounding area as it only spoils his own sport, just as when deerstalking. A punt is only a boat, but one that is operated in a way that specifically tries not to 'disturb', which cannot be said of the ship, the fishing trawler, the yacht, the power boat, the canoe and the wind surfer – all seen in our estuaries during the shooting season.

TODAY AND THE FUTURE

Wildfowling has been described as the pursuit of quarry species of wild duck and geese for sport with the use of a smooth-bore shotgun, either on foot or under certain conditions by boat, this specifically including the use of traditionally built and manually propelled gunning-punts.

Today's small number of punt-gunners have a well-organised and corporate voice through the B.A.S.C., their parent organisation, that rightly provides guidance for those pursuing this sport – an integral part of the whole sport of wildfowling that must stand united if it is to have the future that it deserves.

The sportsman conservationist and pure conservationist have common cause as the destruction of habitats and resultant loss of species is in neither's interest. With goodwill and understanding there is room for both, but the massive contribution made by shooting interests in creating, preserving and managing wetlands over very many years must not be overlooked by the modern protectionist. In the absence of such effort, he might have a great deal less to enjoy today.

It is likely that the decline in punt-gunning that has taken place throughout this century will continue, as more punt-guns pass into collectors' hands, not to be used again. Other guns, punts and their equipment are falling into disrepair through age. However, the future belongs to those who care deeply about it and to those who are prepared to solve the problems of today. The present generation of wildfowlers and punt-gunners hold the sport in trust knowing that its continuance largely depends on their actions, a responsibility I do not believe they will abdicate.

16
INLAND MARSH SHOOTING
THE LATE NOEL M. SEDGWICK

An inland marsh, for the purpose of this chapter, is any low-lying, boggy land, liable to flood, or to part-flood in late summer, autumn or winter, be it well drained or otherwise, and which lies on the other side of the sea wall to the beach, saltmarsh, or muds. It may start directly at the foot of the sea wall itself, when it will not, in fact, be a proper freshwater marsh, but a brackish one, with perhaps a long, narrow channel of water formed by the digging of those builders, lookers, and menders who erected the wall, or keep it in repair. This channel, of course, runs parallel to the wall and lies almost under its shadow.

Nearer the centre of these brackish grazings are often flashes of shallow water to which a number of wildfowl come, frequently resting on them by day when the sea is particularly rough, or using them as temporary sheltered lay-bys when the wind drives off the sea at near gale force. There are times when a hide may be built in the open and left unused until the fowl become accustomed to it. Then, one morning, when the sea is lashed to fury by the wind, the gunner, with his decoys out on the water in front, may enjoy some shooting. The decoys will probably be best set out a hundred yards in front, if this is possible, since any duck flying in from the sea will pass over the flash at a good height (especially if they have been much shot at from behind the sea wall) and, after passing it and the ambushed gunner, will turn back into the wind and drop towards the decoys.

If there is any reed cover on these brackish acres, no hide may be necessary. The water is brackish since, in some cases, waves splash hard against the sea wall and spume is blown high and over it; sometimes, too, there are leaks under the wall, and it is not altogether rare to see spurting fountains of salt water at high tide rising from the floor up to twenty-five yards and more from the wall itself, where rabbits have had their burrows and a ferreting tide has found the weakness.

Thus, while such marshes may be used by duck and wading birds when a full tide has drowned the saltings and a certain amount of flighting and even decoying can be enjoyed then, the usual lack of cover and often the disturbance of people walking along the sea walls keeps the birds very wide awake or scares them off; certainly much shooting does the reverse of encouraging them to use places of this kind.

But while brackish marshes, though wigeon and other duck and waders may be flighted well on occasions, as at high water, both by day and when there is a full moon with plenty of cloud background, it is the true freshwater marshes where bags can be made, and these marshes may lie a mile or so from the sea to a few miles inland.

Farther inland still we get those isolated grazing marshes and water-meadows where sport may be good in hard weather, and where some duck flighting can be had with more or less local birds. On these small, far-inland bits of boggy ground, where there is probably one good channel to take off the water, with a number of narrow runnels emptying themselves into it, sport is almost as local as are the birds, although there are times when extreme climatic conditions will bring southward-migrating duck and snipe, and even, perhaps, a small party of geese to them, adding spice to the more usual odd mallard or few couple of snipe shot by one or more walking guns. Most of these small places are included in the surrounding shooting rights so that only under an exceptional influx of birds, driven out of their usual haunts by frozen ground and water, are they shot with any seriousness. Most of the season they are kept quiet, unless the party shooting the surrounding ground decides to walk them for the odd covey or the few pheasants.

Perhaps some enthusiast among local sporting talent is allowed to walk the marsh land only for duck and snipe, when, if he is a fair shot and knows how to go about his job, he may shoot from a few to ten and more couple of snipe in a morning, walk-

up a few mallard in their favourite sheltered lay-bys, or flight duck going out of, or coming into, the marsh at dusk, from surrounding lakes and ponds, after the stubbles have been ploughed under and there is less feed out on the farms.

What will be said later about making inland marshes more attractive to fowl and how best to shoot them under certain conditions, applies, on a smaller scale, to these little damp spots reaching right into the centre of the country.

Each marsh, of course, like each ballast-pit, stretch of river, lake or pond has to be considered individually up to a point, for none is alike, but the general method of coming to terms with wildfowl forms a pattern on which lesser patterns can be worked out. Mallard and teal, for instance, behave very much alike the country through, and, though they may favour certain marshes and certain portions only of those, their main behaviour and characteristics should be studied, so that it becomes possible to know how to improve the attractions of a marsh to them, and then those methods of shooting them to good effect can be carried out, on a larger scale, on more extensive marshes to which far more birds come.

In short, what advice follows in this chapter regarding larger duck marshes can apply to a great extent to smaller far-inland places, always provided that the rule of thumb is not too strictly followed, but an intimate assessment is made of local conditions, and such conditions may vary considerably in detail the country through. Even the larger fresh marshes close to the coast, or within easy goose- and duck-flighting distance of it, may differ a great deal. One may be the daytime grazing place each winter of a large or small population of pinkfooted or whitefronted geese; another may seldom see a goose, but be well known for its fair-sized wigeon flock, and for a good scattering of pintail, mallard and teal.

There are many good inland marshes which form part of the acreage of private estates, where wildfowl are seldom, and sometimes never, shot. Such places are the true sanctuaries of the country, for, whether the estate itself is shot over privately or by a syndicate, it is the game which is the main concern, and, though the guns may enjoy an occasional duck flight in winter, such flights are carried out with due thought to preserve the flightlines and sanctuary of the fowl. Moreover, the keepers who look after the game and see that no shooting or poaching is done by outsiders, aid the stock of mallard by keeping down the crows and other corvids which would otherwise take countless duck eggs.

The locals, who may envy and even say hard words about the landowner, when they see hundreds of wigeon flying backwards and forwards over this private marsh, and sheltering there the day through, or watch mallard, pintail, shoveler, tufted, pochard, teal, and other duck afloat on its patches of floodwater, should realise that such unofficial sanctuaries are good for both the fowl and for themselves, for neither geese, feeding on the marsh by day, nor the duck resting there in peace, and sheltered from bitter winds, will remain on those few sacred acres. The geese will fly out at dusk and probably make for the coast and the sandy roosts beyond, to return at dawn, while the duck, becoming restless and noisy at dusk, will start to flight as the dusk deepens – flight out over the boundaries to their nocturnal feeding grounds which, in late summer and early autumn, will be the cornfields and barley stubbles. But soon after September, their flightlines will become more settled, as they make for other low-lying ground and lakes and ponds, and generally flying round at night, joined by other duck which have spent the day resting on large waters such as lakes, reservoirs and smaller private marshes.

At dawn, when the geese are thinking of lifting and making inland, the duck of our private marsh will be returning along their flightlines, coming over high with the wind (especially if they have been much shot at), or battling low against it if it is blowing off the marsh. Any gunner, be he local or not quite so local, will watch and study the movements of these fowl, discover their lines of flight, and then seek permission somewhere along them to enjoy a little evening flighting, with perhaps odd morning flights when opportunity allows during the weekends.

Time should never be wasted on attempting to decoy duck flying in or out at dusk or dawn for they have a set purpose then: to get out to their feeding grounds, and to return to their resting ground. Only on rare occasions will they alter course or altitude on seeing decoys set out. There are, nevertheless, exceptions which prove the rule, and occasionally during a morning flight duck will come down to decoys, but this is usually either early on in the season before the birds have formed fixed habits and many of them are still young, or when 'foreign' birds arrive, from stress of weather, which do not belong to local populations. They seem temporarily lost and may drop down to decoys even at flight time. About the countryside, within easy flighting distance to salt water, are disused gravel- and ballast-pits on which some-times really large rafts of duck may be seen resting by day. Some of these pits are rented, for reserves, by local wildfowling clubs; some are 'reserved' by birdwatching societies; others are retained by their owners, or the shooting let to small syndicates; today even a few winter sailing clubs attempt to rent them. These pits are sanctuaries in their own right, except when shot occasionally by any shooting syndicate renting them or when dis-turbed by fishermen; even then little damage is done to the birds, which quickly learn the lesson. The wise coastal gunner, or his brother-in-arms on the other side of the sea wall, should welcome them, for, as in the case of inland marshes, the duck cannot stay on such places, but must flight off at dusk and return at dawn; and there is always the chance of their being disturbed during the day by workmen or chance ramblers, when the gun on the saltings may suddenly see a couple of hundred mallard, or a sprinkling of various kinds of duck, swinging round his field of vision, and perhaps coming within range. Or they may fly inland to marsh or water-meadow and offer sport to any gunner there.

The small pond or marshy bit (unless it lies, like a patch of floodwater, in the open, devoid of cover) may require no artificial hide, the gunner standing *quite still* among natural cover, or even in the open. But should he feel too 'naked', a strip of camouf-laged netting hung between two cut sticks (bamboo canes show up too much, unless stained) will hide him and the dog; or he can string up some rushes, or make a sandwich of them laid between bits of wire netting.

On larger waters, or on completely bare ones, permanent or semi-permanent hides should be built in advance of the shooting season, so that the duck get used to them, and should be sighted with care. Duck will often flight in against the wind, and although, if coming direct from a certain locality each evening, they may arrive with the wind, they will fly on and turn back into it before pitching. They may even give a false run-in or two in acknowledgement of the seasonal baptism of fire.

If the prevailing wind blows from the south-west, hides should face in that direction so that, even if birds flash downwind from the west, they will turn back to settle, and, in doing so, show up for an instant against the rapidly fading patch of light. Therefore, when hide-building, likely wind direction, western sky and touching-down strip should be studied in conjunction with each other, and with any other strictly local points, such as the dark background of trees, a boundary fence, etc.

Whether or not decoys are used or are necessary depends on the ideas of the individual gunner, some of whom seem to like to complicate what need only be a simple situation. To wade out and anchor a dozen decoys, and to have to retrieve them during the tail-end of a flight, just for the sake of using them, is simple foolishness.

On the arable feeding grounds only the tyro can bungle matters once he has found the stubble being used and has sought permission to shoot there. Duck can be shot on laid corn just as pigeon are shot, and wooden or rubber decoys will bring them down quicker if the birds prove a little wild and suspicious after having been shot at a few times. Similarly on the stubbles, decoys, though seemingly used only by the more enterprising gunners, can be of considerable advantage.

Once the actual feeding ground has been lo-cated, the only thing left to do (apart from setting out decoys) is to make a rough hide of rakings, after studying wind direction and light. An open circle of rakings forms a good hide, the sides being added to where greater concealment of movement is necessary, such as the gunner slowly preparing to rise to his feet for steadier shooting. An armful of rakings can help to camouflage him if it is spread over his legs, and the same applies to hiding the dog. He should, of course, sit back to the wind, and, if his dog is facing him, he will see by the movement of its head and eyes if duck are approaching from the rear.

Back now along the shores of firths, lakes, reservoirs, rivers and flashes, gunners are in hiding, keen to taste the fruits of a new season. Many flightlines from resting waters to feeding grounds may be well defined, but where there is a trend towards fresh birds arriving from other places in the north, or from overseas, there may be quite a number of duck flying about in search of feeding or resting grounds, and for some time their

flight lines will be erratic. It is then worth putting out a raft of decoys, or just a spattering of them.

The duck which lie out on big waters will almost certainly have steady flightlines to their feeding grounds, and, though these may differ a little according to change of feeding areas, disturbance, or wind direction, the observant local fowlers will know what to do, and where to go.

If there is no natural cover or artificial hide along a good line of flight a portable hide can be used. This is constructed of camouflage netting, with four stakes (or even sticks) tied into it to make a hide with four 'walls', each a yard wide. The hide is easily carried around and can be used as a 'wading-stick' if there is any doubt about the depth of the water.

On many preserved shoots, where the guns like

to enjoy some early duck shooting, no doubt the keeper has erected comfortable butts, or hides. On some river-banks, edged by swampy ground, semi-permanent hides are built at intervals, with every modern convenience, including pegs to hang bags on, duck-boards to stand on, shelves for cartridges and odd objects, and a 'window' offering a perfect view.

Duck shot are retrieved by pickers-up, or, in a few cases, caught in nets strung across the water downstream. Guns take up their positions quietly before growing dawn, and either wait for morning flight or, in daylight, for birds driven off the river or the surrounding water-meadows.

While duck are shot on the stubbles and on other inland feeding, in England, at least, the shooting and decoying of geese on their feeding grounds is frowned upon by some fowlers and some farmers will not allow geese grazing on their pastures or feeding on the stubble or potato fields to be killed. Nor is it considered sporting to dig-in or stalk them on their roosting grounds out on the sands. The recognised method of shooting geese for sport is as they flight in towards the land at dawn, or fly out to their roosts at dusk; preferably the former.

In Scotland, especially when large concentrations of geese are doing some damage to fields, farmers will allow visitors to lie-up and shoot the big birds over decoys. This method has sometimes been made much of by 'romantic' writers, but, while stalking feeding alert geese may well prove an arduous undertaking, shooting them over decoys, by daylight, or when they feed under a bright moon is quite *infra dig*. Far better a few geese shot battling against a wind, after several disappointing gooseless days, than making a big bag over decoys.

As with the coastal fowler, the inland-marsh shooter does not really consider that his season is beginning to blossom until he hears the first welcome voices high overhead of the first wigeon to arrive. The coastal gunner may first hear the *wheeoo-wheeoo* of cock wigeon riding out on the estuary and the purring or growling note of the hens. But inland, the flight shooter suddenly hears one evening twittering voices far above him – *widget-widget!* – and sees perhaps one or more companies seemingly spying out the land below, searching for signs of flooding. If conditions are satisfactory, the birds may come down to feed. On the other hand, they commonly clear off and may not be seen again for as much as a week. They have discovered no special attraction on the inland marshes, and for a spell may spend their daylight hours in rafts on an estuary or on reservoirs and lochs or lakes, or out on a calm sea. Then the inland gunner sighs and continues to flight his mallard in the evening, filling in his spare time by day walking-up the few snipe which breed locally, and welcoming any early influx that may come to his area.

While mallard and teal remain perhaps the chief target of many minor forays – with the odd shoveler or pintail drawn in – those days at early snipe, when the elms and willows and birches are yellowing and the marsh grasses form a painter's palette behind a wide fringe of tasselled great reeds with their pennants still green, and a breeze is blowing across the soggy ground of marsh and water-meadow, are happy ones for the snipe shot. If the long-bills have been feeding well under a bright moon they usually retire to their sleeping quarters in well-favoured patches of reed-tussocks, or sometimes to 'seats' in a reed-bed, to sleep the sleep of the just. Soon they have digested their food, are rested, and while they may not necessarily be quick off the mark, they are at least alert. If, on the other hand, the night has been dark and wild, or the ground slightly hardened by frost, and the birds started only to feed well as the elements quietened just before dawn, they may seek to probe for food long after daylight, being very much alert, though they will be sluggish for the rest of the morning and sit tight.

There are two schools of thought about how snipe should be walked-up. The first prefers to walk the ground downwind, for birds flushed rise into the wind and so offer an easy going-away shot. The second likes to walk upwind, believing that their approach across splash-splosh ground is less likely to be heard by resting snipe. A small third school will talk about walking across-wind. The answer is, of course, to know your sport and to know your quarry and your ground, when it will become obvious that no hard and fast rule can be right, but that the snipe shooter must be something of an opportunist, guessing (rather than theorising) how birds are likely to behave after a quiet moonlit, or a wild, wet night. Experience of local conditions, as in all shooting, should be the indication of how to set about matters rather than reliance on the written word of authors forced to generalise.

Alert snipe, walked downwind on sploshy ground on a windy day, will obviously hear the approach of human feet, as well as the cart-horse-like ones of a labrador, or hairy-footed spaniel. If a shooter prefers to walk downwind, then let him leave his dog at sit before he comes within hearing range of snipe lying in a patch of reeds. Whether his dog remains seated, or runs-in once his master has got off both barrels, does not seriously matter so far as this kind of stalking is concerned, though he should be sufficiently obedient not to race out too far ahead.

Snipe should be walked-up carefully and slowly, and whether you snap at rising birds or take your time in pulling the trigger is strictly a matter for the individual.

Driven snipe, put up by beaters, or by half a team of guns walking and half standing, can provide excellent sport. Even two experienced guns can enjoy it in lesser degree, if there are plenty of snipe lying out in a chain of water-meadows. One goes forward and stands behind a bush over which flushed birds are known generally to fly; the other zigzags noisily towards him.

Suddenly the fowling season proper is upon us – rain, flooding, frosts, the fall of the leaf, migrant fowl! The whitefronts, the pinks and the greys have become 'educated' as the season advanced, and, with every gunner's barrels against them, they are as wild as ever they will get. The main populations may be still in the vicinity of their earlier haunts or some may have moved farther south.

By this time, a fair-sized marsh may hold many surprises, and flooding will reveal, through the glasses, a great assortment of fowl resting by day. Gulls and plover scold and wail as they fly over the wide wings of water, but a sweep with the glasses shows massed companies of wigeon sheltering under a woodland slope, a tall hedge, or a steep bank. With them, though on their own, are scattered mallard and pintail, pochard, tufted, teal, even the odd smew, perhaps, and a couple of cormorants sitting on submerged gate-posts.

Suddenly the duck are up and flashing low across the marsh. Up and down they race, the teal flocks, like a coastal phalanx of mixed waders, rushing here and there. A peregrine, chasing a pigeon, has caused panic.

But how to come to terms with this great assortment of duck? Much of the marsh is flooded, but odd islands of grass are not yet awash, though recently covered by floodwater. Observation will have shown the duck-shooter to which (if any) accessible (by boat or wading) patches the wigeon are coming at dusk to feed on – accompanied by small parties of other species. Probably the twittering flocks – following a few bolder spirits – decide to drop down, their wings set, on to a strip of grass right out on the open flood, with the nearest drowned gate-post standing up eighty yards from their chosen feeding ground. If it is possible, which it seldom is, to wade out to it, and to set a few decoys near the edge of the island (with perhaps a stuffed wigeon on the grass itself) well and good. But if the floods are not sinking too rapidly, thereby exposing a great deal more marsh within twelve hours, a hide should be built next morning on the strip, being well camouflaged to sink into the surroundings, and plans thought out for the following evening, when the wigeon will return to feed, having left the island soon after dawn.

Before mid-afternoon the gunner should be in his hide with, perhaps, a couple of mallard decoys, or two pairs, well out on the water, and either mallard or wigeon decoys placed as life-like as possible round the edge of the island. If it is necessary to take out a boat, or rubber dinghy, this should form the base of the hide, the latter being tipped-up and propped up, and draped with camouflage netting, with further netting surrounding the gunner, though, under some circumstances, a back door may be left wide open.

It is folly now to shoot at circling, twittering flocks as they pass over or near at extreme range. They should be allowed to come down, if they are showing signs of so doing, and even a few allowed to settle. After a double shot, neither man nor dog should move, for, although the birds will depart, probably out of sight, it is almost ten to one that they will soon return to make another attempt to get down to feed and are sure to be watching the spot.

After a shot or two has eventually been fired and the wigeon seem to have vanished for good, the gunner will glue his eyes on darkening sky for other duck, and presently he will hear once more those thin wigeon whistles far up against where first one and then another star is beginning to twinkle. For some time the companies, now suspicious, will fly round, and may even clear off for a further period, especially if mallard or teal are shot at, and they may not return until it is too dark to see them, or the moonlit sky is cloudless with no background to show up flying duck. If, however, the night is a good shooting one, with a bright, full moon hiding behind a very thin veil of mist, so that the heavens look like an inverted gold-fish bowl, or if a bright moon comes and goes behind sailing masses of cloud, the gunner may well find himself enjoying one of those exceptional, bag-filling occasions when wind, moon, cloud, flood and all else seem to have combined for his benefit.

Thus, when the marshes are in various stages of flooding, observation must be kept to watch where wigeon are feeding as the water rises or recedes, and, in a somewhat lesser sense, the same applies to other duck, and even to teal, which love certain drains or areas of seed-providing marsh and will flight there as soon as these favourite places become uncovered. They also hunt vanishing pools of floodwater for food, and, when they are seen using such pools or flashes, or overfull drains, let the gunner, if possible, sit facing such water when the very last light is draining from the sky (though shooting sitting is not a good plan for overhead flighting), and he will hear the *zip-zip* of teal flighting in behind him like bullets, missing his head by yards or inches, and get a glimpse of them momentarily against the shine of the water. This sport requires very good eyesight, quick reactions, and snap-shooting *par excellence*.

Meanwhile, any gunner, salt- or freshwater, knows how he feels about shooting from a sitting position. In fact, he will get far more misses than if he rose to his feet and swung on to his target. That is learned by experience. But to be able to sit on a dry seat, and to be able to swivel, so that one can, without undue effort, keep a look-out fore and aft is a great advantage, and every shooting man, except the strictly conventional one, should have made for himself the swivel stool. The prototype was invented by 'Johnnie' (Judge) Johnson, sometime Chairman of WAGBI, but was later 're-invented' by one who used four-ply instead of thick, heavy board. The diagram opposite shows how to make this most invaluable seat (which can be used for pigeon shooting among the reeds, or right out on open floods).

The diagram (Figure 31) shows an adjustable stool, but one can also be made without an adjustable seat and requires short and long main tubes, so that one can take out the seat most suitable for the occasions – short tubes for grass; medium for such cover as *Spartina* grass; long tubes for floodwater sitting. These seats, or stools, allow one to hide behind a minimum of cover, and to swivel round without effort to keep a watching brief in the rear. It is felt that one can get good shooting from them at flight, but the 'seater' should, if he wants to make a bag, wait until the birds are coming within good range and then slowly rise from his stool and very gently raise the barrels of his gun.

The stool is of even greater value in mud-gutter or for saltings, for the gunner can sit in the centre of a muddy channel down which water is trickling and remain dry, clean, comfortable, and out of sight.

No apology is needed for emphasising that every marsh, swamp or chain of water-meadows has its own individual 'peculiarities', and what form of shooting applies well to one may not altogether suit another, but it is, of course, quite impossible in a chapter of this kind to cover all and every eventuality throughout the country. There are some marshes to which wigeon seldom if ever come; there are others on which wigeon are regarded as the main objective. There are marshes known for their excellent snipe shooting; there are others which seldom hold a snipe. This chapter, then, applies perhaps more to the general kind of marsh, more often within flight of the coast, to which duck come in considerable quantities when cold weather sends them southwards and floodwater encourages them to settle and to remain for weeks on end, particularly if at least some parts of the marsh, or some neighbouring preserves, form daytime sanctuary and shelter.

All manner of problems arise on narrow strips of marsh or water-meadows bordering small rivers and brooks. To give but one instance, while is it not difficult to walk-up mallard and teal on some twisting brook or stream, simply by coming on them round the bends, or by walking out into the meadow and then stalking back towards the bank at a spot where birds have been seen, such a place may not lend itself easily for snipe shooting. If patches of rushes or reed-tussocks lie near the river's bank and are more favoured by snipe than cover farther from the water, the birds, when flushed, will fly out over the water (especially against a prevailing wind) and if the current is very fast it may be difficult to recover them in numbers,

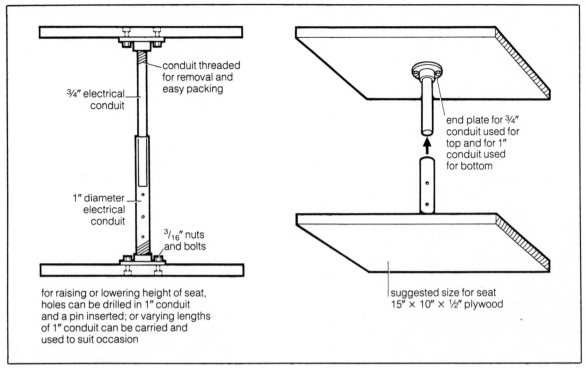

FIGURE 31 *A swivel stool*

even with a good dog. This is just a minor point, but one of many with which local conditions can face the rough shooter.

Another problem which not infrequently arises is when a flight pond has been fed and a flightline induced, and not over-scrupulous neighbours take advantage of it by shooting duck flighting to and from it over their ground.

The real problem of inland marsh shooting, however, is getting upon terms with the fowl there, when others have the same idea, for many marshes are split up so that they are owned or farmed by several men, each of whom may give leave to shoot to one or more of his friends. It is galling to hear a shot suddenly go off close by in the dusk just as a company of wigeon or a big flock of teal are coming down to your decoys. On the other hand, it is equally galling to see quantities of duck flying about and settling at the far end of a marsh where there is no one to put them on wing. Therefore, 'company' can be a two-edged sword and, the 'best bet' of all is when the gunners get to know each other and can come to some mutual understanding, however elastic it may be.

Some marsh shooters who operate only on

Saturday afternoons have an understanding about matters and will even phone each other at a given time to make arrangements for that week, so that each knows the time when the other will be on the marsh, and other details, such as the using of decoys, etc. The extreme limit to such understanding is surely the case of a businessman whose friend phones him when he sees the geese flighting in the direction of his home a mile or two away, giving the former the chance to pick up his gun, run upstairs to the flat roof of his place, and there get a shot in as the skein passes over.

But whether the gunners who 'share' the shooting of a large marsh are friendly or 'distant' with each other, they will usually combine against outsiders who unlawfully encroach on 'their' ground, or who may go so far, say, as to bring a gunning-punt down to a flooded fresh marsh and use, perhaps, a swivel 4-bore against the resting duck by day, or under the moon, and floating over ground on which they have no business to be.

From Christmas till the finish of the duck- and goose-shooting season (which is 31 January except on the foreshore) is the best part of the inland shooter's year, for any prolonged spell of hard weather is likely to send more and more duck southwards; in any case, there is a natural movement south during the colder months, even if winter does not actually harden the land and seal up the water.

'Going afloat' on inland marshes usually implies taking a boat out to a good flighting point, or sometimes attempting to 'punt' up to some geese or duck in a camouflaged boat, but with ordinary shoulder guns – a practice that is not really common and which is frowned upon on many marshes.

At the season's end the gunner's heart often bleeds, for the marsh is flooded and 'black with duck'. The wigeon sit out in great rafts and are flighting at dusk to perfection. Everything seems to have got into full swing – when the gong goes!

The duck shooter who is also a keen ornithologist may lay aside the gun with perhaps less regret than the gunner who shoots for sport and the pot. The more fortunate ones find their way down to the foreshore for the twenty extra days' shooting allowed there. But soon those days, too, have passed, and the marsh gunner is back on his old ground with a strange sense of loss and gain, to start his gunless rounds, perhaps, or carrying a gun to kill vermin.

There are many methods of dealing with pests. Often enough, as he sits in his hide near the water's edge in the fading light of a winter's evening, the gunner will hear the hoarse voice of a homing crow and see that villain pass like a shadow in the gathering gloom. He will most surely take advantage of the situation to down one of his worst enemies. More, should he be aware that homing crows (or even hunting crows during the day) are likely to come near, he will find that a dead duck, placed on its back on the edge of the flood, with a few scattered feathers round it, will bring a crow close in to investigate, and he may, in his patience, even wait for it to call its mate to the feast.

During the season, he will have shot any rat on sight, but now, with the close season on him, he will spend more time, particularly as spring approaches, walking round the channels, drains and ditches, letting his dog hunt out and bolt rats, and then shoot the swimming creatures with a shotgun, rifle or even with a catapult. It is surprising how many rats can be killed like this, even on a short walk round on a Sunday morning.

Now, as he stands with very mixed feelings indeed, watching a thousand wigeon on a pool of receding floodwater, already gay in their courting plumage, and so busy about their affairs that they allow him to get fairly close and stand and watch them; when he hears the first redshank, back from the coast to nest once more in the fresh marsh; as he listens to the rooks talking and sees them building in the wood over the river – he begins to think along the lines of keepering and improving his marsh. Plank bridges have gone afloat in the floods. These can be found and replaced, this time with greater care and attention. To those likely spots for mallard to nest – those rushy, swampy corners – he may well carry a whitethorn branch or two, placing it where the reeds and rushes and grass can grow up round and through it, so that it will make a thorny retreat from vermin. Perhaps he can get permission to wire round similar odd corners of good nesting cover, to save them from trampling cattle, and so encourage duck to nest there.

The wigeon may still be there in March, and even April, when mallard are sitting hard on eggs, or, in a mild season, have already hatched off an early brood or two, but now that restlessness which so assailed him throughout the shooting season is laid. He watches the mating duck with no thought of 'murder' in his heart, but only a fresh awakening to his small duties towards improving his marshland acres.

Then one morning the last drop of surface water has left the marsh and the wigeon have gone. Their lovely piping and whistling are no longer heard; only the noisy gossiping of rooks in the rookery and the belling of a pair of redshank as they race up and down their nesting territory, with perhaps the quacking of an agitated mallard duck as she sees the farmer's dog approaching her nursery.

Plover are wailing and weeping and casting themselves this way and that above where the first milkmaids and moon-daisies are showing pink and white heads above the lush grazing. A pair of snipe rise from the dampness of a patch of yellow kingcups, one circling to drum, wings and stiff outer tail feathers held rigid as the bird tip-tilts in a shallow dive, its bleating heard at a great distance. Before very long, the first family of young mallard will be on wing at dusk, and thoughts will flash ahead to those first September evenings, when the duck will be flighting once more to the barley fields.

Decoys set out on a flooded field (John Paley)

SETTING OUT DECOYS

Some mention of decoys has already been made, but the use and setting out of decoys, especially on inland marshes and flooded water-meadows, deserves more than a few passing remarks. Indeed decoys can, not infrequently, ensure better and surer sport and reasonably larger bags. One of the main functions of decoys is to bring the duck into reasonable range and thus to obviate the temptation to take long shots. In this country the use of excessive numbers of decoys is not looked upon with favour and, when conditions are ideal, one should never be tempted to overshoot. During the last three months of the year, by which time wigeon have arrived in considerable numbers and mallard and teal have become educated to the ways of the man with a gun, thoughts about using decoys during evening flight will have turned to active measures. Later in the season, when most of

the overseas wigeon have arrived, these active measures will assume far more serious and more frequently organised use of decoys. In, say, October and November, the gunner will probably be satisfied to set out perhaps half a dozen mallard decoys, either to attract passing duck during the day, or, more likely, as duck begin to flight as dusk deepens and they scout around for the evening safety of their fellows, having now more or less finished their gleanings on the arables, where already most of the stubble has been turned under.

In this chapter there is space only to generalise in the reasons for and the practice of using decoys. One well-known writer on wildfowling stated that the art is to get within range of the birds, but another argues, and with good sense, that the art of the fowler should be to persuade his quarry to come within range of his gun. In this latter respect, it is obvious that decoying and/or calling must prove the attraction, and very fruitful they can be at times. A would-be user of decoys may learn the elementary facts of decoying from others, but only his own experiences and initiative will make him proficient to deal with varying conditions of fowling grounds, weather, feeding places and so on. It is useless, as has been pointed out, to float decoys haphazardly on a splash pool, wide ditch or dyke, where duck are returning to their daily lay-bys at dawn. On the other hand, decoys set out realistically on and about, say, the edges of a splash of floodwater much used as a landing place by wigeon favouring the lush grazing surrounding it, should attract the twittering companies during the evening at very deepest dusk. The enterprising gunner may even find satisfaction and somewhat better results if he has made for himself life-like wigeon decoys (always matt finished to prevent daylight or moonlight from showing them up for what they are), a few 'swimming'; a few 'standing at ease' on the edge of the pool; a few 'asleep' or 'resting' in obvious security.

Your writer of affairs sporting frequently states that all decoys should be pegged out facing the wind, but watch a party of mallard swimming and feeding and it will be seen that they do not conform to this conventional idea, for they do not swim and peck about in a straight line, do not keep a pattern, and odd numbers may leave the main group and be seen feeding away at the edge of the water, or even landing to waddle about, or to rest. Decoys should, therefore, always be made to look as natural and to 'behave' as naturally as possible. The same applies when decoys are used on flight-ponds, or close to the banks of reservoirs and lakes.

Wigeon coming down to feed at their accustomed time and place may drop in to any decoys, although the more natural the better. They will fly around and down to a few mallard decoys, or even to a zigzag string of self-inflated decoys. The objects of decoying may be said to be threefold:

(1) To bring the birds down to feed on water within range of the gunner lying in ambush.
(2) To bring hard-shot wary duck down more quickly than they would come if no decoys were present.
(3) To bring flighting or passing duck flying round within shot.

As to calling, this is a difficult study of its own and should never be attempted until the gunner has learned for himself by careful study which note and inflection of a note is likely to attract a passing bird, and which will issue a warning to it. All too often tyro gunners can be heard 'quacking like mad' on their newly acquired calls – only to scare away every fowl within hearing, if not to risk getting peppered in the growing darkness by an even less experienced tyro learning duck shooting the hard way!

WILDFOWLING GUNS – THEIR SELECTION AND CARE

DESMOND MILLS AND ERIC BEGBIE

The range of shotguns available to the modern wildfowler is extensive and the newcomer to the sport will be presented with much conflicting advice before he finally makes a selection and writes a cheque to his local gunshop. Each type of gun has its devotees and, wherever wildfowlers gather, arguments will rage around the respective merits of large-bore guns, over-and-under or side-by-side, long barrels or short, magnum or game gun.

Traditionally the larger-bore weapons were favoured for service below the sea wall and many of those mighty fowling pieces have been preserved by proud owners, either as relics of the past or, if still in shootable condition, for occasional use on the marshes. For all practical purposes, the 4-bore and 8-bore are guns for enthusiasts who have the time and inclination to load their own cartridges. In the next chapter David Garrard provides all of the necessary information on this intriguing subject. Such guns, however, do not really offer a serious option to the novice fowler.

In practice, the largest gauge for which commercially loaded cartridges are readily available is the 10-bore magnum and, to be pragmatic, the sportsman wishing anything other than a highly specialised wildfowling gun would be better served by a 12-bore, in either magnum or normal proof. Incidentally, the calibre of shotguns is normally stated as a 'bore number', a figure which is derived from the reciprocal of the weight in pounds of a spherical ball of lead which has a diameter equivalent to that of the gun barrel. Thus a 4-bore has a barrel of the same diameter as a quarter-pound ball of lead, while a 12-bore barrel will allow a ball of lead weighing one-twelfth of a pound to pass along it.

The latterday wildfowler favoured larger bore guns (John Tarlton)

CARTRIDGES

In the previous edition of this book the late Gough Thomas, a man who earned much respect as gun editor of *Shooting Times*, dealt with the topic of cartridges before discussing guns, because it is, after all, a few pellets from the cartridge which kill the quarry. The gun merely detonates the cartridge and directs the shot charge in the desired direction. There would seem to be little reason to depart from his wisdom today.

Because duck and geese frequently fly at or beyond the practical limit of shotgun range, wildfowlers tend to be obsessed with the problem of extracting maximum firepower from their weapons. At this stage it must be emphasised that no gun should ever be used with a cartridge which might generate a pressure greater than that for which the gun is proofed. It is also essential to recognise that the killing power of a cartridge is a function of two factors – pattern density and striking energy – and that the maximum effective range of any cartridge load is determined by which ever of those factors *fails first*. If pattern density falls

away before striking energy, the maximum range at which a clean kill can be expected is dictated by the former parameter. Conversely, if striking energy drops below the necessary minimum, then no advantage can be gained from the fact that the shot pattern might remain sufficiently dense at greater distances.

Put at its simplest, to ensure that the quarry is killed cleanly, the bird must be hit by a sufficient number of pellets and must be struck hard enough by each. In arriving at theoretical figures, a certain margin of error should be allowed as all good wildfowlers hate nothing more than to witness a bird being struck but flying on wounded. The following table employs accepted ballistic data to indicate maximum effective ranges for a selection of popular 12-bore cartridge loads. In each case it is assumed that a full-choke barrel is used and that grey geese are the quarry.

Table 4: Maximum effective range of cartridges for geese.

Shot load (oz)	Shot size	Max. range (yards)	Limiting factor
$1\frac{1}{8}$	4	40	Striking energy
$1\frac{1}{8}$	3	50	Both equally
$1\frac{1}{4}$	3	50	Striking energy
$1\frac{1}{4}$	1	42	Pattern density
$1\frac{1}{4}$	BB	35	Pattern density
$1\frac{1}{2}$	3	50	Striking energy
$1\frac{1}{2}$	1	47	Pattern density
$1\frac{1}{2}$	BB	38	Pattern density
$1\frac{5}{8}$	1	50	Pattern density
$1\frac{5}{8}$	BB	40	Pattern density
$1\frac{7}{8}$	1	53	Pattern density
$1\frac{7}{8}$	BB	43	Pattern density

Note: American No. 2 shot is equivalent to British No. 1.

From this type of information it is possible to make some recommendations about the shot loads and shot sizes which may be favoured by wildfowlers. It is immediately noticeable that a large question mark must hang over the use of BB shot for goose shooting and, indeed, the additional range obtained from very heavy cartridge loads appears not to be as dramatic as many fowlers believe.

The following table is reproduced from the second edition of this book and demonstrates the effects of both shot load and choke boring on maximum effective range. A comparison of the two

tables will show that Table 5 suggests slightly longer ranges than Table 4. This is simply because the data used for Table 5 contain a smaller margin of error.

By averaging the results of both tables it can be deduced that a game load of No. 3 shot will be effective against geese up to a range of about forty-five yards, while an additional six or seven yards will be obtained by using a heavy magnum cartridge with either No. 3 or No. 1 shot. When duck are in prospect, the same ranges will apply if No. 6, No. 5 or No. 4 shot is used. Generally, the larger shot size should be used from a tighter-choked barrel, while smaller shot will provide a denser pattern when fired from an open barrel.

Table 5: Effective ranges of various loads

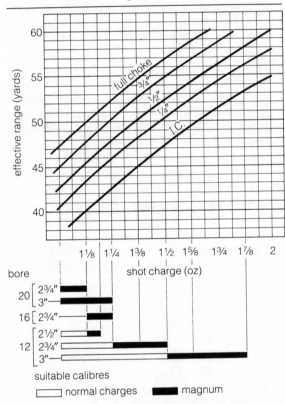

SHOTGUNS

The decision to purchase a specialist wildfowling gun in 10-, 8- or even 4-bore is likely only to be made by someone who has been at the game for many years and who can afford to have a weapon that will serve a single purpose. Many more wildfowlers are likely to wish to use their gun for roughshooting or pigeon decoying as well as for sport involving geese and duck.

For this reason, the majority of fowlers in Britain choose either an ordinary 12-bore game gun or a 12-bore magnum with 3 in. chambers. Whether this gun is a traditional side-by-side, a more modern over-and-under or a 3-shot semi-automatic will not affect its efficiency if it is treated with care and swung in the right direction. It is vitally important, however, that the gun should suit the cartridges that will be used.

The use of light game guns with heavy-loaded cartridge really should not be considered. It is a dangerous practice which should be avoided at all costs. Guns that are built to withstand the pressures of heavy loads may appear to resemble conventional game guns but, in fact, they differ in many ways. Apart from the obvious 3 in. magnum with the long-bodied action, the basic fundamentals are different. Usually the gun is wider across the breech ends. The other main area being the thickness of the back action. This is the measurement taken from the face to the back of the action body. Usually on a heavy gun it is $\frac{5}{8}$ in. deep and its purpose is to give the gun additional strength. Another means of adding strength is the introduction of bolsters. The weakest part of the action is at its root or, in layman's terms, where the flats meet the face. In an endeavour to strengthen the root, protrusions of metal are left on each side of the action body when forged. These are later filed to

8-bore (above) and 12-bore wildfowling guns (Eric Begbie)

shape to give additional strength and weight to the body. Many big game rifles are built in a similar manner.

We should perhaps understand what happens when we fire our gun to appreciate the stress we are placing upon a conventional game gun when using a heavy-loaded cartridge. As shooters, recoil is appreciated as the backward force which is encountered when the gun is discharged, but what is not understood is that the barrels are trying to move forwards and the action rearwards. In simple

FIGURE 32 The critical parts

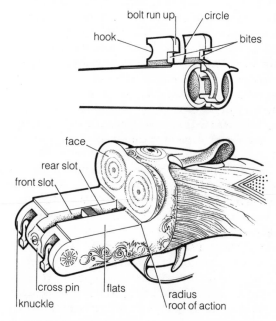

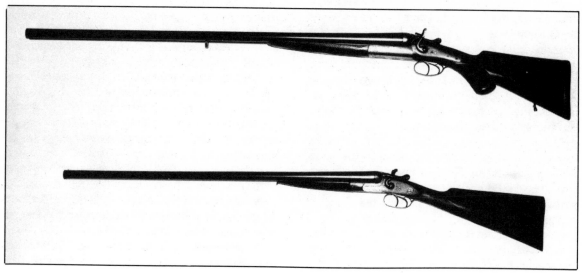

terms the action is trying to part from the face of the barrels. Of course, the lighter the gun, the more excessive the recoil. What holds the action on the face? Not the bolt as many shooters firmly believe. Jointing of action to barrels is a term that is most commonly known but few understand exactly what is entailed.

Jointing is possibly the most skilful operation performed in the manufacture of a shotgun. So many factors have to be considered when jointing the action to the barrels if wanting to effect as near perfect a fit as is possible. It has often been said that the life of any gun is only as good as it's jointing – a statement which most practical gunmakers would most certainly endorse. What keeps the action on the face of the barrels is a combination of many surfaces fitting together and working in perfect harmony. The cross pin, although it allows the barrels to pivot, must fit right around the hook; at the same time the circle of the rear lump (or steel) must just move the smoke black used to show the correct fitting, when the action closes (Figure 32). Of course, the barrel lumps fit correctly into the slots of the action. The same principle applies to boxlocks, sidelocks and over-and-unders. Many old hammer guns that were built for the sole purpose of shooting wildfowl are as tight today as when they were made. An indication of the skill and craftsmanship that few people ever achieve using basic hand tools such as files and chisels.

The function of the fore-end is, of course, to push the cross pin up into the hook and hold it there apart from allowing the gun to open and close. If a gun has been badly jointed in the initial stages of manufacture, and it does happen, then it can never be put right. You may be wondering how to tell if your gun is loose. A simple test will soon put your mind at rest. Remove the fore-end from the barrels, take the small of the stock in the right hand, place the end of the stock on your thigh and shake the barrels. Any looseness will be transmitted through the gun as a distinct vibration.

As previously mentioned, the fore-end pushes the cross pin right up into the hook, at the same time the circle is pulling the action onto the barrel face. Hence the fore-end must be removed otherwise a false impression will be given of the gun being tight.

Having considered all the facts, what should the fowler look for in his gun? There is no single prescription which will cater for every shooter, but

For large bore guns, weight is a consideration. A J. W. Rosier *8-bore weighing* 12½ *lbs* (B. W. Pacey)

there are certain basic fundamentals he needs to consider.

The gun should be suited to the user. Length of stock should take account of the fact that the fowler will wear heavy garments for winter weather. Weight of the gun is another aspect that should be given careful consideration, especially if wanting to use one of the big-bore guns that were once so popular and are now becoming available from manufacturers abroad. In this particular type of gun, a longer barrel should be sought rather than a shorter.

'CHOKE'

What distinguishes the barrel of one gun from another is the degree of choke. The simple explanation of choke is that it is a restriction in the end of a tube. Whilst various gunmakers have fixed ideas on the length of the choke cone they put in the tube, its function is to hold the shot together more tightly as it leaves the end of the barrel. The amount or degree of choke is purely a personal choice, but every shooter should consider its merits. A gun that has a tight choke can be regulated to throw a more open pattern, but a barrel that has been produced to throw open patterns cannot be made to do the reverse. In practice the correct choice of choke is the one which will enable the shooter to place the largest percentage of shot onto the target.

In producing good patterns much depends on the type and make of cartridge used, for some guns throw better patterns using a particular type of cartridge than others. The internal finish of the gun barrel plays a most important part when wanting good shot patterns.

Shotguns may be obtained with single or double trigger and many of the popular wildfowl guns available are single trigger. Good crisp trigger pulls without drag are most important not only in duck and goose guns but game guns as well. If fitted with a fully automatic safety, then the design should be such that it allows for a positive touch. Serrations or chequering, whichever is applied to the safety thumbpiece, should always be crisp so that even in the coldest of weather there is no fear of the finger sliding off.

Always consider your gun in relation to the load of cartridge you want to use. Check the proof marks on the flats of the barrels.

GUN CARE AND MAINTENANCE

Because wildfowlers use their guns in some of the worst conditions shooters ever experience, it is only common sense that they, above all other shooters, should pay particular attention to the cleaning of their guns. Correct gun cleaning will extend its life, improve its appearance as well as maintain its safety and in many cases increase its value. Guns should be cleaned immediately after use and inspected frequently, particularly before the start of a new season.

BARRELS

When cleaning, the intention is to remove all moisture, fouling and deposits to prevent unwanted corrosion taking place. A very important point to remember is that blood and salt water can be the prime causes of rusting on barrels. If either come into contact with the metal, endeavour to clean them as soon as possible, otherwise you can face the possibility of rust and the loss of barrel blueing. Don't forget to inspect your gun daily for at least a week after, since salt, if left, is the enemy of metal and no amount of oil or grease will prevent rusting and corrosion.

There are several ways in which to remove moisture from the barrels. Newspaper or kitchen roll rolled into small balls is ideal. Push the balls down each barrel from the chamber end using your cleaning rod. Carefully examine the 'lead-in' from the chamber to the bore and just behind the chokes for any evidence of lead fouling that has been left adhering to the walls of the tubes. If present, swab the bore with a clean patch or clean rag soaked in one of the bore solvents specially made for the purpose. Allow a couple of minutes for the cleaner to do its job and dislodge the leading and then clean out with a wire brush followed by a clean patch. Check that the fouling has been removed. If it has, a light application of oil placed on a clean patch is all that is needed. Before use, always remove any oil placed in the barrels since excessive oil can become an obstruction, which could cause either a bulge, rivelling, or even a burst barrel.

The extractors and their holes are prime areas for trapping moisture and dirt. They are best cleaned by using a feather. If you have used your gun in heavy rain it is strongly recommended that the extractors be removed, wiped dry and given a light application of grease. Clean the extractor bed and make sure that no water is in the extractor holes. Replace the extractors, not forgetting to clean the rims.

Ventilated and conventional ribs are natural traps for water. Placing a clean piece of cloth on a small Swiss file will enable the area between the barrel and rib to be cleaned and dried. The best method of ensuring that all moisture is removed from the sides of a conventional game rib is to place a piece of clean cloth around a kitchen knife and push up and down each side of the barrel. But make sure no scratches result. An old, stiff shaving brush is also ideal for cleaning the rib sides.

The final task is to wipe the barrels over with an oily rag having made sure that the lumps and bites are cleaned.

The action is far more difficult to clean and many shooters are of the firm belief that the more oil they put into slots and holes the less chance their gun has of being rusty and corroding and so ensure a better service. This is not true. The head of your stock and the fore-end wood in time will cease to absorb oil and will become spongy and ultimately rot.

The slots of your action can be cleaned with the aid of a small file and clean cloth. Make sure that the face and flats are dry and clean. Slots and small holes are best cleaned with a feather. Finally, wipe the action over with an impregnated cleaning cloth, not forgetting the trigger guard and trigger.

If during the season you have had your gun out

on a number of wet days, water may penetrate the action. It can, if neglected, rust internally and possibly cause many problems resulting in costly repairs. With this in mind it's well worth the small cost of getting the gunsmith to strip and clean your gun at the close of the season.

WOODWORK

Your stock will have been given one of several types of finish that are on the market. Among the most popular is French (or button) polish or the traditional oil-finished stock that has been polished by hand.

After a day's shooting in the rain, many shooting men apply oil to their stocks in much the same manner as they do to their boots, thinking that they are doing a very worthwhile job. They may well be adding life to their boots but they are certainly reducing it when it is applied to their gun stock. Wood is rather like a sponge due to its grain structure. In simple terms it is porous. Both will absorb water, the sponge will double in weight and the gun stock will absorb oil in a likewise manner until it can absorb no more. It may well take years, but nevertheless it will happen, with the final result being that the wood rots and cracks. The simple answer is to rub the stock with the palm of your hand. This will help to bring back its life and beauty. Stocks that have been given a polyurethane or sealed type of finish are simply wiped over with a dry clean cloth, since linseed oil will not penetrate this type of finish. The chequering is cleaned with the aid of a soft-bristle nail brush, but not one with plastic teeth. Gently brush backwards and forwards working across the chequering.

STORAGE

At the end of the season take a little extra time in the cleaning of your gun, paying particular attention to those difficult areas, which are normally water traps. Where is the best place to store it? Many problems can result from guns being stored in wet or damp cases and damp rooms. It is most important to ensure that the gun case has been dried properly before placing your gun inside. If your gun is being put away until the start of another season it is not sufficient just to lift the gun case lid and give it a cursory glance now and then. Remove it from the case and closely examine the barrels and action. Look for any telltale signs of

Guns should be stored in a secure place

corrosion and, of course, examine the case. There is a good reason for regular attention as the majority of gun cases are lined with baize or felt. Both materials will absorb moisture, especially if the case has been left in a humid atmosphere. In time the barrels will start to corrode and pitting will set in. In most cases guns should be stored in a rack that is in a well-ventilated room. A wire security cord through the trigger guards will deter thieves.

When transporting guns they need as much protection as possible, especially if placed in the boot of a motor car. Then by all means use a gun case for this will afford it the protection it requires.

SECURITY

It is incumbent on all who shoot or own a shotgun to ensure that guns are stored in a 'SAFE' manner. As a shooter you are morally obligated to ensure that inquisitive hands do not have access to your possessions. They must always be out of the reach of small children and preferably away from prying eyes. Those who have chosen to store guns in steel cabinets have taken very positive steps towards reducing both accidents and thefts.

Gun cabinets can be obtained to store up to fifteen guns. Many are manufactured so as to resemble attractive pieces of furniture that blend in with one's decor. Normally they are made from 14 SWG steel plate with full-length hinges and folded edges for additional strength. Special features include five-lever anti-theft Chubb locks. Although there are other equally well-made models available, thought must be given to where best they should be located. Garage, under the stairs, spare room, loft? – to name but a few places. All are possibly suitable, but would the cabinet be subject to dampness? Choose your place carefully. Many are made to be rawlbolted to the wall, although some models can be fixed to the floor.

INSURANCE

Having gone to the expense of purchasing a gun it makes sense to see that it is adequately insured. You may well have been left a fowling piece that has been passed down through the family and many such guns still in use today may well be classed as works of art never to be repeated, for the skills that were lavished on such pieces have been lost for ever. No amount of money will ever replace such craftsmanship and beauty. Should they be taken to the marsh or foreshore and subjected to the use for which they were made, or should they be encased behind glass and preserved for future generations?

The art of gunmaking as practised by our forefathers lies in the hands of a few. Only those shooters who possess such beautiful guns with lavish Damascus barrels, ornate sculptures in the form of hammers and pieces of wood that have been shaped and polished into exquisite stocks can make the decision. But consideration must still be given to insurance even though the gun may not be used.

There are different types of insurance valuation. The one that we need to consider is replacement value. If your gun is virtually new then it is reasonably easy to estimate its value against a brand new model. This could be done by simply checking a current price list. The most difficult to value is the fowling piece made by one of the late masters of English gunmaking in pristine condition. In such cases great care must be taken in selecting the person or firm to whom the gun will be entrusted to carry out a true and expert valuation.

A valuation of this type is not usually expensive. The cost for such work is either charged as a fixed fee regardless of the value or alternatively as a percentage of the estimated value. You would of course expect to receive a detailed report, which would list the gun's major attributes and special features. It is always a good idea to keep one's insurance up to date, for it could prove costly if your favourite gun was not adequately insured.

18

HOMELOADING WILDFOWLING CARTRIDGES

DAVID GARRARD

Homeloading has a long and honourable tradition in the annals of wildfowling as reference to the writings of Sir Ralph Payne-Gallwey, Henry Sharp, J.C.M. Nicholls and others will confirm. The fowler's needs then (as now) could best be met by relatively small quantities of diverse ammunition. Loaded into brass 'Perfect' cases and backed by black powder they could be put together cheaply and conveniently on the kitchen table. Although the introduction of nitro powders and improved components of every kind has revolutionised the performance and production of shotgun ammunition, the fowler's basic needs remain unaltered. This chapter aims to instruct the novice loader in the modern techniques for meeting those needs, using the sophisticated equipment and wide range of components available to him.

Experienced loaders will be well aware of the advantage of loading ammunition for wildfowling. These are:

(a) *Economy* – The heavier loads favoured by wildfowlers, i.e. 1.3/16 oz. and upwards in 12-bore, the 'big' 10- and 8-bore loads and those 20-bore loads suitable for the sport, can be homeloaded at a fraction of the cost of the factory-loaded ammunition.

(b) *Versatility* – Wildfowling can call for a wide variety of cartridges compared, for instance, with game shooting, where, at most, two loads will cover all eventualities. The fowler may thus require a light load of small shot for a session decoying teal at morning flight and, that same evening, the heaviest load he can handle for flighting grey geese. On other occasions a more versatile load will fill the bill. All those requirements can be met expeditiously and cheaply by the fowler loading his own – and in the relatively small quantities that are often adequate for his needs.

(c) *Specialisation* – Most of the ammunition required by the wildfowler can be described as specialised compared with the needs of the game/pigeon shooter. However, the homeloader can cater for his choice to a far greater extent than those who rely on the factory loads. Many of the latter, for instance, are available only in a quite restricted choice of shot sizes – no constraint here for the homeloader. Owners of lightweight guns may find that the full-velocity 'magnum' loads produce excessive recoil. Homeloading on the well-proven 'low-velocity' principle can overcome this difficulty. Many other examples of such specialised application of the loader's art will spring to mind.

Economy, versatility and specialisation are the advantages that loading his own ammunition offer the wildfowler. In addition, of course, to the interest of an absorbing hobby that adds another dimension to his sport.

RELOADING THE CARTRIDGE

Most shooters are familiar with the construction of the shotgun cartridge and therefore have at least some idea of what is involved in reloading. The usual sequence of operations is summarised below:

(1) To re-size the expanded metal head to its original dimensions by means of a metal die.
(2) To remove the fired primer and replace it with a new unit 'matched' to the powder concerned.
(3) To meter the correct charge of a suitable powder into the case.
(4) To insert the wadding over the powder.
(5) To meter the correct shot charge into the case.
(6) To re-form the closure of the cartridge either with a tapered crimp by machine, or with a hand-operated rolled turn-over tool.

An inexpensive reloading machine (Eric Begbie)

A single-action reloading machine (Peter Doubleday)

The loading machines now available have been designed to perform all these functions efficiently and consistently. The operator has only to use them with common sense and in accordance with the maker's instructions. This, with the careful choice of components, will ensure the production of reloads that inspire the confidence so essential to good shooting.

LOADING EQUIPMENT

The simplest loading equipment comprises the old hand tools originally designed for use with black or bulk powders. They produce cartridges with a rolled turn-over and their use is now confined to reloading the big 10- and 8-bore cartridges. In-structions in their use will be found on page 160. Attention here will concentrate on the modern hand-operated machines designed to produce a crimped closure cartridge using dense nitro powders. They are available in all gauges, including 20- and 10-bore.

Those on the market are all of American manufacture and are intended for reloading plastic cases, the only type worth considering for fowling. There are a number of such machines regularly advertised in the sporting press. Outstanding value for money is the Lee 'Load-all'. It produces a quite well-finished cartridge, especially from compression-formed cases, and though not as durable as the more expensive machines, could be a good first buy. A good many fowlers find that the

Load-all meets all their needs. The choice of the main range of single-stage machines is now currently restricted to the MEC 600 and 700 models, the Pacific 105DL and 155DL and the Redding '16'. Any of these will make a first-class job and last a lifetime of loading. At the top end of the market are the Pacific 266DL and the Ponsness Warren 375, both examples of durable engineering and excellent design. All these machines will turn out 100–200 loaded cartridges per hour according to the energy and skill of the operator. Those shooters who require higher output, or who wish to spend less time at the loading bench, should consider the MEC 'Grabber'. This machine combines an output that approaches that of the expensive fully automatic machines with the simplicity of the single-action versions.

An essential piece of equipment that every loader should possess is a powder scale or balance. With it the essential checking of the powder charges 'thrown' by any bushing can be made conveniently and as frequently as seems desirable. In its absence the help of a friendly pharmacist will need to be enlisted, a very inferior arrangement. The loader with a scale can proceed confident that his powder charges are 'spot on'. He will never regret buying one.

LOADING COMPONENTS

CASES

The cartridge case is the basic component of every load. Only plastic cases need to be considered in relation to wildfowling. They can be divided into 2 types:

(a) *Plastic-tubed case (PT)* – The familiar plastic case used by all British and continental cartridge loaders. They are now all constructed on virtually identical lines. A plastic tube with walls .022 in.–.023 in. thick is locked into a mild steel head with a flat plastic base-wad. The metal head is made resistant to rusting by 'brassing' or tinning. PT cases are excellent all-rounders and generally to be preferred for magnum loads. They can usually be reloaded 3–4 times before the crimp section splits. Supplies of PT cases are so easily obtained that reloading them only once or twice can be practised with advantage.

All Eley cases, together with those by Cheddite,

Fiocchi, SMI, Rottweil, Browning, etc., are essentially similar and can be used with the same loads.

(b) *Compression-formed cases (CF)* – These are all of American origin, being made under patents held by the Winchester or Remington Cartridge Companies. The case consists of a single plastic unit of great durability swaged from a plastic 'slug'. It is fitted with the conventional metal head. The tube section has a marked internal taper which reduces the capacity of the case and tends to produce higher pressures than the PT case, a factor which calls for reduced or modified powder charges. CF cases are therefore not quite so well suited to bulky, high-pressure magnum loads. One of their virtues lies in an exceptionally tough 'skived' (tapered) crimp section, making for a perfect re-crimp which can be repeated up to six or more times. The CF case is thus the re-loader's ideal in many ways. The brands available are: Winchester AA (rare), Winchester Trap 100/200/300, Winner, Premium. Remington RXP (no longer made) and Blue Magic. All are $2\frac{3}{4}$ in. (70 mm) in length. Winchester Ranger and Game Bird are available as $67\frac{1}{2}$ mm cases. All are closed with a 6-fold crimp except for the WW AA and Blue Magic, which feature an 8-fold closure.

POWDERS

There is now a wide range of powders in several brands which, wisely chosen, will meet all the fowler's needs. They are all smokeless and based solely on nitro-cellulose (single based) or on a mixture of nitro-cellulose and nitro-glycerine (double based). The latter type, being entirely non-hydroscopic, can prove more consistent performers under damp, cold conditions.

Powders by Nobel Glasgow (double based)
Nobel 80 A good all-rounder for the general run of 12-bore loads up to $1\frac{1}{8}$ oz. Not suited to small or 'big-bore' loads.

Nobel 82 A slower-burning powder than Nobel 80 suited to the heavier loads in 12-bore and to standard loads in small bores. Can be used for low-velocity loads in all gauges.

Powders by Vectan (SNPE) (single based)
AS Quite a fast burning powder that can be used with up to $1\frac{1}{8}$ oz loads in 12-bore. Not suited to small or 'big-bore' loads.

A selection of reloading components (Peter Doubleday)

AI A versatile powder very well suited to home-loading of 12-bore loads up to 1¼ oz. An excellent powder for low-velocity loads in 12-bore and standard 20-gauge loads.

AO An excellent powder for magnum loads in all gauges. Highly recommended for this purpose.

Powders by Vihtavuori (single based).
N 320 An excellent powder for all 12-bore loads up to 1⅛ oz.

N 340 A 'slower' powder than N 320 which gives excellent consistent results with 1⅛ oz and 1¼ oz. loads in 12-bore in both PT and CF cases, as well as in 20-bore loads.

N 330 A slow-burning pistol powder which has potential for heavy and magnum loads in all gauges.

Powders by SNIA (single based)
GM 3 A powder of similar character to Nobel 80 with a parallel range of uses.

GM 3 (Special) A slower-burning powder than GM 3 with a wide application for heavier loads in all bores.

Powders by Hercules (double based)
These old-established powders of proven performance are imported from the USA and their cost fluctuates with the dollar exchange rate. They are thus usually expensive compared with rival powders and supplies can suffer accordingly.

Green Dot A modern powder giving first-rate results with loads of up to 1⅛ oz in 12-bore.

Unique A very old-established versatile powder that can be used with standard loads in all gauges.

Herco A slow burning powder that is outstanding for use with the 1¼ oz load in 12-bore and in other heavy loads.

Blue Dot A very 'progressive' slow-burning powder ideally suited to heavy and magnum loads in all gauges.

PRIMERS

The function of the primer is to ignite the powder and thus to initiate the 'action' which results in the shot charge acquiring its lethal velocity. All modern primers are 'rustless' and extremely reliable. They can vary in power or 'brissance' and the loader need be only concerned with choosing a primer compatible with the powder in use. Correct matching of primer and powder is of crucial importance in successful cartridge loading so 'stick to the book' here.

Eley battery-cup primer This was introduced a few years ago to replace the old Surefire cap. It is a relatively 'mild' primer specifically designed for use with the Nobel Glasgow powders with which it should normally be matched. It is also useful for matching with other powders where containing breech pressures is a problem.

The Eley primer is around .242 in. in diameter, somewhat less than that of the rival primers designed for reloading (.244 in.–.245 in.) and is, thus, a slack fit in some cartridge cases.

CCl 109 and CCl 209 primers These primers, of American origin, are of identical brissance and are excellent 'all-rounders' that can be used with all the powders listed. Highly recommended.

Winchester 209 primer Another excellent all-rounder that can be regarded as interchangeable with the CCl 109/209 primers. Highly recommended.

Vihtavuori '20' primer A fairly powerful primer specifically designed for use with the Vihtavuori powders. It can be matched with suitable charges or other powders.

Martignoni 586 primer A medium-strength primer from the Martignoni range. Can be used with all powders listed although of slightly greater brissance than the CC1/WW primers.

The Cheddite primer This primer, imported by the Gamebore Cartridge Company, is specifically designed for reloading and has a diameter of .245 in., making it a satisfactory fit in all cases. It is intended for use with the Vectan powders. Tests with these and the Nobel Glasgow powders show that the Cheddite primer can be safely and effectively substituted for CC1/WW primers in all loads.

WADDING

Good-quality wadding is essential for a good load. Do not economise here, the savings are likely to be negligible.

As far as wildfowling is concerned the traditonal felt or fibre wadding is best used only when satisfactory one-piece plastic wadding is unobtainable. This latter type has all the virtues and is strongly recommended for all wildfowling purposes. It maximises pattern density and quality and gives a better velocity/pressure ratio than the traditional wadding – as well as simplifying and speeding the reloading process. The best-known 'native' wads are:

Plaswad Mark III and Plaswad Mark IV Both are designed for use with $1\frac{1}{8}$ oz loads in 70 mm and $67\frac{1}{2}$ mm cases respectively. The latter can be used with heavier loads in 70 mm and 3 in. cases. Both wads are versatile, being designed for use in both PT and CF cases. They have been proven over many years and are a thoroughly reliable component.

The SNIA 'GT' series of wads These are among the best known of the imported wads and can be strongly recommended. The 41/21, 38/18 and 34/16 versions are of greatest value to the loader of fowling ammunition.

Gualandi 'G' wads Another first-class wad available for $1\frac{1}{8}$ oz loads in 12-bore and $\frac{7}{8}$, $\frac{15}{16}$ and 1 oz loads in 20-bore.

Eley GL and TL wads The former is particularly useful to the fowler/loader. It can be used for $1\frac{1}{8}$ oz loads in $67\frac{1}{2}$ mm cases and in a wide spectrum of heavier loads in the longer cases. It is an easily compressed, low-pressure wad. The TL version is restricted to $1\frac{1}{8}$ oz loads in 70 mm cases.

Winchester WW AA12 and WW AA20 wads These are both made specifically for use in CF cases, for which use they are highly recommended. The over-powder (o/p) cup is of smaller diameter than the other wads described here and, for this reason, they are not so well suited to use in PT cases.

SHOT

Up until recently (1986) virtually the only sources of lead shot available to loaders were Eley or Sheldon Bush. Both makers marketed a good quality product in sizes 9-BB which, properly loaded, gave excellent results and printed the 'standard' level of patterns quoted in the *Shooter's Diary* and elsewhere. All this shot contains $\frac{1}{2}$–$\frac{3}{4}$% antimony and by present-day standards is on the 'soft' side. The Gamebore Cartridge Co. now have available shot containing 2% antimony, which is very much harder than the rival brands and can produce patterns 10–15% denser than 'standard'. It is strongly recommended when really dense patterns are required. It is available in sizes 9–4, including No. $7\frac{1}{2}$.

LOADING PROCEDURES

If possible the loading machine should be set up on a really solidly made permanent bench. This is much better than the kitchen table and, by reducing erratic vibration of the machine, will facilitate consistent loading. Under the bench, in drawers and on shelves, the cases and components can be stored conveniently to hand.

Before attempting to start loading the maker's instructional book should be carefully studied, the loader making himself familiar with the mechanics of every stage of the loading process. Most troubles stem from neglecting to do this. It is advisable to make a few 'dry runs' to ensure that the tool at each 'station' is properly adjusted and making a perfect job. Once 'set up' the machine should give faultless service. In particular check that:

(1) The correct type of powder and correct powder bushing are in use.
(2) The correct size of shot and correct shot bushing are in use.
(3) The correct length of sizing die is fitted (Ponsness Warren Machines).
(4) The correct pre-crimping head, 6- or 8-fold, is fitted.

An essential preliminary to the loading process is to make a selection of the cases required for the intended load. Do not attempt to combine this work with the loading sequence, it will lead to erratic delays and prevent the development of a regular loading rhythm which contributes to consistent quality and a high output.

The cases should preferably all be of the same brand. They must all be checked for length and soundness. Reject any with a split tube, splits in the crimp section, or with a bulged or split metal head. Check too for faulty base-wads or for cases in which the tube is loose in the head. Be rigorous in this inspection, remembering that a sound case is the basis of a high-quality cartridge. Before considering loading techniques in detail it is worth emphasising that good loading requires a relaxed yet alert approach. A hasty 'near enough' approach is fatal to high-quality work. It will lead to irritating mistakes and reduced output with a sizeable proportion of reject loads – not the batch of perfect reloads that should be the object of every session at the loading bench. Concentration on the job in hand is essential. The loading sequence can now be considered in detail. Provided that the machine has been properly adjusted little trouble need be anticipated.

Resizing Resizing rarely presents any problem, the main difficulty being the odd case that refuses to enter the die. If forced the metal head will crumple on the mouth of the die and the case must be rejected.

De-primering Occasionally a primer is encountered that is so tight that the force required to punch it out results in a bulged head. An unusual cause of rejection.

Renewal of primer A properly adjusted machine makes this a straightforward operation. Primers should be seated level with the metal head or .002–.003 in. below it. For obvious reasons never proceed any further in loading a case in which the primer protrudes above the head. Avoid loose-fitting primers. Cases in which the primer pocket has been enlarged by repeated reloading can give trouble here, as can the Fley primer (see under Primers, above).

Dropping the powder charge The action of sliding the charging bar across is simple and foolproof. The weight of the powder so dispensed will largely depend on the vibration to which the machine is subjected before the powder is dropped. For this reason a uniform, methodical loading sequence should always be followed. When this is done powder charges within ±.2 grain of nominal charge should be thrown. It is essential to check the charges thrown by any bushing by weighing dropped charges. New powders and renewed bushings should always be checked in this way.

Inserting the wadding The plastic guide fingers fitted to loading machines make this easy enough. Occasionally the obturating cup of a plastic wad will foul one of the crimp folds and is thus very easily damaged. If the slightest suspicion exists that this has happened the wad should be withdrawn and scrapped if damaged. Before replacing the wad the case mouth should be reamed with a tapered wooden plug.

Ramming the wadding Plastic wads present no problem. All that is needed is to seat the wad firmly on the powder; a pressure of 20–30 lb will do this. Greater pressure can be used if it is necessary to compress the wad to provide a wad column of the correct height for a good crimp. The shot column can be lengthened by inserting card wads into the shot-cup before dropping the shot. This may be required, for instance, in some of the 10-bore loads included in the Loading Tables.

The importance of a wad column of the correct height for a good, tight crimp is really crucial to the production of high-quality ammunition. Time is well spent in establishing any adjustment needed to this end. If anything err towards a column slightly on the high side. This will ensure the resistance against which a tight crimp can be folded. A short column will give rise to a weakly formed crimp, often 'dipped', and thus to reduced ballistics.

Dropping the shot The charge dropped is not so sensitive to erratic vibration of the machine as is the powder. No real problem here.

The top of the shot charge when *in situ* should be level with, or very slightly above, the lower crimp folds. Any significant discrepancy at this stage may indicate that an error has occurred somewhere along the line. Therefore check the height of the wad column (see above); that the correct powder and shot charges are being dispensed; that the case in the machine is of the correct length. Check too that powder is not being lost through the primer pocket, the new primer having been omitted. Any of these faults must be remedied before continuing to load.

Pre-crimping Before going ahead check that the correct type of head is fitted, i.e. 6- or 8-fold.

It is at this stage that the most frequent and annoying fault occurs – a split in one or more of the crimp folds of the PT case. It rarely affects the more pliable and tough CF case. The frequency of the fault can be minimised by avoiding an excessive degree of pre-crimping. A light touch will suffice here. Cases embrittled by cold are very prone to splitting at the crimp. In cold conditions therefore cases should be warmed up (in the airing cupboard?) before starting to load.

Crimping and tapering A good, tight crimp, properly tapered, is essential if the cartridge is to develop effective ballistics and give a clean powder burn, particularly with the slow-burning powders that so often feature in fowling ammunition.

Set the crimping head to form a reasonable deep crimp, but not so deep that a central hole is left through which the shot can escape. Persist with trial and error until the best setting is established. A firm pull on the handle should then provide a perfect crimp – if not then check on the pre-crimp and wad column height.

An effective taper ensures a smooth feed into the gun chamber and makes a major contribution to the strength of the circumferential fold of the crimp. It is in this fold where the main strength of the crimp lies. Loading machines incorporate an adjustable tapering device in the crimping head which, when properly set, will produce a beautifully finished cartridge. A below-par taper can be remedied by running the cartridges through the head a second time with the device set at 'full taper'. Above all avoid a crimp finish that is 'mushroomed'. Apart from the difficulties in loading that will ensue, such a closure will be below strength and will give low ballistics, perhaps approaching the 'blooper' level. It is attention to this sort of detail that separates the first-class loader from the 'slap-happy' operators.

THE USE OF HAND TOOLS FOR LOADING 10- AND 8-BORE AMMUNITION

The only commercially loaded 10-bore ammunition now available in this country is that imported at great expense from America in $3\frac{1}{2}$ in.

cases. Rather than purchasing and reloading such cartridges, 10-bore users would do better to load new cases by hand and finish with a rolled turn-over, thereby dispensing with the need to acquire an expensive loading machine.

Since Eley abandoned the marketing of 8-bore ammunition some years ago all 8-bore shooters have had to load their own cartridges by hand and will have to continue to do so. Any fowler taking up loading 8-bore cartridges should acquire a copy of *8-bore Ammunition* by Douglas McDougall. In it will be found detailed instructions on every possible aspect of the subject, together with a wealth of information on 8-bore guns and ammunition in general. The instructions that follow here inevitably include data culled from Douglas McDougall's book.

TOOLS AND EQUIPMENT

Hand loading was extensively practised in black powder days and the same simple tools and techniques can be used today with modern components. These comprise:

Case resizing die(s) These can take the form of a stout steel tube of an appropriate internal diameter into which the case is forced in a vice. It can be punched out with a wooden dowel. Dies can be purchased from specialists.

Punches for de- and re-primering Purpose-made punches are available or a 5 in. nail can be modified to use as a punch to drive out the old primer and the new one seated with a $\frac{3}{16}$ in. hollow punch which bears on the flange of the battery-cup.

Powder measure or hopper These can be obtained from specialist suppliers or can be home-made by sweating a metal bottom onto a length of $\frac{1}{2}$ in.-diameter copper tubing. The hopper must just hold the correct powder charge after the powder has been settled by light tapping.

Dowel Of wood, $\frac{5}{8}$ in. in diameter, for ramming the wadding, etc.

Shot measure or hopper Again available commercially or can be home-made from $\frac{5}{8}$ in.-diameter copper tube – see under 'Powder measure'.

Rolled turn-over machine Used for closing the case. Suitable machines can be purchased in each gauge. A cheaper method is to use a simple rolled turn-over (RTO) head in a hand or electric drill.

Again these are available in the trade.

Powder scale An essential piece of equipment for the hand loader used for making up powder and shot hoppers and for checking on the charges actually loaded.

LOADING PROCEDURE

Cases should not be completely loaded 'one at a time'. Rather all the cases of a batch should be put through each stage in succession. This is the quicker procedure and results in more uniform loading.

(1) Reconditioning the case. New 10-bore cases require no treatment. The mouth of fired 10- and 8-bore cases can be restored 'as new' by inserting a tapered wooden plug into the mouth and exposing the case mouth to the live steam issuing from a boiling kettle. Rotate the plug in the case. The metal head of 10-bore cases can be resized, if found necessary, in a tubular resizer. A great majority of 8-bore loading is done in once-fired Remington industrial cases, $3\frac{1}{4}$ in. in length. These cases have a 'double thickness' metal head that has to be sized down to fit the gun chambers. A stout-walled tubular die can be used for this purpose. Cases already resized can be purchased, possibly the easiest procedure. New Fiocchi industrial cases are also available. These too require sizing before use and can be so bought. These industrial cases do not normally require re-sizing between loadings.

(2) Punch out fired primer. Use a purpose-made or home-made punch.

(3) Seat the new primer using a purpose-made punch or a $\frac{3}{16}$ in. hollow punch. The case should be inverted over a length of dowelling.

(4) Insert the correct powder charge. Use a hopper – see under Tools above.

(5) Insert the wad. For all 10-bore loads the Remington SP 10 plastic wad is very strongly recommended. For all 8-bore loads the Gamebore plastic wad is regarded as essential. The wad should be firmly seated on the powder using a dowel. Do not compress.

(6) Insert the shot charge. Use the correct hopper.

(7) Place the over-shot card in place. There should then be a full $\frac{1}{4}$ in. – $\frac{5}{16}$ in. of 'free' tube above the overshot (o/s) card for a good RTO closure to be formed. If necessary, adjust the wad column to this end.

(8) Form the RTO closure. Use of a hand machine presents no problems. If an RTO 'head' is used in an electric drill, care should be taken not to prolong the operation and overheat the case mouth. If this happens the RTO will 'set' and then will fail to open out on firing. Instead it will be blown off, thereby ruining the case for future use and, incidentally, raising pressures to an horrendous level.

Solid brass cases cannot be 'rolled'. The overshot card is cemented in place with a 'silicone rubber' bath sealant as shown in the diagram below. The sealant takes 24 hours to 'cure'.

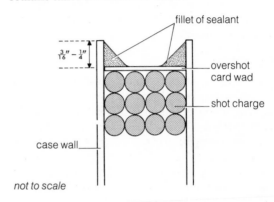

SHOT 'BUFFERING'

This is a technique whereby shot patterns may be increased in density by 10–15% compared with unbuffered charges at all ranges. At the shorter ranges this can lead to a concentration of the shot charge, which leaves little scope for the normal 'aiming errors'. At really long range buffered loads show to great advantage and it is suggested that their use should be restricted to such shooting.

Buffering involves filling the spaces between the shot pellets in a cartridge with a suitable fine-ground powder. Thus insulated from each other the pellets are very much less distorted by the impact of pressure in the breech. They then 'fly' a straighter course than unbuffered, distorted pellets, and so print denser patterns. The technique has been used in the past by our forefathers, who mixed bone-flour with their shot. Subsequently, experiments with domestic flour, 'cream of wheat', etc., have proved successful. These materials, however, are relatively heavy and apt to absorb moisture, which leads to 'caking' and other adverse side-effects. Finely ground polyethylene powder or 'flour' has proved the ideal buffering agent. It adds very little to the total weight of the charge and is virtually free of caking. It is very strongly advised that no other material be used for this purpose.

Note. Reduced powder charges are required in buffered loads. Those recommended have been tested for ballistics and should be followed exactly. No uninformed experiments should be made here.

The use of shot wrappers is recommended with buffered loads. These give total protection to the shot charge and prevent any buffer powder caking on the case walls. Wrappers can be cut from any suitable plastic sheet .007–.010 in. thick. Fertiliser sacks make ideal material.

PROCEDURE

Proceed to the station or stage where the plastic wad has been seated on the powder. If using a machine remove the case therefrom. Insert the plastic wrapper. It should be rolled up 'pencil thin' and placed in the shot-cup. Here it will open up and line the case. Drop the shot charge into a small container or measure out with the hopper. Pour about half this charge into the case and add about a teaspoon of buffer powder. This powder must then be settled or caused to sift down among the shot pellets until the inter-pellet spaces are all filled. *Light* rapid tapping of the case will do this – use the spoon. It should be continued until the buffer is *in situ.* Now add the remainder of the shot and more buffer powder and repeat the process until the buffer is level with the upper pellets composing the charge. A scrap of paper should now be placed on top of the

shot and the case returned to the machine for closure. The paper 'seal' is not needed in hand loads finished with an RTO.

Note. When setting the buffer avoid *heavy blows* which will disturb the shot and cause the buffer to migrate to the base of the charge, where it will be ineffective and will make a proper closure difficult to achieve.

SHOT SIZES

A subject for endless argument and discussion among fowlers where faith often plays as important part as logic when a choice of shot size is made. Those genuinely seeking guidance are advised to use the smallest size that will give adequate striking energy and penetration at sporting range i.e. to maximise pattern density. The larger shot sizes can give spectacular chance kills but lack consistent performance.

A personal choice

For duck
In all 20-bore loads: No. 7 (2.4 mm)
In $1\frac{1}{8}$ oz 12-bore loads: No. 6 (2.6 mm)
In all other 12-bore loads: No. 5 (2.8 mm)
In 'big-bore' loads: No. 4 (3.1 mm)

For geese
In $1\frac{1}{4}$ oz 12-bore loads: No. 3 (3.3 mm)
In all other, heavier loads: No. 1 (3.6 mm)
BB (4.1 mm) could by tried in buffered 10- and 8-bore loads only, particularly for Canada geese.

LOADING TABLES

Not all wildfowling calls for heavy loads. Modern $1\frac{1}{8}$ oz 12-bore loads are powerful medicine and are at least adequate for a wide range of uses. A selection of these loads is included in the tables that follow. They aim to provide a wide spectrum of loads for all fowling purposes and incorporate a fair range of powders and other components. A great majority are for use in the universal 12-gauge gun with a selection to meet the needs of the 10- and 8-bore enthusiasts.

Recommended home loads for wildfowling for $2\frac{1}{2}$ in. guns. 12-bore. MMSP. 3.0 tons/sq. in. ($1\frac{1}{8}$ oz) 850 kg/sq. cm

Case	Primer	Powder charge (grains)	Wadding	Shot charge (oz)
PT $67\frac{1}{2}$ mm	Eley	Nobel 80 23.5	P'wad IV	$1\frac{1}{8}$
PT $67\frac{1}{2}$ mm	CCI 109/WW 209	Nobel 80 21.0	P'wad IV	$1\frac{1}{8}$
PT $67\frac{1}{2}$ mm	Eley	Nobel 82 27.0	P'wad IV	$1\frac{1}{8}$
PT $67\frac{1}{2}$ mm	CCI 109/WW 209	Nobel 82 23.5	P'wad IV	$1\frac{1}{8}$
PT $67\frac{1}{2}$ mm	CCI 109/WW 209	AS 21.0	GT 38/18	$1\frac{1}{8}$
PT $67\frac{1}{2}$ mm	CCI 109/WW 209	A.1. 26.0	GT 38/18	$1\frac{1}{8}$
PT $67\frac{1}{2}$ mm	Viht. '20'	N 320 25.0	P'wad IV	$1\frac{1}{8}$
PT $67\frac{1}{2}$ mm	CCI 109/WW 209	GM 3 23.5	GT 38/18	$1\frac{1}{8}$
PT $67\frac{1}{2}$ mm	CCI 109/WW 209	Green Dot 22.0	P'wad IV	$1\frac{1}{8}$
PT $67\frac{1}{2}$ mm	CCI 109/WW 209	Unique 25.0	P'wad IV	$1\frac{1}{8}$
CF 70 mm	Eley	Nobel 82 26.0	P'wad IV	$1\frac{1}{8}$
CF 70 mm	CCI 109/WW 209	A.1. 23.0	P'wad IV	$1\frac{1}{8}$
CF 70 mm	CCI 109/WW 209	GM 3 22.0	GT 38/18	$1\frac{1}{8}$
PT $67\frac{1}{2}$ mm	Eley	Nobel 82 27.0	Eley GL	$1.\frac{3}{16}$
PT $67\frac{1}{2}$ mm	CCI 109/WW 209	A.1. 26.0	GT 38/18	$1.\frac{3}{16}$

Note: A WW AA12 wad can be substituted for Plaswad IV in $1\frac{1}{8}$ oz loads in the CF case.

For $2\frac{3}{4}$ in. guns. 12-bore. MMSP. $3\frac{1}{4}$ tons/sq. in. ($1\frac{1}{4}$ oz) 900 kg/sq. cm

Case	Primer	Powder charge (grains)	Wadding	Shot charge (oz)
PT 70 mm	Eley	Nobel 82 27.5	P'wad IV	$1\frac{1}{4}$
PT 70 mm	CCI 109/WW 209	Nobel 82 25.0	P'wad IV	$1\frac{1}{4}$
PT 70 mm	CCI 109/WW 209	A.1. 26.0	GT 38/18	$1\frac{1}{4}$
PT 70 mm	Viht. '20'	N 340 30.0	P'wad IV	$1\frac{1}{4}$ H.V.
PT 70 mm	CCI 109/WW 209	GM 3(sp) 25.5	P'wad IV	$1\frac{1}{4}$
PT 70 mm	CCI 109/WW 209	Herco 28.0	P'wad IV	$1\frac{1}{4}$
CF 70 mm	Eley	Nobel 82 26.0	P'wad IV	$1\frac{1}{4}$
CF 70 mm	CCI 109/WW 209	A.1 23.0	Eley GL	$1\frac{1}{4}$
CF 70 mm	Eley	A.1. 28.0	Eley GL	$1\frac{1}{4}$ H.V.
CF 70 mm	Viht. '20'	N 340 24.5	P'wad	$1\frac{1}{4}$
CF 70 mm	CCI 109/WW 209	Herco 26.0	P'wad IV	$1\frac{1}{4}$
PT 70 mm	CCI 109/WW 209	AO 33.0	Eley GL	$1.\frac{3}{8}$
PT 70 mm	CCI 109/WW 209	A.1. 23.0	Eley GL*	$1\frac{1}{2}$ L.V.*

*Compress wad. Use No. 5 or larger.

For $2\frac{3}{4}$ in. guns. 12-bore. Magnum proved. MMSP. $3\frac{1}{2}$ tons/sq. in. 1000 kg/sq. cm

Case	Primer	Powder charge (grains)	Wadding	Shot charge (oz)
PT 70 mm	CCI 109/WW 209	AO 33.0	Eley GL*	$1\frac{1}{2}$
PT 70 mm	CCI 109/WW 209	Blue Dot 35.0	P'wad IV	$1\frac{1}{2}$
CF 70 mm	CCI 109/WW 209	AO 31.0	Eley GL*	$1\frac{1}{2}$
CF 70 mm	Eley	AO 33.0	Eley GL*	$1\frac{1}{2}$
CF 70 mm	CCI 109/WW 209	Blue Dot 32.0	Eley GL*	$1\frac{1}{2}$
PT 70 mm	CCI 109/WW 209	AO 30.0	Eley GL* + $1\frac{1}{4}'' \times 2\frac{1}{4}''$ wrapper + buffer	$1\frac{1}{2}$
PT 70 mm	CCI 109/WW 209	A.1. 21.0	Eley GL* + $1\frac{1}{4}'' \times 2\frac{1}{4}''$ wrapper + buffer	$1\frac{1}{2}$ L.V.

*Compress wad fully especially in C.F. cases.

For 3 in. guns. 12-bore. Magnum proved. 4.0 tons/sq. in. 1200 kg/sq. cm

Case	Primer	Powder charge (grains)	Wadding	Shot charge (oz)
PT 3 in.	CCI 109/WW 209	AO 39.0	Eley GL*	$1\frac{5}{8}$
PT 3 in.	CCI 109/WW 209	AO 37.0	Eley GL*	$1\frac{3}{4}$
PT 3 in.	CCI 109/WW 209	Blue Dot 35.0	P'wad IV	$1\frac{5}{8}$
PT 3 in.	Eley	Nobel 82 26.0	P'wad IV*	$1\frac{5}{8}$ L.V.
CF 3 in.	CCI 109/WW 209	Blue Dot 34.0	Eley GL*	$1\frac{5}{8}$
CF 3 in.	Eley	AO 36.0	Eley GL*	$1\frac{5}{8}$
CF 3 in.	CCI 109/WW 209	AO 35.0	Eley GL*	$1\frac{5}{8}$
PT 3 in.	CCI 109/WW 209	AO 35.0	GL + $1\frac{1}{4}'' \times 2\frac{1}{4}''$ wrapper + buffer	$1\frac{5}{8}$

*Compress wad. WW AA (Red) or GT 34/16 can be substituted.
Note: In all the above 12-bore loads a GT 13/18 or 'G' wad can be substituted for the Plaswad m.IV.

For $3\frac{1}{2}$ in. 10-bore guns. MMSP. 4.0 tons/sq. in.

Case	Primer	Powder charge (grains)	Wadding	Shot charge (oz)
PT $3\frac{1}{2}$ in.	CCI 109/WW 209	AO 52.0	SP 10	2
PT $3\frac{1}{2}$ in.	CCI 109/WW 209	Poudre 'T' 38.0	SP 10	2
PT $3\frac{1}{2}$ in.	CCI 109/WW 209	GM3 (sp) 33.0	SP 10	2 L.V.
PT $3\frac{1}{2}$ in.	CCI 109/WW 209	AO 50.0	SP 10	$2\frac{1}{4}$
PT $3\frac{1}{2}$ in.	CCI 109/WW 209	Blue Dot 43.0	SP 10	$2\frac{1}{4}$
PT $3\frac{1}{2}$ in.	CCI 109/WW 209	AO 45.0	SP 10 + $1\frac{1}{4}'' \times 2\frac{1}{2}''$ wrapper + buffer	$2\frac{1}{4}$

Note: The height of the wad column of any of the above loads may need adjustment for either a rolled turn-over or crimp closure by placing 20-bore filler cards in the base of the shot-cup. Use $\frac{1}{16}$ in. card o/s for RTO.

For $3\frac{1}{4}$ in. 8-bore guns: MMSP. $3\frac{1}{4}$ tons/sq. in. $2\frac{1}{8}$ oz.
All loads utilise the CCI 109 or WW 209 primer and the Gamebore 8-bore plastic wad.

Case	Powder charge (grains)	Shot charge (oz)	
'Original' Rem. Indst.	57.0 Blue Dot	$2\frac{1}{4}$–$2\frac{1}{2}$	Composition base-wad
'Original' Rem. Indst.	57.0 AO	$2\frac{1}{4}$–$2\frac{1}{2}$	Composition base-wad
Rem. Indst. 'Unibody'	50.0 Blue Dot	$2\frac{1}{2}$	'One-piece' plastic case
Rem. Indst. 'Unibody'	52.0 Blue Dot	$2\frac{1}{4}$	'One-piece' plastic case
Rem. Indst. 'Unibody'	47.0 AO	$2\frac{1}{2}$	'One-piece' plastic case
Rem. Indst. 'Unibody'	49.0 AO	$2\frac{1}{4}$	'One-piece' plastic case
Rem. Indst. 'Unibody'	42.0 AO Buffered load**	$2\frac{1}{2}$	'One-piece' plastic case
Rem. Indst. 'Unibody'	45.0 Blue Dot Buffered load**	$2\frac{1}{2}$	'One-piece' plastic case
Modified Rem. Indst.	52.0 Blue Dot	$2\frac{1}{2}$	Case with yellow plastic base-wad
Modified Rem. Indst.	49.0 AO	$2\frac{1}{2}$	Case with yellow plastic base-wad
Henry Indst. No. 8	53.0 Blue Dot	$2\frac{1}{2}$	
Henry Indst. No. 8	50.0 AO	$2\frac{1}{2}$	
Solid brass	45.0 Blue Dot/AO	3	
Solid brass	50.0 Blue Dot/AO	$2\frac{1}{2}$	

** A plastic shot wrapper $1\frac{1}{4}$ in. $\times 2\frac{3}{4}$ in. should be placed in the shot-cup before dropping and buffering the shot charge.
Note: Before loading any of the Remington cases it is important to identify the type. The latest 'Unibody' is of one-piece plastic construction similar to a compression formed case. The others all feature a plastic tube with a separate base-wad as in the table above.

20 bore Loads For $2\frac{3}{4}$ in. 20-bore guns. MMSP. $3\frac{1}{4}$ tons/sq. in. (1 oz). 900 kg./sq. cm.

Case	Primer	Powder charge (grains)	Wadding	Shot charge (ozs)
P.T. $67\frac{1}{2}$ mm Ranger	CCI 109/WW 209	18.5 A.I.	'G' wad	$\frac{15}{16}$
P.T. $67\frac{1}{2}$ mm Ranger	Eley	18.5 Nobel 82	'G' wad	$\frac{15}{16}$
P.T. 70 mm	V 20	21.0 N 340	'G' wad	I
P.T. 70 mm	CCI 109/WW 209	23.0 AO	'G' wad	I
P.T. 70 mm	CCI 109/WW 209	23.0 Blue Dot	'G' wad	I

The loading of hard shot (2 % antimony) is strongly recommended in these 20-bore loads. No. 7 (2.4 mm) shot has proved extremely effective in the field.

Black powder loads

These are included for the information of the owner of guns proofed only for this reliable old propellant. A 'gentle giant' that produces first-class patterns.

Bore	Chamber (in.)	Powder charge (drams)	Shot charge (oz)	Velocity
12	$2\frac{1}{2}$	3	$1\frac{1}{8}$	S Any shot size
12	$2\frac{1}{2}$	$2\frac{3}{4}$	$1\frac{1}{4}$	LV
12	$2\frac{3}{4}$	3	$1\frac{1}{2}$	LV
12	3	$3\frac{1}{4}$	$1\frac{3}{4}$	LV
10	$2\frac{5}{8}$	3	2	LV
10	$2\frac{7}{8}$	$3\frac{1}{4}$	2	LV
10	$3\frac{1}{4}$	$3\frac{3}{4}$	$2\frac{1}{4}$	LV
8	$3\frac{1}{4}$	5**	$2\frac{1}{2}$	LV
8	$3\frac{1}{2}$	$5\frac{3}{4}$	3	LV
8	$3\frac{3}{4}$	6	3	LV
8	4	6	$3\frac{1}{4}$	LV
4	4	8	4	LV

Note: Use felt or fibre and card wadding with black powder, plastic wadding produces excessive plastic fouling. A I/II" card should be used over-powder (o/p) and under-shot (u/s) with a maximum thickness of felt/fibre wadding. Use fine (T.S.2) powder for 12-bore loads and the coarse (T.S.6) for heavy loads in the 'big-bores'.

*No. 4 shot or larger should be used with the low-velocity loads recommended for wildfowling.

**Use 6 drams in the old Remington Indst. case. The base-wad needs reducing in height to accommodate the black powder loads.

SOURCES OF SUPPLY

Powders, primers, shot and wads can be obtained from gunsmiths specialising in their supply. More specifically:

Nobel Glasgow powders, Eley primers, GL and TL wads. Eley agents. Vectan powders, Cheddite primers, hard shot, 8-bore plastic wads. Gamebore agents. Vihtavuori powders and primers. Pacific loading machines. Mountain and Sowden Ltd, P.O. Box 5, Horsforth, Leeds.

Specialists who cater for a wide range of loading components and tools are:

Ballistic Products (Alan Myers),
Vicarage Farm,
New House Lane,
Winmarleigh,
Garstang, Lancs.

MEC loading machines. All powders, CCI & Winchester primers, SP 10 wads. 8-bore plastic wads. New 10-bore cases. Buffering powder. RTO machines. Case re-sizers. Powder scales. Re-sized Rem. Indst. cases. Punches and shot hoppers.

Adams Shooting Supplies,
1 Bridge End,
The High Street,
Annan,
Dumfrieshire DG12 6AD.

RTO machines and 'heads'. Primer punches, powder and shot hoppers, re-sizers, powder bushings (to order). A good contact for any 'one off' machining jobs.

19
CLOTHING AND EQUIPMENT
PETER WHITAKER

Sporting fashions have followed two distinct main lines over the centuries. On the one hand there are the colourful costumes of the chase, the purpose of which was to heighten the spectacle and make the huntsmen more easily identifiable, which gradually became increasingly like uniforms. On the other may be instanced the quieter clothes, subdued of hue, which were designed to enable the hunter to blend inconspicuously with the local scenery, hence the greys and greens which, since the hunter began to wear clothes, have always been so popular.

Wildfowling couture has always belonged to the second category for obvious – or rather not so obvious – reasons. It has never aspired to the *haute classe*, partly because fowling was for centuries identified with the poor man's sport, but equally since the conditions under which the sport is practised hardly equate themselves with finery. At the same time, precisely because of these conditions, wildfowling clothing deserves a great deal more attention than it is sometimes given by those unaccustomed to the marsh in all its moods.

For many years now, a certain type of wildfowler seems to have become steeped in the masochistic idea that, to be a credit to his sport, he must endure all sorts of supreme discomforts and rate as a lively candidate for such unpleasantness as pneumonia, or at least the 'screws' in later life, at the same time running the risk of drowning, or death from exposure each time he goes out. 'It's rough; it's tough; it's rugged' is his proud theme song. And so it is, and it would not be wildfowling if it were not, but it is not half as bad as that – not nowadays, anyway, and a great deal of the discomfort and so-called unpleasantness is due entirely to lack of planning.

Nowadays, there is no excuse for a wildfowler going about his business inadequately clad. With nylon, terylene, Dacron, Gannex, polyester, Gore-tex and similar man-made fibres, one can travel light and relatively cheaply, and still keep warm or cool, according to the climate.

In any consideration of basic requirements, the natural starting-point is boots. Leather boots may be fashionable in some quarters, but on the marsh rubber thigh boots – not the knee-length sort that let in the water as soon as you kneel down, as kneel down you must before long – are the modern answer. The more expensive kind have leather soles with metal studs, and the obvious advantage is that they can be re-soled. Disadvantages are that studs slip on icy surfaces and the 'ledge' provided by the soles can make extrication from deep mud more difficult. Experience of these shows that the tops wear out before the bottoms. Don't expect your rubber boots to last more than two seasons. If they are well cleated to start with, they will wear longer and not slip. If the tops wear out first, cut these off and you have a pair of gum boots that will last you another year.

The life of a pair of thigh-boots depends largely on how they are kept when not in use. Always dry them when you take them off, by stuffing them with newspaper, or by leaving them overnight with a pair of electric boot-dryers working inside the foot. If they are dried in front of a fire, see that only the soles face the fire, but not too close. Never hang up the boots by the tops, which stretches and strains the rubber. Out of season suspend them in the dry from a cord looped round the foot.

Straps which secure the boot to belt or braces are a bore and uncomfortable. Get a pair of boots stiff enough to stand up without this aid. Carry a cycle puncture outfit in a pocket in case of a puncture. Clean the boots before hanging them up. Dirt encourages rot and cracking of the rubber.

Novice fowlers are sometimes advised, when buying their first pair of thigh-boots, to choose a size larger than that of their normal shoes, on the principle that bigger boots can accommodate several pairs of socks. But this leads us to another mistake often made, the wearing of too many or too thick socks which defeat the foot-warming object because they impede circulation and, fitting tight between foot and boot, allow for no passage of insulating air. In a well-fitting – which does not mean tight – boot, a single pair of thin socks may be enough, especially if a 'sock' is included between foot sole and boot.

Layers of newspaper cut to the shape of the foot make a primitive but effective moisture-absorbent sock of this kind, though perhaps better are those made of honeycombed sponge rubber.

Another combination is a thin silk or nylon sock topped by a pair of oiled wool seaman's stockings; it is worth securing the latter below the knee with a garter of some sort, for stockings that slip down round the ankle inside a long boot make walking uncomfortable and legs cold.

Best of all are a pair of thin wool socks and a pair of 'Husky' thermo-insulated bootees. Made of polyester-filled, quilted nylon they are the answer to foot comfort in the coldest weather.

Some support round the ankle and heel is useful and indeed necessary when creek-crawling or stalking fowl out on the saltings. A length of strong cord tied round the instep, and above the heel, prevents boots pulling off in mud and also allows the boot to be withdrawn from it with a minimum of noisy, sucking sound. A rubber band cut from an innertube is a good alternative.

A great boon to wildfowlers as well as fishermen has been the development of lightweight but tough olive green chest waders in which the rubber boot is married to pvc upper parts, fitted with well-secured metal buttons and strong braces. The design allows for comfortable walking over quite long distances without an acute condensation problem, while the waders can be stowed away folded without fear of cracking. In these the gunner can reach new depths in dry comfort, though he must still watch his step, for chest waders of any sort can be dangerous if once they fill with water.

So much, then, for boots and socks. From there we progress upwards to trousers.

These should be primarily windproof, and secondarily water-resistant. Here is to be found, usually, the most vulnerable gap in the fowler's defence against the elements. Impervious to rain and wind and the worst that the weather can do above and below, he is inclined to forget seating arrangements, only to be reminded of his oversight when the inevitable time comes to sit down in the damp.

Thin rubber over-trousers, which are the choice of many, are apt to tear, and overheat the nether regions.

The answer seems to be to choose a 'pliable' pair of trousers of almost any material, so long as they are warm and windproof – breeches are hard to beat, while a pair of dungarees deserve consideration – and to wear over them an additional pair of slacks which are waterproof. Recommended are shorts cut from waxed cotton overtrousers. Worn outside waders, they keep the posterior dry when at squat and at the same time allow enough freedom of movement for unimpeded creek jumping. Pyjama trousers worn next to the skin form a sound windproof base to any type of over-trousers.

Getting nearer the bone, what about underclothes? Remembering that the basis of all effective cold-weather clothing is the provision of an insulating layer of air between flesh and the elements, there is little doubt that the string vest, and pants, proved in action and extreme conditions of wartime, are a good basis, though thermal underwear has now superseded them. There is one proviso here, for best results. The shirt topping this base must be of good, close-weft material which will do its share of keeping out the wind.

On top of this and beneath the outermost garment a seaman's jersey is the favourite winter choice. A point to be made here is that any gap at the neckline is to be avoided, and it matters not whether a tie or scarf or towelling cravat is worn so long as something, not too tight, is included at this level to keep out the draught. It is surprising what a lot of warmth there is in a tie. The simple addition or removal of this item is an additional advantage when a long, wearing walk to the marsh is involved. By leaving it off on the way there, one can move more freely, and clothing is allowed to breathe. Once in position, the donning of a tie or scarf contains the warm air layer, and when the time comes for a strenuous retreat it can be removed.

Clothing restrictions of any sort are to be avoided; bulk under the topmost garment leads to overheating and subsequent chilling of the body. Priority protection from the cold is advisable in the region of the lower back and kidneys, and one of the best ways of ensuring this is to wear a waistcoat, the back of which is made of flannel, or some similarly thick material. If the waistcoat is equipped with four pockets – with flaps – in front, so much the better. Waistcoats have the ad-

Dressed for the marsh (D. T. Frost)

vantage of no sleeves or tightness about the shoulders that impede gun-handling when several layers of clothing are worn. The choice of additional sweaters, etc., is purely a personal one. Such dodges as wearing layers of newspapers to protect the back are now outmoded by modern clothing and here again 'Husky' provide a perfect answer with their thermo-insulated shooting waistcoat.

In the matter of the outermost, overall garment, the choice is fairly wide, and all manner of coats and jackets are seen on the marsh. Selection is governed by weather conditions, availability and price. On fine and balmy days a sweater or battle-dress blouse may be sufficient. Ordinary jackets that droop below the waist are not recommended because their bottoms get wet as soon as the forgetful fowler stoops or bends down in water, and so do the cartridges carried in the side pockets.

The ideal fowling coat must be wind- and waterproof, light and of a neutral colour to blend with the marsh, and long enough to cover the tops of thigh-boots. Smocks are still a favourite choice, and double-texture parkas, many of them surplus American army equipment, remain useful, especially since they are reversible, the outer side being coloured green and the inner white, an asset in snow. The parkas are extremely wind-resistant, but they are by no means waterproof, and even if the fowler does not have to contend with much heavy rain in a season, hiding and lying about in wet places soon leads to uncomfortable saturation.

First choice is one of the various waxed cotton coats, though a more expensive Gore-tex type *provided its seams are soundly tailored and sealed* is better. The lined type are warmer than the unlined. Get one big enough to cover sweaters, etc., and long enough to sit on, on the mud. A three-quarter-length coat is my choice. A belt adds to its warmth and stops it dragging on the shoulders.

Whether a fowling coat is better for a zip or buttoned front, is a moot point. Buttons, even if they do come off from time to time, are more easily replaced than a zip, but the latter makes for easier access to binoculars. Button-fronted coats have an overlapping flap at the join, and appear to keep out the wet as well as a zip. The latter does not simplify access to inner pockets, waistcoat, etc. Very useful indeed for lying in wet ambushes is the pvc camouflaged waterproof suit made by the American Clearwater Corporation and obtainable from Ralph Grant of Leicester.

Two areas worthy of protection remain to be considered; head and hands. Headgear is wide in variety. Something light and waterproof is the choice and a peak fore and aft is not adopted for affectation but to shield face from birds and neck from rain. Hats or hoods that act as ear plugs are not recommended. The fowler relies very largely on his hearing for warning of bird movement. A balaclava knitted helmet is an asset in cold weather and can be rolled up to form an adequate hat. But it is useless and most uncomfortable in rain. A face mask is not affectation. It hides the most noticeable feature of the gunner and helps to keep off the wind.

If anyone can shoot properly in gloves, he is welcome to wear them. They soon get wet and filthy on the marsh, however, and foul up gun and everything else one touches. A better proposition are wristlets – those with leather, fleeced-lined extensions to cover the back of the hands are warm and wear well. Chemical pack handwarmers are preferable to the solid-fuel type, and well worth putting in the pockets. Hands will become acclimatised and stay warm longer if they are dipped in the water early on and allowed to dry naturally. This may be hard to believe, but it's true. Remember, too, that fitness and food make for a good circulation and warmth. No amount of extra clothing will warm an unfit hungry body.

Given a gun, some cartridges and an adequate costume, the game shooter – and even his rougher, inland counterpart – can acquit and enjoy himself with a minimum of trouble. If it rains, he goes home; if he gets caught in the rain, he sends for his waterproof; if his cartridges swell in the damp atmosphere he sends for dry ones from his car; he stops for lunch at a convenient half-way halt when he is hungry or thirsty; if he finds himself or his gun or his dog in some trouble, there is someone close at hand to help him out. But if he is fowling, the chances are that he will have none of these things or people to help him out of a hole; he must depend in the main on himself and, if he is ill-prepared, he may well find himself not only short of sport but indeed short of breath as well; in fact at his last salty gasp.

There is still a tendency, just as there always has been, to talk about wildfowling in terms of extreme danger. Some writers have been inclined in their glamourisation of the sport to make it sound so risky that it should not be undertaken by anyone short of Superman. This, while it is undoubtedly wrong, is an error on the right side, for there are today a larger number of enthusiasts who have been driven to the shore-line for want of any other opportunity so cheap and easily accessible, without appreciating the implications, and they are the ones who inspire the frightening pictures sometimes painted.

Many sports are dangerous if the participant goes in for them without thinking or making the necessary preparation. But wildfowling is no more – and indeed a great deal less – risky than such pastimes as rock climbing and motor racing. A field sport only becomes hazardous when something extraordinary, with fatal or frightening consequences, occurs, and the following suggestions are made with a view to preventing this sort of thing, as well as simplifying what is, of necessity, among the more awkward and uncomfortable sports.

The most formidable basic dangers that confront the shoreshooter are few and elementary. They comprise tide, fog (and snow in that it can be almost equally blinding) and mud. All can be defeated by a pocketful of gadgets.

Tides are treacherous, and their time of rising and falling may, and should, be determined from a tide table obtainable from any local ship's chandler or good local newsagent. Flight times as well as the gunner's safety depend on tide tables, so they are a double necessity. See that you consult a current edition. More than one fowler has got wet by failing to look at the date of his borrowed and dog-eared copy. Do not trust in these tables implicitly. Study them in conjunction with a note of the wind. A strong onshore wind can advance a tide as much as an hour or more and pile it up higher. Similarly vice versa.

Used in conjunction, a reliable watch is an

obvious necessity; best of all one that is waterproof. Unless the timepiece is 100% waterproof, unbreakable and impervious to mud, choose a pocket, as opposed to a wrist, model.

Here we must include the torch, which can be vital in all sorts of situations from signalling to one's fellows, particularly in the case of an emergency, to spotlighting obstacles on the way off the marsh. Most serviceable are the rubber-cased models. Carry a spare bulb Sellotaped inside the reflector. A spare pocket torch of the pencil type is a double insurance.

First line of defence against invisibility, which may be caused by mist, snow, fog, or just plain nightfall, is a compass, and the ability to read it. Learn how to take a forward and back bearing from any Boy Scout's manual, or if this is too much bother, at least know the four main points and the one which spells safety and the sea wall. Creeks running directly to and from the wall are good guides off and on to the marsh, and a compass bearing of the extremity of one of these, out on the mud, will set the wandering fowler on the right track. But let him note on which side of the creek he went out to sea, and head for home on the same side.

Compasses come in all sizes, and those incorporated in whistles, pocket knives, etc., are better than nothing. But the bigger the instrument, the more reliable, and although there is no need for an unwieldy large compass, let it be of

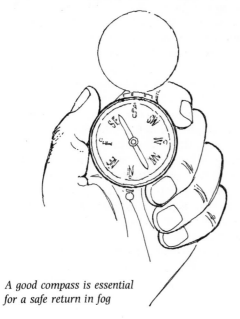

A good compass is essential for a safe return in fog

proportions commensurate with accuracy. One large enough to fit into the eye-piece cover of a pair of field-glasses is sufficient, and this is a good place to carry it. No properly-equipped fowler sets forth without field-glasses or binoculars, and this fitting ensures a vital 'double take'. Don't despise the monocular by the way. It is less bulky, cheaper and highly effective.

There is no easily portable mud extricator within the meaning of the word, but a strong, sharp knife can be used for cutting off boots in an extreme emergency.

The lone fowler who gets into difficulty still has no recognised distress signal on which he can rely to summon help. But no distress signal will ever be an absolute guarantee of rescue, and the best way of avoiding trouble remains a sound knowledge of tides, weather and marsh, not going out alone, or at least leaving word of one's whereabouts before setting out.

Any gun becomes heavy quickly where a march of some distance to the shooting ground is entailed. When the going is as heavy as it usually is hard by or below the sea wall, and the gun on the weighty side, as many fowling pieces are, it is an advantage to be able to rely on some other means of support other than one hand, which would be welcome to preserve balance or break the stumbling fowler's fall, if unencumbered. The answer, which continental shooters of all sorts have been trying to teach us for years, and which we are so slow to learn, is a sling, whereby the weapon may be suspended from the shoulder or across the back, and there are many shooting occasions, far from the wildfowler's world, on which such an appendage proves a boon, as any pigeon shooter will confirm.

Slings and sling fittings need not necessarily spoil the appearance of any gun, a main objection in the eyes of many, for the sling swivel is easily removable from its screw hole in the stock, and the same applies to the fitting screwed into the bottom rib, when the gun is to be used where a sling might be a nuisance. If these minor alterations are still considered undesirable, it is possible to buy a sling which loops over the small of the stock and the barrels. The disadvantages here, however, are that one never feels too certain about the forward fixture, which is liable to slip off unless the barrels are of good length if the fowler is pretty boneless in the shoulder, and also that when the gun is

mounted, the line of sight is interrupted by a thickish band across the barrel(s).

The ideal sling fittings would seem to be those that neither mark the gun nor interrupt the sight plane. Mechanically-minded fowlers may like to experiment with a forward sling fitting in the form of an eye affixed to a section of a slip-on hand-guard, with the backward loop slipped round the small, or grip, of the stock. Ingenious improvisers can work out something on these lines for themselves.

Sooner or later out on the mud the gunner is bound to slip or fall in a creek and block his gun barrels with mud or some similar obstruction. All the old books advise the fowler to carry a pull-through in his pocket with which to dislodge such foreign bodies from his tubes. Anyone who has driven his barrels into a soft creekside will realise how useless a pull-through is for this purpose. If you object to the idea of swilling out the gun barrels in the nearest creek, take with you instead a sectionalised cleaning rod, or better still one of those metal rods with a cord running through the centre on the 'Helvetic' pattern. Such a slender, short-lengthed tool is no trouble to tuck away in pack or bag, and will clear barrel obstructions, or

poke out swollen cartridge cases (if a cartridge extractor has been forgotten) with speed and absolute efficiency. Which reminds us that a cartridge extractor should not be forgotten, for shooting in wet places leads sooner or later to swollen cartridge cases that are awkward to remove unless plastic-case cartridges are being used exclusively. Whatever the type of cartridge extractor chosen – the pliers type has the advantage of being adaptable to any bore – make it a fixture, not to be forgotten, by securing it to cartridge belt or jacket lapel with a length of nylon cord.

Cartridges, including the plastic-cased type, deserve special protection from the elements, but at the same time they should be easily accessible. A favourite way of carrying cartridges on the marsh is in a belt, with a few tucked away in reserve in inside pockets. Nine times out of ten this allows for a more than sufficient supply. On the tenth occasion, few fowlers want to shoot more than this number, anyway.

Only one type of cartridge belt is worth considering and this is the one with closed loops. Two-and-a-half inch cartridges will keep snug and dry in a belt of this sort, and the longer cases also, for they have the extra protection afforded by the deeper brass. A belt like this can be worn with confidence outside one's clothing if necessary, although it is better girt beneath the outer layer. It pays to keep any cartridge belt supple and waterproof by treating it from time to time with saddle soap.

Before adding further to the wildfowler's burden let us now consider how he is going to carry the bulkier items of his paraphernalia which refuse to fit comfortably or safely into pockets.

On the backs of most fowlers one can see what has come to be known somewhat romantically as a 'goose bag', which may be of any material and dimensions – the larger, within reason, the better – the object of which is essentially to contain and carry home the successful hunter's bag. The object remains, but its fulfilment has long been relegated to the realms of wishful thinking in the minds of most fowlers, who carry such a bag just in case, on the one hand, but otherwise for the major reason that into it may be packed a lot of useful oddments on the outward trip, and as Dalgety in his *Wildfowling* excused its part in the scene: 'It is useful to sit upon.'

Game bags, goose bags, bags of any sort which suspend from one's shoulder and flap about against the fowler's rump, eventually working round to the front, unless restricted by diverse cords and straps, are nothing short of an awkward nuisance. Much to be preferred is a pack or haversack of some sort, which fits fairly and squarely on both shoulders, leaves both hands free,

and cannot slip out of place when its wearer comes to jump a creek or slither in the mud. If you have to buy one, the army-style big pack is obtainable at very little cost from most surplus stores. Empty, it will take three pinkfeet easily, and more duck than result from the average flight. The unexpected big bag is never too hard to carry off the marsh, and a roll of string will cope with this and other emergencies.

Half a dozen thin rubber collapsible duck decoys take up next to no room in a big pack. Wear a duck or goose call round the neck, but *only* take one if you know precisely how and when to blow it. Being fairly water resistant, such a pack will also do duty as a seat or cushion in damp places. Other items it may be required to accommodate from time to time include a flask of soup, for long vigils, especially under the moon, a bite to eat, a piece of camouflage netting to drape over the dog and a coal shovel for trimming out a seat or hide in a gutter.

Any type of shooting stool makes a pack in which to carry it essential. Individual gunners may develop their own ideas of other equipment they want to take on the marsh, but it is a sound rule to reduce one's burden to the minimum and travel as light as possible. Those fowlers who take a thumbstick on their forays use it not so much to support their burden as to test water depths in gutters and to help progress over rough going. It is also a very useful support for a camouflage net.

20
THE WILDFOWLER'S DOG

JAMES DOUGLAS

CHOICE OF BREED

Choosing a gundog breed has always been a subject fraught with difficulty. Deciding which dog is best for any particular task is not straightforward and different breed enthusiasts tend to advocate the one that they particularly favour. To add to the confusion individual animals often perform well beyond the norm of their breed, giving rise to a belief amongst the inexperienced that his breed brothers and sisters must possess similar attributes. However, since this book is primarily for the wildfowler, I intend to concentrate on the breeds most suitable for wildfowling and on how the fowler's dog should be chosen and trained. Space does not allow a long preamble about the merits and pitfalls of the numerous other breeds.

The wildfowler aspiring to gundog ownership is likely to be given various confusing claims about the breeds available and it is a difficult decision for the inexperienced to make, particularly when he realises that his new canine friend is to be a family member for at least the next ten years. He therefore must decide what sort of shooting he is likely to do. What experience does he have with dog training and what amount of time does he have to devote to the dog? All these are important factors in his choice.

Gundogs are divided into several separate categories – the spaniels, the HPRs, the pointers and setters and the retrievers. Spaniels are essentially hunting dogs and there is no better breed for the sportsman who wishes to get maximum benefit from any given piece of shooting land. The spaniel, better than any other, will find game and flush it in even the densest hedgerow or thicket. They are however essentially dogs for rough shooters. Whilst individual spaniels are certainly capable of performing well for the wildfowler, they are not generally ideal for the job. Temperamentally they are not suited to sitting patiently in a hide for longish periods of time, preferring to busy about getting things done. Physically they are not designed to withstand very cold temperatures. Their thick coats have little waterproofing or insulation, being designed as protection against thorn rather than cold.

Spaniels, particularly if they are fit, have very little fat reserves, their bodies tending to be more athletic than they might seem, with their thick coats giving the illusion of bulk. A spaniel bustling about on a cold snowy January day is keeping himself warm with his constant movement, very different indeed from immersion in cold water (which transfers heat away from the body much faster than air), then sitting chilling before further immersion. The spaniel is not really suited to this type of work.

The term HPR refers to hunting, pointing, retrieving – the continental breeds developed to perform all three functions. They include the viszla, the weimaraner, the munsterlander, the German wirehaired pointer and, of course, the German shorthaired pointer (GSP), which is the most popular of the continental breeds in this country.

Devotees of the GSP produce some excellent working specimens, but this is one breed of animal

174

which is certainly unsuitable as a first dog. The breed has a tendency to be highly strung and they do require an experienced hand to get the best out of them. Physically they are not designed to withstand repeated entry into cold water and then sitting soaked and cold until they are required to work again. With their very thin coats and streamlined muscular bodies they have no protection whatever against the elements, though, like the spaniel, enthusiastic specimens might mislead you into believing they were impervious to the cold.

I had one particularly big, well-muscled dog, who was very experienced in the field in every way. But even he used to sit shivering quite violently after immersion in cold water on a winter's night, and in his later years became very reluctant to enter cold water.

Pointers and setters were developed for working the moorland and vast field areas for upland game and are totally unsuitable for any form of fowler's work.

There are several breeds of retriever to consider, and they are all suitable candidates as a fowler's dog – golden retriever, flat-coated and curly-coated retrievers, Chesapeake Bay retriever and, of course, the labrador retriever. The choice of breed that you make is a matter of personal taste, and there are a few simple guidelines that apply whichever breed you choose.

CHOOSING A PUPPY

You must choose a dog from proven working stock and not one bred from show animals. Show animals are denoted on their pedigree with the prefix CH or SH CH and all emphasis in their breeding has been on their physical appearance – their instinctive working traits having little or no relevance to the show breeder. It is desirable and an excellent guide to the potential gundog purchaser that the prefix of several of its ancestors in the pedigree should be clearly marked FT CH. This refers to Field Trials Champion and does give an indication of what the young dog's potential is likely to be. However, it is important to remember that a dog, no matter how illustrious its pedigree, must be trained for whatever task you require of it. It will not just happen by magic.

When you choose a puppy it is of vital importance that both parents have been X-rayed and passed the British Veterinary Association hip scheme, giving you a degree of assurance that your young dog is less likely to develop hip displasia. In addition, it is important that the parents are certified clear of PRA (progressive retinal atrophy).

The labrador retriever is by far the most popular of the retriever breeds and the chances of getting a good working specimen are very high since puppies and young dogs are widely available throughout the country. This breed, developed over two centuries in Newfoundland, where it was used as a water dog by the fishing and coastal communities, is the ideal breed for the wildfowler. With its calm temperament, an adult experienced dog will happily sit for long periods in a hide with a fowler, impervious to the coldest winter weather, and be ready to spring into action as required. Physically, a well-bred working labrador is infinitely more suited to withstand repeated immersion in cold water and if properly fed and kept in the right condition, will show no ill effects from working in severe weather.

When choosing a puppy destined to be a wildfowler's dog, it is essential that not only is it of the correct breeding, but that the type of dog must be of the thick, square-set variety, what many people refer to as 'the old-fashioned' type of labrador. You must avoid one of the thin, racy specimens. Having visited the coastal communities of Newfoundland I can assure you that some specimens of the labrador retriever that are commonly used in the modern shooting field would certainly not survive for very long in the environment that shaped their ancestors.

EARLY TRAINING

Once you have chosen your young puppy, very much like a human child, it is sufficient to let it have its formative growing months without expecting anything of it other than that it should be good mannered. It should walk to heel on the lead, and be taught to sit by the simple method of holding its feeding bowl above its head and pushing its bottom down into a sitting position with the other hand, gently repeating the word 'sit'.

Personally I like to encourage a young dog to get used to carrying something in its mouth from an early age. The easiest way of introducing your young dog to this early retrieving is with a small puppy dummy. Gently restraining the young dog with your hand across his chest, throw the dummy and, removing your hand, encourage him to 'fetch'. The instant he runs out and picks up the dummy, encourage him back and make a fuss of him. Once your young dog has shown you that he will pick up a retrieve and bring it to you resist the temptation to ask him to perform this service more than once a day, the idea being to keep the action fresh in his mind whilst avoiding over-emphasising it in his early months.

The most important factor in your young dog's early life is how you feed it, and there are a few simple rules for you to remember. What you put into your young dog in the way of protein will have a direct bearing on the physical development of the dog as it grows. A human takes sixteen to eighteen years to grow from baby to adult – a long time and a vast amount of food, compared to the dog, which will grow from puppy to adult physique in as many months, with huge demands made by its growing body on the supply of nutrients from its food. Therefore, if you are to allow your dog to achieve its maximum potential growth and physical development, you must feed the dog properly and resist trying to do it on the cheap.

A young puppy should be fed little but often, with a diet which includes plenty of milk and meat protein. There are many excellent proprietary complete foods on the market that print their protein contents on the packaging. These should be used as a base, to which meat, fish, milk and an occasional egg should be added. As a general guide, all puppies should be chubby, not bloated and never thin, and since all individual dogs'

metabolism and their requirements vary, there are no hard and fast amounts you should feed. Be guided by the dog's condition. If it is getting too fat, ease off on its food. If it is getting thin, step it up.

If you are in doubt as to the dog's protein requirements or, indeed, if you have a question about the dog's general health and well-being, the best advice is always to consult your veterinary surgeon. Indeed it is he who will guide you as to the correct course of action with vaccination and regular worming of your young dog. It is your vet who is the best guide on supplementary vitamin and mineral additives to your dog's diet.

Apart from walking your young dog on the lead to heel, teaching it to sit and giving it occasional little retrieving exercises, resist trying to start its training too soon.

There are several pieces of equipment that you will need to do the job of dog trainer effectively, a whistle, several hand-thrown dummies, a starting pistol, and a dummy launcher with three dummies.

All dogs, like human beings, have different personalities. Some develop later than others and there is little point in starting a young dog's training regime proper until it is mentally at its most receptive. As a general guide this would normally be between seven and nine months. Once you start your young dog's training schedule you must begin to put a constantly greater emphasis on the command to sit. The cornerstone of all dog training is two commands, sit and recall. Any dog that will sit immediately on command and then, when ordered to do so, return to its handler, cannot get into trouble, nor embarrass its handler.

Once you have got your young dog to sit to voice command and it does so every time, quickly and obediently, then you must begin to add the other commands to make it sit. All young dogs learn by repetition and association of previous tasks. The dog will now sit, since your voice has commanded it. If simultaneously to commanding it to sit you raise your arm towards the dog, palm facing it, the dog will sit since your voice command has told it to do so. It will quickly associate the physical movement of your arm going in the air with the action of sitting, and before long you will discover your dog sits to a hand signal only. Equally, you will find that by giving it the visual command to sit and giving one quiet toot on your whistle the dog will quickly associate the whistle sound with the action

Sitting to command is an important element of basic training (Eric Begbie)

of sitting, and will start to sit to whistle alone.

A dog's concentration level is between fifteen and twenty minutes, so there is no point in going out for long training sessions. This will only result in your young dog becoming bored and increase the temptation for it to misbehave. It is preferable that you set aside a few minutes every day – ten to fifteen minutes in the morning and evening will progress your young dog much more rapidly than four hours on a Sunday afternoon. It is important you constantly remind yourself that dogs learn by repetition and the more often a dog is asked to perform a particular task, the more firmly the requirement will become implanted in its brain.

Decide where you are going to train your dog. Ideally it should be in a situation where there are no other distractions. Walk the dog at heel to your training ground. Make it sit and, with your arm raised again, gently, quietly tell it to sit. Then walk a few yards backwards. If the dog attempts to get

up and follow you, gently but firmly take the dog, without frightening it, put it back in position and repeat the exercise. The object of this lesson is for you to progressively put ever increasing distance between yourself and your young dog. When you leave him in this sitting position, it is of great importance that you return to the young dog nine out of ten times, so that it learns the confidence and independence of being away from you but realises that it is still under your command, that you always return and there is no chance of your running off and leaving it.

Only occasionally will you call it to you, and when you do, encourage it to dash straight up to you. The recall command is three short toots on the whistle, accompanied by a straight-arm, exaggerated thigh-slapping movement. Let it know you are pleased with it and command it to sit. Delay a little between commands so that the dog learns a series of individual tasks as opposed to your stringing them all together, which would have the result of the dog starting to anticipate you – the beginnings of unsteadiness.

INTRODUCTION TO WATER

The wildfowler's dog is going to be required to enter water happily on command and then take direction in the water, so its introduction to water must be correct, as must its directional control. Once you have got your young dog happily walking at heel, sitting on command and allowing you to walk away in a large circle without moving, and when you do call him he comes to you like a rocket, stopping on the whistle and upraised arm, then with that foundation you can move forward.

Introduction to water must always be made with great caution. Never assume that because a dog is of a breed that is expected to swim, it will jump in automatically. Introduce the young dog with great care. Choose a warm day, preferably in summer, when the water temperature should be high, and then employ one of the following methods – put wellington boots on and, walking in the shallows, encourage the young dog into the water, making a game of it, either by throwing small twigs that he can see and wade to get, progressively letting him go deeper until he becomes buoyant and starts to swim, or take him with an older more experienced dog and let him play in the shallows with the older dog. The idea is to make the introduction as natural and pleasant as possible. Most retrieving breeds, once introduced to water, quickly gain confidence. The reason for the caution is that some individuals need extra coaxing and it is wise to assume that yours is one of these.

The labrador is an ideal water dog (James Douglas)

RETRIEVING

Up until now all the retrieving your dog will have done will have been straight retrieves, where you have kept the dog sitting, thrown the dummy out and, after a short pause, sent him after it, using the ground and its natural obstacles such as long grass, contours and bushes to encourage the dog to search for the dummy, always using the command 'fetch' or 'on' when you want him to retrieve.

When you send your young dog out on a retrieve it is important that you squat down beside it and point your straight arm in the direction of the retrieve, lining it out, rather than giving a casual and not particularly direct command. In years to come, if you were on a flat beach or marshland, the benefit of sending your young dog in a straight line will become apparent.

The secret of real steadiness with your dog is that he should never assume a retrieve is automatically his property, but that it is a privilege allowed him occasionally by you. Make him sit, throw the dummy, leaving him sitting, get it yourself. In this way you will get the dog used to the idea that progressively you will increase the distance between the two of you as you throw the dummy all around the field, collecting it yourself. If your dog tries to chase it, blow the stop whistle, stop him before he gets to it. If he does retrieve it, don't make a fuss, take it and start again at the basics of leaving him sitting as you throw the dummy, progressively getting farther. The idea of what you are trying to achieve is that you can leave your dog in a sitting position, throw the dummy all around the field and only once in ten retrieves per session is he allowed to pick a dummy, you collecting the other nine. As you progress with your young dog you can reduce the ratio to five to you one to the dog, and as he is nearing the end of his training this figure can be reduced to four retrieves per session – two each.

It is as important that a wildfowler's dog sits to flush as much as a dog that is to be used for walked-up game, since chasing is a nightmare that must be avoided at all costs. To teach the dog is relatively simple. Ideally enlist the help of a gundog trainer or local keeper who can allow you access to a game pen. If none is available then you will have to make do with wild game. The method in both cases is identical. Walk the dog where game will be disturbed. The instant it appears make the dog sit.

It is important when doing this that you make the dog sit before it starts to chase. If it has any tendency to chase whatsoever, it must be firmly put in its place and convinced of your displeasure. Regular practice with this steadiness to game soon sinks in, but of course success in the game pen is dependent on the fact that up to this stage in the dog's training it should never have met game alive or dead.

DIRECTIONAL CONTROL

Directional control is built in to the retrieving training and should only be started when the foundation of an absolutely rock steady young dog has been achieved. Standing out in front of the dog throw a dummy to the left and send him for it with a big arm directional movement. Then repeat the exercise to the right. In your next training session throw out two dummies, one left and one right. Wait a few moments and then give him a clear directional command to go for the first one you threw, progressively increase these distances between you and the dog and the dog and the dummy.

Introduce your young dog to shot with the assumption that he may be a sensitive individual. Never assume he'll take it in his stride. Stay with the dog, have a companion go 100 yards away and fire a shot, then if there is no untoward reaction from your young dog, let him come progressively closer, firing a shot. If your dog appears to be frightened, stop and repeat the exercise another day. Once your young dog is happy with the sound of shot, standing a good distance from him, fire your starting pistol and throw the dummy.

A wildfowler's dog should regard the sound of shot as a perfectly natural part of the day out and not as the herald of a retrieve. This is particularly important if you are flighting at dusk. You may fire a few shots and miss. The last thing you want your dog to be doing is getting ready to dash off in a futile hunt, so therefore there is an advantage if you have taught him to sit to shot. This is simple. Your dog will by now sit nicely to hand, whistle and voice commands. If you wish to teach him to sit to shot, hold the starting pistol behind your back in your right hand, whistle in mouth, call him in. When he is coming towards you, give him the hand signal to sit as you simultaneously blow the stop and fire the pistol. He will quickly learn to associate the action of sitting with the sound of shot. You can then drop the whistle and eventually the hand signal and sit him to shot alone.

From now on introduce the starting pistol on a regular basis, always prior to throwing a dummy, and then naturally, using the same method, introduce the dummy launcher, first at distance, then working closer until you can stand beside the young dog and shoot the dummy off into the distance, sending it for only the occasional retrieve, which by now should be getting progressively more difficult – over streams, walls, into undergrowth, in other words, giving the dog as much varied retrieving experience as possible.

The importance of distant blind retrieves with good directional control for a water working dog is essential since the environment which most fowling dogs are going to work in is flat. With their low eyeline it is difficult for them to mark a bird, and when you add the factor of moving water, either by current or wind, the ability to stop and redirect is vital.

Retrieving a goose (Eric Begbie)

By concentrating on stopping your dog on the whistle you will compel the dog to pay attention to you. Some trainers think that stopping a dog too often on the whistle, particularly during recall, tends to make the dog ponderous, but this has little bearing on the fowler's dog, since accuracy and obedience are preferable to speed. Leave the dog sitting, walk away let us say a hundred yards, give it the recall and when it is halfway towards you stop it, making it sit. Throw a dummy on either side of the dog, send it for one, stop it, send it for the other. It is of vital importance that you completely master being able to stop the dog on land, get it to look at you, then re-direct it. Indeed this ability must be so well trained into your dog that it reacts automatically to the sound of the whistle, otherwise when it gets to water it will have a tendency to ignore you, and once it discovers you cannot get to it when it is swimming it will quickly learn to do as it pleases. Therefore directional control is vital.

The natural progression is of course distant blind retrieving with hand signals and whistle. Again like all aspects of dog training this is a progressive training skill. The dog having a firm foundation of all the training I have described so far will of course be under control. By the simple expedient of putting your dog against a fence or wall, giving it initially a few visual retrieves along the fence to the right, left and directly away from you, the dog will quickly fall into the pattern of running in straight lines, and as you increase the distance between you and the dog and the dog and the previously hidden dummies you will progressively work the dog on what are, in essence, long blind retrieves.

Throughout the period when you will be training your young dog it is a good idea to repeatedly, say once a week, go over all your dog's training to date, checking that there has been no tendency for the dog to slacken on any individual task. Set yourself an exercise routine and then carefully go through it. Walk the dog to heel, get him to the field, quietly tell him to sit and walk on. Walk a distance away, shoot a dummy right and left, send him for one, stop him halfway, and send him for the other, which he should retrieve to hand and all without you raising your voice. You should be able to line your young dog up on a straight arm and send it running out where it will be hand and whistle directed onto a blind retrieve and it must sit the instant it flushes any game. Your young dog should enter water without hesitation and in every way should be an increasing pleasure to work with, and at all times you should strive to give all commands as quietly as you can.

When you can go out and go through the whole training exercise, start to move towards simulating shooting. Walk around an area, leaving out a false trail of blind retrieves. Then collecting your dog set off around your previous course as though you were rough shooting. Stop when you are the distance you wish to work your dog from the retrieve, fire a shot, then work your dog out to the retrieve, take it and continue. In this way you will naturally find yourself and your dog approaching the shooting season with confidence, and the pleasure you will get from your sport will greatly increase when you are working your dog.

A good retriever is a very necessary companion for the serious wildfowler and time spent on thorough basic training will be rewarded over a period of many fowling seasons. This will result only if you take proper care of your dog on the marsh. Make sure he has a dry seat and, when you have left the marsh, consider the needs of your cold and wet dog before your own.

21

WILDFOWL CONSERVATION – THE WILDFOWLER'S CONTRIBUTION

TONY LAWS

Since the formation of the B.A.S.C., as WAGBI, in 1908 there has been an immense growth in our knowledge about the wildfowl that inhabit or visit our shores. This has resulted in changes in attitudes and management priorities presenting new challenges to be met and overcome by all involved, including the wildfowler. This chapter reviews the history of wildfowl conservation in the United Kingdom and, more particularly, the part played by the wildfowling community and how it has met, and is continuing to meet, these challenges.

WILDFOWL CONSERVATION – A HISTORY

WAGBI was founded to defend the sport of wildfowling against factors that were moving contrary to its interests. It is significant that these not only included the growing enthusiasm of extremists bent on complete bird protection but also an alarming loss through drainage and subsequent development of much excellent wildfowl habitat. Thus wildfowlers registered a pragmatic interest in conservation right from the earliest days. However, voluntary staff serving a modest membership, the intervention of two world wars, and the need to concentrate resources on countering a growing protectionist lobby, meant that the conservation role of the Association was initially forced to take a back seat.

But things changed with the passing of the *Protection of Birds Act* in 1954. The discussions in Parliament and in the press at the time of the Act revealed a horrifying state of ignorance, confusion, suspicion and emotion where wildfowling was concerned and caused deep rifts between wildfowler and conservationist. Ultimately, the provisions in the Act were accepted by the majority of

wildfowlers. However, there had developed a determination that never again would genuine sportsmen find themselves in similar circumstances.

Membership of WAGBI grew dramatically, enabling full-time staff to be employed. In addition, the formation of local clubs and associations became recognised as a way of bringing individuals together to collectively safeguard and manage their sport – thus providing a mechanism for major conservation initiatives in future years. The Act also brought together leading wildfowlers and naturalists in 1955 under the auspices of the then new Nature Conservancy to probe fearlessly and thoroughly into the differences which existed. The work covered by these 'tea parties' has been described elsewhere, not least in the second edition of this book, by Max Nicholson, the then Director General of the Nature Conservancy. However, it is worth mentioning two main points which were discussed then as they embody themes that have continually needed to be addressed to the present day and, no doubt, will need to be addressed in the future.

First, it was recognised that there could be no real progress while the elementary facts about wildfowl numbers and trends were in dispute. This led, in no small part, to the development of the National Wildfowl Counts by the Wildfowl Trust, which enabled wildfowlers also to become involved. Alongside has grown the need to 'find out the facts' over issues relating to shooting, such as the size of the wildfowler's bag and the potential problems of lead shot ingestion or shooting disturbance of wildfowl populations. The wildfowlers' trust in the results of such work is vital if they are to be used in future management strategies. The B.A.S.C.'s contribution to such work is covered in Chapters 27 and 28. Here I would like to emphasise

182

that the wildfowler has a unique part to play in both undertaking such studies and reacting sensibly to their findings.

Secondly, the somewhat conspiratorial atmosphere in which many wildfowlers felt that plots for closing areas to wildfowling were being hatched by various groups up and down the country had to be replaced by open discussion of each project of mutual interest from its earliest stages. Since these early days much has been done to break down this suspicion through increased liaison at national and local level, although, regrettably, it still remains one of the most frequently recurring problems.

In 1960 the 'tea parties' between the Nature Conservancy, WAGBI and the Wildfowl Trust were formalised as the Wildfowl Conservation Committee, which drew up a policy statement for wildfowl conservation under three headings (Atkinson-Willes, 1963):

(1) *The purpose of wildfowl conservation*
To safeguard the species of wildfowl and to maintain existing stocks in at least their present strength and in their present distribution.

(2) *The roles of refuges in wildfowl conservation*
In the case of a species with a limited distribution in this country, refuges may be needed to safeguard some or all of its main resorts. More usually, a refuge will serve as a strong point for a number of species to ensure their status in the district. Special refuges will form wildfowl reservoirs, increasing the stock to the advantage of sportsman and naturalist alike, and will also provide centres from which some of the less common species may be encouraged to extend their range.

Refuges may likewise be used to mitigate the local effects of overshooting or unsporting practice, while still affording controlled shooting to responsible wildfowlers.

(3) *International co-operation*
Finally, as wildfowl are migratory, there is the international aspect and the need for Great Britain to continue to play a full part in the European field of conservation, so that all countries may be brought to fulfil their responsibilities for conserving and increasing the stocks.

With the added emphasis on the need to con-serve breeding stocks, the main justification for the maintenance of wildfowl stocks and distribution as embodied in the 1960 statement – to provide human pleasure and sport without harming bird populations – has recently been restated in the second edition of *Wildfowl in Great Britain* (Owen, Atkinson-Willes and Salmon, 1986), the Wildfowl Trust's definitive survey into wildfowl habits, stocks and prospects in Britain.

The first refuges and reserves with controlled shooting zones were established during the formulation of the policy – the Humber Refuge (1956); Southport Sanctuary (1956); Caerlaverock National Nature Reserve (1957) and the Lindisfarne National Nature Reserve (1960) (Harrison, 1967 and Nicholson, 1970). Wildfowlers were fully involved in the planning of these schemes and today continue to participate in their management (see Chapter 22).

By 1966, there was an extensive network of forty-seven national and regional wildfowl refuges throughout Great Britain, supplemented by local refuges set aside by wildfowling clubs. However, most of these were designed to protect only the roosts (particularly of geese). During the 1970s and 1980s the acceleration of habitat losses, primarily through reclamation for agriculture or industrial development but also through proposals for water storage or tidal power generation, led to the concentration of people's minds on the need to protect decreasing feeding areas as well. This has been tackled at various levels. Criteria were established to identify wetlands of international importance to waterfowl, usually linked to the number of birds which a site regularly supports. This in turn has led to international conventions and directives, such as the Ramsar Convention 1971 (Ramsar Sites) and the European Community Directive on the Conservation of Wild Birds 1979 (Special Protection Areas) with signatory governments (including that of the United Kingdom) undertaking to take special care to safeguard these sites from harmful development. In Great Britain the notification procedures for Sites of Special Scientific Interest (SSSIs), introduced through the *Wildlife and Countryside Act 1981*, provided the Nature Conservancy Council (NCC) with a mechanism for scrutinising activities potentially damaging to these and regionally important wildfowl sites. In Northern Ireland, Areas of Special Scientific Interest (ASSIs), under the *Conservation and*

Amenity Lands (Northern Ireland) Order 1985, have the same purpose, through the auspices of the Department of the Environment (Northern Ireland).

PRESENT-DAY TRENDS

However, the most dramatic effects have been brought about by the upsurge of public interest over the last two decades in conservation and activities such as birdwatching. This has led to the growth of membership and political influence of the voluntary conservation bodies such as the Royal Society for the Protection of Birds (RSPB), the Wildfowl Trust and the Wildlife Trusts. Between them these groups now manage, and in many cases own, many tens of thousands of hectares of wetland reserves with importance for wildfowl. Indeed, their sites hold double the number of wildfowl (excluding migratory geese other than brent) supported on national nature reserves (Owen, Atkinson-Willes and Salmon, 1986).

How then does this situation measure against the objectives set in the 1960s? As for the aim of maintaining stocks, the wildfowl counts show that this has been more than achieved in the last twenty years. The safeguarding of wildfowl sites has no doubt had a major part to play in this. But what of the balance between the requirements of the birds and those of their 'users', both naturalist (for watching) and wildfowler (for harvesting)?

Using figures in *Wildfowl in Great Britain* (1986) it is interesting to note that nearly 42 % of wildfowl (excluding migratory geese other than brent) recorded at peak counts in 1981–2 were found in statutory and voluntary body reserves or refuges, the majority of which are unshot. This demonstrates the large increase in wildfowl reserves of one type or another over the last twenty years (see maps opposite). With the formation of refuges continuing apace, there is perhaps a need to ensure that the necessary 'balance' alluded to above is not overlooked. Not least of the potential problems is that of attracting large numbers of birds to 'honeypot' refuges. While these sites can provide dramatic, but localised, birdwatching opportunities they can also result in a redistribution of birds at local, regional and even national levels, thus decreasing wildfowling opportunities in the 'catchment' areas. The concentration of large

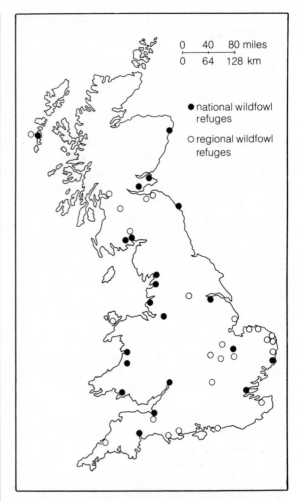

FIGURE 33 *National and regional wildfowl refuges established by 1966 under the joint Nature Conservancy, Wildfowl Trust and WAGBI wildfowl conservation policy (from* The New Wildfowler *in the 1970s)*

sections of populations on a small number of sites could also increase the risk of catastrophic losses by a pollution incident or possibly disease. The conservation interest of formerly inhabited sites may decrease, thus lessening arguments against harmful development.

The distribution and location of refuges themselves obviously becomes a key consideration. We need a far better understanding of factors, both natural and man-induced, affecting wildfowl distribution within and between sites and this is the subject of research currently being undertaken by the Wildfowl Trust and B.A.S.C. Perhaps, ultimately, we need to decide what wildfowl population levels we should seek. This would enable us

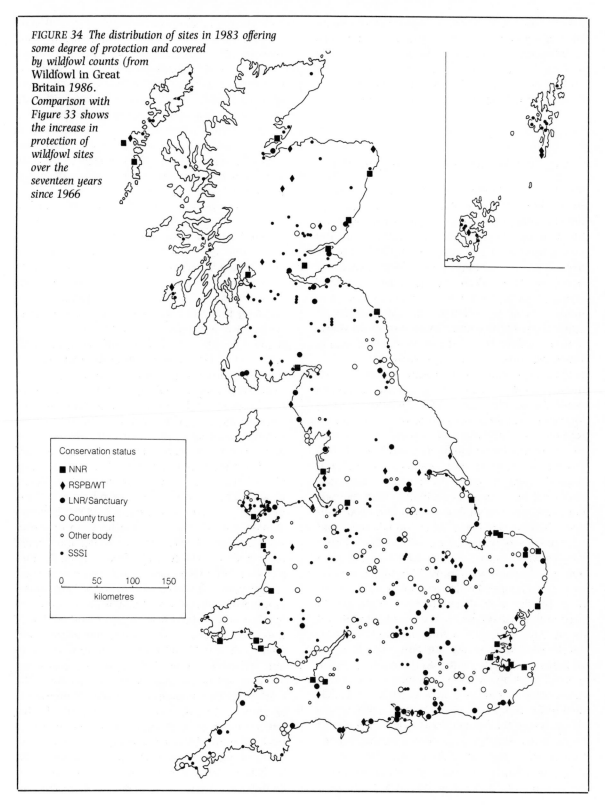

FIGURE 34 *The distribution of sites in 1983 offering some degree of protection and covered by wildfowl counts (from* Wildfowl in Great Britain 1986. *Comparison with Figure 33 shows the increase in protection of wildfowl sites over the seventeen years since 1966*

Conservation status

■ NNR
◆ RSPB/WT
● LNR/Sanctuary
○ County trust
· Other body
· SSSI

0   50   100   150
kilometres

to devise more integrated management strategies, both nationally and at estuary and wetland level, enabling agreement to be reached on the location and positioning of shot and unshot land to the mutual advantage of all user interests while also meeting real wildfowl conservation needs.

THE WILDFOWLING CLUB SYSTEM

We have seen how wildfowlers were involved in the setting up of the refuge network, but this was not the only initiative being pursued in the early 1950s and 1960s. With the increased mobility and lifting of the austerity measures at the end of the Second World War many people were attracted to marsh and foreshore to take advantage of the 'free' shooting there. As a result, it became more and more difficult to reconcile the old 'free-for-all' approach with the maintenance of wildfowl stocks and the enjoyment of the sport of wildfowling. Unsportsmanlike shooters demonstrated that they could make conditions unpleasant or at times even intolerable for others, and gave rise to abuses which harmed the good name of wildfowling and increased calls for greater protectionist measures. Responsible wildfowlers recognised this serious threat to their long-term interests and the trend of forming wildfowling clubs gathered momentum with the aim of acquiring sporting rights and imposing self-regulation. Initially, such actions gave rise to considerable suspicion and opposition from those used to being able to go wherever and do whatever they wished on saltmarsh and mud flats. However, once it became clear that the main aim was to control improper shooting practices, these actions gained wide acceptance and support. Since the first club affiliations to WAGBI, a well-tried and tested system for the establishment and day-to-day running of a shooting club has been developed and there are currently 382 B.A.S.C. affiliated clubs in the United Kingdom, with in the order of 200 being wildfowling clubs. In fact, there are very few wildfowling clubs which are not affiliated to the B.A.S.C. A situation now exists where shooting over the great majority of wildfowl sites in England and Wales and Northern Ireland is controlled either through wildfowling clubs or reserves or refuges. On the few remaining areas action is already in hand by the B.A.S.C. and local

clubs. In Scotland, the public right of recreation on the foreshore means clubs cannot directly hold sporting rights over such areas. However, much progress has been made through the formation of shooting schemes within national and local nature reserves and others will no doubt follow, although only on the basis of full consultation and trust between wildfowlers and conservation bodies. Viewed against the problems of the 1950s and 1960s this regulation of wildfowling by clubs has in itself been, and remains, an immense contribution to wildfowl conservation.

The club system has also provided a medium for other conservation efforts. Again in 1954, WAGBI embarked on the ringing and release of hand-reared mallard as its first concerted conservation effort. The idea was to encourage an interest in conservation in every wildfowler in order to answer those critics who were constantly proclaiming that the wildfowler never attempted to replace any of his quarry, and to augment native mallard populations. The scheme ran until 1977, with over 15,000 birds being released annually at its peak. Other schemes also involved wildfowlers in redistributing Canada geese (taking this work over from the Wildfowl Trust) and extending the range of the greylag goose in the United Kingdom through translocations. Many of the flocks of greylag now to be seen throughout the country are the direct result of this latter scheme, which was phased out in the early 1970s, it having achieved its goal. The success of the duck releasing scheme in adding to wild populations is more doubtful. While some returns from abroad were recorded, such as mallard released near Newmarket being recovered at Verkhayaya-Tayma, Russia, the majority of birds remained in the vicinity of their release point. However, in retrospect this was not as important as the educational aspect. As the late Jeffery Harrison recorded in the second edition of this book: 'Logically the conversion of the wildfowler into a wildfowler-conservationist followed, and in human terms this has been the greatest achievement of the mallard-rearing scheme. The need for his club to manage a reserve, to improve it by planting suitable food and cover plants for his duck, leads to an appreciation of similar efforts by his local naturalists and so on up the scale to the chain of national wildfowl refuges established by the Nature Conservancy.' The wildfowler thus saw for himself the importance of habitat management.

THE MANAGEMENT OF CLUB LAND AND RESERVES

This interest was nurtured by WAGBI adopting a policy that each of its affiliated clubs should come to manage its own local reserve, on which to carry out a full programme of conservation. Clubs were also encouraged to co-operate with any other naturalist organisation in similar enterprises. In order to develop and illustrate the main principles of reserve management, the WAGBI Sevenoaks Gravel Pit Reserve was established and managed in co-operation with the Wildfowl Trust as an experimental reserve for breeding and wintering wildfowl and waders. While firing the enthusiasm of wildfowling clubs, the Sevenoaks Reserve also pioneered work in habitat creation on newly formed wetlands and provided the impetus for many others to experiment with planting programmes on other sites. Today, the reserve is managed by the Jeffery Harrison Memorial Trust. It maintains close links with the B.A.S.C. and boasts a full-time warden and interpretative centre. The latter provides an important educational facility, particularly for local schools.

By the late 1970s wildfowlers and indeed the shooting community as a whole had firmly come to realise that they had a crucial role in ensuring the future of the countryside. In 1978, with the continuing loss of wildlife habitats causing growing concern, the B.A.S.C.'s conservation work developed a step further with the establishment of a Habitat Conservation Programme. It had become apparent that the reserves established by B.A.S.C. members varied greatly in their value, and that the nature conservation needs of other land managed by members should be taken more fully into account. Thus the programme came to have the objective of ensuring, as far as possible, that all land under the influence of B.A.S.C. members was managed in a way that improved not only its shooting interest but also its intrinsic nature conservation value.

To achieve these aims one of the first tasks was to establish comprehensive records on the conservation value of particular sites, together with their current management, future needs and available management resources. This was achieved through a comprehensive survey of B.A.S.C.-affiliated club land, financially assisted by the Nature Conservancy Council in recognition that suitable management of the considerable areas of countryside under the influence of the B.A.S.C. membership would lead to a valuable strengthening of the country's biological stocks – both flora and fauna. This study showed that in England alone a total of over 104,500 hectares of land was under the management influence of B.A.S.C.-affiliated clubs (more than any other conservation organisation), with approaching 70% being designated as SSSIs (some 98% if only coastal wetland is considered).

This land data base is being continually added to and updated and has proved invaluable when advising on management and when liaising with conservation bodies. This is particularly so in the case of SSSIs, where, under the *Wildlife and Countryside Act*, wildfowling clubs (as site owners or occupiers) have an obligation to discuss their site management with the NCC. It is reassuring to note that in the great majority of cases the NCC has simply consented existing club management, thus endorsing its compatibility with the nature conservation interests.

The increasing complexity of the conservation world and our increasing knowledge of wildlife and its management means that the wildfowler must also look towards a more sophisticated and co-ordinated management of his activities. Thus, in recent years an increasing number of clubs, with the assistance of the B.A.S.C., have prepared and adopted management plans clearly setting out management objectives (both for shooting and conservation) and how these are achieved. These plans are used by individual clubs to review their current policies and prove invaluable when consulting other bodies. One of the B.A.S.C.'s objectives is that every club operating on an SSSI or other area of nature conservation value should do so under a management plan.

A B.A.S.C. DEMONSTRATION PROJECT – LLYN YSTUMLLYN

Such careful planning can result in management improving both shooting opportunities and nature conservation interests. In order to demonstrate this integration of interests to mutual benefit, the B.A.S.C. has developed a demonstration project on a 240-hectare site comprising a freshwater marsh SSSI and adjoining scrub and woodland at Llyn

187

The reinstatement of open water at Llyn Ystumllyn SSSI – the B.A.S.C.'s blueprint for integrated management for shooting and nature conservation

Ystumllyn, Gwynedd, North Wales. In the 1940s Llyn Ystumllyn could well have claimed to be one of the most important sites in Wales for breeding and wintering water birds. At the time, the site comprised two large water bodies divided by a low island and fringed with varied and extensive beds of marginal aquatic vegetation. Records of bittern, garganey and shoveler exist during the breeding season, while in winter the site harboured large numbers of wigeon, teal, mallard and shoveler. Whitefronted geese and whooper swans were also regular visitors. It was these large wildfowl populations which gave Llyn Ystumllyn its fame as one of the best duck shoots in North Wales. However, in the 1950s an agricultural reclamation scheme lowered the outfall of the lake, resulting in the almost complete drainage of the site.

A number of schemes designed to reinstate the wetland habitat were considered over the next twenty years, but without success, and it was with the wish to see the site managed to improve its sporting interest as well as to protect and enhance its remaining and still valuable conservation value that the owner of the majority of the site approached the B.A.S.C.. Following extensive survey work, the B.A.S.C. was able to identify those parts of the site of greatest conservation interest and management potential. With assistance from the NCC it proved possible to arrive at agreements with the landowner and farming tenants granting the necessary management rights and responsibilities to the B.A.S.C. This set the scene for the establishment of new water control regimes. Through the provision of feeder ditches and sluices (grant aided by the NCC and constructed by B.A.S.C. conservation volunteers) an area of nearly two hectares can now be kept flooded during the crucial spring and early summer. The results have been encouraging with the return of species which would formerly have inhabited the original lakes and wetlands. In the first year, nesting heron returned to the site, while numbers of breeding teal, snipe and curlew increased. In the second year a pair of shoveler gave the first breeding record of this species for at least nine years. In 1987, as a European Year of the Environment project, the Welsh Water Authority excavated deeper water areas to diversify the habitats and help guard against summer droughts. Islands provide safe nesting sites and loafing areas. Other work is aimed at creating 'swamp' habitat of shallow water, reed bed, islands and willow scrub, providing secure and secluded sites for duck and other species such as the secretive water rail and grasshopper warbler. Other pools will invigorate the existing reed beds, hopefully attracting reed warbler and bearded tits.

The management described is also of benefit to the sporting interests of the site. Shooting for duck and snipe on the marsh and pheasant and woodcock on the adjoining scrub and woodland is undertaken by the owner according to a carefully planned and agreed programme. Thus, Llyn Ystumllyn represents a modern, practical blueprint as to how nature conservation, shooting and indeed farming can be integrated at site level, and the experience gained has already not only benefitted B.A.S.C. members but also other conservation bodies and land-managing agencies from home and abroad. Llyn Ystumllyn has shown the benefits of the co-operation and partnership approach, not least between the B.A.S.C. and NCC, in achieving current nature conservation aims while providing excellent sporting opportunity. This principle is now being extended to projects at wildfowling club level.

LAND PURCHASE AND PROTECTION

The potential for such management obviously increases when clubs have secure tenure over land. In this respect, it is most encouraging to record the steady increase of area of land under the ownership of wildfowling clubs. The setting up of club land purchase funds and the B.A.S.C.'s Wildlife Habitat Trust Fund, designed to provide loans for land purchase and management, will ensure that this trend continues. With land ownership comes increased management responsibilities and the associated need for dissemination and training of management techniques by the B.A.S.C. through courses, advisory literature and events such as the Wildfowling Conference, where club representatives are able to appraise each other of achievements and pitfalls.

But wildfowlers realise that managing their own sites is not enough as the health of wildfowl populations relies on the perpetuation of habitats throughout the locality or indeed their entire range. There have been many examples of wildfowling interests making strong representation against threats to important wetlands. This has included the proposed barrage schemes for the Wash and Morecambe Bay in the 1960s and 1970s, the threat of a refuse tip adjoining Bridgwater Bay

NNR in 1981 and the dumping of power station fly-ash on saltings in the Medway Estuary in the same year. Again, it was the local wildfowling club which played a major part in alerting the authorities to, and monitoring, the organic lead effluent pollution in the Mersey Estuary in 1979 and 1980. More recent concerns have been the barrage proposals for tidal power generation on the Severn and Mersey estuaries. On these and other sites, participation of wildfowling groups and the B.A.S.C. in local estuary conservation groups ensures a co-ordinated approach. Such 'liaison' groups, many instigated by the B.A.S.C., also have a valuable role to play in increasing understanding and trust between shooting and conservation interests, leading to more co-operation and more efficient site management.

A CASE STUDY – THE RIBBLE ESTUARY

I would like to round off this chapter with a brief account of one particular site which puts into context many of the points which have been mentioned.

The Ribble Estuary in Lancashire is of international importance for birds. The mudflats support one of the biggest wintering and passage populations of wading birds in Britain, while the saltmarshes support the largest wintering population of pinkfooted geese in England, together with notable populations of wigeon, mallard, teal and pintail. The estuary is an SSSI and qualifies as a Ramsar Site and SPA.

Of the wildfowling interests, the Southport and District Wildfowlers' Association (SDWA) was one of the first wildfowling clubs to be formed in this country. In addition to controlling its own shooting from an early date, the club pressed for the establishment of the Southport Sanctuary in 1956 to protect the pinkfooted goose roost. The sanctuary is still managed by a committee comprising wildfowlers and naturalists. This strengthens the integration of the management of the sanctuary and the shooting permit scheme administered by the club on adjoining land.

In the face of a reclamation scheme which resulted in a major public outcry, the NCC purchased 2200 hectares of saltmarsh and mud at Banks Marsh on the south side of the estuary in 1979. This was later declared a national nature reserve. The shooting over this area had been held by the SDWA for a number of years and the NCC inherited the benefits of habitat improvement conducted by the club, mainly in the form of created and improved wet flashes on the marsh. Wildfowling has continued under an NCC licence to the club which provides for a central refuge area. This, coupled with careful management of grazing, has increased the number of wildfowl using the area. In December 1987 a record count of 35,000 was recorded for wigeon on the Ribble Estuary. The NCC reserve warden is assisted in running the shooting scheme by the SDWA wardens, who also help out with other management tasks. This contribution has been enhanced by the B.A.S.C. and NCC running a training scheme for club wardens.

To the north and east of Banks Marsh, two other wildfowling clubs, the Preston and District Wildfowlers' Association (PDWA) and the Lytham and District Wildfowlers' Association (LDWA), respectively, have managed sporting rights since the early 1960s. Each manages its own unshot refuge. The PDWA's refuge comprises both tidal and freshwater marsh. On the latter a planting programme of marginal aquatic species has been undertaken based on recommendations from both B.A.S.C. and NCC and attracts numerous wintering birds. On Warton Marsh the LDWA have enhanced the area's conservation value by maintaining summer water levels in the flashes by pumping.

In recognition of the considerable overlap between the shooting and nature conservation interests on the Ribble and working closely with the three wildfowling clubs, the B.A.S.C. prepared a consultative document for the estuary in 1980. This reviewed the situation on the estuary and proposed the formation of a liaison group to bring the two interests closer together. The aims of the liaison group were stated as:

(a) to promote the informal exchange of views and information between the wildfowling and nature conservation interests on the Ribble Estuary;

(b) to promote the successful integration of wildfowling with nature conservation requirements, thereby preserving the tradition of wildfowling and ensuring reasonable provision for its continuation in the future;

(c) to promote the sound management of the wildfowl of the Ribble Estuary as a whole.

The first meeting was held in April 1981 with the group comprising representatives from each of the wildfowling clubs together with those from the B.A.S.C., the NCC, the Wildfowl Trust (there being considerable interaction between the wildfowl of the Ribble and those of the Trust's Martin Mere reserve) and the Southport Sanctuary Committee. Representatives also attend from the various local authorities, who own much of the land in the estuary. The B.A.S.C. provides the secretariat, organises meetings and co-ordinates information as appropriate. Meeting twice a year, the committee provides a valuable forum for open and frank discussion and assists in the development of a greater mutual understanding between the different interests on this internationally important wetland. This has resulted in a greater co-ordination of information gathering, such as wildfowl counts. A co-ordinated approach on threats such as marina proposals and other potentially harmful developments has also been possible.

The situation on the Ribble and elsewhere paves the way for the future. It illustrates how wildfowling interests have adapted to changing priorities. Further, that despite the increasing complexity and sophistication of the conservation world, wildfowlers still have a unique part to play in wetland conservation, not least through their great practical knowledge and management influence over extensive areas. Assisted and guided by the B.A.S.C., wildfowlers will continue to meet this challenge.

REFERENCES

Atkinson-Willes, G. L. (Ed.), 1963. *Wildfowl in Great Britain*. Monographs of the Nature Conservancy Council, 1st edition. HMSO.

Harrison, J., 1967. *Wealth of Wildfowl*. Corgi.

Nicholson, E. M., 1970. 'National Wildfowl Refuges' in *The New Wildfowler in the 1970s*, 2nd edition. Barrie and Jenkins.

Owen, M., Atkinson-Willes, G. L., and Salmon, D. G. 1986. *Wildfowl in Great Britain*. 2nd edition. Cambridge University Press.

Sedgwick, N. M., Whitaker, P., and Harrison, J., 1970. *The New Wildfowler in the 1970s*, 2nd edition. Barrie and Jenkins.

22

WILDFOWLING ON NATURE RESERVES

TONY LAWS AND RICK GOATER

It is often forgotten that many of the country's longest-established and most prestigious nature reserves and wildfowl refuges would not have come about, or at least their conception would have been considerably delayed, had it not been for the initiative and support of wildfowlers.

This is well illustrated by the Lindisfarne National Nature Reserve in Northumberland. In August 1960 the Northumberland and Durham Wildfowlers' Association drew the attention of the Nature Conservancy (now the Nature Conservancy Council) to the great increase in uncontrolled and often indiscriminate shooting in the Holy Island area and asked that consideration be given to the establishment of a wildfowl refuge. This was followed up in 1961 by a similar and independent request from local naturalists. Following discussions with the wildfowlers, naturalists and local landowners it was decided that the Nature Conservancy should combine the proposals by establishing a National Nature Reserve and National Wildfowl Refuge. The reserve was declared in 1964. To this day its management programme provides for the traditional sport of wildfowling to continue over part of the area, where shooting is controlled by a permit system. The remainder of the reserve consists of sanctuary zones where no shooting is allowed. A wildfowl panel which includes representation from local wildfowlers, B.A.S.C. and local naturalists advises the Nature Conservancy Council (NCC) on matters relating to the conservation of wildfowl in the reserve.

A similar story lies behind other sites, including the Humber Wildfowl Refuge and Southport and Wyre Lune Sanctuaries, established to provide protection to goose roosts, and the Local Nature Reserves (LNRs) at Breydon Water (Norfolk), Montrose Basin (Tayside, Scotland) and Traeth Lafan (Gwynedd, Wales).

Many of these, and others, were established as part of the wildfowl refuge system resulting from the wildfowl conservation policy, established in 1960 by the Wildfowl Conservation Committee (Nature Conservancy, WAGBI and Wildfowl Trust). This established an integrated approach, making provision for refuge areas to act as 'wildfowl reservoirs' for the benefit of wildfowler and naturalist alike, as well as areas within reserves for responsible wildfowlers to continue their sport. Whilst the need for the establishment of reserves and refuges primarily to control shooting has declined, not least due to regulation brought about by the growth of the wildfowling club system, the commitment and contribution of wildfowlers to the management of such wildfowl reserves continues into the present day. In 1987, B.A.S.C. affiliated clubs had management interests in 47 reserves and refuges of importance for wildfowl in Scotland, England, Wales and Northern Ireland. These comprised: 13 National Nature Reserves (NNRs), 10 Local Nature Reserves (LNRs), 3 Statutory Wildfowl Sanctuaries, 13 Conservation Trust reserves and 7 Royal Society for the Protection of Birds (RSPB) reserves and the Strangford Lough Wildlife Scheme in Northern Ireland.

The sharing of expertise and knowledge by shooting clubs and other conservation bodies to increase the effectiveness of site management remains a common theme. For example, the sporting rights over the foreshore in the Teign Estuary in Devon are jointly held by the Devon Trust for Nature Conservation and the Devon Wildfowlers' Association, with an agreed scheme for the regulation of shooting within the estuary, including the designation of shooting and refuge zones. A similar joining of forces was undertaken at Broomhill Flash near Wombwell, Barnsley, in South Yorkshire. This small 8-hectare site comprises open water created by mining subsidence surrounded by rough grassland, and has become an important local ornithological site attracting significant numbers of wading and other water birds. Discussions between the Wombwell Gun Club, the farming tenant and the Yorkshire Naturalists' Trust showed a common concern for, and approach to, problems of disturbance, poaching and vandalism on the site. Improved management was brought about by a scheme whereby the site is shot by the club to agreed levels while co-operative management is effected by means of a joint management committee.

The wildfowlers' contribution extends to practical site management. Coastal reserves consisting of wide expanses of saltmarsh and mudflats are notoriously difficult to warden effectively. Controlled shooting by a wildfowling club can greatly increase the wardening coverage. In a number of cases clubs also have responsibilities for wardening designated unshot refuges within a reserve. A notable example is the comprehensive wardening scheme operated by the Langstone and District Wildfowling and Conservation Association on the

RSPB reserve at Langstone Harbour. On the Ribble Marshes NNR, a team of wardens from the Southport and District Wildfowlers' Association has been formed to assist the NCC warden, with candidates attending a training course organised in conjunction with the B.A.S.C. Nor are such activities confined to the shooting season. At Colne Point NNR in Essex the Braintree Wildfowling and Gun Club have assisted with the wardening of vulnerable little tern colonies during the nesting season.

Turning to habitat management, notable examples of tasks in which wildfowling clubs have been involved include maintenance work on tern colony islands in Nutbourne Marshes LNR, the construction of tern nesting platforms at Breydon Water LNR and of wildfowl nesting and roosting rafts at Rutland Water by the Leicestershire Wildfowlers' Association. The latter use is an example of work on a site where no shooting interests exist. The wildfowlers concerned were simply wishing to employ usefully a considerable interest in, and commitment to, practical conservation.

Finally, wildfowling clubs are also involved in the important interpretative and educational role of reserves. At Pagham Harbour LNR, the local wildfowling club have set up their own interpretative centre in an old 'salt house' renovated by the club with considerable effort and at their own expense. Elsewhere, such as at Breydon LNR and Colne Point NNR, wildfowlers have provided the labour for the construction of birdwatching hides.

Against this national background of considerable involvement of wildfowlers in the management of wildfowl reserves and refuges, the remainder of the chapter deals with one particular case study at Montrose Basin LNR. This reserve is an excellent example of the integrated approach to wildfowling and conservation through provision of controlled wildfowling consistent with local conservation needs.

MONTROSE BASIN LOCAL NATURE RESERVE

The South Esk is one of several short rivers draining the western Angus glens. It flows east across fertile Strathmore, through the city of Brechin and reaches the North Sea at Montrose. The Burgh of Montrose is built on a broad sand and clay spit which constricts the estuary of the South Esk, creating an almost circular tidal area, the river leaving it in a channel little wider than the one entering it. This is the Montrose Basin, today a Local Nature Reserve (LNR) administered by Angus District Council (ADC). The management of the LNR is undertaken by the area's major landowner, the Scottish Wildlife Trust (SWT), acting as agent for ADC. The SWT employs a full-time ranger/naturalist there.

Traditionally the Basin has played host to a multitude of largely recreational activities. Apart from being a favourite haunt of walkers and birdwatchers, it caters for Montrose Sailing Club, Montrose Angling Club, bait-diggers, wildfowlers and the commercial interests of Joseph Johnston and Sons, salmon and mussel fishers.

The reserve covers a little over 1000 hectares, of which 800 are tidal mud and sand flats. The river meanders close to the southern shore and a dendritic pattern of lesser channels dissects the main part of the Basin. Most of the area is firm underfoot, just one or two places near the main channel being responsible for the odd lost boot.

At the western end of the reserve, the remaining 200 hectares are a mixture of habitats. Here, land was reclaimed from the estuary in the middle of the nineteenth century and many of the areas called 'sea greens' on the old maps are now medium-quality arable land or wet permanent pasture. Only a narrow strip of saltmarsh remains, bordering the seaward edge of the floodbanks.

Two small reedbeds exist in low-lying sections of this part of the reserve and mark ancient courses of the river. A series of brackish pools adds to the mix of habitats, which has proved attractive to thousands of wetland birds for centuries. The mud of the Basin is extremely rich in invertebrate life, providing food for very large numbers of waders such as oystercatcher, curlew, knot and redshank. In summer the surface turns green with a lush growth of algae and eel grass (*Zostera*), fed upon by a flock of up to 300 moulting mute swans in July and August. The first of nearly 5000 wigeon to arrive in autumn also feed heavily on the vegetation until frosts and rough weather kill it off and wash it to the shore.

The expansive flats are ideal roosting grounds for the wintering pinkfooted geese which flight to and from the cereal and grass fields between Dundee and Aberdeen. In recent times over 12,000 birds have been counted leaving the Basin on October and November morning flights. This is approaching 70% of Iceland's breeding pinkfoot population, the whole of which winters in Britain. It may be that a much larger percentage of the population regularly uses the Basin but that food shortages force birds to move on quickly. In 1987, when stubbles were left unploughed owing to a very wet autumn, food for geese was very plentiful and numbers roosting on the Basin rose to over 35,000. It is easily the Basin's most important species, but just one of eight species for which the area can claim national or international importance.

Wildfowling has been a major part of life on the Montrose Basin for hundreds of years. As early as the thirteenth century the king, when based in Forfar, had his own fowler, who lived at and took the name of Foullerton. Fullerton Farm lies less than a mile to the south of the Basin.

Of course, most of the area comes under the designation 'foreshore', which in Scotland is that land between the high- and low-water marks of ordinary spring tides. As such, until the bye-laws

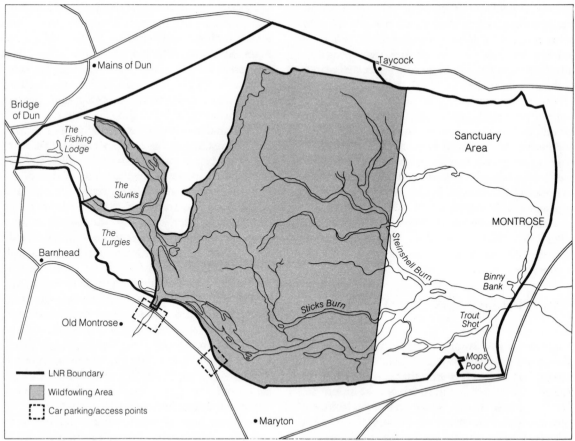

Figure 35 The Montrose Basin

controlling activities on the LNR were confirmed by the Secretary of State for Scotland, the public had a general right to shoot on the Basin. This is the case irrespective of ownership. Although much of the Scottish foreshore still belongs to the Crown, the ownership of many areas, including Montrose Basin, has long since passed into private hands.

The majority of the Basin belonged to an important local family, the Erskines of Dun, until 1976, when it was sold to the Scottish Wildlife Trust. Despite this, certain rights were still held by the Crown for the public and these included wildfowling.

Although there are few reliable records of goose counts on the Montrose Basin before the Second World War, it is clear from what little is written, and from the memories of locals alive at the time, that the roost was of considerable importance, with pinkfeet numbering several thousands, particularly during spring and autumn passage.

In the early 1950s, when he was in the district netting and ringing pinkfeet, Peter Scott counted 4000–5000 using the Basin. It has been suggested that the publicity attached to the ringing programme may have been the root cause of the birds' subsequent decline there, for wildfowlers, many from northern England, were alerted to the potential of the Montrose Basin, and increasing numbers travelled north for the next three decades to benefit from the free foreshore shooting which they were unable to enjoy in the South.

During this period, the pinkfeet roosting on the Basin could be numbered in hundreds only, the peaks in spring and autumn rarely reaching 1500. Members of the local wildfowling club, Montrose and District Wildfowlers' Association (MDWA), witnessed with growing concern the overshooting of their patch. No part of the estuary was left undisturbed. As the years went by, fowling on the Basin became an uncontrolled free-for-all. Protected species were shot, there was shooting from small boats, shooting throughout the night at wildfowl silhouetted by the lights of the town and even shooting out of season.

Something had to be done to solve this problem on safety grounds if for no other reason. Throughout the 1960s and early 1970s informal discussions were held between MDWA, the Nature Conservancy, Angus District Council and the SWT. Even in those early days the Club was pressing for the creation of an LNR with a permit system for wildfowling and a no-shooting sanctuary zone where the geese could roost in peace. The situation was complex as several landowners were involved with the Basin. Possibly because the MDWA was not one of them, agreement was not reached. No solution to the problem seemed to be forthcoming.

Then in 1976 the saltmarsh and mudflats of the Basin owned by the Erskine family were offered to the SWT for the creation of a nature reserve, and the Trust, aided by a grant of £5000 from the World Wildlife Fund, did not hesitate to buy. Many Montrosians wondered what value there was in '1800 acres of stinking mud', but those were less enlightened times. Immediately the MDWA had an ally – the major landowner on the Basin.

In May of that year the Angus and Dundee Branch of the SWT wrote to ADC asking that it exercise powers conferred on it by the *National Parks and Access to the Countryside Act 1949* and declare Montrose Basin a Local Nature Reserve, promulgating bye-laws for its protection. So began four years of negotiations between conservation bodies, relevant landowners and all parties with an interest in, on or by the Basin.

Most of the hard work was done by The Montrose Basin LNR Working Party – a committee of SWT, NCC and ADC representatives who, for the success of their mission, relied upon initial personal and informal discussions with everybody involved.

During this time the interest of British Petroleum plc was attracted by the exciting potential of the plans for the Montrose Basin and to date, since 1980, the company has annually donated a grant large enough to enable the SWT to employ a ranger/naturalist there. With a man on the ground, the activities of the Working Party were enhanced. The boundaries were negotiated and management policies drawn up. Draft bye-laws were produced, advertised and agreed upon. The LNR was statutorily declared in June 1981 and the bye-laws submitted first to the Crown Estate, then

to the Secretary of State for Scotland for confirmation. This occurred in June 1982. Thus was formed an LNR which included not only SWT land but ground and rights belonging to several private farmers as well as major landowners such as the National Trust for Scotland, ADC, Prudential Assurance Company, South Esk Estates and Joseph Johnston and Sons.

The Working Party, its goal achieved, was disbanded, but committees had already been formed to run the reserve. A Reserve Management Committee comprising representatives of the NCC, NTS, SWT, ADC, WAGBI (as it was then called) and MDWA was to manage the reserve through the ranger/naturalist to provide, preserve and enhance, under suitable conditions and control, opportunities for the study of the flora, fauna and geographical and physiographical features of special interest. In addition it was to offer the public, subject to appropriate conditions and control, sporting and related activities not prejudicial to the purposes of the nature reserve.

To further these objectives a Consultative Committee was formed to represent parties having an interest in the Basin and to pass observations and recommendations to the Reserve Committee. This committee approved two sub-committees dealing with scientific research and planning on the one hand and wildfowling on the other. A working group of the Wildfowling Sub-committee was to formulate a system to control shooting within the LNR.

In order to have some data on which to base such a system, the newly appointed ranger/naturalist observed fowling activity on the Basin throughout the 1980–1 season and produced a report for the Working Group, which then gave recommendations to the Reserve Committee. As might be expected, shooting pressure was found to be heaviest from late November until the end of the season and the concentration of people on the mudflats at evening flight was often enough to prevent the incoming geese roosting there at all. Even when the birds could settle to roost they were likely to be put to flight again by late wildfowlers approaching them too closely.

Very few days saw no shooting on the Basin and Saturdays were by far the busiest. Sunday shooting, against the law in Scotland, was noted a few times. Over ten access points to the area were used, and though most wildfowlers took up position by as direct a route as possible, some wandered a great deal, disturbing, in particular, the estuary's wading birds. Individuals would walk around the Basin perimeter during the day, causing considerable disturbance to high-tide roosts. Frequent shooting out of range and poorly controlled dogs added to the unsatisfactory state of affairs.

On the strength of these findings a method of wildfowling control, based on that used by the NCC at Caerlaverock National Nature Reserve on the Solway, was introduced as soon as the bye-laws became effective. The first season of operation was 1982–3. It was felt that the system should bring about a fall in the number of shooters on the Basin at any one time. The eastern end of the mudflats (a little under half the total area) which included the major goose roosting site was declared a no-shooting sanctuary zone and marked on the ground by a series of posts running north–south across the flats. Entry by wildfowlers to this area is forbidden except for the retrieval of shot birds by a person who has left his gun within the shooting zone. Legal access points were reduced to three at the western end. This allows for ease of monitoring by the ranger/naturalist and helps keep people away from the sanctuary zone.

Shooting is allowed only by permits, of which there are two types: seasonal and short period or temporary. A total of ninety permits covering the whole season is available to locals – persons living within the boundaries of Angus District and residents of South Kincardineshire within fifteen miles of the centre of Montrose. Forty are sent to MDWA linked with the condition that the Association provide voluntary wardens when required by the ranger/naturalist.

The remaining fifty are available to any local (including MDWA members who fail to receive one of the block allocation) on a first-come first-served basis. An additional six honorary seasonal permits are issued to landowners, tenants and commercial interests within the LNR.

Temporary permits are available at a rate of five per weekday on a first-come, first-served basis, but with non-locals being given preference over locals. The rationale behind excluding Saturdays is that Saturday was traditionally the day of heaviest wildfowling activity and this measure was necessary to even out pressure. Visitors may have temporary permits for up to five consecutive days but no more than that number within any two-

week period. A maximum of twenty-five permit days can be issued to any visitor during a single season. These stipulations prevent unscrupulous locals who have failed to obtain a seasonal permit booking up long periods in an indirect way.

Wildfowling is limited to six hours each day: between one hour before and two hours after sunrise and between similar hours around sunset. Reasonable walk-on and walk-off time is permitted and is now accepted as being about half an hour. So on a day when sunrise is at 08.38 hrs, fowlers may start walking to position at 07.08 hrs. These rules ensure that disturbance during daylight is kept to an acceptable minimum and the hours usually coincide with maximum flighting by wildfowl to the Basin.

Permits are issued by ADC. Wildfowling arrangements for the reserve and invitations for permit applications are advertised in national sporting journals and the local press during June each year. The deadline for seasonal permit applications is usually 15 July, but temporary permit applications are accepted throughout the season. In practice, all but a few days are taken up well before 1 September.

After 15 July all seasonal permit applications are passed to the Wildfowling Sub-committee, vetted and returned to ADC. Successful applicants receive their permits before 20 August. The number of applicants usually nearly equals the permits available, so few locals are disappointed. A local blacklist does exist; persons on it are unlikely to acquire permits. Wildfowlers on the B.A.S.C. blacklist and those without a shotgun certificate or third party insurance are unable to shoot on the LNR. When permits are sent out they are accompanied by copies of the bye-laws and 'notes for wildfowlers', which explain the set-up on the Basin and encourage sensible behaviour on the reserve.

The permit itself is a 12 in. × 6 in. waterproof card, folded to a pocket-sized 6 in. × 4 in. On one side is printed the dates and hours for which it is valid, the fact that only shotguns up to a maximum size of 4-bore may be used and that the use of decoys, calls and dogs is permitted. The latter are encouraged as those wildfowlers using a well-trained dog lose many fewer birds and cause far less disturbance than individuals rushing all over the place after injured geese because they are without a dog. A map of the LNR showing access points and the wildfowling area is included.

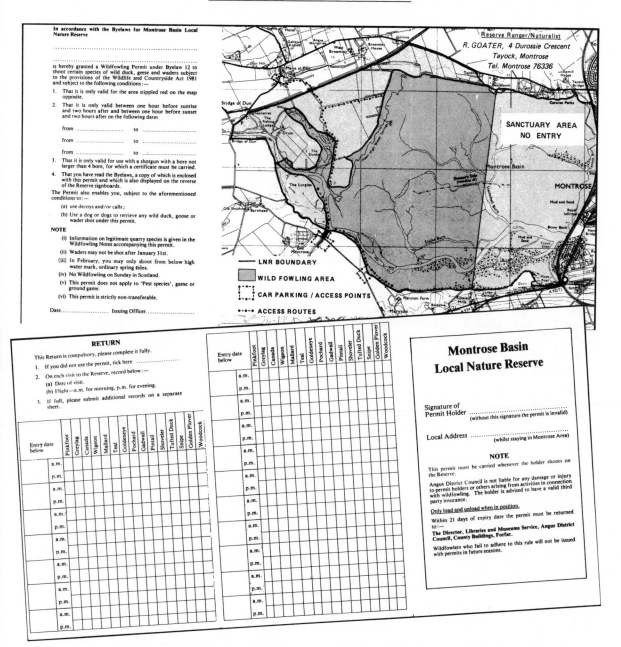

An example of the permit needed before you can shoot on the Montrose Basin

On the other side of the permit is a return listing legitimate quarry species with spaces for the holder to fill in dates when the permit was used and his successes and failures. Within 21 days of the expiry date, permits must be sent back to ADC. From the return the ranger/naturalist compiles a report on the past season which is discussed by the Wildfowling Sub-committee and any changes to the system which seem necessary after these deliberations are put to the Reserve Committee.

Administrative costs are involved and for the first few seasons these were met by ADC and all permits were free of charge. Today only the block allocation to MDWA is free and all other permits cost £4.00. When the principle of charging was introduced it met with some opposition from locals, who had always enjoyed free foreshore shooting. The response by visitors from England, however, was that it was well worth the money – a minute sum to pay for such good sport.

The desired reduction in numbers shooting on the Basin was achieved. A reasonable maximum carrying capacity was reckoned to be about twenty guns and this is very close to the figure reached on the busiest days. On most flights the numbers are far lower. It is possible that the very small charge for permits has indirectly reduced pressure in the Basin further. Only 40% of temporary permit days allocated are actually used and it is assumed that holders of these permits consider it no great loss if weather or commitments prevent them visiting the Basin.

The first few seasons after the introduction of the system saw some problems, caused mostly by non-locals visiting the area 'on spec'. Recognised access points were not used and some shooting occurred during the wrong hours and sometimes within the sanctuary zone. A strong presence established by the ranger/naturalist with the help of volunteers from MDWA soon rendered such activity rare indeed.

The beneficial effects of the rules covering wildfowling are manifold. Permit holders, and particularly members of the Association, have developed a pride in the LNR and the wildfowling set-up, which ensures that they warden the area subconsciously while they themselves are shooting. Unsporting behaviour, not necessarily observed or even under the jurisdiction of the ranger/naturalist, can be most effectively brought to the attention of the malefactor without delay.

The standard of etiquette on the Montrose Basin is now very high and it is therefore a much safer place to shoot than it was a few years ago. No individual wishes to jeopardise his future permit applications by not following the rules of the game. Other users of the Basin, particularly birdwatchers and walkers, now know when and where to expect guns and generally avoid the shooting area within season around dawn and dusk except on Sundays.

In many people's minds the concept of increasing numbers of birds together with thriving wildfowling is a paradox, but this is the situation which the Basin can boast today. Over 40,000 wildfowl and waders now regularly use the estuary in winter. This is double the totals achieved throughout the 1960s and 1970s. Because of its extreme importance for migrants passing through in spring and autumn, the total number of birds relying on the Basin's well-being is truly enormous. That the area can also cope with various operations of man reflects well on the enlightened management policies of the Reserve Committee. Nature conservation is of prime importance, but by limiting certain activities in time, space and magnitude, many potentially conflicting demands on the Montrose Basin are reconciled and wildlife emerges the winner.

The management of the wildfowling illustrates this well. The table below shows that the total number of birds shot remains broadly similar each season but that the four main quarry species on the estuary have increased. Numbers of wildfowl and shooting pressure are nicely balanced, the result being that each season over two hundred fowlers experience some of the best wildfowling in Scotland while their resource flourishes.

The table also shows well the situation of the greylag goose at Montrose. In the days of the decline of the pinkfoot, the grey was the major quarry species of the two. Numbers roosting on the Basin have remained stable and are dependent largely on the weather. When favoured freshwater roosts inland are frozen, the geese tend to use the estuary, preferring the far western end, where they spend the nights on the flunks and its shingle islands.

The birds' predilection for a freshwater roost site, where in this case wildfowlers can reach them far more easily than they can the mudflat-loving pinkfeet, results in a much greater proportion of

Numbers and major species shot on the Montrose Basin. Figures in brackets are peak counts for each season

Season	Total shot	Pinkfoot	Greylag	Wigeon	Mallard
1982–3	1255	182 (6000)	394 (1350)	357 (3860)	219 (393)
1983–4	1417	257 (9500)	331 (1600)	384 (3400)	305 (851)
1984–5	1152	247 (9500)	161 (1600)	327 (4426)	283 (1023)
1985–6	1403	323 (12,000)	307 (1500)	348 (4500)	329 (1534)

the Basin-using greylags being shot than of the pinkfeet. Because the greylag tends to be a cold-weather bird on the Basin, Statutory Wildfowling Suspensions relating to prolonged freezing conditions can markedly reduce the season's bag of this species, as can be seen from the 1984–5 figure.

The Montrose Basin is protected by not only being an LNR but also a Site of Special Scientific Interest under the *Wildlife and Countryside Act 1981*. In many similar situations the laws and bye-laws based on these designations are hopelessly difficult to enforce. The key to the success of operations on the Basin is the ranger/naturalist, who liaises with all parties in the reserve and patrols frequently. Any illegal dumping, effluent disposal, shooting, sailboarding, etc,. is prevented or discovered immediately and the police or NCC alerted.

There is never a shortage of volunteers to carry out management work such as tree planting, litter clearing along the tideline, and path making. Members of MDWA have not only helped with these tasks but have played a large part in creating a car park and tree nursery. This is in addition to more formal and invaluable wildfowling wardening. Volunteer wardens are under the direction of the ranger/naturalist and are issued with written authority by the Reserve Committee. When on duty they do not carry a firearm and their tasks are similar to those carried out by the ranger/naturalist during wildfowling hours. Permits are checked or bona fide individuals recognised by their faces or cars. Unfamiliar vehicles are checked against a list of expected cars.

Wardens ensure that nobody gains an unfair advantage by walking-on too early and they listen for shots fired outside the permitted hours. It is ensured that the sanctuary zone remains undisturbed and that only the correct access points are used. All of the reserve's entry points have a notice board on which are displayed a map of the site, bye-laws and general information. Sunrise and sunset times are posted at the wildfowling entry points, so there is no excuse for shooting at the wrong time.

When the permits are returned, the entries on them can be verified by what the ranger/naturalist and wardens noted during the season. Sometimes the returns do not tally – every year a number of fowlers claim they were shooting on a Sunday. This is typical of the sort of problem arising when returns are filled in several days after the event. Individuals not using their permits are less likely to receive one the following season and this has led to some false claims in the past where a fowler has insisted he was on the Basin when the ranger/naturalist knew very well that he was not. False claimants and owners of unreturned permits may not be able to shoot on the reserve the following year.

Such problems are rare and apart from minor grumbles from individuals who always think the past was better, the Basin and its wildfowling system have received nothing but praise. It is gratifying to hear visitors to the Basin saying how much things have improved and locals saying how much better behaved the visitors are than they used to be! Many groups and individuals have given time, money and expertise to the Montrose Basin LNR and in so doing made it such a fine example of collaborative conservation. It is easy to forget the far-off days when the Montrose and District Wildfowlers' Association was a lone voice crying in the wilderness.

23
SITE MANAGEMENT BY B.A.S.C. CLUBS

PETER MAYHEW

The most fundamental asset of all wildfowling clubs is the land on which they carry out their sport, for without well-managed land there would be no birds and no fowling. In days gone by, when wildfowlers were virtually the only folk to venture beyond the sea wall in winter, ownership or management of the land was almost irrelevant. Wildfowling was 'free' for all to enjoy. Today, however, the conservationist and developer, yachtsman and walker all have their eyes on coastal land and wildfowling can only be carried out in relation to these other land interests. Moreover, if the security of the club on that land is not strong, the wildfowler will soon be ousted by these, often stronger, interests. Thus the recent concern amongst wildfowling clubs for purchasing the freehold of coastal mudflat and saltmarsh.

While some will regret the passing of the 'good old days', the current situation has much to recommend it. Clubs think much more about their land. In many cases it is the main thing that holds them together. They are concerned about its proper management, both for shooting and conservation. They monitor what goes on and how it could be improved for fowler and birder alike. Finally, there is a recognition of the need to plan the management which is required on club land. More and more clubs are using management plans, which set out in black and white a description of the site, the objectives of the club for their land and exactly how those objectives are going to be achieved, whether through changes in shooting regime or new habitat management schemes.

However, probably the most important benefit of a club's interest in, and care for, its fowling land is that it shows that wildfowlers can look after their own affairs. Local regulation of shooting in a responsible manner reduces the possibility of calls for national controls. It allows sensitive, well-founded adjustments to management to be formulated and put into practice by the club itself, rather than blunderbuss regulations being imposed from above. For this reason alone, all clubs need to become keen site managers and to learn how to manage not only their shooting but also the habitats on which it depends.

MANAGEMENT OF SHOOTING

Shooting men have recognised for centuries that their sport needs to be regulated, if it is to be sustainable. This applies particularly to wildfowl, which tend to be sensitive to excessive disturbance. Wildfowlers have often been at the forefront of setting up national or local wildfowl reserves (Chapter 22). What is often not recognised is that most wildfowling clubs carefully regulate the shooting on their own land. This is done through a variety of mechanisms.

The establishment of unshot refuges is probably the most important method available to clubs for managing shooting on their land. These disturbance-free areas tend to ensure that birds do not move off elsewhere, but remain in that particular locality. Traditionally they covered roosting sites, particularly goose roosts on sandflats, but today feeding areas such as saltmarshes, wader roosts and suchlike may also be included. The size, extent and positioning of refuges on club land tend to be dependent on the number of statutory or voluntary conservation body reserves in that area, i.e. club refuges will be extensive if the general locality contains few non-club refuges, and vice versa. Notable examples of club refuges over saltmarsh are the unshot saltings at Skegness, held under lease by the Skegness, Wainfleet and District Wildfowlers' Club, and part of Terrington Marsh, managed by the Fenland Wildfowlers' Association. In Northern Ireland, the Dundrum Inner Bay Wildfowling and Conservation Club have created a refuge area around an important wader roost in the Inner Bay, whilst in Cumbria, the Westmorland Wildfowlers' Association manage the mudflats on part of the River Kent as an unshot goose roost. It should be remembered that refuges can also be created through time limits on shooting. For example, on the Camel Estuary in Cornwall, the Cornwall Association for Shooting and Conservation restrict their shooting to three days per week in order to reduce disturbance levels on the estuary.

There are a number of other ways in which clubs regulate the shooting on their marshes. Related to the above, some clubs restrict shooting to a certain part of the day, e.g. dawn and dusk flighting or, during the night, to the full moon period only. Again, this is designed to provide undisturbed feeding times, particularly for night-feeding wildfowl and wader species. All clubs control the number of members within the club, the maximum figure normally being dependent upon the amount of wildfowling land available to the club. In large clubs, with small fowling sites, very often a permit system is used to ensure that these sites are not overshot, e.g. the Kent Wildfowling and Conservation Association (Chapter 11). On sites which consistently hold large numbers of

birds, bag limits are often imposed to ensure that stocks are not overshot. Finally, on some sites, club members are forbidden from shooting certain wildfowl species, normally because of their small populations in that locality. For example, the clubs shooting on the Dovey Estuary do not shoot the small population of Greenland whitefronted geese that winter in West Wales.

A criticism often levelled at wildfowling in the days of 'free' shooting was that irresponsible or even illegal shooting was all too common on the foreshore. Witnesses recorded incidents of out-of-range shooting, shooting of protected species and so on. On club-managed land, however, such incidents are very rare. All clubs exercise strict control on applicants for membership. Some require prospective members to have completed the B.A.S.C.'s Proficiency Award Scheme, which gives basic instruction to new shooters. Once in membership, many clubs have a continuing education programme, which ensures high standards of proficiency, quarry identification and safety.

Effective wardening is an essential requirement of successful shooting regulation. It is, therefore, one of the most universal forms of management undertaken on club sites. It ensures that no unauthorised persons shoot on the club's land,

Members of Chichester Harbour Wildfowlers' Association clearing a reed bed in Stansted Lake, West Sussex. The reeds in this badly overgrown and silted lake were too soft to take a tracked digger in safety, so the work is being done with silage knives and other hand tools (D. T. Frost)

that no illegal or irresponsible behaviour takes place and that refuge areas remain as such. In most cases, all members act as wardens when shooting on club sites and are empowered to approach any person shooting to check they are a club member or guest. Many clubs also operate a more formal system involving nominated voluntary wardens, mainly at weekends. This is particularly found where permit schemes allow visitors to shoot on club marshes. Such work is often undertaken through a rota system – indeed wardening may be a condition of membership. Where clubs control a number of sites, individual site wardens may be appointed with responsibility for issuing shooting permits, recording bag returns and undertaking general wardening duties.

An increasing interest amongst wildfowling clubs is research and monitoring on their land.

Wildfowlers are often in the best position to carry out certain types of research work, since they are regularly on the marsh and also since they collect an annual 'sample' of wildfowl which can be weighed, measured, eviscerated or whatever. Moreover, successful management of shooting or habitats at a local level can only be undertaken in the light of research into bird numbers, distribution, shooting levels, etc., on that site. This is distinct from the contributions by many club wildfowlers throughout the country to national research projects such as the National Shooting Survey. Clubs need to know what is going on on their land. Thus, some clubs carry out regular bird counts on their marshes. Many clubs now request their members to complete bag returns in order to build up a picture of the total harvest of wildfowl from the club's marshes each winter. For example, a sophisticated bag return system has been run by the Langstone and District Wildfowlers' and Conservation Association for many years and this has been invaluable in discussions on the management of the harbour with other interested parties. In the long term, it may be possible to relate these figures to local wildfowl populations, although bird turn-over (i.e. the fact that individual birds are constantly moving into, and away from, a particular site) is a big problem in this respect. Some clubs request details of all fowling visits made – this gives a precise picture of annual marsh usage. Clearly there is always a danger of surrounding members with too much red tape. However, a balance must be struck if wildfowling research is not to become the prerogative of non-wildfowling organisations.

HABITAT MANAGEMENT

Twenty years ago most wildfowling clubs thought of conservation as primarily duck rearing and ringing. The protection of the land on which wildfowl lived tended to play second fiddle. While the former activities helped to increase local stocks and taught us much about wildfowl movements, today it is recognised that the most pressing need in wildfowl conservation is for habitat protection and correct management.

Many clubs now have a conservation officer heading a team of enthusiastic volunteers who carry out projects ranging from pond cleaning to saltmarsh mowing. These projects are not only of practical benefit to wildlife (quarry and non-quarry alike) but also of tremendous public relations value. The wildfowling club is seen as a positive force for local conservation, rather than an unidentified group of gunmen.

Getting club members involved in conservation work can be difficult. Members often take a while to recognise not only the importance of, but also the enjoyment to be had from, habitat management. Normally, though, a few enthusiasts will be found. More comprehensive schemes may require more organisation to get sufficient labour. One club runs a points system whereby different management tasks carry different numbers of points. A member's points total for the year determines the amount of shooting to which he is entitled during the season. Other clubs waive part of the membership fee in lieu of labour provided. One club, which manages about fourteen sites, recruits labour with military precision. Each site has a manager who is responsible for general wardening, monitoring and small management tasks. Major work is undertaken by club work parties. On average there are three work parties per year for each site, which works out at 43 man days per year per site.

Funds for habitat management are sometimes short. Club subscriptions are often related simply to paying sporting rents and little else. However, more clubs are recognising that funds must be actively sought for this type of work.

B.A.S.C. CLUB PROJECTS

Coastal mud and sand flats would, at first glance, seem to offer little scope for habitat work. Few plants remain rooted in this harsh regime. One plant which does survive is also of great importance for grazing wildfowl, primarily brent geese and wigeon. Eel grass or *Zostera* was originally found in most muddy estuaries. However, in the 1930s, a 'wasting disease' caused its rapid decline. While it has recovered to a certain extent in some estuaries, it remains absent or significantly reduced in many. In the mid-1970s the River Orwell Sporting and Conservation Club observed that the wigeon on the Orwell Estuary were short of feeding sites. The *Zostera* had declined and the saltmarsh was in poor shape. An enthusiastic member saw the potential for a conservation project and organised a *Zostera* transplanting scheme. The work was undertaken by the junior club members, who cut *Zostera* turves from a point farther up the estuary and transported them by rowing boat to the planting site. The choice of site was of critical importance. Many attempts at transplanting have ended with the turves simply being washed away in a strong current. The Orwell Club were, therefore, careful to choose a site where sediment was being deposited rather than eroded. They also placed the turves in groups of four – surrounding a central sheltered area. This acted as a nutrient settling zone, encouraging the turves to root once again. The work was carried out over several March weekends, when the summer growth of the *Zostera* was just starting. Today wigeon can be watched, feeding on the new *Zostera* beds.

Further up the coast, on Breydon Water, the Great Yarmouth and District Wildfowlers' Association have, over a number of years, been heavily involved in the habitat management on this local nature reserve. Cord grass, *Spartina anglica*, is a major problem on many estuaries. This vigorous hybrid has invaded many mudflats and salt-marshes and severely reduced wader and wildfowl feeding areas. Where it has gained a significant hold, the only answer is herbicide spraying as is done on some major coastal reserves. However, where it is only starting to arrive, it is possible to carefully dig up individual plants and remove all fragments as and when they appear. The club have assisted *Spartina* control groups each year to try to prevent this plant becoming established on the flats.

On some estuaries saltmarshes provide essential feeding areas for grazing wildfowl. In the past, these coastal grasslands provided good summer stock grazing for local farmers. Today, however, cattle and sheep numbers have greatly decreased in many parts of lowland Britain, particularly in the east. The saltmarsh grasses have consequently become much ranker and less palatable to wildfowl. On some marshes, cattle have been imported from far afield to restore former grazing levels. A simpler method, if the necessary machinery can be got onto the marsh, is to cut the grass in mid-summer using a gang-mower. This technique has been used successfully by the Dee Wildfowlers' Club for a number of years. They were concerned that the grasses of the extensive Dee saltmarshes were becoming unpalatable to wigeon because of undergrazing. For about two weeks each July they hire a tractor and gang-mower and cut round the main wigeon flashes – to a distance of about 20 m. They also dam certain flashes to ensure that some water remains on the marsh (which is slowly drying out). This type of management has been carried out on both shot and refuge areas, and provides favoured feeding sites for the wigeon.

Islands are very valuable in open estuaries since they provide safe roosts for waders and undisturbed nesting sites for terns. Certain species of the latter have become very rare on British coasts due, in many cases, to disturbance by beach walkers. Unfortunately, shingle islands, which are ideal for terns, are rather rare. On Breydon Water, the local club has, along with local naturalists, constructed common tern nesting platforms. These raft-like structures are anchored to the estuary bed and provide ideal, undisturbed nesting sites. On other estuaries, where saltmarsh islands provide high-tide wader roosts, clubs have been involved in erosion protection schemes using groynes and other structures to prolong the life of these fragile islands.

One outstanding example of coastal site management by a wildfowling club has been the creation of the Moulton Marsh Nature Reserve, by the Spalding and District Wildfowlers' Association, in conjunction with South Lincolnshire Nature Reserves Ltd. For a number of years, the club had kept a linear saltmarsh at the mouth of the River Welland as an unshot area. At the instigation of an enthusiastic committee member, a 21-year lease of the site was negotiated. Talks with the Internal Drainage Board and the Water Authority, who were working on the sea wall along the site anyway, led to the creation of an area of lagoons, scrapes and islands. A system to control water levels on the site was also installed. Wildfowlers, a Manpower Services Commission task force and the local authority have been involved in tree planting on adjoining areas and planting of aquatic reeds, etc., on the site itself. Regular monitoring of the

Members of Chichester Harbour Wildfowlers Association repairing a long stretch of sea wall at Fishbourne in Chichester harbour to protect neighbouring wetland habitats (D. T. Frost)

wildlife on the reserve is carried out, with 90 different species of bird recorded to date. Finally, the site is seen as an important educational resource for conservation and two birdwatching hides have been constructed. Probably the keynote to the success of this project has been the close co-operation between conservationists, wildfowlers and public authorities.

While coastal habitat management is still at the heart of wildfowling club conservation work, increasing attention is being paid to inland wetlands. This reflects the fact that inland sites often offer more scope for intensive habitat work. Moreover, while they have always been important for breeding birds, wintering wildfowl are increasingly tending to use inland wetlands.

One well-known example of inland habitat management is the comprehensive scheme run by the Chichester Harbour Wildfowlers' Association. The club's conservation committee, comprising 30 members, controls the management of 14 small wetlands in West Sussex. The sites, which include village ponds and other locally important inland wetlands, are held under management agreements negotiated with the aid of an outline management plan. Management tasks have included island construction, restoration of derelict ponds, reed cutting, mink control, etc. More recently, efforts have concentrated on wildlife and management recording schemes, allowing annual reports to be produced. The club uses this work to promote the whole concept of shooting and conservation by mounting exhibitions at various local venues and giving illustrated talks to community groups. In recognition of their conservation work, the Countryside Committee of West Sussex County Council presented their annual Conservation Award to the club in 1979.

Farther north, the Leicestershire Wildfowlers' Association have a very active conservation section. For a number of years the club had contacts with a local school – Grace Dieu. Within the grounds of the school was an interesting boggy area which attracted a few snipe and duck. After discussions with the school authorities, it was agreed that the club should take over the management of this site. A plan was drawn up after site visits by B.A.S.C. staff, which concentrated on creating attractive feeding habitat for wintering snipe, mainly by manipulating grazing levels. Improvements for breeding habitat were also suggested. One of the best aspects of this site is that the school pupils are fully involved in the monitoring and management of the bog. The club has now extended its conservation work and negotiated a lease on a 40-acre gravel pit. Again, a management plan has been drawn up with B.A.S.C. assistance and improvements to its wildfowl breeding and wintering capacity are being considered.

Finally, mention should be made of the work of the Holderness and Humber Wildfowlers' Association on Fisherman's Channel. This old estuarine creek, which was cut off from the Humber Estuary many years ago due to a large-scale drainage scheme, now acts as a freshwater haven for wildlife in a desert of intensive agriculture. Primarily because of its winter wildfowl numbers, the NCC have designated it as a Site of Special Scientific Interest. Along with the South Holderness Countryside Society, the club has been monitoring bird numbers through the year. Management proposals to improve the habitat for wintering and breeding birds have been drawn up with help from the B.A.S.C. and it is likely that the two organisations will obtain rights over the site so as to manage it as a nature reserve.

Local site management has, therefore, come a long way since the last edition of this book. Clubs throughout the country are recognising that they must be able to show they can manage land effectively, not just for their sport but for all the wildlife and other interest on their land. Dependent on this is not only the future of wildfowl stocks, but of wildfowling as a sport.

24

NATIONAL WILDFOWL COUNTS

DAVID G. SALMON

The National Wildfowl Counts must represent one of the most remarkable examples of sustained co-ordinated fieldwork by amateur ornithologists in the world. The aim of the counts is to cover as many localities in the UK, coastal and inland, as possible once in each winter month from September to March. All the swans, geese and duck are included, together with great crested and little grebe, coot and cormorant. The scheme was launched in 1947 by the International Wildfowl Inquiry Committee, forebear of the present International Waterfowl and Wetlands Research Bureau (IWRB). The Wildfowl Trust took over responsibility in 1954 and George Atkinson-Willes, who organised the counts from 1952 to 1983, moved to Slimbridge. By the early 1960s more than 2000 sites had been covered at some time, although the average number of counts received was 500–600 in each month. Then in the mid-1960s an International Wildfowl Count scheme was set up by the IWRB at Slimbridge, also co-ordinated by George Atkinson-Willes, aiming to cover the whole of the Western Palearctic in January each year, and in some years in November or March. When this began, with the first full survey in 1967, there was a major impetus to increase the coverage in Britain; the number of counts made in January rose to 1100–1300, and in other months to 700–900. Following further efforts, the number of sites visited in a season had risen to 2000 by 1985–6, with 1700 in January and 1200–1300 in other months. By 1986, nearly 5000 waters had been covered at some time since 1960 – comprising 2100 natural or ornamental lakes, 600 reservoirs, 400 mineral workings and 700 freshwater marshes or lengths of river, plus virtually all estuaries and bays and many stretches of open coast. More than 1500 individual counters are involved. Despite an increasing proportion of professional input, as many of the most important areas have become reserves, the vast majority of counters are still amateurs operating in their own time and at their own expense. Even the Regional Organisers, who are responsible for a major part of the organisation, are almost all amateurs, and are highly experienced field ornithologists closely involved with their county or area societies.

From their onset the organisation of the counts has been funded by the Nature Conservancy, now the Nature Conservancy Council (NCC), who require the information for the formulation of sound national policies of wildfowl and wetland conservation. The data are used to estimate the population levels of each species, detect trends in their numbers and assess the relative importance of individual resorts, enabling the identification of Internationally and Nationally Important sites under the agreed criteria, and thereby the designation of Sites of Special Scientific Interest, Ramsar Sites and EEC Special Protection Areas on the grounds of their importance for wildfowl. The counts are in constant demand to provide evidence against threatened development of important areas, and have also formed a baseline for numerous applied studies, on such topics as population dynamics (e.g. Hill, 1982), the effects of recreational activities on wildfowl populations (e.g. Tuite, 1982), and the importance of man-made habitats (Owen, 1983).

A further boost to the count coverage occurred in 1969, when the British Trust for Ornithology (BTO), NCC/Royal Society for the Protection of Birds (RSPB), Birds of Estuaries Enquiry was launched (Prater, 1981; Salmon et al. 1987). The Enquiry, though concentrating mainly on waders, includes all birds on estuaries by means of monthly

counts organised in a similar way to the wildfowl counts. Many previously uncounted areas have been included. The wildfowl data from the Enquiry have been made available at all times to the Wildfowl Trust (which co-sponsored the scheme for some years).

Figure 36 shows the extent of coverage of Britain's 10 km grid squares by wildfowl counts between the 1960–1 and 1985–6 seasons. (In Northern Ireland the major estuaries and the principal inland area – Lough Neagh – have been counted regularly and efforts are now under way to increase the coverage.) A dot is placed in the square if a count was made there at least once during this period. Where a square has not been covered, a triangle indicates that it contains land above 500 m altitude and an open square that it has no standing water over 0.5 hectares (ha) in extent. In both these cases the area is relatively unlikely to be important for wintering wildfowl.

The advent of the International Wildfowl Counts made the UK figures, which include only part of most regional populations and flyways, much more meaningful. Not only is it possible to gauge the importance of this country as a wintering area for the different species but individual sites can also be assessed in an international context. The coverage of international counts in north-west Europe, the Mediterranean and North Africa has been remarkably good, with 16,800 sites visited in January at least once between 1967 and 1983 (Rüger et al. 1986).

The monthly UK counts received at Slimbridge used to be transcribed from the original forms into ledgers. Hand analysis of the whole of the data was too laborious, so the assessment of trends from year to year was made using a sample of some 200 so-called Priority Sites. Results from these were returned during the winter, trends were assessed for the commoner species by comparison with numbers counted in a 'master' year, and each

counter received a two-page report within a month or two. Although most major concentrations were included in the Priority Counts, the index proved to be a rather variable estimator of trends. Since the Priority Scheme was also rather costly, it came to an end in 1979–80.

Between 1978 and 1980 all the post-1960 counts were entered into the Wildfowl Trust's newly acquired computer. Since then the data have been processed within a few months of the end of each season, and analyses are made for every species, incorporating all sites. Each counter, as well as major organisations such as the NCC, RSPB and British Association for Shooting and Conservation (B.A.S.C.), now receives a 50–60-page annual booklet, *Wildfowl and Wader Counts* (e.g. Salmon *et al.* 1987) published under contract to NCC, which includes the report on the wader counts organised by the BTO through the Birds of Estuaries Enquiry.

Because of their locations or habits some species pose severe problems for regular counting and attempts are made to supplement the standard monthly counts by special surveys. In particular, certain of the geese and swans are usually away from their estuarine or lake roost sites during the day and are frequently missed. Annual censuses of roosts and feeding grounds are therefore undertaken, either by or in conjunction with the Wildfowl Trust, for pinkfooted and greylag geese in the autumn, Greenland whitefronted geese in the autumn and spring, and darkbellied brent geese in December and January (Ogilvie, 1986a; Ogilvie & Boyd, 1976; Stroud, 1984). Periodical surveys of whooper swans in autumn or winter, and mute swans and Canada geese in summer (when assessment of the population is easiest), have also been carried out (Ogilvie, 1976, 1986b; Salmon & Black, 1986).

Barnacle geese are counted monthly in their principal and highly localised winter resorts on the Solway and Islay, but the remainder of the Greenland population, scattered over Ireland and the Hebrides, is censused only occasionally from the air (Ogilvie, 1983).

Sea duck, especially the scoters and longtailed duck, pose special problems in that they are not easily counted from the shore. In addition to the

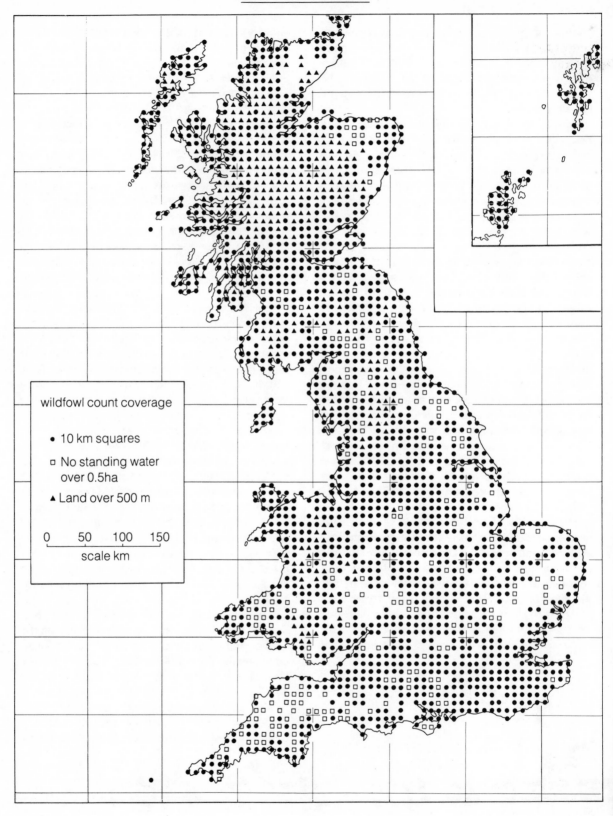

wildfowl count coverage

• 10 km squares

□ No standing water
  over 0.5ha

▲ Land over 500 m

0   50   100   150
        scale km

FIGURE 36 (left) *Coverage of 10km squares in Great Britain by National Wildfowl Counts (updated from Owen et al, 1986; data on standing water from Sharrock, 1976)*

standard counts, boat and aerial surveys have been carried out in northern Scotland by the RSPB and the University of Aberdeen in conjunction with oil companies, and large concentrations have occasionally been located elsewhere (e.g. Carmarthen Bay). It is very likely, however, that there are many flocks, especially off the west coast, which have never been found. The Wildfowl Trust would like to see the survey work expanded to gain a better idea of the national and international populations of these highly vulnerable species.

Regular counts in summer have not been attempted, but a special survey of breeding duck was carried out in the late 1960s (Yarker & Atkinson-Willes, 1972). The BTO's first Breeding Atlas (Sharrock, 1976) was much more comprehensive but not quantitative. A combination of Atlas data with the autumn counts of the most important breeding species has provided an estimate of populations which was better than achieved previously (Owen *et al.* 1986). A sample survey was carried out in 1980 on inland waters as part of a study of the effects of recreational activity, but this did not provide data on national totals. However, a comparison of matched waters with the 1960s indicated increasing trends in most species (Tuite & Owen, 1984), an impression confirmed by many disparate sources, and more intensive work on our breeding populations is planned by the Wildfowl Trust. There are relatively few large concentrations of moulting wildfowl in the UK, but attention is being focused increasingly on the late summer period, particularly with the ever growing demand for water-based recreational facilities. A July/August count in 1985 covered over a thousand waters (Salmon *et al.* 1987), and further surveys may be arranged at least in some areas.

Two massive reviews of the results of the wildfowl counts – entitled *Wildfowl in Great Britain* – have been produced by the Wildfowl Trust's research team, covering the period up to the early 1960s (Atkinson-Willes, 1963) and from 1960 to the early 1980s (Owen *et al.* 1986). These comprise detailed reviews of the numbers of wildfowl recorded in England, Scotland and Wales, both region by region and species by species, and of such subjects as ringing, agriculture, threats to wetlands, the practice and effects of wildfowling, other forms of recreation, the creation of reserves and pollution. An even more expansive review was possible in the 1986 edition than its predecessor, thanks to the great increase in the coverage of counts and other studies – and the advent of the computer age!

ACCURACY AND REPRESENTATIVENESS OF THE COUNTS

Wildfowl counters are experienced ornithologists, many of whom have been involved with bird surveys for a long time. A test of accuracy involving 117 observers of varying experience estimating numbers in photographed goose flocks showed that substantial errors were made even by experienced counters. Since there was no consistent bias, however, errors tended to cancel each other out, and the mean of all counts was within 10 % of the true figure (Matthews, 1960). These observers were asked to make their estimates within 30 seconds and would not be able to make repeat counts as under most field conditions. Another test on counts of waders (Prater, 1979) showed that there was consistent bias, with most observers overestimating numbers when these were small and underestimating large flocks. In another comparison of counts with photographs, underestimating error even with very large wader flocks averaged only 5 % for experienced observers (Hale, 1974).

These tests would tend to exaggerate the errors under most conditions, since birds are difficult to count on photographs in 30 seconds, the time allowed. In the field, many observers make several counts, from different viewpoints or over a period of two or three hours. We can say with some confidence, therefore, that the wildfowl counts provide us with a reasonably accurate picture of numbers and distribution. Where there are errors, numbers are likely to have been underestimated.

It is impossible using volunteers to make very frequent counts on a regular basis, but a test using almost daily counts for three years at Durleigh Reservoir, Somerset, showed that the numbers of wildfowl varied considerably over a monthly period and the counts made on the set monthly dates deviated by up to 50 % from the average for the whole month (Matthews, 1960). The deviation varied with the species, being high for mobile species such as pochard (51 %) and low for the more sedentary ones such as tufted duck (25 %) and mute swan (13 %). However, over a long series of counts fluctuations cancelled each other out and averages gave a good indication of the importance of the site. Most of the fluctuations were short term, so that for most species fortnightly results were no less variable than monthly ones. Even with weekly counts the numbers of mallard and tufted duck remained variable. Much of the variation was removed when adjacent waters were combined, indicating that local movements were partly responsible.

To gain an idea of turnover, i.e. the number of individual birds passing through a site or area, it is necessary to examine the basic counts in relation to such aspects as regional trends, sex ratios, ringing returns, recognition and/or colour marking of individual birds and bag sizes. This has been done on a national scale for wigeon, resulting in an estimate that at least 50 % more 'use' Britain between September and March than are present at any one time (Owen & Mitchell, 1988), and on a local scale for Bewick's swans, the long-term study by the Wildfowl Trust at Slimbridge showing that 60 % more pass through the site in a winter than occur at peak (E. C. Rees). The published estimates of the British populations relate to the peak numbers present *at any one time*. For some species, such as non-migratory ones or those with discrete wintering populations using Britain and not moving on (e.g. most of the geese), these estimates should also reflect the total number of individuals using the country as a whole.

INDIVIDUAL SPECIES ANALYSES

Included in the second edition of *Wildfowl in Great Britain* (Owen *et al.* 1986) are analyses of the trends in numbers of each species, based on the results of the National Wildfowl Counts. Examples of the trend graphs for January are now shown (updated to 1985–6) for four quarry species: European whitefronted goose, wigeon, mallard and pochard.

The trends are expressed by means of index values, calculated by comparing the totals from sites covered in consecutive years. 1970–1 was arbitrarily chosen as the 'anchor' for the indices,

which were obtained by working backwards or forwards from that season (=100) and applying the ratios between the consecutive years' totals to the index for the previous (after 1970–1) or subsequent (before 1970–1) season. This method allows for fluctuations in the count coverage, and gives all years equal weight. (On average 80–90 % of the wildfowl counted in any one year are included in the paired comparisons.)

The graph for the European whitefronted goose (Figure 37) shows a peak period around 1970, when 11,000–13,000 were counted in Britain, coinciding with a run of very good breeding seasons and moderately hard winters. In the mid-1970s the level declined to below that of the early 1960s, and apart from an influx in the cold winter of 1978–9, the numbers have remained remarkably constant, at 5000–6000, though with a hint of a recovery in recent years. In comparison, the numbers in the Netherlands rose dramatically to an average peak of over 250,000 between 1979–80 and 1983–4 (Ebbinge *et al.* 1986).

The trend for wigeon (Figure 38) clearly shows

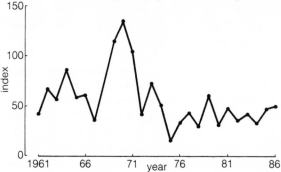

FIGURE 37 *Trend indices for European whitefronted geese in Britain in January, 1961 to 1986, based on 1971 = 100*

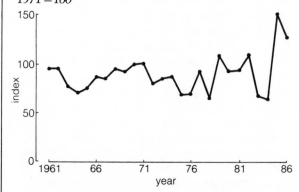

FIGURE 38 *Trend indices for wigeon in Britain in January, 1961 to 1986, based on 1971 = 100*

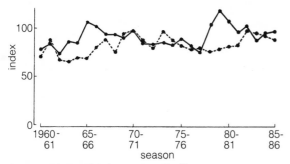

FIGURE 39 *Trend indices for mallard in Britain in September and January, 1960–61 to 1985–86, based on 1970–71 = 100*

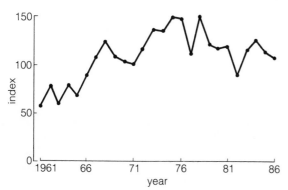

FIGURE 40 *Trend indices for pochard in Britain, 1960–61 to 1985–86; average indices for December and January (based on 1970–71 = 100), to even out irregular movement patterns*

the influxes which occur from the Continent in most hard winters. In the January with the lowest index, 1978 (before the cold snap of February 1978), 114,000 were counted in Britain, in 1985 a remarkable 320,000. Intriguingly, a year later, after a prolonged mild spell, the numbers were not much lower, an example of a partial repetition of a previous winter's movements which is quite common. It is thought highly unlikely that large numbers of wigeon are missed in the counts, since they are highly concentrated on their favoured resorts. The estimated north-west European population in January, based on the results of the International Counts, is 750,000, with a uniform trend broken by reductions in hard winters, when there is a net loss as birds move south towards Mediterranean regions (Rüger *et al.* 1986).

For mallard (Figure 39) there is no discernible trend either in September (the post-breeding British stock) or January (the annual peak). Moreover, there is no correlation between the two indices; i.e. they vary quite independently of one another. This

is not surprising, since the January index includes immigrants, which also makes it much more variable than that of the British breeding population. The stability both of the post-breeding population in Britain and the mid-winter numbers in north-west Europe as a whole (Rüger *et al.* 1986) suggest that there are density-dependent factors operating to regulate the population. These can act in many ways on the productivity of the breeding stock. The main ones are through emigration from crowded areas, an increased proportion of non-breeders, and reduced hatching and rearing success through interference and competition in crowded habitats (Dzubin, 1969).

Evidence from North America indicates that although shooting may account for a relatively high proportion of the mallard population, below a threshold level (around 40%) it is compensated for by a lower natural mortality (Anderson & Burnham, 1976). Thus, provided shooting pressure is not excessive, it appears that our influence on the mallard population either through its mortality rate or its breeding output has hitherto been slight. So scattered are mallard over tiny, uncounted waters, that the number counted in Britain (150,000–200,000) is well below the actual peak winter population, estimated at 600,000–700,000 (Owen *et al.* 1986). Research by the B.A.S.C. suggests that 700,000 are shot annually (Harradine, 1985). Allowing for turnover, the fact that the birds are shot over a number of months and the large number of released birds which are not included in the estimate, these figures are not necessarily inconsistent.

Pochard (Figure 40) increased in Britain in the 1960s and early 1970s, but have declined in both Britain and Europe as a whole since then. The most spectacular change has been at Duddingston Loch, a small water in Edinburgh, where the numbers of roosting pochard rose to a remarkable 8000 in 1975, but have since declined to only a few hundred. The pochard fed in the nearby Firth of Forth, and these changes coincided with a similar pattern in the numbers of sea duck in that part of the firth. During the late 1970s the amount of raw sewage pumped into the firth from Edinburgh was reduced as treatment works were introduced. The outfalls had contained grain from local breweries and also attracted an abundance of invertebrates. The commencement of treatment is thought to have been the main cause for the decline in at least some of the wildfowl involved (Campbell, 1984). The total numbers of pochard in the remainder of Britain showed an almost identical trend, however, and it appears that Duddingston Loch was mirroring rather than governing the national picture. Pochard are certainly highly opportunistic birds, as shown by their sudden appearance on floodland when the level is right for feeding, or on the coast as inland waters freeze, yet they are declining on an international scale in the face of a continuing increase in suitable habitat, with the creation of further reservoirs and gravel pits, and a proliferation of one of their favourite invertebrate food items – the zebra mussel, *Dreissena polymorpha* – in Central Europe (Schifferli, 1983). Adverse factors may involve severe winters or problems on the breeding grounds (Rüger *et al.* 1986), while disturbance through man's recreational activities on artificial waters cannot be helping.

THE FUTURE

With roughly 100,000 individual counts available the possibilities for future analyses of the National Wildfowl Count data are virtually limitless. Work is currently concentrated on 'in-depth' reviews of particular species, further applied studies (on such aspects as disturbance and cold-weather movements) and the development of a Wetland Register for the UK. Meanwhile, as threats to wetlands and wildfowl populations seem if anything to accelerate, with numerous proposals for estuarine barrages, recreational facilities and reclamation projects, the monitoring process must continue, so that the up-to-date picture on all species and sites can be obtained, and the most powerful arguments in dealing with these threats be available.

REFERENCES

Anderson, D. R., & Burnham, K. P., 1976. *Population Ecology of the Mallard: V.* 'The effect of exploitation on survival, recovery and harvest rates'. US Dept. Interior Fish and Wildlife Service Resource Publ. *125*.

Atkinson-Willes, G. L. (ed.), 1963. *Wildfowl in Great Britain*. First Edition. Nature Conservancy Monograph No. 3. HMSO, London.

Campbell, L. H., 1984. 'The impact of changes in sewage treatment on seaducks wintering at Leith and Musselburgh, Scotland'. *Biol. Cons, 14.* 111–23.

Dzubin, A., 1969. *Assessing breeding populations of ducks by ground counts*. Canadian Wildlife Service Report Series 6.

Ebbinge, B., van den Bergh, L., van Haperen, A., Lok, M., Philippona, J., Rooth, J., & Timmerman, A., 1986. 'Numbers and distribution of wild geese in The Netherlands, 1979–1984'. *Wildfowl, 37,* 28–34.

Hale, W. G., 1974. 'Aerial counting of waders'. *Ibis 116,* 412.

Harradine, J., 1985. 'Duck shooting in the United Kingdom'. *Wildfowl, 36,* 81–94.

Hill, D. A., 1982. 'The comparative population ecology of mallard and tufted ducks'. PhD. thesis, University of Oxford.

Matthews, G. V. T., 1960. 'An examination of basic data from wildfowl counts'. *Proc. XII Int. Cong., Helsinki 1958,* 483–91.

Ogilvie, M. A., 1977. 'The numbers of Canada geese in Britain, 1976'. *Wildfowl 28,* 27–34.

Ogilvie, M. A., 1983. 'The numbers of Greenland barnacle geese in Britain and Ireland'. *Wildfowl, 34,* 77–88.

Ogilvie, M. A., 1986a. 'Darkbellied brent geese 1985–6. Numbers in Britain, mid-December 1985 and mid-January 1986'. Unpubl. rep. Wildfowl Trust to Nature Conservancy Council.

Ogilvie, M. A. 1986b. 'The mute swan *Cygnus olor* in Britain 1983'. *Bird Study, 33,* 121–37.

Ogilvie, M. A., & Boyd, H., 1976. 'The number of pink-footed and greylag geese wintering in Britain: observations 1969–75 and predictions 1976–80'. *Wildfowl 27:* 63–75.

Owen, M., 1983. 'The importance of artificial habitats for wildfowl in Britain'. *Proc. Symp. Wildlife on Man-made Wetlands:* 73–97. Great Linford.

Owen, M., & Mitchell, C. 1988 'Movements and migrations of wigeon (*Anas penelope*) wintering in Britain and Ireland'. Bird Study 35, 47–59.

Owen, M., Atkinson-Willes, G. L., & Salmon, D. G., 1986. *Wildfowl in Great Britain*. Second Edition. The University Press, Cambridge.

Prater, A. J., 1979. 'Trends in accuracy of counting birds'. *Bird Study 26:* 198–200.

Prater, A. J., 1981. *Estuary Birds of Britain and Ireland.* Poyser, Calton.

Ruger, A., Prentice, C., & Owen, M., 1986. *Results of the IWRB International Waterfowl Census 1967–1983.* IWRB Special Publication No. 6, Slimbridge.

Salmon, D. G., Moser, M. E., & Kirby, J. S., 1987. *Wildfowl and Wader Counts 1985–86.* Wildfowl Trust, Slimbridge.

Salmon, D. G., & Black, J. M., 1986. 'Results of the January 1986 whooper swan census in Britain, Ireland and Iceland'. *Wildfowl* 37: 172–4.

Schifferli, L., 1983. 'Distribution and numbers of ducks wintering on Swiss waters, 1967–81, and possible factors affecting them'. *First Western Hemisphere Waterfowl and Waterbird Symposium*. Edmonton, Canada 1982: 140–4. Canadian Wildlife Service.

Sharrock, J. T. R. 1976. *The Atlas of Breeding Birds in Britain and Ireland*. BTO, Tring.

Stroud, D. A., 1984. 'Status of Greenland white-fronted geese in Britain, 1982/83'. *Bird Study* 31: 111–16.

Tuite, C. H., 1982. *The Impact of Water-based Recreation on the Waterfowl of Enclosed Inland Waters in Britain*. Report to the Sports Council and the Nature Conservancy Council.

Tuite, C. H., & Owen, M., 1984. 'Breeding waterfowl on British inland waters in 1980'. *Wildfowl* 35: 157–72.

Yarker, B., & Atkinson-Willes, G. L., 1972. 'The numerical distribution of some British breeding ducks'. *Wildfowl* 22: 63–70.

25

INTERNATIONAL CO-OPERATION, CONSERVATION AND WILDFOWLING

COLIN B. SHEDDEN

As earlier chapters of this book have shown, the great majority of the wildfowler's quarry is migratory and the fowler and his quarry are either subject to or the subject of international legislation. It is important, however, to remind readers that not all aspects of wildfowl conservation and wildfowling are determined by restrictive legislation – many of the most important features still come under voluntary agreements and arrangements, or at least the relevant international legislation had its roots in such voluntary agreements. Co-operation is therefore the cornerstone of international conservation.

CONSERVATION

Wildfowl have always been an important group of birds from the point of view of the conservationist and birdwatcher. Not only do they afford a spectacular sight in their large wintering flocks, easily 'laid on' for the visiting public, but individually their plumage can be spectacular. In addition, they illustrate the concept of migration in a simple and classical way as well as being straightforward examples of a group whose survival is closely linked with a particular series of habitats, i.e. wetlands. This, and the associated threat of over-exploitation through commercial shooting, led many world-wide groups to pay particular attention to wildfowl.

One of the most outstanding examples of this was the work of Ducks Unlimited, an American organisation that, in 1937, had the foresight to see that North American waterfowl were threatened not by shooting but by progressive erosion of prime wetland breeding habitat in the northern states and Canada. Between 1937 and 1987 this organisation, backed primarily by American wildfowlers,

has reserved 4 million acres of habitat for wild birds, now has over 600,000 members and can raise, in one year, over $66 million. The contribution of such a massive campaign to manage, restore or create wetland habitat for North American waterfowl cannot be underestimated, and neither can the fact that this is a voluntary initiative aimed at conserving a continent's waterfowl. I shall return to this example later, because there are lessons to be learned for Europe, but Europe is not without its own examples of truly international co-operation, co-operation that has benefited not only our wildfowl but also our wildfowlers.

THE INTERNATIONAL WATERFOWL AND WETLANDS RESEARCH BUREAU (IWRB)

The International Waterfowl and Wetlands Research Bureau (formerly known as the International Waterfowl Research Bureau) is more than its name suggests. Not only does a great deal of research on waterfowl and wetlands go on under its wing, it also stimulates and co-ordinates the conservation of waterfowl and wetlands throughout the world. Founded in 1954 and based in the Wildfowl Trust's headquarters at Slimbridge for the past twenty years, this truly international organisation has thirty-eight national delegations, seven representatives of international organisations, five international and twenty-one national contributor organisations. The B.A.S.C. and a number of other fieldsports organisations fall in the latter category, contributing annually to the IWRB.

Much of the work of the IWRB is carried out from Slimbridge, but an important contribution is made by the Research Group co-ordinators, who deal with either groups of waterfowl, geographical areas of interest or subjects such as feeding ecology or endangered waterfowl. In fact, Dr John Harradine of the B.A.S.C. is currently co-ordinator of the Hunter Harvest Research Group (Wing Survey), where he collates all information currently collected in Europe emanating from the analysis of duck, goose and woodcock wings submitted by hunters. There is also a Hunting Rationalisation Research Group, so the actual representation of shooting interests is well maintained within IWRB and is seen to be an extremely valuable contribution.

Much of IWRB's work relates to wetlands and the waterfowl that utilise them and, both directly and indirectly, IWRB has been responsible for the continued existence of numerous wetlands throughout the world. The main vehicle by which this is achieved is the Ramsar Convention on Wetlands of International Importance Specially as Waterfowl Habitat, which both IWRB and the International Union for Conservation of Nature and Natural Resources (IUCN) administer jointly. This provides a voluntary framework for international co-operation on wetland habitats and, ten years after it came into force in 1975, 300 sites covering more than 20 million hectares were designated for inclusion by more than 50 contracting parties. The contracting parties are 'convinced that wetlands constitute a resource of great economic, cultural, scientific and recreational value, the loss of which would be irreplaceable'.

This view of wetland and waterfowl conservation is endorsed by a large number of other international agencies, such as IUCN, the United Nations Environment Programme (UNEP) and the International Council for Bird Preservation (ICBP), all working in their own way towards securing the future of both wetlands and their waterfowl. In conjunction with this, and with the work of IWRB, the Federation of Fieldsports Associations of the EEC (FACE) is also actively involved, a point to which I will return.

However, another important contribution to waterfowl conservation was made by IWRB in 1986 with the publication of their *Results of the IWRB International Waterfowl Census 1967–1983* (IWRB special publication No. 6). To quote from the preface of this report 'The reason for starting the counts in the first place was the growing concern amongst certain hunters and ornithologists at the apparent decline in the stocks of waterfowl over the previous 25 years. There were many, however, that disagreed on either side and had convincing evidence to support their claims; in some areas there were said to be many fewer birds than formerly, in others as many as ever or even more.'

I am sure that similar arguments have taken place at every fowling site in Great Britain, and indeed in Europe, over the past 25 years. What the results of this report have done is to clarify the situation and, by compiling over 85,000 counts from about 17,000 sites in 38 countries, a good impression of the situation can be obtained.

Overall, the results showed that in western Europe the wintering populations of most dabbling and diving ducks have increased, and, in particular, species such as gadwall and shoveler had shown what can only be described as 'dramatic increases'. Tufted duck increased in central Europe, mallard in the north and west of Europe and, looking at all of Europe, teal and goldeneye showed increases. The major cause for concern occurred in the west Mediterranean areas, and the central European region, where pintail and wigeon were seen to be declining. Additionally, wigeon and pintail in north-west Europe seemed stable, though an increase along with the other common duck species would certainly have been desirable.

The IWRB have, apart from analysing and publishing this extremely valuable data, proposed reasons for these changes. On the positive side we see features such as the increasing number of man-made wetlands in the form of gravel-pits and reservoirs over the past 20 years, mild winters, increase in nutrient content of water bodies through, for instance, agricultural pollution, expansion of the growing of winter cereals, the establishment of reserve areas and, also, the shortening of some European shooting seasons. Against this we have extensive habitat loss and development activity on wetlands, i.e. around the Mediterranean, relatively long hunting seasons in southern Europe in particular, and the effects of the few severe winters experienced during this period.

The continued monitoring of these populations by the IWRB and their co-ordination of national counts, many of which are done by fowlers in both Britain and in the rest of Europe, is essential to the welfare and development of management guidelines for our waterfowl. Therefore, the continued support of this body by hunting associations, other non-governmental organisations and governments themselves is essential. German and French shooting interests have, in recent years, provided staff and funds for the important task of collating these internationally important counts.

SHOOTING ASSOCIATIONS

Nationally, each European country has its own representative associations. The importance of their mutual co-operation is essential, as is their co-operation with both voluntary conservation bodies and national conservation agencies. Only in this way will the future well-being of both wildfowl and wildfowling be assured.

I mentioned Ducks Unlimited earlier, commenting upon their valuable contribution to wetland conservation in North America and, consequently, their contribution to waterfowl conservation. For the past three years or so many European shooting associations have been looking closely at the way this operation works in North America, and indeed in Australia and New Zealand as well. There are, of course, fundamental problems involved in transposing a Ducks Unlimited scheme from North America to Europe, not least the fact that most of our breeding waterfowl are found behind the Iron Curtain. Consequently, fund raising to purchase, rent or manage this breeding habitat is not practical. Instead, a number of European associations and foundations have come together and are seeking, through the formation of national sections, to create a European Wetland Fund to be known as 'Euroducks'. It is hoped that by the time this is published a number of these fund-raising sections will have been formed in European countries, directing their funds to the international fund, which will then allocate money to projects designed to restore, manage or re-create wetlands of importance to European waterfowl.

We know from the IWRB that European waterfowl populations are, broadly speaking, increasing or at least stable, but this fund intends to ensure the long-term conservation of these species, and work towards guaranteeing their future as part of Europe's natural and cultural heritage.

Closely involved with this initiative, and many others in Europe, is FACE. Now 11 years old, FACE is a non-governmental international organisation with its base in Brussels, the headquarters city of the EEC. Its objective is both the promotion and defence of fieldsports in Europe, seeing fieldsports as having an important role to play in protecting wildlife and natural habitats through the 'rational utilisation' of these resources. FACE is now considered by the European Commission as the sole representative of $6\frac{1}{2}$ million hunters in the EEC countries and is consulted each time a matter concerning wildlife and its management is raised politically in Europe.

Both directly and indirectly, FACE has worked under an official contract with the European Commission on an inventory of important wetlands for wildfowl, the effects of modern agriculture on wildlife, the ecological effect of harvesting wildlife, as well as running its own migratory birds programme. In addition FACE has collaborated with a number of international agencies on specific areas of interest, and has achieved, for the sportsmen of Europe, an important and very useful role in international conservation. In fact, in 1987 FACE was officially accepted as a member of IUCN, the 'trade union' of conservation bodies.

An on-going project, partly funded by FACE, illustrates the importance of co-operation between the shooting associations and research and conservation groups. The project is entitled 'Analysis of cold weather movements of waterfowl in western Europe', and is being carried out by Wildfowl Trust scientists on behalf of IWRB. In brief, the study is investigating the extent to which waterfowl shift from their 'normal' wintering areas in north-west Europe to milder regions farther south and west in response to severe winters. The IWRB have already recognised that severe winters may adversely affect European populations of waterfowl and, in an attempt to assist the valuable stocks of these birds, this study hopes to produce management plans for not only severe weather refuge areas but also to rationalise the many procedures for severe weather shooting suspensions already in existence in Europe. Ideally, this research will benefit not only the wildfowl but the wildfowler as well, hence the importance of an input and involvement by European sportsmen.

CONCLUSIONS

As I have briefly outlined, co-operation between all groups interested in wildfowl is not only beneficial to our wildfowl, but maintains the important contribution made by fowlers to conservation in its rightful place. Without this co-operation at an international level, politicians and decision-makers could be either unaware of the importance of the fowler to the conservation of wildfowl or could easily choose to ignore his involvement.

The B.A.S.C., through its prominent role in FACE, its membership of IWRB and ICBP and its close contact with many other organisations, ensures that, at the international level, this constructive co-operation continues. Only in this way can the interests of the fowler on the foreshore be extended as far as the all-important political forums in Europe, which influence so many of our activities in this day and age.

26
CONSERVATION AND BIRD PROTECTION

RICHARD PORTER AND GARETH THOMAS

It is all too easy for people to think that wildfowling and bird conservation and protection do not mix. Although there are a number of practical problems that require resolution, those interested in shooting and conservation should be united about the needs to conserve waterfowl stocks and the habitats that support them.

Ornithologically, Britain is of major international importance for breeding seabirds and our wealth of wintering wildfowl and waders. In the main both have prospered in the 20th century. Our estuaries are amongst the most outstanding and productive wildlife habitats in Europe. Estuarine mud teems with invertebrate life, which in turn supports hundreds of thousands of birds, many of them migrants from their northern breeding grounds in the high Arctic as far apart as Canada and Siberia.

Almost $1\frac{1}{2}$ million waders winter on UK estuaries – 40% of the total that winter in Europe. In addition, huge numbers of waders use our estuaries as stop-over sites for refuelling and moulting when on long migrations between their northern breeding and southern wintering grounds. The number of wildfowl wintering on our estuaries varies with the severity of winter weather, but at times there may be as many as half a million duck, geese and swans when inland sites are frozen – over a quarter of the total number of wildfowl in the UK.

UK estuaries support more than one-third of the north-west European wintering populations of five species of wildfowl: shelduck, wigeon, teal, pintail and the two races of brent geese. They also hold six species of waders: oystercatcher, grey plover, blacktailed godwit, bartailed godwit, knot and dunlin. Twenty-eight estuaries regularly hold over 20,000 waders and/or more than 10,000 wildfowl in winter and are officially recognised as being of international significance.

The government has accepted an international duty to protect these sites against damage. It is required to do this under the Convention on Wetlands of International Importance Especially as Waterfowl Habitat (the 'Ramsar' Convention), and by European Community law under Directive 79/409 on the Conservation of Wild Birds. In Great Britain, both the wetlands listed under the Convention, and the 'Special Protection Areas' (SPAs) designated under the Directive, are protected by means of the provisions of the 1981 *Wildlife and Countryside Act*, which provides for the notification of Sites of Special Scientific Interest (SSSIs). Over 200 sites have been confirmed as qualifying for one or both of these international designations, although progress in formal listing of these has been slow to date. In Northern Ireland the equivalent of GB's SSSIs are Areas of Special Scientific Interest (ASSIs), notified under the *Conservation and Amenity Lands (Northern Ireland) Order 1985*.

SSSIs and ASSIs are thus a crucial mechanism for the protection of waterfowl populations. The Nature Conservancy Council (NCC) (or Department of the Environment in Northern Ireland) is required by law to notify owners and occupiers of sites which meet certain standard criteria of importance. This notification includes a list of operations on which the owner or occupier must consult NCC if it is intended to carry them out. NCC may then consent to the operation or decide that it would damage the interest of the site and should not be carried out, in which case it can offer to enter a management agreement with the owner or tenant. These agreements include payments designed to offset any financial loss which might result.

Payments are now also available under the *Agriculture Act 1986* in areas such as the Somerset Levels and Norfolk Broads which have been designated ESAs (Environmentally Sensitive Areas), to farmers who agree to continue with or adopt particular management practices which benefit wildlife and landscape.

WILDFOWL COUNTS

To help monitor the numbers and distribution of wildfowl and waders using our wetlands, the British Trust for Ornithology (BTO) and the Wildfowl Trust (WT) maintain substantial databases. In the case of monitoring the birds on our estuaries, the Birds of Estuaries Enquiry has been undertaken by the BTO since 1970, funded by the Nature Conservancy Council and the Royal Society for the Protection of Birds (RSPB). It has involved the co-ordination of over 750 counters on a regular basis.

The Wildfowl Trust, also with the help of NCC funding, has been responsible for organising wildfowl counts since 1952. Nearly 5000 waters have been covered at some time since 1960 and in the early 1980s more than 1500 counters were involved. The maintenance of both these databases has occupied one or more full-time officers since counts began.

HABITAT LOSS

For a long time, man's activities have resulted in habitat loss on estuaries. Extensive land claim for agriculture has for example been demonstrated around the Wash, Essex and North Kent. Land claim for industrial purposes has taken up large areas at Seal Sands, Teesmouth and Southampton Water. Sadly, such activities continue. Some recent proposed developments, if implemented, would affect many estuaries, including some of the most important for wintering waterfowl.

Barrages for tidal power generation are under serious consideration at two of the most important estuaries – the Severn and Mersey. Such barrages would result in catastrophic changes in the tidal regimes. They would considerably reduce the area of intertidal mud that is exposed, denying feeding areas to birds. Restricted tides could lead to changes in salinity and an accumulation of pollutants. The loss of intertidal areas would mean that waders and wildfowl would be forced onto the remaining areas at greater densities. This would increase competition for food, depleting the food more rapidly and dispersing birds into areas which are not able to support them. The result, in the long run, will be fewer birds in the population overall. This has already happened for the dunlin and redshank, whose wintering populations in Britain have declined by a frightening 35% and 25% respectively since the mid-1970s.

On inland wetlands, reclamation for agriculture has historically been the main threat, though losses have been partly compensated for by the creation of new habitats, such as reservoirs and gravel pits. Of particular concern has been the conversion of damp lowland pastures into arable areas. Many of these pastures used to flood in winter, providing suitable conditions for mixed flocks of wigeon, teal and pintail as well as the ubiquitous mallard. Better land and river drainage has, for example, allowed about a half of the 6000 hectares of washlands in East Anglia to be converted into arable land, most of which is no longer flooded in winter.

Conservation bodies, together with shooting organisations, are having their success in putting forward their case for wetland conservation to Parliament, through planning enquiries, both to protect individual sites and to influence government policies. The turning point was the Amberley Wildbrooks Public Enquiry of March 1978, where the government rejected Southern Water Authority's application for a pump drainage scheme which would have destroyed a site of national importance for waterfowl. Recent conservation successes have included:

The Wash, Lincolnshire/Norfolk: conservation clause inserted in *Port of Fosdyke Act 1987*, a private bill concerned with the development of Fosdyke Port.

Budle Bay, Lindisfarne, Northumberland: following a public enquiry into a proposed residential development on the edge of this site, planning permission was refused.

Langstone Harbour, Hampshire: following a public enquiry into a proposed marina and residential development at the Kench, planning permission was refused.

Blackwater Estuary, Essex: proposals for marina and residential developments at Heybridge Basin were withdrawn.

Foulness, Essex: an appeal against refusal of permission for a marina development at Barling Magna was dismissed.

Poole Harbour, Dorset: an appeal against refusal of permission for yacht club development was dismissed.

HABITAT PROTECTION

Organisations such as the B.A.S.C. and Game Conservancy recognise and support the importance of habitat protection. Whether this has stemmed more from the threats to species or from the loss of places where shooting can be done is uncertain, but also largely immaterial. Likewise, organisations such as the RSPB and Nature Conservancy Council recognise and acknowledge that many important habitats owe their continued existence to their value for gamebirds and wildfowl. In many places where gamebird shooting has ceased, the loss of habitats such as upland moorland and lowland woodland has been especially severe, and those that have been kept for shooting are now doubly important.

Taking coastal areas alone, wildfowling clubs affiliated to B.A.S.C. now hold or share a management interest in more than 75,000 hectares in England alone. For comparison the RSPB's coastal reserve holdings are 15,000 hectares in the whole of the UK. Conversely the RSPB has over 500,000 members, about five times the number in the B.A.S.C.

Have the holdings of wildfowling clubs failed to stem the tide of loss of wetland habitats? Many clubs specialise in leasing areas, which unfortunately does not guarantee their long-term security. By contrast, purchases by conservation bodies have secured several areas in perpetuity, especially inland and coastal grazing marshes. Often such purchases are viewed as hostile by wildfowling groups, but the habitats and the birds they support would likely have been lost for future generations of wildfowlers and conservationists alike if it were not the fact that they were owned and protected against development. Accordingly, conservationists recognise the advantages in the B.A.S.C.'s recent initiative to establish a fund for land purchase rather than lease. Conservationists do not regard this as competitive provided that one important proviso is allowed for: the provision of adequate sanctuary areas for quarry and protected species alike. Properly planned land ownership by both interest groups can and should be complementary.

Looking towards the future, conservation organisations such as RSPB will continue to seek land at important coasts and inland wetlands where habitats are vulnerable to damage or loss and disturbance-free refuges are inadequate or lacking.

Why do we need sanctuary areas? Preventing habitat loss and damage is vital, but it is insufficient on its own. It is also important that birds have disturbance-free places where they can feed and roost according to their normal behaviour patterns. The RSPB and many other conservation organisations therefore wish to secure sanctuary areas on all major coastal and inland wetland complexes. In such places, disturbance by humans in general would be kept to a minimum. Further work still needs to be done in many cases to determine what constitutes the size and location of adequate sanctuary areas. The advantages have been amply demonstrated at the Ouse Washes, where the management of about 20 % of the 1914-hectare site as undisturbed refuges has allowed the wigeon population to increase threefold and to be enjoyed by at least 50,000 visitors a year. Just as important, biologically, is that the wigeon usage of this site, as measured by days spent at feeding or roosting, has increased fivefold since the refuges were first created in the 1970s.

Normally the RSPB seeks to buy land unencumbered by shooting tenancies or other constraints that make it difficult to establish sound refuge areas. In a few cases at some of our larger holdings, however, the continuation of shooting has been a condition of sale and we have accepted this so as to secure the habitat. Our policy in such cases is to seek to have such tenancies with B.A.S.C.-affiliated rather than non-affiliated clubs. In the case of some smaller holdings, however, it is not possible to satisfy the objectives of field sports and conservation jointly. Old Hall Marshes is a case in point, where one of the main aims is to provide an adequate feeding refuge for some 5000 brent geese which would normally range over cropland in the locality, where they can cause conflict with farmers.

Small sites such as Old Hall Marshes require a single self-contained refuge occupying all of the area. Larger and more complex sites with several replicates of each habitat may require a series of widely spaced refuges, and the ratio of refuge to non-refuge areas may be smaller.

To help determine guidelines for the size, number and location of refuges it is essential that research is undertaken into the effects of shooting disturbance on wildfowl. Such a project is currently being carried out by the WT and B.A.S.C., with the support of the NCC and the RSPB. In the meantime, we have to take a pragmatic approach to refuge size and location, using the collective experience of our scientists, managers, wardens and local people, including wildfowlers.

QUARRY SPECIES

All responsible wildlife conservation bodies recognise the existence of a legitimate quarry list, comprising species which may be killed during the open season. This is certainly true of the RSPB. Nevertheless, we monitor the populations of these species and may argue for some to be removed from the list or against others being added. This is not to be interpreted as being 'anti-wildfowling'. Indeed under the terms of its Royal Charter the RSPB can 'take no part in the question of the killing of gamebirds and other legitimate sport of that character'. Consequently we take a neutral position over the question of wildfowling *per se*. The morality and ethics of shooting are matters quite distinct from the Society's prime aim of bird conservation.

From time to time specific matters arise which might require a change in legislation. The adding or removal of a species from the quarry list or changing the length of the shooting season are examples. In such cases the RSPB, before deciding on its stance, takes into account the following factors (within Europe as well as Britain):

(a) waterfowl population size and trend – the demography of these (sex/age composition and breeding), their mortality patterns and the impact of shooting on them;

(b) threats to local parts of populations or to geographically restricted populations;

(c) trends in habitat loss or damage, and known threats to same;

(d) adequacy of unshot refuges;

(e) consistency with the EC Birds Directive and relevant legislation in other European countries;

(f) Relevance to other interests, particularly birdwatching but also recreation, agriculture and fisheries.

There are bound to be a number of issues to which conservationists and wildfowlers must continually address themselves. We have already given the example of the need for sanctuary areas, but we will now briefly consider two others under current debate.

COLD-WEATHER RESTRAINT

The first is cold-weather bans. In the past the institution of an Order by the Secretary of State banning wildfowling in severe weather was virtually a free-for-all between conservationists and wildfowlers. The ground rules were few and although a constant dialogue between conservationists and wildfowlers existed, the determination of a ban was never easy. In the last ten years, however, wildfowlers and conservationists have worked closely together to establish a set of criteria for determining when a ban should be introduced and a set of procedures to see that it works properly. The criteria are given elsewhere, but it should be remembered that these have only been achieved by constant formal and informal dialogue and it is fair to say that wildfowlers and conservationists (at least those representing the major organisations) are reasonably satisfied with what has been achieved. Now we are in a much clearer position to know when a ban should be introduced and when it should be suspended. There are also voluntary restraints called by B.A.S.C. prior to a statutory ban. Much discussion has gone on recently about the need for regional bans. For example, wildfowlers in south-west England or Wales may argue that because conditions are not inclement there should be no ban in that region. However, the feeling generally is that bans should be national. If the northern part of Britain is frozen the south will assume greater importance for those wildfowl remaining in our country and southern estuaries for example will become more important because of the greater abundance of birds seeking refuge there.

LEAD SHOT

Whilst all may be well in the cold-weather ban sector, not the same can be said of an issue which is likely to assume a greater importance in the years to come. That is, the pollution caused by spent lead shot.

After habitat loss, lead poisoning is the single most important problem facing waterfowl in the United States of America. After 30 years of wrangling, often extremely bitter, the US Government has faced up to the need for waterfowl hunters to use a non-toxic form of shot. Steel shot is the first suitable non-toxic ammunition to be commercially developed. In the RSPB's view new improved steel loads are as ballistically sound as their lead counterparts; barrel wear has been overcome with the provision of plastic shot cups in the cartridge. Some tests have shown that bagging efficiency and the crippling rates of steel-shotted cartridges are the same as the corresponding lead-shotted cartridge. The US Government has decreed that it will be mandatory for all waterfowl hunters nation-wide to use non-toxic shot by 1991. It is worth describing the strategy in some detail as it is bound to be examined closely by many countries.

The US Fish and Wildlife Service has published final regulations establishing zones where non-toxic (steel) shot will be required for waterfowl and coot hunting during the 1987–8 hunting season. The non-toxic shot zones cover 44 states and include counties having an annual waterfowl harvest of 20 or more per square mile in addition to areas where non-toxic shot was required last year and additional areas identified by the states themselves. These areas are expected to account for over 70% of the US waterfowl harvest in the 1987–8 autumn and winter. Five states, Iowa, Minnesota, Mississippi, Nebraska and Wisconsin, have gone all the way and will require non-toxic shot for all waterfowl hunting this autumn. The full schedule for implementing non-toxic shot requirements according to the size of the waterfowl harvest in any given county is as follows:

Number of waterfowl harvested/square mile	Year non-toxic shot required
20 or more	1987–8
15 or more	1988–9
10 or more	1989–90
5 or more	1990–1
Fewer than 5	1991–2

The US Fish and Wildlife Service is requiring for the first time in 1987–8 that non-toxic shot be used when hunters are taking non-waterfowl species in an 'aggregate' or combined bag limit along with waterfowl or coots. Thus, if non-toxic shot is required for one or more species in an aggregate bag limit it must be used for taking all species in the same aggregate.

Waterfowl poisoning by spent lead shot is not as well researched in Britain and Europe as in the USA. However, collaborative studies by the RSPB, WT and the B.A.S.C. have shown that certain species in Britain can be affected, e.g. mallard, pochard and tufted duck. The amount of spent lead shotgun pellets at some sites is a growing cause for concern. For example, 30 pellets per m² have been recovered in the top few centimetres of soil at some inland flight ponds and 16 pellets per m² at the Ouse Washes Ramsar Site. These spent pellets are consumed by quarry and non-quarry birds alike.

In the last few years, die-offs from lead poisoning have been noticed for Bewick's swans, whooper swans and grey geese in Britain. Spent lead pellets were shown to be the cause of death in each case. The RSPB believes such poisoning is preventable. Steel-shotted cartridges should soon be available in this country and the benefits of their use should be promoted to a greater extent. Wildfowling clubs are in perfect positions to carry out trials.

THE WAY FORWARD

The way forward must be through more collaboration between conservationists and wildfowlers to achieve the safeguarding and management of wetland habitats. The formation, in the last decade, of conservation groups to protect five of our major estuaries, in Langstone Harbour, the Mersey, Dee, Thames and Severn, is a good example of co-operation. Supported by major conservation and wildfowling associations, these groups are administered by local people who know the estuaries well and are concerned for their future. Such groups not only act as watch-dogs for undesirable developments but have devised plans for the future protection and enhancement of these important wetlands. They can, of course, call on support when any national political action is necessary.

We have seen how wildfowlers and conservationists can work together in gathering facts. We would like to see them work more closely together in producing arguments that can be put forward in protecting habitats under threat. Despite political protestation, despite scheduling of sites and the addition of those sites to international conventions, their long-term conservation is still not necessarily wholly secure. Who knows what threats will emerge, or in what form, over the next half-century or even decade. One theme that comes through the whole series of the *New Wildfowler* editions is that safeguarding land is vital. It is doubtful if any one organisation (including the government) can buy all the important habitats, so we must, as conservationists and wildfowlers, collaborate in securing land as the ultimate safeguard.

It is in addressing the future conservation problem surrounding waterfowl habitats that the efforts of conservationists and wildfowlers will find their greatest synergy.

27
WILDFOWLERS AND RESEARCH
JOHN HARRADINE

Wildfowlers have always taken a keen interest in the numbers and movements of birds in the estuaries and coastal regions of this country and whether these have changed, and if so, why; how the bags compare with those of previous years; how the condition of duck and geese changes through the season, particularly in relation to severe weather. Consequently they have always been keen to help in studies which are aimed at increasing our understanding of wildfowl biology and behaviour, and which will help tackle any problems or issues that arise.

Wildfowlers are ideally placed to assist in both national and local studies, being so closely attuned to their quarry, its behaviour and movements, as any good and successful hunter needs to be. They can supply material or information from different parts of the country, thereby providing a sample which, in the statistical sense, is more representative of the subjects being studied than could be obtained by a single researcher or research group, and certainly much cheaper. Their own local studies can help their own club's members to manage their shooting better in relation to the needs of both conservation and other recreational users of the area, and to take an active part in discussions with other interested bodies.

Many research studies have been undertaken at the national level in which wildfowlers have played a substantial and valuable role. Some have been conducted by WAGBI or, more recently, the B.A.S.C., on behalf of the shooting community, whilst others have been conducted either by other organisations, with the Association's support, or jointly by shooting and conservation bodies undertaking research of common interest.

The B.A.S.C., in order to represent the interests of its members in the most effective way, has always needed factual information on all aspects of sporting shooting. Those who make decisions which can affect our sport, from local to inter-

national level, increasingly require facts and figures on which to base their decisions. Members of the Association expect their parent body to be well informed and to be able to answer their many questions and, on occasion, problems which may arise on one aspect of their sport or another. Similarly the public at large needs to be correctly informed so that it can see shooting in its true perspective amongst the many activities which take place in the countryside. Wildfowlers, as well as all other members of the Association, have an immensely important role in all this work since it is their support and assistance which ensures the success of much of the work that needs to be done. The need for research has always been present, but perhaps today the need has never been greater.

This natural interest and willingness to help was tapped and enhanced particularly by Dr Jeffery Harrison, Honorary Director of Conservation and Research for WAGBI during the 1960s and 1970s. His enthusiasm and understanding of the many issues involved helped many wildfowlers to appreciate the need for and the value of well-conducted research.

VISCERA STUDY

One of the first projects, begun in 1957, involved a study of the diet of wildfowl, since he recognised that knowledge of the feeding habits of British wildfowl was very scanty, and that it was a prerequisite for any form of wildfowl management. The work was initiated by the Wildfowl Trust and grant-aided by the then Nature Conservancy, and attempted to make a qualitative and quantitative survey of the food and feeding habits of various British wildfowl. As Peter Olney said in *The New Wildfowler in the 1970s*, the success of the scheme depended to a large extent on the close liaison between the wildfowlers and the Wildfowl Trust. As a result, large numbers of wildfowl viscera were sent in by individual members and affiliated clubs

Left: Shelduck are often encountered by wildfowlers on the shore but are protected by law (Julian Novorol)

Below left: Pinkfeet (Julian Novorol)

Below: Evening on the marsh (Eric Begbie)

Bottom: Wintery conditions. Brent geese and wigeon – cold weather brings in the wildfowl (Julian Novorol)

of WAGBI, following instructions on how to remove, preserve and despatch the samples.

Although it was confined to the shooting season this survey produced a considerable amount of information on the foods eaten by wildfowl, including the variations between species, and within seasons, from place to place, and how feeding habits are related to food availability.

The practical application of this research was then demonstrated at the WAGBI/Wildfowl Trust Experimental Wildfowl Reserve in Sevenoaks, Kent. Agreement had been reached between WAGBI and the Kent Sand and Ballast Company in 1957 to manage some flooded gravel pits as a wildfowl reserve. The pits at that time were virtually devoid of vegetation, and in order to make an attractive habitat for wildfowl, a planting programme was necessary which would provide their feeding, cover and nesting requirements. This could not start until the food preferences of the wildfowl likely to use it were known. The results of the diet studies near the pits helped determine which plant species should be introduced. The planting and vegetation management programme has since continued and has resulted in an immensely successful and valuable wildfowl reserve. Its early history is described by Jeffery Harrison in *A Gravel Pit Wildfowl Reserve* published in 1972 by WAGBI.

Another significant exercise in research undertaken by wildfowlers was part of the mallard rearing and release scheme begun in 1954, again the result of the enthusiasm and farsightedness of Jeffery Harrison. Its primary objective was to supplement the wild duck populations from which the shooting community would subsequently benefit, but perhaps its greatest success was the interest the scheme generated in wildlife conservation within the wildfowling community. This has since developed enormously throughout the country, making a very substantial contribution to the management of wildfowl populations and their habitats, both locally and nationally (see, for example, *The Conservation of Wildlife Habitat in England by B.A.S.C. Members* by Laws, 1984).

Each of the ducks released was marked with a WAGBI leg ring and the study of their recoveries

Left: A view of Hamford Water, Essex, showing the complex creek and saltmarsh system – a fine example of wildfowl habitat (Julian Novorol)

over the years since has revealed much about the migratory behaviour of mallard, including the dispersal of birds from their point of release, the distance travelled, range occupied, and the phenomenon of abmigration, which occurs when a resident bird pairs up with a migratory bird and returns with it to the latter's breeding grounds. There is no doubt that the ringing research programme added to the knowledge of the behaviour and migratory patterns of wildfowl, which was essential to help direct the future conservation efforts to best effect. Some of its results are described in *The New Wildfowler in the 1970s* by Jeffery Harrison and John Wardell.

DUCK WING SURVEY

In the 1960s Jeffery Harrison saw the potential for using his fellow wildfowlers to help address an important question about duck populations – to what extent does the production of young each year affect the size of the population wintering in this country? Both the National Wildfowl Counts, organised since 1954 by the Wildfowl Trust, and observation showed there were considerable variations in the numbers of ducks in different places each winter, but it was not known whether the success of the previous summer's breeding season was responsible or whether factors such as weather conditions in Europe or changes in migratory patterns influenced the numbers finally reaching the United Kingdom.

Counting the numbers of birds of each species during the winter was relatively easy, but the determination of the numbers of immature and adult birds, even if their plumages allowed them to be distinguished in the field, was much more difficult. Wildfowlers were in a unique position to provide the means of doing just that, by providing wings from their own duck bags from which the age and sex of the birds could be determined. If enough wildfowlers from all parts of the country contributed samples of wings each season it would be possible to obtain an insight into the importance of production in determining the size of the winter populations, at the same time as providing additional information about duck biology, behaviour and movements as well as something about wildfowlers themselves. The attractiveness of the scheme was heightened by the fact that information of this sort could not be obtained by other means without considerable difficulty and expense.

With the help of similar work in North America a key was developed to enable any given wing of most of the British quarry duck species to be identified as to its species, sex and age (that is first winter or immature, or adult) from their shape, colour and degree of wear on certain feather groups on the wing. The book *Duck Wings: a study in duck production* by Jeffery Harrison, Hugh Boyd and Allan Allison, was published by WAGBI in 1975, and became widely used not just in this country but also in Europe. Now, after many thousands more wings have been studied since its publication, the key needs some revision (and this is planned) but it still provides a good basis for undertaking studies of duck wings by individual wildfowlers and wildfowling clubs.

Over the years of the B.A.S.C.'s study some 70,000 wings have been collected from hundreds of wildfowlers and other shooting men and women from around the country. Each season from 100 to 200 contributors have been sending in up to 5000 wings; most recently the annual sample has averaged around 3000. Most wings are from mallard, teal and wigeon, with the rest coming from the much less commonly shot dabbling and diving duck species (including pintail, tufted duck, pochard, shoveler, gadwall and goldeneye and, before the *Wildlife and Countryside Act 1981*, a few other species like scaup, garganey and longtailed duck). Wings are sent in at the wildfowler's own expense to the B.A.S.C.'s headquarters with the date and place of shooting attached. Nowadays special wing cards are provided to make this recording of details easier and to assist the subsequent computerisation of the results. The determination of the species, sex and age of each wing for many years was undertaken by Jeffery Harrison and Allan Allison until Jeffery Harrison's untimely death in 1978. The analysis continued under Allan Allison until the early 1980s, when Andrew Macfarlane, another keen wildfowler and taxidermist, took over.

Careful study of these wing results has revealed a number of valuable insights into the behaviour and biology of the ducks wintering in the United Kingdom. In fact, though, somewhat ironically it has not proved possible to demonstrate a relationship at the national level between the age ratio (that is, the percentage of immature birds) in the wildfowler's bag for any of the three main species (mallard, teal and wigeon) and the numbers of these ducks wintering here each season, as revealed by the National Wildfowl Counts. Such a relationship would be expected if a successful breeding season resulted in a large autumn population of ducks comprising many young from which the wildfowlers took their bag, and vice versa. On the other hand, there may be other factors more important in determining the number of ducks which winter here, including migratory patterns and weather conditions. Certainly Jeffery Harrison believed, on the basis of his wing studies, that the decline in teal wintering in Britain during the 1960s was due to changes in their migration rather than poorer breeding success. Furthermore, every wildfowler knows the effect the winter's weather on the European continent has on the numbers of duck here each season and that a spell

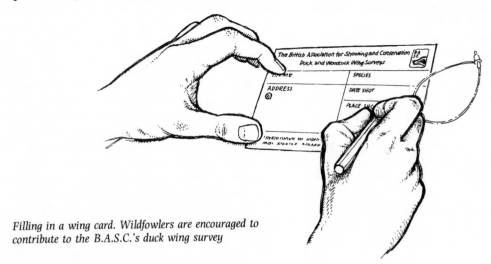

Filling in a wing card. Wildfowlers are encouraged to contribute to the B.A.S.C.'s duck wing survey

of severe wintry weather can markedly increase the numbers of birds, and improve the shooting!

On the more local level, however, some relationships have been found. In Kent itself, where Jeffery Harrison did so much research on duck wings, a good correlation has been found between the age ratio of mallard and the corresponding duck counts from 1965 to 1974 (Owen *et al.* 1986).

It may well be a question of obtaining sufficiently representative samples of wings which has prevented clearer relationships from emerging. Indeed, bearing in mind the huge area of north-west Europe, Scandinavia and northern Russia in which many of our ducks breed, the fact that they are subject to various mortality factors between their nesting and wintering grounds, that wildfowlers tend to shoot more young and inexperienced birds and sometimes 'select' males rather than females, it would be surprising if the age ratio of a relatively small number of wings obtained each shooting season did reflect the success of the previous breeding season! Furthermore, we are still considerably hamstrung by the great lack of knowledge of what happens on the breeding grounds each year since so many of these, particularly those in Russia, are inaccessible. The best indications we have for most species are the counts of birds the following winter.

Over the past twenty years or so, though, the changes in the age ratio from year to year amongst the mallard, teal and wigeon have been closely related (Figure 41). This is encouraging and probably does reflect the fact that these three species breed in the same general, though very extensive, area. Indeed Myrfyn Owen of the Wildfowl Trust, in the new edition of *Wildfowl in Great Britain*, considers that the age ratio as revealed by the Duck Wing Survey does indicate the quality of each year's breeding season across this huge range.

The analysis of the sex ratio over the years of this survey has been even more interesting. Amongst the mallard, teal and wigeon, males have consistently appeared more frequently than females in the wing samples. The average percentage for mallard is 53.5%, teal 56.5% and wigeon 57.5%. In a statistical sense the mallard percentage is significantly lower than that of the other two species. Most duck species in fact show more or less equal proportions of the sexes at hatching, so any difference must arise later or perhaps be due to shooting itself. There is certainly some evidence,

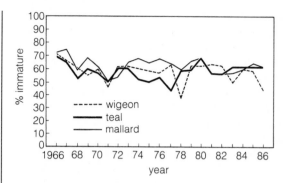

FIGURE 41 *Annual variation in the age ratio of ducks as revealed by the Duck Wing Survey*

particularly from America, that males appear in the hunter's bag more frequently than females – this is likely to be due to the size, plumage or behaviour of the male making it more likely than a female to be shot. It has always seemed unlikely, however, that the imbalance of the sexes observed in the wing samples could be entirely due to this cause.

Also of interest is the finding that the proportion of male teal has increased over the period of the wing survey, from about 53% during the first ten years, to 59% during the last ten years. The reasons for this are unclear but may reflect changes in teal migratory behaviour, or in survival of females, rather than any change in 'hunter selection' of the sexes.

If the wing results are analysed in more detail, further patterns appear when the adult males and females and the immature males and females are separated. Amongst the adults, males dominate females most in wigeon (some two and a half times) and least in mallard. Amongst the immatures the sexes are much more equal.

The remarkable difference between the adult cock and hen wigeon was one of the early discoveries of the Duck Wing Survey, and led Jeffery Harrison in the 1970s to propose that differential migration of the sexes was the main cause. More recently, two other studies strongly support these early findings of the survey. Recoveries of ducks ringed in the Netherlands have shown that males migrate ahead of females in the autumn, when females are still concerned with raising their young, but later on females catch up with and then overtake the males to winter in the more southerly parts of the range. The authors

(Perdeck and Clason, 1983) conclude that their findings confirm the interpretation made by Jeffery Harrison. Teal also show such behaviour but mallard much less, probably because mallard establish their pair bonding between the sexes much earlier than the other species, which thereby keeps the sexes closer together. In a more recent study, Myrfyn Owen and Michael Dix (1986) compared the preliminary counts of sex ratios in British wintering populations of some ducks with the results of the Duck Wing Survey and concluded that the sex ratios revealed by the B.A.S.C.'s Wing Survey give a good indication of the ratios in the populations of our more common species. The authors suggest that competition between the sexes is likely to be the major cause of this differential migration, and that this in turn may lead to greater mortality of the females in the less favourable southerly parts of their range, and hence to the dominance of males in the population at large.

There are many other potential uses of wing collections and these include mapping out the distributions of different species over their wintering grounds; determining flyways and migratory periods; responses of ducks to weather conditions, food availability, disturbance and other factors; sampling ducks for toxic chemicals in the environment and even identifying the geographical origins of birds by analysing the trace elements in their feathers. The benefits of such studies are now widely recognised, thanks to the work of Jeffery Harrison and many other wildfowlers, so much so that the International Waterfowl and Wetlands Research Bureau recently established a new research group based on the B.A.S.C.'s experience in wing studies, and co-ordinated by the B.A.S.C. with the support of the Danish Game Biology Station (where detailed studies of wings are now also undertaken). This Wing Survey Research Group seeks to promote and co-ordinate duck wing studies throughout north-west Europe and Scandinavia in conjunction with ringing and bag studies as a means of making a contribution from the hunting community (used in the European sense) to the management of our migratory ducks. This work, from its humble origins in Sevenoaks through the interest and enthusiasm of a few wildfowlers, has now grown to a study of international dimensions which, with the continued support of wildfowlers, will help to clarify aspects of

duck biology which will be not only of considerable interest but also potentially of importance in guiding the management of our duck populations for both shooting and conservation purposes.

NATIONAL SHOOTING SURVEY

Another major programme of research which depends so much on wildfowlers for its success is the B.A.S.C.'s National Shooting Survey programme. This began in 1979 to collect factual information about sporting shooting in the United Kingdom, particularly on the numbers of people shooting live quarry, the numbers of each quarry species shot each year, as well as when and where this shooting took place. It is essential that the Association has this information so that it can account on behalf of the shooting community for the impact of our sport on wildfowl and also contribute to the understanding of the many factors which affect the quarry species and hence their management needs. Furthermore, it ensures that the Association remains in a strong position to be involved in discussions and policy planning at all levels, with national and international bodies both within and outside government, on a whole range of matters relating to sporting shooting. Being in possession of a considerable quantity of detailed information, it can speak authoritatively. In fact, through this programme, the B.A.S.C. now has a more detailed and comprehensive body of information on shooting in this country, particularly of migratory birds, than anybody else and is consequently able to make very significant contributions to both national and international debate.

The main element of the National Shooting Survey comprises an annual bag return from a large sample of B.A.S.C. members, selected randomly from the membership file. Each member is asked to provide details of his (or her) shooting throughout the season, the numbers of each species shot, for wildfowl and gamebirds the month of shooting and the main county of shooting. For the other so-called 'pest' species, including pigeons, rabbits and hares, and for deer, totals only for the whole year are requested. A shooting diary is provided for the selected members to help them record the necessary details.

It did take a little while for some sportsmen to accept the need to record the details of their own shooting and then make them available for further analysis, since such bag details in this country have tended to be regarded as being personal and not for wider use. But the response rate to this survey, although rather low initially, has more than doubled as members have recognised the benefits of their parent body being armed with this type of information.

One of the main objectives of this research was to obtain the first realistic estimate of the total number of ducks shot each year in this country. Previously only 'guesstimates' had been made with little sound basis.

There has been a growing need to verify that the total duck bag was biologically acceptable particularly given that sporting shooting in the United Kingdom is not regulated to nearly the same degree as in North America. Its successful degree of regulation, however, is achieved partly through the basic legal framework for shooting but mainly through the fact of shooting rights being associated with the ownership of land and the strong sporting traditions which have been passed down the years. The high degree of regulation of the coastal wildfowling in England and Wales has been due largely to the control of the many wildfowling clubs affiliated to the B.A.S.C. (Laws, 1984). In Scotland the situation is less well regulated, on account of the differences in legislation affecting the use of coastal regions, but affiliated clubs still exert some regulating influence over the shooting of ducks and geese.

Through the detailed information supplied by the members of the B.A.S.C. over several years, together with other market research conducted by the Association into the characteristics of the whole shooting community in this country, it proved possible to estimate that perhaps as many as one million ducks are shot annually in the United Kingdom. Mallard are thought to comprise nearly three-quarters of the total, although it should be remembered that several hundred thousand are reared and released each year. Such figures inevitably caused something of a stir since they were several times greater than previous 'guesstimates'. Furthermore, the estimated bags of the most common species of ducks, particularly mallard, teal and wigeon, appeared to comprise a large proportion of the numbers of each of these species currently believed to winter in the UK each year, as revealed by the National Wildfowl Counts.

Whilst the NSS estimates are acknowledged to be still relatively crude, although more realistic than any before, they have had the effect of questioning, in a constructive way, the completeness of the National Wildfowl Counts themselves, since they have raised the important issue of 'turnover' in birds in a given area, that is, movement of birds through that area in between the monthly counts that take place throughout the winter season. It is strongly suggested that, especially for teal and wigeon, there are many more birds than the number actually counted using this country during the winter, a point of considerable interest to both conservation and shooting interests. This, in turn, has stimulated welcome efforts, particularly by the Wildfowl Trust, to determine the extent of this 'turnover' in our wildfowl populations. Indeed, it is now thought that the number of wigeon using Britain during the winter is at least half as many again as is present at the peak (Owen & Mitchell, 1988).

Although total bags of each of the duck species are now being measured in tens or hundreds of thousands, the fact remains that all the main quarry duck populations wintering in the UK are either increasing or at least stable, as is shown in the 20-year review of duck populations, by the Wildfowl Trust (Owen et al. 1986). We may still not know for sure the total number of birds wintering in this country, and hence, as in the American system, how many should be available for 'harvesting' in order to maintain at least a stable population. We are now beginning to get some idea of how many ducks actually are 'harvested' each year, through the NSS. Whatever the level actually is, though, duck shooting in the UK does appear to be biologically acceptable, a finding of reassurance to all those interested in shooting and conservation.

The results of this work, recently published in the Wildfowl Trust's *Wildfowl*, has provided for the first time a comprehensive account of duck shooting in the United Kingdom, including the parts of the country where shooting takes place, patterns through the season, and the importance of wildfowling in February and moonlight shooting (Harradine, 1985). This achievement has been welcomed by the other conservation organisations also concerned with the well-being and future of our wildfowl populations which provide sporting shooting. It has demonstrated that the sporting shooting community does take its responsibilities seriously and is prepared to invest considerable resources accordingly. Its success has been due so much to the willingness of shooting men and women to support the research work of their parent body and to provide details of their shooting activities.

It must be made clear, however, that wildfowlers, quite naturally and rightly, will not support research unless they are satisfied it is necessary to increase our knowledge of wildfowl and their management needs or to address an issue which is causing concern to themselves or to other conservation organisations. Even then there can be some apprehension in wildfowler breasts over how the results of any research might be used in the future, particularly by way of justifying further restrictions on their sport. Sometimes these may indeed be necessary and, if clearly demonstrated, will be accepted. In fact, wildfowling has been faced with an increasing number of restrictions in recent years, some less well founded than others, so it is not surprising that there can be some scepticism when research into controversial matters is proposed.

LEAD SHOT

In 1979 the B.A.S.C. agreed with the Wildfowl Trust and the RSPB to undertake a joint assessment of the extent of ingested lead pellet poisoning in Britain arising from spent shotgun lead pellets.

The subject had been somewhat controversial for some time, particularly in the United States of America, and it was felt useful to ascertain to what extent there was any problem in this country. As before, wildfowlers rallied to support this work and contributed some 2700 gizzards from 24 different species, together with many hundreds of livers and wing bones for lead analysis. In addition some 22 wetland sites around the country were sampled, mainly by wildfowlers over a period of several months, for pellets in the soils.

The results provided a great deal of information about the level of pellet ingestion by wildfowl and the densities of pellets in different types of soil in this country. Difficulties arose, however, when estimates were attempted of the total numbers of ducks possibly dying each year as a direct result of ingested lead pellet poisoning. Methods and assumptions were used which have since been found in America to be inappropriate in estimating mortality from pellet ingestion levels. A figure was produced, however, which has since been used extensively to demonstrate the impact of lead pellet poisoning in British wildfowl. The fact is, though, that there is no evidence of any problem at the national level in this country and this is a view

accepted also by other conservation organisations, including the Wildfowl Trust. Local problems, however, can and, occasionally, do occur which can frequently, but not always, be traced to clay pigeon shooting sites depositing pellets in high densities in areas accessible to waterfowl. The solution to these local problems is local changes in management to prevent further deposition of pellets and possibly removal of those already deposited. This subject is covered more comprehensively in Chapter 28.

DISTURBANCE STUDY

Another issue which wildfowlers have to face is that of the disturbance to wildfowl allegedly caused by wildfowling. As the direct effects of shooting have become better understood, in light of the results of the National Shooting Survey and other research, the question of disturbance caused by the sport has received much more attention. It has often been claimed to be harmful to wildfowl populations and used to justify restrictions on shooting without evidence of harm being produced.

It was not surprising, therefore, that when a major study of the effects of disturbance caused by wildfowling was proposed by the Wildfowl Trust, supported by the Nature Conservancy Council and RSPB, wildfowlers viewed them with some reservation and were unsure to what extent they wished to be involved. In view of the increasing attention given to the whole question of disturbance, however, it became clear that a comprehensive assessment of the whole subject was necessary in order to put it into perspective and, indeed, to identify any aspects of wildfowl and wildfowling management which may need particular attention. For the success of the study, the support of the wildfowling community again was essential, since so much information about the sport could come

only from the wildfowlers themselves. In due course, a joint assessment was agreed between the B.A.S.C., through its Wildfowling Liaison Committee, and the Wildfowl Trust for each to undertake specific studies of different aspects of the disturbance question with a view to producing a joint report at the end. This would enable all interested parties to be better informed on the effects of wildfowling disturbance and how best to manage them, without the difficulties or suspicions being caused by either organisation undertaking such a study on its own.

CLUB RESEARCH

It is perhaps issues such as these and the sharply focused attention which has increasingly been directed at our estuaries and coastal regions in recent years that has emphasised the need for wildfowlers to become more involved in research. Nobody denies the greater pressures nowadays than in the past on wildfowl populations and on their habitats from a whole range of different sources. Few believe that wildfowling can continue in the way that it used to be enjoyed and most accept that changes and adjustments to circumstances today are required, as is management for sound conservation and multiple use of coastal areas for tomorrow.

Wildfowlers are very concerned that any changes that are made should be soundly based and not unduly influenced by protectionist interests, who would simply like to see an end to all shooting. They are increasingly concerned also that the strength and influence of the protectionist lobby can result in persuasive arguments being put forward with the result of further restrictions on their sport being imposed. In response to this many wildfowling clubs have now begun their own research studies in their local areas, collecting detailed facts and figures about the birds as well as their shooting. Numbers of the quarry species, bag sizes, body weight, sex and ages of the birds, changes in habitats, usage of the marsh by club members, are all vital as well as fascinating aspects of wildfowling management to monitor. Their study helps club members not only to safeguard their own shooting and contribute to the conservation management needs of their locality but also can provide club members with a new interest in

their sport and may even make their own shooting more rewarding. Such local studies can also support the national work undertaken on their behalf by their parent body.

Game shooters have traditionally kept a game book to record the details of their shooting, but this practice is less common amongst wildfowlers, perhaps because wildfowling is more of an individual and personal sport. Detailed records of the numbers of each species shot over a particular estuary or marsh, however, can be not only of considerable interest to club members, especially when compared to previous years' bags, but also a valuable indicator of the numbers of quarry species using the area from year to year. Together with the counts of the wildfowl themselves, either as recorded by the National Wildfowl Counts or as undertaken by the club itself, such bag studies can help to put their shooting levels into local perspective. Wildfowlers often find themselves faced with claims of excessive shooting from protectionist interests and consequently under pressure to restrict their shooting or establish new no-shooting reserves. Without information on their own shooting levels, including the numbers of wildfowlers using the area, the numbers of birds shot, the times of the season when they are shot and even the number of nil visits, wildfowlers can be in a weak position to resist such pressures. Such a position prevailed on the Ythan Estuary in north-east Scotland, for example, in the early 1980s when the adjacent Sands of Forvie National Nature Reserve was extended to include the estuary, which has for long been important for wildfowling, particularly for geese. One of the main objectives of reserve management by the Nature Conservancy Council was to minimise human activities, particularly over the sand dune areas, so as to allow the vegetation processes and changes to take place as unhindered as possible. In the face of its proposals to reduce wildfowling activity on the estuary the local wildfowling clubs and the B.A.S.C. undertook a survey of wildfowling for several years, collecting facts and figures on the numbers of wildfowlers, the quarry shot, where wildfowling took place and other aspects, so as to be able to quantify the levels of activity. It was clear at the end of this exercise that wildfowling was by no means excessive for that estuary and helped to satisfy the NCC that no further restrictions were necessary.

In addition to resisting unwarranted pressures to restrict shooting, comprehensive bag records can be a positive aid to management. One club on the south coast of England, which has a shooting licence from the RSPB over one of the latter's reserves, has kept detailed bag records for the past nine years. The club believes that these records demonstrate that the terms of the licence have had the effect of disproportionately increasing the numbers of one of the quarry species shot at the expense of the others. An adjustment in these conditions, therefore, could well achieve a more equitable sharing of the wildfowling over all the main species utilising the site.

Many wildfowling clubs operate some form of bag return in order to collect the type of information which might be helpful to the club in any future negotiations with landowners or those holding the shooting rights. There can be some resistance to establishing a bag return scheme, particularly from the older members of a club who remember the times when wildfowling around the coasts of Britain was less rigorously regulated and under less scrutiny than it is today. It may be easier to institute a simple voluntary scheme initially, but many clubs find that the need for such factual information becomes so great that some form of obligatory bag return is essential to obtain the necessary details, often backed with strict sanctions against those failing to return the information.

Such a bag return form can vary from a simple total number of ducks and geese shot through the whole season by each person, to the numbers of each species shot on each day, or even each flight, throughout the season, on different parts of the shooting zone, with the number of visits made, including those during which nothing was shot. The precise form will depend on the individual club's circumstances and needs, but to be successful it does require a specific member of the club to take responsibility for the scheme, especially for the analysing and presenting of the results correctly after the end of each season.

Some clubs already are required to supply certain details of their members' shooting to the managers of their shooting area, such as the NCC, RSPB or local authorities, as a contribution to the management of all the activities taking place on those particular sites. This does not preclude additional details of particular local interest being collected by the club, however, over and above those required by the agreement.

Related to such bag monitoring is the use of duck wing collections to provide a fuller picture of the club's bag of ducks taken through the season. For many years wildfowling clubs have contributed to the national Duck Wing Survey, but an increasing number now are developing their own schemes, in conjunction with the national scheme, to help determine the proportion of males and females and the ages of the main species being taken in the club's area. It may not always be safe to rely on individual club members to identify correctly the immature male from immature female, even when the whole bird is in the hand. A more accurate assessment of the composition of the bag and how it changes through the season, and from season to season, can often be made by an experienced member of the club collecting a sufficiently large sample of wings, and analysing these in a consistent manner.

The results of such club-based studies can be of considerable interest to the club's members, revealing aspects of wildfowl biology and behaviour perhaps not previously considered. There is also potential value in revealing the patterns of usage of the different parts of the shooting area, and whether any particular type of shooting has the effect of taking more of a given sex or age group than another.

The expertise to undertake such analyses is often already present within a wildfowling club or can be developed through a certain amount of training provided by the B.A.S.C. The 'Duck Wings' key is certainly helpful, but experience built up over the years has shown that additional characters are valuable in determining some species' wings. Without doubt a reference collection of the different types of wings of each species is an invaluable aid to conducting such studies and should certainly be amongst the first of the steps taken. It is important also, if the results of these local studies are to be integrated into the national surveys, that those undertaking the analyses be consistent in their determinations. In the early stages of club-based wing studies, therefore, a certain amount of close co-ordination between local and national studies is sensible so that the results ultimately are comparable. The scope of contributing to the national surveys is considerable, since a series of well-developed club wing study schemes around the coasts enables a more detailed geographical analysis of the sex and age ratios of our duck populations within this country which may well provide a new insight into duck wintering behaviour not previously realised.

SEVERE WEATHER

The subject of severe weather suspensions of wildfowling in recent years (see Chapter 28) has focused attention on the need to learn more about how wildfowl respond to periods of prolonged severe weather and to achieve a sounder basis for determining when any restrictions should take effect. To many wildfowlers the condition of birds under these circumstances is a very pertinent factor and they perhaps are the best placed to monitor the changes in condition which might indicate when ducks and geese reach a point when they cannot obtain sufficient food and when it is then reasonable to minimise unnecessary disturbance until they are able to recover.

Whilst it could prove difficult to obtain sufficient records of wildfowl condition from around the country in time to be able to make the necessary decisions under the current arrangements, the more that is known about wildfowl in cold weather then the closer these arrangements might be tailored in the future to the needs of the birds. A study is currently under way to monitor the condition of wildfowl during the winter to assist in

Under the auspices of the B.A.S.C. wildfowlers are recording duck body weights through the season to develop a greater insight into factors affecting condition

just this way. A number of wildfowlers around the country have been supplied with precision balances, bought with NCC grant aid, for weighing the ducks they shoot through the season. In addition, they are removing a wing from each bird so that its length can be measured as well. This is to provide a 'correction' for the different body size of ducks, which clearly affects the measured weight. Wing length has been found to be closely related to body size, so that its application to the weight measurement is a useful way of reducing one of the variables in this type of investigation.

As in much biological research, the data collected by many of these studies become more valuable with each season that passes. As any wildfowler knows the wildfowl themselves, their habitats and the factors affecting them are extremely variable. As a result the information from one season alone may not be sufficient to enable analysis and interpretation of the results with any confidence. Considerable amounts of data collected from as many different situations as possible are needed to help smooth out some of the variations normally expected, as well as those unexpected, before normal patterns can be determined against which any changes in the particular factors being studied can be related. Hence most of the studies involving wildfowlers may last for several years. This can be somewhat frustrating to those contributors anxious to know the outcome of their efforts. Interim or annual progress reports certainly can help to maintain the interest and support of contributors before the final results become available.

Wildfowlers over the years have contributed a great deal to our knowledge and management of wildfowl populations. There is no doubt that they will continue to do so as they have such a deep interest in the birds, their habitats and their needs.

Wildfowling does have to change in line with the needs of the birds in face of pressures from various sources and this is accepted.

But change for change's sake will not be so sympathetically received and support for research not readily forthcoming if its purposes and methods are not perceived as being necessary or appropriate. Wildfowlers are as concerned as anybody about the future of our coastal areas and their wealth of wildfowl and will be keen to assist where possible, or undertake themselves where necessary, studies which will help secure our wildfowl populations and the opportunities for wildfowling's crafts and pleasures.

REFERENCES

Boyd, H., Harrison, J. & Allison, A., 1975. *Duck Wings – a study of duck production*. WAGBI Conservation Publication.

Harradine, J., 1985. 'Duck shooting in the United Kingdom'. *Wildfowl* 36, 81–94.

Harrison, J., 1972. *A Gravel Pit Wildfowl Reserve*. WAGBI Conservation Publication.

Laws, A. R., 1984. *The Conservation of Wildlife Habitat in England by B.A.S.C. Members*. British Association for Shooting and Conservation, Rossett.

Owen, M., Atkinson-Willes, G. L. & Salmon D. G., 1986. *Wildfowl in Great Britain*. Cambridge University Press.

Owen, M. & Dix, M., 1986. 'Sex ratios in some common British wintering ducks'. *Wildfowl* 37, 104–12.

Owen, M. & Mitchell, C., 1988. 'Movements and migrations of wigeon (Anas penelope) wintering in Britain and Ireland.' *Bird Study* 35, 47–59.

Perdeck, A. C. & Clason, C., 1983. 'Sexual differences in migration and wintering of ducks ringed in the Netherlands'. *Wildfowl* 34, 137–43.

Sedgwick, N. M., Whitaker, P. & Harrison, J., 1970. *The New Wildfowler in the 1970s*. Barrie and Jenkins.

28
TOPICAL ISSUES IN WILDFOWLING
JOHN HARRADINE

DARKBELLIED BRENT GEESE

Of the various issues currently in the minds of wildfowlers the one most deeply felt probably is the loss of quarry species. Losses have taken place over the years, but they have generally coincided with major revisions of the bird protection legislation. Some species formerly shot by wildfowlers have been justifiably removed from the quarry list to help conserve those which clearly have been under pressure, whilst others have been removed as a result of pressure generated by protectionist lobbies taking advantage of the legislative revisions to limit the number of species which can be shot. To date the process has been one of continuing loss, as far as the wildfowler is concerned, since no species have yet been restored to the quarry list. This measure would appear to be entirely appropriate, however, if shooting in this country is to be managed according to sound wildlife management principles. There is no reason why a formerly reduced quarry species, once recovered sufficiently, should not be made available again to enable a 'harvest' to be taken from it.

The darkbellied brent goose (*Branta bernicla bernicla*) epitomises a species which was formerly of considerable importance to coastal wildfowlers, declined drastically in numbers after its food supply declined, was given necessary protection, has since recovered dramatically, but still has not been restored to the quarry list, despite assurances that it would be, once its population had increased sufficiently again. An intriguing species, of considerable interest to wildfowlers, conservationists and farmers, the brent goose has become something of a *cause célèbre*. There is no doubt that its restoration would do much to help repair the damage done, in the eyes of the wildfowling community, to the conservationist movement in this country, in the light of the latter's apparent unwillingness to consider returning a once-protected species to the quarry list.

The darkbellied brent goose breeds in western Siberia and typically migrates via the Baltic and Netherlands to arrive off the Essex coast during October and November, before dispersing farther north and south around the coasts of England. On arrival the geese eat *Zostera* (eel grass) on the mud flats, but then, as the season progresses, move farther inland, eating *Enteromorpha* and other marine algae, marsh grasses and herbs, and, for an increasing number of geese, arable crops and pasture grass above the sea wall. It is this inland feeding which has caused some conflict with farmers in recent years and which has led to the provision of alternative feeding areas in which their feeding is encouraged.

The size of the population was considerable, although unknown, in the earlier years of this century, but in the 1920s and 1930s a 'wasting disease' decimated the *Zostera* foodstocks and the numbers of geese declined dramatically and their distribution altered markedly.

Since its protection in the mid-1950s, when the population was around 16,000, the brent goose has increased rapidly, particularly following its protection in Britain, France, Denmark and parts of West Germany, and has recently reached more than 200,000 birds, although has since declined somewhat from that (Figure 42). It is widely believed that this increase has been largely due to the reduction in shooting mortality. As the numbers have increased the habit of inland feeding has increased also, suggesting that the population has outgrown its wintering estuarine habitat. The fact that the species is adaptable enough to begin feeding inland indicates that much more habitat is now available to it during the winter and this may assist its further increase. On the other hand, it is a matter of mild controversy as to what does regulate the numbers of brent geese, and whether limiting factors are beginning to operate, particularly on the breeding grounds. As these lie within the Soviet Union little is known about them.

FIGURE 42 *North-west European and British population size of the darkbellied brent goose, 1956 to 1986*

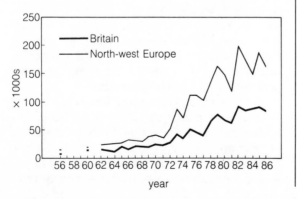

Recent research has indicated the importance of the spring staging areas in the Dutch and German Wadensee, where the birds build up their reserves *en route* to their breeding grounds. If they prove able to expand into inland feeding areas during this critical time of the year as well then it would seem that further population increases are likely.

The brent goose was extensively shot by coastal wildfowlers until its decline. Throughout the debate leading up to its protection in 1954, however, the concept of restoring the brent goose to the quarry list, once its numbers had recovered, was promoted by, amongst others, the then chairman of the Nature Conservancy and Sir Peter Scott. Wildfowlers accepted the need for temporary protection, particularly in view of the assurances given for future reinstatement. Since then the population has increased by some twelve times and appears still to be increasing, and many wildfowlers wish the opportunity to shoot brent again. The wintering UK population is close to the population sizes of both species of grey geese (pinkfooted and greylag) also wintering here for which there has long been a full open season.

Probably more important than the brent being a sporting quarry species *per se* is the issue of a species being protected for conservation reasons but only for as long as that protection is needed. As was said at the time, if the brent goose was not reinstated in the future, once its numbers had recovered, the wildfowling community may be less inclined to support future measures to protect species when there appeared to be some need to do so.

In 1977 the International Waterfowl Research Bureau's First Technical Meeting on Western Palearctic Migratory Bird Management concluded that darkbellied brent goose stocks did not permit any harvesting at present. In 1979, however, during the Second Technical Meeting, and following a population increase of some 40,000 geese, the view was expressed that there were no biological reasons for preventing harvesting (excluding agricultural considerations). Since then the population has increased further. Most recently (1987), Sir Peter Scott of the Wildfowl Trust has publicly agreed that the brent goose could now 'stand some shooting provided this was strictly controlled'. It is clear that a population which can raise anything up to 90,000 or more young per year and which is subject to little hunting pressure anywhere in its range, should be able to sustain the loss of a few thousand birds through shooting. It might well have the helpful effect of at least limiting further population increase, or even somewhat reducing it. This latter effect would certainly be welcomed by many of the farmers currently troubled by brent geese and also by many wildfowlers, who increasingly believe that the rising numbers of brent geese are adversely affecting the numbers and distribution of wigeon through some form of competition between the two species.

Agricultural problems began to develop in the early 1970s, when brent geese started coming over the sea wall to feed on agricultural crops. Nowadays, particularly in years with a high percentage of young, birds are increasingly moving inland even before they exhaust their more traditional coastal foods. The *Wildlife and Countryside Act 1981*, through the Ministry of Agriculture, Fisheries and Food (MAFF), permits the licensed shooting of a limited number of geese on those farms most troubled in the east and south-east of England. Since 1982–3 a few hundred birds have been shot each year under licence. The purpose of this shooting is specifically to reinforce scaring methods, rather than to reduce numbers, within the developing network of alternative feeding areas which has been promoted by the Nature Conservancy Council, MAFF, Royal Society for the Protection of Birds (RSPB) and the National Farmers' Union. Sites of importance to geese, particularly those in Sites of Special Scientific Interest, are being used to attract geese that have been discouraged from vulnerable crops elsewhere by scaring procedures with or without licensed shooting. Depending on the precise designation of these sites it may be possible for farmers to be compensated through management agreements for any loss of yield. This system of refuges helps to provide for the conservation needs of the brent goose as an insurance against any substantial future population declines, but there is disagreement between the conservation and agricultural bodies involved as to the extent to which the brent goose should be regarded as a conservation or agricultural problem and funds made available accordingly.

Currently, the main grounds for opposition to the reinstatement of the brent goose to the quarry list are based on the variability of its breeding success, the current strategy for managing its agricultural depredations, and the absence of any co-ordinated and regulated system for the future shooting of brent geese within Europe.

237

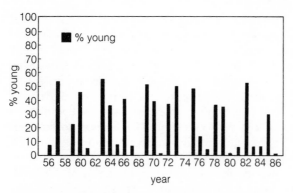

FIGURE 43 Percentage of young darkbellied brent geese in the wintering population, 1956 to 1986

The variability in breeding success is indeed considerable and the cause of a greater degree of uncertainty about the future of this goose population than for other high Arctic breeding goose species. Success varies from 50 % or more young appearing on the wintering grounds to a complete failure of breeding (Figure 43). Some controversy currently surrounds the causes of such variability, but it is widely believed that weather conditions, particularly snow cover, on the breeding grounds are the dominant factor. In Britain, where just under half the total darkbellied brent goose population typically winters, the absence of flexible shooting management regulations, which could vary shooting according to these variations in productivity, does concern conservationists. Inevitable comparisons are made with North America, where population monitoring and control of hunting are highly developed.

Sporting shooting is seen as a threat to the development of the alternative feeding area system, which is deemed to be aimed at balancing the effects of shooting and other disturbance factors rather than accommodating the whole wintering goose populations. Scaring is required to be effective but not to disrupt patterns of traditional dependence of specific groups of brent geese on particular sections of the coast. Furthermore, the view is also held that brent geese should not be allowed to spread farther inland as a result of scaring or disturbance on the coast because the species evolved as a specialised coastal feeder. The conservation and agricultural bodies which are actively promoting this scheme at present fear that patterns of movement and feeding will be disrupted and the birds and their damage dispersed over a wider area and farther inland.

Following its removal from the quarry list by the *Protection of Birds Act 1954* the darkbellied brent goose was then included in Annexe II/2 of Article 7 of the European Commission's Directive on the Conservation of Wild Birds, 1979. This allowed the species to be hunted only in Denmark and the Federal Republic of Germany. Hunting in Denmark had stopped temporarily in 1972, however, and the prohibition has since been continued by Danish government decision. The United Kingdom, Netherlands and France were enabled by Article 9 of the Directive to derogate from the provisions in Article 7 to allow shooting of brent geese '. . . to prevent serious damage to crops . . .', on account of the agricultural problems increasingly being encountered. The *Wildlife and Countryside Act 1981* in Britain, which directly followed the EEC Birds Directive, then incorporated these provisions into British legislation.

The wildfowling community is in no doubt that the brent goose population could sustain a regulated harvest and that wildfowlers should have restored to them the opportunity to shoot brent geese if they so wish. At the same time, however, they recognise that the variable breeding success of the brent goose and the agricultural problems require that any shooting season be carefully tailored to both the characteristics of the species and the needs of the different interests in the bird. Consequently they are prepared to discuss ways in which a shooting season could be flexible in order to respond to dramatic changes in breeding success from year to year, and hence the possibility of limited seasons, confined to those parts of the country where the sub-species occurs. This would avoid any overlap with the much less abundant lightbellied brent goose. Sir Peter Scott has suggested limiting shooting to inland sites, so as to avoid discouraging the birds from utilising to the full the foreshore areas, but many wildfowlers would wish to consider restoring shooting to the foreshore, the site of the traditional shooting of this goose species. Shooting later in the season would then minimise any premature dispersal of geese inland from the foreshore. Clearly, monitoring of each season's shooting and bags, and their effects on the birds, would be necessary, but, at the same time, would be much more easily undertaken nowadays than in the past, with the detailed schemes of bird counts and bag monitoring carried out by the conservation and shooting organisations. Furthermore, in addition to the existing comprehensive system of wildfowl refuges around the country, additional disturbance-free areas are becoming available through the alternative feeding area strategy, where birds would not be disturbed. Opportunities for shooting brent geese would be limited even further, not only because of where and by whom the shooting rights are held but also because not all B.A.S.C.-affiliated clubs, which regulate so much shooting around the coast, wish to shoot the goose. Many of the clubs which do would consider imposing their own conditions on shooting, including bag limits as well as bag returns. The sensitivity of the subject would ensure that careful scrutiny of shooting would take place, helping further to limit any excessive shooting, unsporting practices or commercialisation of goose shooting.

At the same time wildfowlers are under no illusion as to what is required to alter the current protected status of the brent goose. For it to be treated as a sporting quarry species it will have to be added to Schedule 2 Part I of the *Wildlife and Countryside Act 1981* (since wildfowlers in Britain do not wish to have the brent goose treated as a 'pest' species). This will require, in turn, 'Britain' to be added to the list of countries in which the dark-bellied brent goose may be hunted under Article 7 Annexe II/2 of the Birds Directive. In order to achieve such a change a unanimous decision would then be required of the European Commission in favour of allowing sport shooting in this country. Consequently the support of the hunting and conservation organisations as well as the governments from all European countries represented on the Commission would be essential before any such decision was sought. Furthermore, a fundamental requirement of any case put to the European Commission is that Britain has (albeit for the first time) the necessary flexibility in its domestic legislative arrangements to open, close or restrict a shooting season as required by the circumstances, and an effective system of controls and monitoring of the kill of brent geese in any given season.

Clearly much thought and discussion is needed between all interested parties both in Britain and Europe before changes to the present protected status of the darkbellied brent goose could become possible. A practical scheme will be needed which will provide the desired opportunity for sporting shooting, albeit well regulated, but which will not exacerbate, and preferably help to reduce, the current agricultural difficulties encountered by some eastern and southern coastal farmers. It will also have to satisfy conservation bodies both within Britain and Europe that the conservation needs and the future of this fascinating sub-species are safeguarded. This process inevitably will take time, but the evident willingness of some conservation organisations to start discussing practical schemes which recognise the interests of all parties is encouraging.

WILDFOWLING AND SEVERE WEATHER

One of the more contentious issues of recent years amongst wildfowlers has been the suspension of wildfowling during periods of prolonged severe weather. The issue really came to a head after the 1978–9 winter, when a statutory suspension order was signed by the Secretary of State for the Environment under pressure from a protectionist organisation. In light of the ill-feeling and problems that were generated by this action it became clear that an agreed system of managing wildfowling during periods of prolonged severe weather was necessary. Over the intervening years a system has evolved which is now largely accepted by the shooting community. It provides wildfowl and wader populations with freedom from shooting disturbance at times when this may be needed and also shows that the shooting community is responsible in the way it pursues its sport during periods of adverse conditions for wildfowl.

The prolonged severe winter of 1962–3 was the first to reveal the need for restricting wildfowling in view of the problems which birds appeared to suffer (Harrison & Hudson, 1963). Frozen foreshores, exceptional mortality and large bags all pointed to the need for some action and, indeed, many wildfowlers stopped shooting voluntarily before the B.A.S.C. (then WAGBI) itself called for a national voluntary ban on wildfowling. A minority of people, however, did take advantage of the conditions and this led to pressures to provide statutory powers to suspend wildfowling during future periods of severe weather.

The first opportunity to make such provision occurred with the *Protection of Birds Act 1967*. Section 7 of the Act enabled the Secretary of State to make orders protecting any wild bird outside the closed season in Schedule 3 (the so-called 'quarry list') of the *Protection of Birds Act 1954* if this seemed necessary in the event of severe weather. The species covered were the quarry duck, geese and waders, woodcock, snipe, coot, moorhen and the somewhat anomalous capercaillie. Before any such order was signed the Secretary of State was obliged to consult, *inter alia*, a representative of the shooting community. In practice, John Anderton, the B.A.S.C.'s Director, acted as that representative. Some basic guidelines were also prepared for use when severe weather prevailed, centring on the length of time foreshores were frozen, but which relied to a considerable extent on the subjective judgement of those the Secretary of State was obliged to consult.

The first occasion on which these new powers were invoked was in January 1979. A period of hard weather caused problems throughout the country and conditions on the Continent were sufficiently severe for much shooting there to be stopped. In the UK daily discussions were taking place between the B.A.S.C., Nature Conservancy Council (NCC), Wildfowl Trust and RSPB about possible temporary suspensions of shooting. There was disagreement over the extent to which the frequent short thaws were enabling the birds to stay fit. In the event, the Secretary of State was pressurised to suspend wildfowling, without consulting all those who should have been consulted, and, in so doing, caused considerable acrimony and confusion. When the dust had settled it was clear that all the interested parties should seek a practical and agreed means of operating Section 7 of the 1967 Act so as to avoid any further confrontations between shooting and protectionist interests.

During 1979 the B.A.S.C., NCC, Wildfowl Trust, RSPB, British Trust for Ornithology, Game Conservancy and the Department of the Environment met on several occasions to work out some objective criteria for deciding when hard weather was exceptional enough to warrant the use of the Section 7 powers. The Working Group considered also the biological questions involved, the collection and evaluation of the data forming the basis of the criteria, the speed and reliability of the data collection for rapid decision-making and the practicalities of implementing the appropriate decision in a way which would cause the least possible

confusion and scope for misunderstanding. Much attention was directed to the freezing of the foreshore and the body weights of wildfowl as indicators of the need for restricting wildfowling. Considerable problems were found with both approaches, making it difficult to incorporate either into a practical scheme, that was sufficiently speedy in use. For example, freezing may cover only part of the foreshore, depending on tides and currents. Different reports about the extent of freezing could come from neighbouring estuaries subject to similar weather conditions. The gradual freezing of estuaries makes it difficult to decide when freezing has actually started. Was frozen sand or silt adequate or would the tideway itself have to have ice floes or ice cover on it? Finally, there was no system for ensuring that such information would be available in a given winter after several years of mild winters, or that it could be collected in an objective and dispassionate way.

With regard to the condition of birds, which too was clearly an important factor, there proved again to be no system which would ensure that the information could be collected and made available in a crisis in an objectively valid way. Substantial numbers of duck from many parts of the country would have to be shot to provide a statistically acceptable sample for decision-making.

Attention turned to the data collected by the Meteorological Office's coastal stations, which regularly through the day record the 'state-of-ground', in terms of degrees of moisture, freezing or snow cover. Coastal stations were chosen since not only are most estuaries of considerable importance for wildfowl under normal conditions but also, during severe weather, most other wildfowl and waders move towards the coast. Only when coastal stations showed prolonged adverse conditions would action need to be taken.

In order to test the suitability of this type of data for implementing the statutory powers, the B.A.S.C. undertook a substantial research programme to verify that it would give sufficiently realistic indications of the severity of the weather. This research showed that when more than half of an agreed number of coastal meteorological stations had recorded frozen or snow-covered ground for an unbroken period of fourteen days the Nature Conservancy Council, the government's advisory body on conservation, would have a reasonable basis for advising the Secretary of State that an order suspending wildfowling was appropriate. The research concluded that of the times of day when the data were collected, the 09.00 hrs data provided as good an indicator of ground conditions as any other. It was then agreed that periods of one or two days, when fewer than half the stations reported the frozen or snow-covered ground, would not require the fourteen-day sequence to start again, whereas a 'thaw' of three or more days would result in the earlier period of severe weather being disregarded.

A retrospective study of data since 1959 showed that, had these criteria been adopted then, there would have been a basis for statutory suspensions in 1961–2, 1962–3 and, just, in 1978–9. Consequently it was felt that the criteria accorded with political realities and did provide a reasonable basis for deciding when to use this provision of the 1967 Act, subject to the fact that the final decision always lies with the Secretary of State.

Since voluntary restraint has always been part of the normal tradition of wildfowling, having been seen to have worked particularly well during 1962–3, it was agreed that the concept of voluntary restraint be incorporated into the severe weather procedures. Consequently, when 'severe weather' has been recorded for seven consecutive days (or ten days including one or two days of thaw), the B.A.S.C. would call for voluntary restraint from the shooting community in order to encourage responsible shooting behaviour at a time when excesses could be committed. Its call would also serve to warn people of the possibility of a statutory suspension if the weather remained severe for another seven days.

The procedures agreed by the Working Group also covered responsibilities for contacts with the Meteorological Office, communication between the main organisations involved, the need for restrictions on birdwatching and cannon-netting and arrangements for publicising these actions.

Finally, while it was recognised that the weather could affect one part of the country rather than another, it was felt appropriate that any suspension should extend to the whole country. Considerable difficulties were envisaged not only in determining any regional boundaries for different action, but also in publicising and enforcing any regional variations. Moreover, it was recognised that, during such weather conditions, wildfowl frequently seek refuge in regions less badly affected

and they need some respite there too. On the other hand, it was recognised that responses to the call for voluntary restraint would vary regionally depending on local needs.

This new set of procedures received a very thorough and rigorous testing during 1981–2. In early December 1981 'severe weather' began and, in accordance with the agreed procedures, finally led to a statutory suspension beginning on 22 December. Problems arose over ineffective publicity in the pre-Christmas period and from backbench political pressures to delay the introduction of a suspension to enable woodcock shooting over Christmas, causing last-minute delays and confusion and insufficient time to publicise the suspension order. The police appeared also to be quite inadequately informed.

Frustrations began to develop, particularly in the west and south-west of the country, where weather conditions remained 'open' but where sportsmen were unable to enjoy any sport. Calls for regionalisation of suspensions came not just from individuals but also from wildfowling guides and commercial shooting interests, where long-established arrangements for shooting holidays were being thwarted. Pressures also developed to have the woodcock exempted from statutory suspensions on the grounds that the species was far better able to withstand severe weather than wildfowl and other waders.

At the end of December a nationwide thaw set in and the suspension order was expected to be lifted on 5 January 1982. An unexpected return of severe weather, particularly in Scotland, then created considerable confusion, since the procedures had not anticipated such an early return of severe weather after the operation of the suspension procedures. The B.A.S.C. called for continued restraint, particularly in Scotland, after the suspension had lapsed, but it was agreed by all the organisations to reintroduce the Scottish suspension and then the England/Wales suspension on 10 and 12 January, respectively. Considerable efforts were made on all sides to publicise these reimposed suspensions, but they did not result in satisfactory media coverage. A week later a general thaw set in, but, as had been previously found, publicity of the lifting of suspensions proved to be even less effective than that surrounding their imposition.

The Nature Conservancy Council's Working Group duly reviewed the events of the 1981–2 winter. The problems of effective publicity attracted the most attention and changes were made to the arrangements to allow more time for all relevant people to be adequately informed. The existing network of thirteen meteorological stations was upheld, but a suspension order would henceforth be signed after thirteen days of frozen or snow-covered ground, to take effect at 09.00 hrs on the fifteenth day, the intervening time being used to publicise the fact. The government was encouraged to place advertisements in selected national newspapers and to have suitable announcements included in television and radio weather forecasts. Other changes to the arrangements included a minimum period of seven days' 'thaw' before any suspension be lifted, capercaillie should be excluded from any future bans, and further research undertaken to determine the efficacy of wildfowling suspensions and the effects on wildfowl of severe weather. The possibility of excluding woodcock from the arrangements was also carefully considered but was felt neither desirable nor practical.

The operation of these revised arrangements was not realised again until January 1985, when severe weather predominated in the east and south-east of England. In due course a statutory suspension was imposed in England and Wales and, two days later, in Scotland, even though conditions in Scotland were felt by many not to warrant any such action. Considerable dissatisfaction developed through much of the suspension, which finally was lifted just before the end of the inland shooting season. Continuing publicity problems, inadequate enforcement by the police and a growing belief that the criteria were not reflecting the conditions under which wildfowl in reality were living, led to efforts being made by the B.A.S.C., on behalf of its wildfowling members, to have the suspension lifted before the end of the fourteen-day period. Calls for a regional approach to statutory suspensions and the exemption of woodcock were renewed.

The whole matter of wildfowling suspensions received very thorough examination at the B.A.S.C.'s first Wildfowling Conference, held in February 1985. Strong views were expressed and it was clear that the current arrangements were no longer acceptable to the shooting community. In light of this the B.A.S.C. undertook a thorough review of all the arrangements relating to severe weather wildfowling suspensions for the NCC's Working Group, which met in June 1985 to review their recent operation.

The aspects carefully reviewed included the system of monitoring the state-of-ground/weather conditions, other relevant factors affecting wildfowl, a regional rather than national approach, publicity arrangements, and more research involving wildfowlers to understand better the effects of severe weather on wildfowl and the relevance to the birds of the arrangements for imposing shooting suspensions. It was agreed that improvements were necessary so as to ensure that the arrangements for future suspensions of wildfowling were both less restrictive on wildfowlers and more acceptable to them.

The result of this review was a more acceptable and workable system for managing wildfowling during periods of severe weather. One of the main changes was an increase from thirteen to twenty-three of the coastal meteorological stations, giving better coverage of the British coast, the majority of stations in both Scotland and in England/Wales being sited on the milder western side of each country, in contrast to the previous bias towards the colder eastern sides, and eliminating some from inappropriate locations. Scotland would henceforth be treated separately from England/Wales, using nine and England/Wales using fifteen of the stations, with both sharing Carlisle. This separation went some way towards satisfying the call for a more regional approach to the arrangements, since weather conditions frequently are harsher in Scotland than elsewhere. It also recognised that the respective Secretaries of State would wish to make their own decisions. Suspensions also, whilst being imposed for a maximum of fourteen days, would now be re-examined after a maximum of seven days. This change provided the basis for lifting suspensions early if weather conditions changed substantially rather than allowing them to run the full fourteen days.

In order to obtain more detailed and relevant information concerning weather and feeding conditions, condition of wildfowl and other factors, and to involve the wildfowlers who are themselves most affected by these arrangements, a new network of local contact groups, comprising both shooting and conservation people, was established, working through the regional offices of the

B.A.S.C. and NCC. They would monitor such factors as the state of the foreshore, condition of birds, unusual numbers or movements of birds and other factors important to, and best collected from, the shooting community. This system would ensure a much greater human input into the system which had been lacking before, when decisions were based on the somewhat arbitrary state-of-ground data. The information would be particularly helpful in determining where any voluntary initiatives might be appropriate, and during the period when statutory suspensions or their lifting were being considered.

The need for considerably improved publicity was universally accepted and the Department of the Environment and Scottish Development Department undertook to place public notices in a larger selection of national and regional newspapers, and to ensure through the Home Office that police forces were adequately and speedily informed.

In January 1987 yet another spell of particularly severe weather affected much of the country. On this occasion the operation of the arrangements was marked by a considerable measure of acceptance and agreement between all the parties involved. A statutory suspension began in both Scotland and England/Wales on 21 January, preceded by widespread expressions of voluntary restraint by wildfowlers throughout the country. Its imposition, however, coincided with a dramatic change in the weather. It subsequently proved possible, with willing agreement of all parties, to lift the suspension on 26 January, one week after its imposition. The early lifting of the suspension was widely appreciated and had the effect of demonstrating to the shooting community that the new system of arrangements was now flexible enough to respond to unexpected changes in conditions. Wildfowlers accepted the severe weather arrangements more readily as a result, recognising that considerable improvements had been achieved, wildfowlers themselves were now more closely involved, and the arrangements provided for suspensions more closely tuned to the needs of wildfowl populations.

CURRENT ARRANGEMENTS

The arrangements currently applying for suspending the shooting of wildfowl and wader species during periods of severe weather are detailed below. They provide the basis for the Secretary of State, under Section 2(6) and (7) of the *Wildlife and Countryside Act 1981*, to declare any period not exceeding fourteen days as a period of special protection for any birds included in Part I of Schedule 2 with respect to the whole or any specified part of Great Britain. Before making such an order he must consult a person appearing to him to be a representative of persons interested in the shooting of those birds. The species normally covered by such an order are mallard, teal, wigeon, pintail, tufted duck, pochard, shoveler, gadwall, goldeneye, pinkfooted goose, greylag goose, white-fronted goose, Canada goose, golden plover, woodcock, snipe, coot and moorhen.

The criteria for triggering severe weather procedures are based on the state-of-ground data collected daily by twenty-three coastal National Climatological Message Stations around Britain. The locations of the stations are given in Figure 44. They undertake standard climatological recording of state-of-ground at 09.00 hrs, seven days a week, passing the data to Bracknell, London, the same morning.

The state-of-ground is determined according to two series of codes as below:

E – State of the ground without snow or measurable ice cover

0 Surface of ground dry (without cracks and no appreciable amount of dust or loose sand)
1 Surface of ground moist
2 Surface of ground wet (standing water in small or large pools on surface)
3 Flooded
4 Surface of ground frozen
5 Glaze on ground
6 Loose dry dust or sand not covering ground completely
7 Thin cover of loose dry dust or sand covering ground completely
8 Moderate or thick cover of loose dry dust or sand covering ground completely
9 Extremely dry with cracks

E' – State of the ground with snow or measurable ice cover

0 Ground predominantly covered by ice
1 Compact or wet snow (with or without ice) covering less than one-half of the ground

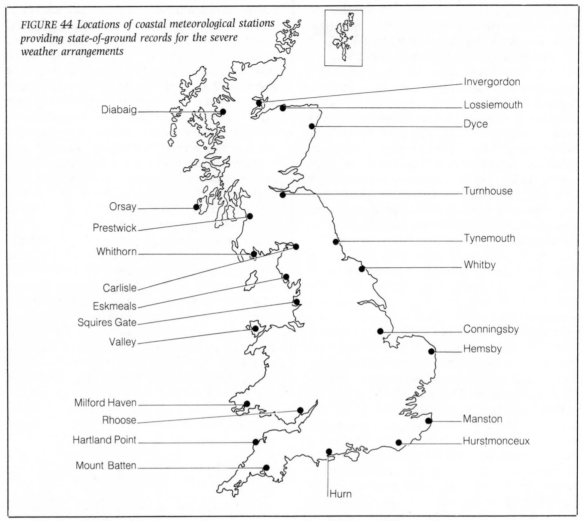

FIGURE 44 *Locations of coastal meteorological stations providing state-of-ground records for the severe weather arrangements*

Invergordon
Lossiemouth
Dyce
Diabaig
Turnhouse
Orsay
Prestwick
Tynemouth
Whithorn
Whitby
Carlisle
Eskmeals
Squires Gate
Conningsby
Valley
Hemsby
Milford Haven
Rhoose
Hartland Point
Manston
Hurstmonceux
Mount Batten
Hurn

2   Compact or wet snow (with or without ice) covering at least one-half of the ground, but ground not completely covered
3   Even layer of compact or wet snow covering ground completely
4   Uneven layer of compact or wet snow covering ground completely
5   Loose dry snow covering less than one-half of the ground
6   Loose dry snow covering at least one-half of the ground (but not completely)
7   Even layer of loose dry snow covering ground completely
8   Uneven layer of loose dry snow covering ground completely
9   Snow covering ground completely; deep drifts

'Severe weather' is defined as occurring when more than half the meteorological stations record state-of-ground E 4 or 5 or E' 0 to 9. 'Thaw' occurs when fewer than half the stations record the above states-of-ground.

When seven days of frozen or snow-covered ground have been so recorded in Scotland or in England/Wales or both, the Nature Conservancy Council informs the B.A.S.C. accordingly. If the severe weather looks likely to continue the B.A.S.C. informs by first-class post the secretaries of its wildfowling and game shooting clubs, Joint Councils and syndicates that, if the severe weather continues for a further seven days, and looks likely to continue, a statutory order suspending the shooting of ducks, geese and waders in the appropriate county is likely to be signed on the thirteenth day to take effect on the fifteenth day, for a maximum period of fourteen days. Press releases are also issued to all press and media outlets.

The B.A.S.C. also calls on the shooting community to exercise voluntary restraint where appropriate. Advice is given that any signs of changes in bird behaviour, or of changes in the numbers or species using a given area, might suggest the need to introduce bag limits or reduce those already existing or to introduce time limits on shooting so as to provide periods of undisturbed feeding. Where evidence appears of very difficult feeding for wildfowl, such as declining body condition, freezing foreshore or snow-covered feeding grounds, then a total ban on wildfowling in the locality might be the appropriate response. The decision, though, is taken by the individual wildfowler or the wildfowling club, perhaps in liaison with other wildfowling groups in the vicinity, in response to local needs.

Should the conditions which necessitated the call for restraint continue until the thirteenth day and look likely to continue, the NCC, having consulted with the B.A.S.C. and other conservation bodies, advises the appropriate Secretary of State to sign a suspension order which would come into effect at 09.00 hrs on the fifteenth day. If a thaw of three or more days occurs within this period then the earlier days of severe weather are disregarded. Before signing, the Secretary of State normally consults with the B.A.S.C., as representing the persons interested in shooting wildfowl and waders.

Once the suspension order has been signed the B.A.S.C. telephones as many as possible of its wildfowling and game shooting club secretaries, Joint Councils and syndicates, issues press releases to all newspapers, sporting magazines, radio and television editors and institutes a 24-hour telephone information service. Similarly the Department of the Environment and Scottish Development Department, as appropriate, issue press releases and place public notices of the suspension in the following national and regional newspapers: *The Times, Daily Telegraph, Daily Express, Daily Mail, Sun, Scotsman, Glasgow Herald, Dundee Courier and Advertiser, Aberdeen Press and Journal, Dumfries and Galloway Standard, Edinburgh Gazette* and the *Western Daily Mail*.

Throughout the period of restraint and any statutory suspension, the local contact groups provide detailed information on local conditions and needs, co-ordinated by the B.A.S.C. and NCC regional offices for their respective headquarters, to be used in monitoring the conditions around the country, where voluntary restraint might be needed and, in due course, when the lifting of any statutory suspension is appropriate. They pay particular attention not only to the foreshore and freezing of inland waters and feeding grounds but also to the condition of birds, bird numbers and movements, appearance of unusual species, significance of wind chill and to snow cover, the last especially in Scotland.

A suspension order is signed for a maximum period of fourteen days, although it is reviewed after a maximum of seven days. This review takes into account not only the state-of-ground information but also the reports from the local contact groups and the weather forecasts. It is undertaken by the NCC in conjunction with the B.A.S.C. and other conservation bodies. The lifting of a statutory suspension before the end of the maximum fourteen-day period takes into account the need for a period of recovery for wildfowl after the end of the severe weather itself. In this event the Department of the Environment or Scottish Development Department and the B.A.S.C. undertake publicity campaigns as extensively as possible to inform the shooting community of the fact. If the suspension runs to the full fourteen days and then lapses it is likely that the B.A.S.C. only will undertake the appropriate publicity. It is clearly the responsibility of all shooting sportsmen to appraise themselves of any restrictions applying during periods of severe weather, and to act accordingly. The most up-to-date information is always available from the B.A.S.C.'s headquarters or regional offices.

If the severe weather continues beyond the end of the first fourteen-day period the appropriate Secretary of State, following agreement between the main organisations, is likely to be asked to sign another suspension order for a further maximum period of fourteen days, which would then be managed in a similar way to the first. Once any suspension order has formally ended there is scope, if the local contact groups indicate the need, for continuing voluntary restraint to be encouraged in any parts of the country still not fully recovered.

After the end of any winter when these arrangements are actually used, the NCC Working Group, comprising all the relevant shooting and conservation organisations and appropriate government departments, reviews the use and considers whether any further amendments are required.

The evolution of an acceptable set of procedures to manage wildfowling when wildfowl may be subject to stress from prolonged severe weather has taken some time. That there is a need for one, under some exceptional conditions, is in no doubt. The shooting community must avoid the risk of (appearing to be) damaging the wildfowl populations. The future of shooting depends on its practitioners being seen to exercise self-discipline and meticulous responsibility for its quarry. Apparently irresponsible or selfish behaviour, and demands for shooting when a large part of the country is suffering prolonged severe weather, does not reflect the true sporting ethic and could readily bring shooting into public disrepute. Secondly, the birds themselves may be in poor condition and simply not worth shooting. Thirdly, they can also be 'unsporting' because they become too easy to shoot. Finally, the shooting community has an international responsibility when severe weather forces continental wintering wildfowl populations temporarily into the UK. Sportsmen in other European countries, where they have undertaken careful management of their own birds, have good reason to expect extra measures to be afforded to 'their' birds once they are forced out of their usual wintering haunts by severe weather into unfamiliar ground in the UK. Under such circumstances the birds need to recover any lost condition so as to be able to return to their breeding grounds to breed successfully. It is appropriate to recall HRH The Prince Philip's views, expressed, as the Association's Patron, in the 1982 Annual Report of the B.A.S.C., that, whilst the shooting suspensions then had not met with universal approval, 'it is worth remembering that it is infinitely better for the shooting fraternity to be seen to be leaning over backwards in the name of conservation than to fall on its face for the sake of a few days' sport in exceptional conditions'.

LEAD SHOT POISONING AND WILDFOWL

Few wildfowlers will be unaware of the controversy surrounding the question of ingested lead shot poisoning in wildfowl. Cases of wildfowl apparently being poisoned by lead have been recorded since the middle of the 19th century but it was not until a major study was undertaken in the United States during the 1950s that a great deal of light was shed on the nature and extent of the problem. Frank Bellrose of the Illinois Natural History Survey estimated that some 2–3 million ducks died each year from lead poisoning in the United States (Bellrose, 1959). His study did not generate very much controversy at the time. In fact, his view then was that such losses did not appear to be sufficiently great to warrant prohibiting lead shot in waterfowl hunting, although if the problem became more serious then he felt that iron shot would provide a means of overcoming it. He did, however, encourage efforts to find an alternative to lead.

In the mid 1970s, new concern arose about the possible impact of lead poisoning losses amongst waterfowl particularly in light of the loss of their habitat and the decline in some populations. The US Government's Fish and Wildlife Service consequently proposed regulations prohibiting the use of lead and requiring the use of steel shot for waterfowl hunting in states where the problem appeared to be greatest. Controversy developed immediately and has raged since. Much research has been undertaken and a great deal more is now known about lead poisoning. However, biologists, wildlife managers and waterfowl hunters continue to disagree over its extent and impact on waterfowl populations. Steel shot has emerged as the only realistic alternative to lead in shotgun cartridges, and is considered likely to be more effective than other remedial measures. Progressively more and more states have now mandated the use of steel, the approach being generally one in favour of conservatism in face of wildfowl population problems. Furthermore, the Fish and Wildlife Service has recently indicated that by 1991 all states will be converted to steel for waterfowl hunting. The controversy continues, however, and centres mainly on whether steel loads wound more birds than lead, the possible damage to wildfowlers' guns and the higher cost of the new loads.

Some studies on the ingestion of lead shot by wildfowl have been undertaken in both the United Kingdom and Europe, mainly to determine the extent to which problems, similar to those claimed to occur in America, exist in Europe. Pellet ingestion rates have been found to vary from species to species and from place to place. A recent review conducted by Shedden (1985), however, concluded that the differences between the incidence of lead pellets in waterfowl on both sides of the Atlantic and the absence of regular die-offs of birds in Europe, indicate that lead poisoning is not as great an issue in Europe as it is in America. Consequently there appeared to be little basis for proposing the mandatory introduction of steel shot for waterfowl hunting in Europe. Since then, the Danish government has legislated against lead shot over its most important wetlands and lead shot is further restricted in use for some types of inland duck and clay pigeon shooting.

The question of lead shot in Europe has been addressed by the FACE (Federation of Field Sports Associations of the EEC) *ad hoc* Working Group on Lead Shot. The working group recognises that some local problems of lead shot poisoning can, and do, occur but that often these are better tackled at the local level, perhaps by altering the management of shooting over the sites in question. If such management remedies prove inadequate then it may be that the local replacement of lead shot is the most appropriate course of action. Accordingly, FACE welcomed the development of steel-loaded cartridges within Europe.

The risk of lead poisoning to ducks and geese depends on the availability of lead shot in their feeding areas. This depends, in turn, on the amount of shooting and the nature of the sediments into which the shot falls, and the susceptibility of the birds to any lead that is ingested. There seems little doubt that a duck or goose (or sometimes, a swan) may ingest lead shot more whilst feeding, in mistake for food items, than whilst gritting. One or more pellets may be ingested at any one time, and, depending on a variety of factors, the bird may be poisoned. If it survives that occasion it may still be at risk if pellets remain available in the locality.

In the United States more than 5 % of ducks contain lead shot at any one time, although it has been estimated that up to 40 % of the duck population ingest shot during the whole season, allowing for a bird to pick up pellets on several different occasions throughout the period. Most waterfowl ingest only one or two pellets at any one time. From very large numbers of birds studied over the years in the U.S. about 64 % found with pellets were shown to pick up one pellet, 14 % two pellets and 7 % three pellets, with the remainder

taking larger numbers of pellets. Broadly similar proportions have been found amongst British waterfowl. Different species of wildfowl can ingest pellets at different rates, this being related to their habitats and feeding habitats. Generally diving ducks can ingest the most shot, and grazers the fewest. In Britain, for example, in a national study by Mudge (1983), about 11 % of shot tufted duck and pochard were each found to contain pellets with a mallard at 4 %, teal 0.5 % and wigeon 0 %. Amongst the greylag and pinkfooted geese some 7 % and 3 %, respectively, contained pellets. Eight of the 17 species studied, though, contained no pellets. Amongst birds from these and other species found dead, varying levels of pellet ingestion were found, although variable sample sizes make their interpretation difficult. Swans, though, did contain rather more lead than most other species, but anglers' split lead shot was also present, particularly in the mute swan.

One of the more obvious factors affecting the ingestion of lead shot by wildfowl is the nature of the habitat and its sediments. The majority of pellets in Britain are generally found in the top two inches of mud and so may be accessible to dabbling ducks in shallow waters and diving ducks in deeper waters. Pellets seem to settle through muds rather slowly but in soft and mobile sediments, particularly those in estuarine and other coastal habitats, they can become unavailable to wildfowl much more quickly, perhaps soon after the shooting season. The sites most likely to show slow settlement of pellets are the small freshwaters with hard sediments that are not subject to physical disturbance. Vegetated sites do not seem to influence pellet availability too much. In America it has sometimes proved possible to reduce availability by cultivating the shot-over land. It is not known how quickly lead pellets disintegrate in different soils but intact pellets continue to be found in the soils of the Wildfowl Trust colleciton at Slimbridge, some 40 years after shooting stopped there. Depending on the particular circumstances, therefore, the annual addition of pellets to the environment may be cumulative.

Although there are other sources of lead in the environment it does seem clear that shotgun pellets and anglers' lead weights are the main source of lead poisoning in wildfowl. The lead has been measured in soils in several countries and shows considerable variations in density from place to place. Bellrose, in the US, found densities from 0 to 118,000 pellets per acre, averaging at 28,000 per acre, and more recent work has revealed up to 350,000 pellets per acre. In Denmark higher densities have been found, namely up to 745,000 pellets in hunting areas, and 1,600,000 pellets per acre in areas used for clay pigeon shooting. In this country Mudge found no pellets in three out of 22 sites, and up to 120,000 per acre at an inland flight pond. The total quantities of lead introduced into the environment by hunting appear considerable – estimated at 3000 tons per year in the US, 1900 tons in the UK and over 900 tons in Denmark. It is important to note, though, that the quantities of lead entering the environment from other sources are many times greater. Indeed, recent research at Oxford University has shown how the background levels of lead, primarily from leaded petrol, can contribute significantly to the contamination of wildfowl, particularly in urban areas. Overall, however, most deaths of wildfowl from lead poisoning do apepar to be caused by the smaller quantities of spent shotgun pellets or anglers' weights.

Lead itself is a poisonous heavy metal, with no known biological function in animals or birds. It manifests its toxicity by inhibiting many of the enzymes required for day-to-day biological functioning, in a wide variety of body systems. For most animals once a lead pellet has been ingested it is normally voided harmlessly from the intestine, or becomes deposited, again harmlessly, in such organs as the appendix. An X-ray of many a wildfowler's appendix can be quite startling! In a bird, however, the muscular gizzard, with its complement of grit essential for grinding down coarse items of food, also grinds down any ingested pellets and this can release soluble lead which is absorbed into the bloodstream, and carried around the body. Typically it will concentrate in such organs as the liver and kidney and also in the bones where, with time, being chemically similar to calcium, it accumulates.

Once lead has been absorbed, it can lead to a wide range of deleterious effects, including weakness, deterioration of nerves and other tissues, muscular paralysis resulting in a loss of flight and the inability to walk, loss of appetite and internal damage to the lining of the gizzard, which can prevent food digestion and hence result in a blockage of the intestine by compacted, undigested

food. In turn these effects can lead to starvation and marked loss of body weight. Anaemia is another common effect. This is due to the destruction of red blood cells and the reduced capacity of bone marrow to produce more. It is this effect of lead on a key enzyme (delta-aminolevulinic acid dehydratase) which is necessary for the manufacture of haemoglobin in blood, that forms the basis for a sensitive test of a bird's blood to determine whether it is affected by lead poisoning. One lead pellet can reduce the activity of this enzyme by 20 % for up to three months subsequently, although the bird may well recover. Typically a bird affected by lead poisoning will show lack of coordination, emaciation, drooping wings, 'kinked' neck (especially in swans) and green-stained faeces. Severe cases may lead to coma and death. Whether sub-lethal levels of lead can have harmful effects on reproduction is not clear.

A considerable number of factors affect the susceptibility of a given duck or goose to lead poisoning once it has ingested one or more pellets of shot. The most important appears to be the bird's diet, but also relevant are the amount of grit and soil ingested, the age, sex and size of the bird, and the time of year. It has long been known that diets high in cereal grains are associated with the greatest losses of waterfowl, whereas more balanced diets, preferably including green forage or aquatic plants, have some sort of protective effect. It now seems that protein, calcium and phosphorus are the components which provide the greatest protection against lead toxicosis, the first two particularly reducing the absorption of lead and lowering the body burden of lead. These findings help to explain some of the differences in mortality from lead ingestion both between species and between the United States and Europe. Thus, in the US mallard is regarded as being vulnerable, not only because it tends to ingest lead pellets quite frequently, but also because it feeds extensively on cereal grains and weed seeds, both of which tend to be low in protein and calcium. Pintails, on the other hand, generally ingest more shot but their animal diet is high in protein which makes them less liable to be poisoned. Amongst the geese, their frequent consumption of green plants normally confers much protection against lead-induced mortality. The generally higher consumption of cereal grains by American waterfowl as a whole may well contribute to the higher incidence of ingested lead poisoning in that country than in Europe (see below).

The beneficial effects of calcium-rich grit in reducing lead toxicosis are well documented. They are related not just to the effects of calcium *per se* but also to the ways in which lead appears to be voided from the intestine without being absorbed into the blood stream. Apart from dietary factors, female ducks tend to be affected by lead poisoning more than males, and adult birds more than immatures. These differences seem to be related to the body size, quantities of food eaten and the metabolism of calcium in the different ages and sexes. Finally, losses from lead poisoning tend to occur most frequently during the winter and spring, at least in the US. This is mainly due to the return of waterfowl to hunted areas after the end of the hunting season in order to utilise the food which is still abundant, but which is then consumed in association with the lead pellets deposited during the season. In the US, incidence of lead poisoning tends to increase through the season, but in the UK and Europe, several studies have indicated a decline from the start of the season. Again many factors are probably responsible for these differences, not least feeding habits and differences in hunting practices.

Whilst there is little doubt that, under some circumstances, the ingestion of lead pellets by ducks and geese can lead to their deaths, it is much less clear how many birds die each year from lead poisoning, and what the consequences are in conservation terms. In the US it is claimed that between one and three million waterfowl die each year. Relatively few of these birds are ever found, however, unless a die-off involving hundreds or, occasionally, thousands of birds occurs. This can happen particularly after the season, when many birds have been exposed to lead pellets and when a stressful factor coincides such as a spell of severe weather. Such obvious losses are then readily detected and recorded. Less easy to record, though, are the day-to-day losses, which many people in the US believe are the most important aspect of lead poisoning. Birds sick or dying from lead tend to seek cover and become more vulnerable to predators and scavengers. Field trials with carcasses in the US have shown how quickly dead waterfowl can be removed from the environment, by a large variety of species including mink, raccoons, foxes, coyotes, eagles, hawks and many others, provided that the numbers of sick waterfowl are not too great at any one time. Consequently these losses of waterfowl can be overlooked.

In the UK, in contrast, die-offs of waterfowl are virtually unknown. By far the largest occurred at Loch Spynie, Morayshire in the autumn of 1986, when some 300 greylag geese were apparently poisoned following their exposure to spent shotgun and some anglers' lead pellets in the Loch's muds in the wake of a temporary lowering of the water level. The few other recorded cases of waterfowl poisoning have usually proved to be related to deposits of lead pellets resulting from clay pigeon shooting. Furthermore, in this country much shooting takes place over designated parts of statutory and non-statutory reserves, which are frequently checked by wardens, often with dogs, immediately after shooting. Little evidence has emerged that significant numbers of waterfowl are being poisoned by lead. Moreover, unlike in the United States, wardens here are not competing with a large predator and scavenger population. Consequently it is virtually impossible to estimate the numbers of waterfowl which may be dying from lead poisoning in Europe each year. The number and complexity of factors operating are considerable, apart from the fact that in contrast to the United States relatively little work on the subject has been carried out. Some estimates have been attempted for individual countries, for example, Mudge (1983) for Britain, based on the incidence of ingested lead pellets in gizzards. This approach, though, is fraught with difficulties and is known not to produce reliable estimates of mortality. For example, some two thirds of the mallard found in Britain containing lead pellets contained only one pellet. Whilst this does not mean that no pellets had previouly been ingested or would not subsequently be ingested, it is frequently found that waterfowl on a nutritionally adequate diet are not seriously affected by the ingestion of a single pellet. Furthermore, whatever the numbers of ducks and geese which do succumb to lead poisoning each year there is the important question of the impact of any such loss. It is currently believed that duck populations normally compensate for most hunting mortality by showing reduced non-hunting mortality, thereby maintaining a steady overall death-rate from year to year. Consequently a reduction in shooting pressure would not be likely to be followed by an increase in the size of the population. It is possible that against this framework of compensatory population dynamics, a small loss of birds through lead poisoning would not be of significance in population terms, and that subsequently removing this particular source of mortality would not have the effect of increasing the total number of birds. On the other hand, it is likely that some birds are dying in this country as a result of lead poisoning, either directly or through a greater vulnerability to predation or disease brought about by poisoning. This is clear not only from the birds which, from time to time, are found with symptoms of lead toxicosis (either from shotgun or anglers' lead) but also from the finding of lead pellets in gizzards, or elevated levels of lead in the tissues and blood of waterfowl shot or found dead. However, there is no evidence that these losses constitute a national problem in conservation terms, a view also expressed recently by the Wildfowl Trust. Locally problems can occur though, which do need to be tackled. Any such losses to lead poisoning would be seen by many as an unnecessary waste of a resource. The issue then becomes how best to tackle any problems that may be occurring.

In the United States, various management techniques have been tried in order to reduce the availability of spent lead pellets to waterfowl, with varying, but generally rather low, degrees of success. They include altering water levels of wetlands subject to substantial shooting according to their use by waterfowl, providing calcium-rich grit in feeding areas, cultivating soils containing pellets, to help bury them out of reach of birds, and promoting the growth of submerged, leafy aquatic plants to provide a diet better able to protect waterfowl against the effects of any poisoning.

Habitat management, in the interests of hunting and game conservation, is practised to a much greater extent in the US than in the UK. In this country, with a much smaller problem arising from lead poisoning anyway, the cause of local problems has usually turned out to be shot deposition in waterfowl feeding sites from clay pigeon shooting. The remedy has then proved relatively simple, namely to alter the direction of shooting so that pellets no longer fall into these areas. Indeed, this principle should be adopted, as far as possible, by all those shooting such disciplines that can deposit substantial quantities of pellets in areas utilised by waterfowl.

The provision of calcium-rich grit in wetland sites subject to significant shooting levels is another option although there is some doubt as to its efficacy. It can have the beneficial effect of reducing susceptibility to lead poisoning, by speeding up the expulsion of pellets from the intestine but in those birds which retain pellets longer, it may give them more time to be eroded by the grit itself.

Clearly, the most potentially effective management practice to prevent future lead shot poisoning is the replacement of lead shot with some non-toxic alternative. This has been the policy in much of the United States for many years now, and, more recently, in Denmark. Whilst a number of possible materials have been tried over the years, including alloys of various metals, coated lead pellets, and a sintered lead/iron shot, none has been found as suitable as soft steel, which, nowadays, is the only commercially viable alternative. To date it has not been found to harm birds once ingested. Development of steel-loaded cartridges has occurred primarily in the US and the product now available is markedly improved on the first cartridges produced in the early 1970s.

Steel pellets cannot simply be substituted for lead. Steel is less dense than lead (30% less, size for size) so a higher muzzle velocity is necessary to help maintain the downrange and striking energies of steel pellets. The size of steel pellets has been increased to help overcome this deficiency, such that a steel pellet two sizes larger is broadly equivalent to a given lead pellet. Ballistically there are also other differences in the behaviour of steel compared with lead pellets. The harder steel deforms less as it travels along the barrel, and so the pattern remains tighter throughout its flight. The higher initial velocity results in the steel load reaching a target up to about 40 yards more quickly than lead, but, thereafter, it tends to slow down more quickly as well. The result of these various differences in performance appears to be the need for an adjustment to shooting technique in order to achieve the best with steel. Thus different forward allowances are necessary with targets at different ranges. In turn this requires a better judgement of range itself (which is no bad thing!).

Innumerable comparisons have been made over the years between steel and lead cartridges, many by individual hunters and some in very large, scientifically-controlled trials, where hundreds of hunters fired thousands of shots at ducks and geese without knowing at the time which type of cartridge they were using. The results continue to be debated, with the emphasis remaining on three main issues – the crippling (wounding) of birds, damage to guns and costs of steel-loaded cartridges.

One of the problems in addressing the issue of 'crippling' (defined as being mortally wounded but unretrieved) is that no single uncontroversial way has been devised to present data on the crippling of waterfowl during hunting. Consequently different conclusions have been drawn from a variety of trials, all conducted differently, which cannot easily be compared. Some of the trials appeared to show an increase in crippling with steel and, although others have not shown such differences, the view generally prevails amongst hunters that steel results in more cripples. Consequently they feel that the benefits of reduced losses of waterfowl to lead poisoning by the use of steel shot may be negated by an increase in crippling losses. However, a recent review of the issue by Sanderson & Bellrose (1986) has concluded that for ducks, fewer birds would be bagged with steel shot if the same number of shots were fired (since generally fewer hits are achieved with the tighter patterns of steel) but that, overall, crippling rates from steel would be much the same as from lead. With geese, however, the authors would expect a slight reduction in crippling losses. Moreover, they show that the widespread use of steel in the US since the mid-1970s has not resulted in an increase in crippling losses at the national level.

Two points need to be borne in mind. Crippling might be expected to be less with steel shot than with lead since the tighter patterns and shorter shot strings of the former tend to result in the bird being either hit hard or missed altogether as it is often the outfliers in a lead pattern which wound a bird. On the other hand, the harder steel pellets may pass through a bird without killing it. The second point is that the above-mentioned trials all utilised hunters who were not as familiar with steel and perhaps had not learned to adjust their shooting technique to its demands. If comparisons of steel and lead cartridges were made by using hunters proficient with both types of cartridge, the results might be more favourable towards steel.

Damage to gun barrels is another issue of concern to the shooting community. Stories abound of expansion of choked barrels and scratching of barrel walls. The latter was a problem to begin with but it was overcome by containing the steel shot in larger plastic cups thus preventing its contact with the barrel walls. The main risk of choke expansion (ring bulging), however, seems to remain for thin-walled guns with half or full choked barrels. Clearly this includes the quality English game guns and has led to much concern in the UK, although presumably not many London or Birmingham guns would be taken out on the marsh. In the US wildfowl shooting is commonly done with relatively cheap, thick-barrelled pump-action guns, for which an increasing choice of replaceable, hardened barrels is now becoming available. It may be that slight choke expansion, as can happen in fact with magnum lead loads, is somewhat academic in terms of subsequent shooting performance and gun value. Recent experience in Denmark, now requiring steel shot for much of its waterfowl shooting, appears to reveal few of the fears of gun barrel damage from steel cartridges. On the other hand in this country ring bulging in quality game guns would be viewed with considerable concern.

The third main issue concerns the cost of steel cartridges which is inevitably higher than lead since it is more expensive to roll steel wire into spheres and load them with different powders and wads. However, the price differential in the United States has declined over the years of increasing steel production, as would be expected. Recently the suggested retail price of steel has varied but is up to 25 % more than lead cartridges. In Europe, the demand for steel-loaded cartridges in Denmark since 1986 has resulted in a marked drop in price, from American-manufactured cartridges initially costing up to two and a half times that of lead, to the European-manufactured cartridges now being produced by some companies as Dan Arms, although still substantially more costly than lead. Loads produced by other companies in Europe, including Eley and Rottweil, are likely to cost somewhat more, although they are not yet being made available in the UK.

Wildfowlers, increasingly, are talking about steel cartridges and some are keen to try them for themselves. If, in due course, they feel that there is a need for the use of steel and they find it an acceptable alternative to lead then the increase in price probably will not worry them too much, particularly in view of the rather small costs of cartridges in relation to the overall costs of wild-fowling. It may be that the inland game shooter who shoots flight ponds for ducks will react more strongly against the price differential and the risks of gun damage, since he may be using rather more cartridges during a season and higher value guns.

In view of the increasing attention being given to lead shot and the interest amongst wildfowlers to the issue, the B.A.S.C. has recently obtained some steel shot cartridges, and, together with some wildfowlers, has begun to assess steel's perform-ance in the field and its effects on shotguns, so that the Association can advise wildfowlers accord-ingly. However, in the absence of any evidence that there is a conservation problem related to the use of lead shot the Association continues to be opposed to the general replacement of lead with some alternative material.

There is one issue outside that concerning effects on waterfowl which has been given little attention until recently, and then mostly in Britain and Europe. This is the question of possible contamin-ation of the environment as a whole by lead originating from shotgun shooting. Increasingly, concern is being expressed at the possibility of lead pellets lodging within crops, and being eaten or incorporated into foodstuffs for livestock or even humans, and of pellets decomposing within the soil, contaminating soil waters and being taken up by plants, which, in turn, are subsequently con-sumed. Landowners and farmers are beginning to question the effects of lead being deposited on their land before they agree to new clay pigeon shooting facilities being set up. Indeed, some environmental lobby groups have launched campaigns to have lead cartridges banned at clay pigeon shooting sites on the grounds that lead is a toxic metal, the effects on the environment of which are not yet fully understood and that they are likely to be harmful. In Denmark the use of lead cartridges is now restricted in clay pigeon shooting within 250 metres of arable crops and even over certain soil types. Work carried out in that country has indicated that, at least under some soil conditions, significant dissolution of lead from pellets can take place and some of this can subsequently find its way into plants.

In view of these developments it is clear that an assessment of this issue is required. Little work of this kind has been undertaken in the UK. There is no doubt that it would be helpful for the shooting community to be aware of the impact of its activities on the countryside at large and also to take an active, influential part in any discussions which are likely to develop on the subject. Accord-ingly, the B.A.S.C.'s recently established Lead Shot Working Group, comprising the main shooting and manufacturing organisations in the UK, has proposed a study of the fate of shotgun pellets in the countryside to be conducted by an environ-mental consultancy. The Association, having ob-tained the necessary funding, began the study in August 1988.

In conclusion, it is clear that lead pellets are already in this country's environment, and are continuing to accumulate. They can be harmful to waterfowl and perhaps other animals , and, occa-sionally, in some localities, do cause actual harm. Only a few European wetlands have revealed any significant problems, and many of these are related to clay pigeon shooting, which can deposit large densities of pellets in such areas. National agencies need to address these sites at a local level, which, in turn, will help to allay fears at both the national and international level. At the same time, how-ever, in any such 'hot-spot' areas the most ap-propriate response may prove to be the replacement of lead shot. Steel-loaded cartridges are being developed and are becoming available in Europe. Recent experience in Denmark has suggested that they may be quite well received and used effect-ively, without some of the ill-effects expected on the basis of earlier experiences in America. On the other hand, widespread concern remains in this country. Wildfowlers are prepared to try steel cartridges for themselves, and perhaps use them, if they prove to be an acceptable alternative to lead, in order to reduce any problems that the continued use of lead may be causing. There are many aspects which need to be investigated, and it will take time before a full assessment of the issue can be made and the wildfowling community ap-praised accordingly.

GEESE AND AGRICULTURE

For the wildfowler of the past and today geese have always held a special place in his life. There are innumerable accounts of 'vast' numbers of both greylag (*Anser anser*) and pinkfooted (*Anser brachy-*

rhynchus) geese in various parts of the country providing unforgettable days of shooting. It was not until the 1950s, however, that any reasonable counts of geese became available and only in the 1960s did the Wildfowl Trust begin its annual November roost counts, from which it has since been possible to monitor closely these goose populations. In the 1950s there were some 20,000 to 30,000 greylag in the British Isles each autumn, and, on average, some 10,000 more pinkfooted geese. No doubt these seemed a lot to the wildfowler then, but, following dramatic changes in both numbers and distribution of these geese in this country since, the opportunities for goose shooting nowadays, both inland and coastal, have changed dramatically. The greylag population has now reached well over 100,000 birds, whilst the pink-footed goose reached a new record total of 172,000 in November 1987. Perhaps somewhat ironically it is widely believed that reductions in shooting mortality over the years have been the main contributory factor, and may well enable the populations to increase yet further in size. Improvements in winter feeding conditions may also be playing a part.

The darkbellied brent goose (*Branta bernicla bernicla*) has also undergone a remarkable increase in numbers, as documented elsewhere in this chapter, with up to 90,000 wintering in Britain each year. Similarly the Canada goose (*Branta canadensis*) is increasing rapidly and looks set to equal the population size of the grey goose species

by the turn of the century.

Whilst the increase in goose numbers, particularly of the quarry species, has been good news for the wildfowler, it has not been so welcomed by the farmer. All these species have come to utilise several of his crops, often to such an extent that substantial changes in cropping patterns now cause marked redistributions of the geese (see Owen (1976) for an account of how goose distribution in historical terms has changed in Britain). The flocking nature of geese, often densely, and their traditional wintering habits, have created problems for farmers in various parts of Britain from the damage caused (or believed to be caused) to pastures, cereals and root crops. Grazing itself is usually regarded as being the most serious source of damage, although compacting of wet, clayey soil (puddling) can also be harmful.

At the national level it is unlikely that agricultural damage by geese is economically significant, but there is little doubt that for individual farmers it can be substantial. Generally the migratory grey geese arrive in the country after the cereal harvest and their widespread feeding on stubbles, consuming the spilt grain, is if anything helpful rather than harmful. Similarly their eating of waste root crops, particularly potatoes, is also useful. As these food sources decline through the winter, pasture grass is increasingly utilised, but there is little evidence of damage being caused.

In recent years, however, considerable changes in farming practice, particularly in Scotland, have

Paley

resulted in substantial increases in autumn-sown cereals, which, in turn, require earlier ground preparation. This reduces the 'stubbling' available to geese in the autumn. Apart from grazing itself, trampling and pulling up of the young barley and wheat plants can also be damaging, although problems remain over what constitutes 'damage', and in demonstrating the losses at harvest actually suffered by farmers.

Under certain circumstances damage and losses can be clearly determined, particularly when adverse weather conditions make crops more vulnerable or the effects of goose activity more serious. The problems suffered by carrot farmers in Lancashire during spells of frost and snow from the pinkfooted geese, which winter in large numbers on the Ribble Estuary and at the Wildfowl Trust's refuge at Martin Mere, are well known, including the reported incident of a frozen carrot falling from height through a motorist's windscreen in February 1982! Similarly, greylag geese can damage brassica root crops when snow leaves the tops particularly vulnerable.

During the spring crop damage in England is slight since the migratory flocks by then have largely left the country. Damage to cereals and to the 'early-bite' of pasture crops as late as April or May in Scotland, however, by geese yet to leave finally for their breeding grounds can be substantial. Losses to farmers can include not just the direct effects of grazing but also problems from the consequent delayed maturing of crops.

Agricultural problems with brent geese did not develop until the 1970s, when the birds first began to cross the sea wall from eating the marine algae like *Zostera*, *Enteromorpha* and *Ulva* on the foreshore, to feed inland on cereal crops and pasture grass. Since then the habit has spread, particularly in winters with a large proportion of young birds in the population, so much so that, nowadays, rather than wait until their traditional foreshore foods are exhausted, geese are increasingly moving inland earlier in the winter to feed.

For them it must make sense, since young cereals and fertilised pastures provide a nutritious source of readily available food. Autumn-sown barley and wheat and new grass leys are the most vulnerable, not just to grazing damage but also to puddling of the soil and uprooting of the young plants. Damage can start late in the autumn and continue into the spring, when 'early-bite' grass

becomes at risk, until the birds return to their high Arctic breeding grounds.

Canada geese can cause somewhat different problems, partly because they are present all the year, unlike the previous species. Their habit of feeding close to their roosting and nesting sites increasingly brings them into conflict with farmers, especially where cereals and other valuable crops adjoin lakes, reservoirs and gravel pits. The bird's preference for walking rather than flying worsens its impact by trampling crops underfoot!

Individual farmers undoubtedly suffer substantial damage, although again it is difficult to determine precisely what the claimed losses may be. Direct losses of grass or grain, delayed maturing or harvesting of crops, or hidden costs from the application of extra fertilisers or re-seeding required to redress earlier damage can all affect farmers. Moreover, the effects of autumn and winter grazing are worsened because it continues through the spring and summer, giving crops no chance to recover.

Problems also occur from flocks of Canada geese in public parks and golf courses when their droppings foul the ground or amenity bodies of water. There may also be adverse effects on other wildlife. A flock readily dominates a small water-body and, in the breeding season, the strongly territorial and aggressive ganders can discourage other species of waterfowl from nesting there. The rapid increase of this non-native species of goose, perhaps competing with the feral greylag goose population, which is also increasing rapidly and which is Britain's only native breeding goose, is also causing some concern.

Agricultural problems with barnacle (*Branta leucopsis*) and Greenland whitefronted (*Anser albifrons flavirostris*) geese on Islay in the Inner Hebrides, have also been well publicised in recent years, the consequence again of growing goose populations and their preference for feeding on agricultural land.

REMEDIES

An obvious means of resolving some of these agricultural and other problems caused by geese would appear to be by shooting. Under the *Wildlife and Countryside Act 1981* a full open season exists for the grey geese and Canada goose to 31 January inland and 20 February below the mean highwater mark. Although it is not known for sure how many geese are shot each year for both sporting and control purposes, it is clear that the total number is not sufficient to prevent the population of each species from continuing to increase. Since the reduction in shooting mortality, brought about by various protection measures over the years, including the comprehensive system of non-shooting refuges throughout the country, is believed to be the major factor in the population increases of several goose species, a substantial increase in shooting could well have a beneficial effect. Indeed, the Wildfowl Trust suggests that an additional 2000 Canada geese would have to be killed each year to maintain the Canada's 1980 population level (Owen *et al.* 1986).

On the other hand, substantial reductions in the total populations of most goose species would not be welcomed by many people. Not only are goose-related agricultural problems generally local in nature but also the UK has international responsibilities for the goose populations which winter here, some of which comprise very large proportions of their total world populations. Furthermore, wildfowlers, as a whole, do not wish to regard geese as pests to be culled. They are fine birds with long sporting shooting traditions.

The Canada goose, though, may be a special case. A non-indigenous species, introduced from North America in the 17th century for ornamental purposes, it has expanded rapidly, occupying many inland water habitats, to the increasing disadvantage of farmers, landowners and perhaps other native wildlife. Widely translocated by sportsmen in the 1950s and 1960s to provide sporting shooting, it still is shot relatively little. This is because the bird became sedentary, remaining often well fed and undisturbed on estates, public grounds and nature reserves. Sportsmen often could not shoot them anyway because they were inaccessible and, even when they were able to do so, found them poor sporting quarry compared with the wild goose of the estuaries and marshes.

Many farming and conservation organisations would welcome firmer controls on the Canada goose. Shooting clearly has a role to play in managing this species, although, again, the shooting community would prefer to see its contribution made through the sporting potential of the bird, rather than as a pest to be killed. Indeed, there must be considerable potential for good goose shooting though sympathetic landowners and farmers, particularly for those sportsmen unable to pursue the coastal wildfowlers' truly wild goose. Whilst the birds may be currently somewhat complacent they should soon become more worthy quarry once subjected to some shooting.

Shooting does have a more specific role to play in managing agricultural problems at the local level. Through the shooting season the need to reduce goose numbers or deter others from damaging a given farm can provide some opportunities for goose shooting which is beneficial to both parties. If remedial measures are required outside the shooting season a licence under the *Wildlife and Countryside Act 1981* is normally required. Section 4(3)(c) does provide for geese to be killed by authorised persons for the purpose of preventing serious damage to, *inter alia*, crops and vegetables. The onus would be very much on the person taking such action to demonstrate, if required, that the action was necessary and could not have been carried out under the terms of a licence. Section 16 of the Act provides for the Ministry of Agriculture, Fisheries and Food, or the Department of Agriculture for Scotland, to grant licences to take or kill geese to prevent serious damage to 'livestock, foodstuffs for livestock, crops, vegetables, fruit, growing timber or fisheries'.

This provision is used to assist farmers to deal with problems arising from pinkfooted, greylag and Canada goose damage after the end of the shooting season, and darkbellied brent goose and barnacle goose damage (on Islay) at any time during the winter and spring. Licences are not issued lightly and generally only after other efforts to scare the troublesome geese away have failed, or as part of a co-ordinated refuge management programme of scaring, for which shooting is used to reinforce the effect of the other scaring techniques. A licence is issued to a named individual who, in turn, may be able to nominate a number of others to assist in the shooting. Conditions are usually attached, including a total limit on the numbers of geese which can be killed, and the requirement to report this number once the licence has expired. It should be stressed that such licences are issued for the specific purpose of controlling damage. The shooting which they authorise of course may be conducted in a sporting fashion, but they are not intended to be used to provide sporting shooting in the normal sense of the term.

Scaring techniques have long been used to deter geese from vulnerable crops and are used with varying degrees of effectiveness. Generally they need to be changed quite frequently in order to maintain their deterrent effects, but geese tend to habituate to them and their effectiveness is reduced. Furthermore, the costs in time and labour to the farmer of scaring operations can be substantial.

In recent years the concept of goose refuges or alternative feeding areas has been developed, particularly by the agricultural and conservation organisations on the principle that birds scared off vulnerable crops are best accommodated within suitably sized and located refuges, where disturbance is minimised and attractive foods provided. Management within such refuges, established preferably near major roosts, is designed to make them more attractive than the surrounding, vulnerable farmland. The desired goose response is then encouraged further by scaring, with or without shooting, outside the refuges.

This approach has been adopted particularly for brent geese in East Anglia and southern England, as well as for the barnacle goose on Islay, and is being considered as a practical management approach to other species of geese causing agricultural problems. It is not without problems of its own, however, one being the risk of attracting considerable populations of geese to them, but which, on occasion, leave the refuge and cause substantial damage to neighbouring farmland. This has already occurred with brent geese in Essex and pinkfooted geese in Lancashire. Another cause

for concern among sportsmen are the implications for them if pressures develop to restrict shooting both within potential future refuge areas or elsewhere, on the grounds that it may interfere with the desired movements and behaviour of geese. Indeed this is linked to the biggest difficulty of this feeding refuge approach, namely, the likely effect of further increasing goose populations particularly by yet more reductions in shooting mortality.

Direct financial compensation to farmers suffering damage from geese is a remedy used in North America and some European countries, notably the Netherlands. It is not used in the UK despite its being intuitively attractive to farmers. Clearly much work would be needed to develop a system capable of determining what constitutes damage, appropriate compensation and for administering a scheme effectively. Little is known as it is about the economic impact of goose feeding in this country.

There is another form of compensation which has recently begun to be used. Under the Sites of Special Scientific Interest (SSSIs) provisions within the *Wildlife and Countryside Act 1981*, management agreements can be arranged over sites of importance for brent geese which lie within SSSIs. These take the form of agreed farming and other practices, including the sowing of 'sacrificial' crops, specifically for geese, for which financial compensation is paid to offset the losses thereby caused to the farmer. This can work where feeding areas and SSSIs coincide. Arable cropland *per se*, however, is not normally notifiable as an SSSI, unless it occurs

close to a site qualifying for the international 'Ramsar' status and is considered essential to maintaining the integrity of the site itself. Under these circumstances other types of management agreements with the farmers are being sought by the NCC to provide for the needs of the geese and thereby reduce agricultural damage. Again, there are implications for the future of sporting shooting on such sites and the future size of the goose populations themselves.

For farmers troubled by geese there are some measures, albeit limited, which can be adopted, at least under some circumstances. Some Canada geese, for example, feed close to the waters on which they roost and nest, such that vulnerable crops sited nearby are most likely to be damaged. Similarly, vulnerable cereals close to the sea wall are particularly attractive to brent geese. Moving such crops farther away can help, as can siting of crops near to sources of disturbance.

There are also measures which, whilst normally prohibited under the *Wildlife and Countryside Act 1981*, can be licensed for use against such species as the Canada goose. These include egg pricking or nest destruction and the selective shooting of nesting birds. The first two are not usually effective and require much effort to have an adequate impact, whilst the third approach can achieve substantial reductions at the local level. Another method is the rounding up and killing of moulting flocks of geese. This can be difficult, however, since the public at large has come to know and appreciate the presence of this goose. A fine, impressive bird on both the wing and water, and often very approachable, it gives many people probably their closest contact with 'wild' geese, especially in town and country parks, estates and nature reserves open to the public. There is consequently an educational and recreational element to the Canada goose problem which must be taken into account in managing its depredations.

The healthy state of most of our goose populations is clearly pleasing, although their continuing success is becoming increasingly embarrassing. Sportsmen, conservationists and agriculturists all have a considerable interest in the well-being of our geese, although, currently, it is mainly the farming community which is suffering most. Conservationists and farmers have the task of deciding when the management of a burgeoning goose population becomes less of a conservation

matter and more of one of more relevance to the farming interests. Sportsmen seem to be in the most favourable position of all since opportunities for goose shooting are likely only to increase.

On the other hand there is clearly a need for a national policy for the management of geese in this country. The agricultural problems are being addressed and management directed at minimising damage to crops. The biggest gap in our knowledge of geese is what actually regulates their populations – factors on their breeding grounds, wintering grounds or migration staging areas. Unless this is understood the effects of any particular management cannot easily be predicted. Indeed, it is likely that the approach being adopted to manage current agricultural problems will lead to more geese and problems in the future.

The shooting community clearly has a major interest in the future management of geese and, indeed, a role to play. All the different interests need to work together, therefore, to develop a sensible strategy for geese – to ensure the future of our goose populations whilst providing sporting shooting opportunity and benefits to other interests, and minimising agricultural problems in this country.

WILDFOWLING AND DISTURBANCE

In recent years the direct effects of shooting, in terms of the total numbers of the different quarry species shot, have become better understood now that reliable shooting statistics have become available. This is due particularly to the B.A.S.C.'s National Shooting Survey programme, which has provided the basis for estimating the total numbers of birds being shot each year in this country. In turn, these have indicated that, in relation to the numbers of birds wintering in the UK and the other indicators, populations generally are in good heart and current shooting levels in the UK do not constitute a threat to the quarry populations.

The question of disturbance caused by shooting, however, has since come to attract increasing attention. More and more it is claimed to be harmful to wildfowl populations and used to justify restrictions on shooting, frequently without evidence of any harm being produced. The claims are not restricted just to the quarry species of wildfowl, but also non-quarry species of ducks, geese and, particularly, waders. It tends to be presumed that

anything which causes unnecessary flight or movement away from the feeding grounds is harmful to the birds concerned, without taking into account the likelihood, for example, that birds are readily able to maintain their food intake by altering their feeding strategy through the day.

Clearly it is important to define what is meant by 'disturbance' with respect to wildfowl. Ducks, geese and waders are subject to disturbing factors from many sources throughout most of their lives. These include aircraft, boats, dogs, predators, a wide range of recreational activities, including shooting, farming operations and many others. Birds are adapted to respond to such disturbance: they may remain in the area apparently unaffected; remain in the area but alter their behaviour or distribution; leave the area but return later, or leave the area permanently. None of these responses is necessarily harmful to the affected birds. If the disturbance is sufficiently severe or prolonged that the winter survival of the birds or their subsequent breeding success is impaired and the population is reduced then this clearly would be harmful in conservation terms. If such effects result in the national or international conservation importance of a site being damaged then this too would be deemed harmful. Provided that the birds' feeding and roosting needs are adequately met, albeit not necessarily on exactly the same site, then wildfowl appear well able to cope with such disturbance. Wildfowlers are rightly concerned that disturbance caused by the practice of their sport, which may amount only to temporary changes in wildfowl distribution or habits without any conservation implications, is not used

to enable those opposed to their sport to restrict it unjustifiably.

In one of the first attempts to help decide whether disturbance is important to wildfowl populations, a seminar was organised by the B.A.S.C. in December 1984. This brought together available information and views from the major sporting and conservation organisations, as well as other interested parties. The seminar addressed the key elements of the issue: how birds behave when disturbed by shooting; the consequences of their responses, in terms of birds being denied feeding or roosting opportunities or being made to utilise more energy in seeking alternative sites; the harm, if any, caused to populations as a result, particularly in terms of reduced winter survival or breeding capacity; the ways in which any harmful effects can be reduced by management; and, finally, the extent to which such disturbance might conflict with other users of the area, including bird-watchers.

A preliminary analysis of the National Wildfowl Count data by the Wildfowl Trust in relation to refuges and non-refuges, during and after the shooting season, showed, not surprisingly, that wildfowl are found more frequently on refuge sites. For several species there was a marked increase on refuges since 1960 and a lesser increase or decrease on non-refuge areas. Numbers in March largely increased in both refuge and non-refuge areas, whilst those in January had increased less. Within the shooting season itself, wildfowl numbers tend to peak around October on shot sites, recovering again after the end of the season, whilst on unshot sites the trend was steadily downwards. On many of the sites where shooting management was known to have changed there was little obvious change in wildfowl numbers, although some sites, like the Ouse Washes, showed an apparent increase in wildfowl usage subsequently.

On this analysis it was clear that shooting does cause disturbance to wildfowl in as much as they can be displaced from sites for a period. On the other hand, it was equally clear that there was no current knowledge on the effect of the wildfowl refuge system in the country on the total numbers of wildfowl in the UK, whether shooting disturbance limits the numbers of wildfowl as a whole or merely re-distributes them around the country, or whether British wintering habitat is being limited by disturbance caused by shooting. Recently, mallard populations have been found to be limited by overwinter losses, such that when their autumn populations are large, perhaps following a successful breeding season, then subsequent losses during the winter are greater, and vice versa (Hill, 1984). This suggests that wintering habitat could be an important factor in the regulation of mallard populations. It is possible, therefore, that if shooting disturbance is restricting the winter use of the available habitat by mallard then this could have an effect on its total population.

Information presented by Durham University, deeply involved in wader research for many years, showed that waders generally can adopt a number of strategies to cope with disturbance. Shooting near roosts may increase the amount of flying or even displace the roost itself, but there was no evidence of harm from such effects. Disturbance of their feeding is potentially more important through the consequential loss of feeding time. While a large proportion of the daylight hours are used by waders for feeding, at least some of the larger species feed for less time than actually is available. If necessary they can obtain their energy requirements in a shorter time by dispensing with some of their time normally set aside watching for predators. Feeding at night can also be used to help acquire sufficient food. Furthermore, deposits of fat, which enable birds to tide over lean periods, generally peak in December and January so that non-continuous disturbance can probably be compensated for in energy terms.

In particularly cold or windy weather, however, disturbance could be more harmful as the time available for successful feeding is reduced. It is known that some smaller wader species, including redshank, can suffer substantial mortality during particularly severe weather. It is precisely at these times, however, that shooting itself can be restricted or even suspended temporarily, as detailed elsewhere in this chapter.

One of the few studies which have yet been done on the effect of recreational disturbance on wildfowl was completed in 1983 for the Severn/Trent Water Authority with respect to inland waters (Watmough, 1983). Shooting was not involved but the various other recreational activities and their effects on the waterfowl populations, as measured by the displacement from their normal feeding or roosting areas and the increased energy expenditure caused by the flying away from the disturbing factors, led to the conclusion that the key is the management of refuges, where birds can escape from disturbance and recover any loss of condition.

It is precisely this form of management which has evolved over the years that currently provides a comprehensive system of refuges around the coast, and inland, in which birds can find freedom from disturbance. In the 1960s the Wildfowl Conservation Committee, comprising the then Nature Conservancy, B.A.S.C. (then WAGBI) and the Wildfowl Trust, prepared a national policy for wildfowl conservation comprising a refuge system 'to form wildfowl reservoirs to increase stocks to the advantage of sportsmen and conservationists alike'. Its second objective was that the refuges be used to mitigate the effects of local over-shooting or unsporting practice whilst still affording controlled shooting to responsible wildfowlers. Since then wildfowlers themselves have been actively involved in establishing and managing controlled shooting and sanctuary reserves, local nature reserves and their own reserves, backing up the national system of refuges (27 coastal refuges comprising 9500 hectares) managed by wildfowling clubs in England alone.

In addition to this system of refuges coastal wildfowling is managed and regulated to a high degree by B.A.S.C.-affiliated clubs, many of which jointly manage sites with voluntary and statutory conservation bodies, two-thirds of the sites being SSSI designated. Over and above the legal framework provided by the *Wildlfe and Countryside Act 1981*, many of these wildfowling clubs regulate their shooting by way of the quarry species that can be shot, bag limits, numbers of guns on the marsh, areas and times of shooting, avoidance of feeding and roosting sites and various other devices appropriate to the specific localities. These are described in considerable detail by Laws (1984).

Whilst the disturbance seminar proved a valuable means of assessing currently available information and views on the question of shooting disturbance, it was clear that a number of questions remained unanswered and that more research was appropriate. On the one hand there was the need to determine whether shooting disturbance had any impact on wildfowl populations at the local and national level, and, on the other, to determine the role and effects of the current refuge system on both wildfowl and the sport of wildfowling. In due course, a joint study evolved between the Wildfowl Trust and the B.A.S.C. to address these and other related questions.

Broadly speaking, the Wildfowl Trust undertook to determine the characteristics of individual wildfowl sites and the practices associated with them so that bird numbers and distribution could be related to them. Field studies to monitor the numbers and distribution of birds during periods when shooting does and does not take place were also to be undertaken. Although displacement and changes in behaviour of birds can be caused by disturbance, detailed studies of feeding behaviour, activity patterns with and without disturbance, and associated energy expenditures, are necessary to determine whether an apparent effect of disturbance has any real harmful impact on the wildfowl populations themselves.

With respect to the current refuge system, a review was clearly timely. Developments over recent years in wildfowl conservation have resulted in an increase in the numbers of statutory and voluntary body refuges, as well as the increasing international designation of sites of importance to wildfowl, including 'Ramsar' sites and Special Protection Areas, under EEC legislation. There is no doubt that wildfowlers' understanding and acceptance of the need for refuges as well as their location and management are of primary importance for the success of any strategy for wildfowl conservation. The cornerstone of the 1960 Wildfowl Conservation Committee policy was the mutual appreciation of the viewpoint of each of the interests involved. There has since been a tendency for this understanding to break down and there is a need for common attitudes to be developed on which to build sound strategies for managing wildfowl and wildfowling in the future.

The B.A.S.C.'s contribution to the overall study is to include an examination of the effects of the current refuge system on wildfowl and wader populations and the sport of wildfowling, with particular emphasis on the management of shooting disturbance. It also includes an assessment of what is understood by 'disturbance' by both users and managers of wildfowl sites, its importance in relation to other disturbing factors affecting wildfowl and wader populations and how it should be managed. Its results will be invaluable for determining any changes that might be appropriate to the current management of wildfowling as well as the need for any more refuges over and above the existing network.

This major study, begun in 1986 and expected to last about three years, undoubtedly will provide a great deal of information about wildfowl numbers and distributions and the extent to which disturbance from shooting and other sources may need more attention. A joint study by the B.A.S.C. and Wildfowl Trust culminating in a jointly produced report was not only necessary, since each organisation holds considerable amounts of information required for a full understanding of the issue, but also entirely appropriate, in accord with the deep interest in the well-being and use of wildfowl populations of each organisation.

In view of the general well-being of most wildfowl species in the UK it would seem unlikely that disturbance caused by shooting is having any significant impact at the national level. At some local sites there may be some problems which need tackling but these, as always, are best resolved at that level in light of local circumstances. There is no doubt that an objective assessment of the whole issue of shooting disturbance will make a far more substantial contribution to the future management of wildfowl and wildfowling than the subjective and emotional attitudes which hitherto have prevailed.

REFERENCES

Bellrose, F. C., 1959. 'Lead poisoning as a mortality factor in wildfowl populations'. *Illinois Natural History Survey Bulletin, 27*(3), 235–88.

Harrison, J. G. & Hudson, M., 1963. 'Some effects of severe weather on wildfowl in Kent in 1962–63'. *Wildfowl Trust 15th Annual Report*, 26–32.

Hill, D. A., 1984. 'Population regulation in the mallard' *J. Anim. Ecol., 53*, 191–202.

Mudge, G. P., 1983. 'The incidence and significance of ingested lead pellet poisoning in British wildfowl'. *Biological Conservation, 27*, 333–72.

Owen, M., 1976. 'Factors affecting the distribution of geese in the British Isles'. *Wildfowl, 27*, 143–7.

Sanderson, G. C., & Bellrose, F. C., 1986. 'A review of the problem of lead poisoning in waterfowl. *Illinois Natural History Survey, Special Publication 4.*

Scott, P., 1987. 'Should the brent be shot?' *Wildfowl World, No. 96, 4.*

Shedden, C., 1985. *An Assessment of European Hunters' Lead Shot as a Source of Contamination.* British Association for Shooting and Conservation, Rossett.

Watmough, B., 1983. *The Effects on Wildfowl of Recreation at Reservoirs in the Mid-Trent Valley.* Severn–Trent Water Authority.

29
WILDFOWL IN CAPTIVITY
ROBERT BAKER

All wildfowlers have a deep respect and admiration for the birds they hunt and many would like to have a closer bond with their quarry by keeping a pair or two of duck in their back garden. Contrary to popular belief it is not necessary to have an ornamental lake and plenty of ground. An average-sized garden with a small pool is quite adequate for many species of wildfowl.

The first requirement to keep waterfowl is water. Water to drink and bathe in. It is possible to keep the odd pair of geese with just an old kitchen sink sunk in the corner of their pen, but, if you wish to keep duck, a reasonable-sized pond will be necessary. Three or four pairs of dabbling duck can be kept on a pool nine feet long by five feet wide and about a foot deep. Diving duck will however require a much larger pool at least three feet deep. If a natural pond is not available then one will have to be made from concrete. Polythene sheeting can be used, but the larger duck and geese will scratch the sides as they climb in and out of the pond and eventually hole it. Before siting a pool, remember it will have to be cleaned out from time to time, so do not build under trees or leaves will foul the water in the autumn and in time the tree roots may damage the pond. (If possible connect the pond to the main drain, though a large soakaway is usually more practicable.) The pond sides will need to be sloped to make it easy for the birds to climb out. Duck may cause problems by dabbling around the edges of the pool and making a terrible mess. This can soon be cured by laying a yard-wide belt of pea shingle or paving stones right around the edge of the pond.

Your birds will either be wing-tipped on the marsh or bought from a waterfowl breeder already pinioned. Being unable to fly you will be responsible for their safety, so a fence will be needed not just to keep them in the pen but also to keep predators out. A fence three feet high and a mesh not bigger than an inch and a half will contain most wildfowl, but, if trouble is expected with rats, stoats, foxes or feral cats, then the fence must be six feet high and dug well into the ground to prevent vermin digging under it. In such circumstances the bottom three feet should be half-inch mesh or alternatively, a solid timber barrier is useful, which will also act as a windbreak.

Ideally there should be an eighteen-inch overhang along the top of the netting, but if you are not careful the pen will look more like a concentration camp. It is a good policy to run a couple of tunnel traps on the outside of the pen and keep a permanent covered site baited with rat poison and, with luck, any vermin will be dealt with before they cause any problems.

Having made the pond and erected the fence the next step is to landscape the pen. A few conifers or evergreen shrubs will provide the fowl with shelter from the winter winds and shade from the summer sun. Clumps of rushes and groups of tussocks will give nesting cover in the spring. It is important to have plenty of open grassy areas especially if there are going to be wigeon or geese in the collection. In fact, any bare earth should be sown with grass seed or the duck will quickly turn your pen into a mudbath in wet weather.

Having completed the pen and given the plants a chance to establish themselves the next step is to stock it. The birds may be obtained from either a breeder or from fowl accidently wounded out shooting. Upon retrieving a wounded duck or goose that you wish to keep alive, immediately check the bird for injury. Only birds hit in the last wing joint should be kept. If the bird is just wing-tipped, cut the flight feathers from the injured wing and, if the bone is broken, cut the end of the wing off at the break and tightly bind the wound. Leave the bird quiet in its pen for three days then cut through the binding, but do not remove the dressing. It will wash off in time. Return the bird to its pen and do not disturb it for a week or so and the wound will heal.

It is far better to start the collection with hand-reared birds. Captive fowl will settle down much more quickly than wild birds and many species will readily breed in the following spring. Hand-reared birds will also give wild duck and geese confidence and help to tame them down. However, hand-reared wildfowl have one drawback – they are quite expensive. When buying duck from a breeder, look for birds which are sharp and active with neat plumage. Always purchase true pairs or problems may occur with cross breeding in the spring.

Come the end of March some of the birds in your collection will be looking for nest sites. With the exception of the sawbills and goldeneyes most British duck and geese nest on the ground amid long grass or in rough cover and bushes. A little thought should be given to nesting areas the previous autumn when the pen is being tidied up. Before cutting back the grass and undergrowth, remember to leave some areas rough, especially along the perimeter fence and behind the bushes and shrubs. Tussocks of coltsfoot or clumps of rush make excellent nest sites. Plant them in groups of four in the quieter parts of the enclosure. They may need a temporary fence around them until they are established to prevent the birds grazing them down.

Hollow logs and disused five-gallon oil drums with a hole cut in one end make good sites, but do remember to thoroughly clean the drums out and make sure that there are no sharp edges around the entrance hole. Drill some drainage holes in the side. Fill the bottom of the drum with a mixture of dry wood shavings and peat. Place them around the pen under bushes, half dug into banks or tucked into the corners next to the fence. If it is possible, face the drums towards the pond and cover them with turf or small branches. Covered nesting drums look more natural and will stop the summer sun from heating them up. Upturned wooden boxes or small casks make good nesting sites as well.

Some duck will nest under conifer or fir branches tied into wigwams. If possible try to provide at least two nest sites for each pair of duck in the pen.

Wild caught fowl are very shy breeders in captivity, but, given sufficient peace and an abundance of nesting cover, some may lay, though they will probably take several years. Eggs can sometimes be purchased from ornamental waterfowl farms. It is illegal to take duck or goose eggs from the wild apart from mallard. Even then you must have

All nesting cover should be put in the pen by mid-March

By early April the first eggs can be expected

permission of the landowner to take the eggs and they have to be picked up before 31 March (10 April in Scotland). When the youngsters have been reared they must be left full winged so that they can be returned to the wild before 31 July, as required under the open general licence to take mallard eggs issued under the *Wildlife and Countryside Act 1981*.

Though ducks incubate their eggs quite well, once the ducklings hatch the mother tends to drag her brood from one end of the pen to the other in search of peace and seclusion. Within a day or two most of the ducklings will die from exhaustion and the cold. The best policy is to pick up the eggs and hatch them under broody bantams or use an incubator.

Incubators produce better results with hot eggs, that is to say eggs that have already started to develop. Fresh eggs often fail to germinate unless left under the mother duck for four or five days. By this time the embryo will have started to develop and any infertile eggs can be discarded. Before setting the eggs, give them a wipe with a clean damp cloth to remove any mud or excrement from the shell. Most geese and many duck eggs look very

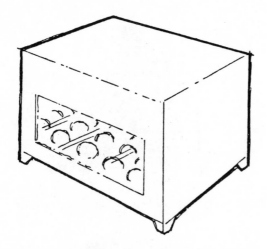

The incubator should be run for a couple of days before setting the first clutch of eggs

similar, so mark them with an indelible pen to show the date they were set and the species.

The incubator temperature should be set at 37.5° celsius and, as duck eggs need higher humidity than chickens or pheasants, put a small dish of water at the bottom of the incubator. Each evening put just enough water in the dish for it to have evaporated by the following morning and top it up again the next evening. As the eggs get close to hatching increase the amount of water to raise the humidity. Some incubators have automatic turners. If not, the eggs will need turning three times a day by hand. Ideally it is best to have a hatcher into which the eggs can be placed when they start to hatch. This will save having to clean the incubator after each clutch hatches. It is amazing the amount of fluff a drying batch of ducklings can produce and it will soon work its way into the mechanism of the incubators.

It is much simpler to use broody bantams to hatch eggs, but you must have the time to take the hen off her eggs once a day in order for her to feed and drink. Settle the bantam for a few days on dummy eggs to make sure she is properly broody before giving her the real eggs. Most hens are capable of turning their own eggs, but they may have difficulty in turning some of the larger waterfowl eggs, so, while the hen is feeding, turn them yourself.

The eggs will need candling after two weeks and any that are infertile thrown out. When placed between finger and thumb and held against a strong light, infertile eggs will appear transparent.

Fertile eggs will seem blacked out with a small clear cell at the top.

Most species of duck hatch after twenty-three to twenty-eight days of incubation, though some geese may take a day or two longer. The day before the eggs hatch, the top end will start to chip as the duckling starts to break out of the shell. When using an incubator now is the time to increase the humidity. However, when using a hen it is better to leave her undisturbed. She will know her job better than you do so leave her alone until the ducklings are ready to move in to their run.

Most duck eggs take between twenty-five and twenty-eight days to hatch

The youngsters will have dried off and gathered their strength after twenty-four hours. They should now be moved into the rearing pens. Ducklings hatched under bantams should be placed in a coop with a run set on short, dry grass. Confine them in the coop for a few hours with their mother hen before allowing them the use of the run in order that they can become accustomed to their surroundings. Youngsters hatched in incubators should be put in a small pen or large cardboard box for the first four or five days, after

Last year's rearing equipment should be thoroughly disinfected

100 watt spotlight bulbs provide ample heat for small clutches of ducklings

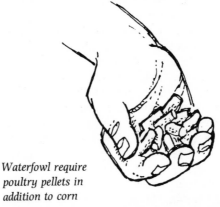

Waterfowl require poultry pellets in addition to corn

which the pen should be enlarged as the birds grow. An infra-red lamp or 100-watt spot-light bulb will be needed to provide heat. Should the ducklings appear to spend all their time under the heater, the bulb should be lowered slightly for more heat. Drinkers of the jam jar type are best to use. The birds may get wet with larger drinkers – a state of affairs to be avoided at all costs in order to prevent pneumonia. Dry wood shavings will help keep the floor dry and absorb the overflow from the water drinkers. For the first couple of weeks the youngsters should be fed on high-protein chick starter crumbs in a shallow dish. The dish should be kept constantly full as ducklings grow very fast and need food available at all times. Young ducklings of different ages should never be mixed as the youngest will be trampled by the older birds. Ducklings will grow faster under heaters than bantam hens as they will have twenty-four hours of daylight in which to feed.

The first quills will start to appear on the flanks and backs of most ducklings by the end of the third week. As more feathers show, the heat can be

steadily reduced and at the end of the fifth week should cease. Some experts are able to harden their ducklings off before this, but, until the beginner is experienced, he would be wise to give his birds some heat until the fifth week. As the quills appear, the crumbs should be gradually replaced with growers' pellets. Up until the fourth week the youngsters should not be allowed to get wet or they may chill, but, from the fifth week onwards, they can be allowed a bath in a shallow pan on warm days.

By their tenth week the youngsters will be able to join the adult birds

Most wildfowl will be fully fledged by their eighth week and be ready to join the main collection a fortnight later. Unless you wish to have the birds full winged they should be pinioned. This is a job best done within a few days of hatching. If you run your finger from the wing tip along the forewing towards the body, you will find a knuckle, known as the alula. With a pair of nail scissors cut the end of one wing off as close as possible to the outside of the alula. This will ensure the bird will be grounded for life. Pinioning is best done in the late evening and the duckling will settle down quickly. A few birds may shed a spot or two

Young ducklings grow very fast

of blood, but they will show no sign of distress and by the following morning will act as though nothing had happened.

Given the correct environment most British wildfowl thrive in captivity, though the sea ducks and the sawbills are not suitable for the novice waterfowl keeper. Once your birds settle down they will quickly become tame. The birds should be fed each morning and evening with a mixture of three-quarters wheat and one-quarter chicken growers' pellets. As the breeding season approaches increase the proportion of pellets to half the total feed. Fine shell grit should be always available to aid the birds' digestion.

Anyone planning to sell live wildfowl should familiarise themselves with the relevant provisions under the *Wildlife and Countryside Act 1981*.

DUCKS

MALLARD

Many wildfowl collectors start with mallard; they are easy to keep and breed readily, but they have several drawbacks. Mallard are very aggressive towards each other and their neighbours during the spring breeding season. They are prolific breeders, having two, three or more clutches of eight to fourteen eggs. The eggs are usually a blue/green, though if your stock has any domestic blood in the strain, the eggs may be cream in colour. It is not unusual to have the odd dusky black or yellow duckling in a brood. Mallard will nest almost anywhere, though under bushes, in clumps of long grass and empty oil drums are preferred. By all means use mallard to gain experience in duck keeping, but I would suggest you let them go free before turning to other species of duck.

TEAL

These small duck are very hard to tame and are notorious escapers. Being so small they can easily squeeze through the narrowest gap, so double check that your fence is secure before introducing them into the enclosure. However, teal are well worth persevering with as, once they are settled, the little drakes become the gems of any wildfowl collection. Their reputation of being hard to breed is not without foundation. They need quiet conditions and an abundance of cover. The clutch of six to ten cream eggs is usually laid in May or June.

WIGEON

Perhaps these are the most delightful of all the British wildfowl and every collection deserves a pair or two. The female is a drab brownish-grey duck with a white underbelly. In contrast, the male has a pale pinkish-brown breast, pale grey vermiculated back and flanks with a white belly and forewings. Its head is chestnut brown with a sulphur yellow crown. On top of his good looks the drake has a magical whistle dear to the heart of every wildfowler. While they may have minor squabbles between themselves, wigeon never molest other species of duck. Wigeon are great grazers and must have access to plenty of grass. They usually nest in long grass or amid tussocks, but will readily lay a clutch of seven to ten cream eggs under a wigwam of fir branches. The ducklings are very distinctive, having a reddish-brown down, and should be given some green food after a couple of weeks.

PINTAIL

These are, for the coastal wildfowler, amongst the wildest and most unobtainable of all the ducks. Only when storms drive them off the sea will he get close views of them. However, in collections pintail are very common and readily become tame. The drake is silent for most of the year, but in the spring he utters a fluting whistle while courting his dowdy mate. Pintail are one of the easiest of the dabbling ducks to breed. By early April the duck will be searching through the tussocks and the long grass for a nest site, where she will lay between six and ten dark olive eggs. Pintail have a shorter incubation that most ducks, taking only twenty-three days before the little dark brown and grey ducklings hatch.

GADWALL

From a distance they look like a rather drab mallard, but, at close quarters, dark grey pencillings overlay a paler grey and ochre on the back flanks. The gadwall has an unusual chestnut brown and white speculum. The drakes have a peculiar call rather like a deep croak. The females breed readily, usually laying in long grass or in thick cover. There may be up to a dozen creamy white eggs in each clutch.

GARGANEY

The garganey is an asset to any collection, but it has one drawback – the drake has the longest eclipse plumage of any duck. It is January before the first feathers of the drake's breeding dress appear. Not until March will he gain his full spring plumage. Within ten short weeks the drake will start his summer moult. Garganey nests can be extraordinarily difficult to find. Unlike most duck, garganeys nest in growing grass which the female pulls over her as she incubates her clutch of six to ten creamy buff eggs. The ducklings are not very hardy and need looking after with care for the first few weeks.

SHOVELER

There are five species of shovelers to be found scattered across the world with the exception of Antarctica. We are fortunate that our European shoveler is the most colourful of them all, though young drakes may take until early March before assuming their full plumage. Shovelers do best when kept on natural pools where they can supplement their diet with small crustaceans and insects. However, they can be kept on artificial ponds provided that they are given plenty of poultry pellets. The drakes can be aggressive towards each other in the breeding season though it is rare for them to fight with any other species of waterfowl. The duck usually lays up to ten buff eggs under a tussock or hidden in thick grass. After twenty-six days' incubation the ducklings hatch, but, like the garganey, they are very delicate and must on no account be allowed to get wet or they may chill. As the youngsters fledge they can be easily sexed as the drakes have pale blue forewings while those of the female are brown.

TUFTED DUCK

Tufties are probably the commonest and easiest diving duck to be kept in captivity. In the wild they feed mainly on freshwater molluscs, so they require a high-protein diet of two-thirds growers' pellets and one-third wheat. They do not breed readily on artificial pools, but provided that there are plenty of rushes and tussocks close to the edge of the pond you may be lucky. Tufted duck lay quite large dark olive green or olive brown eggs, but the clutches are usually small, around six to eight normally, although two females may lay in the same nest resulting in bigger clutches. The sooty black ducklings are impossible to confuse with any other diving duck youngsters; they take a couple of weeks longer to fledge than young dabbling duck.

POCHARD

Like the tufted duck the pochard thrives better on a natural pond where they can forage on the bottom for water weeds and invertebrates. However, pochard can be successfully kept on concrete pools. They usually lay close to the water's edge amidst thick tussocks and reeds. The female usually lays between six and nine large olive eggs. Both pochard and tufted duck are quiet birds, although in the breeding season, the drakes utter a peculiar wheezing call and the females at times have a growling call.

SHELDUCK

There are few sights more breathtaking in an ornamental waterfowl collection than that of a dozen shelduck sunning themselves on a grass bank. Unfortunately shelduck need a lot of space. In a small pen they may become aggressive towards rival pairs of shelduck and other duck. In captivity shelduck need to be fed plenty of pellets, but even with a high-protein diet they rarely attain the size of their wild counterparts. They nest in a most unducklike way, using disused rabbit burrows and hollows in straw stacks. But, in collections, shelduck will use hollow tin drums or an upturned box set in the ground. They normally lay about a dozen large white eggs. The eggs take a little longer than most duck eggs to hatch at around thirty days. The pied youngsters are amongst the easiest duck to rear.

GEESE

Provided you have enough space in your pen it is well worth adding a pair or two of geese to your collection. However, before obtaining any, you should bear in mind that geese are large birds and unless they have plenty of ground they will strip the pen of grass and their droppings will foul the land. You must also spare a thought for your neighbours. Geese can be very noisy – especially in the spring. The clamour of a skein of pinkfeet is marvellous out on the salt marsh but it loses some of its charm outside your bedroom window at three o'clock in the morning.

GREYLAG GEESE

Compared with other grey geese, greylag are rather plain and coarse-looking birds, but they are amongst the cheapest and easiest geese to obtain. They are best kept apart from the smaller geese, which they will dominate. There are no problems in breeding greylag – they usually nest in long grass reeds or under shrubs. Normally greylag lay up to eight off-white eggs which take twenty-eight days to hatch. Like most other grey geese, the goslings are very hardy and easy to rear.

WHITEFRONTED GEESE

There are three species of whitefronts found in Britain. The Greenland whitefront is the most abundant. It is a larger and darker bird than the other two with a distinctive yellow bill. The European whitefront is a greyer goose with a pink bill. The most popular of all the whitefront to be kept in captivity is the lesser whitefront. The lesser is the smallest of the three. Like the European it too has a pink bill, though it can be easily distinguished by its yellow eye ring. All the whitefronts thrive in captivity, though, like other geese, they take at least two or three years before they are old enough to nest. Unfortunately, whitefronts appear rather prone to hybridise with other grey geese. They lay between four and six white eggs in a nest that is usually well concealed amongst vegetation.

PINKFOOTED GEESE

Pinks have a special place in the hearts of many wildfowlers. In the wild they are very shy and seem to have a better idea of how to look after themselves than other grey geese. However, in confinement wild-caught birds become quite tame. At first glance pinkfeet are quietly coloured. They have a very neat appearance when compared with most other grey geese. Unfortunately, pinkfeet are reluctant breeders and may take many years before nesting. There are normally four to six white eggs in a clutch. The young are very hardy. I once had a brood that hatched during a snow storm in mid-April. Despite the cold weather that lasted over a week, the parents reared all the goslings.

BEAN GEESE

There are two races of bean geese which winter in Britain – the western and the smaller Russian. Both races are similar to the pinkfoot, being somewhat larger and browner with a thicker orange banded bill. Their call is much deeper than the pinkfoot and for the most part they are silent birds. Bean geese usually nest amid vegetation and like most grey geese lay between four and six large white eggs.

CANADA GEESE

Unless you have a large enclosure or paddock then Canadas are not to be recommended. They are far too large, too aggressive and too noisy for the average collection. They breed in the early spring and are best left to rear their own young. You may have trouble in getting rid of the young and it is illegal to release Canada geese into the wild.

BARNACLE GEESE

Perhaps the most attractive of all the British geese and certainly the most popular goose to be kept in collections. They are easy to keep, do not need much space and are easy to breed. They do have one drawback – in the breeding season they are very noisy. That apart, barnacles deserve a place in every collection. The nest is usually built amid light cover, often against the fence. They may lay up to seven eggs – however, four or five is more normal. The eggs are white when first laid but they quickly become stained with dirt. Like the brent, barnacle goslings are grey.

BRENT GEESE

Brents unfortunately are not to be recommended for the novice wildfowl keeper. They are not easy to keep, especially in hot summers, and are almost impossible to breed.

30
WILDFOWLING AND CONSERVATION IN EIRE

TURLOUGH J. COFFEY

Ireland's geographical location on the north-westerly tip of Europe with its long inlet shores bathed by the warm waters of the Gulf Stream and its mild wet climate makes it a welcoming haven for migrating wildfowl fleeing the grip of winter. Some of these birds are on passage to warmer climes farther south, but fortunately others stay with us from late autumn until the warmth of spring calls them back to their place of birth to breed. Ireland is the winter home for geese, duck and waders from Greenland, Canada, Iceland, Scandinavia and the European mainland. The saucer-like topography of Ireland with its many lakes, coupled with the high rainfall, results in a lot of inland flooding, particularly in winter. These floods take various forms – some are river callows, some are turloughs, while others are flash floods. These floods vary in size from a waterlogged field to areas around the Shannon River which look like inland seas. These flooded areas provide ideal habitat for wildfowl in winter. The wet summers of 1985 and 1986 gave rise to flooding in June and July and the television news pictures of the tops of the hay-cocks above the water and cattle wading to their chests showed dramatically how these floods cover so much land.

For those readers whose romantic idea of Ireland and its waterfowl is taken from *The Wildfowler in Ireland*, by Sir Ralph Payne-Gallwey, let me state straightaway that things have changed very much since my compatriot went to print over a hundred years ago. Oddly enough a writer up to the 1930s could have reported very little change, but, since the Second World War, things in the Irish wildfowling world have changed a great deal. The greylag goose has all but deserted our island lured by compulsory tillage in Scotland during the war. We have a good fully protected population of palebellied brents and Greenland barnacles. The Green-land whitefronted goose, until recently, was our only quarry goose. Ireland holds 12,000 of the world population of 22,000 of this sub-species, and 8000 are in one location of the Wexford Slobs. The disease which killed the *Zostera* throughout Europe also struck in Ireland and estuaries that were green with wigeon grass (woor) are now bare or hold *Spartina* and sand. The great flocks of wigeon moved from the harbours and estuaries inland, where they now graze on flooded meadows.

The term 'wildfowling' in Ireland is often applied to all branches of shooting and every sportsman carrying a gun is called a fowler, particularly in the west. However, wildfowling is a much neglected sport – the vast majority of Irish game licence holders are rough shooters who pursue the over-rated cock pheasant. The statistics show that grants paid by the Government Forestry & Wildlife Service between 1970 and 1982 were in a ratio of 8 to 1 in favour of pheasants against mallard, which is surprising in a country so unsuited to pheasants and so ideally suited to duck. Much of the Irish wildfowling is done inland on the evening flight when duck fly from the larger bodies of water to the smaller flash floods to feed. This type of shooting is called 'flashing', and can produce great sport. Morning flighting demands more skill and a good knowledge of the flight line of duck to their roosting areas, a type of shooting that depends upon a good wind. Wildfowl are also walked-up in many places with guns stalking-up on sitting wildfowl and shooting the flushing birds. One shot, however, can disturb such a large area that a detailed knowledge of the terrain is needed. For the purist, on the other hand, the only real wildfowling is on the foreshore or estuary and although the bulk of wildfowl have moved inland this still provides great sport, particularly in hard frost when birds seek the open water.

FARMING

Modern developments in farming, particularly since Ireland's entry to the EEC with its insatiable demand for more production of milk, grain and beef to fill its huge stores, have resulted in many changes. Marginal land has been drained and ditches cleared so that we can produce more surplus farm produce. Bogs have been drained, skimmed of their vegetation and turned into peat deserts for fuel production. Afforestation of bogland and mountain has also destroyed the haunts of wildfowl. The main turbary and afforestation has been undertaken by state agencies and forestry is ironically linked with wildlife as a section within the Department of Tourism, Fisheries & Forestry. This exploitation of the land has undoubtedly destroyed the habitat of wildfowl and in some places the change is irreversible.

However, this type of development must be seen in perspective. When the North and South Slobs in Wexford were scheduled for drainage in the mid-1960s the conservationists of the day pleaded for 250 acres to be taken by the state as a wildfowl sanctuary. It was stated by these 'eminent conservationists' at the time that the Greenland whitefronted goose population of 5000 would drop to 250 because only the sanctuary would hold birds. Twenty years on both Slobs are drained, agriculture is intensive, the Greenland whitefronted goose population is 8000, lightbellied brent geese are using the Slobs and mallard numbers in autumn are as high as ever recorded. We should avoid alarmist reaction to these developments. Wigeon will thrive off new-sown Italian ryegrass as they did on the traditional meadow grass and weeds. It is also noticeable that snipe have taken to ploughed fields in winter where bogs have been drained. The wild birds are more adaptable to change than we sometimes give them credit for.

The average farm size in the west of Ireland is under forty acres, with the average in the rest of Ireland not much higher. Therefore, the Irish small farmer has been under great pressure to optimise his farm output, drain his wetland, clear his ditches and groves with substantial capital grants and high intervention (guaranteed) prices for farm produce. It is simply unrealistic and arrogant of sophisticates to preach ecology to families in such an impoverished situation. One cannot expect such families to provide a home for snipe so that we can 'have a shot' or see pretty wildlife programmes on television. The drainage of wetlands, reseeding of meadowland, bulldozing of ditches and woodland can only be stopped when the substantial financial grants to carry out such work are replaced by grants for wildlife management. The regrettable reality of the situation is that we are light years away from such a scenario. The structure of shooting in Ireland also gives rise to other problems as free and uncontrolled shooting is the order of the day. Until recent times it was very unusual to be refused shooting over any land in Ireland except the few large estates which remained intact after the founding of the Irish Free State in 1922. Recent problems on liability insurance may have altered this *laissez-faire* approach.

The majority of organised shooting is administered through the gun clubs or game protection associations which are based upon the parish and are generally open to membership in the parish. The gun clubs are affiliated to the County Regional Game Council, which are in turn affiliated to The National Association of Regional Game Councils. The vast majority of these gun clubs/game protection associations are engaged in rough shooting, pheasant release and predator control, but few have any interest in wildfowling. The membership shoot over the club's lands with the minimum of rules other than the provisions of the *Wildlife Act 1976*. Therefore, wildfowling comes second place and there is little restriction on the times and frequency of shooting. This can lead to undue disturbance and arriving for an evening flight to find the area shot the previous evening or guns in place ahead of you. This can also be dangerous as a gun can slip into place at a flash unseen at dusk. I have often been alerted to such a situation by the glow of a cigarette or a command issued to a dog. It is best to make your presence known in such conditions.

CONSERVATION

The *Wildlife Act 1976* places the responsibility for conservation on the Minister for Tourism, Fisheries & Forestry. Within his Department the Minister has a small Forestry & Wildlife Service which looks after conservation. The Minister also appoints a Wildlife Advisory Council to advise him on matters of conservation. The very diversity of the Minister's portfolio and the inherent conflicts between afforestation and the conservation of flora and fauna is a cause for concern particularly as the Wildlife Section is 'married' to forestry and forestry is the dominant partner. There is much concern amongst those of us interested in conservation about the subordinate status of The Wildlife Section and its lack of budgetary command. Since the passing of the 1976 Act twenty-seven nature reserves have been established of which twenty-six were already the property of The Department of Forestry. Most of these are native woodlands and few have any relevance to wildfowl conservation.

SANCTUARIES

The Minister has also set up sixty-six wildfowl sanctuaries (see Fig. 45) which are simply no-shooting areas. These certainly provide refuge for wintering wildfowl, but they generally lack any system of wildlife management. In these sanctuaries vermin thrive and there is no control over habitat destruction or other disturbance. With the continued pressure for farm expansion and fuel production, the drainage and wetland destruction will continue unabated. The very tight constraints on government expenditure also offer very little hope of state funds for conservation purposes.

The open season for duck is from 1 September to 31 January, and at the time of writing there is a moratorium on goose shooting. The duck species which may be shot are mallard, wigeon, teal, gadwall, shoveler, tufted, pochard, goldeneye, scaup and pintail. Snipe and golden plover are shot from 1 September to 31 January, woodcock and curlew from 1 November to 31 January. A foreshore licence is needed to shoot the foreshore, in addition to the usual firearms certificate.

Mallard release is undertaken by some wildfowl shoots, but the numbers released are very small in relation to the size of the country and the available suitable habitat. In short the potential for the expansion of home-bred mallard shooting is great. Vermin abounds throughout the country as much of the land is unkeepered and greycrows (hooded) and magpies are common. Foxes, rats, feral cats and now feral mink enjoy free rein across much of the land. If mallard release and vermin control were widely practised throughout the country, wildfowling could be improved many fold and be enjoyed by many more sportsmen.

There are many very important areas for wildfowl in Ireland and there are few areas which do not hold some wildfowl. For the wildfowler the most important areas are the Wexford Slobs, which holds 8000 Greenland whitefronted geese and over 4000 duck in autumn. Close by are Tacumshane and Lady's Island lakes. The Little Brosna and Shannon River area holds a very large wigeon and teal population in winter. Lough Cara, a very important lake for breeding mallard, and all the inland lakes hold large wintering duck populations.

It is difficult to assess the status of the Irish wildfowl population in the 1980s compared to other times as reliable census figures are not available and coverage of the whole country is impossible. To rely upon the memories of elderly persons, however well-meaning and accommodating, is a grave mistake as everything came in thousands years ago. The few noughts come too easily! I recall trying to assess the changes in red grouse numbers in County Clare and interviewing several of the kindest and friendliest people I ever met, who all wanted to give me the answers which they thought would please me. I gave up after a long interview with a countryman who finished his story of the great numbers of grouse in the locality by telling me that the bushes were full of them in autumn. To him a grouse was a bird and so was a pigeon or a fieldfare and 'sure it didn't make a lot of difference'. So with wildfowl, the skies were black with duck and geese in the good old days and the truth is we will never know the statistics for those populations. So much also depends upon happenings elsewhere, like the compulsory tillage attracting the geese to Scotland. In the 1970s there was a noticeable drop in the numbers of teal, wigeon and other migratory duck in winter which could be discerned by we wildfowlers. This was due to the reclamation of two large polders in Holland where the duck stayed for those winters. The onset of very hard weather in Europe and Britain drives the birds over to Ireland.

One of the factors which inadvertently conserves our wintering wildfowl is the fact that many of our native shooters do not shoot snipe and teal, some because they are deemed 'too small' for the table, others because they deem them too difficult a shot. However, this has led to a trend of inviting in tourist shooters to shoot these migratory species for little more than the cost of their hotel. On a

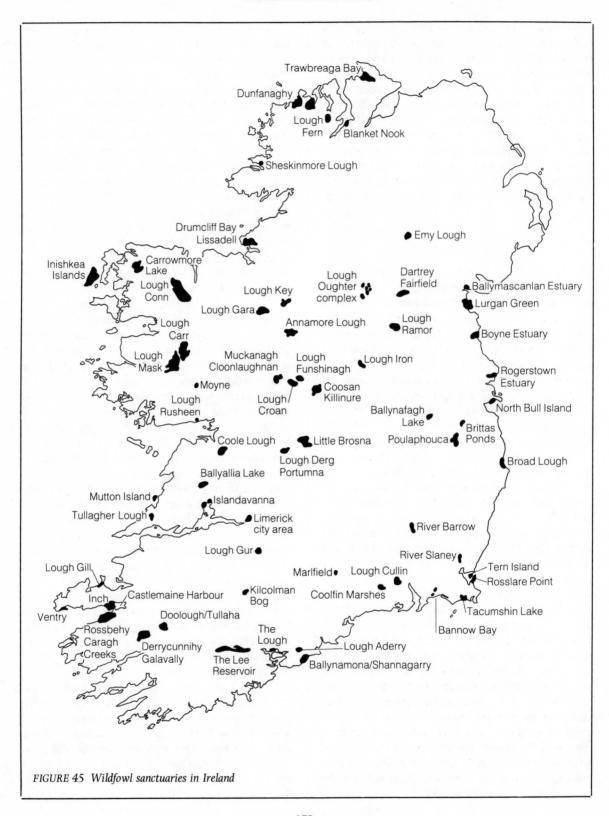

FIGURE 45 Wildfowl sanctuaries in Ireland

small scale and under proper supervision this may not do much harm, but, as there is no artificial rearing of these birds, it could take a long time to reverse a population slide resulting from any overshooting. It is the overwhelming consensus of opinion amongst the Irish shooting fraternity that tourist shooting should be restricted to organised and properly supervised shoots where there is pheasant or mallard release or pigeon shooting to assist in crop protection.

Ireland is still a wild, watery country with an abundance of wildfowl from the brent geese and migratory wild duck in the centre of Dublin (Bull Island) to the Greenland barnacles in Inishkea. This is in spite of modern economic and farming pressures. Conservation is much talked about but little is done to conserve wetlands, improve habitat and promote mallard release. Unfortunately, in the absence of monetary commitment, the wildfowler has been made to suffer. There is a moratorium on goose shooting although the changes in population were not brought about through shooting pressures. Nonetheless, Ireland continues to offer a wide variety of sporting opportunity.

31
WILDFOWLING
IN NORTH AMERICA
NORMAN SEYMOUR

The late Jeffery Harrison's chapter on the North American wildfowl situation in the second edition of *The New Wildfowler* focused on the virtues of what has become the most comprehensive, complex and costly system of wildfowl management in the world. He closed on a note of optimism for the future of North American wildfowl and the wildfowling tradition. However, today this system, which attempts to control both birds and shooters, faces a crisis. Declining duck populations and a growing dissatisfaction with the lack and quality of shooting opportunities have many people wondering how well the system is working.

It is important to understand certain things about North American wildfowl management. The underlying philosophy is that duck and geese are a renewable resource that can sustain an annual harvest, if properly managed. The essential difference between North American and British wildfowl management is that in North America the government takes responsibility for managing the resource and has put in place well-funded agencies to do this.

There are three levels of organization which have an impact on the wildfowling experience. Politicians frame legislation pertaining to management of populations which includes the sport harvest. The actual management is the domain of the biologist-manager, who constantly monitors populations and makes recommendations to the politicians about the nature of legislation governing management. These recommendations should be based on sound biological research and legislation should reflect this, and not pressure by lobbyists from industry and other special interest groups who may seek to further their vested interests. Similarly enforcement should be kept in perspective and should be viewed as a component of management. Those responsible for enforcement should not determine the direction of man-

agement. When the system functions as it is intended to, the biologist-manager has the greatest impact on the decision-making process. He also has considerable independence in determining the details of how populations are managed and on how wildfowling is regulated. Unfortunately, this is not always the case. Politicians and those involved in enforcement are sometimes far more involved than they should be, particularly in parts of the USA.

One of the attractions of this system, when it does function properly, is that management agencies are committed to providing the shooter with the maximum harvest that populations can sustain. This means the management agency, funded from the public coffers, promotes the concept of sport shooting, unlike in Britain where the direction, organization and funding required to defend and safeguard wildfowling must come from the shooting fraternity. Furthermore, without a government-mandated management agency that has the right to make decisions about shooting, representatives of the British shooting fraternity must go directly to government to air their concerns.

It is ironic that the North American management system is at the same time the best mechanism to safeguard the future of wildfowling and the most potentially repressive barrier to the freedom of the shooter to pursue a quality wildfowling experience. The main benefit of the system is the success it has had in maintaining most populations at levels where a sustained harvest has been possible. The main cost has been the often unnecessary regulation and restriction of shooters' activities. The assumption seems to be that the shooter has to be told what to do and then be watched. This creates an adversarial situation and it is the enforcement of regulations that generates the most criticism, controversy and debate among shooters. Sadly, a significant number of shooters disregard regulations, not seeing the relevance of them. This is not so everywhere and many wildfowlers do not feel seriously burdened by regulations and do attempt to follow the spirit of the regulation.

The history of the North American system spans five decades. It was conceived in crisis and implemented in an attempt to reverse a serious decline in duck populations. Concerns about over-harvesting and habitat destruction, and their effects on duck populations, were being voiced as early as the turn of the century. However, it was not until the devastating drought of the thirties on the prairie grasslands, where most of the duck are produced, that the future of wildfowling began to look particularly bleak. This was the catalyst that finally moved enlightened and dynamic people in both government and the private sector to take action to protect the birds and the future of wildfowling.

Government involvement in wildfowl and wildfowling was already a reality when the drought crisis occurred. By 1913 jurisdiction for control of migratory bird populations in the USA had become consolidated with the federal government. This took control away from the many state governments which had been pursuing their parochial interests and politics at the expense of wildfowl and shooters in other regions. In 1916 the Migratory Bird Treaty was signed by the USA and Britain, on behalf of Canada. This treaty now ensured that control of the wildfowl of almost the entire continent was in the hands of two friendly, federal governments. When Mexico later signed the treaty this meant that most species could be managed throughout their range, from the breeding grounds in Canada to the wintering grounds in the USA and Mexico. Today two federal agencies, the Canadian Wildlife Service and the US Fish and Wildlife Service, collaborate to manage wildfowl on a continental basis. The key to understanding how this level of co-operation between the two countries is possible, relates to the fact that they share a common conservation philosophy. Duck and goose populations, which do not respect political boundaries in their migrations, are viewed as a commonly shared, harvestable and renewable resource.

North American society has, for the most part, viewed shooting as a component of conservation.

The concept receives support and frequently active promotion from politicians. The bureaucratic structure and programmes of North American wildfowl management are funded by the taxpayer. In Britain it seems that most people believe the concepts of shooting and conservation are contradictory. This requires the shooting fraternity to sell its case to the public, as well as to the politician.

Biologist-managers in North America monitor wildfowl populations during migration and on the wintering and breeding grounds. It is on the basis of the predicted size of the autumn migration that shooting regulations are set. Although subject to political approval, managers from various regions within each of the four north-south migration corridors, or flyways, annually determine the duration of seasons, daily bag limits, and what species are to be on the quarry list. More specific regulations are tailored to local requirements.

Even though the government has responsibility for setting regulations, the private sector has always had considerable involvement in North American wildfowl management. Millions of dollars have been donated by shooters to organizations like Ducks Unlimited. This money has primarily been used for the leasing and management of habitat. These organizations provide a way for the shooter to make a direct and tangible contribution to the future of his sport. Private sector organizations have considerable influence on the setting of regulations, primarily as a result of their financial clout and vigorous political lobby.

As management techniques were being developed in North America an extensive network of refuges was being established in key locations along the flyways and on the wintering grounds. These refuges, which have become an integral part of management, have always generated controversy because of the way they concentrate birds, thereby making them vulnerable to disease. They do however give managers considerable control over the birds.

The North American management system, through programmes centred on shooting restrictions and habitat acquisition and enhancement, was instrumental in reversing the downhill slide in wildfowl populations during the 1930s. But, despite unquestioned successes and the experience gained by three generations of managers, North American wildfowl management faces another crisis today. Continued high levels of harvest, combined with another protracted prairie drought and general habitat degradation, have resulted in the lowest levels in history for some species of duck. This includes the mallard, which is used by managers as an indicator of continental trends in duck populations. Even though the system has failed to prevent this crisis from happening, it does provide solutions to the problem.

A management plan, which has had broad input from shooters and others with an interest in wildfowl, has been drafted by the management agencies, and is scheduled for implementation by 1990. The North American Waterfowl Management Plan proposes a broadly-based advisory committee to set management goals and objectives for the remainder of this century. There will be five-year performance assessments of the programmes designed to achieve these objectives.

While North Americans debate the relative impact of shooting and habitat loss on duck populations, continental numbers continue to decline. It seems obvious that habitat loss and shooting mortality are inseparable factors that have combined to cause the decline in populations. It is certain that over-exploitation has occurred in many populations. We are not certain of the precise impact of shooting, but it is a mortality factor that can be controlled. It is for this reason that the new plan focuses on the regulation of sport shooting, but the key is regulation and not closure, as some people and organizations have requested. In fact the plan sets a goal of maintaining sufficient breeding stock to produce an annual fall migration of 100 million duck. It is proposed that the 2.2 million North American wildfowlers be allowed to harvest 20 per cent of these birds, the actual number adjusted annually to the size of the fall flight. This level of harvest is considered safe and should avoid the crisis situations that have periodically occurred when harvest levels have not reflected habitat conditions and productivity in the population.

The North American experience has implication for the European harvest, which has been estimated as high as 45 per cent for some populations of duck. Problems in monitoring European populations throughout their range make it difficult to accurately determine population abundance and the size of the sport harvest. Some European populations may not be as stable as they appear and are perhaps being over-exploited without this

being detected. It is difficult to see how such an apparently large harvest can be sustained without integrated management of populations throughout their range.

The North American Waterfowl Management Plan also addresses the other major factor influencing populations. The planners recognize the seriousness of the loss of wintering and breeding habitat to urbanization and agriculture. The plan proposes that 4.5 million acres of breeding and 750,000 acres of wintering habitat be acquired and managed for wildfowl before the turn of the century. The proposal also includes enhancement of the quality of the considerable acreage already controlled. In many parts of the USA much of the critical wintering habitat available to birds is controlled by private wildfowling clubs.

The planners also recognize that there must be realistic mechanisms to achieve their goals, and these mechanisms will be costly. The price tag for habitat acquisition and enhancement is estimated at £700–800 million over the next 15 years. And who will pay for this? Co-ordinated efforts by government agencies and private organizations will raise the largest component of the money required through new and existing legislation and fund-raising endeavours.

Much of this legislation and fund-raising is directed at the users of the resource, particularly shooters. For example, the newly established agency, Wildlife Habitat Canada, is a government-mandated but privately-operated organization which requires every wildfowler to buy a licence. Revenues from this source will be applied directly to habitat acquisition and management. To a large extent this agency was established by the Canadian government to satisfy its responsibility to fund the new plan, and to encourage greater private sector involvement and control in wildfowl management. Some people see an integrated blend of government legal clout and private sector efficiency as the key to the future of North American management.

The control of habitat must be placed in perspective. Managing duck production on the breeding grounds depends on the co-operation and assistance of many people. Even after government and the private sector have spent decades acquiring land, more than 90 per cent of breeding habitat remains in the public domain and is controlled by people like farmers, whose interests are not in producing wildfowl. We fool ourselves if we think we have effective control of duck production, and North Americans have far more control over this than Europeans do.

When the most recent crisis in North American duck populations occurred the wildlife agencies had the structure and funding required to facilitate the implementation of the long-term plan I've been describing. Whether or not the plan is successful remains to be seen, but having such a management system has provided direction in addressing the present crisis which threatens both the future of North American wildfowl populations and wildfowling.

This seems like a good point to identify some management successes and to see how the government agencies attempt to protect the wildfowler's interests, although their primary responsibility is to safeguard wildfowl populations. There are several issues of common concern to British and North American wildfowlers. For example, the use of lead shot in Britain and Europe has become a controversial issue, a ban being in effect in several parts of Denmark. The polarization between shooters and protectionists means that the debate is often bitter.

North American wildlife agencies have investigated the lead shot problem for decades. They have identified specific regions where there is a perennially high risk to birds and wildfowlers must use steel shot there. In reality only relatively few shooters have been affected by localized restriction. This will change in the USA, where the federal government will require the use of steel shot everywhere in the country by 1991. However, nowhere in the vastness of Canada is there a ban on the use of lead. This was a case of the management agency having the responsibility and resources to investigate a problem, identifying where the problem existed, and finding a solution to it.

The North American black brant goose is ecologically identical to its British cousin the dark-bellied brent goose. Both birds suffered the same disastrous population crash earlier this century, but in the last two decades numbers have increased and populations have become abundant. The lack of mechanisms to control the harvest and the consequent reluctance of the Nature Conservancy Council to consider a harvest until this issue is addressed, is an important factor in keeping

the brent off the British quarry list. In North America the brant was quickly reinstated to the quarry list when government biologists became convinced that the constantly monitored population could sustain a harvest. Brant can be shot only in specific areas, but, where they are legal quarry, a significant number of shooters enjoy wonderful sport. Reinstating the brant to the quarry list was one of the objectives of increasing and then maintaining a high level of abundance in the population.

A dramatic increase in the greater snow goose population is claimed as an outstanding example of management success, though other factors outside the influence of man have undoubtedly contributed to this increase. There can be no question that careful regulation of shooting and habitat acquisition and management have combined to enable the population to increase to approximately 300,000 birds, a hundredfold increase in five decades. Now the birds threaten to increase their numbers beyond the carrying capacity of their winter habitat and carefully regulated sport shooting is a major mechanism used to control the population. Not only do wildfowlers reduce the size of the population, but they keep birds moving about the feeding grounds so as to prevent over-grazing and consequently permanent damage to their vital food resources.

Perhaps one can look to the successes of management and feel a degree of guarded optimism for the future of North American wildfowling. However, some shooters are critical of what the system has become. Their main annoyance is the way the paternalistic system, with its plethora of enforced restrictions, has eroded the freedoms of the wildfowler.

One cannot make sweeping generalizations about the impact of regulations and how they are perceived by North American wildfowlers. This depends very much on where they shoot. Generally speaking the continent can be divided into those regions where there is a high density of people, and consequently intense competition for access to shooting, and regions where the opposite situation prevails. For example, Canadian shooters, who represent only ten per cent of the continental wildfowling population and who have the first opportunity to harvest birds, generally enjoy more freedoms and have greater access to shooting than their American counterparts further along the flyways. This is similar to the situation that exists between Scotland and England.

Regulations have been a reality for three generations of shooters and are generally accepted and believed to be a necessary component of management. This is particularly so where people find regulations reasonable, and not unnecessarily restrictive. It is a matter of perception. For example, punt gunning and moonlight shooting, which are in my opinion the two most exciting and unique features of British wildfowling, would be considered unsporting by the responsible North American wildfowler, who has not enjoyed these privileges for fifty years and hence does not consider them part of his traditional wildfowling experience.

It is not any specific regulation that stirs emotional debate and controversy among wildfowlers, but the way in which regulations in general impinge upon the freedom of the shooter. There is no question that the best system exists when tradition, and a type of honour system based on respect for the quarry and other shooters, and on a concept of sharing, regulates the behaviour of shooters. This has been the hallmark of British wildfowling. Enlightened self-regulation eliminates the need for enforcement, but this works only if shooters understand and respect the tradition.

It is worthwhile to consider some of the freedoms that the British wildfowler enjoys, but are denied to the North American fowler because of the way the system intervenes to function as the shooter's conscience. The North American shooter cannot use a gun larger than a 10-bore, thereby eliminating punt gunning. He cannot lure birds by baiting with food and he can shoot only from the half-hour before sunrise to sunset in the USA, and to the half-hour after sunset in Canada. Only under exceptional circumstances can he keep captive wildfowl, and then only under licence. He has daily limits placed on the number of birds he can kill and sale of wild birds is prohibited. There are usually additional restrictions placed on the shooter by local managers. Furthermore, the length of the open season varies geographically, but is rarely longer than three months, and in many parts of the continent hard weather effectively terminates the season before the legal date of closure is reached.

The concept of licensing is also different. The gun ownership certificate required by the British wildfowler is not usually required for ownership of a shotgun anywhere in North America. The British fowler may be required to be a member of the B.A.S.C. in order to shoot in a specific area, but there is no British wildfowling licence as such. Everywhere in North America the wildfowler requires a minimum of two relatively costly government wildfowling permits, but in some places he must have a pocketful of permits before he steps on the marsh. On one stretch of the St Lawrence River five permits are required, a gun ownership permit, a federal wildfowling permit, a provincial wildfowling permit, a permit providing access to shooting on Indian land, and a permit required to use the habitat. If he shoots on a public refuge, the wildfowler requires yet another permit. However, for the most part, revenue generated by the sale of permits goes to some aspect of wildfowl management and this makes it easier for the shooter to dig into his pocket.

The main difficulty with regulations centres on enforcement. Shooters and game wardens, whose responsibility it is to enforce regulations, frequently view each other as adversaries. There is often mutual mistrust with the warden assuming that the shooter is guilty of some infraction of the regulations and the wildfowler believing that the warden is there only to catch him out. The system fails when this ridiculous situation exists. Regulations must be seen to be fair and relevant if they are to be respected. Attempting to fine-tune the system has resulted in many regulations being too complex to be understood or too restrictive to be obeyed. Any system that relies only on enforcement to influence the behaviour of the wildfowler is doomed to failure. Truly effective enforcement is possible only where access to shooting and shooter behaviour are completely controlled, and this is certainly not possible in most of North America.

Perhaps the best way to illustrate to the British wildfowler how his North American counterpart perceives his sport is to describe what it is like to be there, the essential part of wildfowling everywhere. I will describe shooting along the flyways from where the birds breed to their wintering grounds, showing in a general way how restrictions become much more a fact of life where demand for access to birds increases.

In the far north of Canada the native Inuits and Indians harvest wildfowl for food. A few southern sport shooters make 'a trip of a lifetime' to

A Maryland hunter waiting for the Canada geese in a pit blind (Frank H. Meads)

experience shooting on the breeding grounds as the birds, usually geese, prepare to migrate south. If the trip is well organised and timed, the shooter is surrounded by naïve young birds that have never encountered humans and killing the liberal limit requires little more than holding the gun straight. But the real thrill of the experience is being in this wild, harsh, and starkly beautiful land which will soon be locked in icy darkness. The well-being of the southern sportsman depends entirely upon his native guide's skills and knowledge of the flat, featureless landscape, where there is no sign of human life from horizon to horizon. The visitor gets a sense of how important the birds are to the very existence of these people and he leaves the north feeling he's had a glimpse of the past, and much more than just a quality shooting experience.

By mid-September the first waves of migrating birds have reached southern Canada. It is here that they encounter the first serious gunning pressure. On the northern prairie several million duck and geese of twenty or more species congregate before deteriorating weather forces them south. Shooting here has changed little for three generations of wildfowlers. Relatively few people, large numbers of birds and large tracts of public land mean the luxury of ready access to birds and freedom from restrictive regulations. The generous limit of duck and geese may well be a realistic expectation, though weather may force the migrants south after only a few weeks of shooting. In the rural hinterland enforcement is virtually non-existent and, whether or not one respects the regulations, is a matter of conscience. It is here in particular that regulations must be realistic to get the support and cooperation of the shooter just as it is in the British tradition.

Having a legally defined daily limit seems to give some people a questionable goal. Wildfowlers often remain in the field to bag their limit long after they would otherwise have left. This distorts the concept of sport shooting and diminishes the quality of their wildfowling experience. It is almost as if some wildfowlers allow the system to do their thinking for them.

Certainly many shooters abuse the system and the birds. A sentiment one hears expressed is that if they don't get the birds then someone else farther along the flyway will. This is particularly difficult to comprehend where wildfowlers enjoy unrestricted access to large numbers of birds and freedom from restrictive regulations. For many people wildfowling in the rural areas of North America is a wonderfully exciting sport, free of the confinements and stringent regulations that are encountered near urban centres.

To wildfowlers more duck can only be a good thing, but prairie farmers often view duck as vermin. In wet years farmers have problems getting on the land to harvest their grain. They may have the added burden of wildfowl descending on their fields by the thousands, sometimes destroying an entire crop. The wildlife agencies attempt to address this problem by buying or renting land in critical areas and then planting crops attractive to birds to lure them away from the farmers' fields. This is a costly but necessary undertaking since most duck harvested by shooters are produced on privately owned farmland and maintaining the goodwill of the farmer is essential. Providing a surplus of birds for shooting means that periodically these birds cause great concern for others.

Most birds are killed on the southern marshes, where they spend the winter. Birds are vulnerable there because of the length of their stay, combined with heavy shooting pressure and restricted habitat. This situation probably also applies to southern Europe. The number of birds that survive the winter is critical, since it is these birds which will migrate north to breed.

It is on the wintering grounds where cities harbour a large population of mobile wildfowlers. Refuges provide sanctuary for birds where wintering grounds are in close proximity to urban areas, as they frequently are in North America. The full gamut of regulations, including the mandatory use of steel shot, is likely to be encountered here. Enforcement is usually a very tangible reality with shooters having to report to wardens when entering and leaving the marsh, their activities sometimes being monitored by wardens, who patrol on foot, by boat, and even by aeroplane. On some occasions wardens in hides observe the behaviour of shooters to ensure compliance with regulations. With wardens and shooters in such close contact, it is important that wardens are not over-zealous and concerned with legalistic details. They must treat shooters reasonably and not immediately assume they are violating regulations. This is frequently not the case and alienation of the shooter, and the consequential loss of his support and co-operation, is a major problem.

The system attempts to reward the responsible shooter and one way of doing this is by allowing those who can identify males and females of different duck species to potentially harvest more birds. In many parts of the USA where shooting pressure is severe, a different value is assigned to the male, and to the more important female, of each species. The specific value depends on the level of protection needed by that species. For example, this so-called points system might allow a chap who can identify his quarry to take ten male pintail worth ten points each before his quota of one hundred points is reached, while his mate who shares the same hide with him might have to stop shooting after killing one female black duck worth a hundred points.

Of course there is no foolproof system and no regulation or law can completely deter unscrupulous shooters. The points system becomes a sham when shooters kill what they will and then simply retrieve those birds which keep them within their quota. No matter what the system, shooter co-operation and attitude is critical and some North American shooters definitely choose to abuse the system.

Two particularly controversial issues have plagued efforts to maximize shooting opportunities for wildfowlers. One issue is the 'firing line', whereby shooters are allowed to ring the periphery of refuges to shoot at birds entering and leaving.

The atrocious behaviour by many of the shooters on these firing lines makes the well-publicized bad behaviour in places like the Solway Firth seem mild by comparison. Unsporting behaviour by some shooters is a thorny problem in both Britain and North America.

The other issue is the way that commercial interests control farmland around refuges where birds congregate to feed. Some unscrupulous people who own or rent such land see the birds as nothing more than an opportunity for commercial enterprise. Management agencies, funded by tax-payers' money, unwittingly provide these people with birds to shoot. Not only are large numbers of birds legally killed, but shooting is restricted to those who are able to pay for it. Commercial wildfowling in the USA is a multi-million dollar reality. This is something to avoid in Britain, where the relatively small number of wild birds, the vulnerability of duck and geese over cropland and the lack of regulations on how wildfowl are harvested make commercial wildfowling a risk to both the birds and the future of wildfowling.

In an attempt to maintain the quality of wild-fowling where competition to shoot is severe, North American management agencies have taken control of certain traditional shooting areas and have limited access to shooting there. A lottery system provides equal opportunity for public access. These controlled shoots sometimes result in a distortion of the wildfowling tradition, but they can also serve to perpetuate traditions and provide shooters, albeit relatively few, with a quality experience.

The distortion from tradition may be seen on marshes near large American cities, where hopeful shooters sit in a long line of cars for several days waiting to gain access to the marsh for one day on a first come, first served basis. Control may mean that everything is provided for the shooter, from a paved parking lot and toilet facilities, to boats, hides, decoys and a list of instructions on how to behave. The restrictions on what he may shoot, and how he may shoot it, include the number of cartridges allocated to each shooter. Some years there may be daily limits of as few as two birds. The shoot is timed, the shooter must remain within a specific area, and any transgression, however minor, ends his day. This certainly takes the spontaneity and strategy planning out of wildfowl-ing and, even with access controlled, one re-members crowds, litter and surly behaviour on the part of both shooters and wardens. For many people this level of control is so removed from the traditional wildfowling experience that they would rather not participate.

The Canadian Wildlife Service controlled shoot at Cape Tourmente on the north shore of the St Lawrence River provides traditional sport for 480 wildfowlers during a 20-day period in October amidst hundreds of thousands of migrating snow geese. A five-mile by three-mile stretch of prime habitat accommodates 24 shooters each day, and rarely does one see another person. The shooter who has been successful in the lottery, and a mate of his choice, enjoy a two-day shoot, from noon until closure on the evening of the first day, and then from dawn until noon of the second day. Their French-speaking guide takes them by horse-drawn sled far onto the tidal mud flats to the shooting pits, where they are left to enjoy their day. Once they have been briefed on protocol, that is the last they are aware of any government involve-ment in their shooting experience until their guide takes them back to the lodge at the end of the shoot. Unquestionably, what makes this such a quality experience is the attitude of the organizers, and the way this is manifest in their treatment of shooters and others who visit the refuge to witness the spectacle of migration.

It is difficult to make sweeping statements about how wildfowling is pursued across the vast North American continent. There is such a diversity of habitat from the high arctic to the southern coastal marshes, and so many different species of duck and geese, that the details of the wildfowling ex-perience vary considerably. Perhaps a way to illustrate this is to follow one species of duck as it migrates from the breeding to the wintering grounds.

The canvasback is a bird similar in appearance and ecology to the European pochard. These big, elegant diving duck have captured the imagi-nation of generations of shooters all along their migratory flyway. They encounter their first wild-fowlers on the shallow prairie marshes and sloughs of the breeding grounds, where they congregate before migration. Here the fowler, perhaps a local farmer who has decided the night before to go shooting with a mate, finds a place on the marsh where he can hide in the natural cover from the flocks of birds flighting overhead. He has not had to seek permission to shoot on this marsh because many of the prairie marshes are in the public domain and access to shooting is unrestricted. A few rudely carved and hastily painted decoys may serve to draw the birds closer, but the abundance of naïve young birds usually makes this unnecessary. Limits, and other regulations, are probably far from the fowler's mind because he may shoot only once or twice during a season and he feels his impact on the population will be minimal. But the memories of his one or two days on the marsh will be recalled many times during the long, frigid prairie winter.

By the time the birds have left the prairie and stopped for two or three weeks to rest and feed in the deep, wooded lakes of the northern USA, they are wiser and wildfowlers there must lure them with calls and with many more and better decoys than the prairie shooter had. Power boats are required to carry shooters and their gear to their elaborately constructed hides. These wildfowlers may live and work in a nearby town, where they spend the working week waiting for the weekend, when they will go shooting. Or, they may have driven many miles from a city where they have just finished the late shift in a factory and plan to spend all day in search of the canvasback. Successful shooters here must be well organized and they must put considerable time, energy and money into their wildfowling effort.

Now on the Chesapeake Bay of the Atlantic tidewater near the cities of Washington and Baltimore, the canvasback is a very different bird than it was when it encountered the prairie gunner. It is alert to the ways with which the shooter attempts to lure it, keeping to open water and avoiding boats. For his part, the shooter, who may be an urban businessman or a local bayman whose family has lived and shot on the shores of the Chesapeake for generations, has become much more sophisticated in the pursuit of his quarry. Floating 'blinds' that can hide a large power boat and several shooters are surrounded by as many as two hundred skilfully made and precisely positioned decoys. Hides are located on the feeding grounds half a mile or more from shore. Access to shooting areas must be carefully arranged since much of the land and shooting rights are privately owned. Regulations are also much more in evidence here. In some years there are daily limits of only two or three birds and the season may last only a few weeks. This form of shooting requires a serious commitment on the wildfowler's part, but this is necessary if one is to shoot diving duck on the big coastal bays where they winter.

Government involvement in North American wildfowling has been a reality for so long that it is generally accepted, if not always fully understood, by most wildfowlers. While many freedoms enjoyed by the British fowler are denied his North American counterpart, government control of wildfowling in North America means that there is a well-funded management system that attempts to maintain a harvestable surplus of birds. The major criticism of the system is that managers have frequently over-regulated the shooter and have distorted the traditional wildfowling experience. However, this has primarily occurred where demand for access to shooting complicates management. North American wildfowl management faces two challenges in the 1980s. The system must succeed in implementing a new management plan which is designed to reverse a serious decline in duck populations that has occurred. It must also fight to safeguard the concept of wildfowling in a changing social, political and economic environment, while attempting to maintain or enhance the quality of wildfowling through enlightened management of birds and shooters.

North American wildfowl management has undergone considerable change since Jeffery Harrison wrote optimistically about its role in safeguarding the future of wildfowl populations and wildfowling. This system, which requires both government and private sector co-operation to be successful, has functioned relatively effectively for decades, and constantly modifying the system to reflect social and biological realities remains the best bet to ensure a secure future for North American wildfowling.

32
AN INTRODUCTION TO WILDFOWL TAXIDERMY

ANDREW MACFARLANE

Previous editions of *The New Wildfowler* included a chapter on Wildfowl Taxidermy by James Harrison and, while much of the contents are still relevant today, there have in recent years been significant advances in technical practice and changes in the use and availability of certain materials and equipment. In addition, with the enactment of the *Wildlife and Countryside Act 1981*, there are now certain legal obligations on persons undertaking bird taxidermy, particularly in relation to the sale of dead wild birds, including their preserved or mounted skins. Consequently this chapter has been revised and restructured to take account of these various changes.

Before considering becoming involved with bird taxidermy it is essential that the sportsman should familiarise himself with the provisions of the *Wildlife and Countryside Act 1981*, particularly Section 6, which deals with the sale of dead wild birds. If a wildfowler is merely intending to pursue wildfowl taxidermy for his own pleasure then he need not be unduly concerned by this legislation but should at least be aware of the legal effect of the provisions.

The *Wildlife and Countryside Act 1981* prohibits:

(a) the sale, offer or exposure for sale, possession or transport for the purposes of sale, hire, barter and exchange, and,

(b) the publication or causing to be published of any advertisement likely to be understood as the buying or selling or the intention of the buying or selling.

of all dead wild birds (i.e. any bird of a kind which is ordinarily resident in or is a visitor to Great Britain in a wild state, other than poultry or any game bird), or any part of such a wild bird, except those birds included in Part II or Part III of Schedule 3, namely: woodpigeon and feral pigeon at any time

and capercaillie, coot, tufted duck, mallard, pintail, golden plover, pochard, shoveler, common snipe, teal, wigeon and woodcock from 1 September to 28 February inclusive. The sale of these species is prohibited throughout the rest of the year.

The sale provisions of the Act do not extend to game birds, namely pheasant, partridge, grouse (or moor game), black (or heath) game or ptarmigan. *The Game Act 1831*, however, prohibits the sale or purchase of dead game birds from ten days after the start of the close season.

Derived from the EEC Directive on the Conservation of Wild Birds, there is provision under the *Wildlife and Countryside Act 1981* for registration enabling persons to sell dead wild birds, including birds preserved wholly or partly from decay, in small numbers. As previously stated though, this need not concern the wildfowler with an interest in pursuing bird taxidermy as long as he is not offering the products of his work for sale. Further information on any of the legal aspects of taxidermy is available from:

Wildlife Registration Section
Department of the Environment
Tollgate House
Houlton Street
Bristol BS2 9DJ

The purpose of this chapter is to provide the sportsman with an insight into the art and science of wildfowl taxidermy. It is not intended to be a comprehensive guide on the subject and before attempting any taxidermy work it is thoroughly recommended that reference be made to one of the modern manuals currently available. Taxidermy can become an absorbing and rewarding hobby leading to a greater understanding of the anatomy and biology of the subjects and an appreciation of phenomena such as moult sequences, plumage development and colour variation. Indeed the inquiring mind will become fascinated by the subject and a broader interest in wildfowl ecology will hopefully be generated.

It is unfortunate, however, that wildfowl are amongst the most difficult groups of wild birds in which the taxidermist, amateur or professional, may hope to become proficient. This is largely due to the presence, in most species, of extensive subcutaneous fat deposits which are laid down during the autumn and early winter and which act as a source of energy and provide warmth during periods of hard weather. As the shooting season progresses the plumage of dabbling duck, for example, increases in resplendency up until the onset of courtship and breeding in the spring. The wildfowler/taxidermist will often find then that the best specimens for mounting, in terms of plumage, are to be obtained in the period from mid-winter to the end of the shooting season. By this time the adults will show little signs if any of unmoulted feathers from the previous plumage sequence and juveniles in most dabbling duck species will be in well-feathered first winter plumage. Unfortunately the mid-winter period is usually the time of maximum body weight and as body weight is closely related to condition and fat accumulation the problems for the taxidermist should be self-evident. Fat removal and de-greasing are not, however, insurmountable problems and with the skilful use of modern concentrated detergents can be satisfactorily overcome.

PRACTICE

In view of the difficulties likely to be experienced with the preparation and mounting of wildfowl it is strongly recommended that the aspiring taxidermist should first of all learn the basic skills by 'practising' on less fatty and generally easier species. For this purpose some members of the crow family probably offer the best opportunities for the sportsman, most being pest species and readily obtainable. There are one or two differences in technique employed in the skinning of corvids as opposed to wildfowl, but the basics are the same and much will be learnt about the anatomy and structure of the bird, particularly in respect of the articulation of the legs, wings and neck and the positions these can assume dependent upon whether the bird is standing, flying, preening or whatever. It is time well spent examining in detail

a whole bird and also a skinned carcass, experimenting with wing, leg and neck positions.

Care of specimens obtained in the shooting field is important. Specimens intended for mounting should not be left all day in the bottom of a game bag so that feathers become damaged and blood is allowed to exude from wounds or through the bill and nostrils. Similarly, mud-covered birds from the foreshore should receive a preliminary cleaning in the field. This can often be achieved effectively by holding the bird firmly by the bill and waggling the body vigorously in a clean-water pool. The bird should then be dried and set aside from the rest of the bag, preferably wrapped in clean paper. The nostrils, mouth, vent and any obvious shot holes should be plugged with cotton wool to prevent the escape of blood or other body fluids which are always more difficult to remove when dry. This is really all common sense, but it is amazing how often the taxidermist is presented with a bird for mounting which is covered in mud and/or blood and with crumpled or mis-shaped feathers. At home the bird should be cleaned up further if necessary by swabbing with cotton wool and cold water prior to skinning fresh or before refrigeration. If birds are to be refrigerated for an extended period it is useful, particularly in small species with webbed feet, to smear the feet with petroleum jelly and enclose them in tinfoil to prevent dehydration.

With the fresh or defrosted bird lying on its back the process of skinning can now begin. The most usual starting incision would be along the edge of the sternum or breastbone to just short of the vent (Figure 46A). However, with tight-feathered and generally light-bellied birds such as ducks this is not to be recommended and alternative openings can be made either from a position at the front and underneath one wing rearwards to a point just where the leg is attached to the body, or in similar style above the wing and under the scapular feathers (see Figure 46B). Both of these incisions make for more difficult skinning than the sternum to vent incision, hence the recommendation that general skinning competence is first obtained using the easier method. Of the two alternatives the underwing incision is probably the most useful.

Having made the initial incision, taking care not to cut through any feather roots, start freeing the skin from the body by traction and careful use of the scalpel, removing as much fat as possible at the same time. The liberal use of hardwood sawdust

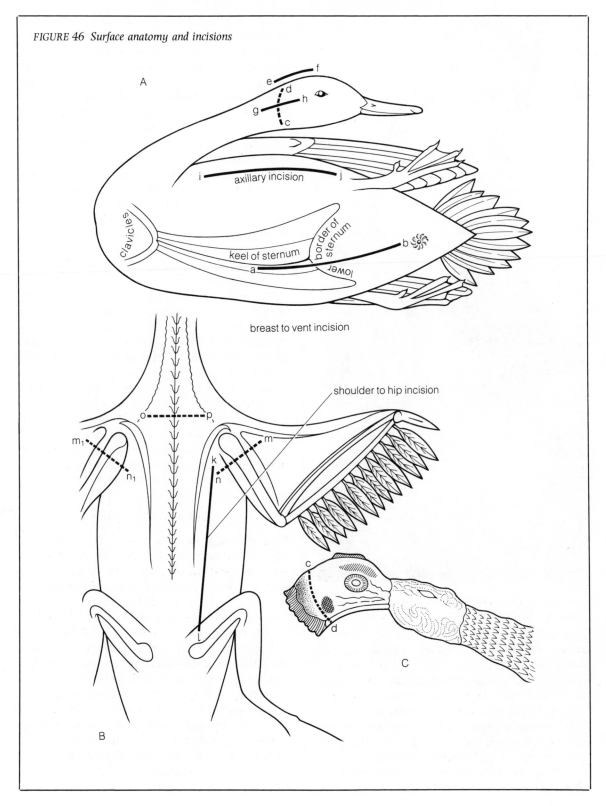

FIGURE 46 Surface anatomy and incisions

A

f
e
d
h
g
c

axillary incision
i   j

clavicles

keel of sternum

border of sternum

lower

a   b

breast to vent incision

shoulder to hip incision

o   p

m₁   m

k
n₁   n

l

c

d

C

B

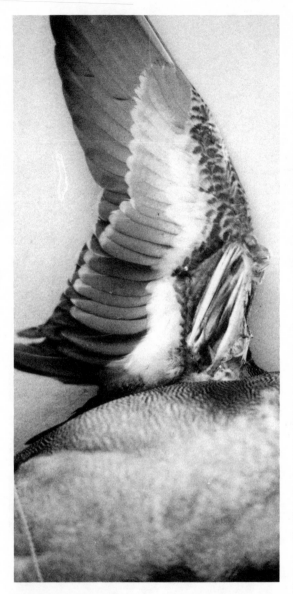

Forewing incision showing exposed muscle tissue
(Andrew Macfarlane)

of the body where the opposing wing and leg can be separated from the body. In birds which have fed prior to shooting the crop is likely to be full and this creates an additional obstacle when the neck is being cut. With care, using strong thread the crop can be closed by tying close to the body. It can then be cut along with the neck, the tying preventing its contents from spilling out.

With the wings, legs and neck severed the last fixed point on the torso is the area around the tail and vent. Great care must be taken here as the skin is apt to tear. Cut across the vent opening as close to the body as possible. Finding the base of the tail, separate it from the body, taking care not to damage the tail feather quills in the process. Once the skin is totally free from the body carefully clean away all flesh attached to the tail and also the oil-filled preen gland.

The next step is to clean the leg and wing bones, which are to be retained as part of the finished mount. By easing back the skin on the legs as far as the heel all flesh and tendons can be removed leaving a clean bone. The humerus on the wing can be treated in the same way, but to clean the forewing bones an incision has to be made on the underside of the wing, allowing access to the bundles of muscle attached to these bones. All of these bones should be thoroughly cleaned by careful cutting and scraping with the scalpel, particular attention being paid to the 'hidden' side of the radius and ulna in the forewing.

NECK AND HEAD

Now the neck must be removed and the head skinned. Because of the relatively large size of wildfowl heads in relation to the diameter of the neck skin it is not possible to invert the skin over the neck and the head. Instead an incision is required along the back of the head enabling the neck to be severed from the head and the skull to be pulled out from the inverted head skin (see Figure 46C). Having made this cut and severed the neck, it can be removed from the body end by inverting the skin along its length until it is free.

Skinning the head is the last stage and this takes some care. By gently pulling and freeing with the scalpel, the back of the skull can be brought out from the head skin, the skin being inverted at the same time. The ears should be carefully cut as close to the skull as possible and when the eyes are

during the skinning of fatty birds will help to absorb grease as well as blood and other exuded body fluids. Shortly the knee joint will become visible and the leg should be severed from the body at this point. Skinning forwards the shoulder of the wing will come into view. This should be separated from the body using scissors, or secateurs in larger species. Continuing forward of the wing the point where the neck joins the body will be exposed. This should be severed at its junction with the body, allowing skinning to proceed round the other side reached the membranes should be cut close to the eyeball taking great care not to cut the eyelids. Having cleared the eyes the head skin is to be inverted right out over to the point where the bill joins the front of the skull (see Figure 46C). The back of the skull now has to be cut away in order to allow the brains to be removed. Following this the tongue, the eyes and all remaining flesh must be removed, leaving the cleaned skull *in situ* to be remodelled prior to mounting. Care should be taken during the cleaning not to separate the lower jaw from the rest of the skull.

The bird is now completely skinned and the next process to be considered is de-greasing. It is sometimes possible with less fatty duck such as wigeon to remove all the fat during the skinning process, but with most duck there will still at this stage be a considerable amount of fat attached to the skin and probably some greasing of the feathers. Late season pintail, for example, tend to be extremely fatty and the combination of this and their fine skins makes them particularly difficult to skin and clean.

In most cases, therefore, it is necessary to remove the fat deposits with the aid of detergent followed by thorough washing of the skin. It is useful at this stage to lightly score the membranes covering the fat deposits with a sharp blade to allow the detergent to penetrate and dissolve the fat, all the while taking care not to cut through the skin or the feather roots. Remember to carry out this process all the way along the inverted neck skin as well. When this has been done concentrated detergent should be well worked into the skin including the legs, wings, underwings, tail, neck and head. A small-headed bronze wire brush is a useful tool for this purpose. The skin should be left for five to ten minutes then immersed in cold water to remove the fat. In very fatty birds this process will have to be repeated until all the grease and fat is removed, followed by a thorough washing in clean water, at which time any blood or other stains can also be removed from the feathers.

Once satisfied that the skin is completely de-greased and the feathers are free from any blood or other stains it should be laid between layers of clean white absorbent paper or towels and lightly pressed to dry it as much as possible. This will need to be repeated several times. The damp feathers can now be fluffed up by very careful use of a hand-held electric hair dryer. Be very careful not to overheat the skin, particularly around the head or any shot holes, or slipping of the feathers may result. After this preliminary drying the whole skin should be placed in a strong plastic bag together with a quantity of heavy magnesium carbonate powder for final drying. Holding the bag closed and shaking the skin around inside will allow the hygroscopic magnesium carbonate to permeate through the feather layer, removing the last of the moisture from the feathers. The skin is then removed from the bag and the magnesium carbonate shaken off, preferably outside! Any remaining traces of the powder can be removed using a soft brush. Now is a useful time to repair any tears or holes in the skin.

PRESERVATION OF SKIN

The skin must now be treated with preservative prior to mounting. There are a number of preservatives available, but, for the amateur, powdered borax is probably as good as any, being safe to use, readily available and relatively inexpensive. The borax should be liberally applied to all exposed skin surfaces, including all around the cleaned skull and the leg and wing bones. The musculature of the wings must now be modelled and this can be achieved using lengths of tow inserted into the wing incision around the radius and ulna bones and by binding tow with thread to the humerus. The wing incision should then be neatly sewn up.

Lengths of galvanised steel wire now require to be cut to the appropriate size for use in fixing the legs and tail to the artificial body and for making the neck. The wings can also be wired if the bird is to be set up in a flying or preening position, but these advanced techniques are beyond the scope of this article. An electric drill with a grinder attachment, or alternatively a hand file, can be used to sharpen the leg and tail wires at one end and the neck wire at both ends. The leg wires should be of sufficient gauge to be able to firmly support the artificial body whilst the neck and tail wires can be of a lighter gauge.

The artificial body can be made using a combination of wood wool and tow or if preferred a rigid expanded polyurethane body available from taxidermy suppliers can be used and adjusted to match exactly the size of the real body by reduction with a rasp or increased by overlaying with modelling compound. When making a body from wood wool the exact dimension of the real body should be reproduced by binding the wood wool tightly with strong thread and finishing off neatly by overlaying it with a layer of fine tow. Most of the indentations in the body can be modelled by pressure from finger and thumb, but more accentuated depressions can be achieved by the use of a stout needle and thread being passed through the body.

Having produced a replica body it is useful to mark on it with a felt-tip pen the positions where the wings, legs and tail are to be fixed to it by reference to the real body. The neck can now be made by twisting and binding tow onto the sharpened wire again to the same length and diameter as the real neck.

The next stage is to model the head using a combination of chopped tow and clay powder mixed with water to form a smooth modelling paste. The addition of a small amount of dextrin to the paste makes it more plastic and manageable.

The cavity of the skull should be packed with chopped tow using blunt-ended forceps, and the cheeks, eye orbits, mouth and throat should be filled using both tow and clay. The artificial neck on its wire, with at this stage the point of the wire not extending beyond the head end, should now be passed up through the neck skin until it comes in contact with the rear of the skull. The wire is then pushed up through the artificial neck, into the cranium, through the top of the skull and the head

FIGURE 47 Wiring to a mannequin

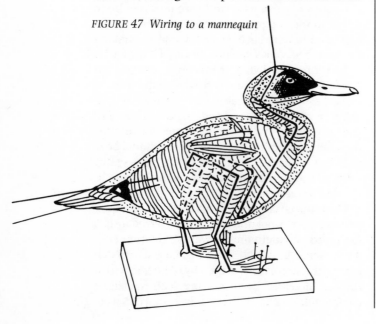

skin and, with pliers, bent back slightly to hold the neck in position. Final modelling of the junction of the head and neck can now be carried out taking care to properly fill out the throat, otherwise unnatural shrinkage will occur. The back of the head incision can now be neatly sown up taking care not to trap any feathers in the process.

The other end of the neck wire is now to be passed through the artificial body at the correct point then turned back and secured into the underside of the body. The two wing bones should now be tied together with thread at the same distance apart as they were on the real body. This can be checked against the marks previously made on the artificial body. The sharpened leg wires are now passed up the legs through the ball of the foot and bound to the cleaned and preserved leg bones with thread, leaving sufficient wire extending beyond the top of the bone to enable the leg to be secured to the artificial body in the same manner as the neck. Tow is then bound onto the wired bone to simulate the natural muscle conformation of the leg. The legs are then fixed to the body using the marked positions as guides and then set at the correct angle for the particular mount required. The root of the tail can now be filled with clay paste and wired to the body at the correct point and angle. The skin should now be arranged in its final position and any last-minute adjustments made to the legs, wings and neck before neatly sewing up, again taking care not to trap any feathers in the closed incision.

Two holes are now drilled in a temporary base and the leg wires passed through and secured underneath either using a power stapler or by bending the free ends of the wires back up through additional holes in the base. At this point the specimen will probably look absolutely ridiculous and you will wonder how it could ever assume natural-looking proportions. From this stage onwards the real skill of the taxidermist and the experience of the field naturalist have to be applied to achieve a lifelike mount. Careful and repeated positioning of the head, neck, wings, legs and tail will eventually result in these appendages lying in the correct position in relation to the body.

When satisfied that this has been achieved the wings and tail can be fixed to the body using sharpened wires, particular attention being paid to the position of the primaries in relation to the tail. The tail feathers should be spread to the required

Method of binding feathers in position until dry (Andrew Macfarlane)

position and fixed in place using two strips of thin card and paper clips.

Glass eyes of the correct diameter and colour are now to be set in position, examining carefully their symmetry from all angles and the positioning of the eyelids. The eyes are fixed into position by bedding them in modelling compound pressed into the orbits. Equal amounts of compound need to be used for both eyes and in quantities which do not cause the eyes either to bulge or look unnaturally sunken. The setting of the eyes is critical to any mount and the job should not be rushed. Once satisfied that the eyes are well set the lids should be held in position until the skin is dry using fine entomological pins.

Finally, individual feathers and groups of feathers will require to be arranged in their natural positions against the body. In wildfowl particular attention has to be paid to the scapulars, tertials and flank feathers. Using sharpened 's'-shaped wires stuck into the dorsal and ventral areas of the body together with thread binding, the feathers can be held in position until the skin is completely dry. Daily inspections of the specimen should be carried out over the following week and any feather movements corrected or other minor adjustments carried out. The webs of the feet should be spread and carefully pinned in position also with fine entomological pins. With the head in its final position the protruding end of the neck wire should be snipped off as close to the skull as possible.

When the specimen is completely dry the bill, legs and feet will have to be painted to reproduce their natural colour. Oil paints were traditionally used, but nowadays well-thinned water-based acrylic paints are more often used as they result in a less shiny, more natural colour and texture. The specimen can now be affixed to its permanent base which can be plain wood or a simulated habitat. If the mount is very special it can be cased, which will certainly prolong its life and reduce the amount of maintenance required.

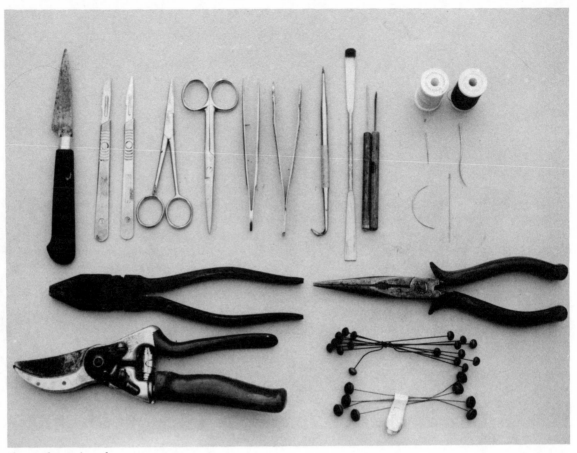

The taxidermist's tools

LIST OF TOOLS AND EQUIPMENT

skinning knives
  (for larger specimens)
Scalpels
Eye hook
Scissors
Secateurs
Pliers
Mounted needles
Files
Electric drill and
  attachments
Electric hair dryer
Needles
Threads
Colour brushes
Soft brushes

Acrylic paints
Tow
Oil paints
Wood wool
Galvanised wires
Absorbent cotton wool
Hardwood sawdust
Borax powder
Petroleum jelly
Powdered clay
Magnesium carbonate
  powder
Dextrin
Glues/adhesives
Glass eyes
Modelling compound

SUPPLIERS OF EQUIPMENT AND MATERIALS

Snowdonia Taxidermy Studios
Llanrwst, North Wales

Starbeck Natural History
The Old Wash House
Church Cottages
Baldersby,
Thirsk, Yorkshire

Watkins and Doncaster,
Four Throws
Hawkhurst, Kent

Karl Lange Glass Eyes,
Mr N.P. Peters
165A Priory Road,
Hornsey, London

33
WILDFOWL COOKERY
VERONICA DOWNING

It seems that no two authorities can agree on the methods of cooking, or even on the eating qualities, of wildfowl. It is fascinating to read accounts of wildfowl cookery from the 18th century down to the present day. Susannah Carter in her *Frugal Colonial Housewife* (1772) described cooking over an open fire, as did Eliza Acton in *Modern Cookery* (1845). Both these authorities served wildfowl cooked rare, after the fashion of the times. The taste today is for comparatively well-done meat. The comforting thought which the novice wildfowl cook can draw from this is that it allows for quite a degree of flexibility.

There are no hard-and-fast rules in preparation and cooking. In fact personal taste, experience and practice will largely decide matters and what follows here can be seen as a set of guidelines. Other factors too will decide on the complexity and care taken over preparing wild duck. For instance, whether it is seen as a luxurious and rarely eaten delicacy or as a regular feature of family fare, alongside scrambled eggs and stews.

Opinions differ over the relative flavour of mallard, teal, wigeon and pintail but, generally, all these can be considered good and enjoyable eating. Diet does affect the flavour of their flesh and grass-fed wigeon from the inland washes is excellent, while birds from the foreshore may have an unpleasant muddy taste. Birds not so good to eat, and sometimes better disguised as pâté, are the shoveler and the tufted duck, goldeneye and other diving duck. If in doubt it is often preferable to use just the breast meat, as the skin and underlying fat tend to hold the unpalatable flavours and affect the whole dish during cooking.

Even in the depths of winter I have rarely found birds to be in anything but good condition and with ample coverings of protective fat. Wild duck are commonly held to need much basting during cooking compared with their domestic counterparts, because of their lack of fat. In fact, many wildfowl have extraordinary amounts of fat and are 'self-basting'. As the fat lies under the skin it is quite easy to both see from a bird's colour and feel after plucking whether or not it is likely to require additional basting.

With regard to hanging wildfowl there is common agreement that this should be kept to a minimum. Personally I do not hang wildfowl and believe that the birds should be dressed as soon as possible. They may lie in the cool of our cellar, head and neck hanging over the shelf edge for two to three days at the most, but early in the season, when the weather is still warm, they should be prepared within twenty-four hours. Badly shot birds with ruptured guts do not want to be left either. For those who do wish to hang their birds, it is the usual practice to suspend them either from the neck or from one leg. Snipe should not hang, but should be plucked, not drawn, and eaten for breakfast the next day.

PLUCKING AND DRAWING

Plucking and drawing duck need not be difficult, but care should be taken when plucking damaged areas of skin so as not to tear it further. Snipe, with its tender skin, also needs to be handled gently. Geese on the other hand are harder work, although the method of plucking and dressing is the same. If you don't want to pluck duck out of doors, then come inside, shut the kitchen door and windows, use a good-sized swing-top bin with liner and pluck carefully into it. Be prepared for a certain amount of flying feathers. I feel that children should be encouraged to see the preparation of game and wildfowl. As a result of regular contact with game in the kitchen, even my toddlers are quite knowledgeable about shooting. They accept the fact that their father brings back food for the table. Only recently my three-year-old asked whether the joint of beef had been 'shot by Daddy', which is understandable when during winter months we eat more wildfowl than beef.

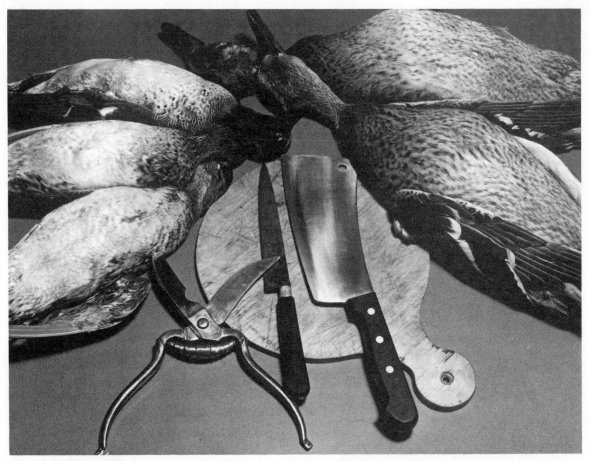

Mallard and teal awaiting preparation (G. Downing)

Plucking is done by pinching the feathers between the thumb and side of the index finger as in gripping a key. A sharp tug removes them easily, and by resting the bird over the knee and bin edge feathers are directed straight into the bin. With apron donned and sleeves rolled up the bird is taken and a start is made by removing the flight feathers from the wing. It may be that you wish to participate in the B.A.S.C. duck wing survey. In that case remove one whole wing from each bird before preparation, ensuring that full details of where and when it was shot are recorded on an appropriate label. After plucking the wings clean, continue with the neck, breast and abdomen. Next turn the bird round and carry on with the back and tail. The bird is then drawn by making an incision over the cavity area. Put your hand right inside to remove heart, lungs, kidneys, liver and intestines with a good tug. Care should be taken when detaching the gut from the anus to remove it completely, with contents. After reserving the liver minus the greenish gall bladder (care to be taken here not to rupture it and release the bitter gall) the cavity can be wiped out with a clean cloth or kitchen towel. Birds with abdominal injuries may have a lot of blood in the cavity. Feet, ends of wings and heads are then removed either with a cleaver or a very sharp knife.

Some people like to singe the remaining down from the skin. I don't bother, as a gentle rub with the fingers removes it quite easily. In the early part of the season, birds coming out of eclipse can be fiddly, as the half-grown feathers enclosed in a soft sheath have to be removed individually.

Once dressed, birds can remain in the fridge for a week if the air is allowed to circulate freely around them. When presented with a surfeit of birds, many cooks will want to freeze the excess for use at a later date. Freezing wildfowl successfully is something I have found tricky in the past if their

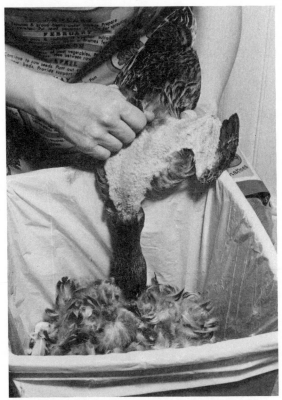

Pluck into a good sized bin with liner (G. Downing)

Pull out the innards with a good tug (G. Downing)

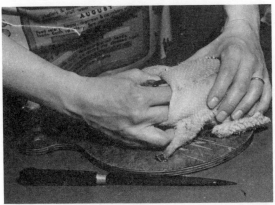

freezer taste and will pass on to the freezer a contaminating odour. All game should be well labelled with species, name and, for interest and comparison, the date and place where shot.

COOKING

Recipes for wildfowl range from the plain and simple to the festive. As with other food, a busy housewife wants meals that are easy to prepare and appreciated by fussy toddlers and pernickety youngsters. There is no reason why baked beans shouldn't boost a wildfowl casserole or duck be served with interesting noodles. Much use can be made of the various forms of modern appliance. Wildfowl can be cooked in a pressure cooker or slow-cooker as well as in the conventional ovens. They will roast well on a spit and provide unusual barbecue fare. Wildfowl can be cooked in a micro-wave oven following the manufacturer's instructions. The amount of lead shot present in the meat is usually too small to affect the efficiency of microwave cooking. Any obvious pellets under the skin should be removed. If the bird is heavily shot, then it is advisable to allow a further one minute per pound to ensure that it is properly cooked through.

Cooking times vary with age, condition of the bird and method of cooking. Early cooks roasting birds next to a 'clear and brisk fire' favoured fast cooking, and keeping the flesh fairly rare. Certainly wildfowl does not want to be over-roasted as it dries out and toughens. If a well-cooked bird is required and it needs longer in the oven, the bird should be covered with foil or butter-paper for part of the cooking time.

To absorb suspect flavours, it is usual to place either an apple or an onion, or both, in the cavity. When fresh herbs are plentiful early in the season I add sage leaves. I also dispense with basting, preferring to place strips of fatty bacon on the top of the bird. If the birds are on a rack, water, stock, cider or leftover wine can be added to the roasting pan to help keep the flesh moist. A little salt rubbed into the skin also helps to make it crisp.

Finally, if one is fortunate enough to have a wildfowling partner who does not like to come back empty-handed, then why not try cooking samphire, sea spinach or mussels? Not only do they make for a good dinner party, but they also provide the ingredients for some interesting conversation.

eating quality is not to be impaired. I personally would recommend against freezing beyond three months for reliable eating and would certainly not want to keep birds for more than six months. To preserve wildfowl at their best I recommend removing the fatty parson's nose and oil gland before double wrapping individual birds in foil and in freezer-quality polythene bags. Birds not adequately wrapped quickly take on that distinctive

RECIPES

MALLARD IN A JACKET (Serves 2)

The accompanying sharp and fruity 'coat' goes well with the meat. The buttery juices and liquor from cooking provide a good gravy.

1 mallard
small onion and apple for the cavity
2 medium-sized cooking apples, peeled and cored
2 carrots
1 large onion
2 oz butter
fresh thyme
stock/water/wine or cider

Fill the cavity of the bird with onion and apple and place in a greased roasting pan, breast upwards. Process the apples, carrots, onion, butter and herbs in a food processor to a coarse paste. Apply the vegetable paste over the breast and legs of the bird to make a jacket.

Roast in a high oven (approximately 200–220°C) for 20 minutes, lower heat and cook for a further 50–60 minutes until cooked through. Add stock or other liquor to the pan about 3 times during the cooking, and this will make the gravy. Serve with green vegetables, potatoes and redcurrant jelly.

OVEN-GRILLED WILD DUCK (Serves 2)

A delicious and less usual way of serving mallard.

Mallard – split into two with wings and skin removed
1 level dessertspoon cornflour
top of the milk
$\frac{1}{2}$ tsp yeast or beef extract

Marinade
4 fl oz of red wine
2 tbsp gin
12 green peppercorns lightly crushed
2 tbsp olive oil
juice of $\frac{1}{2}$ lemon

Mix the marinate ingredients and marinade duck pieces overnight. Place duck pieces on a rack in a roasting pan. Cook at 200° (400°F) Gas Mark 6 for 30 minutes at the top of the oven. Blend marinade with cornflour in a saucepan. Bring to the boil, stirring until thickened. Add top of the milk and extract. Deglaze the roasting pan with some boiling water and add this to the sauce.

Serve with rice and the sauce separately. Garnish with prettily cut tomatoes, chopped parsley and sorrel.

Preparing 'mallard in a jacket' (G. Downing)

WIGEON WITH CHERRIES (Serves 6)

Bottled cherries in a light syrup are ideal for this dish as they are not over-sweetened.

3 wigeon
olive oil
1 medium onion
carrot
clove of garlic
duck livers
wine glass of cherry juice
wine glass of water
wine glass of red wine
bottled morello cherries
5 fl oz double cream
pepper and salt
sprigs of fresh thyme
parsley for garnish

Roast oven-ready birds in high oven (200–220°C) for 30 minutes. Meanwhile heat olive oil in a pan. Cook finely chopped or processed onion, carrot, garlic and livers in the oil for a few minutes. Add seasoning, thyme leaves and liquor. Cook until vegetables are soft. Purée in food processor, return to the pan and reduce sauce.

Take roasted birds and remove breasts and legs. Arrange in an oval dish. Pour over the sauce. Return to the oven for a further 30 minutes.

Serve with a garnish of cherries and parsley. Red cabbage and rice go well with this dish.

PRESSURE COOKER CASSEROLE

Using a pressure cooker is time-saving. This recipe takes about 45 minutes from preparation to presentation.

one mallard
2 tbsp oil
2 onions
clove of garlic
4 rashers of smoked streaky bacon
15 oz tin tomatoes
4 oz mushrooms
4 carrots

Using the pressure cooker without trivet, fry onions, garlic and bacon cut into pieces until browned. Remove these and then brown the mallard on all sides. Return onions and bacon to pressure cooker and add remaining ingredients. Put on the lid and bring up to full pressure. Reduce heat and cook at high pressure for 30 minutes.

If in doubt about the age or condition of the bird allow an extra 5 minutes' cooking time.

FAMILY WIGEON CASSEROLE (Serves 4)

2 wigeon
2 tbsp oil
1 large onion
1 clove garlic
1 parsnip, sliced
4 carrots, sliced
1 cooking apple, peeled and sliced
1 green pepper cut in strips
2 oz mushrooms
2 meat cubes
½ pint water
salt and pepper
sprigs of thyme

Using a casserole, sauté onion and garlic in the oil. Add the wigeon and brown on all sides. Add all the vegetables and stock made with meat cubes and water, seasoning and herbs.

Cook in a moderate oven 180°C (350°F) Gas Mark 4 for one hour or until tender.

Serve with mashed potatoes.

Baked beans added to this casserole make it more appealing to small children as well as extending the quantity for an extra helping.

WILDFOWL RISOTTO (Serves 2)

2 small onions
large clove of garlic
2 tbsp oil
1 mug of long-grain rice
1 each of small red and green peppers
a few sliced button mushrooms
stock/water
white wine (optional)
pieces of cooked duck
1 mug of cooked mussels
seasoning and fresh herbs to taste

Finely chop onion and garlic. Fry in oil until browned and add rice. Stir, and when the rice is just browning remove from heat and slowly add liquor to cover. Add remaining ingredients and cook over a moderate heat, stirring occasionally until the liquid is absorbed and the rice is tender. Add more liquid if required during cooking.

ON ROASTING WILD DUCK

Eliza Acton's recipe 'To roast Wild Ducks'.

This offers an alternative to the usual apple or onion in the cavity, by using 'a bit of soft bread soaked in port, wine or claret' and nothing more. The duck are floured well, cooked on a spit and turned rapidly. Basting is done 'plentifully and constantly' with butter and at a high heat so that the duck are quickly browned and rare. Teal need about 10 minutes, wigeon 15 minutes and mallard about 20 minutes.

Solid-fuel ovens are sometimes less easily controlled than gas or electric ovens. I find the following method for roasting duck in a solid-fuel oven works well. By using the high oven and warming oven you can gain a well crisped skin while keeping the flesh moist.

Cover the bird with streaky bacon and roast in the high oven about 220°C (450°F): 30 minutes for mallard, 20 minutes for wigeon. Remove for between 10 and 15 minutes to the warming oven. Remove bacon and return to top oven for about 10 minutes to crisp the skin.

Full use of the hot oven can be made by roasting parsnips, potatoes or baking a pastry flan.

SNIPE ON TOAST FOR BREAKFAST (for one person)

Snipe – plucked but not drawn
1 rasher of smoked streaky bacon cut into two pieces
1 round of bread toasted on one side
knob of butter
ground black pepper

Place snipe on uncooked side of toast and put on a grill pan. Cover with streaky bacon. Grill under hot grill until the bacon is crispy. Remove bacon and keep. Baste with butter. Season with pepper. Return to grill on reduced heat and cook until juices run clear when pricked. (Total cooking time is about 15 minutes.) Serve on toast with bacon. If not cooked thoroughly snipe are bitter to taste.

GOOSE WITH PRUNE AND APPLE STUFFING

1 wild goose
salt and pepper
¾ lb prunes soaked overnight or the 'no-need-to-soak' variety, stoned and chopped
1 tbsp soft brown sugar
2 large cooking apples, peeled, cored and chopped
½ pint poultry stock
½ pint dry cider
1 tbsp redcurrant jelly

Rub the dressed goose inside and out with salt and ground pepper. Prick the skin all over.

Mix the prunes, apples and sugar together and spoon into the cavity. Secure with a skewer or trussing needle and fine string. Place the goose on a rack in a roasting pan and cook at about 180°C (350°F) Gas Mark 4, allowing 20 minutes per pound, until juices run clear when bird is pierced.

Baste frequently during cooking with the stock and cider liquor.

When goose is cooked remove to a warmed serving dish and strain the excess fat off the pan. Put the liquor from the pan into a saucepan and reduce. Stir in redcurrant jelly. If more gravy is required add extra dry cider.

SIMPLE DUCK LIVER PATE

6–8 duck livers
8 oz of chicken livers
1 thick piece of smoked bacon
2 cloves of garlic, chopped
salt and pepper
olive oil
1 tbsp brandy
bay leaves
clarified butter

Fry the livers, chopped bacon and garlic in the oil until cooked through. Process this in a food processor until the preferred consistency is obtained together with the brandy and seasoning.

Press into a dish or individual ramekins. Press the bay leaves on top, and cover with clarified butter.

ORANGE SALAD (to serve with duck)

4 large sweet oranges
1–2 tbsp French dressing
chopped tarragon and chervil or chopped mint or
  chopped chives

Peel oranges, removing pith, and leave whole. Slice oranges with a sharp serrated knife about ¼ in. thick. Arrange in a salad bowl. Pour over dressing and sprinkle with chopped herbs.

BAKED RED CABBAGE (to serve with goose or duck)

1 red cabbage, shredded
1 chopped onion
seasoning
3 tbsp vinegar
3 tbsp water
4 sour apples, peeled and sliced
1 tbsp brown sugar
a piece of softened butter blended with flour to a
  paste

In a buttered casserole, put the finely shredded cabbage with the onion. Season well and pour over the vinegar and water. Cover and cook gently for one hour. Add apples and sugar. Continue cooking gently for a further hour. When cooked, and just before serving, blend the butter and flour with a little of the liquid and stir this into the cabbage to thicken it.

Baked red cabbage freezes well, and it is time-saving to have a ready-prepared accompanying vegetable especially if doing the above goose recipe for a dinner or lunch party.

SAMPHIRE (OR SEA ASPARAGUS)

This is good as an hors-d'oeuvre before a main course of early season duck, when the samphire is still bright green.

Allow a good-size bunch per person. Rinse it well in cold water and cut off lower stem and roots. In a large pan cook the samphire in fast-boiling un-salted water for 5 minutes. (Extra salt is not needed as samphire is naturally salty.)

Serve with fresh brown bread (preferably home-baked) and plenty of butter.

SEA SPINACH

Like samphire, sea spinach does not need to be salted. It also reduces considerably in volume through cooking.

Take as much as will fill a large saucepan before cooking. Prepare by stripping the leaves from the stems and rinsing well. Cook with a little unsalted water with the lid on until the spinach has collapsed and is tender. Strain. Chop finely and stir with a knob of butter.

MUSSELS

When using mussels without their shells in a recipe, I reduce the preparation time by not scraping all the barnacles off the shells. They make better eating too it they are allowed to rid them-selves of the sand in their digestive tracts. To do this place mussels in a bucket of fresh water with a handful of oatmeal overnight. Before cooking them remove the beards and adhering stones and shells. Having discarded loose or open mussels, place in a large pan and pour in boiling water. Cook for about 5 minutes until the shells are opened. Adding a small amount of bicarbonate of soda (about $\frac{1}{2}$ tsp.) to the cooking water is considered to neutralize the toxins of any suspect mussels, a precaution I take anyhow as it doesn't seem to impair the flavour!

The mussels are then removed from the shells, which are discarded for use in the recipe. Once cooked they also freeze well when packed in small polythene boxes.

34
FAMOUS WILDFOWLERS
OF THE PAST
THE LATE HENRY JAMES, UPDATED BY JOHN RICHARDS

COLONEL PETER HAWKER

While it might be questioned that Hawker was the first to 'discover' wildfowling as a sport, there is no doubt that he was the first to write a comprehensive treatise on the subject. His *Instructions to Young Sportsmen* and his 'Diaries' are to be found wherever English is spoken and constitute a 'monument more enduring than bronze'. Born on 24 December 1786, he was gazetted Cornet of the 1st Royal Dragoons in 1801. Six years later he fought under Wellington in the Peninsular War, and at the battle of Talavera received a severe wound of the thigh which troubled him all his life, and as early as 1813 put an end to his active career in the army. Instead of soldiering in the Low Countries and being present at Wellington's final victory at Waterloo in 1815, we find him almost every day of the season, and many nights as well, engaged in his beloved wildfowling and game shooting.

From the age of sixteen he kept a diary and recorded almost everything that happened to him, not only shooting, angling, matters of health, travel and visits to gunsmiths, but even music, of which he was a skilled exponent. This record he kept in detailed manner for fifty years – almost to the day of his death on 4 August 1853.

Sir Ralph Payne-Gallwey writing in *Instructions to Young Sportsmen* many years later, stated, 'It is a book which for terseness, accuracy and original information is without an equal'. This is a rather singular comment for, as will be seen later, Payne-Gallwey himself in editing the Hawker 'Diaries' in 1893 is shown to be anything but accurate, if not, indeed, misleading. Whether this was intentional or not, we can only surmise – if intentional, the reason must always remain obscure. However this may be, a false impression of Hawker was created which portrayed him, in the words of a modern wildfowling author, as a 'butcher and nothing

else'. This latter writer adds that at times Hawker's Diary is 'quite sickening'. However, it is pleasant to record that this acidulous impression did not last, for five years later this same sportsman described Hawker as 'so lovable, so English, so Pickwickian'.

Eric Parker in his edition of the Hawker 'Diaries' (1931), which was based on the original typescript, shows that unfavourable conclusions regarding Hawker are extravagant and unjust.

Hawker lived in the days of the muzzle-loader–flintlock and percussion. It is interesting to note that it was in 1853, the year of his death, that the first breech-loader, the Lefaucheux pinfire gun, was put on the English market. Hawker never tired of experiments in the manufacture of guns and punts, and on days when he could not go shooting owing to his thigh wound, he was querulous and unhappy. He writes that when 'almost fainting' and as 'nervous as a cat' he would still go out and in spite of his physical suffering handle his gun effectively. On another occasion he records that 'though half dead I never made more extraordinary shots'. He cared little what the weather was like. Apparently gales had no terror for him – he describes some of them as Siberian!

One entry in his diary reads: 'Confined to my bedroom and for the greater part of the time to my bed, in spite of cupping poultices, fomentations, colchicum and calomel.' Another: 'Weathercock with head where tail ought to be; dark, damp, rotten, cut-throat-looking weather . . . doctors galloping in every direction; an armistice from guns and shooting; the poor punters driven to oyster dredging, eel picking, day labour or beggary; not even the pop-off of a Milford snob to be heard in that unrivalled garrison of tit shooters.'

Hawker was a keen student of the science of shooting and ballistics – slow to adopt a new device till he had thoroughly weighed up its worth. As a marksman he was supreme. One must remember the handicaps under which he shot. His guns were heavy and long barrelled, and he had to reload from the muzzle after each shot. To these must be added the suffering from his wound, which was liable to constantly recurring discharges of pus. Throughout his writings, his advice to the shooting novice is clear, crisp and concise. If, as Eric Parker remarks, the word breech-loader is substituted for muzzle-loader, it would do for the modern shooter all that it did for our forefathers one hundred years ago.

Eleven editions of the *Instructions* were published, the first in 1814, the tenth and eleventh, after his death, by his son. The ninth and best edition was published in 1853, shortly before his death. It is the 'Diaries', however, which have the greater interest for the majority of wildfowlers. Let us here consider briefly their history.

A certain amount of mystery attaches to their survival. They remained unread and unknown for forty years after Hawker's death. In 1893 Sir Ralph Payne-Gallwey was asked, apparently by the Hawker family, to write an Introductory Notice of the author and edit extracts from the original volumes. There were in all thirty-four of these! When published it was assumed that the Payne-Gallwey edition was a digest of the recordings of Hawker himself, and that the numbers of wildfowl and game killed were actually shot by Hawker to his own gun; indeed on reading the text it is impossible to arrive at any other conclusion.

It should be remembered that Hawker's original records were never intended for publication. The Payne-Gallwey edition consisted of two handsome volumes which soon went out of print. Eric Parker relates that even after the First World War he had difficulty in finding a copy. He thought it lamentable that such a wealth of shooting lore should remain more or less a closed book to the modern shooting man. He recounts further how that when he had read them, he was at a loss to solve the mystery of why a man so 'genial and high spirited' as Hawker should always prefer to go shooting alone and shun the company of his friends, not even taking with him his henchmen or his gamekeepers. If for no other reason the size and weight of his bags would seem to demand an attendant. His wound, too, which caused him such physical suffering, would almost necessitate a companion.

Eric Parker determined to search for anyone who might be able to clear up this obscurity and eventually discovered a great-grandson – Peter Ryves Hawker, then living in France. This Mr Hawker when he returned to England found amongst his possessions portraits, books, various papers dealing with his great-grandfather and unexpectedly the typescript copy of the 'Diaries' from which Payne-Gallwey had worked, together with proofs from printers. Eric Parker then goes on to say that here was the answer to a riddle that had puzzled him ever since he first read the Payne-Gallwey volumes published in 1893. He discovered that for some unaccountable reason Payne-Gallwey had not only omitted to a great extent the names of the Colonel's shooting companions, including the second Mrs Hawker, but ascribed to Hawker alone the total head of wildfowl or game killed. He gives numerous instances in the Diaries of where this occurred.

To quote an example, Payne-Gallwey (1893) records Hawker's entry in his diary for 7 September 1850 as follows: 'My bag was 12 partridges and 2 hares. Scent worse than ever but no reason to complain as I killed all that it was possible to kill and took the lead of other parties.'

Eric Parker (1931) records Hawker's entry *for the same date*: 'Sent Charles Heath to scour Bullingham again but did not follow him till the afternoon. My bag was 12 partridges and 2 hares – *his 10 birds*. Scent worse than ever, but no reason to complain as *we* killed all that it was possible to kill and took the lead of other parties.' This is one of scores of occasions where Payne-Gallwey fails to make it clear that Heath, Hawker's banking friend, was present, although, in this instance, he does not credit Heath's birds to Hawker's gun.

Let it be remembered that both these commentators took their information from the same source. Thus it is not surprising that some who have read only the account given by Payne-Gallwey have concluded that Hawker was an egotist and boasted of his own accomplishments. Through his researches Eric Parker has produced evidence to dispel this unsavoury impression.

In 1943 he further discovered that the original 'Diaries', which for long were supposed lost, had, like so many of our treasures, found their way to the United States. J. C. Gow relates that the late David Wagstaff, a noted American collector of sporting works, bought them from a London bookseller and presented them in 1945 to the library of Yale University. It is interesting to speculate how they came into the bookseller's hands!

CHARLES ST JOHN

Charles St John, a name inseparably connected with that entrancing record of natural history *Wild Sports and Natural History of the Highlands*, was born at Chailey in Sussex on 3 December 1809. He was grandson of the second Viscount Bolingbroke. A schoolfellow described him as having from early days a zoological 'bump'. At his boarding school he at various times kept squirrels, guinea-pigs or rabbits and was never without livestock of some kind. He was in due course appointed to a clerkship in the Treasury, but this sort of life had no appeal to him and after a few years he settled down at Rosehall in Sutherland in a house left him by his cousin, the late Lord Bolingbroke. He lived here a more or less secluded life, and could indulge to his heart's content in shooting and fishing. Impecunious, he married at an early age a woman of fortune, and so was enabled to live the life of a sportsman and naturalist in the Highlands.

Morayshire was soon to claim him and, surrounded by mountain sport and a game country, the sea and numerous lochs, here spent a great part of his active life. After a time a neighbour of similar tastes who had spent much time in his company, and noted his keen sporting outlook and quality of accurate observation, induced him to write short essays on mixed sport and natural history. At first St John ridiculed the suggestion and did not think he could write anything which people would want to read. However, during the following winter he agreed to try his hand.

The friend, who occasionally wrote articles for *The Edinburgh Quarterly Review*, was short of 'copy', and with his consent embodied some of St John's material. Thus was born a story of world-wide fame – 'The Muckle Hart of Benmore'. The editor of the journal was delighted with it and wrote in such a complimentary strain that it served as seasoning for the shooting lunch which St John and his friend Jeans shared next day amongst the whins! Jeans relates that St John rejoiced greatly in the first money he had ever made by his own exertions, for of course they shared the proceeds. On his next visit to London the series of chapters was sold to John Murray, who published them as

Wild Sports and Natural History of the Highlands. I wonder if there is any shooting man who has not read this fascinating volume!

After a few years (1849) St John moved his household to Elgin and here in the three following years he reached the summit of his sport and literary pursuits. Every walk furnished instances to record in his diary of nature study. His boys, when school permitted, were his constant companions, and both inherited his flair for drawing, sketching and water-colour painting of birds and fishes. Although leading a healthy and temperate life, when on his way out to shoot in December 1853, he was struck down by cerebral haemorrhage and became paralysed down his left side. He never recovered the use of his limbs, but he rallied sufficiently to allow his moving to Brighton and later Southampton.

Until the last he hoped to return to his native heath and the scenes of his early sport, but this was not to be. He died at Woolston near Southampton on 12 July 1856. He had asked to have the skull of Leo, his favourite retriever, placed within his coffin and this was done. Like many who have been devoted to animals, he was a most lovable man of broad views – an outstanding naturalist, a meticulous observer, and one who never recorded a fact of which he was not absolutely sure. St John has been severely criticised over the matter of the osprey – that he had a part in the destruction of this great predator cannot be denied. He was a man of strong likes and dislikes, and with strange contradictions. The odd thing is that St John realised the importance of its preservation, and yet, when opportunity presented, this side of his nature seemed to desert him and he put forward plausible reasons for its destruction. He had said that he knew no reason why the 'poor osprey should be persecuted as it is quite harmless and lives wholly on fish', but later excused his shooting it by enlarging on the price put on its skin and the commercial interest that was involved.

Strangely enough, whilst vowing vengeance on the hooded crow, St John speaks in glowing terms of the great black-headed gull – surely one of the worst predators we have? He stated that the 'hoodie' was the only bird against whom he waged an unpitying warfare. Many regard *A Tour of Sutherland* as St John's greatest literary work. It is noted for the recording of many interesting observations of natural history.

COLONEL CHAMPION RUSSELL

Colonel Russell was one of the greatest of the wildfowlers of the nineteenth century. An Essex man, he was a keen naturalist, especially where wildfowl were concerned, and all his life devoted much time to the welfare of birds and animals. It is strange that, like Marryat in the fly-fishing world, he left no personal record of his interests in this direction – no papers, not even notes of ornithological interest with the exception of some letters to *The Times* and the *Field*.

In his day, making a collection of rare birds was a popular hobby, and he had visited both Africa and America on this quest. Counties and County Boroughs still made their own close seasons and he took a leading part in having the close time for Essex altered. The commonest species of wild geese frequenting the estuary of the Essex Blackwater and adjacent coasts was the brent, and in hard winters enormous numbers would congregate on that coast. Fishermen-fowlers were heard to remark: 'There are acres of them.' Punt-gunning was a very popular pastime and would frequently account for huge bags. It is recorded that on an occasion in the winter of 1860 when 'punting' with thirty other gunners, all firing together at an arranged signal, Colonel Russell killed 704 geese besides a large number of cripples which escaped and afterwards fell prey to beachcombers and gulls. At these times he would be the 'Admiral' of this creeping flotilla. This is usually regarded as the British punt-gunning record.

Christy, writing in 1890, records that even in Russell's day it was commonly said that the brent geese were not so plentiful as they used to be. This remark repeated *ad nauseam* in immediate post-war years no doubt accounted to a large extent for brent being placed on the protected list in 1954. It should be remembered that brent are essentially sea geese, and that in many instances, whilst the coastal areas may appear deserted, large numbers have been identified some miles from land [This was written in 1961 – Editor]. Col. Russell remarked that brent geese used sometimes to remain all the winter without coming within sight of land. He also stated that he never saw a brent goose asleep – day and night they were always alert whether near the coast or far out at sea. He was a noted wildfowl shot, and had one of the biggest guns used on the Essex coast. It is said that in forty-five years of sport, he lost only one season when absent in America. Versatile in the extreme, he was a skilled photographer, yachtsman and chemist.

Col. Russell was also an excellent taxidermist, had punts built to his own design and to the poor homeless vagabond was kindly and generous almost to a fault. With his wide experience, it is much to be regretted that he left no records of ornithological interest. He died in 1887, in his sixty-seventh year.

SNOWDEN SLIGHTS

Snowden Slights, who was called the 'last of the Yorkshire wildfowlers', lived at East Cottingwith in the Derwent Valley. He left no notes, and so it fell to one of his friends to tell us most of what we know about him. Second son of John Slights who taught the village school, Snowden first saw the light in July 1830, and from about the age of nine years accompanied his father when he went punt-gunning. He started work as a basket maker. This precarious calling showed poor returns, and when winter came he spent every available hour in the pursuit of wildfowl to help his livelihood.

For a time the years were ones of struggle. A planting of osiers which he had scraped up his savings to purchase was destroyed by floods, and he was thrown back more than ever on wildfowling to obtain a living. However, as the years passed, his reputation as a man of high principles was established. When he landed on hard times, the local landowners gave him facilities which helped him to weather the difficult years. A man of few words, benign and generous, he was a most astute observer, and there was little in the habits of wildfowl with which he was not familiar. Added to this was an iron constitution and first-rate skill as a weather prophet. Nature was kind to him, and even when in the 'sere and yellow', and the years had shrunk his figure, his back was still straight, his mind alert and his eyes were bright.

Towards the end he was heard to remark that a professional fowler's life though full of hardships was also full of charm. Sometimes after a fruitless expedition he would come home, his clothes frozen on him and feeling half dead; he would have to be assisted to the fire and thawed out. Then after something to sustain the inner man he would turn in and sleep the clock round.

Owing to its formation the Derwent Valley was subject to floods and the river had a long tidal course. Both factors contributed to form an isolated area at East Cottingwith which is flat and offered sanctuary to duck and waders arriving from the coast. Snowden Slights was primarily and outstandingly a punt-gunner; flighting had little or no appeal for him, and it was seldom that he engaged in it. He always maintained that one shot at flight did more to unsettle the fowl than half a dozen from a punt. Others have suggested that the reason for this may be that duck have settled down before a punt-gun is fired at them, whereas at flight they are *en route* to their destination and their senses are strained in watchfulness.

Snowden Slights used to say: 'I like the sport but I don't shoot for sport as much as for a living.' His favourite shot with the punt-gun was at the duck on the ice at a range of thirty-five to forty yards – next to this a shot at similar range as they were rising from the water. Notwithstanding his fondness for punting he was a keen lover of guns of all types and was an accomplished shot with a shoulder gun.

His cottage was a veritable armoury and as long as he could scrape the necessary funds together he was constantly buying or exchanging fowling pieces. These varied from one weighing 140 lb used solely for punt-gunning, down to a little double fourteen-bore muzzle-loader which was his favourite fowling-piece. Snowden collected in all twenty-eight guns, and it is said that they occupied a part of his heart comparable with that of his children. Some of them eventually came to rest in the museum at York – amongst the number an old blunderbuss, short-barrelled and bell-mouthed, which had been used for coach protection.

HENRY COLEMAN FOLKARD

Henry Coleman Folkard, barrister-at-law, was responsible in 1859 for a bulky volume entitled *The Wildfowler*. In the preface he gives his reasons for launching this treatise on the public and takes pains to show that it is not inconsistent with the dignity of a lawyer to follow a sport like wildfowling and to write about it! In the introduction to the fourth edition published thirty-eight years later (1897) he exhibits a querulous outlook, firstly complaining that though he was the sole inventor of this title another purloined it and for several years wrote a series of articles to the *Field* and other newspapers under the same title, and secondly, after pointing out that works on wildfowling were scarce and that Hawker's *Instructions to Young Sportsmen* was almost the only one, he attacks Hawker, declaring that he cannot be relied upon, and that many of his views are erroneous.

Strangely enough he states that Hawker's work was first published in 1824, whereas the first edition saw the light exactly ten years previously. The above series of articles was republished later by the *Field* in a volume entitled *Modern Wildfowling* (1880) by 'Wildfowler'. This was the *nom de plume* of Lewis Clement, founder and first editor of the *Shooting Times*.

The book is a charming account of the sport, full of common sense and excellent precepts. It has now become extremely scarce. That Folkard did not agree with the theories advanced in these articles is evidenced by the fact that he described them as impracticable. After discussing why comparatively few took up wildfowling as a distinct branch of sport, he came to the conclusion that it was 'because it was in reality so little understood'. Most amusingly he adds: 'In this impression I am borne out by the opinion of Colonel Hawker who says that "many of the greatest field sportsmen know no more about wildfowl shooting than children".' It will thus be seen that the kindly qualities which we associate with many sportsmen could hardly be attributed to Folkard. He was cantankerous and had an acidulous tongue, or perhaps I should say pen!

As an author and authority on wildfowling he had no small opinion of his own qualifications. He even criticised Daniel's *Rural Sports*, saying that the few intelligible remarks are so cramped and inaccurate that they tend rather to mislead than to instruct the inquirer! It may, however, be said that, although at times responsible for erratic statements, he was an astute observer and recorded many facts not mentioned by other writers.

He was one of the first to emphasise that non-diving and therefore non-fish-feeding waterfowl cannot have a fishy flavour. He also dwelt on the risks attaching to a fall on soft and deep mud if unaccompanied, pointing out that 'the only practicable method of getting up from a fall on the ooze is by rolling over on the back so as to draw the arms out of the mud and then by placing one foot with the mud patten firmly and flatly on the ooze, at the same time pressing both hands on the knee of the leg so raised and giving a cautious but determined spring and so bringing himself on to his legs again.' He naïvely adds: 'Care should be taken not to fall!'

Other examples of his potted wisdom include: 'When away from the mainland don't go far from your punt and never lose sight of it in foggy weather.'

'Brent geese when on the wing are known by their black-looking bodies and white rumps.' A mere glance through the pages of Folkard's work quickly emphasises that he was first and foremost a punt-gunner. That he was given to erratic statement will also be noted.

In the company of great wildfowlers of the past where are we to place Folkard? It is difficult to escape the conclusion that though he gave a very comprehensive account of wildfowling in many parts of the world, much of the subject matter is academic and seems to lack the personal touch. One searches almost in vain for an instance where he is quoted by later writers on the sport – in fact I can call to mind only one who acknowledged him in this way, and, oddly enough, this was Lewis Clement, whom he attacked.

SIR RALPH PAYNE-GALLWEY, BART

In the annals of British sport there are not many wildfowlers with a reputation which could be compared with that of Sir Ralph Payne-Gallwey. As an all-round shooting man he had few equals, and was the foremost authority on gunning punts and their design. His specifications for the building of these craft are still widely followed.

Born in 1848 this 'Eccentric Irish Genius', as he has been called, was a sportsman of many parts. A large photograph taken at his home, Thirkleby Park in Yorkshire, shows him in his gunroom surrounded by the implements of his sport. The photograph is autographed by him, and on the reverse he explains the reason why it was taken.

Payne-Gallwey was the author of several works – his first and most famous being *The Fowler in Ireland* written in 1882 when he was thirty-four. This is an exhaustive treatise on wildfowling, packed with instructive fowling episodes. It has now become scarce. His *Letters to Young Shooters* in three volumes (1890–6) deals with shooting in its several branches, the third volume being given entirely to wildfowling. In this series he left us a

wealth of shooting doctrine, a treasure in itself, and without which no shooting library would be complete.

As an exponent of the art of shooting Payne-Gallwey had few, if any, equals. One often hears eminent shooting men say, 'I cannot explain exactly what I do, or how I do it.' In contrast, Payne-Gallwey's instructions are clear and comprehensive and leave the reader in no doubt as to the methods he employed.

Payne-Gallwey's *Book of Duck Decoys* appeared in 1886, and about the same time he collaborated with the late Lord Walsingham in the well-known 'Badminton' volumes on shooting. His place in the art of shooting and ballistics is exemplified in a work of outstanding merit – *High Pheasants in Theory and Practice* (1913) – the last of his researches to be given to his fellow sportsmen and one which leaves no doubt of his immense experience of shooting and the zeal with which he carried out his ballistic experiments.

I have referred elsewhere to Payne-Gallwey's editing of the 'Hawker Diaries'. He died at Thirkleby Park, Yorkshire, at the age of sixty-eight.

ABEL CHAPMAN

To students of big-game hunting, shooting, wildfowling and natural history, a glamour still hangs about the name of Abel Chapman. One of the greatest sportsmen of all time, it is recorded that every moment of his leisure he spent in shooting, fishing and the study of wild nature.

A Northcountryman, he was born at Silkworth Hall, Co. Durham, in 1851, and was the eldest of six sons. From early childhood Chapman was keen to learn. It is said that at ten years old he was an industrious student of the classics and showed a strong bent for natural history. At fourteen he went to Rugby, where he formed a lifelong friendship with F. C. Selous. Here his love of the classics was further developed, and even to the end of his life he liked to quote passages from Greek and Latin literature and discuss them with his friends. After leaving Rugby he entered the business of his father – a brewer and wine importer in Sunderland. Shortly afterwards he made journeys to Spain, Portugal and southern France primarily concerned with the business, but also including sporting interludes of shooting and collecting birds and beasts in the places he visited.

It must not be thought that he was merely a collector of specimens. Shooting was a fetish with him from the first. As soon as he could carry a gun it became almost an object of worship and by means of it he was able to further his study of wild-life. He shot his first grouse on 12 August 1866, when less than fifteen years old. At twenty-one he accounted for his first big game, a wild boar in Sierra de Ronda, Spain.

In his *Wild Spain*, written in collaboration with Walter J. Buck (1893), considered by many to be Chapman's greatest work, he gives an amusing account of the arrival of his gunning punt in Spain and states how the Spanish Customs were as much concerned as if a hostile fleet had appeared off Malaga! They had never seen or heard of anything like it before! Chapman was the first ornithologist to locate the breeding grounds of the flamingo in the marismas of Guadalquivir; in South Africa he was responsible for the founding of the Sabi Game Reserve, now known as the Kruger National Park.

Chapman was known for never making a statement unless he had absolute proof of its truth. His huge collection of trophies he bequeathed to the Hancock Museum in Newcastle upon Tyne.

Always an enthusiastic student of the natural history of the Border Country, he made a per-manent home for himself on the North Tyne in 1898. It could scarcely be said that Chapman settled down here, but the quiet and secluded house at Houxty was his home for the remainder of his life.

Chapman was one who took a serious view of life, and maintained a strict self-discipline through-out his long years of activity. Like Oliver Crom-well, he was 'thorough' in everything he under-took, a doughty fighter, and one who delighted in argument – but a staunch and loyal friend. Sensitive and tender-hearted, and like some who have spent much of their lives in the wild places of the earth, he was of a shy and retiring nature.

Abel Chapman was unmarried. He died on 23 January 1929, a great sportsman and naturalist of the old school – perhaps one of the greatest.

JOHN GUILLE MILLAIS

In the days before films were discovered and photography was in its infancy, the institutes of sport and kindred pursuits were conveyed to many from the brush of the great painters of the Vic-torian Era – Sir Edwin Landseer and Sir John Everett Millais. Both were accomplished sports-men, but whilst Landseer was an incomparable animal painter, Millais was a far greater sportsman – angler, game shooter and deerstalker – but even he was surpassed in this respect by his son, John G. Millais, who was in turn soldier, sailor, a British Consul, artist, zoologist, author and landscape gardener.

This versatile Scot had a philosophy all his own and lived it to the full. 'If variety is the spice of life, and a living can be made, give me the open spaces. It is far better than grinding all one's days at an office stool to amass wealth which once gained cannot always be enjoyed. The great thing in life is to live.' Here we have in his own words the principles which underlay the life of one of the greatest big-game hunters, wildfowlers and natu-ralists of all time. Calm, collected and determined, he seems to have held fast to this doctrine all his life. That he had most indulgent parents even in early youth is obvious.

Born in 1865, he became a collector of British birds at nine years old and began to procure these with a catapult. At ten years he met with an accident when using an old 12-bore muzzle-loader. He was firing at an oystercatcher in the River Tay, when the nipple was blown out and cut his cheek. Soon afterwards he was presented by his father with a 20-bore fully choked, with which he shot the greater part of his collection in the estuaries of the Eden and Tay.

Between the years 1880 and 1890 he made many visits to the Orkneys, at that time shooting grounds little known to the public, and at twenty-two he had already killed a pair or two of almost all the birds resident in summer in the British Isles.

Millais soon became a brilliant shot. In 1885 his old flat-coated retriever 'Jet' pointed in some bracken. Up got a brace of woodcock which he shot with a right and left. Hardly had he reloaded when another brace rose and he got both. Just as he was reloading and commenting to the keeper on his luck, a fifth bird rose, which he killed with a long shot.

About 1886 he began to illustrate books and from then onwards his interests in this direction increased. He got opportunities to develop as an artist and naturalist – callings which he afterwards so greatly adorned. His father wished him to enter the army, and after a crammer course in London, to the surprise of his tutor, he qualified in the preliminary examination and was commissioned in the Seaforth Highlanders. He was fortunate in having an indulgent Colonel where sport was concerned and leave was readily granted.

Previous to this, at the age of eleven he went to Marlborough, where a fellow pupil gave him special tuition in the art of catapulting and its ballistics! Commenting on his four years there he relates: 'I worked so hard to improve my shooting – being perfectly absorbed in the hunting and preservation of my specimens – that I soon surpassed my master and became the leader of a gang of what my tutors described as undisciplined young reprobates.' He naïvely adds, 'I was the only boy who ever went through Marlborough and was birched by the headmaster four times (all for catapulting) without being expelled!'

He served five years in the Seaforths, during which period he published the well-known *Game Birds and Shooting Sketches*. However, he soon began to realise that a military life was not his *métier*. He became restless and had set his heart on Africa.

If Millais could be with us today, seventy years later, his confidence in the trusteeship of the white man would sustain a severe shock! He makes the interesting comment that 'Like my friend, F. C. Selous, the book that first influenced me was Baldwin's *African Hunting*', adding that this volume used to be read to him and his brother on Sunday afternoons at Queen's Gate, when they would sit entranced and listen to adventures in Africa.

Strangely enough, though a man of sanguine temperament, Millais had in common with Selous and Neumann a sense of the supernatural, as may be seen from reading his *Newfoundland and its Untrodden Ways*.

One of Millais's best-known works and one of much charm is his *Wildfowler in Scotland* (1900). This details many of his early wildfowling experiences and has now become scarce. Much wildfowling lore can be gleaned from its pages and it embodies the conclusions of one who weighed his words carefully.

He writes: 'It is commonly accepted that big-game hunting, especially the chase of the lion, buffalo and elephant, is the most dangerous of all forms of sport. Personally I am inclined to doubt it, and should say that wildfowling in a punt in the northern firths is almost equally, if not quite, as easy a method of losing one's life. English and Irish waters are comparatively safe, but in the northern firths the wildfowler will often be caught in sudden squalls when off poling ground and then nothing but skill and luck can save him. Never venture off poling ground in a punt in Scotland when the wind is in the south and be slow to do so if it is in the north. The game is not worth the candle, even though the firth may for the moment be as still as glass, and a big tempting pack may be floating down with the tide. . . . In a few seconds the placid waters may be lashed into a seething sheet of foam. As in big-game hunting rashness is the ever-present danger, and if pluck overrides judgement there is sometimes no second chance.' If proof of this is needed, a walk through the cemetery in Nairobi will be convincing!

In wild-goose shooting Millais was an advocate of heavy bores and recorded many exciting occasions with his favourite 8-bore. It is interesting in this connection to remember that there are about as many pellets of No. 2 shot in an 8-bore $3\frac{1}{2}$-inch case as there are No. 6 shot pellets in a 12-bore case, with the additional advantage that a pellet of No. 2 is far more likely to stop a goose. Thus wounding is much less likely to occur here than in countries like America, where 8-bores are prohibited.

STANLEY DUNCAN, FZS

Son of an engineer, wildfowler and naturalist, not surprisingly Stanley Duncan followed these occupations. Further advances in these fields and for himself an international reputation as an authority in his subjects, were due solely to his conscientious sincerity in everything he did.

At the age of sixteen he began contributing to the *Shooting Times* and other sporting magazines and papers, thereby making friends throughout the British Isles who supported him when, with his personal friends, he founded the Wildfowlers' Association of Great Britain and Ireland in 1908.

WAGBI had Stanley Duncan as its secretary for over forty years and throughout the two world wars. He was helped by his executive committees with clerical assistance firstly from a Mr Dunderdale, then in turn from four daughters of an original member and, for some time, his eldest son Cyril.

Realising that wildfowling problems were a national matter, he dealt with any trouble by correspondence with the appropriate authority wherever and whenever it arose.

Although an engineer, he spent most of his spare time wildfowling, or attending meetings in the interests of WAGBI. Being descended from the Downeys, the Victorian Royal Photographers, he was able to illustrate *The Complete Wildfowler*, his classic book written jointly with Guy Thorne, and other writings with his own paintings, drawings and photographs.

He made, or modified, most of his punt-guns, having made two single guns from Sir Ralph Payne-Gallwey's double breech-loading punt-gun, and he designed no less than ten duck punts. He even began a motorised submersible one which he never completed. His last punt, a large double boat to carry the now famous two-inch-bore gun which he made, was eventually sold to James Robertson Justice, who entertained the Duke of Edinburgh to a morning's punt-gun shooting.

In the middle 1920s he rented two acres of land near Hull, employed a man full-time, made his own incubators and brooders and, with the help of his three sons and their friends, built pens for his

Stanley Duncan

hand-reared wild geese and duck. He experimented in rearing partridge, and pheasant, releasing the birds on to the 500-acre shoot that he shared with his friend, Trevor Field. The shoot was ideally situated, adjoining the Upper Humber just below the confluence of the Trent and Ouse. These waters are now The Humber Wildfowl Refuge.

In 1923, along with many other famous names, Stanley Duncan started 'The Sports Protection Association', later taken under the wing of Nicholas Everett's 'Field Sports and Game Guild' from which evolved 'The British Field Sports Society' as we know it today.

Stanley Duncan broadcast five times on his subject of wildfowling, giving, without artificial aids, the bird calls used to bring his quarry within range, a gift that made him and his brother Norman famous. He tested prototype sporting guns for firms such as BSA, and for many years ran the 'Information Bureau' for the *Shooting Times*, a magazine to which he contributed regularly for sixty years. He bred and trained many retrievers, some of which he exported to America, kept a loft of top-strain homing pigeons, started a successful gunsmith business for his sons and founded, with Trevor Field, 'The Hull Gun Club' with one of the first skeet layouts outside London. He was also an able taxidermist.

As age took its toll, he relinquished his secretaryship of WAGBI, having made a brave effort to take over and re-establish for the Association defunct duck decoys at Ashby Golf Course, near Scunthorpe, and another near Selby, for the catching and ringing of wildfowl. The task proved too much for him, but until his death he attended the meetings concerning the Wild Birds Protection Bill as the representative for WAGBI, his brainchild.

DR JEFFREY HARRISON, OBE

Jeffery Harrison was born in 1922, son of James Harrison, general practitioner and much respected sportsman and ornithologist. His father had a profound influence on his life: Jeffery followed in his footsteps. He was educated at Malvern College and later went to Clare College, Cambridge, and St Thomas's Hospital, where he qualified and served as a doctor. He later joined his father and brother David in a practice at Sevenoaks, Kent. Jeffery became interested in wildlife conservation, particularly wildfowl, at a very early age. He was to

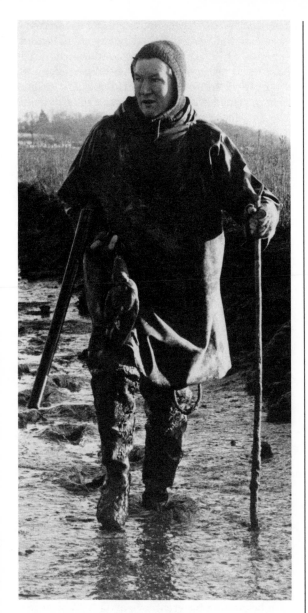

Jeffery Harrison (Pamela Harrison)

write his first book while still at school – *Handbook of Birds of the Malvern District* – which was published in 1941, then *The Wildfowl of the Elbe Estuary* whilst serving in Germany as a surgeon lieutenant RNVR. In 1952 he wrote *Estuary Saga* and in 1954 *Pastures New*.

Jeff was no armchair ornithologist and, in the early 1950s, the Harrison family negotiated with the Kent Sand and Ballast Company a management lease of gravel pits at Sevenoaks. The success-

ful development of the Sevenoaks Reserve was later to be documented in one of a number of important WAGBI conservation publications. Today the Reserve is run by the Jeffery Harrison Memorial Trust and attracts many visitors each year.

In the 1960s Jeffery Harrison, like his father, became involved with the Wildfowlers' Association of Great Britain and Ireland. He initially held the post of Honorary Scientific Adviser and later became Honorary Director Conservation/ Research. In this book *A Wealth of Wildfowl* published in 1967 there is a lucid account of the extraordinary meetings which brought wildfowlers and naturalists together to ensure that wildfowl would flourish in an ever-changing environment. Not only did Jeffery talk sense, he was also able to demonstrate to others the strength of his arguments. His scientific and technical knowledge was immense and he delighted many audiences with his lectures on the wildfowl and wildlife of places he had visited throughout the world. Wherever he travelled he was accompanied by his wife, Pamela, who became one of the most successful photographers of wildfowl in Britain and whose photographs so brilliantly illustrated Jeff's articles, lectures and books. He was one of the original co-editors of *The New Wildfowler* and *The New Wildfowler in the 1970s*.

Because of his sound technical knowledge Jeff was often called upon to represent sportsmen at international level. He acted as a representative for Her Majesty's Government at the Ramsar Convention on Wetlands and Waterfowl. He also attended meetings of the International Waterfowl Research Bureau and the International Council for Bird Preservation. Many of the projects which Jeff pioneered, such as the Duck Wing Survey, were to become of international importance. It is fitting that the seal was set on his endeavours when Her Majesty The Queen bestowed on him the OBE.

Jeffery Harrison was a wildfowler, author and artist but, perhaps above all things, he was a family man. To have accompanied him and benefited from his remarkable knowledge was a privilege. Jeff's wisdom and infectious enthusiasm was an example to all who knew him. He was a truly great wildfowler/conservationist. He died on 1 September 1978, following a morning flight in the company of his friend Jimper Sutton. He would not have wished it otherwise, nor would his friends.

MACKENZIE THORPE ('KENZIE')

In every sport characters emerge and the name of 'Kenzie' has become a legend. His father, Machenzay Thorpe, was a pure Romany gypsy who came south from Yorkshire in the early 1900s to work on the Lincolnshire farmland. It was here that he met Kenzie's mother, a Sutton Bridge girl. Kenzie was born in 1908 and had three sisters, Mabel, Leiler and Lana (who died young), and four brothers, Bob, Donny, Lewis and Verdon. He left school at twelve and went to work on a local farm. He quickly learnt to poach roosting pheasants and coveys of partridges from the fields, but soon he was in trouble with the law and by the age of sixteen he was in court, charged with poaching and threatening a policeman in the course of his duty. At the age of seventeen Kenzie went to work on the Schooner *The Alert*. He hated life at sea, but it taught him to use his fists and when he returned to Lincolnshire it was not long before he turned to professional fighting. He became middleweight champion of Lincolnshire, winning fifty-seven fights, many of which were won with his powerful right hand, which had already got him in trouble with the police! Kenzie's interest in wildfowl had started in the winter of 1924 and throughout the twenties

Kenzie Thorpe (Pamela Harrison)

the marsh and its neighbouring farmland were the scenes of many glorious wildfowling and poaching exploits. All are well documented in Colin Willock's biography of *Kenzie – the Wild Goose Man*. In the early thirties Kenzie met Peter Scott, helping him to establish a private collection of wildfowl at the East Lighthouse on the channel of the River Nene. By 1936 the Lighthouse collection had become a mini 'Wildfowl Trust' and Kenzie was signed on as full-time caretaker. He became a fine practical naturalist and authority on all wildfowl that visited the Wash. By 1940 Kenzie was out of a job again and his efforts to join the Navy were thwarted. He immediately turned his talent to providing food for the nation! It is said that he carted three barrow loads of fowl up to the butcher's shop each week. Not only did he shoot the marsh but he continued to poach and by June 1956 had been convicted of twenty-nine charges.

Kenzie by this time was changing his philosophy. Instead of poaching he turned his attention to wildfowling. Guiding visiting guns on the marsh or inland on the farms which he knew so well from his poaching adventures. Many fowlers today will have fond memories of accompanying Kenzie Thorpe on dawn and dusk forays for ducks and geese. His houseboat at Shep Whites was a landmark until his death. Soon after he was buried it was to be burned with his possessions in true Romany style. Kenzie Thorpe lived a hard life, but by his own admission he, given the choice, would do it all again just the same for, in his own words 'its the sport man' that he enjoyed.

CHRISTOPHER DALGETY

Christopher Dalgety was born at Lockerby Hall, Hampshire, in 1907, where his skill with rod and gun began and his great love of all wild creatures germinated. He read forestry at Cambridge and his intense interest in natural history resulted in his appointment as expedition ornithologist to five important Cambridge expeditions to the Arctic: 1927 to Edge Island, 1930–1 to Spitsbergen, 1932–4 to Greenland and Baffinland. Whenever Christopher took up an interest he did so with complete dedication, and with the most precise attention to detail. During these expeditions and afterwards he pioneered work on the nesting areas and migrations of wildfowl. He became a keen and excellent wildfowler and above all his love was to

Christopher Dalgety afloat in a gunning punt (F. W. Dalgety)

be afloat in a gunning punt. He was a Life Fellow of the Royal Geographical Society and a Fellow of the Zoological Society, he also had a deep interest in entomology. He contributed many articles to the sporting press and was perhaps best known for his articles which appeared in *The Shooting Times and Country Magazine*. In 1937 his book *Wildfowling* was published by the Sporting Press. It contains much practical advice and is regarded as one of the classics on the subject. During the war he was in the RASC Motorboat Section. His knowledge of small boats led him to specialising in the design of canoes of canvas and aluminium which were used on many sorties against the enemy.

After the war Christopher Dalgety and Peter Scott made a study of the whitefronts which inhabited some of the acid peat bogs of Britain. This later resulted in the establishment of the Greenland whitefronted goose (*Anser anser flavirostris*) as a separate race. He was also associated closely with the foundation of The Wildfowl Trust. In 1949 he bought a farm in Hertfordshire, where he established a five-acre sanctuary. He then converted a trout hatchery into a breeding area for ornamental waterfowl. Conservation was always a mainstay of his life and he understood all the ecological factors which spelt success or failure for any particular species.

He returned to the New Forest in 1954 where he took an active part in the life of the forest. He served on the committees of The New Forest Association and The New Forest Buck Hounds. He hunted regularly, always enjoying the thrill of the chase.

In 1974 he moved to Inverness and in this, the autumn of his life, he spent most of his time casting his home-tied flies for salmon, in due season, or stalking the red deer, both with no little success. He died in 1980 on 4 January in his 63rd year.

JAMES WENTWORTH DAY

James Wentworth Day was born in Exning on 21 April 1899, the son of J. T. Wentworth Day. At his home in Wicken his family owned 'Adventurers' Fen', last remnant of the old fen of Hereward and haunt of swallowtails, harriers, bitterns, countless wildfowl and little wild marsh pheasants. During the Second World War his beloved marsh was drained by the 'War Ag', whom James never forgave for what he considered a monumental piece of bureaucratic vandalism.

The marsh was subsequently reflooded and made into a National Nature Reserve, but, for James, it had lost its wild magic. Later he moved to Essex where he fell in love with the country and the people and there he made his home. As a boy he was often to be found in the company of local poachers, fishermen, fowlers, dyke-diddlers and fen slodgers. His first gun, a single-barrel percussion converted from flint, was confiscated by his father and thrown into the river on account of the too many hours it was felt James spent in its company.

He had a natural flair for words and his ability to communicate brought the marshes, coverts and the extravagant characters who haunted them into thousands of suburban lounges. He had a passion for ghosts, of which East Anglia boasts more than its share. James met and shot with many of the legendary names of the covert-side, but wildfowling was his great love. In his book *The Modern 'Fowler* published in 1934 sound advice is given, but blended with it is the romance linking the saltmarsh Vikings with the 'rum owd boys' who lived in the marsh-side villages. The book has become a wildfowling classic and first editions are extremely scarce. He knew every gunner worth knowing and had been afloat with many of them in their gunning punts. The stories he told had often been recounted when out flight shooting or chasing snipe on the bogs near his home. As a journalist he was both volatile and versatile. He had occupied important positions in *Country Life*, *The Field*, *The Illustrated Sporting and Dramatic News* and a number of Fleet Street dailies.

For a time he was Editor and owner of *Saturday Review*, which he used to alert the apathetic British public to the dangers of German rearmament in the 1930s. Almost to his death he wrote a regular countryside column in the *Daily Mail*. James Wentworth Day was an ardent Royalist: he wrote the official biography of George V, he also researched and wrote the biography of Princess Marina, Duchess of Kent, and, latterly, *The Queen Mother's Family Story*. He wrote on all manner of subjects, including the life of Sir Donald Campbell. He was, perhaps, best known in sporting circles for the series of which *Sporting Adventure* and *Farming Adventure* are two of the classics. In his remarkable career he saw service in two world wars, in one as a war correspondent, and later, in 1950 and 1951, he stood for Parliament, slashing the Hornchurch Socialist majority. He was 83 when he died and remained, until his death, an extraordinary rumbustious, colourful character the like of which will never be seen again.

John Richards wishes to express his thanks to Arthur Cadman and John Humphreys for the assistance which they gave to him in the updating of this chapter.

35
A FUTURE
FOR WILDFOWLING

JOHN SWIFT

In his article *The Threatened Extinction of Shore Shooting* Stanley Duncan, shortly after becoming Honorary Secretary of WAGBI in 1908, wrote 'it would be a thousand pities if the wildfowler with all his qualities of energy and perseverance should fail to use them for the protection, purification and perpetuation of his sport' (see Marchington, 1980).

This same spirit in which WAGBI was born, which has enabled the Association to keep the flame alive between the wars and to achieve so much since, is the basis for the sport's future. We have seen that, even now, at the end of the 1980s, the threats, even the issues themselves, are largely unchanged. The need is just as great and the cause – wildfowling – equally worth fighting for.

In looking to the future it is important not only to look back at the lessons learned in the past but also to think strategically. Strategy is designed to work on a large scale and in the long term. It makes efficient use of what you have in order to achieve the defined objective which, in this case, is that defined by Stanley Duncan himself: the protection, purification and perpetuation of wild-fowling.

In recent years, however, the Association has changed its name from WAGBI to the B.A.S.C. The *Wildlife and Countryside Act 1981*, has been brought in and there has been a fall-out of suspicion created by it. Furthermore, the growth of the voluntary and governmental conservation organisations, the amount of money now deployed by such organisations to secure important wild-fowl sites for their own purposes, and the domestic and international pressures for extra legislation have all grown dramatically.

Although this chapter is written seven years after the introduction of the *Wildlife and Countryside Act 1981*, there is still suspicion. Similar suspicion was generated by the *Protection of Birds Act 1954*, but this time it has persisted rather longer. Perhaps the 1981 Act resulted in more bureaucracy which has tended to keep old wounds open. In 1954 outright 'antis' were just as vociferous as they are today. But there were then, as now, a similar number of men and women on both sides who knew that practical co-operation and good-will were necessary, not only for the sake of conservation but also for society's tolerance of wildfowling. Long may that balance continue: but much rests on the shoulders of the wildfowler.

The need to be 'whiter than white' in the public eye was a constant theme throughout WAGBI's growth and Sir Peter Scott has stressed it again in his preface to this book. Stanley Duncan knew that wildfowlers were being driven off traditionally free coastal shooting by farmers and landowners who very often had cause to complain. He wrote: 'It is hoped that by the weeding out of undesirables, benefit will accrue, not only to the wildfowlers themselves but also to those whose lands immediately adjoin free shootings. The rules will be strictly enforced so that any farmer who has just ground for complaint may, by lodging his grievance before the proper authority, secure dismissal of the offender from the Association.' Nowadays, this important lesson applies not only to neighbouring farmers but, increasingly, to landowning conservation bodies. They should be given the same confidence.

The other element in the battle for the hearts and minds of non-sportsmen rested, thanks to the late Dr. Jeffery Harrison, in the field of conservation and science. 'The truth is that over the years the wildfowling community has won two victories, leading the outside world to view wildfowlers as responsible people, deeply concerned with conservation as well as sport, and quietly and discreetly leading some of its less thoughtful members to think and act in this way (Marchington, 1980).

311

So what has changed since the 1954 Act? The same problems and imperatives undoubtedly apply, but there have been fundamental changes, particularly of scale. The protection and nature conservation lobby now has a centralised annual spending budget of many millions of pounds, and some of this has been spent on buying prime wildfowl and wildfowling land. The *Wildlife and Countryside Act, 1981* and the European Community have introduced what many regard as a bureaucratic tyranny which is not as amenable to the 'tea party' method of problem solving. But, on the positive side, the B.A.S.C. has itself come of age as the organisation for all field shooting. It has been able to increase and extend its membership to encompass all 'live quarry' shooting and related target disciplines where these touch on training or an introduction to the sport. The Association has not, however, claimed exclusivity in any area and has sought to work closely with the many other organisations involved in the field of shooting and conservation. The Association has thus become pivotal to the defence of the sport but within this extended area of work the voice and contribution of the wildfowler has been maintained undiminished, not only by strong representation on the Association's Council, but more latterly through the Wildfowling Liaison Committee and the Wildfowling Conferences.

The Wildfowling Liaison Committee, for example, is the only Special Committee of the B.A.S.C.'s Council which has the specific function of operating in two directions at once, not just advising Council but also seeking the views of the local wildfowling membership on important issues. The conferences, for their part, bring wildfowlers and representatives together and help in planning policy.

Thus the situation has changed by degree. The task has become bigger and more complicated, the whole process more political and we also have Europe with which to contend. The amount of money required and that being spent is considerably larger but the essential issues are exactly the same as those facing Stanley Duncan in 1908.

So how is the B.A.S.C. now set to fulfil this pivotal role in the representation of sporting shooting, whilst at the same time keeping faith with its wildfowling roots? The solution breaks down into three main areas: the 'outside world';

the organisation of the B.A.S.C. programmes; and affiliated clubs and their work.

The 'outside world'

The B.A.S.C. is not a warship sailing alone on the high seas, carrying an enormous cannon with which to threaten and, if necessary, blast its political opponents. The Association occupies, as has already been described, a pivotal role at the centre of the defence of sporting shooting and has to consider the views of other organisations with overlapping interests. In certain instances this co-ordination is channelled through the umbrella organisations such as the British Shooting Sports Council, the Council for Country Sports, the Federation of Hunting Associations of the EEC and the Standing Conference on Countryside Sports.

The Association also has responsibilities in conservation and operates through other umbrella organisations for purposes of planning, co-ordination and effecting a political lobby. The International Waterfowl and Wetlands Research Bureau and the Nature Conservancy Council's (NCC) Advisory Committee on Birds, for example, each has its own responsibilities to which the B.A.S.C. contributes.

It is one thing to voice the views of wildfowlers in public through such organisations, and to co-operate in agreed activities, but political action ultimately requires the support of politicians who in turn can use the political process, in an appropriate way, to achieve the desired legislative result whether that be to thwart an attack or to promote a change. Thus the B.A.S.C. itself is required to participate in and organise a suitable lobby, and to enlist the understanding of political representatives who will say what is possible and what is not.

The political process, however, does not begin and end with political representatives at the Palace of Westminster. Links have to be forged for Scottish, Welsh and Northern Irish institutions and for international parliamentary assemblies as well as at regional and county council level. Furthermore, elected political representatives are served by officials, be they civil servants in Whitehall or of the European Commission, who organise consultation and advise on the formulation of policy and decision-making. In the fulfilment of these duties the officials seek advice from the 'voluntary sector' and can, in some instances, come to rely heavily upon it. Certain non-controversial functions may even be passed to voluntary organisations. Such reliance on the voluntary sector and even delegation of authority can be additionally attractive to the government for reasons of finance. It could be very expensive for officials to employ their own professional experts and advisors. There is thus a vacuum to be filled, and consequently the Association pays considerable attention to ensuring that officials are willing to come to the Association for information and advice.

The Association also has to maintain links with official bodies and the so-called 'quangos' which have specific jobs that overlap with shooting. Examples are the police, the Sports Councils, the Nature Conservancy Council, the Countryside Commission, the Crown Estate, the Water Authorities, the Forestry Commission and the agricultural organisations.

Thus the Association exists within a framework of inter-relationships with political, official and voluntary organisations. Many of these relationships are informal and not explicit. They evolve continually and subtly in response to circumstances and personalities. Others are more clearly defined, such as the recent statement of common interest between the B.A.S.C. and the NCC. It goes without saying that the nature of the Association's relations has been a major influence in moulding the Association itself and is vitally important to the future of the sport.

Organisation of B.A.S.C. programmes

In order to meet the responsibilities which Stanley Duncan foresaw in 1908, the Association's work has been divided into programmes run by Headquarters which, nevertheless, almost invariably involve a substantial element of volunteer support. These programmes make up a major part of the total Headquarters function. They may involve special committees of Council in an advisory capacity.

Only a very small number of activities are orientated towards a particular type of shooting. Each programme is geared to work flexibly and without duplication in all branches of shooting where it is applicable. To set out the full range of the Association's work is beyond the scope of this chapter, but some of the main programmes for wildfowling can be outlined as follows:

Political: The Association makes political representations on wildfowling, at all levels, at Westminster, Brussels, Luxembourg and Strasbourg. The wide membership support creates more political contacts.

Conservation and land management: This department assists clubs in the acquisition and management of wildfowling rights through the lease and purchase of land. It also encourages clubs to take all forms of wildlife into account when managing their land, primarily through management plans.

Research: The B.A.S.C. collects, evaluates and disseminates information on wildfowling e.g. national wildfowl bags. More specifically however, it carries out research into wildfowling problems e.g. lead poisoning, shooting disturbance of wildfowl and the effects of severe weather on wildfowl. It organises meetings on topics of interest to wildfowlers e.g. wigeon movements, and assists clubs in setting up local studies on their own marshes, aimed at improving their management.

Education and training: This department runs a nationwide network of Proficiency Award Schemes each of which provides special courses on coastal duck and goose shooting, quarry identification and the law. It also assists clubs to set up their own education and training schemes for new and junior members, and runs specialist wildfowling courses around the country.

International affairs: The B.A.S.C. organises a wildfowling lobby (through FACE) to the European Parliament and the Council of Europe etc. It also advises the European Commission and other official institutions on wildfowling matters in Britain.

Firearms: The Association safeguards the wildfowlers freedom to acquire, own and use the weapon of his choice for the pursuit of his sport.

Press and public relations: The B.A.S.C. maintains links with the press, radio and TV for the dissemination of information on wildfowling.

The above list sets out some of the Association's general work programmes and shows what the Association does for wildfowlers as a special group within the organisation. It will readily be seen that the programmes and services support each other and, as such, make up a comprehensive strategy in their own right for the protection, purification and perpetuation of the sport.

The development and role of affiliated clubs

Throughout its long history WAGBI worked very much through, and with its affiliated wildfowling clubs. Staff and resources were far too small to allow the vast amount of work necessary to be undertaken in any other way. The same is true for the B.A.S.C. today, particularly in the area of conservation and land management. The B.A.S.C.'s principal management force is its clubs.

Thus, in 1979 the B.A.S.C. began a programme to assess the land under the influence of its membership, in particular its clubs in England (*The Conservation of Wildlife Habitat in England by B.A.S.C. Members* by Laws, 1984). The objects of that study were to assess the land under the influence of the B.A.S.C. membership in terms of type and habitat, to identify the sites' nature conservation importance and to assess the effectiveness of any management programmes presently in· hand. The project also assessed the management resources available to the B.A.S.C. membership groups and studied other factors such as site tenure, governing effective conservation management. Finally, the study attempted to determine the most effective ways of promoting management projects and assisting membership groups in the preparation of management plans. In other words, the study was to provide a basis for assessing the position and role of clubs with regard to the B.A.S.C.'s wildfowling strategy.

The study revealed trends in the affiliated clubs' influence over land management. Up to 1956, for example, affiliated clubs were exclusively concerned with wildfowling. However, since then there has been a steady increase in the number of game shooting clubs. Little potential in fact now exists to increase the number of wildfowling clubs, particularly those operating on the coast. In order to expand their facilities wildfowling clubs are now acquiring inland sites to diversify their shooting. It is thus envisaged that the proportion of inland habitats coming under the influence of clubs will continue to increase, both through the establishment of new game shooting clubs, and further acquisitions by existing clubs. However, coastal and major inland wetlands remain a very important element of club land and will continue to warrant priority attention.

The study also identified that, at that time, only a small number of sites controlled by clubs were held by freehold, whether of the site in its entirety or just the shooting rights. The most frequent way of securing an interest in the land was through the holding of shooting rights, by lease or licence. A large number of sites were also held simply by agreement with the landowner. In addition, it was found that the terms of agreements, leases and licences tended to be rather short and many of them were soon coming up for renewal.

Club sites are held from a wide range of landowners and other controlling authorities. Most are held from private landowners like the Crown Estate and the Duchies of Lancaster and Cornwall. Much club land is also held from nature conservation bodies, such as the Nature Conservancy Council and the county conservation trusts and so on.

The survey identified the consequences of the generally increasing costs of land and sporting rights as a result of increasing competition for the acquisition of sites, particularly in coastal areas. Alarmingly, few clubs were then prepared to invest time and financial resources in the management of sites even when the future security of tenure was in doubt. However, certain clubs were increasingly looking to ways of increasing their security and in some cases, this involved serious consideration being given to the purchase of freehold over the land. Since the survey was done, however, many clubs have made major advances in this area and are much more active in devoting time and raising financial resources to secure their sporting rights. An increasing number of clubs have now purchased the freehold of land.

The survey identified the different ways that clubs exercise control over their shooting. The principal methods are to make restrictions on areas to be shot, and the times of shooting. Restrictions on the number of members shooting at any one time or on species to be shot (over and above the law) are also common. Finally some clubs have introduced a bag limit i.e. a limit on the number of quarry to be shot by any one member during any one site visit. Many clubs require members to give bag returns of the number of quarry shot.

A large number of clubs are involved in the management of no-shooting zones; the management of coastal refuges in conjunction with other conservation bodies; the establishment of their own unshot reserves; detailed projects for planning and monitoring their activities and wildfowl numbers; wardening; habitat management; special habitat management on Sites of Special Scientific Interest; and the protection of vulnerable sites through representations at public enquiries; re-stocking programmes of released duck; partici-pation in biological surveys.

The study thus confirmed that clubs have a management influence over considerable areas of Britain. It was found that a high proportion of the land was of high nature conservation value and that clubs make a significant contribution to habitat conservation. As regards the management of the land, whilst labour was generally available, the funding of site acquisition and its management presented a major problem to many clubs.

The attraction of a general policy for manage-ment planning was reinforced by the need to identify site features of nature conservation value which required careful management. The wider adoption of habitat management principles and techniques of benefit to both quarry and non-quarry wildlife would also increase the wildfowler's contribution to conservation.

The foregoing survey and conclusions are ob-viously designed to deal with the important con-tacts between wildfowling and conservation inter-ests. Many clubs have, however, been particularly active in education and training schemes, setting up special arrangements for young sportsmen and for those who wish to take up wildfowling. Many have also been engaged in public relations and charitable work, as well as exercising strict disci-plinary control over their members.

This survey identified where B.A.S.C. and club resources needed to be concentrated. In recent years much progress has been made, not least since the first Wildfowling Conference in 1985. Giving assistance to clubs to achieve these aims will remain central to the B.A.S.C.'s work.

Looking forward

The issues arising over the *Wildlife and Countryside Act, 1981* undoubtedly created a defensive image. There was, however, little alternative. Not withstanding some losses that defensive action was largely successful as far as the wildfowler was concerned. On the other hand, much that is positive is now being done. Achievements are being made on all fronts. With respect to education and training, the Proficiency Award Scheme and

the various club education projects are attracting a considerable amount of positive attention and significantly improving behaviour on the marsh, so that irresponsible shooting by club members is largely a thing of the past. The Association's regional officer network has greatly increased the resources available to clubs in many areas, par-ticularly over publicity and general club assistance.

But it is probably in the fields of conservation and research that most has been achieved al-though much remains to be done. Chapter 21 outlined the historical links between WAGBI and the rest of the conservation movement, particu-larly the Nature Conservancy (as was), Wildfowl Trust, RSPB, and county conservation trusts. There is no doubt that the goodwill and joint ventures of the 1960s and early '70s did suffer somewhat after the 1981 Act and as a result of the enormous expansion of these organisations. How-ever, there are distinct signs that we are now entering a new era – one of protection of our sport linked with appropriate partnerships. A 'State-ment of Common Interest and Co-operation' has just been signed between the B.A.S.C. and NCC. This has led to new initiatives in several areas, not least the recognition that wildfowling clubs have a significant contribution to make to modern nature conservation and are therefore eligible for govern-mental grant aid for the purchase of sites of high conservation interest. Discussions on improved research liaison have been held with the Wildfowl Trust and NCC and a joint research project with the Trust on shooting disturbance is well underway. Meetings with others such as the RSPB will continue, seeking an improved understanding of each other's interests in the future.

This must be the way forward. The wildfowling community cannot stand on its own. Wildfowlers have always been part of the conservation move-ment and will continue to play an essential role in the future. By working in partnership, the wild-fowling community and conservation bodies can together ensure that advances continue to be made for a healthy countryside and the good of the sport.

REFERENCE

Marchington, J., 1980. *The History of Wildfowling*. A. & C. Black.

THE B.A.S.C. WILDFOWLER'S CODE OF CONDUCT

WILDFOWLING AND THE LAW

England and Wales

In England and Wales the foreshore is that part of the seashore which is more often than not covered by the flux and reflux of the four ordinary tides occurring midway between springs and neaps. The foreshore may be in Crown or private ownership. In England and Wales the B.A.S.C. has an agreement with the Crown Estate Commissioners giving B.A.S.C. members a defence against prosecution for carrying guns on the Crown foreshore. **You need permission to shoot on private foreshore.** The onus is on the wildfowler to establish whether the foreshore is private. Access and egress must be by public right of way unless otherwise authorised.

The shooting of wildfowl on Sundays is illegal in some counties:

Counties in England and Wales in which there is no Sunday shooting of Schedule 2 Part I birds.
Anglesey; Brecknock; Caernarvon; Carmarthen; Cardigan; Cornwall; Denbigh; Devon; Doncaster; Glamorgan; Gt. Yarmouth (County Borough); Isle of Ely; Leeds (County Borough); Merioneth; Norfolk; Pembroke; Somerset; Yorkshire (North Riding); Yorkshire (West Riding).

Scotland

In Scotland the foreshore is the area of land between the high and low water marks of ordinary spring tides. In Scotland, whether the foreshore is in Crown or private ownership, the Crown retains in trust certain rights on the foreshore (except in Orkney and Shetland) by virtue of which members of the public may engage in wildfowling. The public right may, in certain cases, be taken away by statute, e.g. nature reserves. The onus is on the wildfowler to establish whether such reserves exist. There is no shooting of wildfowl in Scotland on Sundays or Christmas Day.

Northern Ireland

The shooting seasons and quarry species differ from those in England, Wales and Scotland and are subject to yearly change.

There is no shooting on the foreshore after the 31st January and night shooting is prohibited.

General points

Those who shoot on the foreshore can only legally take the birds listed in Schedule 2 Part I of the Wildlife and Countryside Act 1981, unless otherwise authorised, during the open season.

Schedule 2 Part I

Duck: mallard, teal, wigeon, pintail, tufted duck, pochard, shoveler, goldeneye, gadwall. *Geese:* pinkfooted, greylag, whitefronted (England and Wales only) Canada. *Wader:* golden plover. *Others:* coot, moorhen, woodcock, snipe.

Schedule 2 Part II refers to those wild birds which may be killed or taken, by authorised persons, at any time including woodpigeons, crows and some gulls. You should be aware that some bye-laws, for example, on nature reserves, do not include the shooting of birds in Schedule 2 Part II.

Under certain circumstances some other species not listed in the above Schedule may be shot under special licence. *Details are available from the B.A.S.C. Headquarters.*

Only the wildfowl species listed in Schedule 3 Part III of the Wildlife and Countryside Act 1981 may be offered for sale, dead, from 1st September to 28th February, inclusive:

Duck: mallard, teal, wigeon, pintail, tufted duck, pochard, shoveler. *Wader:* golden plover. *Others:* coot, woodcock, snipe.

The sale of all dead wildfowl is currently prohibited in Northern Ireland.

The B.A.S.C. does not encourage the sale of dead migratory quarry species.

It is illegal to sell dead wild geese.

It is illegal to shoot from a mechanically propelled boat in pursuit of wildfowl. The prudent wildfowler will, therefore, dispense with the engine altogether.

THE WILDFOWLER'S OBLIGATION

Always remember that your main quarry, wild geese and duck, are largely migrants and we have a responsibility to safeguard them and their environment.

Always remember that others judge the sport by your behaviour.

A responsible shot will have Third Party Liability Insurance cover, but an excellent insurance is to follow the B.A.S.C. Shotgun Safety code.

Always remember that it is the wildfowler's responsibility to understand the laws relating to his sport; in particular to be able to recognise his quarry and know when and where he may shoot.

CONSIDERATION FOR YOUR QUARRY

Always condemn unsporting shooting, i.e. at poor fliers and at birds out of range.

Remember a marsh can be spoilt by continual human disturbance – and you need not be shooting to cause a disturbance.

Always mark wounded quarry and ensure that it is picked up and humanely dispatched as soon as possible. A sharp knock on the head with a suitably heavy stick or priest is most effective.

Always remember that a dog is essential for tide shooting and picking up after dark – keep it under control at all times.

SEASONS

Inland September 1st–January 31st, inclusive.
Below the mean high water mark of ordinary spring tides. September 1st–February 20th inclusive.

N.B. Geese and duck *only* after January 31st.

GUNS AND CARTRIDGES

A double-barreled twelve--bore is a suitable all-round shotgun. If your fieldcraft is good you will be successful with the standard 2½″ cartridge (correctly loaded).

Traditionally, wildfowlers prefer a 3″ chambered gun which enables them to shoot heavier shot more effectively. Big-bore guns, i.e. 10-, 8- and 4-bores, although capable of handling big shot very effectively, can be cumbersome and a burden. Choke only marginally increases your range and is no excuse for attempting out-of-range shots.

The B.A.S.C. discourages the use, by its members, of any gun or rifle firing a single bullet or projectile for the purpose of killing wildfowl.

The *Wildlife and Countryside Act 1981* makes the use of self-loading or repeating shotguns illegal for shooting wildfowl unless fitted with a device to prevent the firing of more than 3 cartridges in succession without reloading.

Shot size	Quarry	Maximum effective range
No. 4/5	Duck	40 yards
No. 6	Teal/waders	40 yards
No. 3	Geese	40 yards

PLANNING

When you go on the foreshore for the first time go in daylight with someone who knows the area and can point out marsh boundaries and inherent dangers which occur.

When wildfowling away from home, it is courteous to make contact with the secretaries of the local wildfowling clubs, to ensure you don't inadvertently encroach on private ground.

Always tell someone where you have gone wild-fowling and don't forget to tell them you have returned safely.

Make sure you know of local rules and restrictions, particularly those that may be operating in a nature reserve shooting area.

Always avoid the more distant parts of the marsh when a big tide is expected.

Always consult the tide tables before going on the marsh. Remember that the figures stated will be altered by the prevailing weather conditions.

If you are out all day carry some food and a thermos containing a hot drink.

Wear comfortable, inconspicuous warm water-proof clothing.

Waders are normally recommended.

Always take a large canvas bag – it is often useful to sit on.

Make sure your equipment is sensibly distributed about you and leaves you freedom of movement.

Make sure you carry your shotgun certificate with you.

A game licence is needed for common snipe and woodcock.

EQUIPMENT

Always carry a waterproof wristwatch, it is essential for judging the state of the tide.

Remember, if British Summer Time is in force, to make the necessary correction to your Tide Table.

Always carry a waterproof torch **but remember** torch flashing is **only** justified in an **emergency**.

A pair of binoculars will enhance the day and be useful for identification purposes.

A six-foot wading pole will greatly assist you to walk on the marsh and can be used to sound gutters and crossing places.

Always carry a pocket compass, go straight to your chosen point and note the compass bearing for a safe return route.

Always carry at least a 'pull through'; it is all too easy to get mud or snow into the muzzle of your gun.

ON THE MARSH

Do not disturb the locality or other sportsmen by making a noise, banging car doors when arriving early in the morning or leaving late at night.

Never arrive late, or depart early, and so disturb the shooting of those who have taken the trouble to get into position in good time.

Do not shoot in the immediate vicinity of houses adjoining the shore.

Make sure you are well hidden. Camouflage yourself to suit your surroundings.

Try to make your dog comfortable – if you sit on your game bag make sure he has a dry seat.

Look through your gun barrels to make sure they are clear whenever an obstruction may have entered.

Range judging when wildfowling is particularly difficult. As the flight develops, don't spoil it by shooting at out-of-range birds.

Send your dog to retrieve birds as they are shot.

Take care to recognise legal quarry. If in doubt don't shoot.

Never leave cartridge cases or unsightly pit holes on the marsh.

Dogging the tideline will often recover lost birds.

Never try to be clever waiting for the last moment to leave the marsh when the incoming tide is approaching. Channels fill quickly and in a very short time they will become a torrent.

On leaving the marsh your dog will be cold and wet – consider his needs before your own.

Take care of your quarry – don't waste it.

Pay special attention to cleaning your gun – sand and saltwater will quickly erode it. Check it for faults which may need rectifying.

A BIBLIOGRAPHY
OF WILDFOWL
AND WILDFOWLING
COMPILED BY JOHN RICHARDS

1486
BERNERS, DAME JULIANA *The Boke of St. Albans*

1621
MARKHAM, GERVASE *Hungers Prevention or the Whole Arte of Fowling by Water and Land*

1674
COX, NICHOLAS, *The Gentleman's Recreation*

1686
BLOME, RICHARD (Ed.) *The Gentleman's Recreation*

1697
GENT, J.S. *The Experienced Fowler or the Gentleman, Citizen and Countryman's Pleasant and Profitable Recreation*

1709
PROCLAMATION *The Laws of the Forest and Game and also of Hunting, Hawking, Fishing and Fowling*

1712
MARKHAM, GERVASE *The Young Sportsmans Instructor in Angling, Fowling, Hawking, Hunting, Etc.*

1717
MARKLAND, GEORGE *Pteryplegia or the Art of Shooting Flying*

1735
The Sportsman's Dictionary or the Country Gentleman's Companion in all Rural Recreations

1770
EDIE, GEORGE *The Art of English Shooting*

1778
The Sportsman's Dictionary or the Gentleman's Companion for Town and Country

1797
COX, E. NICHOLAS *The Fowler*

1800
PYE, H.J. *The Sportsman's Dictionary*

1801
DANIEL, REV. W.B. *Rural Sports*
HAWKER, P. *The Sportsman's Pocket Companion, nos I to VI*

1804
THORNHILL, R.B. *The Shooting Directory*
THORNTON, COL. THOMAS *A Sporting Tour through the Northern Parts of England and a Great Part of the Highlands of Scotland*

1808
VINCENT, REV. JOHN *Fowling*

1809
THOMAS, B. (JOHNSON, T.B.) *The Shooter's Guide*

1811
HEWITT, SAMUEL *Groups of Animals*

1814
HANGER, COL. GEORGE *To All Sportsmen and Particularly to Farmers and Gamekeepers*
HAWKER, PETER *Instructions to Young Sportsmen*

1815
MAYER, JOHN *Sportsmans Directory*

1819
JOHNSON, T.B. *The Shooters Companion by 'B. Thomas'*

1820
SCOTT, WM. HENRY *British Field Sports*

1823
HASSALL, J. *Shooting on the Thames*

1832
MAXWELL, W.H. *Wild Sports of the West of Ireland*

1833
MAXWELL, G.S. *Field Book of Sports and Pastimes*

1835
The Old Sports of England
NIMROD (C.J. APPERLEY) *Memoirs of the Life of the Late John Mytton, Esq*

1837
TYLER, JAMES *The Shooters Manual or the Art of Shooting Flying*

1838
JOHNSON, T.B. *The Shooters Preceptor*

1840
A COSMOPOLITE (ROBERT ALLEN) *The Sportsman in Ireland*
COLQUHOUN, JOHN *The Moor and the Loch*
DELABERE, BLAINE *Encyclopedia of Rural Sports*
WILSON, JAMES 'THOMAS OAKLEIGH' *The Rod and the Gun*

1841
COLQUHOUN, J. *The Moor and the Loch*

1842
CARLETON, J.W. (Ed.) *The Sporting Sketch Book*
LACY, CAPT. R. *The Modern Shooter*

1844
MAXWELL, W.H. *Wanderings in the Highlands and Islands*

1845
LUBBOCK, REV. RICHARD *Observations on the Fauna of Norfolk*

1846
CRAVEN (J.W. CARLETON) *Recreations in Shooting by Craven*
ST. JOHN, CHARLES *Short Sketches of the Wild Sports and Natural History of the Highlands*

1849
ST. JOHN, CHARLES *Tour in Sutherland*
THOMPSON *The Natural History of Ireland*

1850
KNOX, A.E. *Game Birds and Wildfowl, Their Friends and Foes*
MORRIS, B.R. *British Game Birds and Wildfowl*

1853
MAXWELL, W.H. *Wild Sports and Adventures in the Highlands and Islands of Scotland*
ST. JOHN, HON. F. *Rambles in Germany, France, Italy and Russia in Search of Sport*

1855
IDLE, CHRISTOPHER *Hints on Shooting and Fishing on Sea and Land*
MILLS, JOHN *The Sportsman's Library*

1856
STONEHENGE (J.H. WALSH) *Manual of British Rural Sports*

1859
BROWN, T. *The Taxidermists Manual*

FOLKARD, H.C. *The Wildfowler*

1860
HAMILTON, COL. J.P. *Reminiscences of an Old Sportsman*
MARKSMAN *The Dead Shot*
MARTINGALE (CHARLES WHITE) *Sporting Scenes and Country Characters*
MILES, H.D. (Ed.) *Book of Field Sports*

1862
LENNOX, LORD WILLIAM *Recreation of Sportsmen (Including Wildfowling in Canada)*

1863
ST. JOHN, CHARLES *Natural History and Sport in Moray*

1864
VERDON, T.C. *The Game Birds and Wildfowl of India*

1866
COLQUHOUN, J. *Sporting Days*
COX, HORACE *Facts and Useful Hints Relating to Shooting and Fishing*
WHEELWRIGHT, HORACE W. *Sporting Sketches at Home and Abroad by 'The Old Bushman'*

1867
LLOYD, L.L. *The Game Birds and Wildfowl of Sweden and Norway*

1871
BARRY, W. *Moorland and Stream*
HARTING, J.E. *Hints on Shore Shooting*
SIXTY-ONE (REV. H. HELY HUTCHINSON) *Twenty Years Reminiscences of the Lews*

1872
DENISON, ALFRED *Fowling and Fishing*
PEARCE, THOMAS *The Idstone Papers*

1873
UBIQUE (PARKER GILLMORE) *Adventures, Afloat and Ashore*

1874
ADAMSON, C.M. *Sundry Natural History Scraps*
LONG, WM. J. *Wildfowl Shooting in the USA*
NORTH, OLIVER (MULLEN W.) *Rambles after Sport, or Travels and Adventures in the Americas and at Home by Oliver North*

1876
HEATHCOTE, J.M. *Reminiscences of Fen and Mere*
OLD SHEKARRY (H.A. LEVESON) *Sport in Many Lands, Europe, Asia, Africa, America, etc.*
WILDFOWLER (LEWIS CLEMENT) *Shooting and Fishing Trips in England, France Alsace, Belgium, Holland and Bavaria (two vols.)*

1877
WILDFOWLER (LEWIS CLEMENT) *Shooting, Yachting, Sea Fishing Trips at Home and on the Continent* (two vols.)

1879
BAGATELLE (A.G. BAGOT) *Sporting Sketches at Home and Abroad*
WILDFOWLER (LEWIS CLEMENT) *Shooting Adventures, Canine Lore and Sea Fishing Trips*

1880
ADAMSON, C.M. *Some Scraps About Birds*
MANLEY, J.J. *Notes on Game and Game Shooting*
WILDFOWLER (LEWIS CLEMENT) *Modern Wildfowling*
WILDFOWLER (LEWIS CLEMENT) *Table of Loads for Shoulder Guns of All Sizes Chokes and Cylinders and for Punt Guns*

1881
BOOTH, E.T. *Rough Notes on Birds Observed During 25 Years Shooting and Collecting in the British Isles*
GREENER, W.W. *The Gun and Its Development*
PHILLIPS-WOLLEY, CLIVE *Sport in the Crimea and the Caucasus*
WILDFOWLER (LEWIS CLEMENT) *Public Shooting Quarters*

1882
ADAMSON, C.M. *Another Book of Scraps*
PAYNE-GALLWEY, SIR RALPH *The Fowler in Ireland*
ST. JOHN, CHARLES *Natural History and Sport in Moray*
STONEHENGE (J.H. WALSH) *The Modern Sportsman's Gun and Rifle*
STONEHENGE (J.H. WALSH) *The Modern Sportsman's Gun and Rifle* Vol. I *Game and Wildfowl Guns*

1883
DAVIES, G. CHRISTOPHER *Norfolk Broads and Rivers*

1884
CHAPMAN, ABEL *A Voyage to Spitsbergen and Arctic Seas*
DAVIES, G. CHRISTOPHER *Peter Penniless, Gamekeeper and Gentleman*
MAYER, A.M. (Ed.) *Sport with Gun and Rod in American Woods and Water*
RICE, MAJOR GEN. W. *Indian Game (from Quail to Tiger)*

1885
BROMLEY-DAVENPORT, W. *Sport*
CLEMENT, LEWIS *Rational Loading* (Table of loads for wildfowling guns)

1886
PAYNE-GALLWEY, SIR RALPH *The Book of Duck Decoys*

REYNARDSON, C.T.S.B. *Sports and Anecdotes of Bygone Days*
WALSINGHAM, LORD (PAYNE-GALLWEY, SIR R.) *Shooting* (Badminton Library)

1887
ADAMSON, C.M. *More Illustrations of Birds*
TOZER, BAZIL *Practical Hints on Shooting (Wildfowl and Trap Shooting)*

1888
20-BORE (BASIL TOZER) *Practical Hints on Shooting*
BAGOT, A.G. *Shooting and yachting in the Mediterranean*
EDWARDS-MOSS, J.E. *A Season in Sutherland*
LEFFINGWELL, WM. D. *Shooting on Upland Marsh and Stream*
LEFFINGWELL, WM. D. *Wildfowl Shooting*
MOORE, STUART A. *A History of the Foreshore and the Law Relating Thereto*

1889
CHAPMAN, ABEL *Bird Life of the Borders*
THE OLD SHEKARRY *Sport in Many Lands*

1890
BARROWS, WILLIAM *The General or Twelve Nights in a Hunters Camp*
CRADOCK, LT. C. *Sporting Notes in the Far East*
MILLER, CHRISTY *The Birds of Essex*
MORRIS, B.R. *British Game Birds and Wildfowl*
PAYNE-GALLWEY, SIR RALPH *Letters to Young Shooter* (3 vols.)
READY, OLIVER *Life and Sport on the Norfolk Broads*

1891
SON OF THE MARSHES (D. JORDAN) *Annals of a Fishing Village*
WATSON, J. *Poachers and Poaching*

1892
GRIMBLE, AUGUSTUS *Shooting and Salmon Fishing*
MITCHELL, F.S. *The Birds of Lancashire*
OWEN, J.A. (Ed.) *Within an Hour of London Town*
SON OF THE MARSHES (D. JORDAN) *Among Wild Birds and their Haunts*

1893
CHAPMAN, ABEL; BUCK, W.J. *Wild Spain 'España Agreste'*
DIXON, CHARLES *Game Birds and Wildfowl of the British Isles*
HAWKER, COL. PETER *The Diary of Col. Peter Hawker 1802–1850* (2 vols.)
SON OF THE MARSHES (D. JORDAN) *With the Woodlanders and by the Tide*
UBIQUE (PARKER GILLMORE) *Leaves from a Sportsman's Diary*

1895
CORNISH, JAMES *Wild England of Today*
CRAWFORD, O. (Ed.) *A Year of Sport and Natural History Shooting, Hunting, Coursing, Falconry and Fishing*
ELLIOTT, D.G. *North American Shore Birds*
EMERSON, P.H. *Birds, Beasts and Fishes of the Norfolk Broads*
NYE, E. SCUDDER *Scientific Duck Shooting* (USA)
SHARP, H. *Practical Wildfowling*
SON OF THE MARSHES (JORDAN, D.) *The Wildfowl and Seafowl of Great Britain*
SUFFLING, E.R. *The Land of the Broads*

1896
CHAPMAN, ABEL *First Lessons in the Art of Wildfowling*
CRAWFORD, J.H. *Wild Life of Scotland*
SON OF THE MARSHES (JORDAN, D.) *In the Green Leaf and the Sere, Woodland Moor and Stream*

1897
BICKERDYKE, J. (C.H. COOK) *Wild Sports in Ireland*
CHAPMAN, ABEL *Wild Norway*
CORNISH, C.J. *Nights with an Old Gunner*
MACPHERSON, REV. H.A. *A History of Fowling*
SHAND, ALEX INNES *Mountain Stream and Cover*
SUFFOLK AND BERKSHIRE, EARL OF (Ed.) *Encyclopedia of Sport*

1898
A SON OF THE MARSHES, (JORDAN D.) *Drift from Longshore by a Son of the Marshes*
ELLIOT, D.G. *The Wildfowl of the United States and British Possessions*
KEARTON, RICHARD *With Nature and a Camera*
MORGAN, W.A. (Ed.) *'The House' on Sport by Members of the London Stock Exchange*

1899
HAMBLEN, J. *Fur and Feather Tales by Hamblen Sears*
LONG, WM. J. *Fowl of the Air*
PRINGLE, J.J. *Twenty Years Snipe Shooting*

1900
CORNISH, C.J. *Wild England Today*
HARTING, J.E. *Essays on Sport and Natural History*
MARTINDALE, THOMAS *Sport Indeed*

1901
BRADFORD, CHARLES *The Wildfowlers*
CONWAY, JAMES *Recollections of Sport Among Fin, Fur and Feather*
GRINNELL, GEORGE B. *American Duck Shooting* (USA)
MILLAIS, J.G. *The Wildfowler in Scotland*
PEEL, C.V.A. *Wild Sport in the Outer Hebrides*

1902
EVERITT, NICHOLAS *Broadland Sport*

HASLUCK, P.N. *Taxidermy*
MILLAIS, J.G. *The Natural History of Surface Feeding Ducks*
SHAND, ALEX INNES *Shooting* (Hadden Hall Library)

1903
DUTT, W.A. *The Norfolk Broads*
HARTLEY, GILFRED W. *Wild Sport with Gun, Rifle and Salmon rod*
HUTCHINSON, H.G. (Ed.) *Shooting*
SHAW, L.H. DE VISME *Snipe and Woodcock*

1904
BRYDEN, H.A. *Nature and Sport in Britain*
PATTERSON, A.H. *Notes of an East Coast Naturalist*
SCOLOPAX (M.H. GRANT) *Book of the Snipe*
SHARP, HENRY *The Gun, Afield and Afloat*
WALKER A. STODART; MACKIE, P. JEFFREY *The Keeper's Book*

1905
ALPHERAKY, S. *Geese of Europe and Asia*
DUTT, W.A. *The Norfolk Broads*
OATES, W. COAPE CAPT. *Wild Ducks, How to Rear and Shoot Them*
PATTERSON, A.H. *Nature in Eastern Norfolk*
SHAW, L. DE VISME *Wildfowl*

1906
DEWAR, D. *Bombay Duck*
DUTT, W.A. *Wild Life in East Anglia*
FINN, FRANK *How to Know the Indian Waders*
HARTING, J.E. *Recreations of a Naturalist*
PATTEN, C.J. *The Aquatic Birds of Great Britain and Ireland*
SHARP, HENRY *Modern Sporting Gunnery*

1907
BENSUSAN, S.L. *A Countryside Chronicle*
FALLON, W.J. *Practical Wildfowler: A complete guide to the art of the fowler with a description of the birds usually met with*
FORREST, H.E. *Fauna of North Wales*
LONG, WM. J. *Whose Home is the Wilderness*
PATTERSON, A.H. *Wild Life on a Norfolk Estuary*

1908
BAKER, E.C. STUART *The Game Birds of India, Burma and Ceylon.* Vol. I *The Indian Ducks and their allies;* Vol. II *Snipe, Bustards and Sandgrouse*
DEWAR, G.A.B. *Life and Sport in Hampshire*

1909
CUMING, E.D. *British Sport, Past and Present*
HALLIDAY, W. *The Book of Migratory Birds*
HIGSON, D. *Seafowl Shooting Sketches*
HOOD, MAJOR A. *Shooting – Notes on Shooting in the British Isles*
PATTERSON, A.H. *Man and Nature on Tidal Waters*

1910

CHAPMAN, ABEL; BUCK, J.W. *Unexplored Spain – Wildlife in a Wild Country*

COWARD, T.A. *The Vertebrate Fauna of Cheshire and Liverpool Bay*

DURHAM, J.M.M.B. (MARSHMAN) *A Medley of Sport*

1911

DUNCAN, STANLEY; THORNE, GUY (C.A.E.R.) *The Complete Wildfowler*

HUTCHINSON, H.G. *When Life Was New*

1912

BOLAM, G. *Birds of Northumberland and the Eastern Borders*

CHAPMAN, MILLAIS, HARTING, SELOUS INC'D *The Gun at Home and Abroad*

HARTLEY, G.W. *Wild Sport and Some Stories*

QUINTIN, COL. T.A. ST. *Chances of Sport of Sorts*

SMITH, SYDNEY, H. *Snowden Slights, Wildfowler*

SPORTSMAN *Encyclopedia of Sports and Games* (4 vols.) – *Wildfowling* Vol. 2)

1913

DURHAM, J.M.M.B.; RICHARDSON, R.J. *Melton and Homespun – Prose and Verse*

MILLAIS, J.G. *British Diving Ducks*

STREATFIELD, F.N. *Sporting Recollections of an Old 'Un*

1918

PARKER, ERIC *Shooting Days*

WHITAKER, J. *British Duck Decoys of Today*

1919

MILLAIS, J.G. *Wanderings and Memories*

PARKER, ERIC AND OTHERS *Shooting by Moor, Field and Shore*

1920

DAWSON, MAJ. K. *Letter to Young Sportsmen*

PATTERSON, A.H. *Through Broadland in a Breydon Punt by 'John Knowlittle'*

READY, O.G. *Life and Sport on the Norfolk Broads*

ROWLEY, J. *The Art of Taxidermy*

SPEEDY, TOM *Natural History and Sport in Scotland*

1921

BERNSEN, P.S. *The North American Waterfowler* (USA)

HAZELTON, WM.C. *Wildfowling Tales* (USA)

PRICHARD, H. HESKETH *Sport in Wildest Britain*

1922

BANDERAS *Sporting Reminiscences of South America 1919–1921*

BATTEN, H. MORTIMER *Woodlore for Young Sportsmen*

COWARD, T.A. *Bird Haunts and Nature Memories*

GLADSTONE, HUGH S. *Record Bags and Shooting Records*

PARKER, ERIC (Ed.) *Instructions to Young Sportsmen in All That Relates to Guns and Shooting by Lt. Col. Peter Hawker*

1923

DUTT, W.A. *A Guide to the Norfolk Broads*

FINN, FRANK *Wildfowl of the World*

HAMILTON, G.W. *Shooting over Decoys* (USA)

MINER, J. *Jack Miner and His Birds*

PATTERSON, A.H. *Cruise of 'The Walrus' on the Broads*

PIERS, SIR CHARLES P. *Sport and Life in British Columbia*

THORBURN, A. *Game Birds and Wildfowl of Great Britain and Ireland*

1924

ARNOLD, E.C. *British Waders*

CHAPMAN, ABEL *The Borders and Beyond*

HAYNES, WM. BARBER *Ducks and Duck Shooting* (USA)

KIRKMAN, F.B.; HUTCHINSON, H.G. *British Sporting Birds*

ROBINSON, BEVERLEY W. *With Shotgun and Rifle in North America* (USA)

WILSON, LT. COL. ALBAN *Sport and Service in Assam and Elsewhere*

1925

WRIGHT, R.G.; DEWAR, D. *The Ducks of India*

1926

NICHOLLS, J.C.M. *Birds of Marsh and Mere and How to Shoot Them*

1927

DOBIE, W.G.M. *Game Bag and Creel*

1928

CHAPMAN, ABEL *Retrospect*

POLLARD, HUGH B.C. *Wildfowl and Waders*

SEIGNE, J.W. *Irish Bogs*

1929

NICHOLS, J.C.M. *Shooting by Moor, Field and Shore*

PATTERSON, ARTHUR H. *Wildfowlers and Poachers, Fifty Years on the East Coast*

1930

BOLSTER, R.C. *Driven Duck*

CHAPMAN, ABEL *Memories of Four Score Years Less Two*

PATTERSON, A.H. *A Norfolk Naturalist*

PATTERSON, A.H. *In Norfolk Bird Haunts in A.D. 1755*

PATTERSON, A.H. *Through Broadland by Sail and Motor*

PHILLIPS, J.C.; LINCOLN, F.C. *American Waterfowl, Their Present Situation and the Outlook for Their Future*

SEIGNE, J.W. *A Bird Watcher's Note Book*

1931
BURRARD, MAJ. J. *The Modern Shotgun*
DAWSON, MAJ. K. *Marsh and Mudflat*
PARKER, ERIC (Ed.) *Colonel Hawker's Shooting Diaries*

1932
DAVIES, G.C. *The Swan and Her Crew*

1934
BARBER, JOEL *Wildfowl Decoys* (USA)
DAY, J. WENTWORTH *The Modern Fowler*
LEMMON, H. GALLIENNE, M.A. LLM *Public Rights on the Seashore*
RUGGLES BRISE, A.W. *Shooting Reminiscences in Essex and Elsewhere*

1935
CHALMERS, PATRICK R. *Birds Ashore and Aforeshore*
DAWSON, MAJOR K. *Son of a Gun*
DE WITT, J. *Chasse de Briere – Paris*
SCOTT, PETER *Morning Flight*
YEATES, G.K.; WINNAL, R.N. *Rough Shooting*

1936
HAIG-THOMAS, DAVID *I Leap Before I Look, Sport at Home and Abroad*
ROSS, COL. E.J. *Duck Shooting in India*
SEIGNE, J.W.; KEITH E.C. *Woodcock and Snipe*

1937
BENSUSAN, L. *Marshland Echoes*
DALGETY, C.T. *Wildfowling*
DAY, J. WENTWORTH *Sporting Adventure*
DROUGHT, J.B. *Green Memory*
DUNSANY, LORD *My Ireland*
KEITH, E.C. *Gun for Company*
WATKINS-PITCHFORD, D.J. *The Sportsman's Bedside Book*

1938
BENSUSAN, S.L. *Marshland Calling*
BONELTE, W. *American Duck, Goose and Brant Shooting* (USA)
BRUETTE, W. *American Duck, Goose and Brant Shooting*
DAY, J. WENTWORTH *Sport in Egypt*
DOBIE, W.G.M. *Winter and Rough Weather*
FARRAR, G.B. *The Feathered Folk of an Estuary*
FITZGERALD, GERALD *Pot Luck – Rough Shooting in West of Ireland*
KEITH, E.C. *A Countryman's Creed*
PERRY, RICHARD *At the Turn of the Tide*
SCOTT, PETER *Wild Chorus*
SQUIRE, L. *Wildfowling with a Camera*
TENNYSON, JULIAN *Rough Shooting*

1939
ALEXANDER, W.B. *The Woodcock in the British Isles*

BRATBY, MICHAEL *Grey Goose*
VESEY-FITZGERALD B. *A Book of British Waders*
WILDFOWL ENQUIRY *The Status and Distribution of Wild Geese and Wild Duck*

1940
SEDGWICK, NOEL M. *The Young Shots*
WHITE, S.E. *Wild Geese Calling*

1941
B.B. (WATKINS PRITCHARD) *The Countryman's Bedside Book*
BRATBY, M.; SCOTT, P. *Through the Air*
MACINTYRE, D. *Highland Gamekeeper*
YATES, G.K.; WITNALL, R.M. *Roughshooting*

1942
B.B. (WATKINS PRITCHARD) *Sky Gypsy*
LYNN, ALLEN *Roughshooting*
PARKER, ERIC *The Shooting Weekend Book*

1943
B.B. (WATKINS PRITCHARD) *The Idle Countryman*
HAILNER, VAN CAMPEN *A Book on Duck Shooting*
KORTRIGHT, FRANCIS H. *The Ducks and Geese and Swans of North America*

1944
HOCHBAUM, A.L. *The Canvasback on a Prairie Marsh* (USA)

1945
B.B. (WATKINS PRITCHARD) *The Wayfaring Tree*
BUCHAN-HEPBURN, SIR JOHN (BART) *Lowlander in the Field – The Time of Life*
HOLLAND, RAY P. *Shotgunning in the Lowlands*

1946
DAY, J. WENTWORTH *Harvest Adventure*
PERRY, RICHARD *A Naturalist on Lindisfarne*
SCHALDACK, W.J. *Upland Gunning*
SEDGWICK, NOEL M. *A Shooting Man's Year*
SEDGWICK, NOEL M. *By Covert, Field and Marsh*

1947
CONNETT, E.W. *Duck Shooting Along the Atlantic Tide Water*
FARRINGTON, S.K. (JNR) *The Ducks Came Back*
HORSLEY, TERENCE *Sporting Pageant*
KENNARD, C.H. *What Sport*
PITMAN, E.N. *And Clouds Flying*
QUEENY, E.M. *Prairie Wings*
SALISBURY, HOWARD M. *Duck Guns, Shooting and Decoying*

1948
DAY, J. WENTWORTH *Wild Wings and Some Footsteps*
DROUGHT, J.B. *Successful Shooting*
RICHARDS, COMBE *Wild Goose Chase*
ROSS, ROBERT ERSKINE *Wings Over the Marshes*

SCOLOPAX (W.H.T. LONG) *The Gun in the Field*
SEDGWICK, NOEL M. *The Shooting Man's Year*
WATCHER, JOHN *Pleasures Without Change*
WITNALL, R.N. *Shore Shooting*

1949

DAY, J. WENTWORTH *Coastal Adventure*
NMEMMIONE A.R. *Adventures' Fen*
SCOTT, PETER *Wild Geese and Eskimos*
SEDGWICK, NOEL M. *The Gun on Saltings and Stubble*
TEMPLEWOOD, VISCOUNT *The Unbroken Thread*

1950

B.B. *Tides Ending*
B.B. (WATKINS PRITCHARD) *Letters from Compton
    Dervill*
BRATBY, M. *Notes on Some British and Foreign
    Wildfowl*
DAY, J. WENTWORTH *Marshland Adventure*
DUNCAN, STANLEY; THORNE, GUY *The Complete
    Wildfowler, Revised Edition*
NICHOLS, J.C.M. *Wildfowling*
SEDGWICK, NOEL M. *Wildfowling and Roughshooting*

1951

BARCLAY-SMITH, PHYLLIS *A Book of Ducks*
DAY, J. WENTWORTH *Broadland Adventure*
SEDGWICK, NOEL M. *With Dog and Gun*
SHACKLETON, K. *Tidelines*

1952

DAY, J. WENTWORTH *The Modern Shooter*
HARRISON, JEFFERY, G. *Estuary Saga*
SEDGWICK, NOEL M. *Shooting Round the Year*
TRYON, AYLMER; MONAHAN, HUGH *The
    Wildfowler's Year*

1953

ARNOLD, RICHARD *The Shore Shooter*
B.B. (WATKINS PRITCHARD) *Dark Estuary*
B.B. (WATKINS PRITCHARD) *Tides Ending*
MACKENTY, J.G. *Duck Hunting*
SAVORY, A. *Fisherman Fowler*
SAVORY, A. *Norfolk Fowler*
SCOTT, PETER; FISHER, JAMES *A Thousand Geese*
SCOTT, PETER, *Wildfowl and Eskimos*
SEDGWICK, NOEL M. *Shooting Wildfowl and Game*
SHEPHERD, MICHAEL *Come Wildfowling*

1954

DAY, J. WENTWORTH *A History of the Fens*
DELACOUR, J. *The Waterfowl of the World 1954–1964*
DROUGHT, CAPT. J.B. *A Sportsman Looks at Eire*
HARRISON, JEFFERY, G. *Pastures New*
JAMES, EDWARD C. *Hunting Ducks and Geese (USA)*
POWELL, BILL *My Wild Goose Chase*
SHACKLETON, KEITH *Wake*
WHITAKER, PETER H. *Approach to Shooting*

1955

BENHAM, HERVEY *Once Upon a Tide*
BUXTON, A. *The King in His Country*
HOCHBAUM, A.L. *Travels and Traditions of Wildfowl*
SAVORY, ALAN *Lazy Rivers*
SMITH, PETER J. (Ed.) *The Northwestern Wildfowler*
THORNEYCROFT, NIGEL *Fowler's Moon*

1956

CADIEUX, C.L. *Goose Hunting*
ELMAN, R. & OSBORNE, W. *The Atlantic Flyway (USA)*
HALLIDAY, W. *The Book of Migratory Birds Met With
    on Holy Island and the Northumberland Coast Plus
    Accounts of Wildfowling on the Mud Flats*
POWELL, BILL *The Grey Geese Call*
ROBERTS, E.L. *Happy Countryman*
SMITH, PETER, J. (Ed.) *The Northwestern Wildfowler*

1957

CADMAN, ARTHUR *Tales of a Wildfowler*
ERRINGTON, T.L. *Of Men and Marshes (USA)*
SCOTT, PETER *Coloured Key to the Wildfowl of the
    World*
SCOTT, PETER *Wildfowl of the British Isles*
SMITH, PETER J. *The Wildfowler Magazine, Published
    by Dee Wildfowlers' Club*
TICEHURST, NORMAN F. *The Mute Swan in England*

1958

ARNOLD, RICHARD *The Shoreshooter*
FREUCHUM PAD SALMONSEN F. *The Arctic Year*
WILLOCK, COLIN *The Puntgun Adventure*

1959

RIPLEY, B.A. *A Paddling of Ducks*

1960

WALSH, ROY, E. *Gunning the Chesapeake*

1961

SCHNEIDAUER, T.R. *Cyges et Oies Sauvages*
SCOTT, PETER *The Eye of the Wind*
SEDGWICK/WHITAKER/HARRISON (Eds.) *The New
    Wildfowler*
WILLOCK, COLIN *The Bedside Wildfowler*

1962

TAVERNER, J.H. *Wildfowl in Hampshire*
WILLOCK, COLIN *'Kenzie'*
WILLOCK, COLIN *Duck Shooting*

1963

ATKINSON-WILLES (Ed.) *Wildfowl in Great Britain*
CADMAN, ARTHUR *Goose Shooting*
CADMAN, ARTHUR *Shoulder Gunning for Duck*
HOFFMAN, L. (Ed.) *Proceedings of the Mar Conference*
SEDGWICK, NOEL M. *Wader Shooting*
STOKES, TED *A Sailor's Guide to Ocean Birds (Atlantic
    and Mediterranean)*

SWIFT, J. *Proceedings on the First European Meeting on Wildfowl Conservation*
WALSH, ROY E. *Sanctuary Pond*

1964
HARRISON, JAMES M. *Bird Taxidermy*
LINDUSKA, J.P.; NELSON, A.L. (Eds.) *Wildfowl Tomorrow*
OLNEY, P. *List of European and North American Wetlands of International Importance*

1965
BARRETT, W.H. *A Fenman's Story*
BROWN, P. *Birds in the Balance*
EARNEST, A. *The Art of Decoy – American Bird Carvings*
HANSON, H. *Canada Goose*
MACKEY, W.J. *American Bird Decoys*

1966
EDINBURGH, HRH PRINCE PHILIP, DUKE OF *Birds from the Britannia*
EINARSON, ARTHUR S. *Brant Sea Goose of the Pacific*
SALVADA, Z. *Proceedings of the Second European Meeting on Wildfowl Conservation*

1967
COY, KUNDALL; RALPH, W. *Wildfowling at a Glance*
FRITH, H.J. *Waterfowl in Australia*
HARRISON, J. *A Wealth of Wildfowl*
JOHNSGARD, PAUL *Waterfowl, Their Biology and Natural History*
STEARNS, HYDE J. *Duck Stamps* (USA)

1968
COLES, C. *Game Conservation in the Changing Countryside*
FINLAY, E. *Down the Creek*
HINE, R.L.; SCHOFIELD, CLAY *Canada Goose Management*
JOHNSGARD, PAUL *Waterfowl*
JOHNSON, A.A.; PAYN, W.H. *Ornamental Waterfowl*
NIALL, IAN *A Fowler's World*

1969
BARSKE, P. *The Black Duck*

1970
SEDGWICK/WHITAKER/HARRISON (Eds.) *The New Wildfowler in the 1970s*

1971
Walsh, H.M. *The Outlaw Gunner* (USA)

1972
McDOUGALL, D. *Goose Fever*
WATKINS, PRITCHARD, D.J. *The Best of B.B. – An Anthology*

1973
LE GRESHAM, C.T. *The Complete Wildfowler* (USA)
RICHARDSON, R.H. (Ed.) *Chesapeake Bay Decoys*

1974
BYRNE, JACK *Duck Hunting in Australia and New Zealand*
CADMAN, A. *A Guide to Roughshooting*
CARTIER, J.O. *Getting the Most Out of Modern Waterfowling*
CARTIER, JOHN O. *Modern Waterfowling* (USA)

1975
COLES, C, (Ed.) *The Complete Book of Game Conservation* (2nd edition)
WILLOCK, COLIN *The ABC of Shooting*

1976
B.B. (WATKINS PRITCHARD) *Recollections of a Longshore Gunner*
HARRISION, JEFFERY; GRANT, PETER *The Thames Transformed*
JOHNSGARD, P.A. *The Bird Decoy, An American Artform*
MARLOWE, CHRISTOPHER *Legends of the Fenland People* (1926)
SAVORY, ALAN *Fisherman Fowler*

1977
MARCHINGTON, JOHN *The Practical Wildfowler*

1978
RUFFER, J.G. *The Big Shots*
WATSON, N.P. *Victorian and Edwardian Field Sports From Old Photographs*

1979
FLECKENSTEIN, H.A. *Decoys of the Wild Atlantic Region* (USA)
HUMPHREYS, JOHN *Hides, Calls and Decoys*
HUTCHINSON, CLIVE *Ireland's Wetlands and Their Birds*
McDOUGALL, D. *8 Bore Guns and Cartridges*
OGILVIE, M.A. *The Wetlands of Britain*

1980
BEGBIE, ERIC *Modern Wildfowling*
CADIEUX, C.L. *Goose Shooting* (USA)
DELPH, J. & S. *Factory Decoys of Mason, Stevens, Dodge and Peterson* (USA)
DELPH, J. & S. *New England Decoys* (USA)
FLECKENSTEIN, H.A. *Shore Bird Decoys* (USA)
MARCHINGTON, JOHN *The History of Wildfowling*
SCOTT, G.H. (JOSH) *From Guns to Binoculars*
WILLOCK, COLIN *Landscape with Solitary Figures*

1981
BEGBIE, ERIC *The Sportsman's Companion*
FLECKENSTEIN, H.A. *American Factory Decoys* (USA)

HAID, A.G. *Decoys of the Mississippi Flyway* (USA)
McDOUGALL, D. *More 8 Bore Loads*
SMALL, A. *Masters of Decorative Bird Carving* (USA)

1982
BROCKBANK, L. *Dee Wildfowler – the Last Professional, Harold Gill*
COLES, CHARLES (Ed.) *Shooting and Stalking*
HUSTER, H. & KNIGHT, D. *Floating Sculpture, the decoys of the Delaware River*
JACKSON, A. *Shotguns and Shooting*
THE WILDFOWLER (ROGER MORAN) *A Tale of the Shannon Estuary*

1983
BISHOP, B. *Cley Marsh and Its Birds*
DOUGLAS, JAMES *The Sporting Gun*
FLECKENSTEIN, H.A. *New Jersey Decoys* (USA)
FLECKENSTEIN, H.A. *Southern Decoys of Virginia and Carolina* (USA)
HUMPHREYS, J. *Stanley Duncan – Wildfowler*
TURNER, G.D. *(Ed.) Handbook of Shooting – The Sporting Shotgun*

1984
MARTIN, BRIAN P. *Sporting Birds of the British Isles*

1985
KING, PETER *The Shooting Field*
McDOUGALL, D. *8 Bore Ammunition*

1986
HUMPHREYS, J. *Hunter's Fen*
JAMES, A. *Memories of a Fen Tiger*
OWEN, M.; ATKINSON-WILLES, G.L.; SLAMON, D.G. *Wildfowl in Great Britain*

1987
BEGBIE, ERIC *Fowler in the Wild*

1988
JARRETT, A. *Wildfowling – One Winter's Tale*
SKINNER, J. *Through the lens with Stanley Duncan*
SWAN, M. *Fowling for duck – a guide to successful duck fighting*

INDEX

punt-gunning (*cont.*)
  see also gunning-punts

quarry list: alterations to, 221, 235
  North America: determination of, 275
quarry species 111, 120–1
  conservation of, 221
  disturbance from shooting, 257ff.
  effect of EEC legislation on, 94, 95
  in Eire 269, 271
  in Northern Ireland, 92–3
  numbers shot annually, 228–30

ragworm: habitat, 74–5
Ramsar Convention, 97, 183, 215
  and estuary protection, 218
  and wetland conservation, 97
recipes: cooking samphire, 293, 297
  cooking sea spinach, 293, 297
  family wigeon casserole, 295
  goose with prune and apple stuffing, 296
  mallard in a jacket, 294, *294*
  oven-grilled wild duck, 294
  pressure cooker casserole, 295
  simple duck liver pâté, 296
  wigeon with cherries, 295
  wildfowl risotto, 295
recoil, 149–50
red-breasted goose, 24
Redding '16', 156
redshank: Birds Directive and, 95
  effect on wintering numbers, 219
refuge areas, *184*
  achieving balance in, 184
  for darkbellied brent, 237
  distribution/location, 184–6, *185*
  effect on wildfowling, 260
  effects of disturbance, 258–9
  for geese: effects on goose movements, 256
    management of, 256
  establishing, 220–1
  management, 259
  North American, 275
    legal killing around, 281
    siting, 280
  Northern Ireland provisions, 93
  purpose/objectives of, 191, 259
  review of current, 260
  unshot, 200–1
Remington Cartridge Co. cases, 156
re-primering punches, 160
research/monitoring, 315
  B.A.S.C. and, 313
  by clubs, 202–3
  wildfowlers, 224ff.
reserves: establishment of first, 183
  experimental *see* Sevenoaks Gravel Pit
  management of, 187, 259
  and population increases, 56
  results of counts on, 184
  shooting schemes, 186
  vegetation programme, 225
  see also refuges
reservoirs, 219
  increase in, 216

restocking programmes, 20
Results of the IWRB International Waterfowl Census 1967–1983, 215
retrievers, 174
retrieving: distant blind, 179, 180
  puppy training, 176
Ribble Estuary, 189–90
ring bulging *see* choke expansion
ringing/ringing studies: hand-reared mallard, 186
  and breeding/wintering distributions, 30ff.
  and migration studies, 30
  research programme, 225
Rottweil cases, 156
Royal Society for the Protection of Birds, 20, 184
  habitat protection policies, 220
  land holdings, 220
  and quarry species, 221
Russell, Colonel Champion, 310
rust/corrosion: preventing, 151

'sacrificial' crops, 256
Salicornia, 112
saltings: and foreshore shooting, 81
  ambush point in, 112
  1–20 February, 84
saltmarsh: active erosion of, 74
  below the sea wall, 111
  ecology, 70, 74
  effects of enclosure/reclamation, 77
  management of mature, 77
  mowing, 77, 203, 204
  plant succession, 112
  Spartina on, 76
  shooting over: identifying access, 114
    safety when, 113–14
  unshot refuges, 200
  use of compass on, 109
  wardening, 192
sanctuaries: in Eire, 271–3
  in Montrose Basin, 196
  unofficial, 137, 138, 139
Sanderson and Bellrose: steel shot review, 251
sandflats, *70*
  habitat work on, 203
scaup, 24
  Birds Directive and, 95
  breeding/wintering distribution, 46, *46*
  identifying, 65
Scoloplos armiger, 75
scoter 24
  feeding habits, 74
  methods of counting, 207, 209
scoter, common: Birds Directive and, 95
scoter, velvet: Birds Directive and, 95
Scott, Peter, 194
  on darkbellied brent, 236
  on wildfowling, 311
Scottish Wildlife Trust: and Montrose Basin, 193
sea ducks: feeding habits, 24
sea purslane: habitat, 112
sea wall: ambush point on, 112
  duck shooting below, 111ff.
  repairing, *204*

rights of way over, 81–2
Sedgwick, 'Tim', 19
setters, 174, 175
setting-poles, *130*, 130–1
Sevenoaks Gravel Pit Reserve, 187
  survival/breeding performance, 52–3, *53*
Shannon River, 271
Sharp, Henry, 154
Sheldon Bush shot, 158
shelduck, 24
  Berne Convention and, 96
  in captivity, 267
  feeding habits, 74
  moulting migrations, 28
  population: density dependence, 54–5
  wintering sites, 218
shelgeese, 24
shirts, 168
shooting: claiming birds, 108–9
  cold weather restraints, 222
  conduct/conditions on Crown Estate, 20
  compensating for *see* compensatory survival
  prohibition on night, 117
  Sunday regulations, 84
  time limits on, 109
shooting permits *see* permits
shooting rights: buying leasing, 20
  see also clubs
Shooting Times: and legislation, 19
'shore': defining, 111
shot, lead: ban for clay shooting, 252
  density per acre, 248
  homeloading, 158
    'buffering', 161–2
    dropping the, 159–60
    effective ranges, 148
    load/size recommendations, 148
  ingestion: problem of, 182
    effects on birds, 248
    estimating mortality from, 230–1
    studies into, 246–7
  North America: restrictions on, 277
  pattern density, 147–8
    see also shot 'buffering'
  poisoning from, 246ff.
    blood test for, 248
  pollution from, 222–3
  punt-gunning, 131–2
  reducing availability to birds, 250
  replacing with non-toxic, 250
  size and effectiveness, 148
    for geese, 126
    recommendations, 162–5
  striking energy, 147–8
shot, steel, 222, 246
  and muzzle velocity, 250
  North American regulations, 280
  performance trials, 250–1
shotgun certificate: applying for, 78
  photographs, 81
  and cartridge purchase, 81
  exceptions to holding, 78
  minors holding, 80
  obtaining in Scotland, 88
  penalties for not holding, 79
  police powers, 78, 81